Financial Times Pitman Publishing books

We work with leading authors to develop the strongest ideas in business and finance, bringing cutting-edge thinking and best practice to a global market.

We craft high quality books which help readers to understand and apply their content, whether studying or at work

To find out more about Financial Times Pitman Publishing books, wisit our website:

www.ftmanagement.com

EUROPEAN BUSINESS

An Issue-Based Approach

THIRD EDITION

Richard Welford

Kate Prescott

FINANCIAL TIMES
PITMAN PUBLISHING

FINANCIAL TIMES

MANAGEMENT

LONDON · SAN FRANCISCO
KUALA LUMPUR · JOHANNESBURG

*Financial Times Management delivers the knowledge,
skills and understanding that enable students,
managers and organisations to achieve their ambitions,
whatever their needs, wherever they are.*

London Office:
128 Long Acre, London WC2E 9AN
Tel: +44 (0)171 447 2000
Fax: +44 (0)171 240 5771
Website: www.ftmanagement.com

A Division of Financial Times Professional Limited

First published in Great Britain in 1992
Second edition 1994
Third edition 1996

© Richard Welford and Kate Prescott 1996

The right of Richard Welford and Kate Prescott to be identified
as Authors of this Work has been asserted by them in accordance
with the Copyright, Designs and Patents Act 1988.

ISBN 0 273 61989 6

British Library Cataloguing in Publication Data
A CIP catalogue record for this book can be obtained from the British Library

10 9 8 7 6 5 4

Typeset by M Rules
Printed and bound in Great Britain by Redwood Books, Trowbridge, Wiltshire

The Publishers' policy is to use paper manufactured from sustainable forests.

CONTENTS

For our families, friends and all those close to us who unquestioningly give their encouragement and support.

PREFACE

The emerging European marketplace

The Single Market of Europe is a continually changing and evolving entity. Two years ago, when the last edition of this book was published, people were talking in terms of a European Community, driven by common trade and intra-Community business practices, but lacking a common framework for economic union. Since that time, the new initiatives introduced by the Maastricht Treaty establishing the convergence criteria for monetary union mean a policy framework is in place for creating one of the largest economic unions in today's global marketplace.

The accession of Finland, Sweden and Austria to the European Union has also extended the scope of power and influence of Europe as a whole. Combined with Norway, Liechtenstein and Iceland, the European Economic Area (which embraces EU principles) represents the largest economic group in the world economy. Other countries, too, have set up their stall to become members of the new economic group – Turkey, Cyprus, Poland and Hungary are all negotiating with the European Commission to secure access in the near future.

Although consolidation of the Single Market and further plans for expansion are beset with uncertainty, particularly in relation to a new common currency and perhaps, in time, political union between the 12 Member States, it is hard to deny that a great deal has already been achieved by Euro-policy makers creating a new business and social environment for the people of Europe.

The Maastricht Treaty set the foundations for much of the new direction to be pursued, and the 1996 Intergovernmental Conference is likely to further consolidate unity and common driving principles for a EU which could, ultimately, include as many as 20 separate Member States.

Events in Eastern Europe in recent years have also demonstrated radical change. While less than a decade ago the dismantling of communism would have been unthinkable, we are now seeing previously centrally-planned economies taking radical steps to develop market economies along the lines enjoyed in the West. Here too, the outcome of the new era is far from certain as we were reminded by the continuing turmoil in the Soviet Union.

The new competitive agenda

So what does the future of the Community hold in store for the Members States? To a great extent it is impossible to say. Nevertheless, it is clear that new business opportunities exist now which have never existed before. Markets are not only opening up, but the communication networks which for so long carved up the EC are being integrated and co-ordinated, providing an environment in which institutions enjoy new freedoms.

Nevertheless, the new European market is dominated by intense competition which raises the stakes for European firms to improve both their efficiency and effectiveness (their competitiveness). At the same time, consumers are enjoying more choice and, in some cases, lower prices as a result of the price competition engendered by the aggressive strategies of the major industrial players. It is inevitable that this new environment will encourage survival of the fittest, and those firms unable to face up to the new challenges posed will perish. Despite such harsh realities though, the firms that adapt to the new operating environment will emerge from the battlefield fitter, leaner and potentially offering more advanced technological products.

Technological development is one of the mainstays of long-term growth in the Community and, to this extent, a variety of policies are being adopted to promote innovation and new technological development to allow European firms to compete in the world arena where new product development, and lead times on innovation, are taking on greater significance. Before the Single European Act (SEA) there was a great deal of concern that European firms were slipping behind their Japanese and American counterparts in the world marketplace. The new impetus to competition in the internal market and a clearer focus on future directions for growth and development provided by the Commission is actively addressing this problem. Although the ultimate success of the initiatives will depend upon the ability of firms to react to the changes brought about by the removal of barriers, the frameworks of legislative change have been carefully designed to foster development of this nature.

Growing talk is of the establishment of flexible organisations, better able to develop systems and structures which permit both adaptability and improved efficiency. This is far from an easy task, although the signs are that firms are embracing this new challenge and employing new, innovative techniques in their management and strategic planning.

Towards economic and social cohesion

Perhaps more importantly, however, the Community is now clearly focused on the issues of monetary and social union, factors which set the EU aside from other leading economic groups. The policy directions outlined in the Treaties extend these concerns into the realm of national sovereign rule, creating a degree of conflict between the Community institutions and the Member States, but providing a clear and all-embracing framework for future development. Indeed, there are those outside of the EC who look with envy at the comprehensive nature of the initiatives proposed to achieve union, recognising its potential to effect the kind of change needed to support a prosperous and buoyant market.

Limitations of the text

German reunification has changed the face of the EU as well as Europe as a whole. However, whilst we recognise the creation of a new Federal Republic of Germany, throughout the book it has often been necessary to refer to East Germany (the GDR) and West Germany as constituted before 3 October 1990. These two parts of Germany remain divided economically and socially; reliable statistics for a united Germany are still unavailable, and this situation is likely to remain so for some time to come.

In addition, much of the comparative data which exists excludes Finland, Austria and Sweden. This has been addressed wherever possible, although some data continues to refer to the 12 Member States in existence prior to 1995.

No book on European business can seek to be prescriptive or to provide all the answers; the rapidity of change within the EU, and indeed in the world beyond, makes that impossible. Our aim, therefore, has been to raise the issues facing European businesses now and in the future, and to provide a general overview of the key topics for people interested in understanding some of the complexities of the Single Market as well as those doing business in Europe.

The history of the EU, institutions and Member States

The book begins in Chapter 1 with an overview of the development of the EU, establishing a context for the current stages of development. Chapter 2 extends the contextual underpinning of the review by providing a background to the Community institutions and their role in shaping the new legislative environment. No business can act in a vacuum, and the EU itself, via its various institutions, will have an impact on every firm and every individual. While this takes a broad EC-wide perspective on the new operating environment, Chapter 3 highlights the particular economic conditions currently dominating the business environments in the individual Member States and looks at the issue of regional policy as a supporting mechanism for development.

Policy review: Monetary union, rules for competition and social integration

Chapter 4 focuses on macroeconomic issues, in particular, the move towards developing a single European currency. Within the current proposals for the Single Market, it will not be possible to achieve full integration without a supporting economic mechanism – the EMU, and greater alignment in Community-wide macroeconomic policy making.

Member States' governments and the Commission have always been keen to monitor mergers between firms and control those with dominant market positions. The Commission is also keen to ensure that there are no impediments to free trade and has, therefore, created a strict framework for competitive behaviour designed to curtail practices which are deemed not to be in the interest of the Community. Chapter 5, focusing on competition policy, covers all these issues and forms a body of knowledge vital to doing business in Europe. Change in the Community is taking place at all levels, including microeconomics, which will have a pervasive effect on every business (and indeed every individual) residing within the 15 Member States. Chapter 6 focuses on workplace issues which will be introduced as part of the Social Charter, ranging from changes in manufacturing techniques to changing relationships between trade unions and firms.

European strategy development

As firms are facing up to new competitive pressures, strategic management in the EU is taking on a new perspective. Firms are employing new techniques and are looking to adopt strategies of 'best practice' as they move from federated organisational structures (based on serving the needs of individual Member States) to more flexible integrated strategic solutions which allow a pan-European vision and strategic objective. These new directions are explored in Chapter 7, which focuses on the challenges ahead for firms operating on EU soil. Chapter 8, which focuses on marketing management in a European context follows on directly from Chapter 7. Although marketing is an integral part of firms' strategy development, change in the marketing discipline as a whole, along with new challenges posed by integration, mean that this topic is worthy of separate comment.

It is not possible for firms to plan and implement their strategies independent of the cultural environment; the Single European Act attempts to remove physical, technical and fiscal barriers but there are no policies which can be introduced to remove cultural barriers between the Member States. These barriers will remain long after the principle policies of the EU have been accepted and catered for. Firms which assume that the Single Market means a homogeneous group of customers with the same demands and wants may be sadly mistaken. Failure to take account of cultural nuances between markets may potentially result in expensive mistakes and, while standardisation may be possible in a variety of business functions, firms need to look closely at the markets of Europe to identify both the commonalities and differences. These issues are discussed in Chapter 9 along with some prescriptions for managing cultural diversity and adopting new business practices.

Europe and beyond

Although the above issues relate specifically to the operations of firms within the EU, it is not possible to attain a comprehensive understanding of the workings of the Single market without addressing some of the wider issues pertinent to the current business environment. The final three chapters of the book consequently broadens the scope of analysis. An issue which is gradually finding its way up the industrial agenda is the environment; global warming, the depletion of the ozone layer and acid rain are largely products of industrialisation. Ethically, businesses have a duty to respond to the environmental challenge, although those who choose to ignore their moral duty to the welfare of the EU will be forced into compliance by new EC legislation. Environmental management is increasingly becoming a part of firm's strategic focus and, as pollution and the threat to the environment of industrial activity observes no physical boundaries, it is more pertinent to examine the environment within a European context. This is the subject of Chapter 10.

Chapter 11 examines the changes in Central and Eastern Europe, and considers both strategies for Western businesses looking East, and Eastern businesses looking towards the markets of the EU. Finally, Chapter 12 examines the EU in a global context and assesses how the Single European Market is impacting on the new world economic order where business is increasingly being dominated by the activities of the global triad (Europe, America and Asia-Pacific). It principally focuses on the activities of non-EU firms within the Community, although some attention is paid to the global arena and its overriding impact on all world business.

Intended market

The book provides a useful resource for introductory courses on European business, and we would envisage its use on specific European business courses at undergraduate, postgraduate and MBA level. It should also be seen as a vital background resource for anyone studying business subjects in the 1990s. European integration will have an impact on all business activities, and any student of business who is not aware of the important issues surrounding the Single Market is not equipped to enter the business world.

CHAPTER 1

The Development of the European Community and the European Union

A BRIEF HISTORY

The idea of creating a political and economic union in Europe is not a new one. Even before the Second World War there were those who thought that there was a need to create a unified Europe to maintain peace in the region and to create a common European culture. Prior to 1945, the forces of nationalism – which we once again see today in Eastern Europe – won and the consequences were not surprising.

Since 1945, the task of creating a secure union of countries in Western Europe has gathered pace. The realisation of interdependence of the defence of Western Europe was marked by the signing of the North Atlantic Treaty in 1949. In many ways, this led to further integration by recognising that, after the Second World War, Western Europe was part of a larger military grouping which separated military decisions from political and economic developments within individual countries. Interestingly, the defence issue is still not fully resolved, with differences of opinion between Member States of the European Union as to the need for a common defence and security policy.

When West Germany's economic recovery began after 1945, it was recognised that there was a need to include the country, not only in the defence of the West, but also in its economic prosperity. This need was heightened by the onset of the Cold War. However, the integration of West Germany had to be achieved without reawakening the nationalism which had torn Europe apart in the past. In particular, some sort of reconciliation acceptable to France was required.

In part, the beginnings of the solution were found by Jean Monet, who is now often seen as the 'father' of the EC. Jean Monet was instrumental in creating the European Coal and Steel Community (ECSC) between France, West Germany, Belgium, the Netherlands, Italy and Luxembourg in 1952. It was argued that it would be more rational to treat the coal and steel industries of the area as a single entity and reap the benefits of a unified market and greater efficiency. Politically, it was also a means of monitoring and supervising the essentials of war-making capacity.

The continuation of the Cold War meant that Western Europe was continually forced to consider its security position, and it was clearly acknowledged that West Germany had to play a part in that. This led to the signing of a European Defence Community (EDC) Treaty in which West Germany was rearmed subject to a number of conditions, and a type of European army was created where small units could be merged into an integrated force under the control of NATO.

The establishment of the ECSC and the EDC led to their member states considering the practicalities of further integrating their economic activities, at the same time as preserving their own economic, domestic and foreign policies. Almost inevitably, it was felt that the 'European experiment' had to be enlarged. In June 1955, foreign affairs ministers of the six ECSC Member Countries met in Messina, Sicily, to investigate the possibilities of further integration. In turn, a committee under the chairmanship of the Foreign Affairs Minister of Belgium, Paul-Henri Spaak, was established, and it is largely their ideas which lay behind the Treaty of Rome. The United Kingdom was invited to participate in the work of the committee but, when it became clear that what was being planned was a union whereby countries would sacrifice a degree of sovereignty to a supranational body, the UK left.

The Spaak Report envisaged a European society with a common economic policy to ensure general economic expansion and measures to develop and fully utilise Europe's basic resources, including human resources. The resulting Treaty of Rome, creating the European Economic Community (EEC), contained detailed plans for the creation of a common market among its signatories but never went as far as creating a political union.

The Treaty was signed in 1957 by the six ECSC members, and the EEC was subsequently established in 1958. The UK opted out and, in effect, eliminated countries such as Ireland and Scandinavia, for which, at that time, the UK was a much more important trading partner than were the six signatories. Austria, Sweden and Switzerland regarded the Treaty as having political overtones incompatible with their status as independent, politically neutral countries. Spain and Portugal were ruled out of membership since they were considered to have undemocratic governments.

Early success in the operation of the common market was demonstrated by the first round of enlargement when the UK, Ireland and Denmark joined in 1973. For the UK, in particular, this was a significant change of policy. However, this change was not brought about by any ideological commitment but by some harsh economic facts. Industries within the EEC were expanding at twice the rate of British industry, and, as a single entity, the UK was lacking its former influence over world affairs. The view amongst many politicians within the UK, therefore, was that outside of the EEC the UK would become weak, isolated and relatively unprosperous.

In 1981, Greece joined the Community, followed by Spain and Portugal in 1986. In 1987 the Single European Act (SEA) became operative. New areas of policy development centred on the intention of having a single internal market in place by the end of 1992, with the free movement of capital, human resources, goods and services. The SEA also strengthened other policy fields, particularly in the areas of competition, social and economic cohesion, health and safety, and the environment.

In 1994, following the meeting in Maastricht, and the signing of the Maastricht Treaty, new plans were laid for realising the objective of monetary union. With legislative proposals in place, the European Community became the European Union, a reflection of its move towards common economic goals.

The next countries to join the Union did so in 1995; Finland, Austria and Sweden, recognising the growing power of the Community, applied for, and were granted, access. In effect, there is now a queue forming to join. Cyprus and Turkey have made formal applications, and Poland and Hungary are in constant negotiation with European officials. Former East Germany became part of the Community upon reunification in 1990.

Increasingly, the EU members have become part of a broader European movement bounded by common histories, both diverse and common cultural values, and a recognition that there is a need to promote compatible political systems. The Maastricht Treaty, the most recent attempt to orchestrate this kind of comprehensive inter-state co-operation, has now emerged as the mainstay of EU policy change and, given the pervasive effect of its proposals, deserves some comment. Before this, however, it is necessary to outline the main objectives of the Single Market and the overall proposals for the future shape of the EU.

OBJECTIVES OF THE SINGLE EUROPEAN MARKET

The real genesis of European integration was brought about in 1985 with the launch of the Commission's White Paper *Completing the Internal Market*. It included a seven year timeframe for completion – a period which was to see numerous legislative proposals designed to create the Single European Market. After a number of false starts, the race for a harmonised Europe was really on.

The White Paper also served as a catalyst; it brought about a period of reassessment amongst EU Member State policy makers and companies who were confronted with the reality of change. Firms and Ministers were forced to wake up quickly to the reality of adapting to a new Single Market and thus everybody became embroiled in the specific details of legislative change. In the headlong charge for the 1992 winning post, the overriding objectives of the creation of the Single Market tended to become obscured.

Generic objectives

Whereas the motivation for the creation of the European Community in 1957 was essentially political, effecting a long-term commitment to a Europe-wide peace by Member States, the driving force for the 1985 reforms was economic. The competitiveness of the EU had been continually falling behind that of Japan and the USA, the world's leading trading nations. This manifested itself in a slowdown in absolute output, high rates of inflation and unemployment, and slow growth in investment and productivity. More seriously, however, Europe exhibited a failure to perform well in new emerging technologies on which the future development of world economic business looked likely to rest.

Unlike their Japanese and American counterparts, European firms were constrained to competition in small national markets. Any attempt to broaden their competitive scope by expanding into other EU nations was hampered by a broad array of barriers, which raised costs and undermined efficiency.

Unlike tariff barriers in the past, these new non-tariff barriers were less obvious and more insidious: not only were technical and legislative differences identified as hindering competition, it also emerged that these differences were being exploited by firms and governments to sustain differential advantages between markets. This meant limiting cross-border expansion by biasing business towards indigenous firms and effectively discriminating against foreign entrants. The blame did not stop here. Restrictions on the free movement of goods, people and capital were equally accused as being detrimental to the economic success of the EU.

Specific objectives

In order to achieve the underlying objective of improving performance it was necessary for the Commission to set more specific targets for the creation of the Single Market. At the head of the list was promoting an improvement in economic performance by lowering costs of operating across Europe.

Cost savings are not achievable overnight and are not direct. Much of the cost saving designed for Europe depends on companies reacting to changes brought about by the new legislation. In the short-term, this means their reacting to the impetus provided by the lowering of barriers by increasing their penetration of the European Union. In the long-term, it requires their reacting to the increased competition effected by their earlier actions, and lowering their prices. Ultimately, price falls will, hopefully, initiate greater demand and greater economic performance. Clearly this complex chain of events provides a great deal of scope for distortion and potential failure. European firms are being targeted as the key *change agents*, the linchpin for the success or failure of Single Market objectives.

Change is being imposed on firms by confronting them with a number of supply-side shocks. Paradoxically, then, deregulation is being prompted through greater regulation. The Commission hopes that this reform is without loopholes for evasion. Like people, however, companies rarely behave quite as expected. Indeed, as they are staffed by people, quirks of character are reflected in company behaviour and consequently the future for Europe is uncertain.

Not all objectives, however, depend on the actions and reactions of European firms. Some of the features of Single Market legislation centre on macroeconomic policy issues. European monetary union – potentially the spearhead of true economic union – gives firms further impetus to respond proactively to the challenges of the Single Market. Monetary union provides the potential to standardise competition through the creation of a single currency and, in so doing, bring about price competition with prices falling to meet the lowest EU common denominator. If coercive supply-side pressures fail to produce the desired reaction from firms, it is unlikely that they will be able to avoid the macroeconomic incentive to change. Similarly, the provisions for social policy across the Community have the power to shape business practices quite considerably, although this is seen by some countries as eroding sovereignty, and even the foundations of their business culture, providing a common framework for social rights will make nations more accountable to their people than has ever been the case in the past.

THE TOOLS FOR ACHIEVING GROWTH

The European Commission has tackled the barriers to pan-EU competition in a number of ways by:

- removing physical barriers
- removing fiscal barriers
- removing technical barriers
- liberalising internal competition through strict competition policy.

Physical barriers

Physical barriers include those that restrict the movement of goods and the movement of people. Frontier controls, for a long time, frustrated European businesses by causing delays and excessive amounts of documentation, raising the costs of moving product across borders.

The elimination of border controls is not possible: countries need to be protected against terrorism and smuggling, and checks need to be made to ensure goods comply with health and hygiene regulations. However, a reduction in paperwork and border 'red tape' has been effected. The introduction of the Single Administrative Document (SAD) in 1988 meant that one form replaced 70 separate sets of paperwork. This too, has now been removed, giving firms complete, document free, movement of goods across borders.

Physical barriers also relate to people. Within the new Single Market people will be free to move around to find work, and companies must be allowed to recruit employees from whichever markets they choose. The major hurdles to this freedom in the past stemmed from the imposition of work permits, personal taxation, differences in social security provisions and non-recognition of qualifications from other Member States.

The opening of border controls for people raises a number of risks concerning national security. A degree of continued regulation is essential to protect countries from international terrorists and the import of drugs and criminals. These issues, in turn, are likely to bring about greater co-operation between police forces in the 15 Member States in a combined effort to crack down on undesirable behaviour within the EU.

Removal of fiscal barriers

Fiscal barriers include restrictions on capital movements as well as differences between tax levels and excise duties. In the former case, greater freedoms in the provision of capital are opening up financial markets to more competition, stimulating a convergence in the cost of capital across the EU. This is an important factor in the achievement of a level playing field. Further, liberalisation of capital movements allows firms unrestricted access to investment in EU markets.

Two particular issues related to fiscal harmonisation are posing problems: Monetary Compensatory Amounts and VAT. Monetary Compensatory Amounts (MCAs) are subsidies designed to eliminate distortions in currency rates between countries in the cross-border movement of agricultural products. Without them, currency differences would cause price differentials between the markets, providing incentives to export goods and disturb the competitive balance of business in agriculture. By removing frontier controls the Commission is removing the check point for managing administration of these funds.

VAT, while posing similar difficulties, is more complicated as it embraces a wide array of sectors. Different VAT rates apply to products between EU markets. Approximating these rates (and establishing common bands) is fraught with difficulties. This is not only because wide differences exist in the amount of tax applied to various products, prompting disagreements over levels, but also the fact that open frontiers changes the way that VAT is levied. Because border controls can no longer be used as the administrative zone for collecting VAT, alternative systems have had to be developed to provide for taxing exports. The solution has been to collect VAT on products as if they were domestic sales with net trade flows being used to determine which country owes what to whom. Although there remain fears that this system will be difficult to police it allows VAT to be collected without intruding on the new found border freedoms.

The removal of technical barriers

Technical barriers, the divergence between technical standards and testing procedures, are seen as an important breeding grounds for inefficiency. With firms adapting products to suit different technological requirements in the 15 Member States, duplication of effort and sub-optimal manufacturing scale works against the kind of efficiency which Japanese and American firms can attain in producing for large domestic markets. These barriers are often regarded as the real culprits in the perpetuation of fragmented markets across Europe. Differences exist across numerous industries and various Member States:

> ... the standard for windscreens ... stops a car built to West German standards being automati-cally sellable in France; the particular way headlights and sidelights must be wired in cars sold in Britain; the way French buildings are insurable unless tiled with French standard tiles; the national favouritism in government for procurement which so often means foreign companies' tenders are unsuccessful; the local banking rule banning the service that a foreign bank is adept at providing.

> (Colchester and Buchan, 1990 p. 80)

Removal of these technical disparities is, more than any other legislative change, likely to facilitate the attainment of greater scale economies.

Liberalisation of competition

While the removal of barriers across Europe is designed to promote increased business, cost savings and greater efficiency, liberalisation of this kind would be pointless without shoring up the rules of competition. Physical, technical and fiscal barriers have all served to protect markets from competition for a long time. Their removal opens up markets to the realities of competition, and in so doing, raises the incentive for governments and firms to look for new forms of protectionism.

Combining the removal of barriers with a rigorous competition policy is essential to the development of the Single European Market. This involves the Commission encroaching on areas of sovereign rule, for instance, governments are no longer allowed to spend money on supporting local industries. This kind of behaviour is seen as distorting market forces and competition and supporting inefficiency.

WHAT THE SINGLE EUROPEAN ACT HOPES TO ACHIEVE

The Cecchini Report (1988) is the most comprehensive document outlining expected achievements of the Single Market. The research team, under the direction of Lord Cockfield, Vice President of the European Commission, set out to determine the economic effects of the completion of the internal market on Members States of the EU. Their overall findings were quite staggering. The identified costs of non-Europe (the inefficiencies brought about by separate, fragmented markets) were estimated to be as much as Ecu 200 billion. Effectively, completing the Single Market, therefore, is expected to produce an equal level of cost saving.

Many of the estimations made by Cecchini have since been challenged, and few observers of the Single Market expect the impact on the EU of 1992 to be any where near as impressive. Nevertheless, the report provides a foundation for the type of benefits which are likely to be realised. Overall, four major consequences are envisaged:

- a reduction in costs resulting from exploitation of economies of scale in production and business organisation

- improved efficiency within companies, industrial re-organisation and a downward pressure on prices under increased competition
- new patterns of industrial competition arising out of a reallocation of resources with real comparative advantages playing the key role
- improved innovation affecting new business processes and products in the dynamic internal market.

Specifically, Cecchini's report lays the foundation for the virtuous circle which the Single Market is expected to achieve. The arguments goes as follows:

1 Removing barriers to intra-EU trade will allow firms to operate, unhindered in a wider Europe. As they take up the opportunities of expanding their European coverage, increasing their output, they are better placed to raise the scale of their manufacturing units (closing the gap between the average scale of EU and USA plants).
2 The lowering of barriers and the stimulus for EU expansion will intensify competition across the markets of the Community.
3 The combined effect of the above two issues is to reduce costs. In the first instance, efficiency provides the scope for cost reductions. In the second, increased rivalry among firms will stimulate price competition.
4 As prices fall, consumers' purchasing power will rise which will increase demand and raise the volume of EU business. Despite greater levels of trade, the downward pressure on prices initiated by greater competition will stifle inflation.
5 Competition encourages firms to innovate and develop new technologies as a way of sustaining long-term advantages.
6 In turn, new technologies will expand through Europe, be produced in larger scale units, face a downward price trend and stimulate further innovation.

The argument is that, once the circle is completed it will roll inexorably on, producing a competitive environment in which EU firms may develop their potential to match that of their leading international rivals.

The downward pressure on prices is also likely to prompt industry rationalisation. As prices fall there will be firms which are unable to react quickly and firms will not be able to produce profits and, consequently, likely to atrophy and die.

Benefits of the Single Market are seen as being particularly pertinent in several industry sectors. Cecchini (1988) highlights financial services, telecommunications services and equipment, automobiles, foodstuffs, building products, textiles and clothing and pharmaceuticals as being those industries where the impact may be most felt. These sectors have traditionally been characterised by a high degree of government regulation and protection and have, through a lack of competition, become inefficient.

The major benefactors from these improvements are customers (which effectively includes everybody in the EU) and firms themselves. Consumers will reap the benefits of lower prices, increased choice and ultimately improved innovation and technological development.

Firms may equally benefit from lower costs. As customers save money through lower prices in finished products, so firms will find cost savings in lower prices for raw materials and intermediate goods. Further cost savings may be made in labour and capital factor inputs as the freedoms in these markets ultimately result in price harmonisation around the lowest industry level. Despite this downward pressure on price, firms are expected to preserve profit margins through improved internal efficiency – in particular, the removal of X-inefficiencies.

WHAT IS ACHIEVABLE?

In the final analysis, what is the Single European Act likely to achieve? There are so many uncertainties associated with the Single European Act and the long-term effects of changing legislation that it is impossible to provide anything but very broad prescriptions for the future of the EU.

What is unquestionable is that the Single European Act will initiate greater harmonisation among the Member States. By standardising technical regulations and removing competitive bias through unfair practices there will be a convergence of conditions between European markets. Nevertheless, the Cecchini Report and other 'promotional' publications choose to ignore those factors that will continue to support fragmentation of markets across the EU. Cultural differences, which are deeply seated within the societies which make up the EU, will not disappear in the wake of 1992. There are certain elements which may never disappear and which may continue to support different consumer attitudes and behaviour and perpetuate a degree of fragmentation across Europe. Indeed, some observers expect an increase in nationalistic behaviour as organisations and individuals attempt to preserve the identity of their culture.

Notwithstanding these sustained barriers to integration, the Single European Act has catalysed interest in the European market and potential opportunities for expansion. As the profile of Europe has been raised on the world stage, firms within the EU, and indeed those from Japan and America, have taken a renewed interest in Europe. This has resulted in a spate of takeovers, particularly by American firms, keen to play an active role in what is now the largest market in the world. It is this, as much as the change in legislation, that is effecting increased competition in the EU.

The encroachment on the EU by foreign firms, supported to an extent by the Commission's external trade policies which have restricted imports and have promoted direct investment, provide an equal opportunity for global multinationals, regardless of their country of origin, to benefit from the potential gains offered by the Single Market.

Monetary Union may provide the key impetus for change within the EU, not only because of the macroeconomic effects brought about by its introduction, but also the fact that this will more effectively link Member States to common policies and directions and prevent firms and governments seeing the Single Market as a way of sub-optimising benefits. Evidence exists among Member States to suggest that full commitment to Europe, with the inherent belief that individual country futures are inextricably linked with European developments, is not a reality. Recent experience, particularly some of the concerns voiced over elements of the Maastricht Treaty, demonstrates that there is still a long way to go before Member States implicitly accept the ethos of a Single Market.

THE MAASTRICHT TREATY

Having set the wheels in motion for economic and social change within the EU, the SEA gave rise to an agenda of momentous change. Developments since that date, however, threw up some important gaps in proposed policy and key problems associated with the process of integration. The Treaty on European union agreed in Maastricht in December 1991 (the so-called Maastricht Treaty) therefore broadens the scope of policy for European union and is now regarded as the most ambitious plan yet to draw together the activities of the 15 Member States of Europe. Amending and adding to the Articles outlined in the Treaty of Rome, the new Treaty has established the guidelines for future development. In particular, EU leaders agreed on protocols to support the new policy, which have, in effect, further empowered the institutions of the EC (the Commission, the European Parliament, the Council of Ministers and the European Court of Justice) to act as the over-riding decision making centre for the 15 Member States.

Absent from earlier proposals were any provisions for a common defence policy and an integrated approach to external affairs. The latter omission, in particular, was regarded as a significant problem given the EU's power in the world economic order and the international political arena. With this in mind, the Treaty has forcefully outlined the intention of the new provisions to assert the identity of the EU on the international scene by implementing a common foreign and security policy ultimately leading to a framework for a common defence policy. Lying at the heart of this new policy is the intention of safeguarding the independence of the EU, strengthening security, promoting international co-operation and preserving peace in line with the United Nations Charter. The new Articles demand greater transparency of information between the Member States on all issues related to security so that the Council may define a common position. Member States will, in future, find that joint decisions made at an EU level are binding (pursuant on a unanimous decision by the Council of Ministers).

This lays the foundation for a common defence policy for the EU wherein it has been confirmed that European policies will not prejudice national defence and will be developed within NATO obligations but will, undoubtedly, mean closer military co-operation between the Member States. While this may potentially touch a nerve with certain Member States, particularly those for whom the armed forces are an integral part of their national heritage, recent global unrest and resultant co-operation between nations has already laid the groundwork for moves in this direction.

If the new Articles are to provide a legal framework for a *United States of Europe*, which is arguably their intent, it is not surprising that economic union is high on the agenda. The Maastricht Treaty outlines three clear stages towards the achievement of economic and monetary union by the 1 January 1999. Stage 1 was launched under existing EU powers with action being taken to improve co-operation and co-ordination between Member States in economic policy, strengthening the European Monetary System and extending the work of the Committee of Central Bank Governors. Conversely, Stages 2 and 3 require new, formal, policy measures provided by the Treaty, principally because they involve setting up new institutions – in particular a European System of Central Banks comprising the European Central Bank and its national counterparts. Within the new Articles, a special protocol has been outlined for the UK, giving it the right to *opt out* unless a decision to proceed to Stage 3 has been agreed by its government and parliament.

Regarding social policy, the UK's failure to accept the new draft provisions mean there will be no change to the existing Articles outlined in the Treaty of Rome as modified by the SEA. The remaining Member States have also agreed to implement the new Social Charter. The UK's failure to accept new policies effectively means it has been excluded from the decision-making process which may potentially serve to widen the gap between the UK and Continental European provisions and make it more difficult for the UK to accept policy change at a later date. It is for this reason, and also the fact that the Maastricht Treaty outlines such a comprehensive and wide-ranging package of policies, that there is some fear that this ardent attempt to unify the Member States of Europe will actually result in a break up of the Community and the backward step in the achievement of real economic union. The results of the Danish referendum rocked the foundations of the economic monolith and resulted in growing divergence between the Member States. France and Germany, on the one hand, have taken these retrogressive steps to catalyse renewed determination to maintain the momentum for the creation of a Single Market. The UK and Italy, on the other hand, took some comfort in the fact that the Danes' public show of reluctance to accept such embracing legislative change gave greater voice to their concerns, in particular those relating to the loss of sovereignty.

The UK's greatest fear concerning economic union, since the early inception of the Single Market, is loss of sovereign rule. This fear has once again reared its head, although this time it is heightened by the fact that the institutions of the EC are continuing to expand their powers and assert their dominance over national authorities. Aware of this concern, and keen not to allow the new agenda to undermine the steps that have already been successfully taken in the establishment of the Single Market, legislators have reaffirmed the concept of subsidiarity. A new Article states *any action by the Community shall not go beyond what is necessary to achieve the objectives of the Treaty*. The basis of subsidiarity is that decision making will be made at the most appropriate level, which recognises that some decisions should remain within the hands of national authorities, particularly those relating to regional development. To this extent, it was hoped subsidiarity would guarantee democracy and diversity. Nevertheless, the concept of subsidiarity is not a panacea for countries who see the loss of sovereignty as concomitant with the demise of national supremacy. Members of the EU implicitly accept that membership equates with EU legal supremacy. Consequently, as the legal framework is extended to incorporate an ever-growing number of key policy areas, an increasing number of key decisions will inevitably be made at EU rather than national level. To an extent, much depends on the ability of national authorities to embrace the ethos of the Single Market in their decisions and encourage shared political commitment. Continuing failure of Member States to incorporate new EC directives in their national legal frameworks will undermine new freedoms of subsidiarity, although the EU would prefer decisions to be made at a national level, the perpetuation of national interest over EU-wide objectives makes such a system potentially ineffectual.

Despite these reservations, the new Treaty further empowers the institutions of the EC to make EU-wide decisions. Most importantly, the European Parliament has been afforded new powers of co-decision with the Council of Ministers. This allows them to reject proposals (by majority vote) if agreement cannot be achieved in a Joint Conciliation Committee. The procedures apply mainly to those policies where are qualified majority on the part of the Council is necessary, covering internal market legislation (including the free movement of goods, services, people and capital) as well as issues related to research and development, trans-European networks (telecommunications, energy and transport infrastructure), education, health, consumer affairs and the multi-annual environment programme.

The Maastricht Treaty has initiated a new momentum for economic union and a small step towards greater political union. Those countries that are finding it difficult to accept the pervasive influence of the new policy agenda, the UK in particular, are faced with a very difficult decision: either accept that change is inevitable and establish national policies to complement those being introduced at EU level or consider the prospect of being left out of one of the major economic dramas ever staged. Sitting on the fence runs the risk of being excluded from decision making to the extent that national interest will go unheard as the European machine ploughs through its economic union furrow. Much uncertainty still remains, not least the future of Eastern Europe, although one thing is eminently clear: the process has come too far to be reversed. The Intergovernmental Conference in 1996 will address many of the concerns which the Maastricht Treaty has raised and will endeavour to promote further unification of the Member States. Central to the agenda is discussion of the long-term development of the EU – the deepening of policies and the widening of its geography.

FURTHER READING

Cecchini, P., *1992: The Benefits of the Single Market*, Wildwood House 1988. This is the abridged version of the full report 'Research on the Cost of non-Europe', published in 12 volumes by the European Commission (1988) and will give further details on the architecture of the Single European Market and the rationale for integration.

El-Agraa, A.M. (1990) *Economics of the European Community*, Third Edition, Phillip Allan. This text takes an economic perspective on European integration including the economic benefits to be derived and the overall impact on European and international competition.

McDonald, F. and Dearden, S., (1992) *European Economic Integration*, Longman. This text outlines the historical perspective of Europe's development and the main areas of policy being introduced for the realisation of a common union.

Roney, A. (1995) *The EC/EU Fact Book*, Fourth Edition, Kogan Page in association with the London Chamber of Commerce. The text looks at topics such as the Treaties of the European Union, legislation, a range of policy issues and a discussion of commercial strategies in Europe.

REFERENCES

Cecchini, P., *1992: The Benefits of the Single Market*, Wildwood House, 1988.

Colchester, N. and Buchan, D., *Europe Relaunched: Truths and Illusions on the Way to 1992*, Economist Books, Hutchinson, 1990.

CHAPTER 2

European Community Law

INTRODUCTION

The creation of the Single European Market – a market which is devoid of barriers to business and offers up a level playing field for competition – has necessitated the creation of a new legal framework for regulating European Union-wide economic activity. This is where the EU differs markedly from other regions and economic groups where the law remains within the bounds of the individual nation state.

In order to achieve the overall objectives of the EU, primacy of European Community law over national rulings was deemed essential. The intention was that new European law would be written into national law, translating EU-wide aims into Member State legal frameworks. This process of translation is beset with problems, not least because new directives are not always seen as being beneficial at national level.

The following discussion focuses on the problems associated with the development of Community law, the systems created to support legal rulings as well as some of the main areas of legal change which will impinge upon the behaviour of institutions across the Single European Market.

PROBLEMS WITH IMPLEMENTING COMMUNITY LAW

Scope of new legislation and the process of adoption

The main problem associated with developing laws which provide a common EU framework is that many developments are detrimental to individual Member State objectives. This has resulted in a degree of reluctance to accept new laws and directives and a consequent time lag in the achievement of EU-wide aims as Member State governments drag their feet in adopting new principles.

It is hardly surprising that attempts to provide a common framework which cuts across 15 separate legal systems face problems of integration. One striking difference between the Member States of the EU is that which exists between English law and that pertaining in the rest of Europe (Scotland, for historical reasons, uses the Continental system of law). English common law emerged as a series of devices aimed at settling disputes, whereas Continental law originated as a system for establishing which rights and duties ought to be accepted as an 'ideal for justice'. To this end, a large body of law in England was created by the courts through rulings on individual cases which had the power to set legal precedence. Alternatively, Continental law was laid down by scholars and then codified through practice.

It is for this reason that many governments have criticised the actions of the European Court of Justice which has, in some cases, pushed through new legislation by making binding decisions. It is arguable that many of these decisions have speeded up EU-wide legal reform which would invariably have ended in stalemate had they been left to political negotiation. The European Court of Justice's ruling in the 1979 *Cassis de Dijon* case provides a good example. West Germany attempted to block French imports of Cassis de Dijon (a blackcurrent flavoured liqueur), as it failed to comply with German law, which laid down a minimum alcohol content of 25 per cent for spirits. Cassis produced in France showed alcohol levels of only 15–20 per cent, significantly lower than the German standard. The European Court of Justice held that German law contravened Article 30 of the Treaty of Rome, prohibiting quantitative restrictions on imports. Although the German ruling did not prohibit import quantities per se, it was considered that all trading rules which hindered intra-EC trade could be considered as imposing quantitative restrictions. The European Court of Justice rejected German claims that the import of such goods would be detrimental to public health (as the low alcohol limit would encourage increased consumption) and without further proof that barring entry was justifiable on such grounds as tax policing, fair trading or consumer protection the European Court of Justice overruled the German ruling.

The essence of the European Court of Justice's ruling in the *Cassis de Dijon* case centred on the notion of *mutual recognition* which compels governments to observe rulings made by other Member States over the activities of foreign firms operating on their soil. This extended the definition of the Single Market beyond a simple free trade area without barriers into a more comprehensive collection of states where legal obligations were to be observed across borders.

The issue of mutual recognition has since been incorporated into legislation dictating the future of many industrial sectors. Mutual recognition of testing procedures and licenses in the pharmaceutical industry, and guidelines for financial instruments in financial services are an important part of the process of opening up markets and actively encouraging European expansion. It is difficult in sectors, such as these, to adopt a common approach to legislation without invoking reaction due to political sensitivity. Mutual recognition importantly establishes new freedoms without requiring immediate harmonisation of standards and practices which, due to pervasive differences in local regulations, would potentially result in a protracted period of negotiation, slowing down the process of liberalisation.

Perhaps more importantly, however, the *Cassis de Dijon* case set a precedent for supranational Community law; pan-European provision superseding individual Member State considerations. This provided one of the most important blows to national sovereignty: the ruling effectively precluded governments from refusing access to goods emanating from other European countries. It is now only possible for governments to bar access to goods if they can show that morality, health, safety or the environment are at risk.

Other test cases have also allowed the European Court of Justice to set new directions for a comprehensive Community legal framework. The *Nouvelles Frontiers* case in 1986 suggested that competition rules could be applied to government run air transport which, like the *Cassis de Dijon* case, has significantly shaped future developments in the area of competition policy. Control of government owned national services have come under fire in recent years as the European Commission has sought ways to break down national monopolies and foster competition in sectors which have usually been shielded from the rigours of competitive pressures and have consequently become 'fat and lazy'.

As a result of this case approach to Community law provision, the UK is understandably satisfied with the process. Other countries are less approving of the system, and question whether the European Court should be given the freedom to shape new legislation. Part of the argument against this kind of development is that it precludes 'fair' representation from the Member States, or even the regions. With Community-wide law increasingly dictating social, environmental and cultural policies, there is great scope for local dissatisfaction over new rulings. The inclusion of regional representatives in the decision making process is not feasible, principally because it would result in too many conflicting interests. The Treaty of Rome, therefore, only recognises central governments who are responsible for adopting Community directives in local laws at both a national and regional level.

The process of national adoption is typically slow. Although the issuance of *regulations* requires immediate action, being automatically applicable from the moment they are published, *directives*, which permit Member States discretion of how they should incorporate new objectives into national law, take time. Therefore, while the results to be achieved through the imposition of new directives are binding, the form and methods of their imposition are left up to the individual state. As a consequence, directives are understandably preferred by the Member States as they allow greater freedom over their incorporation into local legal systems. There is therefore a time clause involved in the issuance of directives which gives governments a period of adjustment to the new legislation.

Nevertheless, there are some countries which have continued to dally in the adoption of new rulings. Italy stands out as the worst offender, and while the government shows great willingness to accept new proposals, the failure to put new directives into practice has resulted in the European Court of Justice issuing second rulings in a number of cases, for example, the ruling made in 1987 ordering compliance on a 1983 ruling regarding the inspection of fruit and vegetables had still not been met in 1992. This highlights one of the key limitations of the European Court of Justice; it has no dedicated policing mechanism to enforce rulings. This raises the second key problem associated with the imposition of European law, the fact that penalties imposed for breaking laws are left up to the Member States.

Divergence in imposed penalties

Individual Member States are the arbiters of fines and penalties which results in a wide disparity in the sanctions imposed for breaking laws. The problems associated with such broad differences in penal interpretation goes far further than antagonising firms and institutions which are treated more harshly than their foreign counterparts. Variance in the imposition of penalties has the potential to cause conflict between those Member States taking a hard line against domestic offenders (supporting the EU's objectives) and those taking a lenient stance or failing to act on specific judgements. It is easy to imagine such conflict resulting in a renewed period of reciprocity demands and covert protectionism, which is quite clearly out of keeping with the major objectives of the Single European Market. But what are the answers? The Commission has ruled against coercion and preferred to rely on policing by the individual or the institution. This means that compliance with the law and the impact of public opinion on the setting of fines and penalties is regarded as critical to the effective development of an EU-wide framework.

There is evidence of this kind of activity in the realm of competition policy (*see* Chapter 5) where firms which have borne the brunt of unfair practices are flagging offenders to the Commission. The Commission's lawyers hope that this kind of vehemence will be shown in other areas of Community law and that self-policing will become the essence of the translation of centrally established directives into local constitution. It should be noted, however, that competition law differs from other areas of new provision in that the Commission imposes fines which fosters greater commonality and overall acceptance.

Incompatibility with sovereign rule

Running in parallel with EU concerns are those pertinent to the individual Member States. Many of these are not compatible with wider European objectives, which can raise tensions between the Commission and the Member States. Although no country has flagrantly refused to comply with Community rulings (as this would effectively mean their rejecting their membership of the Union) many cases exist where individual countries have challenged the supremacy of Community law by claiming that it contravenes local legal provisions. Notwithstanding these tensions, however, membership of the Union involves governments accepting Community legal supremacy which suggests that finding ways to incorporate Community law in local frameworks is more beneficial than challenging new legislation.

The UK, through the House of Lords and the 'rule of construction approach' has demonstrated a willingness to adapt legal guidelines to comply with Community rulings. A test case regarding Article 119 of the Treaty of Rome demonstrates this principle. Article 119 asserts that men and women should receive equal pay for equal work. *Pay* is defined as ordinary wages or salary and any other considerations whether they be in cash or in kind received directly or indirectly by the employee. The case between *Garland v British Rail Engineering Ltd* concerned the provision of special travel facilities offered by British Rail to its workers. In the event, there was a clash between the UK's Equal Pay Act 1970 and Article 119. The former makes no provision in connection with death or retirement while the latter provides the basis for entitlement of special travel facilities to former employees after retirement, even though there was no formal contract stipulating such an arrangement. The House of Lords ruled in this case that provisions laid down in the Equal Pay Act 1970 must be construed so as to conform with Article 119.

Thus, in situations where Community law is not seen to be directly effective, the UK courts can accord priority to Community law by interpreting UK law *purposively* to comply with the spirit and purpose of the Union's provisions. By accepting the supremacy of Community law over Acts of Parliament, the UK has implicitly indicated its commitment to the new European agenda and adapted its approach in line with the overall intentions of the Single Market. To an extent, it means the UK has relinquished sovereign rule.

Conversely, in Belgium, Community law is incorporated into domestic law through statute. Until a legal ruling in 1972 on the importation of dairy products, there was no provision in the constitution for the supremacy of international law. It was ruled that the Belgian government had contravened Article 12 (which prohibits governments introducing any new customs or excise duties on imports). The Belgian courts accepted the abolition of the duties, and in so doing, implicitly accepted that in disputes between national law and the Union Treaty, the Treaty must prevail.

The French have continued to find it difficult to accept the supremacy of Community law, possibly as a result of their propensity to reinterpret legal statutes and find loopholes in the law. With the Single Market now a reality, the French have had to review their legal systems, once adjudged as being inaccessible and archaic. Test cases, in rulings made by both Cour de Cassation and the Conseil de Etat, mean that acceptance of Community legal supremacy has been achieved, albeit through a degree of enforcement rather than ready compliance. This was particularly the case with the Conseil de Etat which refused to accept the supremacy of the Community Treaty until representatives were elected to the European Parliament in 1977.

The supremacy of Community law posed severe challenges to German constitution which has traditionally been applied with great rigour. Germany challenged Community provisions for failing to provide adequate protection of fundamental rights, the constitutional court ruling that until such provisions were made, German constitution would continue to be observed. The European Court of Justice, however, found that no proposed measures contravened the German constitution, resulting in an overruling of the German decision. However, acceptance of supremacy is not universal in the German legal system. In 1981 and 1986 the German Federal Tax Court refused to observe directives, refusing to permit tax payers exemptions laid down in Community law. While the decision was overturned in the Constitutional Court, it provides evidence of the problems associated with integration of Community legal statutes into local law.

Although resistance to Community legal supremacy is apparent in most Member States, membership of the Union means that ultimate acceptance is inevitable. This reinforces the need for national governing bodies to develop systems to integrate new Community Treaty provisions into local frameworks in order to facilitate the process of unification. By continuing to challenge new legislation local authorities simply slow down the momentum of change and add to the already heavy burden on the European Court of Justice.

Subsidiarity

Before moving on, it is important to look briefly at the concept of subsidiarity which has been introduced to counterbalance concerns over loss of sovereign rule. It is arguable that the concept of subsidiarity has been introduced to placate Member States and its actual effect is limited. Prior to the Edinburgh summit in 1992 a European Commissioner is reported as suggesting the EU would be able to agree

> a text sufficiently meaningless to everyone on subsidiarity, to get through the artificially pumped-up debate on how to divide power between the Union and the Member States.

While the introduction of the concept may potentially serve as a reminder to the Commission that some policies are best left to national authorities, the Commission remains the arbiter of the most appropriate level of decision making. In addition, as the Commission's main role is establishing policies which draw together the 15 Member States, it is likely that their concerns will be most effectively debated and concluded at a supranational rather than national level. The key question, therefore, appears to be – does subsidiarity offer any succour to national authorities concerned about a loss of sovereignty?

Article 3b of the Maastricht Treaty asserts:

> The Community shall act within the limits of the powers conferred upon it by the Treaty and of the objectives assigned to it therein. In the areas which do not fall within its exclusive competence, the Community shall take action, in accordance with the principle of subsidiarity, only if and in so far as the objectives for the proposed action cannot be sufficiently achieved by the Member States and can therefore, by reason of scale or effects of the proposed action, be better achieved by the Community. Any action by the Community shall not go beyond what is necessary to achieve the objectives of this Treaty.

The ambiguity of this statement (described by Lord Mackenzie-Stuart, former president of the European Court of Justice, as '*a disgraceful piece of sloppy draftsmanship, so bad that one is forced to assume it must be deliberate*') gives little comfort to those who believe that some sort of counter-measure is necessary to dilute the overriding power of the Commission. To an extent, however, the technical minutiae of many of the policies which have been debated by the Community's institutions (such as noise levels for lawn mowers, specifications for tractor wheels, or what does and what does not constitute a sausage), have tended to obscure the real point of unification – a common set of operating standards – and raised concerns at a national level over the Commission's powers and intent, making more locally based decisions desirable.

There is also some fear that the notion of subsidiarity will encourage national governments to take a retrogressive step, challenging new policies (such as new competition rules) and arguing that the support of national institutions is legitimate to national sovereign concerns. It also has the potential to encourage greater regional autonomy. In the UK, for instance, subsidiarity has been defined in the new national constitution to suggest '*functions should be exercised at the lowest practicable level of government*' and '*decisions must be taken as closely as possible to the citizen*'. This means that Scotland, Wales and Ireland see new opportunities for greater local decision-making power, which is clearly at odds with central government's rejection of local democracy.

Clearly, then, there remains a great deal of confusion over what the concept of subsidiarity actually offers the Member States. At the Edinburgh summit it was suggested that the completion of an internal market should be based on a notion of *quasi-federalism* in which '*national legislation will not be replaced but framed in a way that respects minimum Community requirements*'. Sir Leon Brittan suggested:

> If the decision does not need to be taken at Community level, the Commission will be wise to set out the general objective, but leave it to the individual Member State to achieve that as they wish, according to their own traditions and their own laws.

This implies that the new legal framework for Europe will arise from 'directives' rather than *regulations* which allows a degree of flexibility in the adoption of new laws. This kind of thinking is confirmed in the Maastricht Treaty through the desire '*to deepen the solidarity between their peoples, while respecting their history, their culture and their traditions*'.

As the Single Market programme is dynamic, and the role and power of the institutions continually changing, it is possible that subsidiarity will taken on greater effect in the future once the Member States have been drawn together to a sufficient degree. At the moment, failure of nations to demonstrate true commitment to the new Europe and lack of mutual trust between the 15 Member States as well as between the European institutions, necessitates the Commission taking a firm hand against offenders. As attitudes change, and the notion of a single market is readily embraced by national governments, more power may be afforded to nations and, indeed, the regions, as governments and organisations work willingly within a common framework. Until that time, it is probable that a degree of conflict will remain between national governments and central decision-making bodies as a result of concerns over sovereignty. Nevertheless, subsidiarity offers the potential to accommodate both uniformity through supranational co-operation and the desire to retain sufficient control at a local level. Much, therefore, depends on the way in which the Commission chooses to interpret the ambiguity of the subsidiarity provision. It could well be argued that they would be wise to heed the concerns of the Member States as the continuing sovereignty debate potentially threatens the momentum of the Single Market programme. Equally, they need to carefully consider the role of the Commission and look more towards developing systems which prompt political co-operation between different levels of government and decision-making authorities, rather than concern themselves with drawing lines of demarcation.

THE INSTITUTIONS AND MECHANISMS RESPONSIBLE FOR LEGAL CHANGE

There are four principal Community institutions responsible for developing and implementing law: the European Parliament, the Commission, the Council of Ministers and the European Court of Justice. In order to understand the workings of the Community it is necessary to outline the role and activities of each institution.

The European Parliament

The European Parliament represents the voice of the people in EU decision making. Originally, the European Parliament was afforded certain supervisory powers (particularly over the Commission) and the right of participation in the legislative process. In conjunction with the EU 'deepening' these powers has been the further extension of them, incorporating budgetary powers, European political co-operation, culture and education, giving Parliament far greater influence in the Community system. Nevertheless, it has generally been accepted that the Parliament has limited constitutional power vis-à-vis national legislation, and it is more of a symbolic Parliament than governing body. Unlike national Parliaments, it does not elect a government (no 'traditional' government existing at Community-level), governmental style decision making being performed by the Commission and the Council of Ministers.

The basic mechanism for supervision rests on addressing questions to the Commission and the Council. Equally, Members and senior officials of the Commission are often present at the European Parliament's committee meetings which enhances a two-way flow of information and provides greater integration of the Parliament into the decision-making body of the Community. The role of Parliament has also been extended by the submission of the Commission's annual programme of work which enables on-going supervision of policies rather than simple retrospective checks on the Commission's activities.

Parliament also has the ultimate power of sanction over the Commission which permits a motion to be sanctioned if a two-thirds majority of votes cast is obtained. In such an event, the Commission would be compelled to resign as a body. In relation to the Council of Ministers, there are a number of areas outlined in the Treaties in which the Council cannot enact legislation without first consulting the European Parliament (mandatory consultation). A practice of non-mandatory consultation has also developed (optional consultation) wherein the Council consults Parliament on issues even when it is not obligatory. This has helped to strengthen Parliament's position in the decision-making process. Despite this, however, Parliament's decisions are not officially binding. The Commission has attempted to adopt amendments made by Parliament wherever possible, submitting them to the Council, and has undertaken to explain in detail their reasoning behind failure to adopt proposed amendments. A similar undertaking has also been given by the Council of Ministers.

Perhaps most importantly, however, is the necessity of the Council consulting Parliament on the most significant Council legislation. If the Council acts without requesting Parliament's opinion, then laws passed will be deemed invalid by the European Court of Justice. This is not to suggest that Parliament's approval is necessary for the passing of legislation, just that their opinions must be sought before rulings can be made. In 1980, the European Court of Justice wielded its power in this way, stating that the Council's ruling on the *Isoglucose* case was invalid because of the failure to consult Parliament on the matter. The court ruled that consultation with Parliament is a fundamental democratic principle which allows the people of the EU, through their European Parliamentary representatives, to exercise their sovereign power.

Similarly, in 1985, Parliament ruled that the Council had violated the Treaty of Rome in relation to the common transport policy. The Court welcomed the MEPs' action and ruled against the council for failing to establish a common transport policy in two areas. The reverse side of the coin is that the European Court of Justice is able to review the legality of acts by Parliament.

It is still the norm for most Treaty Articles to require one reading or consultation. Once a common position has been achieved on new legislation by the Commission, it is communicated to the European Parliament which is then given three months to comment on the proposal and suggest amendments. Where no amendments are made or the common position approved, the Council adopts the Act in question definitively. If within the time limit, however, amendments are recommended by an absolute majority of MEPs', the Council's common position is rejected. The Commission then has one month to review the proposal in the light of the proposed amendments, and the Council must than accept the proposal unless further amendments are deemed necessary by unanimous decision. The European Parliament's power, then, is limited and can be exerted only where the Commission adopts its amendments. This power of influence may be extended by pressuring the Commission, which usually takes the form of Parliamentary voting on amendments. If the amendments are accepted Parliament then votes for the legislative resolution of the amendments leading to their incorporation in the Commission's proposal. If, however, the amendments are rejected, Parliament has the right to judge the Commission's position 'unsatisfactory', delaying the progress of the proposal by referring it back to the appropriate Parliamentary Committee for further comment.

For 10 Community Treaty Articles, extra legislative stages have been added to give Parliament second readings. Once amendments have been made by the Commission, the proposal is passed to the Council to adopt a 'common position' and then referred back to Parliament for further comment. Although, once again, Parliament lacks any real legislative power, this process persuades the Commission and the Council to take the opinions of Parliament seriously. The most notable area included under this new ruling relates to the area of harmonisation measures specifically designed to achieve the objectives of the Single Market.

Three other key roles are also accorded to Parliament:

1 Parliament is permitted to participate in policy discussions with the Commission at the pre-proposal legislative stage. The Commission may test out feelings towards a proposed policy by consulting Parliament at an early stage in policy development as a means of ensuring later acceptability. Parliamentary committees can also directly suggest potential initiatives to the Commission. Alternatively, Parliament can itself, take the initiative and present proposal reports for legislative formulation.
2 Parliament can intervene on budgetary matters, amending proposals and delaying

implementation. The Commission is responsible for drawing up a draft budget which is then sent to the Council for formal establishment before being sent on to Parliament for approval or amendment. Parliament is given 45 days to suggest amendments before handing it back to the Council for final ratification. Parliament requires a majority of 315 votes to accept the final budgetary proposals, failure to reach this consensus leading to overall rejection of the budget, as occurred in 1979 and 1984.

3 Parliament has a key role to play in EU enlargement where absolute consent (260 votes) is required before a new Member can be accepted.

Members of the European Parliament (MEPs) were first elected in June 1979 before which time they were nominated by national Parliaments. Nevertheless, even now an electoral approach has been adopted, there is no common electoral systems with the UK maintaining its 'first past the post' philosophy and the remaining 11 Member States each adopting some form of proportional representation. Until the UK sees fit to change its approach, it is unlikely that a uniform electoral system will be achieved. Each elected MEP serves a five-year term of office.

Most activity in the European Parliament is channelled via individual political groups. These can be established with a minimum of 26 MEPs if originating in a single state, 21 from two Member States and 16 from three or 13 from four or more. To an extent, it is unsurprising that these groups have formed given the propensity of MEPs to gravitate towards others with similar political ideals. There is also great incentive to widen the group given that funds distribution for political groups is partly based on numbers.

In the 1994 elections, the number of people in the Parliament was raised from 518 to 572, and following the accession of Finland, Austria and Sweden this was raised to 626 (comprising 16 for both Austria and Finland and 22 for Sweden). The breakdown of the European Parliament as at 17 January 1995 is shown in Table 2.1.

Table 2.1. Distribution of seats in the European Parliament

Party	B	DK	D	GR	E	F	IRL	I	L	NL	A	P	FIN	S	UK	Total
PES	6	3	40	10	22	15	1	18	2	8	8	10	4	11	63	221
EPP	7	3	47	9	30	13	4	12	2	10	6	1	4	6	19	173
ELDR	6	5	–	–	2	1	1	6	1	10	1	8	6	3	2	52
EUL	–	1	–	4	9	7	–	5	–	–	–	3	1	1	–	31
FE	–	–	–	–	–	–	–	29	–	–	–	–	–	–	–	29
EDA	–	–	–	2	–	14	7	–	–	–	–	3	–	–	–	26
Greens	2	–	12	–	–	–	2	4	1	1	1	–	1	1	–	25
ERA	1	–	–	–	1	13	–	2	–	–	–	–	–	–	2	19
EN	–	4	–	–	–	13	–	–	2	–	–	–	–	–	–	19
IND	3	–	–	–	–	11	–	11	–	–	5	–	–	–	1	31
Total	25	16	99	25	64	87	15	87	6	21	16	25	16	22	87	626

PES	Groups of the Party of European Socialists	EDA	Groups of the Economic Democractic Alliance
EPP	Group of the European People's Party	Greens	Green Group in the European Parliament
ELDR	Group of the European Liberal Democratic and Reformist Party	ERA	Group of the European Radical Alliances
		EN	Europe of Nations Group
EUL	Confederal Group of the European United Left	IND	Not Attached
FE	Forza Europa Group		

The Groups of the party of European Socialists (PES) is clearly the largest group with 198 members, over a third of which are from the UK, headed by Pauline Green. The Group of the European People's Party (EPP), with 157 members, is headed by the former Belgian Prime Minister, Wilfried Martens. The group comprises just 19 UK Conservatives. In the last round of elections the Group of European Liberal Democratic and Reformist Party (ELDR) lost a significant number of seats (down to 52 from 122) and now have no German Members.

The European Parliament holds, on average, a one week part-session every month with additional sessions being run on specific topics. These sessions are complemented by plenary sessions held each year (since 1985) in Strasbourg, as well as meetings of the 50 working bodies, committees, sub-committees, working parties and delegations.

There has, in recent years, been increased co-operation between parliamentary committees and their national counterparts, most usually in the form of small national delegations from both parties. In recognition of the fact that EC Treaties have the power to place national powers in the hands of the Council of Ministers, national Parliaments have created specialist bodies to ensure information exchange with their MEPs who are, importantly, their formal representatives in EU issues. With this key role to play, most Member States choose their own candidates for European elections to ensure adequate representation and ensure party concerns are represented. As a result of this factor, MEPs can find themselves caught between the desires of their national political party on the one hand, and their European political affiliations on the other.

Finally, the growing power of the European Parliament should be stressed. Although it has no real legislative power, its consultative power should not be overlooked. As the pace of unification accelerates the Parliament is taking on a more deterministic role in EU destiny, partly as a result of greater power invested upon it, but also because it has attempted to find ways of extending its influence. Although it remains a long way from being a true parliament with the decision-making authority traditionally associated with national parliamentary bodies, its pivotal role in policy making makes it an essential actor in the Single Market initiative. With talk of political union being a long-term reality, the potential for radical change is not out of the question. As the EU becomes more involved with representing the needs of the people rather than the needs of nations, a ruling Parliament, directly elected and wielding real power, will be essential. Equally, with the move towards European Monetary Union increased, concentration of public spending will be afforded to Brussels which reinforces the need for a central administrative body.

The Council of Ministers

The Treaty of Rome established a grouping of independent sovereign states, but did not establish a new federal state. Therefore, the key European institution is the Council of Ministers which represents the interests of the 15 Member States. It was originally intended by the architects of the Single European Market that power would ultimately pass to a democratically elected assembly as trust between the Member States increased and the importance of sovereign rule diminished. This has not happened with issues of sovereignty continuing to dog the unification process and tensions between individual states being, in some cases at least, revitalised by Single Market initiatives which favour one state over another. Consequently, the Council remains the key decision-making body.

The main function of the Council is to formulate Community law. Although the Commission has some power in this respect, the Council presides alone in key, politically driven and sensitive, legislation. The Treaty of Rome rules that the Council should only act on Commission proposals which it may then turn into legal Acts. Nevertheless in practice, the Council acts as an important initiator of policy directions. This has resulted partly from the numerous grey areas which have emerged since the Treaty was drafted with policies being outside of specific provisions, but also the fact that the Council has developed its own dynamism which makes it a fairly sophisticated decision-making body which is respected by the Member States as being representative and fair.

The Council is made up, in essence, of several councils which are representative of different ministries, for example, the Ministry of Agriculture and the Ministry of Transport (*Technical Councils*) as well as Foreign Ministries (*General Councils*). Meetings of the latter group are generally believed to hold higher status than the technical councils which reflects the critical role of the Council in external EU policy development (a role from which the European Parliament is exempted altogether).

As Council membership varies, and members continue to hold down full-time posts within their own nations, most of the actual work is conducted by the Committee of Permanent Representatives (COREPOR) whose function it is to filter through the proposals before passing them on to the Council for a final decision. COREPOR was established in 1958 and comprises of ambassadorial civil servants who liaise between national officials and the Commission. The complexities of this liaison role has resulted in a high degree of bureaucracy in which the division between national and EU interests often becomes blurred.

Whereas the Commission remains a neutral agent in orchestrating EU policy, the same cannot be said for the Council, where individual representatives are intent on getting the best deals for their own state. Similarly, the six month presidency rotation system enables Member States to push through those policies it wishes to see adopted. However, this is not necessarily detrimental to the overall achievement of a unified Europe as it ensures that the policy directives are reflective of key national agendas and means that conflicting ideologies are well catered for in the process of change.

In the run up to 1992, pressure on the Council to effect rapid change meant that the voting procedure had to be adapted. Originally, the Treaty laid down that all decisions required a unanimous vote before implementation was possible. It is not surprising, given the problems of unifying the objectives of, then, 12, separate nations with distinct political and economic agendas, that consensus was often difficult to achieve. This led the Council to consider a system of compromise. Disagreement between France and the other Member States on the future organisation of the EU meant that some kind of compromise was essential. The basis for this is the *Luxembourg Compromise* which suggests:

> Where, in the case of decisions which may be taken by a majority vote on a proposal from the Commission, very important interests of one or more partners are at stake, the Members of the Council will endeavour, within a reasonable time, to reach solutions which can be adopted by all the Members of the Council while respecting their mutual interests and those of the Union.

> (European Parliament Fact Sheet En I/B/2)

This threw into relief the inadequacies of the Council's decision-making process and resulted, in 1985, in agreement being reached on the abolition of unanimity and replacement with a system of qualified majority. The qualified voting system is based on a weighting procedure which gives the 'big four' ten votes, Spain eight votes, Belgium, Greece, Portugal and the Netherlands five votes, Austria and Sweden four votes, Denmark, Finland and Ireland three and Luxembourg two. A qualified majority requires a minimum of 62 votes out of a total of 87. It is, therefore, now only in relation to fiscal measures, free movement of people and social rights that unanimity is required.

This relaxation of decision-making strictures has undoubtedly undermined national control over the activities of ministers in the Council. With the new voting system enabling ministers to be outvoted in the Council, national interests may go unheard. This has led to countries questioning the *democratic deficit* where decisions are made with little consultation of national Parliaments. This has led some to argue in favour of granting the European Parliament greater power although this solution too has its detractors particularly those who continue to argue for retention of sovereignty and increased involvement of national governments in EU decision making.

The relationship between the Council and the Commission was, to a great extent, described in the above section. Stated simply, the Council acts on proposals issued by the Commission in the establishment of EC legislation, with the European Parliament providing a 'sounding board' for the acceptance of new regulations and directives.

The Council of Ministers should not be confused with the European Council which is a regular summit of Heads of State and their Foreign Ministers. While there was no legal basis for the European Council in the Treaty of Rome, it arose out of Summit Conferences of Heads of State as a means of discussing the problems of achieving European unity. Meetings are held at least twice a year and, while they are expressly informal, they do initiate decisions and directives for future action. They are also often able to settle problems which the Council of Ministers has failed to resolve because of the status of their participants. The European Council is an important step forward in inter-EU co-operation at the highest level and, while its activities are not regulated by the Treaty of Rome, it has the power to establish the main economic and political guidelines for the future development of the EU. Its proposals are passed on to the Council of Ministers to be translated into formal Community guidelines.

Over its history, the European Council has addressed a wide range of issues including implementation procedures, trade relations with Japan and the USA, unemployment in the EU and amendments to the original Treaty. On many occasions it has not been possible for the European Council to come to an agreement on issues (notably the draft budget for 1988, elimination of farm surpluses, structural fund resources) although the on-going dialogue between political heads means that there is a growing commitment towards EU policy. Unlike other agents of change, the European Council is an inter-governmental policy initiator rather than a supranational actor and while some theorists argue that this is detrimental to the development of a single unified market, others argue vehemently that the European Council provides an important 'safety valve' when alternative channels of decision making fail.

The Commission

The Commission is now headed by 20 civil servants representing the 15 Member States who are chosen to represent the interests of the EU rather than individual countries. As a result, the Commission is the most supranational body involved in the machinery of the Single Market. Each Member State must be represented by at least one Commissioner, but no Member State may have more than two nationals. In essence, this results in the largest nations – 'the big four', plus Spain, sending two Commissioners and the smaller states one each. Commission members are appointed by common agreement of the Member States to serve a four-year term, which is renewable. On appointment, the Commissioners are compelled to swear an oath of allegiance to the EU promising to put EU interests before national objectives.

Theoretically at least, the Commission is independent of national governments although, as national nominees, they are chosen as much for their national loyalty as their potential to demonstrate loyalty to the EU. This was clearly apparent in the refusal of Margaret Thatcher to renew Lord Cockfield's term of office, as she argued he had 'gone native' and put EU considerations above those of the UK. To an extent, however, it is useful for Commissioners to retain a degree of national concern as it permits national interests to be brought to the fore in Commission decisions which aids the integration of Member States.

The distribution of policy roles between the Commissioners is achieved via negotiation although ministers actively lobby the President in order to attain key roles, as observed from a national perspective. The Commission members are assisted by a group of political officials ('a cabinet') who perform an advisory and co-ordinating function. Comprising around six members, the cabinet is usually made up of fellow nationals, with the stipulation that at least one should come from another Member State. The Commission is organised into 23 Directorates General, each of which covers a particular area of policy and a number of specialist units and support services (outlined in Table 2.2). Beneath this executive level, the Commission employs around 15 000 permanently employed civil servants.

Commissioners are responsible for a portfolio of policies and therefore preside over various Directorates General which means that lines of responsibility and accountability are often blurred. This adds to the bureaucratic nightmare of managing such a huge operation which has resulted in many accusations of inefficiency. Nevertheless, the enormity of the task of attempting to integrate 15 Member States, as well as having to work in 11 different languages it is not surprising that decision-making procedures are often complicated and take a long time.

The Commission undertakes three basic tasks: initiating EU action, acting as 'guardian of the Treaties', and implementing policies. While it was pointed out earlier that both Parliament and the Council of Ministers play a subsidiary role in initiating new policy measures, the bulk of this activity rests with the Commission. It is through the formulation of legislative measures that the Commission advances the development of the Single European Market. It is for this reason that the Commission is often described as the 'driving force' of the EU.

The Commission has an almost free hand over the development of policy agendas and it is not untypical for the Commission to pass between 700–800 proposals, recommendations and drafts to the Council each year. However, as a result of the institutional crisis of 1965 (resulting from France's unwillingness to accept supranationalism), proposals have been importantly influenced by the likelihood of adoption by the Council. In this particular instance, the Commission had announced a proposal for introducing import levies on agricultural goods (to be paid directly to the Commission) and the granting of greater power of budgetary decision to the European Parliament (then the European Assembly). This would have effectively enhanced the powers of both the Commission and Parliament at the expense of the Council, wherein lies the most national influence. This move was rejected by the French government who feared the loss of national sovereignty concomitant with this shift in power and the provision for a system of majority voting. The French, as a result, boycotted the Community. The situation was resolved through the *Luxembourg Compromise* (discussed above) which laid the foundation for consultation with Member State governments before the issuance of new proposals:

> Before adopting any particular important proposal, it is desirable that the Commission should establish the appropriate contacts with the Governments of the Member States through the Permanent Representatives, without this procedure compromising the right of initiative which the Commission derives from the Treaty.

Table 2.2. Directorates General and Special Units of the Commission

Directorates General

DGI	External Relations
DGII	Economic and Financial Affairs
DGIII	Internal Market and Industrial Affairs
DGIV	Competition
DGV	Employment, Industrial Relations and Social Affairs
DGVI	Agriculture
DGVII	Transport
DGVIII	Development
DGIX	Personnel and Administration
DGX	Information, Communication and Culture
DGXI	Environment, Nuclear Safety and Civil Protection
DGXII	Science, Research and Development
DGXIII	Telecommunications, Information Industry and Innovation
DGXIV	Fisheries
DGXV	Financial Institutions and Company Law
DGXVI	Regional Policies
DGXVII	Energy
DGXVIII	Credit and Investments
DGXIX	Budgets
DGXX	Financial Control
DGXXI	Customs Union and Indirect Taxation
DGXXII	Co-ordination and Structural Policies
DGXXIII	Enterprises' Policy, Distributive Trades, Tourism and Social Economy

Special Units and Services

Secretariat General of the Commission
Legal Service
Spokesman's Service
Translation Service
Joint Interpretation and Conference Service
Statistical Office
Consumer Policy Service
Joint Research Centre
Task Force 'Human Resources, Education, Training and Youth'
Euratom Supply Agency
Security Office
Office of Official Publications of the European Communities

A variety of advisory committees and consultative bodies provide the major sounding board for new policy initiation. Such institutions as the expert committees (which usually discuss initiatives at the pre-proposal stage, that is, before they are passed on to the Council), and the consultative committees (including general groups such as the Union of Industries in the EU, and specialised organisations, such as the Committee of Transport Unions in the EU), provide the impetus for policy generation.

Acting as guardian to the Treaties, the Commission is responsible for ensuring that obligations are met, and that infringements of Community law are investigated and, if necessary, taken to the European Court of Justice. This role extends the Commission's sole responsibility for the implementation of Competition Policy (including state aid and subsidies) and the right to sanction and penalise offenders. This power does not extend to other areas of infringement where the Commission has to rely on the goodwill and judgement of the Member States. A number of obstacles also exist which prevent the Commission total freedom to exercise its legal obligations of guardian:

- limited resources mean that not all allegations of infringement can be investigated
- problems of collecting information which either does not exist, or is deliberately hidden
- and political sensitivity which may result in the Commission being lenient in certain instances for fear of 'upsetting the apple cart'.

The Commission implements policies decided by the Council. It may do this directly in some areas, for instance, in the field of competition policy, although in other areas the implementation process is supported by a system of Management Committees, comprising representatives from national governments, wherein a majority voting system (identical to that applied in the Council) ensures overall acceptability.

Embracing these three areas of activity, the Commission acts as the executive of the EU which affords it further power in the management of EU finances, overseeing the collection of income and ensuring proper payments as well as managing the European Agricultural Guidance and Guarantee Fund (which takes up around 55 per cent of the annual budget) and the various structural funds (the European Regional Development Fund and the European Social Fund). Some responsibility is also granted in respect of environmental and technological research programmes. Similarly, the Commission oversees policy implementation which is outside of its own authority by delegating the implementation procedure to national authorities such as the Customs and Excise Authorities and the Ministry of Agriculture. The Commission has an important function to play in external representation. It negotiates with key institutions, principally the United Nations, the General Agreement on Tariffs and Trade (GATT), the Council of Europe, and the Organisation of European Economic Co-operation (OECD), and non-Member States. The latter role importantly includes the determination and implementation of the EU's external trade policy with agreements being passed onto the Council after consultation with Parliament.

The Commission also has responsibility for the various special external agreements of the EU including The Lomé Convention Institutions and the European Investment Bank. This latter institution has an important role to play in its own right in shaping the development of the EU. The main task of the bank is to enhance the balanced development of the EU. Operating as a non-profit making concern, the bank makes long-term loans to help finance specific investment projects to promote:

- economic development in less privileged regions
- improved communication (including transport and telecommunications) between the 15 Member States
- environmental protection
- energy policy objectives including development of indigenous resources, energy saving initiatives and import diversification
- technical development in advanced technologies to enhance EU competitiveness.

Acting in conjunction with the European Regional Development Fund (ERDF), the European Social Fund (ESF), the Guidance Section of the European Agricultural Guidance and Guarantee Fund (EAGGF) and the various R&D funding programmes, the European Investment Bank serves as one of the major financiers in the EU.

It should be emphasised that freedom of the Commission to act on its own authority is not total. The Commission has been brought before the European Court of Justice on several occasions, for example, in 1989 France accused the Commission of going too far in enforcing liberalisation in the telecommunications sector without prior consultation with Member States. As an institution, it therefore remains accountable to the Member States. Nevertheless, it is due to its embracing power that the issue of subsidiarity was first raised. The Commission generally prefers to rely on advisory bodies (usually chaired by Commission Members and offering advice which can be ignored) to support the process of policy development whereas Member States prefer supervision by Management Committees, whose opinions are binding. These differences offer great scope for continued tensions between the Commission and the Member States.

The Commissioners appointed at the beginning of 1995 have a clear agenda, laid out at the Essen summit of the EU Heads of State or government at the end of 1994:

1 To continue to follow through a strategy of growth competitiveness and employment set out in the recent White Paper, in particular, aiding structural changes to facilitate improved competitiveness and employment conditions.
2 Monitoring convergence between the Member States as a means of improving the potential for monetary union.
3 To prepare for further expansion of the EU, in particular the inclusion of Central and Eastern European countries. To identify areas where Eastern neighbours can align their policies and agenda for their achieving this.
4 To participate in the preparation for the 1996 Intergovernmental conference (IGC) which has been charged with revising the Maastricht Treaty to define the future development of the EU which could include as many as 25 Member States ten years from now.

The European Court of Justice

Article 164 of the EC Treaty asserts that the European Court of Justice '*shall ensure that in the interpretation and application of this Treaty the law is observed*'. Its main responsibilities are to:

● settle disputes between Member States
● settle disputes between the EU and Member States
● settle disputes between Community institutions
● settle disputes between individuals and the EU
● give opinions and recommendations on international rulings
● give preliminary rulings on disputes which are referred to the European Court of Justice by national courts.

The judgements of the Court have had a pervasive effect on shaping Community law, particularly in respect of relations between the Member States and the EU and legal protection of individuals. The Court is made up of 16 judges (at least one from each Member State, with the remaining one being appointed by the largest Member States in rotation) and six advocates general who are responsible for investigating cases with complete impartiality and independence, and submitting their judgements to the Court. The judgements of the Advocates General are *not* binding on the Court. Both the judges and advocates general are appointed by common accord of the Member State governments for a term of six years. Every three years there is partial replacement of the judges, although terms may be renewed.

European Community legislation can take a variety of forms: the Treaties of the European Community, Regulations, Directives, Decisions and Opinions. The Treaties are made up of the three founding Treaties, plus the Acts and amendments which have since been made to the existing legislation. They are generally regarded as the primary legislation of the EU. Treaties have *direct effect*, that is they are immediately binding on the Member States and are actionable in the national courts. They cover such issues as the free movement of goods, services, people and capital, and the promotion of competition. Regulations, on the other hand, cover specific technical adjustments particularly in relation to the Common Agricultural Policy. These are also binding and *directly applicable*.

Directives, as described earlier, are also binding in the result to be achieved, although their form and method of their implementation is left to the national authorities. As a result, they are more concerned with general policy principles as opposed to strict regulations. In practice, however, the distinction between the effects of regulations and directives is often blurred, mainly as a result of the fact that directives are usually issued to all Member States – often because they are concerned with harmonisation of laws – but also because they may be written in such a way that there is little scope for national interpretation. Decisions are binding on those to whom they are issued, that is, a Member State, institution or individual and cover a broad array of areas, both specific and general. In some instances, they are more akin to administrative rather than legislative acts. Opinions and recommendations are not legally binding. Their main function is to provide a point of reference for binding decisions rather than a legal device for enforcement.

Although the Court's role is primarily one of interpreting EU Treaties and enforcing Community law, it is also involved in policy development by forging new laws and binding legislation emerging from individual judgements. Rulings in the early 1980s against Asia-Pacific firms and the imposition of harsh anti-dumping duties (particularly against low priced Japanese imports) were highly criticised as being too harsh and beyond the juridical scope of the Court. Issues such as this, as well as the ever growing case load of the Commission, led to new legislation providing for a Court of First Instance to determine certain classes of actions. It is, however, exempt from dealing with actions brought by Member States or one Community institution against another. The overall result is reducing the ever burgeoning number of cases brought in front of the Court as well as providing a mechanism for further juridical review.

One of the great merits of the European Court is its interest in promoting flexibility in interpretation of the Treaties, which allows it to legislate in areas not expressly covered by the Treaties. Nevertheless, its role is restricted: it is not able to intervene in matters unless it is requested to do so and it has no real power of sanction beyond that of reprimand which means that rulings have not always been respected.

Nevertheless, probably the most significant aspect of rulings of the European Court is their supremacy over national law. The implications of this were discussed earlier. Principally, the Single Market has provided for a new legal order in the realm of international law which requires Member States of the EU to give up their national sovereignty in certain fields in favour of an all-embracing EU-wide framework. Recent inclusion in the Maastricht Treaty of the notion of subsidiarity does not equate with devolution of power to the Member States. The inclusion of this provision is to ensure that decisions are made at the most suitable level and, to this extent, it is unlikely that it will effect the operations of the Court in any significant way since its role centres on disputes related to the EU and not the Member State.

MAIN AREAS OF LEGAL CHANGE

The new legislative framework covers all activities associated with the development of the Single Market. To this extent it is impossible to provide a comprehensive review of all areas of new legislation. The following sections therefore attempt a very broad overview of the main areas of decision making in an attempt to characterise the essence of the new legislative framework across the EU. Many of these themes are referred to in later chapters. Where appropriate, examples are provided to illustrate the complexities and problems associated with achieving a pan-European legal structure which supersedes national jurisdiction.

The guiding principles of the single market

Unification is derived from a dual process which involves *negative integration*, limiting the imposition of restraints by Member States, and *positive integration* which centres on harmonising laws at the level of the Member State under EU control. This requires considerable power being afforded to the Community institutions.

Early attempts at developing a common market involved the abolition of quotas and customs duties along with the establishment of a common customs tariff. In negotiations with third countries, the EU also developed a comprehensive external trade policy. At the same time, there was also evidence of co-operation between states in areas such as customs, agriculture, transport, competition, research and development, social adjustment and harmonisation of indirect taxes (VAT). However, in the early 1980s it was eminently apparent that barriers to trade remained and markets continued to be fragmented. Combining both negative and positive aspects of integration had led to a high degree of tension between the Member States and the Commission and meant that liberalisation was slow and often hard to achieve.

These problems were compounded by fierce international competition which reinforced a need to co-ordinate Member State policies more closely. This led to the renewed impetus for European liberalisation and a detailed programme of policies to complete the internal market by 1992. At the meeting of Heads of State in Brussels in 1985, the main approaches to this were agreed. Lying at the heart of the creation of the Single European Market is the provision of a liberal framework for the free functioning of the internal market. The Commission's white paper outlined the following areas of liberalisation:

- the removal of physical barriers (to people, goods and capital)
- the removal of technical barriers
- the removal of fiscal barriers.

The SEA sets out the appropriate legal framework for the achievement of these objectives involving a widening of the powers of the institutions and the processes for policy development.

Freedom of movement and establishment

The removal of physical barriers affords two fundamental rights to EU citizens: the freedom of movement between Member States and the freedom of access to professional activities. It is obviously not possible, however, to remove all border controls over night.

A number of interim measures were therefore adopted to facilitate the progress towards true liberalisation including provision for approximating arms and drugs controls, rights of asylum for non-EU persons and co-ordination of visa controls. Reluctance to accept the removal of border controls as a result of national security concerns has resulted in a renewed focus on inter-state legal co-operation and the establishment of a European legal area rather than the complete removal of controls.

Certain directives have also been adopted which have raised (to Ecu 350) tax relief on the import of small volumes of non-commercial goods. Coupled with this, elimination of double taxation and greater freedom for the movement of personal property or goods across borders (such as cars) and house removals within the EU have supported the freedom of personal movement ethos.

Perhaps more importantly, however, new legislation supports the right of individuals to live and work in Member States other than the country of their citizenship. This has always proved to be a sensitive area, not least because there are inherent problems associated with acceptability of legal qualifications between Member States. The Commission has proposed a system of mutual recognition of qualifications with the proviso that qualifications which differ markedly in scope and content from those pertaining in the local market may be supported by probationary periods or aptitude tests or alignment courses. However, the measures must be justified to the Commission. The directive introduced in 1992, relating to non-academic qualifications (especially crafts and trades), also follows this line. Ultimately, the outlined aim is to introduce a European vocational training card which outlines the nature and scope of the holders' qualifications.

The Treaties confer rights on individuals to enter and reside in any Member State without any need to attain a residency permit, and they cannot be deported from that country unless they represent a public security or health risk, or on grounds of public policy. Importantly, this means that only laws which can be applied to nationals can be invoked to prevent entry and residency. The right to work (and the right to remain in the territory even after employment has ceased) is, perhaps, more problematic. The Treaties apply no definition to the term *worker* and many instances the Court has chosen to use the term liberally to include:

- part-time workers, so long as the work undertaken is truly economic in nature and not nominal
- EU nationals employed in international organisations
- a worker who has been made redundant but is capable of finding further work.

For example, in relation to part-time work, in 1982 a UK citizen, Mrs Levin, was refused a residence permit for the Netherlands as her earnings fell below the national minimum subsistence level. However, it was ruled that no distinction can be made between workers who supplement their earnings with other income (such as that of a spouse). This notion was also applied to a part-time music teacher from Germany working in the Netherlands (1985) who was permitted to raise his income through supplementary benefit. The ruling which permits spouses the right to residency was extended to incorporate 'common-law' partners, following a test case in 1986 where Ms Reed, a UK national, was granted the right to remain in the Netherlands with her partner (an EU worker) on the grounds that cohabitees are, to all intents and purposes, indistinguishable from married partners and should therefore be given the same rights.

Social security is available to the employed, the self-employed, families and their survivors, stateless persons and refugees, with the regulations stipulating:

1 Non-discrimination on grounds of nationality, which requires equal treatment being given to all residents regardless of their nationality.
2 Payment regardless of residence, which allows individuals to claim benefits when residing in a country other than that making payments.
3 No overlapping benefits, meaning an individual cannot claim twice – once in their country of origin and again in the country of domicile. Where, however, people find they are subject to loss because of differences between payments in the two states, several rulings have suggested the individual is entitled to the difference – to be paid by the 'competent institution of the state', i.e. the institution responsible for insurance, paying the larger amount.
4 The above effectively means that individuals are only subject to the regulations in a single Member State.
5 Aggregation – social security systems should regard periods of employment undertaken in other Member States in calculating benefits.

These stipulations apply to a wide range of social security provisions, including: unemployment benefits, old age benefits, accidents at work, invalidity benefits, and family benefits. Specifically related to unemployment benefit, the state responsible for payment is that in which the individual was last employed and paid insurance contributions. This effectively prevents individuals moving to countries which offer higher unemployment benefit. Special provisions are, however, made to migrant workers who travel to other Member States in search of employment. The competent state, i.e. the country where the person last paid insurance contributions, is required to continue to pay benefits as long as the individual made him/herself available for work at least four weeks after becoming unemployed. The individual is then required to register in each state he/she visits within seven days of the date he/she ceased to be available for work in the state just left. By complying with these stipulations the individual is entitled to unemployment benefits from the competent state for up to three months.

Free movement of goods

Despite early attempts to architect a free market for goods there remained important barriers, most specifically border controls and differences in local standards and specifications. Border controls (passport checks, export documentation, spot checks, veterinary checks, etc.) and the inherent delays of such bureaucratic systems were estimated to cost up to Ecu 1 billion. The necessity to simplify documentation and co-ordinate national controls was clear. Achieving such co-operation and compliance has, however, proved very slow and while it is hoped that there will eventually be mutual recognition of national checks (with states accepting checks made at the point of departure) progress in this area has been limited.

Technical barriers also posed a key problem. While legislation was developed to ensure no quantitative restrictions on imports or actions having equivalent effect, the 'get-out clause' permitted nations to ban goods which posed a risk to health and safety or national security. This was used to good effect, particularly up until the *Cassis de Dijon* ruling, with the 'measure' of potential risk to the nation state being left up to the individual country. As a result, the Commission implemented legislation to harmonise health and safety regulations, although rapid technological developments made this kind of approach unsatisfactory. Ultimately, therefore, the Commission have opted for a dual approach to technical harmonisation which provides for mutual recognition of goods until common standards have been agreed. In addition, all new regulations are subject to Commission monitoring and approval.

More specifically, the free movement of goods requires the abolition of customs duties and other measures having equivalent effect. The transitional period for abolishing all duties has now passed (extended to Spain and Portugal up to 1 January 1993) and the imposition of new duties has effectively been barred. It is also not possible for any monetary charges to be imposed on imported goods. The case of reprographic equipment in France (1981) provides a good example of this latter ruling. The French government introduced a three per cent tax on imports and domestically produced reprographic machinery with the aim of compensating for the widespread practice of reproducing books. Authors who were affected by this practice did not, however, receive any benefit from this new tax. As the tax was applied equally to imported goods and locally produced products, the tax did not contravene Article 13 which clearly states that only measures which are unfairly applied to imported goods, with no equivalent for domestic products, can be seen to have an equivalent effect to customs duties.

Similarly, quantitative restrictions (and measures having equivalent effect) are also banned under the new rulings. As mentioned earlier, it was under this ruling that German actions against *Cassis de Dijon* were deemed to contravene existing legislation. Basically, any action which is applied arbitrarily with the potential of discriminating against imports are subject to scrutiny. The case of *Procureur du Roi v Dassonville* (1974) set a precedent for rulings of this nature and led to the notion of the *Dassonville formula*. There was a Belgian ruling which prohibited sale of spirits not covered by a 'certificate of origin'. Scottish whisky, sold in Belgium, therefore had to possess a certificate of origin issued by the UK customs authorities. Mr Dassonville had imported Scotch whisky into Belgium from France, and as he was not in possession of the necessary certificate of origin, manufactured his own. When taken to court for fraud, he did not deny he had contravened Belgian law, but asserted that the courts, by insisting on certificates of origin, were acting counter to the principles of free trade. The European Court of Justice ruled in favour of Mr Dassonville, concluding that the Belgian requirement had an equivalent effect to quantitative restrictions.

It still remains possible for countries to ban imports of goods based on certain justifiable grounds. For example, a ban on imports of pornographic material into the UK from the Netherlands was upheld in the Court on the grounds of public morality (the material being adjudged more obscene than that publicly available in the domestic market), and an import licence on milk was allowed due to the need to regulate the heat treatment process of milk along with the importance of identifying sources of contamination. The latter ruling was made on the grounds of national health and safety provisions.

Perhaps more importantly, however, there is scope for countries to derogate from the free movement of goods for the protection of industrial and commercial property. As owners of a particular type of proprietary technology have the potential to write into their licensing contracts stipulations on geographic market coverage, licensing firms may carve up markets. This acts against the notion of free movement of goods. Consequently, holders of patents or trademarks are not permitted to restrict the import of goods into their own national market, legally produced by licensed firms, in other Member States. This does not apply, however, to compulsory licenses granted in respect of a parallel patent as the originating firm has no control over the conditions of manufacture outside his Member State.

Some comment must also be made on the liberalisation of services. Supported by recent steps taken by GATT to liberalise services on a global scale, the Commission has concerned itself with freeing up the market for services on a pan-European scale. Interestingly, despite new legislation, organisations have shown a degree of reluctance to take advantage of the new freedoms being offered. Rights of establishment, that is complete freedom to set up service provisions in other Member States, subject to host country law, now apply in the service sector. Particular sectors have been singled out for special treatment as a result of their potential contribution to cost saving benefits on an EU-wide scale. Financial services is possibly top of the list with the Commission taking the stance that minimum co-ordination of rules and mutual recognition is the most advantageous means of achieving objectives. Nevertheless, problems still remain regarding consumer protection as well as the degree to which financial service firms should be subject to the same regulations which apply in industrial sectors (particularly with regard to competition policy).

National transport systems have also figured large in the Commission's considerations as a result of their effect on the free movement of goods across the EU. It is only by opening up transportation that the major cost savings expected from enhanced logistics efficiency can be derived. (The competition policy implications for civil aviation are set out in the case study at the end of Chapter 5.) Road haulage liberalisation has been hampered by the system of national and EU quotas and licences (with the former often being evoked on a bilateral basis). Elimination of these quotas is essential to true liberalisation in this sector.

Liberalisation of capital movements

The Commission has outlined three objectives for the liberalisation of capital movements:

- access to more efficient financial services
- the more effective allocation of European savings
- to make the financial system more competitive.

This includes the abolition of restrictions on the movement of capital belonging to individuals resident in the Member States along with discrimination based on nationality or place of residence in respect of the place where capital is invested. In 1986 the Commission's White Paper extended early measures to include long-term credit, acquisition of securities (not quoted on the stock market) and the admission of securities from one Member State to the capital markets of another. In order to further enhance liberalisation, the Commission submitted further proposals in 1987 for the complete liberalisation of capital movements to include short-term securities, current and deposit accounts, loans and credits. The directive also stipulates that all transactions must be made at the same exchange rate as those used for current payments. The only exception to this is where countries are experiencing severe problems with their balance of payments. In such instances firms are permitted to introduce a number of controls on short-term capital movements. There are also guidelines laid down for the establishment of a single instrument for short-term financial support including EU loans and medium-term financial assistance, the latter of which may also be provided to firms suffering severe balance of payment difficulties. These proposals were approved by the Council in 1988.

Coupled with financial liberalisation is the issue of the exchange rate mechanism which cannot be disassociated from other capital measures. Achievement of a workable exchange rate mechanism has the power to enhance the balanced movement of capital as it removes distortions between exchange rates. This should open up the potential for the movement of capital based on market forces rather than governmentally induced economic conditions. Equally, freeing up capital movements cannot be considered independently of certain fiscal matters, in particular, wide differences in taxation between various Member States. Investment decisions are critically determined by taxation levels which has led the Commission to reconsider measures used for taxing parent companies and their subsidiaries as well as measures to prevent tax fraud.

The removal of fiscal barriers

The sole concern under this heading is levels of indirect tax – VAT and excise duty (imposed on e.g. tobacco, alcohol and mineral oils). Despite differences in national rates of VAT, there is no distortion for manufacturers who are reimbursed via a system of import levies and export refunds which prevent dual taxation for goods which are manufactured in one country and sold in another. Generally, EC law stipulates that Member States can set their own VAT levels on imported goods so long as the same level is applied to domestically produced products. Nevertheless, consideration must be made of VAT already paid in the exporting country to ensure that imported goods are not unfairly burdened. For the future, a harmonised rate of VAT is seen as desirable (nigh essential) if a true common market is to be established. Based on the experience in the USA, it was adduced that differences between Member States could exist so long as they did not differ by more than six per cent. With many goods being taxed at between 14–20 per cent (and a range of more essential goods between 4–9 per cent) the Commission felt these rates were acceptable – but should be maintained within those bands. Differences in excise rates are, however, much greater which has led to proposals to align them along an average rate. This would prevent tax evasion as well as distortions in trade.

The proposals have, however, met with great resistance, for example, the UK government has rejected any move towards imposing VAT on children's clothes and food, and the French government has categorically stated that they could not afford the loss of revenue from reducing rates of tax on luxury goods such as cars. Other, more general concerns, have been voiced with regard to loss of fiscal sovereignty as well as the potential for tax differences to result in healthy competition between the Member States. While there is no clear solution to these difficulties, it is possible that Member States will continue to be afforded a degree of flexibility in the establishment of VAT levels on the basis that the existing differences do not pose a serious enough threat to justify continuance of border controls.

Competition policy

Chapter 5 provides a thorough review of competition policy measures designed to enhance the effective workings of the Single Market. Acting in conjunction with liberalisation measures, competition policy directives are designed to provide a common set of rules of conduct for firms competing in the EU. Basically, the directives cover such issues as anti-competitive practice (cartels and market rigging), exploitation of a dominant position (incorporating mergers and acquisitions), state aid and subsidies and public procurement.

Industrial policy

Although the Treaty of Rome explicitly outlined objectives for agriculture, competition, trade and fiscal harmonisation, it contained no formal plan for a common industrial policy. However, some of the 'generic' principles for European integration laid down in

Article 2 concerning *balanced expansion* and *harmonious development* were directly applicable to industry. The Treaty also included open-ended clauses for setting up an industrial development programme although no mention was made of an all-embracing industrial policy.

The first indication of industrial policy emerged as far back as 1964 with the introduction of the *medium-term economic policy*. The second programme, covering the 1968–1992 period included provision for intervention to improve the industrial structure of Europe, a Directorate for Industrial Policy being established charged with the formulation of common objectives for Europe-wide industrial policy. This was a deliberate backlash against the growing trend for governments to support 'national champions', often declining industries in the steel, textiles and shipbuilding industries. By diverting funds into supporting ailing businesses, it was believed governments were not acting in the spirit of the Single Market. However, lack of clear policy guidelines and a lack of purpose to intervene, rendered the Directorate obsolete. Local firms preferred to lobby at the national level and local governments were intent on supporting domestic businesses as a means of preserving local economic welfare, despite subsidies causing a serious drain on national resources.

In the late 1960s, a Memorandum on *The Industrial Policy of the Community* outlined the proposal to 'allow industry to derive maximum advantages from the existence and size of the Common market', through minimal intervention. Nevertheless, the following Programme for Industrial and Technological Policy mixed intervention with non-intervention and set the scene for an unformalised, but necessary, review of industrial policy along a number of key dimensions:

- the elimination of barriers
- approximation and harmonisation of national industrial policies
- the establishment of stronger European undertakings through mergers and alliances
- the introduction of EU financing for certain ventures of major technological interest
- co-ordinated policies for industries either ailing or in a position to set common Europe-wide standards.

The effect of these was limited, and little was achieved in terms of real integration. Industrial policy remained centred on issues of competition and non-intervention. The Union of Industries of the European Community (UNICE) could agree on little except the benefits of private enterprises, and the Commission was dogged by governments' insistence on supporting national industries to preserve their economic base.

Article 130 of the Maastricht Treaty highlights the need for policies designed to encourage an open and competitive industrial sector, smooth adjustments to structural change, promotion of small and medium-sized enterprises and co-operation in R&D. Nevertheless, while a large number of policies exist for promoting Europe-wide industrial activity, this does not equate with a comprehensive industrial policy. Indeed, the debate is still raging on whether or not Europe needs an industrial policy at all. Germany and France stand on different sides of the fence when it comes to the future of industrial provision in the EU. Germany, based on their system of *Ordnungspolitik*, is keen to combine elements of *laissez faire* with corporatist elements, whereas France is in favour of economic planning. The UK too are keen for the Commission to take a guiding hand in setting overall objectives for competition policy, but to allow individual Member States to pursue their own industrial policies, so long as they do not contravene EC law.

Uncomfortably placed between these two divergent groups, the Commission currently seems intent on designing policies for improved efficiency and fairer competition without formalising a framework for an integrated industrial policy. These include economic and monetary union, external trade policies, social and regional policies, competition policies, research and development initiatives and fostering co-operation between Member States. Some of the parallels between the EU's approach and that pertaining in Japan (in particular) and the USA (to a lesser extent) are discussed in detail in Chapter 12. Overall, the fact that many directives are being initiated expressly to raise the competitiveness of European firms vis-à-vis their international rivals is indicative of a move towards a loose industrial federation.

The European Parliament has, on several occasions, addressed the issue of industrial policy, reinforcing the importance of establishing a common market without barriers to achieve economic growth. Similarly, attention to the removal of technical barriers and fostering growth in advanced technologies is seen as a central tenet of industrial policy. It has also been recognised that industrial policy initiatives have increasingly come within the scope of EU structural funds which are set to double following agreements made during the Brussels Summit in 1988. With these concerns in mind, Parliament has addressed their deliberations towards certain sectors which have experienced poor performance, both in the EU market as well as internationally. It is not possible within the confines of this chapter to discuss these issues in detail but they include: the European steel industry, shipbuilding, the aircraft and space industry, the textile and clothing industry, chemicals and pharmaceuticals and the automobile industry.

Perhaps top of the agenda for improved competitiveness is the promotion of research and technological development. The Fourth Framework Programme, (covering the period 1994–1998) divides key activities into four groups:

1 *First activity*: research and technologial development (Ecu 13.1 bn) in information and communications, industrial technologies, (e.g. engineering, manufacturing systems, materials, etc.), biotechnology, the environment (particularly technologies that aid environmental protection), energy (especially technologies that promote efficient use of resources), European transport systems and socio-economic problems.
2 *Second activity*: co-operation with non-EU countries (Ecu 790 m).
3 *Third activity*: dissemination and application of results (Ecu 600 m) particularly to small and medium sized enterprises.
4 *Fourth activity*: training and mobility of researchers (Ecu 785 m).

The overriding aim is to:

make the Community activities more selective so as to increase the economic spin-offs from Community research, in particular by concentrating on generic technologies which will enable European industry and its subcontractors to go back on the offensive in international competition

(Commission, 1993)

Two other issues deserve some comment, that is the application of laws and regulations to Multinational Enterprises (MNEs) and Small and Medium-sized Enterprises (SMEs).

Multinational enterprises

Although there is no specific provision in the Treaties to control the activities of multinational enterprises, there is scope though the implementation of labour laws, fiscal, company and competition legislation to influence codes of conduct of these organisations. With their power to influence both the economic and social arena, it is important that multinationals operate within the spirit of the Single Market initiative. Indeed, many international institutions are intent on providing regulations for international production on a worldwide scale as a result of such a sphere of influence. The OECD already operates a code of practice, based on voluntary acceptance, designed to influence the activities of MNE's, three-quarters of which are carried out within the OECD area. While it is not the Commission's intention to discriminate against MNEs, some of its proposals clearly have more impact on this sector than others.

Discussion on the activities of MNEs date back to 1973 when the Commission published a Communication outlining its views on foreign manufacturing, foreign direct investment and the role of MNEs within a unified Europe. Building on this Communication, several proposals have emerged, for example, employees must be consulted on major policy changes within the firm and be given the right to participate in the company's decision making. A number of directives have also been passed: collective redundancies require consultation between social partners prior to the proposed move with authorities having the right to extend the deadline for dismissal if local labour market conditions make this desirable. Similarly, in an attempt to safeguard employee rights, provision has been made for takeover activity: takeovers may not harm the rights of employees in any way and must not be cause for dismissals. Equally, employees must be kept informed and consulted with regard to the proposed takeover. However, the Commission, through the application of competition policy, actively encourages mergers and takeovers in so far as they do not result in a concentration and the resultant abuse of a dominant position. This raises an important paradox for the Commission in regulating the activities of MNEs: on the one hand, they are intent on providing a free market for goods and services to benefit the growth of multinational enterprises, essential if the EU is to spawn leading global firms with the potential to compete with Japanese and American multinational giants. On the other, they are concerned with regulating the activities of MNEs to ensure protection of the public and workers' interests as well a maintaining open and free competition in key industrial sectors.

It is perhaps in the area of fiscal measures that the Commission sees the need for tighter regulation of multinational firms. Multinationals have the potential, as a result of their extensive business networks, to find ways and means to evade taxes. In 1975, the Council drew up a directive concerning *mutual assistance* by Member States authorities to pool information on direct taxation and VAT. It is through such mutual assistance that the Commission can monitor the practice of transfer pricing (*see* Chapter 7) which allows firms to declare profits in the lowest tax areas through a process of internal price manipulation. The European Court of Justice has passed rulings on transfer pricing at the EU's external frontiers (in relation to *Caterpillar and Sandoz* in 1980) while internal considerations have focused on proposals for establishing common tax systems for parent companies and their subsidiaries (and merged firms) as well as the elimination of double taxation for organisations moving profits between subsidiaries based in different Member States. Relating to activities outside of the EU, Parliament has urged the USA's Administration to support legislation which exempts firms from unitary taxation – a practice wherein subsidiaries are taxed on the basis of their international activities rather than their local investments – as this is regarded as unfair discrimination and tantamount to protectionism.

Finally, co-ordination of regional support programmes is attempted by the Commission, intent on removing unfair incentives for inward investment into certain areas and eliminating the process of outbidding. However, progress in this area of activity is slow, mainly because support is difficult to quantify and cross comparison between Member States highly complex.

Small and medium-sized enterprises

There is no single definition of SMEs within the EU. Various Member States apply different criteria and guidelines which makes approval of an EU-wide definition almost impossible. However, Community institutions generally focus on operational criteria including the number of employees, fixed assets and parental company control. Under certain definitions, it has been concluded that over 95 per cent of Community institutions fall into this category which makes it a key area of concern for policy making.

The European Parliament had continued to voice its opinion that the SME sector has a major contribution to make in the achievement of Single Market objectives through its contribution to growth, employment, quality, diversification and flexibility. Principally, SMEs are regarded as being better able to react quickly to changes in policy and economic/social conditions, which make them an important *change agent* within the EU.

While many SMEs only operate within their own national market they are no less subject to change in Community law than their larger rivals with respect to competition policy, social policy, regional policy, labour law and taxation. Nevertheless, some of the barriers which have beset the free movement of goods and services across the EU have perhaps been felt more acutely by these institutions who lack the 'deep pocket' advantages of larger institutions to overcome the hurdles of operating across frontiers. With this in mind, the Commission have addressed much of their deliberation towards the specific needs of this sector in an attempt to initiate further expansion, establishing a separate Commissioner post for the purpose.

A new action programme for SMEs was launched in 1986 with two overriding aims: creating a favourable environment for SME activities and providing services to support growth and maintain their flexibility. On the first point, the Commission is concerning itself with fostering entrepreneurship, improving the administrative, competitive and fiscal environment, modifying company law and improving social conditions. On the second, training and information sources figure large, particularly in relation to export procedures, company formation and growth, innovation and co-operative agreements. Equally, overcoming problems of capitalisation are top of the agenda.

The Commission have also provided certain exceptions for SMEs which allow them to derogate from general EU-wide rules. These include proposals for: amending directives on annual and consolidated accounts (focusing on the scope of included information); introducing company law in the Member States for one-man businesses; group exemptions in competition law to enable SMEs to achieve scale economies through specialisation agreements, R&D agreements, patents and exclusive marketing and purchasing agreements; opening up public procurement; and, providing tax exemptions to very small firms.

Although some Member States provide a range of information for small and medium-sized enterprises, the Commission has taken it upon itself to co-ordinate information provision to ensure that firms are fully aware of their rights and opportunities. This resulted in the establishment of European Business Information Centres across the EU, often linked to existing organisations such as trade corporations and chambers of commerce which had existing links with the small business sector. Centrally linked to the

Commission, and each other, they provide a very coherent network of activities designed to provide comprehensive information and support. Similarly, a number of business and innovation centres have been established across the EU to provide support services for independent SMEs and partnerships. Over 50 of these were in existence in 1991.

Co-operation initiatives have also been paid considerable attention with the formation of the Business Co-operation Centre (part of the SMU Task Force) responsible for creating a service infrastructure for SMEs. Its role is to provide contact between businesses in different Member States to foster international and inter-regional co-operation. Certain pilot projects have also been undertaken to enhance business co-operation including *Europartnerships* which were designed to improve growth and development in less privileged regions by way of joint ventures. The first project of this kind 'Europartnerships 1988' was based in Ireland, where co-operation was considered to be a major cornerstone of regional development policy.

Technological development by SMEs is afforded high priority, with the Commission actively encouraging the inclusion of SMEs in the emerging R&D programmes such as BRITE, ESPRIT and RACE. Although some theorists argue that research monies should be focused into larger grants to ensure that projects are of such a scale to enhance the potential for major new technological break-throughs, as there is no proof that larger institutions are better placed than smaller ones to develop new technologies, this kind of thinking has been rejected by the EU. Indeed, the greater flexibility of SMEs affords them greater potential to side-step bureaucratic systems which are often regarded as a major hindrance to R&D effort. However, the SPRINT technology transfer programme is the only one to have been specifically designed for SMEs.

Social policy

Many of the issues related to social policy are outlined in Chapter 6. Social provisions are principally concerned with the achievement of full employment, improvements in living and working conditions, proper social protection, the promotion of a dialogue between management and workers and the development of human resources. These should be considered in conjunction with the free movement of individuals, the rights of establishment and social security provisions (all discussed earlier) which sets out a framework for EU citizenship, above and beyond national regulations and requirements.

Environmental policy

Environmental policy considerations are discussed in Chapter 10. As early as 1972, heads of state recognised that it was necessary to implement a common policy on the environment. By 1985, 105 environmental policies had already been enacted, designed to provide preventative solutions to a wide range of problems identified. By 1990, this figure had risen to 160. To this extent, environmental policy is seen as being a critical element in the EU's economic and social policies. Nevertheless, problems have been encountered in the incorporation of directives into national law in several instances which led the European Parliament to propose more stringent measures for monitoring compliance. This principally resulted from the fact that most environmental measures took the form of directives, rather than regulations, which are not immediately actionable. Problems have also been experienced with regard to common agreement between the Member States which has led to the provision of certain decisions being made by qualified majority as opposed to unanimous vote. The Parliament has also proposed that the European Court of Justice be empowered to impose sanctions on those firms failing to comply with new legislative measures.

The Common Agricultural Policy

One glaring omission from the above discussion is the issue of the Common Agricultural Policy. The vast complexities of this sector make a full analysis of the emerging legal framework far too complicated to undertake here. Some comment, however, is necessary to attain an understanding of the importance of this sector in the Single Market initiative.

Intervention in agricultural policy between the 15 Member States occurred long before the genesis of the Single Market. Indeed, intervention and protectionism have been a feature of the agricultural sector on a global scale for many years. The main problems associated with agriculture stem from the fact that there is an imbalance between supply and demand on a world scale with vast differences existing between the developed and less developed world. As food is a fundamental need of all individuals, the political sensitivity of agricultural issues must also not be overlooked. Added to this are a plethora of physical, economic and social factors, such as:

- unpredictable climatic conditions
- differences in production between regions based on physical factors such as climate, soil, altitude and irrigation
- changes in the nature of farming and in the sophistication of farming technology
- the importance of farming to rural communities and the low return on agricultural investment.

Consequently, the vested interest of many parties in the agricultural sector on a worldwide scale make it very hard to regulate.

In 1986, GATT ventured into the field of world agriculture for the first time as a result of vast overcapacity in certain foodstuffs resulting in enormous surpluses in many countries and the resultant propensity of countries to consider exporting surpluses (at low prices). This was seen as having a potentially dangerous effect on world agricultural prices placing an increasing burden on nations subsidising farming activity. The potential stalemate in talks in late 1992 are indicative of the conflicting interests of nations in respect of agricultural policy with the threat of agricultural trade wars reinforcing the political sensitivity of establishing common guidelines to global agricultural management.

Within the EU, policies clearly address the multi-faceted nature of agriculture, with new proposals specifically taking account of:

- a gradual reduction of surpluses which have heavily burdened the tax payer
- encouraging diversification and improved quality for goods destined both for EU and global markets
- maintaining agricultural activity in communities which rely almost exclusively on farming
- enhancing profitability for small, often family-owned, farms
- increasing awareness to environmental issues
- introducing new technologies into food processing industries.

This list is by no means exhaustive, but it does throw into relief the varying challenges faced by policy makers in developing an overriding framework for the maintenance of the agricultural sector.

Two of the clearest instruments available to policy makers are the imposition of controls on markets and prices. In terms of markets, over 91 per cent of all activity is now covered by regulations which include three key elements: free movement of goods, financial guarantees, and Community preference.

In line with the new freedoms which apply to goods and services across the EU, the new agricultural policy provides a framework for the free movement of agricultural goods. This is supported by common guaranteed prices, aimed at removing the incentive for firms to 'dump' surpluses in foreign markets with the potential of wiping out profits for all but a few organisations. This policy was, however, threatened by changes in exchange rates which led to the introduction of Monetary Compensation Amounts (MCAs) a system of levies and subsidies designed to compensate for currency-related distortions in inter-EU agricultural trade. This raises an important question: why is agriculture singled out for such compensatory measures when differences in prices between Member States in other industries are viewed as promoting efficiency rather than being detrimental to the welfare of the EU? The answer lies in the political sensitivity of the sector and the broad differences between the Member States agricultural portfolios which makes the establishment of a 'common' market in agriculture all but impossible. It would not be possible, for example, for Scottish farmers to consider mass production of oranges as the climate militates against it. Therefore specialisation at a national level will always remain, which detracts from the potential of liberalisation to create inter-EU competition in the same way as is possible in other fields.

Although most agricultural prices are quoted in Ecus, to ensure standardisation, payments made to farmers are converted into national currencies. With currencies fluctuating against the Ecu, this means that differences arise in farmers' incomes which has an impact on food prices and trade patterns. The big question is what will happen to MCAs in the event of abolition of border controls? An attempt at a solution to this problem was agreed in 1984 with currency alignments being based on the currency which was revalued the most – the Deutschmark. This would enable prices to be fixed to a stable currency rather than one subject to fluctuations. In the event, however, the effect was to tie farm prices to the rising Deutschmark leading to rapid inflation in agricultural goods. As this has not proved a satisfactory means of establishing common prices, the Commission is now looking towards measures which parallel the new approach to VAT collection (based on blanket national adjustments of VAT levies resulting from trade volume). Obviously, the establishment of a single currency would remove the need for MCAs altogether, although the problems which have beset this move mean that more effective interim measures are essential.

Financial guarantees, expressed through the European Agricultural Guidance and Guarantee Fund ensure that farmers are guaranteed payment for the goods they produce. Burgeoning over-capacity in the industry, however, led to major reforms in 1988 to encourage farmers to produce less. *Stabilisers* were introduced which effected price cuts once a particular threshold was reached. Unfortunately, these measures failed to have the desired impact. As they could not force farmers to produce less, there was still the potential for individuals to carry on production after the threshold had been reached to continue receiving payments, albeit at a lower level. With such high fragmentation in the industry, individual farmers are aware that their own output restraints cannot maintain price levels. There is, therefore, a tendency to produce more, rather than less, to ensure payments and maintain income. The cost to the EU is huge, accounting for an average of 75 per cent of the total EU budget.

Preference emerges directly out of financial guarantees. With so much money pouring into the maintenance of the agriculture sector it is no surprise that the Commission is anxious to protect the EU from international imports. This is reinforced by the fact that EU prices are usually higher than corresponding international prices – an 'open door' policy potentially leading to major losses and the collapse of the whole CAP system. Preferential treatment takes a variety of forms, but basically includes:

- levies – which automatically protect the EU market by aligning import and domestic prices. In theory, these levies can be removed where import prices are higher than those in the EU, although such instances tend to be the exception
- customs duties – which extend to the prohibition of imports altogether
- minimum-price levels – fixed periodically by the Commission.

These policies do not apply to all importing countries. Special agreements negotiated with third countries, particularly less developed countries, provide for free access for a variety of agricultural products. However, it should be stressed that with many agreements, such as the Lomé Convention, these measures do not equate with overriding generosity. Most of the products in question are tropical and are thus not in direct competition with EU produce.

The Commission also undertakes a number of export measures which assist EU firms entering other world markets including export aids and refunds.

The Commission also concerns itself with structural issues related to the agricultural sector. In recent years this has particularly centred on regional structural reform to cater for Europe-wide supply and demand conditions rather than those pertaining to national interests including the conversion of land to new farming types, a trend towards larger scale production, extension of allowances to farmers in less favoured areas and a scheme to encourage the cessation of farming.

Although CAP has been apparently successful in terms of attaining its objectives (raising productivity levels, stabilising markets and providing for EU self-sufficiency), it is not without its critics. In particular, it is accused of overly protecting the EU and preventing consumers from taking advantage of lower world prices, destabilising world markets through the provision of export grants and refunds, producing surpluses and overburdening the EU budget. The 1988 reforms provided the first step in counterbalancing some of these arguments although the failure of guarantee ceilings to reduce output raises doubts over the effectiveness of these measures. Nevertheless, some advance has been made in terms of pricing policies where tight price controls have lowered the average annual price rises from a staggering 12.1 per cent in 1982/83 to 0.3 per cent in 1991 (measured in national currencies).

CONCLUSION

What is clearly apparent from the above discussions (and those included in later sections of the book), is the complexity of the process of developing a comprehensive legal framework for the achievement of the objectives of the Single Market. This is not only because the overriding ethos of a single market – a union of countries with no barriers, where competition between economic actors can be conducted on equal terms, where social provisions are applicable to all and co-ordinated between Member States and where there is a genuine concern for the environment in which we live – involves the development of policies to cover a myriad of differing economic, social and structural issues. It also results from the fact that 15 individual Member States are trying to be moulded into one. The potential for national versus supranational conflict is accordingly immense, and while the legal framework is developing slowly, the hurdles to achieving a comprehensive package of policies which provide for true unification is still a long way off.

Lying at the centre of this inherent conflict is the issue of sovereignty which remains an unresolved issue. Handing over decision-making power to a centralised Council, while theoretically providing for local representation at the EU level, has severely shaken many Member States who have seen their power to influence economic and social provisions for their people ebbing away. Although early in the development, some of these problems were somewhat overlooked and experience has brought the issue of sovereignty into sharp focus to the extent that decision-making mechanisms have been adjusted to cater for national reservations. This has partly taken the form of affording the European Parliament more consultative power to provide a safety net of commenting on proposals, along with the establishment of more formal mechanisms for consultation with national governments. Perhaps more important, though, in the current Maastricht Treaty, is the issue of subsidiarity which determines that all decisions should be made 'at the most appropriate level' which effectively recognises that some decisions are better left to the nation state.

These provisions do not, however, minimise the growing power of Community institutions – the Commission, the Council of Ministers, the European Council, the European Parliament and the European Court of Justice – to shape the new Europe. Little-by-little they are chipping away at national authority and developing a more comprehensive and co-ordinated decision making and legal framework. While progress is inevitably slow, the wheels are continuing to turn to the extent that failure of Member States to adjust to the new proposals will mean their falling behind in the inexorable progress towards real unification.

Questions for discussion

1 What are the main areas of conflict between Member States and the various institutions of the European Community?

2 To what extent do you imagine the issue of subsidiarity will diminish national concerns over loss of sovereignty?

3 How likely is it that the new freedoms related to movement and establishment will result in large numbers of European Union individuals relocating in other Member States?

4 If the Commission has no power of sanction (except in the area of Competition Policy) how successful are the legal provisions likely to be in creating a common framework?

5 If, as is expected, there is an increasing move towards political union, in what way will the European Parliament need to adjust?

6 To what extent do individual Member States wield power over European Union decision making?

7 Do you think that it is necessary for the European Union to adopt a more formalised and comprehensive industrial policy?

8 How are problems related to the Common Agricultural Policy different to those pertaining in other areas of policy making?

9 Given the scale and scope of the areas on which European Union decisions are now being made, how can the institutions avoid becoming bureaucratic monoliths?

CASE STUDY

Commission of the European Communities v Grand Duchy of Luxembourg

Taxation of beer

In Luxembourg, the system of taxation on beer concerns excise duties levied on the hot wort, rather than the finished product, regardless of wastage in subsequent stages of the manufacturing process. As it is impossible to judge *a posteriori* the actual wastage of hot wort in the manufacturing process, it is therefore necessary to tax imported beer on the basis of the finished product. A flat-rate adjustment is applied to take account of the presumed volume of hot wort used and the amount of wastage. Exports of beer from Luxembourg are afforded excise duty refunds calculated at a flat-rate.

Facts of the case

The calculation of hot wort wastage for exports, and thus the basis for calculating the duty to be levied, is based on a multiplier of 10/9, corresponding to a wastage rate of 10 per cent. This leads to an increase in the refund of export duty afforded to Luxembourg beer exporters of 11.11 per cent. However, for importers, the duty is calculated on the basis of export volumes (in hectolitre/degrees). The proportion of wastage thus calculated is increased by five per cent leading to a wastage rate of 4.76 per cent.

As the wastage percentages adopted by the authorities was deemed to exceed the real wastage rate the European Commission wrote to the authorities accusing them of breaching Articles 95 and 96 of the Treaty of Rome. Basically, in the Luxembourg system, export refunds were higher than the amount of tax levied on the finished product and the burden of taxation on imports was higher than that levied on domestically produced beer. Considered in conjunction with the fact that the Commission were informed that the wastage rate in a modern brewery could be as low as two per cent, the Luxembourg authorities were required to submit their observations on the matter within one month of the notice.

The Luxembourg government's reply focused on the poorly equipped nature of the Luxembourg brewing industry maintaining that it was not possible for domestic firms to reduce wastage levels below 10 per cent. The Commission were not satisfied with this response and therefore brought an action against the Luxembourg government.

The cases of the two parties

The Commission asserted that this particular case had been brought to the European Court of Justice not because Luxembourg had decided to levy taxes on the wort rather than the finished product, but because of the manipulation of the system as regards exports and imports. They believed that the Luxembourg government had failed to prove that a 10 per cent wastage level was justified, claiming that their expert report concluded a wastage level in the region of 4.95 per cent. To this end, the Commission believed that the Luxembourg authorities applied a taxation system on exports and imports which differed markedly from that levied on local production.

Domestic brewers, reducing wastage below the flat-rate average, will receive a refund of duty in respect of higher quantities of wort than actually required for production. Thus, they are in breach of Article 96. Equally they asserted that the brewing industry does not constitute multi-stage production extending the breach to Article 97.

The Luxembourg government, on the other hand, suggested that the expert opinions were based on wastage of cold wort and could not therefore be considered. It maintained that Luxembourg brewers had a higher wastage rate than many of their international counterparts and suggested that the Commission had not proved that a 10 per cent wastage rate was excessive. Furthermore, the Commission, who had originally believed that a two per cent wastage rate was possible, had not regarded the complexities of the brewing process and had ignored the fact that their own expert had suggested that in the case of low fermentation beers exported in bottles (like Luxembourg's exported beer) a higher wastage rate was normal – up to 10.25 per cent in hot wort.

The Court's considerations
Article 96 states that:

> Where products are exported to the territory of any Member State, any repayment of internal taxation shall not exceed the internal taxation imposed on them whether directly or indirectly.

Because producers operating below the 10 per cent wastage level would benefit from the applied flat rate, the amount of duty reimbursed may exceed the amount that was charged. Alternatively, Article 95 suggests:

> No Member State shall impose, directly or indirectly, on the products of other Member States any internal taxation of any kind in excess of that imposed directly or indirectly on similar domestic products.

Thus, if there are breweries in Luxembourg with a wastage factor of less than 4.76 per cent, the amount of duty charged on each litre of beer brewed by them will be less than that charged per litre of imported beer and would thus contravene Article 95.

In connection with Article 95, it was pointed out that country's taxation systems should be transparent in that it must be possible to determine, objectively, whether the tax burden on imported beers exceeds that on domestically produced products. In addition, the system must be capable of being applied equally to imported and domestic goods. Some doubt about whether the Luxembourg system met these criteria was expressed.

More importantly, however, as different systems of calculation are applied to domestic and imported goods there is potential scope to suggest discrimination. As domestic production tax is based on the amount of hot wort used, efficient producers enjoy fiscal rewards. Efficient foreign producers do not enjoy the same treatment, because taxes are based on volume of finished product although some quantity adjustments are made for notional volumes of hot wort. However, the adjustments do not take into account the efficiency of the producers.

This case was seen to resemble two others (Case 45/75 *REWE v Hauptzollamt Landau* [1976] ECR 181 and Case 127/75 *Bobie v Hauptzollamt Aachen-Nord* [1976] ECR 1079) in a number of respects. These cases established the following principles:

1 Member States are free to choose the system of taxation they consider most suitable.
2 The system applied to domestic goods constitutes the point of reference for determining whether or not imports have been unfairly discriminated against in the light of imposed taxation.
3 Article 95 is infringed even if it is applicable to a small number of isolated cases.
4 Community law looks with suspicion on national legislation which applies a graded system to domestically produced goods and a flat-rate system to imported products. If a graduated system is applied domestically then governments are left with one of two options: it must apply the same system to imports or the rate applied to imports must be equated with the lowest charged in the graduated domestic system.

Because of the obvious problems in calculating the comparability of the system applied to domestic goods with that applied to imported goods it was clearly difficult to assess whether or not imported beer had been taxed at a higher rate than domestic beer (even in the light of a number of expert reports). However, the Court suggested that it was sufficient for the Commission to establish that the system was liable to have that result. Therefore, the burden of proof was seen to rest on the Luxembourg authorities because of the lack of transparency of the system. Nevertheless, it was deemed necessary to reach a view based on the evidence before the court. To this end, submitted reports by the experts were used to adjudge a fair average level of wastage. It was finally concluded that the 4.76 per cent level (that applied to imported beers) was probably a fair approximation.

With regard to Article 96, it was also concluded that it was sufficient for the Commission to show that the taxation system employed is liable to result in differences between internal taxation and export reimbursement amounts. Once the Commission had therefore proved that it was possible to achieve a wastage rate of lower than 10 per cent, it was therefore left to the Luxembourg authorities to prove that no brewers within their territory achieve such efficiency and thus the repayment of tax never exceeds the amount imposed.

The same considerations which were relevant to the assessment of Article 95 apply here. The 10 per cent figure was regarded as excessive and no proof could be provided to show that no producers manufacture with lower wastage rates. The 10.25 percentage rate which was suggested by one expert's report was disregarded on two grounds: because other reports showed this to be far in excess of other estimates and the fact that there were strong grounds to suggest that some brewers could operate at a considerably lower level.

The Judgement
The European Court of Justice ruled against the Luxembourg government in both instances for failing to fulfil its obligations under Articles 95 and 96 of the Treaty.

Case Study Questions

1 Why do you think the Luxembourg authorities chose a system of taxation based on hot wort rather than the finished product?

2 Is arguing a case for favourable treatment based on the inefficiency of domestic firms in keeping with the spirit of the Single European Market initiative?

3 Could you imagine any cases where applying different taxation systems to internal firms and importers could be justifiable?

4 What approach to taxation do you think the Luxembourg Government should adopt in the future?

5 How does this case compare with the *Cassis de Dijon* ruling?

6 Can you think of any other areas where lack of transparency may pose problems in comparing legislation applied to national firms and that applied to importers?

FURTHER READING

Budd, S. (1987) *The EEC: A Guide Through the Maze*, Kogan Page. This text gives a review of the European institutions and areas of policy reform. Many of the issues discussed are still relevant today, and the author clearly outlines, for the layperson, the workings of the main participants and their role in the shaping of the new European marketplace.

Lodge, J. (1990) *The European Community and the Challenge of the Future*, Pinter. This text provides an overview of many of the problems facing the leading European institutions in creating a common market and a level playing field. Of particular interest are the chapters on the new dynamics of EC integration, policy making, the European Parliament, free movement of goods, services and capital, the Common Agricultural Policy and Political Co-operation.

REFERENCES

The authors recognise the contribution made by the following texts in compiling this chapter:

European Parliament, *Fact Sheets on the European Parliament and the Activities of the European Community*, Directorate General for Research, 1988.

Kent, Penelope, *European Community Law*, the M&E Handbook Series, 1992.

Nugent, Niel, *The Government and Politics of the European Community*, 2nd edn, Macmillan, 1991.

Rasmussen, Hjalte, *The European Community Constitution: Summaries of Leading EC Court Cases*, Nyt Nordisk Forlag Arnold Busck, 1989.

CHAPTER 3

The Member States, Regions and Regional Policy

Although the European Union is becoming more integrated and many key economic variables are moving closer together, there are still discrepancies in the economic performance of Member States. This will increasingly be an issue which will have to be tackled as the area becomes more and more integrated. Whilst macroeconomic policy is controlled domestically it is inevitable that differences will exist as some countries' economic policies will be more successful than others. But even if we see fully integrated macroeconomic policies some time in the future there will still be differences, much as there are regional differences in particular countries: whatever the path of development of the EU the central importance of regional policy will therefore continue.

Differences are bound to exist, due simply to the physical characteristics of the country, such as size, population and natural resources as well as cultural diversity. But during the 1980s disparities actually grew, particularly with the entry of the less developed countries of Spain, Portugal and Greece into the European Community. In 1995, when Finland, Austria and Sweden joined, their relative wealth also changed the balance between Member States. The central issue when considering these discrepancies is that some people fear that unless discrepancies can be reduced, Europe will end up having a core of economic activity and a periphery which is continually less developed.

It is important for businesses to be aware of the environments in which they do business and in particular to have information on economies in which they are based, or with which they have trading links. The establishment of a business in an economy where there are unsuitable productive resources, or where there is little market for the product or service would be unwise. Even within the EU the significant differences between the economies of the Member States makes the location decision vital to the success of a firm.

THE EUROPEAN UNION AND THE EUROPEAN ECONOMIC AREA

This book is not solely about the European Union and we must recognise that even with the entry of Sweden, Austria and Finland into the EU in 1995, there still exist other very developed countries outside the EU, but within the European Economic Area (EEA). In 1991, a new European Economic Area (EEA) Treaty was signed and at the time this was seen as a half-way house to full membership of the EU for some European Free Trade Association (EFTA) states (in 1991, these comprised, Austria, Finland, Sweden, Norway, Iceland, Liechtenstein and Switzerland). The Treaty covered the unification of product standards which are central to market unification. This agreement amounted to the EFTA countries accepting the fundamental principles of the Community's internal market programme, namely, free movement of goods, services, people and capital. It therefore represented a substantial milestone in the drive to deepen and widen European economic integration.

In 1992, Switzerland declared its intention not to join the European Economic Area and with the entry of Austria, Finland and Sweden in to the EU in 1995, the number of countries in the EEA but not in the EU has obviously fallen. Essentially, it leaves only two large countries, Norway and Iceland. Nevertheless, within the EEA there is an expansive network of economic links which are increasingly interdependent. The EEA accounts for almost 30 per cent of the world's gross domestic product and constitutes by far the largest global trading area, with close to 45 per cent of world trade. Well developed and similar economic structures, institutional arrangements, geographical proximity and cultural affinity have all been the driving forces behind creating strong, mutually beneficial ties between the two regions.

The physical characteristics, in terms of size and population of a country clearly have some bearing on its place within the EU and EEA. But the country's economic development in terms of national product and its industrial structure will also impact upon the role it plays in an increasingly integrated European economy. Economic structures in countries change over time and this is particularly true of the EU where the economy and trading relationships are being redefined.

Table 3.1 provides information about the physical size and population of the EEA.

Table 3.1. Area, population and density of main EEA countries, 1994

	Total area km^2	Population (000s)	Inhabitants per km^2	Projected population (2020)
EUR 15	3 234 200	368 450	114	390 020
EEA	3 660 900	373 047	102	395 580
Belgium	30 500	10 068	330	10 554
Denmark	43 100	5 181	120	5 458
Germany	356 900	80 614	226	81 880
Greece	132 000	10 346	78	11 226
Spain	504 800	39 112	78	41 544
France	544 000	57 529	106	63 915
Ireland	70 300	3 560	51	3 828
Italy	301 300	56 932	189	58 688
Luxembourg	2 600	395	153	454
Netherlands	41 200	15 239	370	17 394
Portugal	92 400	9 859	107	11 723
United Kingdom	244 100	57 959	237	61 350
Austria	83 900	7 909	94	8 227
Finland	337 100	5 055	15	4 984
Sweden	450 000	8 692	19	9 397
Iceland	103 000	262	3	307
Norway	323 900	4 299	13	4 653

Source: derived from Eurostat, Basic Statistics of the European Community, 1994.

Traditionally, the EU has been dominated in terms of population by the 'big four' countries, namely Germany, Italy, France and the United Kingdom. These countries are also amongst the most developed. In effect, the decisions of the 'big four' have dominated policy in the EU as a whole up until now. Spain, with its large population is also increasingly important and its overall economic growth has been significant since joining the EU. Sweden, Finland and Austria since joining the EU in 1995, have also been influential as relatively wealthy members of the EU. Belgium and the Netherlands are characterised by their small size but very dense populations. Such density often leads to land shortages and a relatively high price of land, which can lead to a disincentive to invest. At the other end of the spectrum, Spain, Ireland and Greece have low population densities and this has enabled them to pursue relatively large agricultural sectors (see Table 3.3).

With a total population of over 368 million, a single EU economy far outstrips the USA, with a population of 255 million, and Japan with a population of 124 million. It is for this reason that the EU is seen as a huge potential market for sellers outside the EU and indeed we have witnessed significant inward investment, particularly from the USA and Japan leading up to the creation of the Single European Market. In common with many industrialised economies, birth rates in the EU are falling, but people are living longer. Estimates of the population in the year 2020 suggest that there will be around 390 million inhabitants.

Table 3.2 shows the Gross Domestic Product (GDP) of the EU. GDP measures the net output or value added of an economy by measuring goods and services purchased with money. The table shows the dominance of Germany, producing around one quarter of the total EU's GDP. Not only has this resulted in higher standards of living for the population but it has also led to the strengthening of German enterprises. As the EU has developed it has often been German firms which, helped by their profitability and a relatively strong Deutschmark, have been most 'bullish', seizing opportunities for new investment, mergers and takeovers. This has led to accusations of German domination over the EU economy which, on the one hand, is tautologous but is also a product of relative efficiency. Ultimately, it is argued that the spread of this efficiency can only be to the good of the EU as a whole so long as it is not environmentally damaging (*see* Chapter 10).

With a purchasing power standard measurement of GDP per head significantly lower than the average, Greece, Ireland, Portugal and Spain demonstrate their relative under-development. As expected, the less developed countries of the EU have more people still working on the land – over one-fifth in the case of Greece, for example (*see* Table 3.3). It is clear that Spain, Portugal and Ireland all have significant agricultural sectors as well. Italy has the largest agricultural sector in terms of people employed, the figure stands at slightly over two million.

It seems from the figures that the more developed the country, the greater the tendency towards a large service sector. The one possible exception to this is Germany. Here it is interesting to note the relatively high proportion of the population working in industry. Even the former Soviet Union had a smaller percentage of its population working directly in industry (39.4 per cent in 1988). This is one of the reasons that Germany has such a high GDP. It is often argued that only a manufacturing sector, where raw materials and semi-finished products have value added to them in their processing, can generate significant wealth in an economy.

Over time we should expect further structural change within the EU. In particular, the pattern of demand for a country's products will change with the incomes and tastes of the population. For instance, if growth occurs resulting in an increase in real incomes then demand for goods and services which have high and positive income elasticities will tend

Table 3.2. Gross domestic product at market prices

Country	1992 total (Ecu 1000 million)	1990 total	1992 per head (purchasing power standard[1])	1990 per head
EUR 15	5 837.1	5 152.3	n.a.	n.a.
EUR 12	5 421.3	4 738.5	15 616	14 549
EEA	5 929.5	5 268.6	n.a.	14 612
Belgium	169.1	151.5	17 130	15 167
Denmark	110.1	102.2	16 812	15 380
Germany	1 498.5	1 181.8[2]	16 777	17 078[2]
Greece	60.1	52.4	7 851	6 877
Spain	444.1	387.6	12 121	10 927
France	1 020.2	940.9	17 646	16 199
Ireland	38.7	34.9	12 029	10 291
Italy	944.8	862.1	16 497	14 902
Luxembourg	8.2	7.1	20 538	18 413
Netherlands	247.6	223.3	16 061	14 829
Portugal	74.3	53.6	10 532	8 810
United Kingdom	805.6	769.4	15 422	14 566
Austria	143.2	125.0	17 067	15 446
Finland	81.9	108.7	13 853	15 397
Sweden	190.7	180.1	15 820	15 732
Iceland	5.1	5.0	15 727	15 528
Norway	87.3	83.5	16 912	14 941
USA	4 586.2	4 311.6	22 257	20 338
Japan	2 833.7	2 311.3	18 771	16 272

Notes:
[1] Purchasing Power Standard (PPS) is a unit of measurement which cancels out differences in price levels and can be used to make comparisons in real terms.
[2] West Germany only.

Source: Eurostat, Basic Statistics of the Community, 1994.

to increase relative to other goods and services, for example, this means that industries such as leisure and entertainment, with their high income elasticities, will expand relative to those for staple food products.

It is not only the demand side that will affect the structure of the economy however. Technical progress leads to new goods and services being produced and to new innovations, meaning that some goods can be produced more efficiently or at lower cost. The provision of services can also be improved via technical progress and via developments such as text processing and computerised accounts processes. International competition itself is also a force for change in any economy. The demise of some industries in the more developed economies (motorcycle manufacture in the UK, for example) is a result of other countries being able to satisfy changing consumer tastes at lower prices.

A growing trend over the last decade has been towards part-time employment. Table 3.4 shows the pattern of employment across the EU by gender. In every country but Spain, there

Table 3.3. Percentage of the civilian population working in main sectors of economic activity (1990 and 1992)

Country	Agriculture 1990	1992	Industry 1990	1992	Services 1990	1992
EUR 12	6.6	5.8	32.5	32.8	60.9	61.4
Belgium	2.7	2.9	28.7	30.9	68.5	66.2
Denmark	5.7	5.2	25.6	27.4	68.7	67.4
Germany	3.4	3.7	39.8	39.1	56.8	57.2
Greece	25.3	21.9	27.5	25.4	47.1	52.8
Spain	11.8	10.1	33.4	32.7	54.8	57.2
France	6.1	5.9	29.9	29.6	64.0	64.5
Ireland	15.0	13.8	28.7	28.9	56.3	57.1
Italy	9.0	7.9	32.4	33.2	58.6	59.0
Luxembourg	3.2	3.1	30.7	29.6	66.1	67.3
Netherlands	4.6	3.9	26.3	25.2	69.1	70.9
Portugal	17.8	11.5	34.9	32.6	47.4	56.0
United Kingdom	2.2	2.2	29.5	30.2	68.3	67.5
Austria	7.9	7.1	36.8	35.6	55.3	57.4
Finland	8.4	8.6	31.0	27.8	60.6	63.5
Sweden	3.3	3.2	29.2	26.6	67.5	70.1
Norway	6.5	5.6	24.7	23.5	68.8	70.9
USA	2.8	2.9	26.2	24.6	70.9	72.5
Japan	7.2	6.4	34.1	34.6	58.7	59.0

Source: Eurostat, Basic Statistics of the Community, 1994.

Table: 3.4. Structure of the workforce in industry in selected countries (1990)

Country	Structure of male workforce (% of employees) Full-time	Part-time	Skilled	Structure of female workforce (% of employees) Full-time	Part-time	Skilled	Structure of total workforce (% of employees) Full-time	Part-time	Skilled
Belgium	99	1	66	87	13	42	97	3	62
Germany	99	1	71	80	20	40	94	6	62
Greece	98	2	74	89	11	54	95	5	67
Spain	84	16	55	81	19	58	82	18	56
France	99	1	84	95	5	73	97	3	80
Ireland	98	2	66	92	8	44	96	4	59
Italy	100	0	80	96	4	74	99	1	79
Netherlands	97	3	77	73	27	70	91	9	76
Portugal	98	2	56	96	4	47	97	3	50
United Kingdom	98	2	44	77	23	24	91	9	38

Source: European Economy, No. 47, March 1991, p. 35.

are very few men working part-time, but when we examine statistics on the employment of women the picture is different. Women with domestic responsibilities often chose to work part-time, but as we shall see in Chapter 6, there is also a trend towards more flexible working patterns (sometimes at significantly lower wages). The variations which we observe in these statistics must, at least in part, be explained by cultural differences across the EU countries. Table 3.4 also provides a measure of the degree of skill in industry in the different countries. Increasingly advanced technology combined with the availability of cheap labour outside the EU means that it is imperative that skills are increased across the Community if such changes are not to lead to unemployment. However, the statistics tend to suggest that skills levels are extremely variable and that women employed in industry are often less skilled. France leads the league table when it comes to the proportion of skilled workers in industry (70 per cent of the total workforce). It is particularly interesting that the country which lags behind is the UK with a comparable figure of only 38 per cent.

A common way of examining the development of a country is to look at the provision of some luxury items (televisions and cars, for example) and the provision of infrastructure or communications links (e.g. telephone lines). Whilst this is only one very specific measure (or more correctly, indicator) of economic development, it is nevertheless one which is often quoted. It can be seen from Table 3.5 that there are fewer people than the European

Table 3.5. Television sets, telephone lines and private cars in use per 1000 population (1991)

Country	Television receivers	Telephone lines	Private cars
EUR 12	460	470	361
EEA	461	n.a.	374
Belgium	451	375	398
Denmark	536	555	310
Germany	556	474	458
Greece	197	378	176
Spain	400	304	322
France	407	473	419
Ireland	276	259	235
Italy	421	370	488
Luxembourg	267	464	498
Netherlands	485	451	371
Portugal	187	201	281
United Kingdom	434	446	374
Austria	478	427	394
Finland	501	542	380
Sweden	468	690	419
Iceland	319	525	465
Norway	423	515	378
USA	813	533	564
Japan	610	432	299

Source: Eurostat, Basic Statistics of the Community, 1992 and 1994.

average using televisions and telephones in Portugal and Greece, for example. However, there are significant cultural influences here which should not be allowed to cloud the picture too much. To suggest, for example, that people in the USA are twice as well off as people in West Germany just because there is twice the density of television ownership would be spurious. The Americans clearly like the television! In relation to car ownership, we see the highest rates in the USA, Italy, Luxembourg, Germany and Iceland. Given the environmental damage caused by cars, however, many would question whether car ownership is an appropriate measure of wealth.

We may also be interested in examining the future productive potential of an economy. A key factor here will be the education and skills of the workforce. Businesses will not wish to build plants needing highly skilled labour if that labour potential is not present, for example. Table 3.6 contains information on the number of pupils and students in full-time and part-time education in the EEA. Since education at primary and secondary levels is almost entirely compulsory any significant difference in percentages must be made up by those in further and higher education. Countries where the level is below the European average are more likely to suffer skills shortages in the future. Other countries may also have a competitive advantage related to a more highly skilled workforce. However, such considerations imply that the quality of education is equivalent across countries, which it clearly is not. With free movement of labour generated by the Single European Market skills shortages may be less likely though as labour with specific skills is attracted to where it is needed most, by higher wages.

Table 3.6. Young people in full-time or part-time education as a percentage of the population (5–24 years)

Country	1985/86	1989/90	1991/2
EUR 12	67	69	72
Belgium	74	77	80
Denmark	69	71	72
Germany	67	68	71
Greece	65	65	65
Spain	70	74	74
France	68	72	72
Ireland	64	68	68
Italy	60	61	64
Luxembourg	52	53	55
Netherlands	74	74	87
Portugal	59	61	63
United Kingdom	70	74	76
Austria	63	65	66
Finland	68	75	79
Sweden	65	65	65
Iceland	67	70	74
Norway	67	72	75

Source: Eurostat, Basic Statistics of the Community, 1992 and 1994.

MACROECONOMIC PROFILES

The study of macroeconomics is concerned with the behaviour of broad aggregates in the economy. These provide us with general background information about the past, present and future performance of an economy which is vital before considering the more specific issues relating to establishing business in a particular country. There is a need, therefore, to examine a country's key macroeconomic variables in order to get information on the economic stability, potential strength, resource use or capacity and size and growth of potential markets. Information about inflation, wage levels, unemployment and growth are therefore vital. In such an examination it will often be possible to group together certain countries with common characteristics.

Inflation

The Single European Market means that all firms become subject to international competition. Price is a key factor in this competition and, in turn, price is influenced by input costs, wage bills and capital costs. Many of these items are directly linked to domestic inflation and, therefore, countries with high inflation will be less competitive. One of the ways in which we may categorise European countries is therefore by inflation rates. The European Consumer Price Index (which provides a comparable inflation measure) for EU Member States for 1989 and 1990 gives the following observed inflation statistics:

Table 3.7. Inflation rates (percentage)

Country	1994	1993	1992	1991	1990	Average 1990–94	Observations above the EUR 12 average
Denmark	2.2	1.2	1.5	2.3	2.5	1.9	0
France	1.7	2.2	2.0	3.1	3.5	2.5	0
Ireland	2.5	1.3	2.3	3.6	3.5	2.6	0
Belgium	2.4	3.2	2.4	2.8	3.3	2.8	0
Luxembourg	2.0	3.7	2.9	2.6	3.3	2.9	0
Netherlands	2.6	3.0	2.9	4.9	2.4	3.2	1
Germany (West)	3.0	4.2	3.7	4.2	2.8	3.6	1
United Kingdom	2.4	1.7	2.6	4.5	10.6	4.4	2
Italy	3.8	4.5	4.6	6.1	6.6	5.1	5
Spain	4.8	4.6	5.4	5.6	6.5	5.4	5
Portugal	4.8	5.6	8.4	8.9	12.7	8.1	5
Greece	11.1	14.6	14.4	18.0	21.9	16.0	5
EUR 12 Average	3.1	3.5	3.7	4.3	5.9	4.1	
Austria	3.2	3.4					
Finland	1.9	2.1					
Sweden	2.6	4.8					
Norway	1.6	2.2					

Sources: European Research (March 1990 and January 1991) and Eurostat, Eurostatistics for short-term economic analysis, No. 2, 1993 and No. 10, 1994.

Comparisons of observations of domestic inflation rates with the Community average inflation rate between 1990–1994 provide us with a benchmark with which to divide the figures into low inflation and high inflation economies. As can be seen from Table 3.7, this sort of comparison provides very consistent data. Thus countries which have had an inflation problem include Spain, Italy, Portugal and Greece. The UK had relatively high inflation in 1990 and 1991 but this was subsequently brought under control. An interesting characteristic is that all the Southern European economies fall into the high inflation category. This can be explained by a number of factors:

1 Southern European economies have experienced significant growth since joining the EU and fast growth and consequential increases in aggregate demand does cause prices to rise. This is shown clearly in Fig. 3.1 where using conventional aggregate supply and demand schedules we can see the effect of an increase in aggregate demand. AD_1 represents the initial total demand in an economy. This is a downward sloping function since we assume that the lower the price level the more consumers will wish to purchase. AS is the aggregate supply function which is simply the sum of all individual supply functions based on the assumption that the higher the price of a good the more firms will be willing to produce. As the economy expands, national income or output (since the two are equivalent), Y, grows and at any price level consumers will demand more goods. This increases aggregate demand to AD_2. The effect is to increase national output in the economy from Y_1 to Y_2 but also to increase the price level from P_1 to P_2 (i.e. causing inflation).

2 Because of the less developed nature of their economies, government institutions and banking sectors, it has been more difficult to control key policy instruments such as the money supply and fiscal policy. Since there is a direct link between an economy's money supply and inflation, and demand management is less easy in such an economy the power of the government to reduce price rises is decreased. The relative ineffectiveness of government macroeconomic policy is also related to the size and number of parallel (black) markets. With significant, unofficial sectors in an economy it is particularly difficult to control economic activity by means of aggregate demand management policies.

The fact that the UK has experienced high inflation in the past cannot be explained by the factors above. But as we can see from Table 3.8, the UK has had a relative inflation problem. The continuation of this problem in the late 1980s may have been explained by the UK delaying its entry into the Exchange Rate Mechanism (ERM) until late 1990 (the

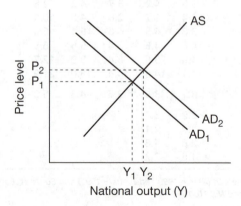

Fig. 3.1 The effect of an increase in aggregate demand on prices and output

significance of this is more fully explained in Chapter 4). Certainly, when France entered the ERM its relatively high inflation rate was brought under control quite quickly.

Table 3.8. Consumer price index for EEA countries (1985 = 100)

Country	1989	1990	1991	1992	1993
EUR 12	116.3	129.9	129.1	134.6	139.1
Belgium	107.3	111.0	114.6	117.4	120.6
Denmark	118.1	121.2	124.1	126.7	128.3
Germany	104.2	107.0	110.7	115.1	119.9
Greece	184.9	222.6	266.0	308.1	352.6
Spain	128.2	136.8	145.0	153.5	160.6
France	112.7	116.5	120.0	123.0	124.8
Ireland	113.9	117.6	121.3	125.1	126.9
Italy	123.8	131.8	140.0	147.3	153.8
Luxembourg	105.1	109.0	112.4	115.9	120.1
Netherlands	101.7	104.2	108.4	112.5	114.9
Portugal	151.0	170.9	189.6	206.7	220.0
United Kingdom	121.8	133.3	141.1	146.4	148.7
Austria	107.8	111.3	115.1	119.7	124.0
Finland	120.0	127.4	132.6	136.7	139.7
Sweden	122.3	135.1	147.8	151.1	158.2
Iceland	216.8	250.5	267.5	278.1	289.5
Norway	130.0	135.1	147.8	151.1	158.2
Japan	103.7	106.9	110.4	n.a.	n.a.
USA	115.3	121.5	126.6	130.5	134.3

Source: Eurostat, Basic Statistics of the Community, 1994.

We need, therefore, to explain why an advanced industrialised economy with mature institutions may still suffer continued inflation. There are four common reasons for this in any industrialised country.

1 Domestic citizens and trade unions often become used to and expect inflation linked wage and salary increases which perpetuates any problem. Such increases simply lead to a wage-price spiral where firms maintain their profitability by putting up prices, increasing inflation and leading to further wage demands. The cycle continues spiralling upwards.
2 Such a wage-price spiral can be avoided if wage increases can be matched by productivity increases, maintaining a firm's profitability. But, commonly, an inability to match high wage increases with productivity increases will result in a need for firms to increase their prices once again leading to inflation.
3 Advanced industrialised countries are often characterised by a high degree of oligopolisation. In other words, there exists a large number of mature, large (often conglomerate) firms with high market shares, brand loyalty and monopoly power. This results in the firms achieving an inelastic demand for their products and enables them to increase their profitability by increasing prices (which is inflationary) without significantly reducing their total revenue.

4 Industrialised economies often become quite specialised in their productive activities or indeed even substitute manufacturing sectors for service industries over time. This sometimes means that they become reliant on certain imported goods as they specialise in their own 'best' products. With a high propensity to import and inelastic demand for imports caused by high living standards, external price increases can therefore result in imported inflation.

As well as price inflation, a key variable in the international competitiveness of countries will be their wage rates and wage inflation. Worldwide, countries in South East Asia have often based much of their growth and international competitive advantage on the ability to produce goods at lower costs than their competitors because of low wage rates. Table 3.9 shows relative wage rates amongst the EU Member States and this accords with the sort of scenario given above where new capital investment may be attracted towards countries where the wage bill is relatively low. Indeed, this incentive is one of the reasons why some investment within the EU has been diverted to Eastern European countries. This issue is dealt with in more detail in Chapter 11.

Table 3.9. Wages in industry (manual workers)

Country	Average gross hourly earnings (Ecu)		Wage inflation (index, 1985=100)	
	1990	1992	1990	1992
Belgium	8.06	9.40	114.3	128.3
Denmark	12.03	13.42	130.2	141.7
Germany	10.17	11.74	120.0	139.4
Greece	3.33	3.65	195.5	261.4
Spain	5.90	6.49	146.6	172.9
France	6.53	7.36	n.a.	n.a.
Ireland	7.10	7.95	128.8	146.1
Luxembourg	8.58	9.01	120.1	n.a.
Netherlands	8.24	9.45	114.4	122.3
Portugal	1.83	2.50	178.0	237.9
United Kingdom	7.81	7.82	140.3	164.1

Source: Eurostat, Basic Statistics of the Community, 1992 and 1994.

The table shows the relative advantage of the southern European countries with respect to wage rates. However, those countries have been subject to significant wage inflation (almost 100 per cent in Greece, for example, between 1985–1990) which will erode their attractiveness if it is sustained. Nevertheless, there are distinct advantages to establishing a presence in the Southern European countries within the EU rather than elsewhere. These include:

● low wage rates
● nearness to a rapidly growing markets in the EU
● the development of common EU standards and legislation which provides a firm with more certainty
● a greater general availability of capital in the EU and a potentially well-trained workforce with freedom of movement allowing for highly specialised staff and management to be moved to where they are needed.

In addition, southern Europe still provides large potential markets itself as its economies continue to develop rapidly and has relatively low land prices which attracts inward investment. Portugal is an attractive proposition for US firms, shipping semi-finished products or exporting to the EU, because of its Atlantic ports, for example.

Unemployment

Unemployment in an economy represents a significant waste of resources which could be used to produce goods and services. It also represents a drain on a government's funds through the payment of unemployment and social benefits. If there is unemployment in an economy there is, consequently, a lower aggregate disposable income with which to purchase goods and services and markets will be consequently smaller. There will also be social costs associated with unemployment which are less quantifiable. Therefore a productive and efficient economy needs to strive to have the lowest possible unemployment. To some extent, a fully employed economy can be self-perpetuating as firms enter economies where there are large markets and avoid investment in less successful economies where uncertainty is greatest. Comparative unemployment rates for EEA countries are shown in Table 3.10.

Table 3.10. Unemployment rates (percentage)

Country	1989	1990	1991	1992	1993	1994	Observations above EUR 12 average
EUR 12	8.9	8.3	8.9	9.6	10.6	10.9	
Belgium	8.5	7.8	8.3	8.2	9.4	10.0	0
Denmark	7.7	8.0	8.6	9.5	10.4	10.5	0
Germany	5.5	4.8	5.6	6.4	7.2	7.8	0
Greece	7.5	7.0	7.7	7.7	10.0[1]	10.0[1]	0
Spain	17.1	16.1	15.9	18.2	21.5	22.9	6
France	9.4	9.1	9.7	10.2	10.8	11.2	6
Ireland	15.7	14.5	16.1	17.8	18.4	18.0	6
Italy	10.7	9.8	10.3	10.1	11.1	11.3	6
Luxembourg	1.8	2.0	2.0	1.9	2.6	3.2	0
Netherlands	8.7	7.5	7.0	7.2	8.8	10.7	0
Portugal	4.8	4.5	4.0	3.9	5.0	6.1	0
United Kingdom	7.1	7.1	9.4	10.2	10.5	10.0	2
Austria	3.3	3.2	3.5	3.6	4.4	6.5	0
Finland	3.4	3.4	7.6	13.0	17.3	17.6	3
Sweden	1.4	1.5	2.7	4.8	7.7	7.3	0
Norway	4.9	5.2	5.5	5.9	6.2	5.8	0
USA	5.3	5.4	6.7	7.3	7.2	6.5	0
Japan	2.3	2.1	2.1	2.2	2.5	3.0	0

[1] Official Rate declared by the Greek Labour Office.

Sources: Eurostat, Basic Statistics of the Community, 1992 and 1994 and Eurostat, Eurostatistics for short-term economic analysis, 1995 and Economist Intelligence Unit, Country Reports for Austria, Finland, Sweden and Norway, 1995.

Overall, the figures clearly demonstrate the effects of the recession in the early 1990s. But they also show, very clearly, how the Community can be characterised into low unemployment and high unemployment areas (in a similar way to that done with inflation statistics in Table 3.9).

What is interesting here though is the relatively good performance with respect to unemployment of countries which have had high inflation. Portugal, for example, with high inflation figures has below average unemployment figures. This phenomenon has to be seen in the context of both the growth strategies and the underlying economic policies of the countries involved. Rapid growth strategies facilitated by expansionary government policies will often provide increasing employment opportunities, but often at the expense of price stability. Ultimately, it returns to policy makers to make a decision about the inflation/unemployment trade-off which they are willing to tolerate.

The figures also demonstrate the relatively poor employment performance of the UK compared with its more advanced counterparts in the EU. Coupled with its equally poor inflation record over time, a significant question mark must be placed over the well being of the UK economy. It has demonstrated neither rapid growth nor price stability but has suffered from periods of high unemployment.

Explanations of the existence of unemployment are very much associated with the 'school of thought' to which one belongs. Essentially, there are two competing approaches embodied in the Keynesian and monetarist critiques. These critiques are not necessarily mutually exclusive but the dominant reason for unemployment in any particular country has to be established before suitable policy can be implemented.

1 The Keynesian critique suggests that unemployment is caused by insufficient aggregate demand for goods and services to provide every worker with a job. Therefore, one way of reducing unemployment is for the government to take steps to increase the amount of demand in an economy. This can be done by increasing government expenditure or cutting taxes, for example. Increasing aggregate demand by too much can be inflationary however.

2 The monetarist approach argues that unemployment is generally caused because wages are too high and that unemployment will be reduced if workers accept lower wage levels, therefore making their services more attractive to employers. Monetarists have often blamed trade unions for pushing up wages and some have even gone as far as to suggest that unemployment and social benefits have created a floor below which wages will not fall, causing a lack of demand for some jobs.

A major reason for the existence of unemployment in some countries, and particularly for the problem of regional unemployment, is the mismatch between the type of vacancies which exist and the type of skills which the unemployed have. This is structural unemployment, for example, there are many unemployed steel workers throughout Europe whose particular skills are no longer in demand. This implies a need for retraining programmes which are in existence to one degree or another in all EU countries. But a key reason for the continuation of structural unemployment is the barriers imposed on the free movement of labour by higher housing and living costs in areas of high industrial concentration (around London and Paris, for example). Structural unemployment is therefore a direct function of longer term changes in the structure of an economy. Thus the rapid development of some parts of the EU is a source of a potential unemployment problem. Evidence for structural unemployment can be found by looking at unemployment figures during periods of relative economic prosperity. In the period 1990–1993 high levels of unemployment can be explained, in part, by cyclical fluctuation but when we examine unemployment in 1986–1987, for example, we can see a large structural unemployment problem.

In the southern European countries, unemployment has been caused as a process of urbanisation has progressed. People leaving the land, either by choice or because automation has reduced the need for agricultural workers, have not always found permanent work in the cities. A characteristic of European agriculture is that output has increased steadily with less and less labour. For those who have found jobs, a common characteristic is that they are of fixed duration or essentially part-time. The growth of part-time working is most significant amongst women.

Further analysis of unemployment rates shows that the impact of unemployment is often very uneven. Table 3.11 breaks figures down for men, women and young people (under 25 years of age). It can be seen that women are more likely to be unemployed than men and that, for young people, employment prospects are often very bad. Putting the two problems together reveals even more disturbing figures, for example, percentages for unemployed women under 25 years of age stand at 26 per cent in Ireland, 37 per cent in Italy and 43 per cent in Spain.

Table 3.11. Unemployment rates (percentage) among men, women and young people (March 1994)

Country	Total	Men	Women	Under 25 years
EUR 12	11.1	9.7	13.0	20.3
Belgium	10.0	7.1	14.4	20.7
Denmark	10.5	9.6	11.6	11.3
Germany	7.8	6.5	9.5	6.7
Spain	22.9	19.7	28.9	38.9
France	11.2	9.4	13.5	23.7
Ireland	18.0	17.0	19.9	27.5
Italy	11.3	7.9	17.0	31.7
Luxembourg	3.2	2.6	4.3	7.2
Netherlands	10.7	8.6	13.7	18.2
Portugal	6.1	5.2	7.2	11.8
United Kingdom	10.0	11.6	7.8	15.4

Source: Eurostat, Eurostatistics for short-term economic analysis, December, 1994.

Growth and industrialisation

Economic growth can be defined as an increase in a country's productive capacity, identifiable by a sustained rise in real national income over a period of years. Table 3.12 indicates that the economies with the highest growth rates are Spain, Ireland, Luxembourg and Portugal, which all experience consistently higher growth rates than the average for the EU. In the cases of Spain and Portugal, membership of the EU in 1986, economic aid (particularly in the case of Portugal) and improvements in the infrastructure and communications are key factors in the growth equation. Ireland is dealt with in detail in a case study at the end of this chapter.

Table 3.12. Growth in gross domestic product (at market prices, 1985 = 100)

Country	1989	1990	1991	1992	1993	1994
EUR 12	113.5	116.7	118.3	120.2	119.8	121.6
Belgium	112.7	117.0	118.6	119.8	118.3	119.8
Denmark	104.2	107.0	109.0	109.8	111.3	115.6
Germany	111.4	116.2	123.4	125.3	122.9	123.9
Greece	108.0	109.5	110.5	112.8	112.6	113.4
Spain	120.3	124.5	127.6	128.2	126.9	128.3
France	112.1	115.5	116.9	119.4	118.3	120.2
Ireland	114.4	123.9	126.3	142.6	146.1	152.2
Italy	113.5	116.0	117.7	118.4	117.6	119.4
Luxembourg	120.7	123.6	127.2	130.9	132.2	134.3
Netherlands	109.8	114.1	116.6	118.0	120.7	122.2
Portugal	120.1	125.1	127.3	128.5	126.9	128.3
United Kingdom	116.2	117.1	114.5	115.2	116.8	119.7
USA	114.8	115.9	115.8	117.2	120.0	123.6
Japan	118.6	125.4	130.9	131.4	131.5	132.5

Source: Eurostat, Statistics for short-term economic analysis, 1992 and 1994.

Once again, however, these statistics are affected by the recession of the early 1990s which affected the EU countries in different ways and at different times. Prior to that recession, we did see quite spectacular growth rates particularly in the least developed regions of the Community. Table 3.13 shows that Spain, Ireland and Portugal led the league table for the fastest growing economies. Even compared with Japanese growth rates they are very

Table 3.13. Annual average rates of growth of gross domestic product at market prices (percentage)

Country	1985–1990	1987–1992	1989–1994
Belgium	3.2	2.8	1.3
Denmark	1.5	1.1	2.2
Germany	3.1[1]	4.7	2.2
Greece	1.7	1.8	0.7
Spain	4.5	3.7	1.3
France	2.9	2.4	1.4
Ireland	4.4	5.3	6.6
Italy	3.0	2.4	1.0
Luxembourg	4.3	3.9	2.2
Netherlands	2.7	2.7	2.3
Portugal	4.6	3.5	1.4
United Kingdom	3.2	1.6	0.6
USA	3.0	2.1	1.5
Japan	4.6	4.2	2.3

[1] West Germany

Sources: derived from Eurostat, Basic Statistics of the Community, 1992 and 1994, and Eurostat, Eurostatistics for short-term economic analysis, 1994.

impressive. Looking at the period 1989–94 we can see the impact of the recession and the fact that its impact on different countries was often quite different.

Growth should not always be seen as necessarily good, however, it does have some negative aspects. Experience suggests that rapid growth can cause externalities such as pollution and other environmental damage (this issue is dealt with in more detail in Chapter 10) and it has already suggested that too high a rate of growth can be inflationary.

Industrialisation is the process of the development of new industries and changing industries leading to the creation of an industrialised economy – in other words, one where the source of economic activity is largely industrially based rather than agriculturally based. The industrialisation process means that there will be organisational change both within firms and within economies.

The UK is generally viewed as the first industrialised country, but it is interesting to note that the rate of economic growth during the UK's period of industrialisation was less than in many of the economies which industrialised later. Levels of income and production per capita in the UK were double those in the rest of Western Europe in the 1850s. The UK produced over half of the world's output of coal and iron. Raw cotton and energy consumption were 48 per cent and 30 per cent respectively of world consumption. What remains interesting is the way in which the UK lost this leadership in the later nineteenth and twentieth centuries. Other countries have industrialised faster than the UK, attained greater levels of output and have managed to hold on to their position to a greater extent. It is interesting to consider the experiences of Japan and Germany, but it also important to consider what might be the next wave of significant growth and industrialisation in countries such as Korea, Malaysia and some of their South East Asian neighbours.

One of the most interesting concepts which arises from a consideration of industrialisation is the process of de-industrialisation. Whilst this *does not* mean that economies go into absolute decline. What it *does* imply is that manufacturing sectors go into relative decline both in terms of the major competitors of that country and also in terms of other sectors in the economy (most notably the service sector). Evidence supporting this can be found in Table 3.3. The experience of many European countries has been that the service sector has grown, manufacturing has become less important and many industries have actually disappeared. This has resulted in structural unemployment and balance of payment deficits as imports are substituted for the goods which are no longer produced domestically.

The question which arises is whether or not this process actually matters. There are those who would argue along the lines of traditional international economic theory that countries with a comparative advantage in the production of a particular good or service should specialise in that area. Some economists have therefore argued that, in the case of the UK, for example, comparative advantage exists in the areas of financial markets, banking and insurance and that the UK should specialise in those areas. The truth is somewhat different however: financial markets are increasingly globalised with the massive advances made in information and communications technologies, the largest banks in the world are now to be found in Japan and the same sort of trend of movement towards the most economically active countries is occurring with the insurance business as well. Whether or not a country which has a declining industrial sector is a sustainable proposition in the long run remains to be seen. Some pessimists argue that the industrialisation and de-industrialisation process has a cyclical nature and that, because the UK was the first country to be industrialised it will also be the first to return to the ranks of the underdeveloped countries.

A PICTURE OF DIVERSITY: THE EUROPEAN UNION'S REGIONAL PROBLEMS

As well as finding significant differences between countries in the EU, we can also identify regional differences within those countries. Because of that, we find that regional disparity is even greater than national statistics can reveal. Table 3.14 provides selected statistics on regional economic indicators. This shows significant differences not only between countries but also within countries. Particular regions, even within the wealthiest countries, have local GDPs well below the EU average.

Table 3.14. Gross domestic product at market prices: selected regional indicators for 1991 (EUR 12 = 100)

Germany	**119.8**
Hamburg	202.8
Düsseldorf	134.1
Trier	86.9
Spain	**77.3**
Madrid	96.6
Rioja	84.7
Extremadura	50.5
France	**111.5**
Ile-de-France	166.7
Aquitaine	103.2
Corse	80.3
Italy	**102.7**
Lombardia	134.4
Toscana	109.3
Sicillia	67.9
Netherlands	**100.5**
Groningen	135.2
Utrecht	105.9
Friesland	82.7
United Kingdom	**95.2**
Greater London	143.6
West Yorkshire	88.8
Northern Ireland	72.2

The origin of the regional problem in the EU is very much tied up with four fundamental characteristics of a modern capitalist economy.

First, there is a declining use of labour relative to capital in agriculture and a corresponding urbanisation process. This has led to the continuing depopulation of peripheral regions.

Second, there is a declining reliance of manufacturing industry on natural materials and the consequence is that the location decision often has to be to establish enterprises near to final markets. This, again, has reinforced urbanisation trends and left regions rich in natural resources nevertheless underdeveloped.

Third, service activities continue to be important and they tend to serve large urbanised populations, further increasing the pull to a centre.

Fourth, there is fierce competition from lesser developed economies for labour-intensive production leaving some traditional industries unable to compete and in decline. Where these industries have previously been regionally based, they disappear and there is nothing to replace them.

It has been argued by some economists (*see*, for example, Mair, 1991) that regional disparities in Europe have widened throughout the 1980s. This is due to two main reasons: first, the beginning of the 1980s saw a worldwide recession, but the recession hit hardest in the less developed regions of the Community where growth rates fell substantially and unemployment reached its highest post-war levels. The recession of the early 1990s also hit different regions to differing degrees with the economies already experiencing significant unemployment faring the worst. It is a trend that the less resilient economies will be hardest hit during times of downturn and firms have to bear this in mind in their strategic planning (*see* Chapter 7). Second, the entry of Spain, Portugal and Greece into the European Community, each with a per capita national income lower than the average and a wider internal spread of economic activity, lowered the average Community income and led to a widening of the disparities.

It is possible to identify a number of specific regional problems which require attention. These can be divided up in terms of their geographical characteristics and it is worth looking at each one in turn:

Urban areas

About 80 per cent of the population of the EU live in towns and cities. These areas have undergone substantial changes in terms of size and function. Economic change and development has been responsible for increasing urbanisation, particularly in the south of Europe. Severe problems of unemployment, poverty and poor housing nevertheless exist in many inner cities and this is often because of concentrations of migrants in certain parts of major cities.

During the 1980s we saw an interesting trend in urbanisation in Europe. The large urban areas tended, on average, to be stable, either growing very slowly or in some cases losing population. However, we saw a more rapid growth in small and medium sized cities with good connections or within close proximity to the metropolitan areas. These smaller urban areas were able to attract skilled workers by offering them a good location, easy communication and shorter travelling distances, in a cleaner and less congested environment.

During the 1990s, the overall urban map of Europe will not change dramatically. Much more rapid rates of growth will occur outside of Europe. In 1980, Paris and London were among the 15 biggest cities in the world, but estimates suggest that no European city will be in the top 20 by the year 2000. Changes in Central and Eastern Europe are likely to increase the importance of cities such as Vienna and Berlin.

Although size may not change significantly the function of some cities may. Growth in the past has largely been a result of socio-economic developments. Present developments include the ongoing transition from a manufacturing to a service economy, the completion of the single market through the removal of internal frontiers, the development of telecommunications and high-speed transport networks. These developments may be accompanied by increased competition between cities to attract investment.

As economic activities develop and change so will the relative position of individual cities. For example, in financial services, although the role of London as a leading world centre is unlikely to be challenged in the next ten years, there are a number of other cities such as Dublin, Brussels, Copenhagen, Barcelona, Lisbon, Luxembourg and Edinburgh attempting to develop financial services which will take business away from the established centres such as London, Paris and Frankfurt. Monetary Union will accelerate competition between these centres to serve European-wide markets, which might affect medium-sized cities providing financial services to a regional or national market.

While the structural funds are not specifically targeted at urban areas, the more peripheral towns and cities are clearly in need of some support. Large cities falling within Objective 1 Support Frameworks include Belfast, Dublin, Lisbon, Oporto, Athens, Palmero, Naples and Seville.

Rural areas

About 80 per cent of the land in the EU is rural, containing under 20 per cent of its population. Rural areas are characterised by considerable diversity but, for policy reasons, the European Commission has suggested a division of rural areas into three types:

- those under pressure from modern development, near to or easily accessible from large conurbations
- those in decline whose survival is threatened
- remote and isolated areas which are depopulated (such as mountain regions and small islands).

As this implies, there is a clear distinction between rural areas which are relatively prosperous, and economically weaker regions, which are home to the rural poor, more vulnerable, very dependent on traditional agriculture and experiencing outward migration. It is, above all, the degree of peripherality which is determining the development of rural areas. The less favoured the region, the greater we find the importance of agriculture in the social and economic structure. Most of these regions, in turn, are located on the periphery of the EU, particularly on the Mediterranean.

Although agriculture is considerably less important in employment terms than it was, it still accounts for 57 per cent of land use in the EU. It therefore continues to be a major influence on Community life. We have seen throughout the 1980s that agricultural produce has consistently outstripped demand leading to surpluses. Despite a more restrictive pricing policy and measures to restrict supply, agricultural production is still rising at around two per cent a year because of the advances of technology. At the same time, consumption of agricultural products is likely to remain stable because of stagnating populations and changes in consumer tastes (e.g. less meat consumption). It is somewhat inevitable that land will be taken out of production in the future.

The development of new businesses and the availability of employment outside agriculture are vital for the survival of these more peripheral rural regions. The development of forestry and tourism and recreation offer some alternatives to the current position but special attention must be given to any degradation of the environment which new industry or activities may bring. Environmental protection and landscape management can, of course, also provide jobs. With the growth in telecommunications networks there is also some scope for the development of the service sector.

Border cities and regions

There are essentially two types of border regions, those within the EU on a border of two Member States, and those on the periphery of the EU which border non-EU countries. Traditionally, border regions have been disadvantaged, not simply because they are peripheral but also because of the constraints imposed by the juxtaposition of different legal and administrative systems, reinforced by poor cross-border communications. In many cases, border areas have also had a poor infrastructure because they are located on the extremities of national transport and communications networks.

The combined effect of these influences is that border areas tend to have lower levels of income per head and higher rates of unemployment than other regions in their countries. This is particularly the case in the border regions of Portugal, Ireland and Greece where GDP per head is around 50 per cent of the EU average. With increasing integration over time, the border areas internal to the EU will lose much of their previous significance. Indeed some regions which are now peripheral in their national context will become more central in a more integrated EU. Such a process may not happen with regions bordering third countries but there will be significant new opportunities from many of these which border Central and Eastern Europe as the process of reform and the development of new markets gathers momentum.

Considerable numbers of people already live in one Member State and work in another, despite the obstacles created by different fiscal regimes, social legislation, culture and language. Steps taken to facilitate the free movement of citizens should increase this cross-border mobility and lead to the emergence of new employment areas extending across national boundaries. Such freedom of movement does, however, bring with it a freer movement for migrants, moving from poorer regions to richer ones, without jobs.

To attempt to alleviate the problems of border regions the European Commission plans to organise actions around three main axes:

1 substantial investment in infrastructure and industrial development, including special measures to tackle the problems of environmental pollution on both sides of a border;
2 a major programme of cross-border co-operation to gain the considerable benefits of co-ordinated physical and economic planning and the sharing of public services and facilities;
3 co-operation to manage immigration and the free flow of cross-border workers.

Coastal areas and islands

The coastal areas are among the most important but most environmentally fragile parts of the EU. In many regions, particularly the less developed peripheral ones, they represent a great development potential. Although new residential, commercial and tourist developments have been bringing inward investment to these areas, the environmental impact of these developments and the seasonal nature of tourism creates other problems.

In the west Mediterranean region, these problems can be seen in terms of heavy congestion. In Provence more than 60 per cent of the coastline has been urbanised, for example. In Spain, over half of the Mediterranean coastline is taken up with intensive housing and industrial and tourist development. In addition, rates of population growth are usually considerably higher than in interior regions. In the Mediterranean coastal areas of France and Spain, these rates of growth are about three times the EU average.

The situation on the North Atlantic and North Sea coastlines is less acute, with many sections of the coastline remaining undeveloped. Urban areas and industry are clustered around important development centres such as Dublin, Rotterdam and Copenhagen. However, certain stretches of these seaboards, such as the Belgian coast are almost entirely built up.

With the entry of Finland and Sweden in to the EU there is also an Arctic coastal region to consider. This is sparsely populated and relatively undeveloped. It has unique environmental characteristics and has a special place in maintaining balance within many ecosystems. As a potentially significant tourist destination in the future, there will be a need to develop sensitive development plans for the area.

The EU's 400 inhabited islands share many of the problems of the coastal areas, such as those arising from the need to reduce overcapacity in the fishing industry which calls for new efforts to encourage diversification. Their generally small size and geographical isolation are major obstacles to be overcome in promoting their economic development. Support for the development of new technologies, transport and telecommunications on the islands are of great importance in helping to make it viable for new enterprises to locate in remote areas.

Of all the EU's islands, only 21 of them have more than 50 000 inhabitants, Sicily and Sardinia have populations of over one million. In general, the islands are characterised by agricultural sectors bigger than the EU average, underdeveloped industrial sectors and a large service sector often dominated by tourism. In the Scottish islands, there has been some development success through diversifying into shellfish and fish farming but, in general, the islands are becoming more marginalised as economic integration increases.

The regional problems, possible solutions and policies for the coastal areas and islands are examined in greater detail in a case study at the end of this chapter.

Mountain and upland regions

Almost 30 per cent of the EU's territory consists of upland and mountainous areas, but only around 7.5 per cent of the population live there. The average population density (42 people per square kilometre) is only one third of the average for the six upland countries and in certain peripheral upland areas the figure can be as low as two or three people per square kilometre. Although these regions are diverse there are some common elements:

- poor soils, more extreme climatic conditions, limited natural resources, but considerable natural attractiveness
- a poor level of economic integration
- a narrow economic base often dependent on agriculture and/or tourism, remoteness and higher investment costs for infrastructure
- ecological richness and vulnerability.

Upland areas can be broadly split into three categories: *extreme peripheral* uplands, *intermediate* uplands and *developed* uplands. The most extreme areas include the northern Highlands of Scotland, the Greek uplands, southern Italian uplands, north-eastern Portugal and the Sierra de Gredos and the western Corillera of Spain. These are peripheral areas, far from economic centres and suffer inadequate communications. In the absence of economic opportunities, their populations have been in long-term decline.

THE CORE–PERIPHERY DEBATE

It has often been argued that one of the consequences of European integration could be the creation of a core of economic activity in the centre of Europe. This core would stretch between northern France, Southern Germany and northern Italy, exacerbating the problems of peripheral regions. The scenario is similar to that which has created a core of activity in the south-east of England and relatively depressed areas in the north. Firms see advantages of being near to other firms and close to the more affluent consumer markets created by higher levels of employment and higher wage rates. The consequence of a core of activity in Europe and the relocation of companies into that core is to leave some areas in Europe in a state of decline. Countries which may be worst affected include the UK and Ireland which, apart from being on the geographical edge of the Community, have the physical obstacle of the English Channel, North Sea and Irish Sea to contend with. The additional transport costs which this creates can act as a competitive disadvantage.

Free market theory would suggest that in time the core will become an expensive area in which to locate and that there will be profitable opportunities associated with locating in peripheral areas where land prices will be cheaper and wage rates lower. A free functioning market would therefore cause factors of production to move out of high cost regions into low cost regions until cost differences are minimised and profits roughly equalised. Even if one accepts the free market argument, there may still be a role for intervention by governments for three reasons:

1 The relocation response may be very slow and there may be a role for speeding up the process via additional relocation incentives.
2 The movement of capital and labour to new locations will be based on private cost assessments and not on social cost. Thus costs associated with congestion, pollution and personal utility will not be taken into account. There may therefore be a role for government in discouraging movement towards a core and promoting peripheral development. This is likely to be achieved with appropriate taxes, subsidies and grants.
3 The mobility of labour is not equal within any workforce. It is generally younger, more able and more enterprising individuals without strong family ties who are able to move. This can result in a population being left behind in a peripheral location which is not only reduced in size but also in competitive ability.

Trends in technology and communications have made the dispersal of economic activity technologically easier. Because of the existence of electronic communications links, remote monitoring processes, computerised stock control and the speed and reliability of such electronic systems, it is possible for the management function to be physically separate from the manufacturing function. Thus, there may be an incentive for firms to establish manufacturing bases where wages are lower and where land prices are cheaper whilst maintaining links with the core at the management level. However, there is a more worrying aspect to this, which is that if firms can locate their manufacturing plants in lower cost areas then why should they choose areas within the EU at all? Why not, for example, chose Eastern European locations which have even lower costs but retain their locational advantages with respect to western Europe? If costs are substantially lower and can even make large transportation costs viable then there may an incentive to locate to the Third World as well. Such scenarios will do little to cure a potential peripheral problem.

The service and information sectors of an economy may also become decentralised over time as providers of services and information have more and more electronically generated information available to them and where electronic communications becomes the norm. Already large databases of information with remote access to them via the telecommunications network have meant that firms no longer have to be near to the centre of economic activity.

It remains to be seen which forces in the core–periphery debate will dominate in the long run and in any case there will be significant governmental pressure to avoid the creation of a periphery. Nevertheless, this is a major issue which has to be addressed in a regional context and the EU has developed a number of instruments aimed at alleviating current and potential regional problems.

REGIONAL POLICY

The EU's response to regional disparities was the establishment of a new set of Structural Funds in 1994. Approximately 80 per cent of the Structural Funds are allocated to the Objective 1 areas (*see* Table 3.16). The amounts which were allocated to the other objective areas can be seen in Table 3.17.

Table 3.15. The main Objective Areas as defined by Regional Policy (1994–1999)

Objective 1:	Economic adjustment of regions whose development is lagging behind.
Objective 2:	Economic conversion of declining industrial areas.
Objective 3:	Combating long term unemployed and facilitating the integration into working life of young people and of persons exposed to exclusion from the labour market.
Objective 4:	Facilitating the adaption of workers to industrial change and to changes in production systems.
Objective 5a:	Adjustment of the processing and marketing structures for agriculture and fisheries products.
Objective 5b:	Economic diversification of rural areas.

The instruments of regional policy

Most regional policies have operated on the principle of subsidies and grants. Although, in the EU, direct subsidies to labour are prohibited, indirect labour subsidies via training and capital subsidies via grants are operated widely. There is also considerable interest in developing infrastructures which will be of direct benefit to firms operating in the more depressed areas of the EU, and since subsidies for infrastructure do not offer direct differential assistance to individual industries, they do not conflict with the aims of EU Competition Policy. The so-called Structural Funds of the EU which provide the monies needed to carry out regional policy initiatives are divided into the following operational areas:

The European Regional Development Fund

The European Regional Development Fund (ERDF) operates on the basis of the principle of additionality. This means that funds are meant to add to, rather than replace, national assistance which is already in place. Problem regions which typically suffer regional problems and require structural adjustment can bid for this money. Thus the ERDF focuses particularly, although not entirely, on Objective areas 1 and 2.

Table 3.16. Regions eligible under Objective 1 (1993)

Portugal	The whole country
Ireland	The whole country
Greece	The whole country
Germany	Former East Germany
France	French Overseas Departments
	Douai-Valenciennes
	Avesnes
	Corsica
United Kingdom	Northern Ireland
	The Highlands and islands of Scotland
	Merseyside
Italy	Abruzzi
	Basilicata
	Calabria
	Campania
	Molise
	Apulla
	Sardinia
	Sicily
Spain	Andalusia
	Asturias
	Cantabria
	Castile-Leon
	Castile-La Mancha
	Ceuta y Melilla
	Valencia
	Extremadura
	Galicia
	Canary Islands
	Murcia
Netherlands	Flevoland
Belgium	Hainaut

Table 3.17. Allocation of structural funds (Ecu bn)

	1989	1993
Objective 1	5.8	9.2
Objective 2	1.0	1.5
Objectives 3 & 4	1.2	1.8
Objective 5a	0.7	0.7
Objective 5b	0.3	0.9

The European Social Fund

The European Social Fund (ESF) has the principal aim of encouraging job creation in areas of high unemployment and providing assistance for the development of new appropriate skills. Thus its main emphasis is on supporting training and retraining schemes. The fund also provides money to help to retrain employees unfamiliar with new technologies, migrant workers and women who are returning to full- or part-time employment.

The European Agricultural Guidance and Guarantee Fund

The bulk of the European Agricultural Guidance and Guarantee Fund (EAGGF) money is spent on intervention and export subsidies in the agricultural sector. Guidance section cash is designed to help rural communities to diversify away from traditional forms of production to new areas of agricultural activity such as forestry, whilst, at the same time preserving the fabric of rural society.

Although most regional aid is provided through these three funds, there are some other programmes which deal with specific industries which are identified as having problems, for example, RECHAR, RESIDER, RETEX and RENAVAL are funds aimed at promoting new technologies and training in the coal, steel, textile and shipbuilding industries respectively.

National governments also continue to provide aid for their own regions, both as part of the additionality requirement alongside EU funds and independently. The EU does, however, have the power to control the amount of funds being allocated as assistance to industry on competition grounds. Certain measures, such as the creation of Enterprise Zones, therefore require clearance by the Commission before their introduction.

THE REGIONS AND ECONOMIC POLICY

It has often been asserted that the EU, as currently being constructed, is moving ahead rapidly in mercantile, financial and monetary matters but is moving at a slower pace in terms of fiscal, budgetary and political issues (Curbelo, 1993). This has brought with it regional tensions because of the unequal economic development of different countries. Moreover, if European monetary union (EMU) requires a number of strict macroeconomic targets to be achieved, the so-called convergence criteria (see Chapter 4), then this will tend to have the effect of excluding certain countries from full participation in the single market.

The language of convergence itself has come to mean convergence of a monetary and financial nature. Other economic issues such as unemployment (a severe regional problem) and production is sometimes added to this, but rarely do we consider political and social convergence. Moreover, that emphasis on the monetary side of the equation has led to a dominant ideology espoused by the greatest economic power, Germany, to become generally accepted. Priority is given to anti-inflationary policies above all else. This sort of policy may well be contradictory to the aims of the less developed part of the Community which would wish to place greater emphasis on growth policies (which are sometimes seen as inflationary) necessary for the reduction of structural inequalities. Many of these economies see convergence more in terms of both economic and social criteria.

It is clear, therefore, that the dominant economic policy in the future will not favour traditional Keynesian fiscal expansion as a strategy for alleviating the regional problem. In an attempt to address regional disparities without such fiscal intervention the EU has identified three basic supply-side measures to focus on, namely:

- mobility of factors of production
- salary flexibility
- competition policies.

It is, therefore, worth examining the regional impact of economic policies in these three areas.

In relation to factors of production, economic theory would tend to argue that labour will be drawn towards areas where there are high salaries (the core) whilst capital, in search of greater profitability would be drawn to peripheral regions where it is a more scarce factor. Over time, capital investment in the peripheral area will lead to the demand for labour increasing, salaries increasing and labour moving back again. Thus, in the long run, we would expect approximate equalities spreading across the whole of the EU.

However, we know that there are important barriers which may prevent this mobility. In terms of labour, we know that there are barriers caused by the eleven official languages of the EU as well as all the minority languages. Cultural differentiation is often cited as another reason for labour not wishing to move location. Moreover, even if there was perfect mobility of capital even the theory would predict that the peripheral regions will suffer in the short run as its most skilled labour is drawn away. In relation to capital, we have argued above that it may be drawn towards a centre of economic activity and actually away from the peripheral regions and we cannot, therefore, assume what theory might predict.

The second issue concerns salary flexibility and it is argued that there will be advantages associated with the low salary levels in some peripheral regions since this will attract new businesses. It is clear from Table 3.18 that there are significant differences in those salary levels but this has led to rather less inward investment from Japan, the USA and Northern Europe than we might have expected to date.

Table 3.18. Average hourly labour costs in industry (US$), 1986–87

Germany	16.3
Netherlands	13.8
Belgium	13.4
Denmark	13.3
Italy	12.2
France	11.4
Ireland	9.1
United Kingdom	9.0
Spain	8.6
Greece	4.3
Portugal	3.0
United States	13.5
Japan	12.8

Source: Gallego, J. A. 'La tercera Europea: Union Economica y Monetaria y dessarrollo regional' in Cuadrado (ed) 'El Crecimiento Regional Espanol Ante la Integracion Europea' Ministerio de Economia y Hacienda: Madrid.

One of the explanations of this phenomena is that the relative costs of labour is increasingly less important when it comes to new investment decisions because new labour saving technology makes labour an ever smaller part of total production costs. In other words, the relative advantages of lower salaries are diminishing all the time. Moreover, the type of labour which is increasingly demanded to operate new technology is that with sophisticated scientific and technical skills: precisely the type of labour which is most lacking in the less developed regions.

When it comes to competition policies (discussed in detail in Chapter 5) we must recognise that the dominant ideology in Europe is based on the intensification of government deregulation and the promotion of economic liberalisation. Thus the intention through the promotion of competition is to expand markets, increase efficiency and reduce prices to the benefit of the whole community. However, central to the notion of deregulation and liberalisation is the elimination of subsidies which give industry in one country a competitive advantage over that in another country. On the other hand though, subsidies are often used as a means of promoting regional growth and development and their elimination removes this instrument of government policy.

There are clearly contradictions between the aims of economic policy and the aims of regional policy. In particular, there are tensions in the less developed countries in relation to financial convergence as a preparation for EMU and wider convergence issues. The idea of a two speed EMU, where the less developed economies would join in the EMU process at a later date, might be a sensible policy if monetary union is to be achieved in the next ten years. But it would further disadvantage those Member States who already lag behind. Indeed, such an EMU process might even reinforce the regional imbalances and differences with respect to the distribution of income.

CONCLUSION

Large differences in the EU do exist and there have been periods (most notably during the 1980s) when those disparities have actually increased. There are severe regional problems in the EU and whilst trying to encourage economic development in them, integration itself poses the threat that economic union might result in the development of a core and periphery of economic activity, thus exacerbating the problem. Moreover, we know that many of the regions of the EU also have severe environmental problems and that rapid economic growth will only make them worse. Regional policy therefore needs to seek a balance between economic development policies and environmental protection.

Nevertheless the integration and unification trend is in motion and to many that trend seems unstoppable. The subsequent major debate therefore surrounds just how wide (in terms of membership) and how integrated the EU will become. Central here is the key debate surrounding whether the EU should be widened (in terms of its membership) before it is further deepened (in terms of economic and political unification) or deepened before it is widened. There is a queue of countries wanting to join the Community. For long standing applicants such as Turkey and for Central and Eastern European countries there is likely to be a long transitional period. But, with the entry of some EFTA countries in 1995, the EU will clearly become both wider and deeper. Although we now have a clear time frame associated with further economic integration, the difficult issue of political union may well become a more central focus.

Whatever the future size and direction of the EU, regional policy will have to be a key policy instrument if integration and harmonisation are to be achieved. The success of that regional policy will be based on the European Commission's ability to use its structural funds in an effective and targeted way and on the commitment of all Member States to putting in place measures which are in the interest of the EU as a whole. However, we must always be aware of the close links between economic policy and regional policy. The next chapter demonstrates that they may not be as consistent as we might imagine.

Questions for discussion

1 To what extent, and why, is the European Union dominated by four large economies?

2 How might you account for the fact that West Germany contributes about 25 per cent to the European Union's Gross Domestic Product whilst it has only 19 per cent of its population?

3 Outline the reasons why some countries may have relatively high inflation compared to their counterparts.

4 How might you account for consistently high unemployment rates in the Republic of Ireland?

5 Which countries have had the highest growth rates within the European Union? How do you explain this?

6 Is there evidence of a core and a periphery of economic activity in the European Union? To what extent will this continue?

7 Describe the types of areas which suffer most from underdevelopment. What can be done about increasing economic activity in these areas?

8 Outline the apparent contradictions between European Union economic and regional policies.

APPENDIX: EUROPEAN COMMUNITY STATISTICAL SOURCES

Eurostat statistical sources

Eurostat is a series of publications which together provide a detailed and comprehensive picture of the European Union. They are easily accessed at any of the many European Documentation Centres situated in all Member States. In the United Kingdom these are mostly situated in the universities of most large cities. The statistics are divided into nine themes as follows:

Theme 1: General statistics
Theme 2: Economy and finance
Theme 3: Population and social conditions
Theme 4: Energy and industry
Theme 5: Agriculture, forestry and fisheries
Theme 6: Foreign trade
Theme 7: Services and transport
Theme 8: Environment
Theme 9: Miscellaneous

For those people wanting general statistical indicators, there are five general publications in Theme 1 which will be of particular interest:

Eurostatistics: Data for short-term economic analysis

Published monthly, this publication contains key statistics on economic and social trends in the EU, USA and Japan including exchange rates, interest rates, inflation, unemployment, balance of payments, national income, money supply, industrial production and foreign trade. Four types of information are given:

1 an 'in brief' section which provides a commentary of the main events emerging from recent trends;
2 graphs illustrating the most significant economic series in the Member States, USA and Japan;
3 Community tables providing comparative country data harmonised on the basis of common criteria;
4 tables by country, providing a selection of the most common economic indicators used in each country.

Basic statistics of the Community

This annual publication covers more general statistics such as population, national accounts, industrial and agricultural production, external trade, prices and wages, employment and unemployment, finance, consumption and expenditure patterns, social indicators, external aid and standard of living. Statistics are provided not only for EU countries but other European countries including Turkey and EFTA members as well.

Eurostat review

Another annual publication but published with a three year data lag covering ten year trends for the EU, Member States, the USA and Japan. The yearbook is divided into seven sections: general statistics; economics and finance; population and social conditions; energy and industry; agriculture, forestry and fisheries; foreign trade; and, services and transport.

Europe in figures

This is full colour presentation of basic EU statistics in graphical format containing brief explanatory notes. Only the most basic statistics are provided but reference is made to the more specialised publications.

Regions

The purpose of this annually published source is to provide an overview of the regions within the EU Member States. It contains the most recent regional statistics including data on population, employment, unemployment, economic and financial aggregates, education and health.

Other (non-Eurostat) sources of statistics and information on the European Community

European access

A current awareness bulletin published by Chadwyck Healey in association with the UK offices of the European Commission. It contains information on policies, activities and events relating to the EU, Member States and related European issues. It prints recent references relating to EU issues and policies from a wide range of printed sources.

Available from:
Chadwyck-Healey Ltd, Cambridge Place, Cambridge, CB2 1NR. England.

CASE STUDY

The Republic of Ireland: A statistical overview

The Republic of Ireland, surprising to many, is not unlike Spain in its type and level of economic development. Agriculture continues to be important and per capita income puts Ireland amongst the middle income countries. But Ireland has experienced high rates of growth of manufacturing output and exports and Ireland is proving to be quite a popular target for inward investment. Helped, no doubt, by considerable financial assistance from its Objective 1 status, commitment in Ireland to the European Community is high and the government is seen to be a major advocate of Monetary Union. Up until now, Ireland's key economic partner has been the United Kingdom but now Ireland is turning away from some of its more traditional links and looking in particular towards other countries in the European Union.

The last ten years have seen some major economic problems in Ireland but some significant positive signs have also emerged. During the period 1972–82 GDP growth averaged a respectable four per cent per annum. In 1983 and 1984, growth began to fall back and in 1985 and 1986 virtual stagnation set in. Strong growth resumed in 1987, with levels rising to 5.8 per cent in 1989 and peaking at 7.1 per cent in 1990, led by an export boom. Slackening growth in both domestic demand and exports brought GDP expansion down to 2.5 per cent in 1991, although there was rapid growth again in 1992 of 4.9 per cent.

Unlike many of its EU partners, a key feature of the Republic of Ireland's current economic situation has been the growth rate of its labour force and the consequent need for an annual increase in job availability. But the economy has not succeeded in doing this for two main reasons. First, the high levels of government borrowing forcing government spending to be reduced. After 15 years of dissipated living, between 1972–1987, when the country borrowed more than I£20 billion ($35.8 billion) to little obvious benefit, the country then went through a period where the borrowing requirement was slashed from 12.8 per cent of GNP in 1986 to 2.4 per cent by 1989. This did have the effect of depressing demand but, even now, the debt to GNP ratio is twice that of the OECD average. It absorbs 79 per cent of income tax yield. Second, rapid growth in the industrial sector has been led by the high technology and pharmaceutical industries where the growth rate of labour productivity is high and where consequently, high rates of output growth are not accompanied by high rates of labour employment.

One of the key problems facing the Irish government is the trade-off between the control of public spending and borrowing, and controlling the high unemployment levels. In order to join in the EMU process, the Irish government will be forced to cut government borrowing and reduce its total debt.

National output

For a small economy, Ireland has seen periods of quite rapid growth, for example, GDP growth in 1990 was high at above seven per cent although it came tumbling back down to 2.5 per cent by 1991. Rising to 4.9 per cent in 1992, it fell again to 2.5 per cent in 1993. In 1994 growth returned to a very healthy 4.1 per cent.

Ireland is one of the most export oriented economies in the West. It is heavily dependent on foreign trade with exports and imports equal to 116 per cent of GDP in 1990. Its ratio of exports to GNP has been around 70 per cent and Table 3.19 indicates that this is growing. Although this figure is probably artificially high because of the substantial agricultural stocks put into by EU intervention, most industrialised economies have export ratios of between 20–30 per cent of GNP. In 1989 a merchandise trade surplus of I£2 315 million, equivalent to 10 per cent of GDP was achieved. The pattern of import growth is expected to mirror that of export growth. Continued growth in business investment and in private consumption are the main factors here.

Table 3.19. Expenditure on GNP (current prices)

	1985 I£ mn	1985 % of GNP	1992 I£ mn	1992 % of GNP
Private consumption	10 598	67.0	17 106	65.1
Government consumption	3 301	20.9	4 773	18.2
Gross fixed capital formation	3 377	21.3	4 676	17.8
Change in stocks	173	1.1	−60	−0.2
Exports of goods and services	10 738	67.9	18 673	71.0
Imports of goods and services	−10 397	−65.7	−15 721	−60.0
GDP	17 790	112.4	29 448	112.0
Net factor income from abroad	−1 966	−12.4	−3 158	−12.0
GNP	15 824	100.0	26 290	100.0

Note: GNP is normally below GDP, due mainly to debt servicing costs and the remittance of profits of multinational subsidiaries to their parent companies.

Sources: Central Statistics Office, National Income and Expenditure and Central Bank of Ireland, Quarterly Bulletin.

Employment and unemployment

The unemployment rate in Ireland was 14.5 per cent in 1990 compared with an EU average of 8.3 per cent, and an OECD average of 6.1 per cent but, in 1994 it rose to 18.0 per cent of the workforce. There are significant structural problems in the Irish economy brought on by high levels of migration amongst younger people in the last decade. Ironically though, the rise in unemployment is partly due to this migration slowing and some emigrants beginning to return. A survey of 1989 university graduates, for example, indicates that record numbers have found work in Ireland. But overall, the total numbers at work fell by an average of 2 600 per annum between 1984–1989 with unemployment rising quite steadily (*see* Table 3.20).

Table 3.20. Trends in the labour force (000)

	1988	1989	1990	1991	1992	1993
Labour force	1 310	1 292	1 305	1 338	1 360	1 375
Employed	1 091	1 090	1 126	1 126	1 139	1 146
Unemployed (%)	16.7	15.6	13.7	15.9	16.3	16.7

Source: Central Statistics Office, Labour Force Survey.

Table 3.21 indicates that the structure of employment has remained quite constant during the 1980s, although agriculture whilst still relatively important has continued its long term decline. One major worry is that any move of industry, labour and capital away from Ireland in an attempt to be nearer to a core of economic activity in Europe, could give rise to a vicious circle of secular regional decline with unemployment accelerating.

Table 3.21. Structure of employment (percentage)

	1984	1986	1989	1991	1993
Agriculture forestry and fishing	16.4	15.5	15.0	13.8	12.6
Extraction	0.9	0.7	0.6	0.6	0.4
Manufacturing	19.1	19.5	19.7	19.6	19.5
Construction	7.5	6.7	6.4	6.9	6.2
Electricity, gas and water	1.4	1.4	1.3	1.2	1.0
Commerce, insurance and finance	19.0	19.6	20.5	20.5	21.4
Transport and communications	6.3	6.0	6.1	5.9	6.1
Public administration	6.5	6.6	6.1	6.2	5.8
Other services	22.8	23.9	24.2	25.3	27.0

Sources: Department of Finance, Economic Review and Outlook and Central Statistics Office, Labour Force Survey.

Inflation

Consumer prices rose at an average rate of 16.2 per cent between 1975–1983, reaching a peak of 20.4 per cent in 1981. Since then Ireland has had a good track record on inflation compared with the rest of the EU with inflation as low as 1.3 per cent in 1993. Wholesale prices actually fell in 1986 and 1990 (*see* Table 3.22) but at other times have resumed a strong upward trend. Real average weekly earnings have risen continuously since 1983, albeit at a declining rate. But despite this, wage costs in Ireland are still low by EU standards and are likely to remain so whilst the consensus governing wage constraint is sustained.

Table 3.22. Price and wage increases (percentage increase on previous year)

	1986	1987	1988	1989	1990	1991	1992	1993
Consumer prices	3.8	3.2	2.1	4.0	3.4	3.2	3.0	1.3
Wholesale prices	−2.2	0.6	4.1	5.6	−2.8	2.7	0.8	0.9
Manufacturing wages	8.2	7.3	5.0	4.0	3.9	3.9	4.4	5.5

Source: Central Statistics Office, Economic Series.

Production

The primary sector, consisting mainly of agriculture has declined in importance in the Irish economy in the last decade. But in 1992 it was still large enough to generate about seven per cent of GDP, account for 22 per cent of merchandise exports and employ about 10 per cent of the workforce. Over half the value of agricultural production is exported; for live cattle and beef the export proportion is higher, at around 70 per cent.

Manufacturing industry in the Republic of Ireland falls into two broad categories. There are the newer, largely foreign owned and export oriented firms, producing in the more technology intensive oriented sectors of industry and the often more traditional smaller Irish owned firms usually supplying, in the main, the domestic market. Many sectors are now dominated by foreign employers. This reflects industrial development policies in the last two decades where foreign firms have been encouraged to establish subsidiaries in Ireland. But because this industry has been typically technology intensive, whilst output and exports have grown significantly, employment growth has been rather modest. Moreover, although foreign owned firms created about 12 000 new jobs between 1986–1989, they have developed few linkages with the indigenous economy and the indirect creation of jobs has been limited.

Like the UK, Ireland is an attractive location for non-EU firms to situate with a mind to jumping over any protectionist barriers in the future, for example, the Hualon Corporation of Taiwan invested I£52 million in two manufacturing plants in Limerick in 1990. Hualon produces synthetic yarns for European markets.

In 1984, the government's White Paper on Industrial Policy decided on new direction for industrial policy, emphasising research, technology, indigenous company development and improving national linkages. Partially due to this stress, the fastest growing sectors of Irish manufacturing industry over the last five years have been chemicals and metals and engineering (predominantly foreign owned), whilst traditional sectors such as clothing and textiles have declined somewhat (*see* Table 3.23).

Table 3.23. Indices of production (1985 = 100)

	1989	1991	1993
Chemicals	144.8	181.5	212.9
Metals and engineering	178.1	185.1	205.7
Textiles	111.1	119.0	125.5
Clothing, footwear and leather	87.0	77.2	73.6
Total manufacturing industries	142.5	154.3	169.6

Source: Central Statistics Office.

Services

Fifty-nine per cent of total employment in Ireland was employed in service activities in 1992. By far the most important sector is tourism, which earned I£1 741 million in 1992. Around three-quarters of this came from foreign visitors and the rest was domestic tourist expenditure. Total tourist expenditure accounted for 7.7 per cent of GNP.

Tourism increased substantially in 1989, and still further in 1990 when in the first nine months visitors increased 13.6 per cent above the equivalent period a year earlier. The biggest increase was in the number of visitors from Continental Europe which rose by 37 per cent. There was a nine per cent increase in visitors from the UK. Earnings from tourism rose during the first nine months of 1992 by 2.2 per cent on the same period in 1991, and expenditure by those tourists was 13.1 per cent higher than in 1991. The number of visitors to Ireland in 1992 was in excess of three million.

Transport and communications

Ireland is well served by road and rail links and no part of Ireland is more than 110 kilometres from a harbour or airport. Cork is the most important port with a throughput of 6.7 million tons in 1992, followed by Dublin with a throughput of 6.4 million tons. The government has been keen to maintain good transport and communications links with Europe and North America and the four international airports handled about seven million passengers in 1990 compared with 4.4 million in 1987. There are fears that the geographical position of Ireland puts it at a disadvantage in a single European market and, therefore, investment in communications infrastructure is a priority.

Table 3.24 indicates that the main trading partners are indeed the EU although Ireland's western ports make trade not only attractive and accessible to the USA but also makes Ireland a staging post for some goods. The low rates of inflation in Ireland is expected to assist Irish exports to the EU.

Table 3.24. Main trading partners (percentage of total).

Exports to:	1980	1988	1990	1992
United Kingdom	42.7	35.5	28.0	31.5
Germany (West)	9.6	11.1	11.7	12.8
France	7.7	9.1	10.5	9.6
USA	5.2	7.7	8.2	8.2
Netherlands	5.5	7.0	5.8	7.0
Belgium/Luxembourg	5.0	4.4	4.4	4.9
EC total	74.4	74.0	74.7	74.1
Imports from:				
United Kingdom	50.8	42.1	38.2	42.4
USA	8.7	15.9	14.5	14.2
Germany (West)	6.9	8.6	8.3	8.3
Japan	2.5	4.9	5.6	5.0
France	5.2	4.1	4.6	4.5
Netherlands	2.8	4.0	4.1	4.4
EC total	72.7	66.0	66.6	66.5

Source: Central Statistics Office, Trade Statistics of the Republic of Ireland.

Debt
Ireland's debt burden has already been noted but it should be added that the external debt (33.5 per cent of total public debt in 1990) is largely denominated in dollars, Deutschmarks, Swiss francs and yen. Because of the relative weakness of the Irish pound as well as new borrowings and interest rate rises the costs of servicing the debt have rise dramatically. But the Irish government's reliance on foreign banks for finance has been declining since 1986.

Table 3.25. Government debt (I£ mn)

	1986	1988	1990	1992
Outstanding external debt	9 754	9 498	8 862	10 856
Interest payments abroad	716	703	730	736

Source: Central Statistics Office, Trade Statistics of the Republic of Ireland.

Trade with the European Union
The current economic situation could work to Ireland's advantage within the EU. Its low inflation rate does make Irish exports attractive. If economic activity gains strength in the rest of the EU, Ireland may also have a strong incentive to switch the direction of its own export activity. The marketing of Irish goods in the EU may yet become more vigorous. Germany, for example, could absorb considerably more Irish goods. On the import side, trade could be stepped up with other low inflation countries such as the Netherlands and France.

Ireland remains a major EU beneficiary in direct financial terms. The whole of Ireland is among the areas defined under Objective 1 of the EU structural funds. Objective 1 regions will receive the bulk of EU structural fund aid up until 1999. During the five years 1989–93, Ireland received a total of Ecu 3.7 billion.

Conclusion
Like Spain and the other middle income economies in the EU, Ireland has experienced manufacturing growth and success in the service areas – particularly with tourism. Its agriculture remains an important contributor to GDP but it has been suggested here that there are some particular problems in this sector. Ireland's farmers have often been accused of producing goods with the highest EU subsidies, rather than meeting consumers' demands, and any further significant reform of CAP will leave Irish agriculture with even more problems.

Ireland's most significant problem has to be unemployment and its associated opportunity and real costs hardly help Ireland's need to service its significant debt.

Case Study Questions

1 How might you account for the trends in employment and unemployment in the Republic of Ireland displayed in Table 3.20?

2 By examining the statistics presented do you consider that there is a trade-off between inflation and unemployment in the case of the Republic of Ireland?

3 Does the Republic of Ireland display the traditional characteristics of de-industrialisation?

4 The Republic of Ireland, as a small economy, is often compared with Belgium and the Netherlands. What is your assessment of the relative economic performances of these countries? Do you consider that this is a fair comparison?

5 Explain why the case study asserts that the economic situation, as described, could work to the Republic of Ireland's advantage.

6 Which countries form the Republic of Ireland's major trading partners? To what extent and why do you think this might change over time?

CASE STUDY

Regional development, tourism and the European Union's coastal areas and islands

The coastline which surrounds the European Union is very varied in its stage of development and unevenly split between the Member States. Where there is a high density of population or intensive use of land, whether for economic reasons or because the area is attractive to tourists, excessive pressures are often exerted on the marine and land environment, which is often particularly diverse and vulnerable. However, for many peripheral regions in the EU, it is their coastline which offers significant development potential. With the entry of Finland and Sweden into the EU, the Arctic coastline, environmentally fragile as it is, requires special attention.

In addition to the coastal areas, there are around 400 inhabited islands in the EU. These vary significantly in terms of size, development, geographical characteristics and remoteness. Those which are most geographically isolated tend to be under-developed and, compared with the continental regions, they have much larger problems with respect to transport, energy supply and communications. Both coastal areas and islands, therefore, demand a planning strategy for realising their potential for development whilst recognising the need to protect the very special natural environments often found in these areas.

Coastal areas
In terms of their land use, we can identify three general kinds of land area:

1 Areas with a high concentration of people and business, with a strong influence on the surrounding region. These areas are characterised by the disappearance of the natural environment.
2 Areas with a mixture of urban, agriculture, fishing, aquaculture and tourist activities and which are characterised both by conflicts over land and sea use between different kinds of development. There are often great seasonal differences in activity.
3 Areas which are relatively unspoilt, because their physical features limit the possibilities for development, such as certain sectors of rocky coastline, or areas

protected by law because of their ecological importance or a remote location which is not favourable for economic development.

The highly developed areas (only about five per cent of the total coastline) continue to develop whilst the mixed areas are seeing new developments, gradually reducing open space. The relatively unspoilt areas are being encroached on, mainly by tourist development, especially in the Mediterranean and are often subject to the effects of pollution produced elsewhere. Moreover, there is scientific consensus that all marine resources in coastal areas depend almost entirely on the environmental quality of the first kilometre of land from the shore.

In some Member States the situation is even more acute. In Spain, for example, nearly 35 per cent of the population is concentrated around the coast in only seven per cent of the land area. In certain Mediterranean areas this gets even higher, for example, 75 per cent of the population of Provence Cote d'Azur live in the coastal districts. In addition, coastal areas are often subject to rapid population growth: in the coastal areas of Spain and France population growth is three times the EU average.

Islands

Around 5 per cent of the EU's land mass is made up of islands. They have a population of around 13 million (four per cent of the total). Islands account for 19 per cent of the land mass of Greece (with 14 per cent of the population), 17 per cent of Italy (12 per cent of the population) and 4.5 per cent of the United Kingdom (three per cent of the population). In general, islands are characterised by a larger than average primary sector (often 20–25 per cent of employment), an underdeveloped industrial sector and an over-enlarged service sector. The importance of the primary sector is a reflection of large numbers of small farmers or a dependence on fishing. This sector is however in decline. In 1971, the primary sector accounted for 55 per cent of activity on the Greek islands. By 1985 this had fallen to 30 per cent.

One common characteristic of all the Community islands is the importance of tourism and, therefore, the variation in population throughout the year especially in the smaller islands, for example, the population of Rhodes doubles each spring, while that of Mykonos increases seven-fold in the summer. For numerous small islands, the tourist high season population can be ten times the local permanent population.

Intensive tourism development

A growing consequence of the attractiveness of coastal areas and islands, coupled with rising real incomes, is a high level of tourism. The principle destination of tourists is the southern coasts of the EU, although there is also a growth in tourism towards islands, mountainous areas and the northern coastal areas. The number of international tourists in the Mediterranean coastal areas doubled between 1970 and the mid 1980s from 58–117 million. Growth rates were particularly high in the countries where tourism was less developed at the beginning of this period. In Greece, the growth was five-fold.

It is the growth of tourism which has been the major factor behind the urbanisation of the coastal region. Over two-thirds of the Spanish Mediterranean coastline, for example, is now directly affected by tourist activities. Moreover, with the massive increases in population which occur during the summer, the local infrastructure and facilities often fall well short of that required.

The success of tourism relies to a great extent on the quality of the environment where it takes place. Tourism is, therefore, influenced by the environment, but it must also be recognised that the environment is equally influenced by tourist activities. Tourism, therefore, requires proper planning and management and the industry itself has a responsibility to respond to the environmental challenge for its own well-being as well as the well-being of society as a whole. Moreover, tourist activities today can destroy the potential earning capacity of a tourist destination in the future.

Intensive tourism, whilst bringing development opportunities with it, has undoubtedly damaged the environment. Tourists, particularly those with higher incomes, are often turning away from destinations which have become overcrowded and spoilt. The number of tourists in the Valencia region of Spain declined by 10 per cent between 1988–1989, for example. However, although the Mediterranean regions may lose out on their share of tourism, because of the rapid growth in tourism as a whole, the number of visitors visiting these areas will not fall. Environmental degradation is therefore set to continue.

Tourism as an instrument of regional policy

We have seen that tourism can indeed create economic development in areas which would otherwise be poorer peripheral areas. Even in the less popular destinations such as the Western islands of Scotland, tourism plays an important part in bringing seasonal incomes into the local economy. Indeed, in areas such as these the potential of earning tourist income often acts as an incentive to protect the natural environment and beauty.

However, where tourism has been at its densest, environmental damage and insensitive building development has been severe, which could, in time, actually threaten the future viability of the area as a tourist destination. Development will then go into decline, with very little other industry for local populations to fall back on.

For the future development of coastal areas and islands, tourism does have a role to play, but tourism policy must find a way of being ecologically sensitive. 'Ecotourism' alongside the development of more mixed local economies is more important than the rapid growth experienced in some Mediterranean areas.

The EU's policy framework to try to deal with these problems falls into three parts:

1 the planning of zones of tourism within a wider strategic framework which takes into account the environmental effects of tourist activity;
2 innovative tourist services such as ecological holidays, out-of-season facilities and the provision of conference facilities; and,
3 the provision of measures to promote ecological and economic diversity, and to preserve open and natural spaces.

Conclusion

The general picture for many of the more southern coastlines and islands of the EU could be one of increasing failure of these areas to accommodate the pressure of new developments. This trend needs to be reversed without plunging these peripheral areas into depression. Tourism and other developments with a higher added value which are less environmentally destructive will be important.

Meanwhile many of the North Atlantic and Arctic coastlines and islands, which have not had the benefits (and costs) of rapid development through tourism still require some attention because of their underdeveloped and peripheral nature. Here, strategies associated with *eco-tourism*, the improvement of communications aimed at increasing the service sector and the encouragement of local economic diversification, will ensure that the depopulation trend of many of these regions is halted.

Case Study Questions

1 What problems are usually associated with the growth of tourism in the peripheral areas of the European Union?

2 To what extent can the encouragement of tourism development be used as an instrument of European Union regional policy?

3 What do you understand by the term *'eco-tourism'*?

4 Why are tourism and environmental management inextricably linked?

5 What other strategies might be used to halt the economic decline of peripheral areas?

FURTHER READING

Nugent, N. and O'Donnell, R. (eds.) (1994) *European Business Environment*, Macmillan. This text has a chapter on the political and economic dimension of the EU, the legal environment, labour markets and industrial relations, finance, marketing and technology.

Regular overviews of the economic and business environment in Europe is provided in the annual *The World of Information Europe Review*, Kogan Page and Walden Publishing. This provides basic information on 50 countries including economic profiles, political analysis, regional profiles and useful maps.

Molle, W. and William, T. (1993) *The Economics of European Integration: Theory, Practice and Policy*, Dartmouth Publishing. This text provides a good introduction to the process of European integration.

Tsoukalis, L. (1993) *The New European Economy: The Politics and Economics of Integration*, Second edition, Oxford University Press. This text provides a discussion on European integration which looks at some of the more political dimensions of the process (including regional aspects).

REFERENCES

Curbelo, J. L., 'The Treaty of Maastricht and the European Peripheral Regions' *European Business and Economic Development*, 1993, 1, 5.

Mair, D., 'European Regional Development: An Analysis of the Reformed Structural Funds', *European Research*, 1991, 2, 3.

CHAPTER 4

Macroeconomic Policy Integration

MAKE IT INTERESTING

(1)

FIRMS AND THE ECONOMY

Firms do not only have to respond to internal change and to changes in trading relationships, they are also influenced by the economy in which they operate and, therefore, to changing macroeconomic policies and the government. With European integration itself having a greater impact on the environment in which the firm operates and with the consequent changes caused by harmonisation, it has never been more necessary for firms to be aware of the operation of the wider economy in which they operate than at the present.

Governments will often try to change the performance and conduct of firms directly via industrial policy and competition policy (*see* Chapter 5), but firms will also be affected by government policies which impact upon interest rates, inflation, taxation, wages and economic growth in particular. The general impact of European integration should be to move macroeconomic variables together. In time, it is possible that complete economic and monetary integration will mean that these variables become equalised because Europe will become a single economy, and just as we do not distinguish between inflation rates in England and Scotland, neither will we do so between England and Italy, for example.

The main tools of a government's economic policy can be divided into monetary policy and fiscal policy. For a detailed examination of these, the reader is referred to any intermediate economics textbook. The main consideration in this chapter is on how monetary and fiscal policy will change over time as monetary and fiscal harmonisation occurs among the Member States.

(2)

OBJECTIVES OF ECONOMIC POLICY

Article 104 of the Single European Act sets out the fundamental goals of the economic policy of the Member States. These are:

- to ensure the equilibrium of the overall balance of payments
- to maintain confidence in the currency
- to ensure a high level of employment
- to ensure a stable level of prices.

Article 105 stresses that these policies have to be co-ordinated and that there needs to be close co-operation between the financial departments of the Member States' governments.

In particular, central banks are encouraged to co-ordinate their policies on monetary and credit matters and establish general guidelines to be followed by governments.

A considerable amount of co-operation already occurs between many of the government institutions in the Member States. Clearly, there are considerable spillovers in the effect of macroeconomic policy between countries, and co-operation is required to ensure that one country's policies will not have a negative effect on another's. As the process of integration continues, this becomes more and more important because the spillovers will become more pronounced.

THE ECONOMICS OF INTEGRATION

The study of economic integration is the study of arrangements between two or more sovereign states as a result of which trade and economic transactions between them is conducted on a basis more favourable to them than to states outside the agreement. Agreements of this kind can range from preferential tariff arrangements to full economic union and different models involving an ascending order of degrees of integration can be characterised on a five point scale.

1 One of the most basic forms of integration or co-operation is that of the preferential tariff on a particular good or range of goods. In this case, participating countries agree to levy a lower rate of taxation on imports from each other than that levied on countries outside the agreement. Such an agreement is common amongst countries which have political links and existed in the United Kingdom, for example, between members of the Commonwealth until the UK entered the European Economic Community (EEC) in 1973.

2 A form of integration extends the preferential tariff to cover all imports between the countries involved in the agreement. Commonly all imports from one country party to the agreement will be at a zero tariff while comparable imports from countries outside the agreement will be subject to a tariff barrier. This sort of arrangement is often referred to as a *free trade area* and characterises the arrangement for industrial products made between the countries involved in the European Economic Area (EEA). Tariffs levied on products imported from non-participating countries are levied at whatever rate the individual country chooses.

3 There is a type of arrangement known as the *customs union*. Here there is completely free trade in all products between the members of the union and a common external tariff levied on imports from non-Member States. Tariff revenues become common property and are subsequently shared out according to some agreed set of rules.

4 There is another level of integration which carries this process one step further and leads to the creation of a single internal market. Free trade between member countries is not only ensured by the elimination of tariffs, but also by the removal of all other obstacles (non-tariff barriers) to free trade in goods and services. Thus licences, foreign exchange controls, customs procedures, standards and indirect taxes other than tariffs have to be harmonised or eliminated. An internal market also operates with respect to production as well as exchange and therefore freedom of mobility for labour and capital is also required.

5 The ultimate level of economic integration is complete economic union. This implies a high degree of co-operation between members of the union and will include the

co-ordination of monetary and fiscal policies and macroeconomic planning across all member countries. This would usually result in a single currency being used. When this is achieved, while countries may remain individual political units, they cease to be independent economic units. In time, many argue, it is likely that their political independence will be reduced and political and economic decisions will be made at the centre, although a degree of devolvement to regions is likely. The USA is a collection of separate states, and while a degree of political and legal sovereignty is maintained by each state, they share a single monetary system and are subservient to a federal government with control over most, though not all, taxation and public expenditure.

The European Union has progressed slowly from being a customs union towards the creation of a single internal market. Progression towards full economic and monetary union looked at one time like being a more speedy process but recent technical, political and economic obstacles have slowed that pace somewhat. There are those who see the move from model 4 to model 5 as an inevitability, but the fundamental basis on which such a move will be made surrounds macroeconomic co-operation and particularly monetary integration. It is to this topic which we now turn our attention.

THE EUROPEAN MONETARY SYSTEM AND EXCHANGE RATE MECHANISM

Whilst there was no specific mention of the establishment of a unified monetary system within the original Treaty of Rome, this has become one of the central issues in the EU. On the one hand, there are those who argue that a single currency is a logical stage in the creation of a single internal market, but there are others who see the creation of a single currency for 15 Member States as leading necessarily to economic unification and a consequent loss of sovereignty for individual governments.

In the early 1990s, the European Monetary System (EMS) developed into quite a different system in its operation than it was initially. During the first five years of its existence, there were frequent appreciations or depreciations (realignments) of currencies within the system, and the credibility of the system was brought into question. Then there followed a period of stability. However, a wave of realignments in 1992 and 1993 and the UK's and Italy's departure from the Exchange Rate Mechanism (ERM) brought about further instability. Since then further depreciations of weaker currencies within the system has meant that credibility has been further reduced and the credibility of the fixity of exchange rates within the ERM has decreased. The question now focuses on when and if the exchange rate mechanism will evolve into a single currency system, whether we will see a hard core of stronger countries adopting a single currency and others being left outside of that system, or whether, for the foreseeable future, the EU will remain a country of 15 different currencies.

Background to the system

The first steps towards monetary union were outlined as early as 1969 with the Barre Plan. This plan required Member States to consult before making changes to their domestic economic policy. In effect, this was the point at which the EEC of only six members began to recognise the interdependence between their economic strategies. A consultation process was also established to begin negotiations over monetary stability in order to consolidate the first decade of the common market.

Early attempts at linking the main currencies in the world had proved to be unsuccessful. The management of exchange rates, known as the Bretton Woods system, in 1972, was quickly revised and with much USA influence turned into the 'Snake' where exchange rates could rise or fall within predetermined limits. This system also had limited success. It was hampered by some members, including the UK, departing from the agreement in 1974.

In 1977, Roy Jenkins, the President of the European Commission once again raised the issue of monetary union. This signalled that the Commission had recognised that currency movements could have a destabilising effect on the economies of Member States. It was felt that the linkage of exchange rates would be beneficial for business confidence and make trade between countries more likely. Consequently, the EMS was born with three main elements:

1 the European Currency Unit (Ecu), the denominator used for fixing exchange rates and for operations within the system;
2 the Exchange Rate Mechanism (ERM) which links domestic currencies to the Ecu; and,
3 financial support mechanisms.

Some form of monetary union was formally recognised as being advantageous by the European Commission within the Single European Act.

The Ecu

The Ecu is a basket of all the Member States' currencies. It is revised from time to time in line with underlying economic criteria upon the consent of all the members. Although the Ecu does not exist in note and coin form, Ecu bank accounts are available and the Ecu can therefore be used as an instrument of settlement between monetary authorities, institutions, firms and even individuals.

The Exchange Rate Mechanism

The central element of the EMS is the ERM. Within this system, each Member State's currency has an exchange rate against the Ecu, called the *central rate*, and therefore against each other via the Ecu. The ultimate aim is that currencies are allowed to fluctuate against the Ecu by up to 2.25 per cent. Central rates can be changed, that is, a currency can appreciate or depreciate within the mechanism subject to the agreement of the other member countries. Originally a six per cent band was allowed for a transitional period although, in August 1993, this had to be widened to 15 per cent to prevent the ERM falling apart (*see* below).

Financial support mechanisms

Short and medium-term support for Member States with balance of payments difficulties can be provided via the granting of credit to those countries. To date, less use has been made of this system than the creators had in mind. Indeed, between 1979–1992 the system was not used at all and it is therefore not pursued further in this chapter.

The Delors Plan

In 1988 Jacques Delors, the President of the European Commission was asked by the Council of Finance Ministers to investigate the process of monetary policy links. His report outlined a three stage transition to full EMU:

Stage 1

This requires that all national currencies join the EMS. Within the system currencies are allowed to fluctuate in exchange rates relative to the value of the Ecu. During this stage, all currencies of the EU join the ERM. The central theme of Stage 1 is the convergence of economic performance of the Member States by providing greater co-ordination of monetary policy between nations and to remove obstacles to financial integration. Capital movements are derestricted to provide a free flow of currency within the EU.

Stage 2

In Stage 2, as defined by the Maastricht Treaty, the structure of EMU is to be established. This is very much a transitional stage with macroeconomic policy decisions remaining with national governments. In the monetary field, the most significant feature of this stage is the establishment of the European System of Central Banks (ESCB). The ESCB would start the transition by beginning to co-ordinate the independent monetary policies through a committee of Central Bank Governors.

The second stage requires three main actions:

1 National monetary policies should be executed in accordance with the general monetary orientations set up for the EU as a whole.
2 A proportion of all foreign exchange reserves will be pooled and would be used by the ESCB to intervene in exchange markets.
3 The ESCB will establish the structure of a European monetary and banking system to achieve some harmonisation of basic provisions (such as cross-border payment arrangements).

Stage 3

The final stage of the plan would begin with the irrevocable fixing of Member States' exchange rates. Central Community institutions would take over the control of monetary instruments. During this stage, national currencies would be replaced by a single EU currency. Thus this stage requires the following key changes to the present system:

1 The EU will take over from the individual Member States the role of international economic policy co-operation.
2 The EU will establish macroeconomic policy rules which would become binding.
3 The ESCB will formulate and implement monetary policy in negotiation with finance ministers of the Member States.
4 Exchange rate interventions will be managed by the ESCB, keeping the Ecu at its required rate against the other key world currencies.
5 All foreign exchange reserves will be pooled and managed by the ESCB.
6 The ESCB will manage the technical and regulatory preparations for transition to a single currency.

7 In order to smooth out the transition process and the disparate effects which monetary union would create, there will be a need to strengthen the structural and regional funds of the EU.
8 The ESCB would then hand over the day to day running of monetary policy to an independent central bank.

The Delors Report satisfies all the requirements of a true economic and monetary union. Nevertheless, whether such a system will actually be implemented in detail is not a certainty and despite a timetable being established in the Maastricht Treaty, the real time scale over which integration will occur is still unclear.

Advantages and disadvantages of monetary co-ordination

Like most policy changes there will be many costs and benefits associated with monetary co-ordination. It is never easy to consider whether the benefits outweigh the costs, or vice-versa, and the considerations should not only be economic ones. There will be political and social ramifications of monetary union which are beyond the scope of this chapter but have to be considered by policy makers. Let us consider the key advantages and disadvantages of monetary co-ordination as they will affect businesses in particular.

Advantages

Certainty and planning

With free floating exchange rates the value of a Member State's currency changes as its economic performance changes, most notably in respect of balance of payments performance and the price level. If these fluctuations are large or very frequent it means that firms, who are involved in importing and exporting, face considerable uncertainty. Indeed, an adverse exchange rate fluctuation can result in a firm's expected profit being turned into a substantial loss. Therefore, whilst freely floating exchange rates maintain a degree of equilibrium for a country it means that international trade activity may be curtailed. The alternatives include fixing exchange rates or doing away with them all together through the use of a single currency.

The key advantage of fixed exchange rates is that they provide certainty in that exchange rate fluctuations are eliminated. Whilst the ERM is not a completely fixed system and small fluctuations are allowed, these fluctuations are small enough to be built into firms' export plans and prices, therefore, firms can quote prices in the knowledge that exchange rate changes will not result in losses being made. Thus the risk of loss is substantially reduced and the increased certainty not only increases the planning horizons of the firm but encourages firms who were risk averse to trade across national boundaries.

Some form of fixed exchange rate is therefore a minimum requirement for a Single European Market. Only with the certainty which fixed exchange rates provide do firms have an incentive to import and export. Thus competition across the EU is increased and markets become European based rather than country based. Arguably, it is even better for businesses to have the use of a single currency where there is no uncertainty at all.

Counter inflationary policy

The claim made for the EMS is that it provides a framework in which counter inflationary policies can be aided. The way in which inflation is created is quite simply by firms' raising the prices of their products. Entry into the ERM means that firms will not be able to continue to raise their prices higher than their European competitors and remain competitive. In the past, countries, such as the UK, which had suffered from a higher level of inflation than their European counterparts, have been able to continually depreciate their currencies. This has meant that the price of their exports on foreign markets has fallen and that the price of their imports which could include competitors' products has risen. Despite price increases domestically, individual firms have still been able to maintain their competitiveness and therefore their markets. But with the ERM, which is a semi-fixed exchange rate regime, this is no longer possible and domestic price rises above the European average will simply result in the loss of markets. There is, therefore, an incentive for firms to keep their prices down. This need for firms to keep their price increases in line with those of their European competitors is often referred to as the *exchange rate discipline* and its effect is to create a convergence of European inflation rates.

Wage rises have often been cited as a major reason for the existence of price inflation, but, within the ERM, if wage rises do result in an inflation rate higher than the average the exchange rate discipline will ensure that firms lose their markets and workers therefore lose their jobs. Thus there is an incentive for workers and trade unions to moderate their wage claims.

Inflation can often be sustained simply by inflationary expectations. If all economic agents (firms, individuals, trade unions, etc.) expect inflation to continue then they adjust their prices and wage claims to match. This in itself then causes the inflation to happen. In other words, inflation expectations are a self-fulfilling prophecy. The value of the EMS is that it helps to persuade economic agents that inflation really will fall. In the past, governments have lost credibility when their counter inflationary policies seem not to have worked, but the exchange rate discipline provides an impetus for people to believe that inflation rates must be convergent across Member States, so that in economies where inflation rates have been traditionally above average, expectations are driven downwards. In general, the effect of these influences will be to drive inflation down towards the levels of the low inflation economies.

It is argued that lower inflation can be achieved without the need for deflationary policies which governments have traditionally used. A deflationary policy squeezes aggregate demand by lowering government expenditure, by increasing taxes, or by increasing interest rates so that less consumption and investment takes place. The effect of such deflationary pressure is not only to reduce the price level, but also to reduce output and, therefore, create lower sales for firms and consequent unemployment.

Reductions in the cost of financial management

Another source of gain of monetary integration could be a reduction in the cost of financial management. With a complete monetary union in place, the costs of currency transactions within the EU could be eliminated, and some of the activities of the institutions dealing in foreign exchanges could be discontinued, leading to a saving in the use of resources.

Disadvantages

Maintenance of exchange rate values

There is a need for Member States' governments to maintain the value of their currency within the ERM. This means that when and if a currency gets close to its upper or lower boundaries, action has to be taken to move the currency in the opposite direction. Traditionally, this has been done by changes in interest rates, for example, if an exchange rate hits its upper limit, then interest rates will be reduced. This will lead to some investors finding another country in which to place their money, and to the demand for that currency consequently decreasing leading to a fall in the exchange rate. Conversely, if exchange rates need to be raised from the lower floor, then interest rates will be raised attracting new funds into the economy, an increased demand for the currency in question and an increase in the exchange rate.

The problem is that this can cause conflict with any anti-inflation policy based on the control of interest rates. The need to lower inflation rates, for example, could run counter to a government's attempts to keep inflation low by the maintenance of high interest rates. It should be obvious that it is therefore not possible to control two objectives of macroeconomic policy (i.e. inflation and exchange rates) with the use of only one instrument of policy (interest rates). In effect, governments lose their ability to use interest rates in a fight against inflation.

Sovereignty

Monetary integration does require co-ordination on the part of governments and central banks. Complete monetary union and a single currency would require a single monetary policy. This has led some governments, most notably in the UK, to argue that moves towards monetary integration involve a loss of sovereignty with respect to macroeconomic policy. The government of Margaret Thatcher, between 1979–1990, held the line that they did not want to relinquish power over the control of monetary aggregates and of the money supply itself, which had been at the centre of their monetarist-based financial strategies. Being monetarists, the supremacy of monetary policy in the determination of economic activity and the price level still means that many do not want to see that important policy instrument in the hands of the EU as a whole.

Two strong counter arguments can be made against this sort of stance, however. First, the economic performance of the UK was inferior to that of many other Member States throughout the 1980s, and it would seem somewhat arrogant to suggest that monetary policy could be *better* operated by the UK government than any other. Second, the whole issue of sovereignty might be re-examined to the extent that monetary integration might imply a pooling of sovereignty rather than a loss of sovereignty. Indeed, the operation of the Single European Market requires that countries increase the amount of co-ordination of their macroeconomic policies, and joint decisions and policies relating to monetary policy might be seen simply as an extension of this.

The successes and failures of the EMS

Despite the experience of the UK (*see* the appendix to this chapter), there are still those who would argue that the EMS has been something of a success. However, the experiences of 1992 and 1993 when speculators 'ram-raided' one currency after another, leading to instability and a re-definition of the ERM, needs to be assessed. Beginning with successes, however, there are four key areas where this has been most apparent.

1 Despite the realignments and fluctuations of currencies within their pre-set bands, the EMS has succeeded in stabilising exchange rates over relatively long periods of time and thereby providing more certainty.
2 There is evidence to suggest that the EMS has provided a framework whereby Member States have been able to pursue counter-inflationary policies at a lesser cost in terms of unemployment and lost output than would have been possible otherwise.
3 Points 1 and 2, together, have ensured that Member States' firms have not put prices up significantly above the European average, and that certainty over exchange rates has increased their ability to plan ahead. This, in turn, has meant that drastic changes in the competitiveness of one ERM Member State, with respect to another have been avoided.
4 The Ecu has become established as a significant currency of denomination and this seems to confirm that the EMS is seen as credible.

Despite these benefits, however, the experiences of 1992 and 1993 when a number of countries were forced to realign their currencies, after intense speculation had forced the value of the currency below its lower limit, along with the departure of the UK and Italy from the ERM, has led to some criticism of the operation of the ERM. It must be recognised, however, that these experiences cannot be separated from the recession of the early 1990s which affected different Member States in different ways, leading to a period of divergence rather than convergence of macroeconomic indicators. Neither should we ignore the economic costs of German reunification which, because Germany was borrowing so much money, had led to relatively high German interest rates, which were attractive to investors.

The speculative attacks which eventually forced many countries to realign their currencies were significantly assisted by the relaxation of capital controls required in the Delors plan. Despite the countries of currencies under attack pushing up interest rates, speculators often pursued their relentless attack on the chosen currency in the certain knowledge that realignment would follow and a large profit made.

It would be naive, however, solely to blame what was often referred to as the 'greed of the speculators'. Were the economic performance of countries such as the UK, Ireland, Spain, Portugal and Italy not fundamentally poor, relative to others at the time, making their exchange rates overvalued, then there would have been no motive for a speculative attack, since the equilibrium value of the exchange rate would not have been outside the ERM bands.

It was, however, somewhat of a surprise that more co-ordinated efforts on the part of all Member States were not made, in order to prevent the realignment of some currencies. It has always been the practice that individual Member States had to maintain the value of their own currencies within the ERM, but many countries often assumed that in times of considerable pressure, other (stronger) countries would come to their aid. In the realignments of 1992 and 1993 very little co-operation and co-ordination was evident.

Since August 1993 there have not been fundamental changes in the operation of the ERM, which is still seen as central to the creation of the single market and necessary for the control of inflation. We have seen a more flexible ERM system though, where realignments have again become more frequent. The operation of the system has, therefore, lost some of its advantages associated with certainty.

At the beginning of August 1993, with German interest rates still high, many of the weaker currencies left in the ERM once again came under significant downward pressure at the hands of the speculators. There were many options open to the finance ministers of the Member States including the complete abandonment of the ERM. However, the ERM with its central position in the European Monetary System, if abandoned would have put the whole process of European Monetary Union out of sight. The compromise was to widen the bands for all currencies (except the German and Dutch currencies which remained at 2.25 per cent) to 15 per cent.

For all its flaws and inflexibilities, the original version of the ERM, based on semi-fixed exchange rates was abandoned. It was a simple system but clearly failed to deal with the economic divergence of Europe as a result of both the recession and Germany's unwillingness to cut interest rates because of their own domestic difficulties. It was replaced by a less simplistic, but more flexible, ERM which itself placed doubts on the ability of Europe to move forward on the original EMU timetable (*see* below). In effect, in 1993, the new ERM divided the main European countries into four distinct groups as follows:

Hard ERM core
Germany
Netherlands

Soft ERM core
Belgium
Denmark
France

ERM periphery
Ireland
Portugal
Spain

Outside of the ERM
Italy
United Kingdom
Greece

The hard core, where 2.25 per cent fluctuations were allowed, was reduced from seven members to only two. The countries which were always commonly thought of as joining Germany and Netherlands in the two-speed model became the soft core where, after the changes in the system, interest rates fell substantially. Ireland, Spain and Portugal are really left on the edge of the ERM because of their poor economic performance and failure to come near to any of the EMU convergence criteria (*see* below). Previously, two of these countries (Spain and Portugal) were within the ERM at the six per cent fluctuation level. The restructured ERM left open the possibility for Italy and the UK to rejoin the system more easily.

The new flexible ERM has allowed countries to pursue monetary policies which are less co-ordinated but, at the same time, more suited to the domestic situations left as a result of the recession in the early 1990s. With the freedom to appreciate and depreciate by as much as 15 per cent either side of the old parities, national banks have had much more discretion to cut interest rates below those of Germany, thus boosting their own domestic economies while remaining within the ERM.

In 1993, the finance ministers of the EU were, nevertheless, at pains to stress that the widening of the ERM bands was a temporary measure and that it would be expected that, over time, countries would begin to move back towards the narrow bands that would enable the next step to be made towards monetary union. In effect, such a widening does not have an impact on the plans to move towards Stage 2 of monetary union, although the original convergence criteria for monetary union will inevitably have to be fine-tuned to the new situation. According to the rules (as outlined in this chapter) for EMU, in order to move to monetary union by 1997 (the earliest possible date outlined in the Maastricht Treaty), a majority of currencies would have had to have returned to the narrow 2.25 per cent bands by the end of 1994. This did not happen.

EUROPEAN MONETARY UNION

Complete European Monetary Union (EMU) was first discussed even before the creation of the EMS. With complete monetary union, exchange rates are indissolubly locked, and a consequential next step is the creation of a common currency. Advocates of EMU argue that it maintains all the advantages of the ERM in terms of certainty and planning and an inflation discipline, but adds more. First, it means that the ability to use interest rates to reduce inflation is restored, so that one of the disadvantages of the ERM are removed. Second, it means that currency exchange transactions and their consequent transactions costs are eliminated. With a Single European Market and increased levels of inter-European trade, such transactions costs could become very large as a proportion of Gross Domestic Product (GDP) and their elimination should imply a resource gain.

EMU necessarily implies further co-ordination of macroeconomic policy. There will be a need for a single monetary policy, which in turn implies common base interest rates and an agreed path for the money supply. Sovereignty over monetary policy is, therefore, completely resigned to a central European agency or central European bank, although Member States would still have a voice in the operation of that monetary policy.

Monetary Union and the Maastricht Treaty

The Maastricht Treaty now forms the basis of plans for monetary union. Even though the UK opted out of this part of the Treaty, its plans are well developed and do not require unanimity to progress. The Treaty envisages the creation of a European Central Bank (ECB) which would issue a single currency and make monetary policy for the whole of the EU. That ECB will be independent of Member States' governments and will be charged with a statutory obligation to pursue price stability. As a direct consequence Member States will be subject to binding rules for budget deficits and public debt to income ratios. Specifically, budget deficits must be less than three per cent of GDP and public debt must be less than 60 per cent of GDP. Unless these two criteria can be met, the Maastricht Treaty makes it clear that a Member State will not be allowed to 'enter' monetary union. These conditions represent the first two conditions of the so-called *convergence criteria* which Member States will be required to adhere to before they can join in with the EMU process.

The other convergence criteria require the following aims to be achieved:

- *price stability*: a rate of inflation no more than 1.5 per cent above the average of the three best performing Member States

- *exchange rates*: domestic currency values must have been within the narrow bands of the ERM for two years
- *interest rates*: rates should be no more than two percentage points above the three best performing Member States for the previous year.

What is clear from these criteria is that monetary union may actually begin without all Member States being involved in that union. Indeed, with a tight timetable for monetary union established within the Treaty, it is impossible that all Member States could indeed meet all the criteria, even if they wanted to.

The original European Monetary Union timetable

As we know, progress towards Economic and Monetary Union is in three stages. The first stage, which started in 1990, has concentrated on improving co-operation and co-ordination between Member States. Stages 2 and 3 involve the establishment of new institutions and indicative dates for key decisions to be made.

Stage 2 (from January 1994) involves the establishment of institutions in order to:

- strengthen cooperation between the national central banks and the co-ordination of monetary policies
- monitor the EMS
- facilitate the use of the Ecu and to oversee the development of the Ecu
- examine and evaluate the technical difficulties involved with replacing domestic currencies with the Ecu
- prepare for Stage 3 of monetary union.

The European Commission reports on the progress of Member States towards achieving the convergence criteria. In the original timetable their findings were to be presented to the Council by 31 December 1996, which would have then decided whether a majority of Member States had met the convergence criteria. This possibility has clearly been missed but, if no date for Stage 3 has been fixed by the end of 1997 then, according to the Maastricht Treaty, the European System of Central Banks (ESCB) must be established by July 1998, and Stage 3 will begin on 1 January 1999. The Council will decide which Member States are then able to join in the process.

At the end of 1994, however, there was no single Member State of the EU which met all the convergence criteria required to join the process of monetary union. It had become increasingly clear that either some relaxation of the tough conditions in the Maastricht Treaty, for judging whether countries would be eligible to move towards full monetary union between 1997–1999 was needed, or that the timetable had to be reassessed (or both). With the effects of the recession of the early 1990s biting hard in borrowing requirements, and other poor economic indicators, it was clear even in 1995 that only a handful of countries would have any hope whatsoever of achieving the targets in the short-term and that could undermine the philosophy of the single market, creating severe divisions. Germany, seen as the cornerstone of the single currency, has often not met the convergence criteria because of the soaring costs of reunification and relatively high inflation since 1993.

Up until 1993, the Commission and advocates of EMU, stressed the need for strict convergence with a view to an early EMU, despite the scepticism of the financial markets and the German government. The Commission's changing stance on this issue reflected the fact that adherence to strict convergence criteria was increasingly unlikely. Although no formal change will be made to the criteria, for convergence there were suggestions relating both to a reassessment of the criteria, to take into account cyclical fluctuations arising out of the recession in the early 1990s, and to the extension of the timescale beyond 1999. In particular, it is likely that greater account will be taken of unemployment and the effects which this has on budget deficits. This left open the possibility of a delay in economic and monetary union. The Maastricht Treaty had always made provision for political judgement about the application of the convergence rules. This, for example, would allow for judgement relating to the extent to which a country's budget deficit was structural or was caused by cyclical problems.

In June 1995 the European Commission launched a revised plan for monetary union. Despite growing scepticism surrounding whether the EMU process could continue at all, it laid out plans for a single currency to be in partial operation by the year 2000. The political decision on which countries join the monetary union would be made between January 1997–July 1998. Actual monetary union would begin in 1999 amongst those countries which met the convergence criteria. After 1999, as soon as a country meets those criteria then it would join in the process. However the EMU process is not going to be a 'big bang'. There will be a phased introduction of bank accounts and Ecu trading relationships until a *critical mass* of trade was being done in Ecus. General circulation of Ecu notes and coins would not occur for three to four years after 1999 however (which could take the process to 2003).

The Commission proposes a three phase transition to the new currency:

Phase A: By July 1998, countries meeting the convergence criteria must make it clear whether or not they will participate in the monetary union process which will begin in 1999. An irrevocable locking of exchange rates would follow.

Phase B: The European Central Bank would begin operating a single monetary policy. Public debt will be converted into Ecus and the ECB would deal exclusively in Ecus vis-à-vis third currencies such as the yen and dollar.

Phase C: The final change-over to the single currency would occur after about three years on a pre-determined date. It would last several weeks as national notes and coins are phased out.

Each phase is very complicated and will be very expensive. There are many technical and legal hurdles to be overcome. Every cash dispenser will have to be adjusted, for example, and legislation will be required in order that every contract written in domestic currencies retains its legality. Most importantly, however, by announcing a definite timetable for EMU the European Commission managed to allay many of the doubts which had been growing as to whether EMU would happen at all.

It is clear from the plans however, that the European Commission is still happy to progress with a timetable which means that some Member States will eventually be using a common currency and others will not. Arguably, this will create a single market within the Single Market. The stronger economies will operate between themselves without the financial costs associated with currency exchange, while the weaker (peripheral) countries will be left out of the process until such time as they can adhere to the convergence criteria. Many argue forcefully that such a divisive policy is hardly in keeping with the Single Market philosophy.

The regional impact of fixed exchange rates and European Monetary Union

In terms of its regional impact, the requirement for fixed exchange rates converts balance of payments problems into a regional problem, primarily for the least developed economies in the EU. This has led to calls from those countries for more economic and social cohesion as well as increased regional assistance before giving up monetary sovereignty. The requirement to balance external accounts could lead to a temptation to concentrate on activities which are currency capturing. Such activities would include the further development of tourism and agricultural production for export, which might be seen as inconsistent with the wish for long term regional development based on more wealth creating activities such as industrial production (Jacobs, 1985). This risk increases as the external deficits rise and is a justification for delaying EMU until there is closer convergence in non-monetary areas.

The mandatory ceiling on public deficits implied by the EMU convergence criteria will also have a regional impact. The policy itself is based on a monetarist ideology which promotes the subordination of fiscal policy and public spending to monetary policy (Curbelo, 1993). In effect, this implies limiting the powers of national and regional governments to decide their own budgetary policies. As discussed in Chapter 3, this again means that the less developed economies in the EU may be prevented from following the growth strategies needed to change structural imbalances.

European Monetary Union and political union

It was never the intention of the original Delors Plan to necessarily go down the path of political union after EMU had been attained. The view was that even after attaining EMU, the EU would continue to consist of individual nations with differing economic, social, cultural and political characteristics. The preservation of this plurality will require a degree of autonomy in decision making to remain with individual countries, and a balance to be struck between national and EU competencies. Clearly, therefore, any link between the two different types of union are more tenuous than the opponents of EMU might wish us to believe. Indeed, if the model adopted for the operation and functioning of the Central Bank is similar to that of the Bundesbank (i.e. free from short-term political interference), then that further distances the two processes.

On the other hand, it is clear that monetary union would require increased co-ordination of the fiscal policies carried out by Member States and, therefore, make some degree of fiscal harmonisation more likely. As we argue below, this may imply political union if such policies are to be the result of ultimate democratic control. In addition, it must be recognised that the independence of the European Central Bank with an emphasis on the establishment of long-term rules and procedures is largely a monetarist model based on a targeted control of the money supply and associated monetary measures. We have already noted in the previous chapter that, the dominant ideology, stemming from the power of the Bundesbank, is far from fully accepted by all Member States. An alternative model, where the Central Bank had a more proactive role in stabilisation and demand management policies, would require much fuller economic union and closer links with other government policies. At the very least, this implies a greater day to day role in monetary policy for the Council of Finance Ministers, or means giving the European Parliament greater power over economic policy. In the longer term, it may actually necessitate political union if the differing policy objectives of the Member States are not to be in conflict.

We must also note that as the central country to the EMS, Germany has tended to perceive that its interests are well guarded by existing forms of policy co-ordination in the EU, and that there may be more risks than additional opportunities in replacing it with EMU. It is a reality that German policy makers have shown less interest in EMU than some of their partners. This has made them insist on not only the tough entry requirements (the convergence criteria), but also on linkage to advances in political integration and federalism to which they attach greater importance. Thus, the Germans, who are perhaps the main advocates of political union, may have a powerful agenda, somewhat different to that of other advocates of EMU.

(5)

FISCAL HARMONISATION

Fiscal policy entails the management of public finance. That is, it deals with both taxation and government expenditure as well as the allocation of public sector tasks amongst the various tiers and departments of government. Because taxation and government expenditure can be used to control the level of activity in an economy, it consists of a number of powerful policy instruments. Unlike the operation of monetary policy, there is already less harmonisation of fiscal policy within the EU and significantly less planned.

In theory, at least, fiscal harmonisation, like monetary union, is required to ensure a single market. The establishment of free intra-EU trade necessitates the removal of all tariff and non-tariff distortions. The removal of tariffs alone may give the impression of a free market but the existence of differential sales taxes, excise duties, income taxes and corporation taxes simply provide equivalent distortions. Significant differences in comparable tax rates, therefore, interfere with the optimal allocation of resources and distort otherwise normal trading relationships.

Substantial differences in indirect tax rates favour producers in low tax countries and discriminate against those in high tax countries. Countries with low rates of direct taxation have an inbuilt advantage in attracting factors of production (particularly labour) and new enterprise to their country even though, if the taxation system was neutral, this might not have been the optimal location. Therefore a non-neutral taxation system implies welfare losses to the EU as a whole, although it may result in welfare gains in some countries.

At present, wide disparities exist in the effective rates of taxation in the Member States of the EU. This applies to both direct taxes (e.g. income and corporation taxes) and indirect taxes (e.g. sales taxes). Sales tax rates, for example, vary within the EU from 0 per cent on many goods to 38 per cent on some luxury goods in Italy. With respect to excise duties, the discrepancies are even greater, reflecting a degree of protectionism, which still exists in the EU, where countries want to protect their own producers, for example, wine is not taxed in Greece, Italy, Portugal and Spain whilst extremely high rates of taxation are imposed in Denmark, Sweden and the UK.

It is not simply the rate of tax which requires harmonisation in order to bring about the free market. With respect to income and corporation taxes, for example, there is a wide disparity in allowances, exemptions and depreciation rates. This means that differential tax systems often impede mergers between firms in different Member States. It is meaningless, therefore, simply to compare the 'declared' tax rates in each country without reference to their base and operation.

Steps towards fiscal harmonisation

The question which arises is how can harmonisation actually be achieved? A possible half-way house, or first stage of a harmonisation programme, could involve the harmonisation of indirect taxation alone. There would be short-term costs, however, even if the partial solution was to be imposed, for example, wine growers in Italy and Spain may find themselves out of work if sales and excise duties were to be imposed on their products.

Apart from these obvious macroeconomic outcomes, one has also to consider the effect of harmonisation on government budgets. If harmonisation became roughly equivalent to an averaging out of tax rates across all countries, then high taxation rate countries would find themselves with budget deficits, as a particular tax rate is forced down, unless it can be offset from elsewhere. Countries such as Denmark and Ireland, which have relatively high taxation rates, would therefore suffer major indirect tax revenue decreases, resulting in a need to raise direct taxes which might be politically unacceptable. With full fiscal harmonisation, such a balance could not be achieved and governments could be faced with imposed tax rates in all areas and could face non-financable deficits.

If all taxation rates were ultimately averaged, then presumably the budget deficits should equal the surpluses and there could be transitory transfers between Member States. But over time, as macroeconomic performance between Member States becomes differentiated and countries do not have the individual power to alter their own budgets, then the central operation of fiscal policy becomes a necessity. For example, if in one country unemployment rises, necessitating the increased payment of benefits, this will result in a budget outflow if taxation cannot be raised to pay for this. If taxation can only be changed unilaterally, then the payment of that benefit will have to be made from the centre and not from the individual Member State. This implies a centralisation of fiscal policy, a centralisation of government budgets and a centralisation of control. Many would argue that this is only really possible with full political union.

The breakdown of the tax burden between direct and indirect taxation has an important bearing on the EU's ability to move towards a unified taxation system in any period of time. Generally speaking, the common tax base is fairly broad for indirect taxation and relatively narrow for direct taxation (*see* Table 4.1). In the case of direct taxes, in 1986, the tax burden measured as a proportion of GDP was highest in Denmark at 28.4 per cent, followed by Belgium and Luxembourg. At the bottom of the league were the Southern European economies and France. In the case of indirect taxation, the highest average rates are to be found in Greece, Portugal, Ireland and Denmark, and the lowest in Spain, Germany and Italy (despite its high level on taxation of luxury goods).

The experience so far

In the period leading up to the Single European Act, the main driving force on the fiscal side was Article 99 of the Treaty of Rome, which specifically called for the harmonisation of indirect taxes in order to remove intra-EU trade distortion. Most of the progress actually made was in respect of value added tax (VAT). It was agreed by all the Member States that the coverage of VAT should be the same and that raw materials and bought-in elements in the production process should be deductible from the tax computation. There was agreement about the general principle of VAT exemptions, but even now the precise nature of these varies from country to country, making the tax base non-equivalent between Member States.

Table 4.1. Taxation burdens in European Union Member States as a percentage of GDP

Country	Direct taxes (1986)	Indirect taxes (1987)
Belgium	18.3	11.4
Denmark	24.4	17.6
France	8.0	13.1
West Germany	13.0	9.6
Greece	6.4	18.3
Ireland	14.5	16.7
Italy	13.7	9.6
Luxembourg	18.3	12.3
Netherlands	12.6	12.6
Portugal	6.9	15.5
Spain	7.6	10.0
United Kingdom	14.9	11.6
EUR12 average	13.6	11.3

Source: Eurostat.

As far as excise duties are concerned, progress has been very slow. One of the reasons for this is the very wide disparities between the rates on different commodities under consideration. While there was been some convergence of rates, a wide divergence still exists. The greatest progress has been achieved with respect to tobacco where a new harmonised system was adopted in January 1987. The essential elements of this system were the abolition of taxes on raw tobacco leaf and the adoption of a sales tax at the manufacturing level, combined with a specific tax per cigarette. Differential rates of VAT nevertheless maintained a price differential between countries.

The adoption of the Single European Act (SEA) reiterated the basic principles of the Treaty of Rome in that it called for the free movement of goods, capital, services and persons. The SEA called for the approximation and ultimately the harmonisation of legislation concerning turnover or sales taxes, excise duties, other forms of indirect taxation and company taxation. The initial emphasis was on indirect taxation harmonisation with the elimination of cross-border customs. In the assessment of the costs of non-Europe (*see* below), the costs of customs procedures amount to about 8000 million Ecu, equivalent to 1.6 per cent of the total value of EU trade. It can also be argued that the abandonment of customs formalities encourages trade to grow as more small firms and private individuals find it easier to sell to and to buy from other Member States.

Indirect taxation

Customs posts at borders are in place partly to act as an indirect taxation containment device. Customs controls protect the indirect taxes of one country from relative tax bargains that are available elsewhere. Moreover, customs controls mean that countries can collect the VAT or other sales tax which belongs to them. A frontier free EU undermines these factors unless tax rates are equalised or at least brought closer together. Rates may not have to be completely equalised, since the experience of the USA indicates that contiguous states can maintain differentials in sales taxes, of up to about five per cent, without the tax leakage becoming unbearable (El-Agraa, 1990).

In order to treat EU transactions crossing frontiers within the EU in exactly the same manner as transactions within an EU Member State with differential VAT and excise rates, a number of measures to ensure fiscal sovereignty have to be adopted in the short run. In 1987, the European Commission proposed moving towards a system which established two VAT rate bands. The lower or reduced rate was to be set at between four per cent–nine per cent, and the upper or standard rate set at between 14 per cent–20 per cent. The lower rate would cover foodstuffs, energy products, water supplies, pharmaceuticals, books, newspapers, periodicals and passenger transport. However, this proposal was not accepted by Member States because it was seen as too constraining, and from 1 January 1993 a more flexible approach was adopted. This requires that the standard rate of VAT should be set at a minimum of 15 per cent and the reduced rate at a minimum of five per cent. However, zero VAT rating of goods is allowed if that rate was in existence prior to 1 January 1991.

When customs posts were in place, the tax collection system involved the refund of VAT when a product is exported, and charging of VAT when the product enters the importing country. This has the effect of guaranteeing the neutrality of taxation but requires customs posts to be used. The replacement of the system of refunding tax on exportation and collecting it on importation, by a system of tax collection by the country of origin, has therefore been proposed and will be implemented from 1997. This also entails the introduction of an EU clearing mechanism to ensure that revenues would continue to accrue to the EU country where consumption takes place. Until 1997, taxation still takes place in the country of destination, although individuals are free to purchase goods (excluding motor vehicles) in the Member State of their choice and use them freely in their state of residence.

The issue of excise duties is even more complex than that of VAT: the situation is characterised by wide disparities, not only in terms of tax levels, but also in terms of coverage. Three main excise duties exist: those on mineral oils, especially on petrol, heating fuels and diesel; those on alcoholic beverages, such as wine, beer and spirits; and, those on tobacco products, especially cigarettes. Following the neutrality principle, taxation is in the country of destination.

With the abolition of fiscal frontiers it is essential to bring excise duties into line to avoid distortions. In addition, it has long been felt that some Member States have used excise duties as a form of protectionism which should also be eliminated. For this reason, in 1987, the Commission proposed a complete harmonisation of excise duties. This was, not surprisingly, rejected by the Member States, because it would imply too radical an upheaval. However, from 1 January 1993, minimum excise duty rates were established. In 1993, for example, this required a minimum tax of Ecu 0.337 per litre of petrol and a requirement that the total tax on cigarettes should be at least 57 per cent of the retail price.

Direct taxation of companies

Tax law in the EU is much more limited in the field of direct taxation than indirect taxation. Company taxation, essentially profit taxes, remains the sole responsibility of Member States. Nevertheless, there are a number of ways in which direct taxation is set to change, in order mainly to prevent cross-border barriers involving both firms and capital. These are designed primarily to prevent the problem of double taxation. The intention is that a common system of taxation applying to both companies and subsidiaries in the EU should be adopted. At the moment, a subsidiary can be taxed in both its own country and the country of its parent company. Such double taxation will be eliminated with subsidiaries being taxed only in the country declared as its tax domicile.

Actual rates of taxation, particularly in terms of corporation tax, will nevertheless have an impact on a firm's location decision, and therefore, in terms of the single market objectives, there are good arguments in favour of harmonising corporation tax. The report of the Ruding Committee, established in 1990 to examine this issue provides some important findings (Ruding, 1992). A survey of companies based in 17 European countries (including the EUR12) indicated that multinational firms' decisions concerning the location of investment are indeed influenced by tax considerations. Such evidence suggests that tax differences among Member States do have an impact on foreign location decisions of firms and thus can cause distortions in competition, especially in the area of financial activities.

Arguments against harmonisation

Opponents of fiscal harmonisation suggest that the developments leading to the equalisation, or at least the narrowing, of tax rates are not necessary to achieve the aims of the internal market. They point out that the factors which influence price are far more numerous and significant than taxes alone. It has been shown that even in a tightly administered market, such as the USA, fiscal differentiation is possible within limits and equalisation of rates is not necessary. Moreover, in the case of goods subject to excise duty, consumption largely takes place in the country of purchase and the present fiscal arrangements are therefore fiscally neutral.

Future prospects

The lack of significant progress on fiscal harmonisation, to date, is no surprise: there are three main reasons for this. First, the EU involves the harmonisation of developed countries with diverse and complicated economic systems. This complexity is growing and harmonisation is extremely difficult. Second, tax harmonisation impacts upon the very foundations of a governments' control and management of its economy. The harmonisation procedure upsets the status quo and any move towards it requires careful and staged progress, if it is not to threaten the basis of macro-economic policy. Third, tax harmonisation is inevitably linked to political unification. If decisions are to be made about uniform taxation policies across Europe, then the question arises as to who makes this decision and how this decision is democratically accountable. Moreover, changes in Community taxation legislation (unlike other areas of economic policy), requires the unanimous approval of all Member States.

THE EUROPEAN UNION BUDGET

The General Budget of the EU forms an important part of the EU's fiscal policy. The Budget is necessarily functional, i.e. the EU is endowed with revenues which it is empowered to discharge for certain specified functions. The EU provides for two types of expenditures. First, there are administrative expenses of the institutions of the EU: the Commission, the Council, the European Parliament, the European Court of Justice, etc. Second, there are the operational expenditures of the EU such as intervention in agriculture, regional aid and grants under the social fund. The total size of the Budget is the same order of magnitude as a large UK government department such as Education and Science.

Fiscal policy is usually thought to have a key role to play in three main areas:

1 It can be used to promote what a government would consider to be an efficient alloca- tion of resources. Market allocation is not always optimal because producers and consumers tend to base their decisions on private costs and do not add in the social costs associated with a good (e.g. pollution – *see* Chapter 10). Fiscal policy can, therefore, be used to tax some goods and subsidise others in order to change the allocation of resources.

2 Fiscal policy can also be used to provide more equity in a country. Governments might consider it desirable to change the personal and/or geographical distribution of income. Thus fiscal policy can be used to tax richer individuals and redistribute that via social benefits to poorer individuals. The government may also use taxes collected across the country to regenerate or develop regions.

3 Fiscal policy has a role to play in the management of the economy by promoting employment, price stability, balance of payments equilibrium and economic growth. Just how great this role is rather depends on the economic perspective of the policy makers. Prior to 1979 and the increased importance given to monetary policy, and policies asso- ciated with deregulation and the free functioning of markets (supply side policies), Keynesians viewed fiscal policy as the main instrument of economic management.

The pattern of the EU's budgetary revenues and expenditures have changed over time. For the first decade expenditures were modest – less than 0.1 per cent of EU GDP. It was roughly evenly distributed amongst administration, agriculture, research and energy and aid for developing countries. The introduction of the Common Agricultural Policy in 1968, whereby a guaranteed price system for farm products was established, transformed this situation. Not only did total expenditure rise dramatically, the great bulk of that expenditure was absorbed by agricultural policy.

Revenue

Essentially, budgetary funds emanate from three sources. First, the duties that Member States collect on imports into the EU are paid centrally. These consist principally of gen- eral customs duties, agricultural tariffs and levies on sugar imports. Second, a proportion of VAT receipts levied by Member States are paid over to the EU. Since 1986 this has been 1.4 per cent of VAT revenues raised on 55 per cent of GNP at market prices. Third, since 1988, the difference between what is raised from the first two revenue sources and what is required to meet EU expenditure is raised form Member States in proportion to their national income.

The EU Budget revenues are based on the principle of *own resources*. This means that the EU has its own independent and clearly defined revenue sources such that the Member States pay to it what actually belongs to it. But revenue still represents less than one per cent of EU GDP and, therefore, the Budget is not a powerful macroeconomic instrument of policy. Moreover, with further integration inevitable, it is not yet central to any federal system. There is therefore considerable doubt as to whether the EU Budget represents a 'proper' budget at all.

In terms of macroeconomic policy, key roles for a budget include an ability to perform stabilising functions between countries and between regions, and the ability to stimulate demand on the fiscal side. The Budget is certainly inadequate for the second purpose and, although attempts are made at evening out disparities via the regional and structural funds, many would argue that the sums involved are not sufficient to make a lot of difference.

The MacDougal Report (1977) recommended that the EU Budget should be at least 2.5 per cent of EU GDP as a precondition for monetary union. It was argued that such revenues should be financed by traditional methods plus an income tax. The burden of income tax must fall among the Member States in a progressive way and in turn Member States need to levy the tax on individuals progressively. It is argued, therefore, that rich people in rich countries will pay more than rich people in poor countries and poor people in rich countries. Quite simply, such an income tax would help to reduce disparities within the EU as well as providing an increased Budget revenue. Both of these factors, it is argued, are required before true economic and monetary union can be realised. With regard to efficiency such a system of taxation introduces a strong fiscal incentive to reduce disparities between the Member States. In particular, the stronger countries will have an incentive to see the weaker countries' growth rates increase since, when convergence occurs, their own tax burden is reduced. Meanwhile, the weaker countries have no incentive to slacken their efforts in reducing disparities, since increases in taxation from the EU will be affordable with significantly increased incomes.

Expenditure

Since 1988 expenditure has been divided into six broad categories:

1 European Agricultural Guarantee and Guidance Fund (EAGGF)
2 The Structural Funds
3 Policies with multi-annual allocation (e.g. research)
4 Other policies
5 Repayments and administration
6 Monetary reserve

The annual increases of expenditure on each category have to be contained within an agreed rate of increase. Political priorities have been reflected in allowing the rates of increase to differ between categories. For example, between 1988–1992 Categories 2 and 3 were allowed to expand more rapidly than others.

European Union expenditure is still dominated by agriculture and, in particular, by the price support given under the Common Agricultural Policy. While this amount has been significant (commonly around two-thirds of the total budget), it will fall in the future as the emphasis is shifted away from price support towards structural support. One important consequence of the massive expenditure on agriculture is that little is left to fund all the other areas of EU activity.

Regional policy, for example, has accounted for well under ten per cent of the budget in recent years, and social policy operated through the European Social Fund (ESF) has received only around seven per cent of the EU Budget. Key areas, such as education and the environment, which are central to quality of life, to the creation of an internal market and to business are seen as minor items of social spending, accounting for only four per cent and one per cent of total social policy expenditure in 1990.

It is often argued that the EU is excessively bureaucratic, but it should be noted that only five per cent of the EU Budget is spent on administration, which is probably not excessive for any organisation of its size. Two-thirds of this expenditure goes to the European Commission.

7 THE COSTS OF 'NON-EUROPE'

There have been a number of attempts by the European Commission to estimate the costs involved of not having European integration. Much of this work has been summarised in the Ceccini Report (Ceccini, 1989), which examined two types of costs associated with what it calls *non-Europe*, i.e. a return to having European countries and markets separated by physical, technical and fiscal barriers. The establishment of an internal market therefore eliminates these costs and creates the following savings:

1 immediate savings due to the removal of barriers; and
2 savings which are spread over time due to the removal of the barriers.

Using a variety of methods, the Ceccini Report came up with significant benefits which would accrue to the EU as a result of integration. These included:

- total gains of around Ecu 216 billion at 1988 prices (around five per cent of EU Gross)
- price deflation of an average 6.1 per cent
- an improvement in the EU's external trade by about one per cent
- an improvement in budget balances of about 2.2 per cent
- around 1.8 million new jobs (equivalent to a reduction in unemployment of around 1.5 per cent).

According to the Ceccini Report, the completion of the internal market will regenerate both goods and services industries. The study estimates that the potential gains for the EU would be in the region of Ecu 200 billion, at 1988 prices. This would increase EU GDP by five per cent. It is argued that the gains will come not only from the elimination of costs of barriers of intra-EU trade, but also from the exploitation of economies of large scale production. With appropriate and co-ordinated macroeconomic policies on the part of Member States, the gains could be as high as seven per cent of EU GDP, and one assumes that with a complete harmonisation of monetary, fiscal macroeconomic policies the gains could be still higher.

8 CONCLUSION

Debates surrounding macroeconomic policy are fierce, with monetarist and Keynesian solutions often being at considerable odds. Moreover, it is impossible to separate the operation of macroeconomic policy from political ideologies. The days of positive economics (if there ever truly was such a thing) are long gone. When one begins to discuss the harmonisation of macroeconomic policy, the politics involved are further heightened, and ultimately the decisions which still have to be taken regarding the degree of harmonisation (particularly in the fiscal area) are likely to be taken on political grounds.

Central to the debate is the issue of sovereignty. There are those who regard sovereignty as being lost upon any type of economic unification. There are those who see sovereignty as being pooled for the greater benefit of all. There are even those, particularly who live in regions of the EU where populations would like increased self-determination, who see the process of unification as giving them sovereignty over their regions if power is devolved back to regional assemblies.

At the very least, though, some sort of limited monetary union seems inevitable, and that would seem to be consistent with the development of an internal market economy with at least some barriers removed. The Maastricht Treaty has made it clear that monetary union can go ahead as long as a majority of countries adhere to the convergence criteria. Whether these criteria are appropriate to all Member States and whether the possibility of a two-speed Europe is in the interests of EU integration are issues which are very questionable. Plans for EMU have stretched the original timetable for monetary union but still create a single market within the Single Market.

What is still uncertain however, is the degree to which other areas of policy will be harmonised, particularly on the fiscal side. Although post-1992, we have seen the beginnings of harmonisation, we have argued in this chapter that to a very large extent, the decision relating to further harmonisation is very much related to the whole question of political as well as economic union.

Questions for discussion

1 Outline the main macroeconomic aims of the European Union.

2 In general, outline the policies open to governments to attain these aims.

3 Explain and distinguish between the European Monetary Systems, Exchange Rate Mechanism and European Monetary Union.

4 To what extent do you consider monetary union to be inevitable?

5 Outline the costs and benefits of the Exchange Rate mechanism. Do any of these change upon the adoption of a single currency?

6 Do you consider that European Monetary Union would lead to a loss of sovereignty for Member States?

7 How might European Monetary Union be of advantage to businesses?

8 Do you consider that the convergence criteria for monetary union are based on a particular ideology? Is that ideology consistent with the aims of all Member States?

9 What sorts of barriers do different fiscal regimes in Member States impose upon the creation of an internal market?

10 Do you consider that complete monetary and fiscal harmonisation is possible without political unification?

CASE STUDY

The United Kingdom, the European Union and the Exchange Rate Mechanism

Background

The United Kingdom economy is the sixth largest in the Organisation for Co-operation and Development (OECD), behind the USA, Japan, Germany and France. In 1989, the UK's GDP was one-sixth that of the USA, and one-third that of Japan. In 1990, exports accounted for slightly under 25 per cent of total GDP. Manufacturing is very important in the economy, although its importance has been declining as the service sector has grown in size. This demise of manufacturing has been particularly acute in the regions where heavy industry was prevalent and this has caused pockets of particularly high unemployment and a decline in average income levels. This has led to a gulf between the more prosperous south and a relatively depressed north.

Along with the other industrialised countries in Europe, the UK experienced a period of rapid growth after the Second World War. Between 1950–1973, GDP grew at an average rate of 3.0 per cent per annum, while retail prices increased at an annual rate of only 4.6 per cent. This strong performance was, however, less marked than some competitors in Europe and growth was often hampered by a balance of payments constraint: as GDP expanded so rising demand led to rising imports, causing a trade deficit. The economy was often forced into a deflationary period in order to attempt to correct this deficit, but ultimately it was necessary to devalue sterling in 1968.

In the 1970s, the UK fared badly after the quadrupling of oil prices in 1973. Inflation in mid-1975 stood at 25 per cent and growth was slow, caused both by the oil price shock and government's attempts to solve the inflation problem. The second oil shock in 1979 doubled oil prices and caused inflation to rise once more, standing at 22 per cent in May 1980. Between 1973–1979 GDP grew by an average of 1.4 per cent per annum.

Economic performance in the 1980s

The combination of high inflation, government policy and a worldwide recession led to a sharp recession in the UK in 1980–81, with GDP falling by 2.7 per cent over two years and unemployment on a strong upward path. After the recession, there was a period of rapid growth, with GDP expanding at an average rate of 2.4 per cent per annum between 1982–1988. Nevertheless, unemployment grew to a peak of 3.1 million in 1986. As unemployment began to fall (to 1.7 million in 1989) inflation rose to eight per cent in 1989 and, at the end of 1990, stood at 10.9 per cent.

Central to government policy since 1979 has been a commitment towards reducing inflation. This policy was largely successful between 1981–1987. Between 1983–mid 1988 the annual inflation rate was around five per cent. But after a large increase in consumer demand in 1987, inflation accelerated until the end of 1990. High interest rates were used throughout 1989–1990 in an attempt to bring consumer expenditure down, but it is uncertain whether this policy, or the deep recession between 1991–1993, caused inflation to fall swiftly to under two per cent. In 1992 unemployment rose, once again, to over three million.

Industrial structure

The UK was the world's leading manufacturing nation during the 19th century. The value of its output has now been surpassed by several economies and much of British industry has been unable to compete with international and European competitors. The industries which have been most severely affected by international competition include iron and steel, motor vehicles and textiles. In 1983, the UK became a net importer of manufactured goods for the first time since the industrial revolution.

As exports of manufactured goods have assumed less importance in overall UK trade, so there has been a shift in relative competitiveness towards services. For a long time London was considered the centre of world banking, insurance and financial markets. But, while important, even these service sectors are beginning to shift. The largest banks in the world are Japanese and the growth of information and communications technology has meant that financial markets and financial transactions have taken on a transnational characteristic with several centres other than London becoming increasingly important.

The United Kingdom in Europe

That the EU is centrally important to the UK is beyond doubt. Table 4.2 shows that more than half of the UK's trade is with its fellow Member States. Nevertheless,

Table 4.2. The United Kingdom's main trading partners (per cent of total value)

Exports to:	1979	1989
European Community	43.0	50.6
Rest of Western Europe	13.7	8.7
North America	11.8	15.4
Centrally planned economies	2.9	1.9
Other developed countries	6.1	5.8
Oil exporting countries	9.0	6.2
Developing countries	13.2	10.4
Imports from:	*1979*	*1989*
European Community	44.5	52.6
Rest of Western Europe	15.3	12.7
North America	13.2	12.6
Centrally planned economies	2.5	1.9
Other developed countries	6.5	7.7
Oil exporting countries	6.8	1.9
Developing countries	10.9	10.0

Note: columns do not necessarily add to 100 per cent because of the existence of traded goods of low value whose country of destination or import is not recorded.

Source: Derived from Monthly Digest of Statistics, 1990.

throughout the 1980s, the UK seems to have been branded as a somewhat reticent member of the EU. It has held up progress of the Social Charter, arguing that such a Charter would place barriers on the free working of the labour market and could therefore cost jobs rather than protect them. It delayed its entry into the ERM until the end of 1990 and, some would say, only entered then because of internal political pressure and until John Major took over as Prime Minister in 1990, was vociferously sceptical about monetary union.

The UK did join the ERM in October 1990. Prior to entry into the mechanism sterling was in a strong position and in the previous months had stood at around DM3.0. However, at the time, the rate at which the entry rate into the ERM was pegged (£1 = DM2.95), was subject to much debate at the time. There are three possibilities, either the rate was right, or it should have been higher, or it should have been lower. Let us examine the case for each argument in turn:

1 **The rate was right.** The government chose DM2.95 because, at the time, it was the market rate. If markets are efficient, and it is often argued that financial markets probably are amongst the most efficient, in general, then this rate was appropriate.
2 **The rate should have been higher** (e.g. £1 = DM3.05). Those who were arguing for a higher rate were pointing to the need to bring the UK's inflation down quickly. Table 4.3 shows the comparative inflation rates amongst member states at the end of 1990. It can be seen that there is a large differential between the UK's rate of inflation and the other countries'. Those who thought that the exchange rate discipline would be an effective tool suggested that it could be made even tougher by entering the ERM at a higher rate. This would make exports relatively more expensive and force domestic firms to keep the price of their goods down.
3 **The rate should have been lower.** Those who were arguing for a lower rate were doing so for two reasons. First, they suggested that the market rate for sterling was artificially high because of high domestic interest rates, pulling in foreign investors as well as the prospect of high oil prices, because of the Gulf conflict in the latter part of 1990. Thus, in time, when interest rates fell and the Gulf conflict was

Table 4.3. Consumer price index for European Union Member States (December 1990)

Denmark	2.2%
Ireland	2.7%
Netherlands	2.9%
Germany	3.0%
France	3.4%
Belgium	4.0%
Luxembourg	4.5%
Spain	6.7%
Italy	6.8%
United Kingdom	10.9%
Portugal	14.1%
Greece	22.9%
EUR12	5.9%

concluded, it was argued that the exchange rate would fall. Second, these people also pointed to the large differential in comparative inflation rates and suggested that a five per cent differential between the UK rate and the average EU rate was too large a gap to close quickly. Thus, it was argued, the exchange rate discipline would have both price and output effects. Those firms which could not keep their prices sufficiently low would lose customers and be forced to cut output and create unemployment. An entry rate which was commonly suggested at the time was DM2.80, which at five per cent lower, would give firms longer to adjust prices although might not bring inflation down quite so quickly.

Throughout most of the period 1990–1992 inflation did fall in the UK. But, as is typical in the social sciences, the extent to which this was caused by entry into the ERM is not clear. Neither is it clear whether the rapidly expanding level of unemployment in the UK was in any way due to firms failing to adhere to the exchange rate discipline. The recession in the UK between 1991–1993, which many argued was deeper than in the rest of the EU, certainly had an impact on these macroeconomic variables.

Sterling under pressure

One of the consequences of the derestricted capital movements which accompanied the development of the EMS, was that speculators found it easier to put pressure on currencies which they expected to depreciate. The poor performance of the UK (and other countries) during the recession of the early 1990s was the underlying reason why, despite the commitment to stable currencies, implied by membership of the ERM, the speculators did not believe that those exchange rate levels were appropriate. Thus, on the days leading up to 16 September 1992, later known as 'Black Wednesday', despite the UK government's attempts to express its commitment to no realignments within the ERM, the speculators continued their relentless selling of sterling.

On Wednesday 16 September, UK domestic interest rates were increased by five per cent in an attempt to keep sterling within its ERM bands. But by the end of the day, sterling's ERM membership had been suspended and the value of the currency allowed to float downwards. Over the coming weeks the devaluation of sterling amounted to 20 per cent against the Deutschmark.

Why did the United Kingdom leave the Exchange Rate Mechanism?

The power of the speculators and the weakness of the UK government in a new era of derestricted capital movements were the direct triggers for the exit of sterling from the ERM. However, the underlying reasons for that departure were threefold:

1 Undoubtedly, with hindsight, the entry rate of sterling into the ERM was too high as a result of the short term characteristics outlined above and an over-reliance on the accuracy of the market.
2 The underlying performance of the UK during the recession had been poor with domestic output falling dramatically and unemployment soaring. Speculators clearly felt that the UK's economic performance would continue to be poor relative to other Member States.

3 German interest rates were high as a result of the costs of reunification and when it came to a decision about whether to lower those interest rates to help maintain the value of sterling and the other currencies under threat, the Bundesbank clearly put domestic considerations before European ones.

After leaving the UK, interest rates in the UK fell, and by May 1993, the recession had been declared at an end. At that time, there seemed little prospect of the UK rejoining the ERM and the UK government had opted out of signing the Maastricht Treaty Chapter on Monetary Union.

Case Study Questions

1 In what way might the high interest rate policy of the United Kingdom government, during 1989 and 1990, have been at odds with maintenance of sterling within the exchange rate mechanism?

2 A basic theory in economics is associated with what is known as the Phillips curve. This suggests that there is a trade-off between inflation and unemployment. To what extent do you think there is evidence from the United Kingdom to support this premise?

3 Why is the rate at which a country joins the Exchange Rate Mechanism so crucial? Do you consider that the United Kingdom entered the ERM at the most appropriate rate?

4 At the time of entry into the Exchange Rate Mechanism, United Kingdom inflation was in double figures. Do you consider that the exchange rate discipline helped to bring inflation down or were there other more important effects pushing the price level down?

5 It was argued by many economists, in 1993, that the United Kingdom's recession was deeper than that of the European Union in general. Can you suggest reasons why this might be so?

6 Do you consider that the United Kingdom's departure from the Exchange Rate Mechanism in 1992 will lead inevitably to its rejection of the other stages of the Delors plan?

7 Given the figures in Table 4.2 what sort of pattern of trade would you expect in 1999?

8 Outline the reasons why the United Kingdom left the Exchange Rate Mechanism.

9 If the United Kingdom does not join in with the process of European Monetary Union, what do you consider will be the consequences?

10 Outline the United Kingdom government's current position on Exchange Rate Mechanism and European Monetary Union membership.

FURTHER READING

Ulff-Moller Nielsen, J., Heinrich, H. and Drud Hansen, J. (1991) *An Economic analysis of the EC*, McGraw-Hill. This text gives a good economic analysis of the European Union, with chapters covering the theory of economic integration and a thorough macroeconomic analysis of the EU.

Nolling, W. (1993) *Monetary Policy in Europe after Maastricht*, Macmillan. This text contains a discussion of the economics and politics associated with monetary union.

Spahn, P. (1993) *The Community Budget for an Economic and Monetary Union*, Macmillan. This text gives an assessment of the fiscal and budgetary implications resulting from monetary union.

Artis, M. J. and Lee, N. (1994) *The Economics of the European Union*, Oxford University Press. This is a very thorough and clear text covering a number of economic dimensions of the European Union.

El-Agraa, A. M. (1990) *Economics of the European Community*, Third edition, Phillip Allan. This is a more advanced text covering economic dimensions of Europe.

REFERENCES

Ceccini, P. *The Benefits of a Single Market*, Wildwood House, 1989.

Curbelo, J. L. 'The Treaty of Maastricht and the European Peripheral Regions', *European Business and Economic Development*, 1, 5, 1993.

El-Agraa, A. M. *Economics of the European Community*, Phillip Allan, 1990.

Jacobs, J. *Cities and the Wealth of Nations,* Vintage Books, New York, 1985.

Ruding, O. *Report on Guidelines for business taxatio*n, Publication of the European Communities, Brussels, 1992.

CHAPTER 5

Competition Policy

INTRODUCTION

In economic terms, competition is associated with the promotion of efficiency which in turn brings with it lower prices, streamlined and productive organisations and technological developments. European Competition Policy is concerned with promoting free markets and healthy competition within a firm regulatory regime. The intention is to broaden the range and lower the price of products offered to the European Union and raise the competitiveness of European firms vis-à-vis their international competitors. While the removal of physical barriers, notably border controls, divergent technical standards and different fiscal regimes is an important part of EU liberalisation, the removal of barriers to competition in Europe will promote the most efficient use of resources and consequently increase the benefits to firms and consumers.

Stimulating competition (and thus efficiency) relies on all firms being given an equal chance to compete across Europe. Peter Sutherland, in charge of EU Competition Policy between 1985 and 1988, described the task as one of developing

> … a level playing field where individual talent, effort and comparative advantage lead to victory, rather than an inclined pitch with moving goalposts, a biased referee and an opposing team full of steroids.

> (Colchester and Buchan, 1990).

In other words, creating an environment in which individual governments' policies do not create unfair advantages and stifle competition.

Efforts are being specifically directed against such issues as state aid, which tends to foster inefficiency and unfairly protect firms from the realities of difficult market conditions, and monopoly and merger policies which can produce national monopolies and cartelised oligopolies. The Commission is also concerning itself with more contentious controls on the activities of nationalised industries and government procurement and thus imposing its authority on traditional areas of sovereign rule. While there is much consensus between governments and firms that competition policy is a key element in ultimately realising a single European market, the path to its achievement is likely to be rocky.

COMPETITION, FREE MARKETS AND EFFICIENCY

It is not hard to find cases in which competition has caused the demise of a firm or indeed a particular national industry. It is only necessary to look as far as the British Motorcycle industry to find an example of aggressive competition from Japanese firms having an adverse effect. How then can the Commission assert with such conviction that competition is beneficial to the EU?

Free markets versus protected markets

As far back as the 18th century, Adam Smith proposed that the widest possible freedom for the exchange of goods promotes economic growth. A nation which relies on protection avoids the discipline provided by competition and inevitably misdirects its resources. Equally, in 1817, Ricardo proposed that free trade among nations increases the total production and availability of goods as each nation concentrates on those products in which it has a comparative advantage. Along with the expansion of worldwide trade, free markets also promote efficiency in production and the allocation of resources, improvements in the quality of goods and higher national living standards. By protecting domestic industries and creating barriers to competition from other EU based firms, governments, rather than acting in the public good, perpetuate inefficiency and reduce living standards for their nation.

Nevertheless, there are strong arguments for protecting local markets:

- in nascent high technology industries protection serves to preserve profits during the early years of development
- protection of employment in declining sectors helps to prevent major regional problems and a drain on state benefits
- protection of industries serving national security needs is in the public interest
- supporting industrial development, particularly the shift away from agriculture and mining, and promoting capital intensive as opposed to labour intensive sectors, parallels world economic developments
- protection of highly visible industries can win government support.

Conversely, arguments against protection can be proposed in all cases

- protection of infant industries involves 'backing winners' which may not succeed and can lead to monopolies which are inefficient
- protection of employment fails to sustain the industry in the long run and involves customers paying for inefficient production. It also obscures the need for retraining workforces from declining industries in new skills required in growth sectors
- with changing world political conditions many would argue that supporting large defence budgets is not in the public interest
- supporting industrial development involves making decisions about areas of expansion. This kind of diversification can involve a serious misallocation of resources, for example, the replacement of labour intensive sectors with capital intensive industries is damaging rather than beneficial to countries which have a large labour force
- whilst governments may gain support through protection of highly visible industries in the short term, they run the risk of long-term inefficiency and the demise of their credibility.

It is clear from these counterbalancing arguments that protection results in inefficiency. What is less clear is how this occurs. By analysing different types of competitive market structure the effects of increased competition on the efficiency of the industry and its inherent firms can be assessed.

Technical efficiency

The theoretical comparison of a firm facing no competition (a monopolist) and a firm operating in a highly competitive market where there are many buyers and suppliers, where products are homogeneous, where there is free market entry and exit and where there is perfect knowledge of the market (perfect competition) is shown in Fig. 5.1.

Perfect competition dictates that the price for the industry (and thus for the firm) is determined by the intersection of the supply curve (which is also the marginal cost curve) and demand (which equates with average revenue) and is shown as P_0 in Fig. 5.1. If, however, the industry were to be taken over by a single firm (a monopolist) and costs and demand are initially unchanged, the marginal revenue curve for the industry must lie within the original average revenue (demand curve). Thus the price charged by the profit maximising monopolist is P_m, higher than under perfect competition, and the output Q_m lower than under competitive conditions. The monopolist therefore charges higher prices to the market and has no incentive to increase levels of output. Equally, there is no incentive to reduce costs and promote internal efficiency to raise price/cost margins as the firm is already earning supernormal profits.

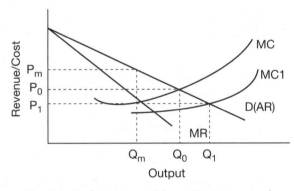

Fig. 5.1 Perfect competition v Pure monopoly

In reality, the price charged by the monopolist may or may not be higher than under perfectly competitive conditions. Much depends on whether or not the monopolist benefits from economies of scale. Where they do, the marginal cost curve moves to MC_1 and the price charged would be lower than under perfect competition.

Within the EU, the only firms that could feasibly be considered as perfect monopolies are the nationalised industries. These firms, often regarded as political policy instruments, are renowned for their inefficiency. Diseconomies of scale, bureaucratic systems, and poor management by civil servants rather than trained business people have all been cited as factors resulting in poor productivity, profits and overpriced goods and services. Such X-inefficiency (the gap between actual costs and those theoretically attainable) is often postulated as a problem specifically associated with large nationalised organisations. Overcoming these problems, however, is not merely a question of privatisation. Turning public monopolies into privately owned monopolies is likely to be more detrimental than beneficial to the public good. Private monopolies unlike their public counterparts are not compelled to provide goods and services which are unprofitable – postal and rail services to remote districts, for instance, could be threatened with the privatisation of the post office and railways. What is more important is that rigorous competition is introduced into these markets by freeing cross-border trade with the effect of promoting price competition, product differentiation and innovation.

Where the industry is characterised by a large number of small players, that is, competition is imperfect (monopolistic), firms face a downward sloping demand curve (*see* Figure 5.2) as products are differentiated from their competitors' and thus not complete substitutes. The small scale of firms also means limited scope for generating scale economies in production.

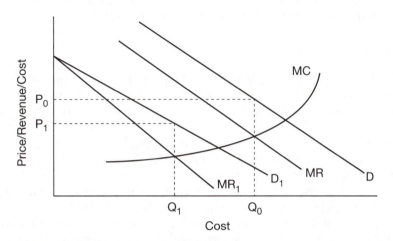

Fig. 5.2 Imperfect competition v New entry

The industry demand curve reflects total demand for industry output at all prices assuming all firms in the industry charge that price. An increase in the number of firms in the industry will shift the demand curve for each firm to the left as market share falls. Thus, in the EU, as new entrants are encouraged to enter markets and stimulate competition, demand for each individual firm will fall along with their corresponding level of market share. In Fig. 5.2, the firm's marginal revenue curve is shown as MR, its marginal cost curve MC and its demand curve D. As the firm is a profit maximiser it will set MC equal to MR and produce output Q_0 at price P_0. With new competitors entering the market (which is likely given the above-normal profits being earned by established companies), the firm's demand is reduced. The demand curve moves to D_1, marginal revenue curve to MR_1 and price falls to P_1 and output to Q_1.

Profit maximising firms under these conditions are likely to reduce their costs and improve their internal technical efficiency as a way of preserving cost price margins and thus levels of profitability. Quite unequivocally, the theoretical model of intensified competition predicts increased efficiency.

Alternatively, in oligopolised markets decisions are made on the understanding that any change in strategy is likely to meet competitor reaction. This raises the likelihood of firms colluding – establishing explicit or implicit agreements with their competitors to actively avoid competition. By co-operating on levels of shared output oligopolists may behave as monopolists aggregating marginal costs and equating them with marginal revenue for the whole industry. Collusion of this kind involves explicit agreement and a high degree of co-ordination, which, as the number of players increases, is hard to sustain. Any increase in output by one player will immediately depress prices and prevent the realisation of opti-mised profits.

More commonly, firms in oligopolised markets do not, as a matter of course, involve themselves in aggressive price competition which can potentially lead to price wars and be damaging for all players. Instead, oligopolised markets are characterised by competition based on differentiation rather than on prices. As collusion and cartels curb the extent to which firms engage in price competition and promote heightened technical efficiency the Commission has specifically targeted these practices as detrimental to competition and the achievement of a Single European Market. However, because oligopolised firms are not exempt from competition they do not ignore efficiency altogether.

Dynamic efficiency

The stimulation of differentiation and new product development are also critical elements in the promotion of efficiency through competition. Dynamic efficiency, which refers to the rapid development of new technologies and products, is essential for firms to keep one step ahead of their rivals in highly competitive markets. Improvements in organisational form, production techniques, management systems, products and services, and distribution sys-tems, performed continuously, all contribute to enhancing the competitive potential of firms to compete both in the EU and in other international markets. Whilst technical effi-ciency involves establishing the most appropriate processes to facilitate best practices, dynamic efficiency concerns the ongoing evolutionary development of the organisation. Both are fostered through competition which means that firms who do not continue to develop in line with other competitors will either be taken over or simply fail to survive.

Many economists fail to agree on whether the propensity to innovate is greater in monopolies or small and medium-sized competitive firms. Obviously large monopolies benefit from 'deep pocket advantages' as they are in possession of greater resources to fund innovation and support its diffusion. With excess profits being earned for each innovation, they are also better placed to dedicate resources to research and development initiatives.

Monopolies are in a more powerful position to protect their innovations through patents and/or the erection of barriers to entry. However, the absence of competition is thought by some economists to dampen the urge to innovate. Because they earn excess profits and can raise barriers to entry, their privileged, protected position gives them less incentive to inno-vate. Conversely, small firms operating in competitive markets without the same privileges need to innovate to survive. Obviously, resources for research and development are limited, but through non-bureaucratic systems and entrepreneurial talents small firms may be as likely (if not more so) to develop new products and systems to enhance their efficiency.

Given the barriers to entry which large monopolies can construct it is clearly question-able whether competition can be introduced to these sectors. Can small firms lacking the same economies of scale and resources survive against such entrenched competition? However, it could be argued their success or failure is less important than the fact that they pressurise the large firms into designing clear policies for continual business improvements (Pelkmans and Winters, 1988).

EUROPEAN UNION COMPETITION POLICY

Competition and efficiency within the EU

European Union Competition Policy, is not designed to protect the firms in Europe. It is expected that the new policies and increased, fairer competition will result in there being both winners and losers. Overall, the aim is to prevent sub-optimisation at national level in favour of promoting competition and efficiency to benefit the EU as a whole.

From what has been outlined so far it is possible to distinguish the specific intentions of the various types of policy being implemented by the Commission:

1 Preventing firms from colluding by price fixing, cartels and other collaborative anti-competitive strategies to stimulate price competition and prevent oligopolists from behaving in a quasi-monopolistic way. As they lower prices, firms will be faced with the challenge of improving their internal technical efficiency and allocating resources more effectively.

2 Controlling the size to which firms grow through acquisition and merger is aimed at ensuring that the acquisitions do not remove competition from the marketplace. In this way, the Commission is ensuring that acquisitions do not result in monopolies reaping supernormal profits and lacking the incentive to lower prices and innovate.

3 Breaking down state-owned monopolies is intended to launch these organisations into the competitive arena – with the effect of removing X-inefficiency and ultimately offering lower priced, and more desirable products and services to customers.

4 The latter issue also relies on freeing up competition particularly in the area of public procurement. Governments show a great tendency to buy from indigenous firms, regardless of whether they supply more cost effective products and services than foreign competitors. By opening up competition in this way governments should be able to make major cost savings by buying from the lowest cost producer (static trade effect) and through competitive bidding, long-term costs should fall further and firms innovate and improve their products and services (dynamic trade effect).

5 Finally, by restricting state aid to indigenous firms the Commission aims to prevent certain institutions having an unfair advantage over their EU counterparts. In addition, as these firms are shielded, to an extent, from the real competitive pressures bearing on the market, they are often 'fat and lazy' and inefficient, a problem which the directives aim to tackle.

Of particular importance are the policies themselves and the strides taken to date to free inter EU trade and promote competition.

European Union competition rules

There are a number of EU rules which stand out as having the most pervasive impact on competitive activity. Articles 85 and 86 relate to anti-competitive behaviour which has an effect on trade between the Member States. Article 85 focuses on concerted practices between two or more institutions, while Article 86 concerns abusive exploitation of monopoly power. Article 92 focuses on governments' role in distorting competition through the provision of state aid.

Article 85

The focus of this Article is on agreements drawn up between firms which act to distort competition, and anti-competitive behaviour which impacts on trade between Member States. It incorporates such practices as price fixing, establishment of quotas, dividing market share between competitors and tie-in clauses between suppliers and buyers. Consequently, the article applies to both horizontal agreements (between competing organisations) and vertical agreements (between, for example, manufacturers and their customers or suppliers). It is important to stress that agreements need not be written. Oral or 'implicit' agreements may also be subject to scrutiny if they are deemed to have an adverse effect on competition.

Not all agreements, however, are considered detrimental to the economic health of the EU. It is possible for institutions to receive *negative clearance* on specific agreements where they are deemed to be 'safe' by the Commission. These include agreements of minor importance, the *de minimis* rule, where the economic effects are not considered to be significant (accounting for less than five per cent of the EU market, where the agreement has effect and where the aggregate turnover of the involved parties is less than Ecu 200 million).

Automatic exemptions also apply to agreements between principals and commercial agents (defined as institutions taking no financial risk in the sale of goods, holding no stock, having no power to determine price and offering no services). The key question is whether or not the agent is economically integrated with the principal and given the ever-growing complexity of relationships between principals and agents, the Commission are looking to review their approach in this area. Also exempt are activities between parent companies and their subsidiaries or between the subsidiaries themselves. As these activities involve one economic unit, they fall outside the scope of Article 85 except where the subsidiary is deemed to have freedom to determine its own course of action, the main criterion for judgement being the size of the parent company's shareholding. Similarly, co-operation agreements between firms (including such issues as joint research and development, joint market research, joint selling arrangements between non-competing firms and joint after-sales services) and sub-contracting arrangements are also exempt.

Special exemptions may also be awarded where the harmful effects of restrictive agreements are more than compensated for by particular benefits. Article 85 identifies four conditions for the granting of such exemptions:

1 where improvements are made in production, distribution or economic progress such as cost reductions or capacity increases;
2 where a fair share of the benefits accrue to consumers (be they final consumers or trading companies) such as lower prices or the improved quality of goods and services;
3 only agreements which actively contribute to the additional benefits will be permitted;
4 a degree of competition must exist in a substantial part of the goods and services supplied.

One further feature of Article 85 is the existence of group exemptions which, unlike individual exemptions, require no prior notification to the Commission. These currently cover:

(a) **Specialisation agreements** – horizontal production agreements which involve the participating firms each specialising in the production of a particular product or product group. The justification for permitting this kind of activity is to allow small and medium-size firms the potential to rationalise production efforts, improve their efficiency and strengthen their competitive position vis-à-vis larger firms. Consequently the exemption only covers agreements between small and medium-sized firms based on market share and turnover. Twenty per cent market share on specialised products and combined turnover of Ecu 500 million are currently applied. Other stipulations dictate that agreements must be reciprocal, and must only apply to the nature of products and not to the volume of production or prices.

(b) **Exclusive distribution agreements** – where stipulations are made by the manufacturer on the permissible sales territory and the sale of competitor products. These are sometimes considered beneficial as a result of their ability to promote efficiency in distribution as well as facilitate unification. The concept of parallel imports is critical here, as traders other than exclusive distributors who buy from third parties in other markets, provide competition for the firm which has been granted exclusive rights. Any attempts to hinder parallel importing therefore render the group exemption inapplicable. No restrictions, however, may be applied in respect of prices or customers and agreements cannot be made between competing firms as this will lead to market sharing, except where one or both parties have an annual turnover of less than Ecu 100 million.

(c) **Exclusive purchasing agreements** – which involve the reseller agreeing to buy exclusively from a specific manufacturer can make it difficult for competitors to penetrate the market. There are consequent limitations on the duration of such obligations (five years) and the nature of products covered (applying only to those which are connected to each other). In addition to these provisions, those relating to exclusive distribution also apply.

(d) **Patent licensing agreements** – which may pose restrictions in terms of territorial rights and the exclusivity conferred on the licensee, do provide access to technologies for those firms without the potential to innovate, and market access for small innovating firms lacking the capacity to sell on a pan-European scale. Three main principles cover the group exemption in this case: a degree of protection afforded to both the licensor and licensee to ensure continued R&D effort by the innovator and ensure a favourable environment for technology transfer; assurance of effective competition and intra-EU trade for patented products; and legal security of the contract partners. Territorial restrictions cannot be enforced, although licensees may only sell in other licensees' territories in response to unsolicited orders, they may not actively sell or manufacture. Regulations do not exempt obligations for licensees to buy materials and components from the licensor (often undertaken to protect the invention) to pay a minimum royalty, to observe technological secrecy and use the technology only in connection with production of the designated product.

(e) **Research and development agreements** – which have always been regarded favourably by the Commission, are permissible so long as competition in the final consumer market is preserved. This means that controls are applied to competing firms who jointly exploit technologies (limiting them to 20 per cent joint market share for products which may be improved or replaced by the new technology), and all parties are afforded right of access to results and freedom of distribution.

(f) **Franchising agreements** – which have become more prevalent in the EU in recent years, usually involve licences covering industrial or intellectual property rights (trademarks, brandnames or know-how). They are regarded as having a generally positive effect on competition allowing franchisors to develop a wide and uniform distribution network without major investment. This has the potential to introduce new competition (particularly for small and medium-size firms), allows rapid expansion and extends inter-brand competition. This clearly benefits consumers as it offers them wider choice and the advantages which result from standardised, efficient distribution. Franchise operations are seen as being very different from exclusive distribution and purchasing agreements as a result of the advantages offered, although the block exemption applies only to distribution and service franchises and not to those in the manufacturing sector.

(g) **Know-how licensing** – like patent licensing, benefits the economy by facilitating technology transfer and innovation although territorial restrictions can stifle competition. As a result of the irreversible nature of knowledge transfer (once attained it cannot be retracted), the Commission were keen to provide greater legal certainty for involved parties on how agreements fit into existing competition policy. The policies which apply to patent licensing also apply here with provision being made for restrictions which are not considered to be damaging to competition: obligations to maintain the secrecy of know-how by the licensee after termination of the agreement; obligations that the licensee divulge any experience gained in exploiting the know-how and the granting of non-exclusive licences to the licensor when improvements and new applications are revealed. By permitting such arrangements the potential to maintain a degree of monopoly over know-how is designed to facilitate its licensing (and implicitly its sharing).

Article 86

Article 86 addresses a rather different problem: the abuse of a dominant position – although having a dominant position is not, in itself, prohibited. Article 86 may be applied where:

1 The parties involved are in a dominant position. Market share is the major determinant (with a watershed of 40 per cent being applied) although this is by no means the only consideration. Other factors, such as beneficial access to raw materials or capital, may also be deemed to allow the firm the freedom to operate without consideration for the competition.

2 The dominant position is in the EU or a substantial part of it. The determination of what constitutes a 'substantial part' depends on a variety of factors, but most importantly the nature of the product market under consideration.

3 There is an abuse of the dominant position – that is actions taken by a dominant firm are damaging to third parties. Examples of such abuse include:
   (a) monopoly pricing, detrimental to customers or market limit pricing designed to deter new entrants;
   (b) discriminatory pricing between or within Member States;
   (c) refusal to sell to a particular customer without valid reason;
   (d) attempts to retain customers by granting fidelity rebates;
   (e) acquisition of firms which affects the competitive structure of the EU market.

The final point in this list brings into question market concentrations brought about by merger and acquisition activity. This has become increasingly important within the Single Market as new competitive pressures and search for European opportunities has led firms to embark on mergers and takeovers as a means of securing market entry in the other Member States in order to spread their Europe-wide activities.

Article 92

As a general rule, Article 92 determines that all state aid to business is illegal in so far as it affects trade between the Member States of the EU. State aid refers to much more than government grants, cheap loans and subsidies: it also involves such issues as tax concessions, provision of goods and services on preferential terms and the acquisition of public shareholdings in private businesses.

Certain types of aid are, however, permissible – particularly aid which supports social improvements, aid which allows recovery from natural disasters and aid provided to certain economically disadvantaged regions (in particular that granted to the Federal Republic of Germany). Similarly, aid provided to support the execution of particular projects in the interest of the EU as a whole or to support economic developments which do not adversely affect trade is considered compatible with EU competition objectives.

The Commission also recognises the importance of supporting small and medium-size companies within the EU and have outlined a series of provisions for support to this sector:

- grants and low interest loans for small business start-ups
- low interest loans and loan guarantees for small business investment in line with those which the largest firms are able to obtain on the open capital market or from banks
- public support to encourage the flow of risk capital to small firms. Encouraging private venture capital firms to invest in small firms by offering them government guarantees and the granting of subordinated government loans on which banks loans may be secured
- grants for research and development by small firms
- grants or low interest loans to support innovation programmes which would otherwise not be entered into as a result of high costs and risks
- grants or low interest loans for projects designed to reduce energy consumption or switch from oil to alternative energy sources
- grants for management improvement covering the costs of consultancy and computerisation.

The Commission are aware that a strong network of small and medium-sized firms is essential to the promotion of economic benefits within the EU. Small business start-up and growth provides new employment opportunities (often in economically depressed regions) adds to competition, provides greater consumer choice and often facilitates economic development in growth sectors and new technology.

The enforcement of rules

Rules may be enforced as a result of direct intervention by the Commission, or as a result of specific complaints made by third parties. In both cases, the Commission has the power to collect information, impose fines for failure to comply with competition rules (payable to the Commission, not injured parties) and take interim action to bring damaging behaviour to an immediate halt. The Commission expects agreements between firms which may be potentially detrimental to the economic welfare of the EU to be notified to the Commission for approval. This applies to those agreements which do not fall under Article 85 and for which firms seek negative clearance as well as those which do fall under Article 85 but which meet the conditions of outlined exemptions. It does not apply to situations where agreements are covered by group exemptions. Nevertheless, there are numerous instances which are not brought to the notice of the Commission and in these instances the enforcement of rules relies on Commission intervention and complaints.

Commission intervention

There are a variety of ways in which the flouting of competition rules may come to the attention of the Commission. Issues raised in the European Parliament, newspaper articles, information received from Member State authorities and contact with various interest groups (such as consumer organisations) all provide a valuable source of information. The Commission is not compelled to act on all information received from these sources but it will react to all situations which are deemed to pose a serious infringement of rules. The first stage of assessment normally involves the collection of information either through direct requests or formal investigations. This not only involves firms suspected of infringing rules, but also third parties who are in a position to clarify certain information as a result of their proximity to the market. Investigation teams have complete freedom to enter firms and consult company documents and take copies of any records they consider pertinent to the case. Although companies do not have to admit investigators, failure to do so will result in the Commission ordering the firm to comply by a formal decision. Visits are usually unannounced to prevent documents being destroyed in the interim.

Complaints

Member State authorities, companies and trade associations may all bring complaints to the Commission. An essential requirement is the legitimate interest of the complainant in the termination of the behaviour under question. This normally means they can show that they are being damaged (or may potentially be damaged) by the behaviour. Where complaints are made formally, in writing, and the complainant demonstrates their legitimate interest, the Commission is obliged to investigate the situation. Where investigations show the complainant has a legitimate claim, the Commission takes the necessary steps to put an end to the infringement. Where, however, no proof of infringement can be found, the Commission is obliged to inform the complainant of its decision, the reasoning behind it, and give him the chance to provide further information. Failure to do so results in automatic rejection of the claim.

Complaints may be made informally, or anonymously, although the Commission has no obligation to act on information so provided.

EVIDENCE FROM THE EUROPEAN UNION

Collusion and market fixing – the application of Article 85

In some industries there are stronger incentives to collude than to compete, particularly those in a state of decline or those in which the actions of one firm cause other players to react aggressively. The building industry is renowned for its anti-competitive activities across various sectors including ready-mixed concrete, steel and associated products, glass and road surfacing materials. Certain characteristics of the industry contribute to this tendency for collusion:

1 there are a relatively small number of suppliers in each national market making it easier to negotiate co-operative market sharing and price fixing;
2 material costs are a relatively small proportion of total development costs which means customers are more concerned about delivery schedules than price;
3 many of the materials are bulky raising transportation costs, localising competition and severely restricting cross-border trade
4 customers are often able to hand on price rises to end-users and demand tends to be inelastic.

Quite unequivocally, the nature of the industry militates against competition, but provides no excuse for further restricting rivalry through the establishment of cartels. Sir Gordon Borrie, Director General of Fair Trading in the United Kingdom commenting on such actions noted:

> Cartels are pernicious arrangements which invariably lead to higher prices for the goods or services involved. Those engaged in this sort of behaviour damage not only their customers but also themselves by restricting efficiency and innovation.

> (*Financial Times*, 25 July 1990)

As Article 85 of the Treaty of Rome is designed to ban practices 'preventing, restricting or distorting competition', except where these contribute to efficiency without inhibiting consumers'… fair share of the resulting benefit' and without elimination of competition activities of this kind can obviously not be condoned within the competitive ethos of the new European market.

Although private cartels are by no means easy to uncover, the Commission relies on customers faced with continual price rises from all producers and rival firms being squeezed by the actions of large groups of market players to flag offenders. These tip-offs in the building industry have resulted in industry scrutiny, dawn raids on firms suspected of being involved resulting in confiscation of documentation. In the building sector, thermal insulation, stainless steel and ready-mixed concrete provide examples of sectors which have come under scrutiny. A wide variety of other sectors have also faced the same kind of analysis – carton-boards, sugar and plastics to name but a few with some cases resulting in heavy fines of up to ten per cent of a company's annual turnover.

The plastics cartel was possibly one of the most spectacular illicit cartels to have been blown open by the Commission involving 23 of Europe's top chemical companies from the UK, France, West Germany, Belgium, Italy, Spain, the Netherlands, Finland, Norway and Austria. Accounting for up to 90 per cent of the EU's supply of PVC and 80 per cent of low density polyethylene (LdPE) they were in a strong position, through collusion, to sustain levels of profitability in an industry suffering from severe overcapacity.

The motivations for collusion are quite clear. Untimely expansion of capacity, just prior to the 1970 oil price crisis, left firms with severely reduced profits in the face of falling demand and increased prices. Quotas were consequently set to ensure firms did not attempt to gain additional market share through aggressive price competition and prices were fixed to harmonise the differences between countries to discourage customers from shopping around for the cheapest deals.

Although the cartels did not always run smoothly, with firms exceeding their quotas, continuing to compete on price and overstating their past sales levels to get larger quotas, frequent meetings were set to continually overcome the difficulties and sustain a co-operative rather than competitive environment for PVC and LdPE plastics. Indeed, in an ICI internal memo in 1983, the failure of price fixing to prevent competitive behaviour was noted.

> It is widely acknowledged that these posted levels will not be achieved in a slack market ... but the announcement does have a psychological effect upon the buyer. An analogy is the car purchase where 'list price' is set at such a level that the purchaser is satisfied when he obtains his 10–15 per cent discount, he has struck a 'good deal' but the car producer/garage has still an adequate margin.

(Reported in the *Financial Times*, 12 April 1989)

The question which must be asked is why, given the failure of the cartel to achieve its objectives of restricting price competition and rivalry for increasing market share, was it sustained over such a long period? At the height of the cartel in 1983 many of the key members were failing to make a profit. Atochem (formerly Chloe) of France was reported to have made a loss of Ffr1bn (£93m), Montedison of Spain L203bn (£87m) and profits for BASF, one of Germany's largest chemical firms, failed to exceed those of the previous year by any significant amount. In addition, they paid the price for being caught out with fines of up to Ecu 6.8 million bringing the total of fines levied on plastics companies between 1984–1987 to Ecu 120m (£184m). However, continuance of the cartel did allow firms to delay inevitable rationalisation and business closure.

Following the Commission's raid in January 1987 on the firms involved in the cartel, the industry has been encouraged to get rid of most of its over-capacity and although it meant a lot of plant closures and redundancies, the result has been to improve profitability beyond the scope ever achievable under cartel conditions. Demand has also risen to a sufficient level to limit the temptation for firms to embark on further co-operative arrangements of this kind. Instead, ICI (of the UK) and EniChem (of Italy) announced a joint venture operation on 13 February 1986. The underlying intent of this venture was to preserve the activities of both companies in a market burgeoned by over-capacity. The joint venture involved the closure of old, inefficient production plants, a reduction in capacity of 300 000 tonnes and a shedding of 1 200 staff (rationalisation only possible for EniChem under the guise of an international joint venture).

In many respects, the scale of this case, involving a large proportion of the EU's major multinational chemical companies, was a powerful exemplar to any firms contemplating collusion under the noses of the EU's cartel busters. Recent experience in the industry has also demonstrated that legal means of co-operation, via alliances and formal co-operation can provide a better solution than carving up markets and behaving in a restrictive way.

Nevertheless, firms appear determined to continue anti-competitive practices. The UK's two sugar giants Tate & Lyle and British Sugar saw their four year price-fixing agreement come to a head in July 1990, entered into following aggressive price wars in the early 1980s. Regardless of their motivations and the fact that Tate & Lyle brought the case to the attention of the Office of Fair Trading (OFT) themselves, Sir Gordon Borrie (director general of the OFT) decided to refer them to the Restrictive Practices Court. As a result of their combined 92 per cent UK market share, they had had 'significant effects on competition in the sugar market over a four-year period'. One of the important effects was preventing competitive pricing and thus artificially raising prices charged to their customers. While loss is difficult to prove firms like Cadbury and United Biscuits, major industrial users, have been urged to sue the sugar companies.

Generally, the reluctance of customers to sue firms which have engaged in anti-competitive practices is thought by the OFT to be one of the reasons for the persistence of cartels. Where the industry is dominated by a relatively small number of suppliers, this reluctance can easily be explained by firms' fear of antagonising suppliers and closing the only sources of supply available to them. Nevertheless, if industrial customers join forces with the European and national officials this may prove a more powerful deterrent than simply fining those firms who get caught.

The activities of the OFT in the UK show the affinity between national authorities and the Brussels based Commission in cracking down on anti-competitive practices. Equally, the Competition Council in France and the German Bundeskartellamt are both concerned with supporting the Commission's activities on preventing the exploitation of monopoly power by their domestic firms. For example, at the end of 1989, the French Competition Council imposed anti-cartel fines on 80 construction firms totalling Ffr166m (£17.3m) and on 43 electrical engineering firms fines of Ff128m (£13.3m). These moves also laid to rest accusations by other EU Member States that Paris had failed to embrace the concept of competition and was insistent on continuing its interventionist and protectionist stance. So, while the European Commission concerns itself with the restriction of anti-competitive practices between Member States, the individual Member States themselves are mirroring the developments at a national level.

Abuse of a dominant position – Article 86

While a dominant position is not, in itself, considered to be detrimental to the economic health of the EU, abuse of that position, hindering the maintenance of effective competition by acting independently of competitors and customers, runs contrary to EU objectives. The soda ash industry in Europe, dominated by ICI (of the UK) and Solvay (of France) came under EU scrutiny in the late 1980s as a result of their 'concerted practice of long standing by which Solvay and ICI divided the European market between them so that neither competed with the other' (EC Report on Competition Policy, 1991). Solvay also provided ICI with large tonnages to allow ICI to continue to service the UK and Irish markets. In return, ICI agreed not to enter Continental Europe. Under Article 85, the two firms' collusive behaviour resulted in ICI being fined Ecu 17 million and Solvay Ecu 30 million. The effect of these agreements was to permit both firms a dominant position within their respective geographical areas, a position which was further exploited by attempts to hold on to their customers. Both firms put in place a system of exclusionary rebates designed to induce consumers to obtain the major part of their soda ash from the dominant firms. In the event, this had the reverse effect, buyers looked to non-EU firms to source their soda-ash requirements, opening up the market to foreign competition. This resulted in a change in pricing policy by ICI and Solvay wherein large soda-ash users were offered a *top-slice* discount on tonnage supplied by ICI or Solvay which would normally have been supplied by non-EU firms. This top-slice was offered after a certain tonnage level was reached which forced non-EU firms to lower their prices in order to compete. Although the detrimental effect of this latter action is felt by non-EU firms, attempts to tie-in customers in this way is not in keeping with overall EU objectives.

Coca-Cola, too, was accused of attempting to tie-in distributors by disallowing them to purchase other cola beverages, or granting rebates where they did not. The latter are referred to as *fidelity rebates* which are ruled to constitute abuse of dominant position (here, manufacturer over distributor).

Relating back to the basic ruling, it has to be proved that the firm is abusing its dominant position in the product market or a major proportion of it. But what constitutes the product market? The case of United Brands provides an interesting case which demonstrates the difficulty of defining the market. United Brands were accused of charging unfairly high prices for bananas in some Member States. The court therefore had to determine what constituted the *product market* for bananas and, thus, whether the firm could be charged with abusing a dominant position. Essentially, the Court had to suggest whether the banana market was a unique market, or one in which consumers would readily switch their buying behaviour to other fruits if the price of bananas rose (whether there were interchangeable substitutes). Ultimately, the court determined that as bananas cater for different dietary requirements, their specific qualities influence customer preference and substitution to other fruits unlikely. Thus the market for bananas is distinct.

Mergers and acquisitions

There is growing concern among some governments, most notably the French, and a large number of corporate petitioners that the EU should be actively promoting 'Eurochampions' – firms with greater capability to take on major international competitors. The decision to judge mergers and acquisitions on competition grounds – restricting those arrangements which distort intra-EU competition – militates against the development of such firms. Nevertheless, there is good cause for the Commission to be concerned about allowing merged firms to attain a dominant position in the EU just as institutions like the Monopolies and Mergers Commission in the UK and the German Federal Cartel Office have prevented the development of national monopolies over a number of years. There is an inherent fear that mergers and acquisitions can result in firms becoming quasi-monopolies with the potential to exploit market power, specifically by charging higher prices.

Article 86 of the Treaty of Rome allows the Commission to 'block mergers which so strengthen a company's dominant position that the only undertakings left in the market are those which are dependent on the dominant undertakings with regard to their market behaviour'. While this provides some broad definitions for the control of takeover and merger activity, more specific regulations were deemed necessary, particularly in the light of the growing trend towards mergers in the Single Market. In December 1989, the specific nature of the controls afforded to the European Commission were agreed, the so-called Merger Control Regulation, to come into effect nine months later in September 1990. Above all, the new regulations are designed to provide a 'one stop shop' for merger vetting removing the need for firms to gain approval from both domestic and EU-wide authorities and clarify the specific nature of the factors on which mergers and acquisitions are judged.

The nature of the applications procedure has been very clearly outlined. Within a week of announcing the merger the firms involved must complete and return to the Commission a notification form which comprises 66 detailed questions covering a wide range of aspects including prices charged in the EU and relative market shares. Although the detailed nature of the questions included on the form has caused a certain amount of dissent amongst firms, the Commission asserts that it is necessary if they are to make a decision within the time limit of one month. Once the Commission has been notified, they are then required to answer three important questions:

1 Does the proposed merger create a 'concentration'? By this they mean a takeover or joint venture which results in a single autonomous entity.

2 Does the proposed deal have an effect on the EU? Specifically, does the formed concentration have annual worldwide sales of more than Ecu 5 billion ($6.6 billion) and do the EU-wide sales account for more than Ecu 250 million. Excepted from this are cases where each party derives more than two-thirds of their overall sales from one and the same country wherein it will come under national competition policy rather than EU regulation. This is likely to bring the Commission around 50 mergers per year to vet – quite a considerable number. Nevertheless they are keen to lower the threshold to Ecu 2 billion to ensure tight restriction over EU mergers and acquisitions.

3 Does the created European concentration impede competition? The strengthening of a dominant position in a market is seen as potentially distorting competition and thus not within the public interest.

Whereas the first two questions are relatively simple to answer the third requires a great deal of analysis. Again, the task force has to decide what constitutes the market. On the surface this appears to be an easy task, whereas in practice it can be highly complex. The Commission has traditionally taken a narrow view of what constitutes a market, building on the concept of demand side substitutability. The Commission's *Notification of Acquisitions* form provides the following definition:

> A relevant product market comprises all those products and/ or services which are regarded as interchangeable or substitutable by the consumer by reason of the products' characteristics, their prices and their intended use.

Nevertheless, supply side factors have also been considered. The case of metal containers serves to highlight this point. In the takeover of the British company Metal Box Packaging by the French concern Carnaud, the market was, initially, taken to be metal containers. Conversely, in parallel mergers between USA metal packaging companies the product market was defined as metal containers and glass bottles in 1964 and was further extended to include plastic containers in 1988. The Commission's argument for taking a narrower definition of the market centred on production switching difficulties in the context of glass, plastic and metal packaging. Calculations of market share, highly dependent on the definition of market boundaries, showed a wide disparity in the Metal Box case. Whereas the merged firm would have had a combined turnover of £2 billion in a packaging market worth £35 billion, in the more narrowly defined metal packaging market it would have had a dominant position and thus have been rejected under new legislation. Similar claims were made by the Commission in the merger of Metallgesellshaft and Safic Alcan (1991), where the differing production techniques of natural rubber and latex meant they were treated as separate products resulting in a narrow definition of the market.

If markets are defined too narrowly this can prevent mergers which do not distort competition and which may rather increase efficiency. Alternatively, if markets are defined too broadly then they will permit mergers to go ahead which act against the public interest by permitting a dominant market position to be attained.

Along with product market definitions, there are also geographic boundaries to be considered. These are shaped by transportation costs which dictate the distance goods may be moved economically, market entry barriers including cultural preferences which suggest whether or not goods stand a chance of penetrating foreign markets, and differing competitive conditions. For example, the cost of transporting industrial gases is very high, not because the gas itself is heavy or bulky, but because the containers in which the gas is stored and transported are metal, raising the costs considerably. Consequently, the geographic boundaries of the market are restricted. Alternatively, the preference for indigenously produced beer in Germany means that any domestic price rises will not result in increased imports. Different cases have resulted in very different geographic market definitions: in the merger between Promodes/Dirsa (1990) in grocery retailing the market was defined on a regional basis whereas in the commuter aircraft sector, the Aerospatiale/De Havilland (1991) merger was considered within the bounds of the global market.

Equally, deciding whether a merger distorts competition is by no means an easy undertaking. For example, assessing whether the merger serves to raise barriers to entry through promoting scale economies or determining whether or not the new merged firm is in a position to behave as a monopolist, requires some degree of subjective judgement and speculation. The task force has to make a rapid decision, in a month, on whether the merger can go ahead, on the grounds that it does not distort competition, or whether proceedings should begin. In that event, where the task force fears that competition will be distorted, they have a further four months to gather information (potentially by seizing documents) and make proposals to the 17 Commissioners whose task it is to make the final decision to clear the deal, stop it, or allow it to proceed with certain amendments. Once this decision has been made it cannot then be undermined by national authorities except where the case challenges national *legitimate interests* – defined as 'public security, plurality of the media and prudential rules'. Further areas thought to be 'legitimate' by national governments may also be considered where a case can be justified for their inclusion.

By taking the upper hand and outlining the procedures and regulations for merger policy, the Commission has simplified the process and made the rulings more transparent for the increasing number of firms contemplating mergers in the EU. In so doing they have taken much power out of the hands of the local authorities for mergers over a particular size, which has naturally caused problems with certain Member States. The French and Southern European governments, in particular, rejected the new regulations on the grounds that the sole criterion of judgement is competition. This, they asserted, fails to take into account the social effects of certain mergers – their arguments being specifically concerned with providing for those firms with the potential to become 'Euro-champions'. Although their arguments were rejected as being against the spirit of free EU competition, a clause was included in the new proposals stating that the Commission should take into account 'the development of technical and economic progress provided that it is to consumers' advantage and does not form an obstacle to competition'. In many ways this simply confirms that joint activities for technological developments are to be encouraged so long as they do not result in higher prices.

On the other hand, the German government was not happy with the fact that their own cartel office could not block mergers after the Commission had made its final ruling. In response, the new legislation allows governments to make a request for their own authorities to take over a case if there are fears that a dominant position can be attained in a 'distinct' market within their territory. Although this threatens, to an extent, the 'one-stop-shopping' approach to the new EU-wide merger laws, as they are undermined by national concerns, the final decision still rests in the hands of the Commission who may refuse intervention by governments if they are not in keeping with the Commission's underlying principles and Community law.

The Commission has made it quite clear that attempts to sway decisions by pressure from national political interests will be rejected. However, co-operation between the

Commission and national authorities is being actively encouraged. National anti-trust authorities are not seen as rivals and adversaries, but are rather regarded as an important source of information and advice. They are provided with documentation concerning proposed mergers under Commission jurisdiction and act as an Advisory Committee to express their views. Overall, the underlying objective of the new legislation and 'one-stop-shopping' approach is not designed to take authority away from national control but to draw clear lines of demarcation between the functions of the Commission and the Member States.

It is interesting that the merger between GEC and Plessey of the UK – prevented by the UK Monopolies and Mergers Commission in 1986 was later allowed to go ahead, in a revised format by the European Commission. The new deal, a joint bid between GEC and Siemens of West Germany, was ruled as not posing a threat to competition and offering considerable scope for economies of scale. Not that these advantages were not highlighted in the case of the former bid. Mr Colin Baillieu, one of the six members of the UK Monopolies and Mergers Commission who supported the original merger, argued that sufficient weight had not been given to:

1 the monopolistic character of the two major UK customers – British Telecom and the Ministry of Defence – demanding a relatively large scale powerful supplier;
2 the international nature of the two key markets – defence electronics and telecommunications demanding considerable financial commitment to price and product quality (efficiency);
3 the size of the R&D investment required to carry firms in both telecommunications and electronics into the future – incapable of being sourced by a single firm.

Mr Baillieu is quoted as saying

> To take an excessively purist line about a small loss of domestic competition is to perpetuate the Balkanisation of an important sector of British industry.

It would seem that the Commission have taken these considerations into account in their recommendation that the revised bid should be permitted to go ahead. This reveals a difference in focus between national authorities and the Commission in which the latter is more concerned with the good of the EU as a whole, the former the individual Member State. If, however, European firms are going to survive in increasingly competitive international sectors, a wider view of competition is preferable to permit firms to grow to the scale necessary to take on leading international rivals.

What is apparent in certain rulings is the fact that the Commission does take into account political considerations. The takeover bid by France's state-owned Aerospatiale and Italy's state-owned Alenia for De Havilland, the Canadian commuter turbo-prop subsidiary of Boeing, was not approved on the grounds that the merged firm would have eventually become a monopoly. It was argued by the firms that the product market was that of commuter aircraft with 20–70 seats. The Commission, however, chose to break the product market into three sectors based on the number of seats in various types of commuter aircraft. On this basis, they calculated that the merged firm would have an overall EU market share of 50 per cent, with over 75 per cent for aircraft over 40 seats. On the world stage, they would have a 50 per cent share between 20–70 seats. The Commission rejected claims that the merger would lead to improved technical efficiency and would only lead to improved competition in the passenger market of 20–39 seats.

The merger might potentially have driven out of the market two privately owned EU companies – British Aerospace and Fokker of the Netherlands – and critics suggested that the underlying intent had been protection of political interests and not the wider concerns of the EU industry. It was argued their considerations had failed to take into account competition from developing countries and the fact that many EU firms were moving over to small jets which would have changed the market share figures significantly. Nevertheless, the political motivations for preserving the status quo and preventing private firms being squeezed out by state-run concerns are apparent.

Perhaps more importantly, however, objections are continually being raised that merger policy should be extended to encompass the fact that over half of all mergers and takeovers are estimated to be unsuccessful and fail to enhance efficiency in any way. As the number of mergers and acquisitions continues to rise and firms embrace the strategy as an important way of securing a firm foothold in many EU markets this issue takes on greater significance.

Table 5.1 highlights cross-border mergers in Europe in 1993 and the first nine months of 1994 from both the acquirors' and sellers' points of view. With the value of many mergers being of a significant scale (Commercial Union of the UK buying the French insurer, Victoire, for £1.5 billion and Guinness paying £894 million for a 34 per cent stake in one of France's leading champagne and cognac producers, Moet-Hennessy), the number of deals coming under EU jurisdiction is significant. European giants such as Rhone Poulenc, British Airways, Allianz, and Phillips have all jumped on the acquisition bandwagon, but little attention has been paid by the Commission as to whether acquisitions involving these leading European and, indeed, international firms raise efficiency.

In the past, firms such as Pabst-Falstaff-General, Heileman and Stroh in the USA brewing industry who have all grown through acquisition have suffered poor consumer acceptance of acquired brands whereas Anheuser-Busch and Miller, who have expanded organically, developing their own brands, are dominant in the industry. This, and other examples, bring into question the efficiency claims being made by merging firms and suggest that the European Commission and EU national anti-trust authorities should consider carefully the experience of American firms when assessing the potential impact of a particular merger.

The challenges of different languages, cultures, customs and business practices, inherent in cross-border mergers often hamper the amalgamation of the two separate organisations from different Member States limiting the achievement of efficiency gains. The result may be large transaction fees and a great deal of managerial disruption and restructuring being incurred for no reason. The failure of major EU mergers in the 1970s – notably between Hoechst and Hoogovens (steel) and Dunlop and Pirelli (rubber) – reinforce the argument that takeovers may not be the ideal medium for attaining efficiency.

Nevertheless, research by McKinsey management consultants between 1981–1987 suggests that firms have drawn on the past experience of mergers which have failed. Out of a sample of 319 separate deals, over half are adjudged to have been a success in terms of post acquisition return on equity and assets, and whether or not they exceeded acquirors' cost of capital. Although the measures are arguably biased towards short-term financial performance rather than long-term strategic gain (market share in particular), they reveal the fact that there are gains to be made from acquisitions.

Strengthening R&D capabilities, more efficient production, better marketing effort, a wider distribution network may all result from the pooling of resources following a merger. Whilst countering the argument that there are no efficiency gains accruing from

Table 5.1. Cross-border acquisitions of United Kingdom companies
The Acquirors

Bidder country	First 9 months 1994 No.	Value £m	First 9 months 1993 No.	Value £m	Total No.	1993 Value £m
USA	283	5 616	213	3 094	300	5 773
United Kingdom	146	4 722	128	2 676	175	3 056
Germany	99	3 256	81	1 693	114	2 292
France	137	1 688	121	1 528	163	4 136
Switzerland	81	1 037	58	620	80	525
Ireland	30	873	21	130	31	209
Netherlands	72	791	67	406	97	589
Belgium	28	619	29	116	32	114
Multi-Europe	39	460	26	1 283	45	1 913
Australia	15	385	10	118	120	13
Saudi Arabia	2	291	1	—	3	—
Canada	30	248	15	59	22	114
Italy	22	122	30	400	42	573
Japan	17	119	35	83	41	191
Luxembourg	15	112	7	185	13	284
Others	216	1 339	157	3 035	102	2 316
Total	1 232	21 678	999	15 426	1 380	22 128

The Sellers

Target country	First 9 months 1994 No.	Value £m	First 9 months 1993 No.	Value £m	Total No.	1993 Value £m
United Kingdom	225	5 615	169	3 986	234	5 827
France	204	5 529	146	2 869	197	3 407
Italy	89	2 682	89	1 158	121	2 745
Spain	108	2 080	94	1 262	126	1 614
Germany	347	1 941	259	1 415	367	2 257
Netherlands	96	1 095	77	929	119	3 203
Multi-European Union	16	1 026	26	2 033	29	695
Belgium	59	673	62	861	82	1 293
Luxembourg	10	536	7	324	10	351
Ireland	10	271	7	63	13	207
Portugal	7	122	12	205	18	205
Denmark	58	108	47	296	60	303
Greece	3	n/a	4	21	4	21
Total	1 232	21 678	999	15 424	1 380	22 128

Source: Acquisitions Monthly, November 1994 p. 31.

mergers, it does not side-step the issue that a degree of caution is required in assessing firms' claims of increased competitiveness and efficiency. The European Commission and national authorities alike are being encouraged by certain interest groups to ensure that would-be merger partners provide substantial proof of the efficiency gains to be made from the merger to the extent that some parties are eager to build clauses into the new regulations to cover the likelihood of successful stimulation of competition and efficiency.

Table 5.1 shows the degree of interest being shown in European acquisitions by non-European firms. Since the mid to late 1980s US firms have dominated the league table of acquisitions. While, in the run-up to 1992, the trend was arguably the result of fears over the creation of a *Fortress Europe* (*see* Chapter 12) which encouraged non-EU firms to gain a foothold in the EU before the barriers went up, recent activity rather reflects the growing intent of leading global organisations to consolidate business activities in the world's main trading areas. It is interesting to note, however, the lack of activity by Japanese firms. More will be said about this in Chapter 12. At this stage, it is simply worth pointing out that culturally, Japanese firms are reluctant acquirors.

Growing trends in acquisition by non-EU firms brings into question the ability of EU merger and acquisition law to control the activities of non-EU firms. In early 1991, two cases of this nature arose: first, Gillette (an American company) was asked to end its shareholding in Swedish Match (a Dutch company) by the British Monopolies and Mergers Commission (MMC) as a result of the monopoly position this gave the joint company in the UK. Swedish Match's subsidiary company, Wilkinson Sword, is Gillette's only substantial competitor in the UK market for wet shavings products.

Second, the Swiss company Tetra-Pak was told that its deal to acquire Alfa-Laval of Sweden was likely to cause competition problems in the EU. The proposed SKr16.25 billion (£1.52 billion) bid by the liquid packaging group Tetra-Pak for the food processing equipment company Alfa-Laval was the first deal between (then) non-EU firms to go to a full enquiry under new Community legislation. Naturally, these decisions are politically sensitive; nevertheless the Commission and the MMC are confident that their legal rights cover non-EU deals.

Under the principle 'when in Rome do as the Romans' those firms who choose to do business within the EU implicitly agree that they will comply with Community law. Deals which take place outside the EU, but which have a direct effect on activities within one or more of the 12 Member States, therefore, are legitimately part of EU jurisdiction. In addition, as the firms often depend for a large part of their business on their activities within the boundaries of the EU it is unlikely that they will refuse to comply with EU, or individual Member State rulings. What this suggests is that the power of EU competition policy has far wider implications than merely affecting internal competition. The new legislation has the potential of shaping competition on a worldwide basis and consequently of playing a role in determining the power of Europe as a major player in the new world economic order dominated by the triad powers of the USA, Europe and East Asia. This theme is returned to in Chapter 12.

State aid and subsidies – Article 92

More open and more competitive markets bring with them greater incentive for governments to protect key national industries. With public procurement and national industrial standards under attack, state aid is one of the only remaining policy instruments for shielding national industries from the rigours of new competition.

Added incentives may also arise from recessionary conditions which place further pressures on governments to support their own national economies through turbulent times. The Commission has prepared itself for this eventuality and has placed the restriction of state aid and subsidies high on their agenda for completing the internal market.

The scale of the problem came to light following a survey completed in 1989 which found that for the period 1981–1986 for the then existing 10 EU Members States aid averaged Ecus 82 billion per year, equivalent to three per cent of the EU's GNP. Within this agriculture accounted for Ecus 10 billion, coal 12 billion, railways 23 billion and manufacturing the remaining 37 billion. It is obviously state aid to the manufacturing sector which is the specific concern of the EU's competition policy. Figure 5.3 outlines the relative average position for European countries between 1988–1990.

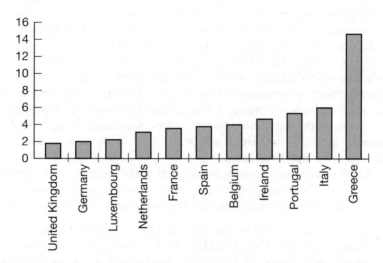

Fig. 5.3 State aid to manufacturing as a percentage of value-added (1988–1990)

In November 1989 the Commission's commitment to preventing state aid became quite clear when it held its ground against the French government regarding state aid given to Renault. It formed an important example of the tough line being taken against governments who deliberately flout Commission legislation and continue to protect their domestic industries. In 1988, the Commission agreed with the Chirac government that the ailing French car company, Renault, could keep a state grant of Ffr12 billion in return for the abandonment of Renault's special legal status (*regie*), protecting it from bankruptcy, by the end of 1988. The French government also agreed to cut car capacity by the end of the year by 15 per cent. In this respect, the government felt that the grant would not distort competition, but would allow Renault to restructure their organisation without a major upheaval.

The instatement of the socialist Rocard government in France, reluctant to be associated with the closure of car plants, meant that the promises were not kept. Despite the Commission demanding that Renault be turned into an ordinary company and enforcing capacity cutbacks the French refused and asserted that cutbacks, during a boom in the car market would be foolhardy. The Commission promptly countered the argument by pointing out the aid for restructuring had never been needed and should, therefore be repaid.

Other car makers had already been ordered to repay state aid – including Peugeot, Alfa Romeo and Rover – and therefore the decision was consistent with previous rulings and also suggested that no European car makers should be given preferential treatment over and above their competitors.

The major underlying arguments in favour of state aid purported by governments are generally to increase international competitiveness and create jobs. In addition, there are a variety of instances where, as a result of market imperfections, state aid may be justifiable. First, where the social benefit may be greater than the benefit derived by the individual firm, that is, there are externalities; for example, it is argued that some research and development (R&D) initiatives result in greater social benefits than returns to the individual organisation. Pharmaceutical research, for instance, which may yield new cures for serious diseases may be worthy of support. Equally, public transport, which potentially eases traffic congestion and reduces the emission of serious pollutants may be a just recipient.

Second, in high technology sectors, which are consumptive of up-front capital and R&D costs there are high returns to scale which make it difficult for firms to compete with incumbents. This reiterates the argument for positive discrimination proposed earlier, but while beneficial at the national level may be more questionable in the wider EU context. Finally, there are instances where, as a result of imperfections in information in the capital market, firms are more able to assess the risks of new projects and new investments than the credit institutions. This results in lenders charging high interest rates making socially desirable investments unprofitable for the private firm and providing a case for government supported loans.

The Renault case suggests, however, that the line being taken by the Commission is that any aid which distorts or prevents competition is not permissible under the new rulings. Several counter-arguments against the benefits of subsidies exist to support this stance:

1 governments tend to be less able to pick winners than the private sector because their decisions are often obscured by social pressures, in particular job creation;
2 government supported R&D may simply replace private sector R&D and may not add to a net overall increase in activity;
3 even if there appears to be an economic case for a subsidy, calculating the exact amount is difficult and can result in too much subsidy being paid which can worsen the distortion;
4 export subsidies paid to firms in one country are likely to be matched by governments in others, leading to a subsidy war which acts as a drain on national resources;
5 the economic costs of subsidies can be high. As governments compensate for state aid through their taxation policies, this impacts on individuals' incentives to work;
6 aid is often a way for governments to delay or prevent the demise of failing industries with no long-term benefits as it simply puts off inevitable closures and redundancies.

The survey on state aid in the 1980s also served to highlight the disparity between official figures on subsidies which cover only cash grants and the real value of aid which also includes soft loans, tax concessions, debt write-offs and government equity participation. By uncovering aid given above and beyond cash grants, the research team found in most cases that the national accounts data could be more than doubled. The biggest disparity was found in Italy, where national accounts data revealed state aid somewhere in the region of three per cent of output, whereas the revealed value of aid was nearer 18 per cent.

In countries with a large public sector – Spain, Italy and France, in particular, the incentives for state aid and intervention are obviously greatest although it would be unfair to single out these countries as all governments have, and continue to find, covert ways to give support to indigenous firms, particularly those which play a key role in the economic welfare of the state. The Commission is, therefore, equally active in attempting to stamp out state aid in its various guises.

In 1988, the Commission intervened in the takeover of the Rover Group by British Aerospace (BAe) following the exclusive deal between the government and BAe to write-off £800 million of the Rover Group's debt. While the Commission did not object to the debt write-off in itself, it did question the fact that the government had failed to secure competitive bids for the Rover Group which could have produced a higher price and a lower agreed debt write-off. When the Commission agreed to a debt write-off of £469 million without deterring BAe from the takeover, the original deal clearly suggested that the takeover pill had been sugared.

Equally, the Commission were critical of Fiat's takeover of Alfa-Romeo in Italy in 1986 not, surprisingly, because the Fiat offer had been accepted despite a higher bid by Ford, but because Finmeccanica, part of the state-owned holding company which owned Alfa Romeo, had injected L615 billion (£269 million) into the company between 1985–1986, despite the fact that the company was losing money and operating at less than half its capacity. The Commission's objection here was the support of an ailing firm with few prospects of producing long-term returns. Ultimately, it ordered Finmeccanica to repay the L615 billion to the state.

What the latter case serves to highlight is the inherent dichotomy in Commission policy which suggests that state aid is all right for firms who don't need it, but restricted for firms who do (Colchester and Buchan, 1990). This fact is reinforced by EU policy on state investment in national companies which asserts that state investment is permissible if it behaves like any other investor by backing companies whose prospects are reasonable. This raises an important question: do the new clamp-downs on state aid mean that no assistance can be given to firms who, through short-term assistance, would benefit in the long term? Manfred Caspari, Director General for competition policy throughout most of the 1980s is quoted as saying 'You can always negotiate with us; you can't negotiate with the market'. Whereas state aid, which distorts competition and protects firms against the reality of competitive pressures, will result in long-term defeat by failing to stimulate efficiency, a certain degree of state aid to assist firms to overcome temporary hurdles can be arranged with the blessing of the Commission.

Although the car industry has come under heavy pressure in the new tough regime, it is by no means the only industry which has been scrutinised and penalised. Equally, it is not only aid directed at specific large national organisations which is being restricted. In July 1990 the Commission took steps to put an end to government investment aid programmes in the UK, Italy, Belgium and the Netherlands. The major argument against this kind of assistance, which has accounted for some Ecu seven billion (£4.8 billion) in subsidies since 1981, is that it allows governments to subsidise any company they wish without gaining the agreement of the Commission. The selectivity and ad hoc nature of these broad brush subsidy schemes is seen as less beneficial than clearly targeted schemes of regional and sectoral aid being given elsewhere in the EU. Investigations are not being restricted to large organisations and cover the whole spectrum of subsidies and grants across the EU.

Unlike other areas of anti-trust policy, control of state aid by the European Commission has no parallel at national level. This makes the process a tough challenge for the Commission as it requires breaking the government habit of bailing out industries in trouble and supporting their national champions on whom national pride is often heaped.

Equally, it is important to make firms aware that the government can no longer provide a buffer when competition intensifies and times get tough. As markets continue to open up it is likely that the Commission will become less lenient towards requests for subsidies to support 'special cases'. While a favourable attitude is currently shown to companies which face little competition from within the EU it is likely that this preferential treatment will disappear as cross-border trade intensifies.

Restrictions on export subsidies and import incentives are also likely to feature high on the Commission's list of clamp-downs in the future. Aid to support non-EU exports obviously have knock-on effects for intra-EU trade. As the volume of business is increased, scale economies give firms greater competitive strengths in all their dealings. Investment incentives provided on an individual country basis, while supporting economically depressed national regions, fail to address the problem of underdeveloped EU areas, particularly those on the periphery. As was suggested in Chapter 2 in the discussion of the Core-Periphery debate, unless European regional policy is centralised, outlying regions of Europe may become devoid of key industries and services. It is critical that incentives be provided to induce investment in areas such as southern Italy, Ireland and the Highlands of Scotland which otherwise may become economically depressed as the major proportion of Europe's industry gravitates towards the centre. Despite this, however, individual company measures designed to attract inward investment remain in place (*see* Table 7.5).

Consequently, future aid and incentives will come under Commission rule. In November 1990 EU governments unanimously agreed a set of Commission guidelines which reject sectoral intervention in favour of an industrial policy based on free markets, firm regulation and competition. Regardless of this commitment, however, harsh economic conditions from enhanced competition from within the EU (particularly under the recessionary conditions in the early 1990s) and unremitting pressure from Japanese competition are raising government concerns over the welfare of leading national firms.

In France, the government is keen to support the Renault car company and the electronics groups Bull and Thomson, who are making losses in the aggressive competitive environment and, in Germany pressure by Siemens and Daimler Benz on the government to grant aid to support ailing sectors and inject funds into new developments, all reveal that the issue of state aid is not simply going to go away because the Commission are ruling against it. However, the hard line being taken by the Commission shows that national firms such as these will have to be content with support granted from EU regional and social funds.

Between 1989–1993, Ecu 6.7 billion was allocated to 'increase business competitiveness' and Ecu 2.8 billion to build 'infrastructure in support of economic activity'. The EU also earmarked Ecu 5.6 billion to fund R&D projects between 1990–1994 and Ecu 13.1 billion for research and technological development between 1994–1998.

Forty per cent of the money set aside between 1990–1994 was targeted at collaborate research in information technology. Critics argue that the way in which it was spent was relatively ineffectual as it was spread across a large number of small projects and argue that in the future it would be better to fund a smaller number of larger projects. The Commission, however, are keen not to alienate small firms, and the likelihood is that future grants will be awarded to small bids. As firms in some countries will inevitably fail to secure grants this obviously has the potential of leading to accusations of favouritism and preferential treatment. However, if funds are to be directed towards those projects most likely to succeed in creating new innovative technologies, the Commission needs to be as hard nosed about who receives funds as they have been about who should give them. In the final analysis, the intent is to ensure national government subsidies and other covert aid arrangements will be replaced by EU-centred grants designed to support new developments and not ailing sectors guzzling much of EU tax-payers' money.

Breaking down state monopolies

Extending beyond the provision of state aid to companies under Article 92, the Commission has also concerned itself with initiating programmes to eliminate state-owned monopolies from the EU marketplace. Governments play an important role in many EU industrial sectors – particularly nationalised utilities such as power, transport and telecommunications. While their spending in key domestic industries supports the development of local infrastructure, the reverse side of the same coin suggests that these often inefficient public monopolies work against the public interest. Lack of competition means high prices, poor services and little incentive for innovation and the development of new technologies.

The EU telecommunications industry was the first to come under fire with the new initiative to break down state-run sectors. Article 90 of the Treaty of Rome, concerned with state monopolies, proposes 'progressive adjustment until no discrimination remains between nationals of member states'. What is explicitly prevented under this article in the telecommunications sector is the affording of exclusive rights to local monopolies for the provision of subscribers' equipment. While this is fairly easy to achieve in areas such as modems, private exchanges and second and subsequent telephones it is much harder to realise in the area of first telephone provision and networks where the monopolies hold most store.

Except for France and the UK, the provision of a first telephone set was under monopoly control in all member states before the new initiative. A gradual erosion of local monopoly power was therefore essential beginning with the value added periphery products and services (e.g. electronic mail, facsimile machines and videotext) followed by some of the more entrenched new technologies (e.g. telex terminals, data transmission equipment, mobile telephones and satellite receivers) and, finally, the provision of first telephone sets.

Achievement of liberalisation involved removing restrictive practices concerning the import of equipment, distribution, maintenance and connection, the only proviso being that equipment can be refused if it fails to meet required technical specifications. For the UK, the adjustments were minimal as the government had already deregulated the telecommunications industry and had taken steps to break up the British Telecom monopoly under Post Office control. For other countries, liberalisation required major upheavals. Generally, however, the directives were welcomed by the Member States as a necessary, and unavoidable, step to improve telecommunications services across Europe.

As technology in telecommunications is rapidly changing and the market growing at an estimated seven per cent per year, many firms feel that to embrace the new competitive challenges they need to expand and thus enhance their capacity for investment in research and development. It is not surprising, therefore, that liberalisation has brought with it a number of international mergers and joint agreements. In the early stages of liberalisation it was the telecom equipment manufacturers who showed the greatest propensity to follow this route (GEC and Plessey, the takeover of CGCT of France by Ericsson of Sweden, and the acquisition of ITT's European telecommunications interests by Alcatel of France). More recently, however, joint ventures have begun to emerge between Public Telephony Organisations (PTOs): Deutsche Telecom have established a joint venture with France

Telecom – Eunetcom (designed to strengthen their joint position against the likes of British Telecommunications); British Telecommunications has established links with MCI of the USA (designed to extend its ability to service the needs of multinational companies); PTT Telecom Netherlands, Sweden Telias and Swiss Telecom PTT have established a joint venture – Unisource (to extend their coverage and compete with the larger PTOs in Europe). Spain's Telefonica has also participated in this latter venture, and it is rumoured that AT&T of the USA are eager to joint the consortium. Fuelled by a need to expand, but hampered by the fact that markets were, in the recent past, monopolised by leading state-owned players, firms are finding new ways of overcoming market barriers and entering into traditionally protected markets.

The only serious bone of contention of this liberalisation concerned the manner in which the new directives were introduced where the authorities issued the directives without first consulting the Council of Ministers and MEPs (permissible under Article 90). This was seen as a ploy by the Commission to show the power it now holds over the Member States and resented as a matter of blatant flouting of sovereign rule. What it clearly demonstrates is the seriousness with which the Commission now approaches its task of removing barriers to competition across Europe.

Notwithstanding the positive effects of such liberalisation, notably the incidence of cross-border activity and thus the breaking down of national preserves held by the post and telecommunications authorities, promotion of efficiency, elimination of restrictive pricing policies and the harmonisation of diverse technical standards, the experience of deregulation in the UK brought with it some cause for concern. The privatisation programme of the Thatcher government between 1979–1990 has often been accused of transferring the power of public monopolies into private monopolies. Following deregulation in the UK, British Telecommunications, despite the efforts of Mercury (who were placed to enter the market after privatisation), still retained a dominant position in the marketplace and was accused of earning excessive profits in the first couple of years following privatisation. As Mercury are required to rent the network systems of British Telecommunications to provide their services, the former state-monopoly is thus earning profits from the new competition.

Proponents of privatisation, however, argue that competition from Mercury has fostered a degree of competitive pressure and has forced British Telecommunications to compete on price and re-invest profits in the development of new products, services and systems – thus enhancing both technical and dynamic efficiency. Indeed, British Telecommunications continues to boast real reductions in the price of telephone services, major investments, particularly in new digital systems and exchanges and improvements in services such as the time for complaint call-outs and mending of line faults (95 per cent of line faults are now cleared the same day as they occur with customers given the right to claim compensation if they are not cleared within two days). There have also been improvements to one of their notoriously poor services, public telephones, where the number of working phones in use is estimated to have risen from somewhere in the region of 50–95 per cent. It is claimed that the figure is still rising!

More recently, the tables have turned on British Telecommunications. The liberal and open nature of the UK marketplace has attracted large amounts of investment from foreign companies (particularly US firms) keen to expand their position in the UK in many of the new emerging telecoms technologies. The mobile telecommunications market in the UK is now one of the most competitive in the world, with numerous firms slogging it out for a slice of the cake. Perhaps more of a concern for British Telecommunications, however, is the granting of licences to cable operators for the provision of telephone services (often at prices 15 per cent below the British Telecommunications rate) which is posing a direct challenge to British Telecommunication's traditional monopoly over basic line provision. Although some would argue that this is healthy competition, it does raise some questions about British Telecommunications' future ability to compete, not just in the UK, but on a worldwide basis where it requires profits for expansion and investment. Governments in other Member States, seem set to take heed of this situation and curb the pace and nature of their own liberalisation programmes.

Although the UK has actively embraced the challenge of privatisation and deregulation, other countries have proved slow to follow suit. Local regulations must be developed to complement Article 86. Harsh penalties are required to deter ex-monopolies from exploiting their position of dominance, particularly in the short term, when foreign expansion is still at an early stage and indigenous firms faced with limited competition from overseas markets. Positive discrimination in favour of overseas firms or new entrants would enhance the process of eroding the privileged position of indigenous firms. Whether this would be permissible in the new regime where market forces are to work to the exclusion of intervention is debatable.

Targeted for future deregulation are energy and air transport. The energy sector brings with it all kinds of difficulties, not least the highly regionalised nature of energy provision, the large amounts of government money currently invested in existing grid systems and the obligation of local authorities to secure national provision of energy to all. Subsidised production of coal in Germany, overcapacity and cheap nuclear energy in France results in a wide disparity in prices and distorts the market for energy across Europe. Alternatively, the air transport industry is already well in the throes of deregulation. The apparent benefit to USA consumers of deregulation of US airlines is supporting the move towards a deregulated European airline industry where monopoly exploitation is eradicated and customers, at last, will witness price cuts in European air travel. (Deregulation and competition in the airline industry is addressed in the case study at the end of the chapter.)

Liberalising public procurement

Outside of the highlighted competition policy directives, but no less important to the creation of a 'level playing field' is the issue of public procurement. Paolo Cecchini in his report to the Commission on the benefits of a single market placed a great deal of emphasis on the cost savings to be derived from opening up public procurement contracts. In 1986, the size of the EU procurement market totalled some Ecu 530 billion with an estimated Ecu 240–340 billion being made up of goods and services which are tradable. This amounts to between seven–ten per cent of EU GDP. However, it is estimated that less than five per cent of contracts are awarded to companies from other EU countries and many are awarded without the benefit of competitive bids on a single tender basis. This quite plainly works against the spirit of competition and is something which the Commission have been keen to stamp out for many years. Why then do these practices persist?

First, national governments see a number of benefits accruing from their policies of buying from local suppliers, not least, lower transport and trading costs, better after-sales service and quicker delivery. Nevertheless, these benefits may be traded off against higher prices and are not sufficient in themselves to have supported incestuous national favouritism for so long. Combined with these factors are the social benefits derived from buying locally, supporting employment, sustaining ailing industries and firms, bolstering emerging high-tech sectors and ensuring that profits are earned by local firms to support new investment and development.

The Commission asserts that national procurement damages both suppliers and buyers. Buyers are faced with higher prices, a limited choice of goods and services and poor value for money from often inefficient local monopolies. Suppliers, on the other hand, suffer from the effects of closed domestic markets which have produced a highly fragmented European market for many goods characterised by over-capacity and large numbers of small producers unable to benefit from scale economies and make a major play for world markets in competition with their much larger Japanese and US rivals.

Second, past public procurement rules proved ineffectual for a number of reasons:

1 They were never watertight. Governments were still able to influence the choice of supplier when evaluating bids on a variety of apparently justifiable criteria.
2 Remaining barriers to cross-border trade. Because differences existed in technical standards between the Member States governments were able to continue buying from local suppliers whose technology was compatible with existing equipment.
3 Purchasing is often highly decentralised. In certain sectors, purchasing is done by agents in widely dispersed regions making the adoption of a central consistent policy difficult and enforcement of rulings almost impossible.

Third, the conflicting interests of buyers, suppliers and governments make designing legislation to satisfy a variety of needs a highly complex task. With these factors in mind, the Commission were aware of the need to amend their regulations and take a much firmer and more transparent stance against governments continuing their restrictive practices. The first task was to tighten up existing regulations. An amended version of the 1977 rulings on equipment purchase were introduced in 1989 and others covering construction and civil engineering took effect in 1990. In conjunction with these new rulings, two additional changes were deemed necessary – more stringent sanctions and powers of enforcement and an extension of the rulings into traditionally protected areas such as energy, transport, telecommunications and water industries.

Because the procedures for taking offenders to court were so cumbersome and time consuming, the Commission proposed a set of guidelines under the control of its own enforcement department. Local agencies are being encouraged to monitor and review practices and it is hoped that they will be given the power to correct violations and award damages. The Commission is also free to challenge national activities and demand an explanation or corrective action within 21 days of the infringement. Much depends, however, on the willingness of customers to report infringements to the Commission or their local authority. Although firms are the damaged party, fear of government reprisal is thought likely to prevent firms from flagging government malpractice.

A test case early in 1989 in which Bouygues, France's leading construction company, suggested what may become commonplace in the future. Bouygues complained to the Commission that the Danish government broke Community law by specifying that local materials and labour had to be used in the construction of a local bridge. The Commission ruled in favour of Bouygues, allowing them to make a renewed bid, and the Danish government agreed that they had infringed Community law and agreed to allow Bouygues to claim damages.

The size of sectors such as energy, telecommunications and water are such that recommendations to break down these traditional state monopolies were almost inevitable in the new pro-competition environment. They were originally excluded because of their public ownership status, but the Commission has disregarded ownership as a preclusive factor and is now concerned with regulating firms who face no competition, enjoy a *special or exclusive right* and operate a network. Although these stipulations appear simple, they overlook the importance these sectors play in individual national economies, and thus the resistance likely to be put up by Member State governments. Other problems, such as the difficulty of developing a single directive for all sectors, and the problems of adjudging all contracts of a certain size on the same criteria have raised government concern over the legitimacy of new regulations.

Regardless of government objections, however, there does appear to be some evidence that things are changing. Privatisation and deregulation of national utilities in many Member States have fostered a growing awareness of the need to stimulate competition and budgetary constraints are continually making state purchasers more concerned about quality and value for money. Increased numbers of takeovers, mergers, joint alliances and co-operative arrangements are additionally serving to break down national boundaries which augers well for competition in traditionally closed sectors as foreign firms gain access to markets through the distribution channels of their partners.

Many would argue that these changes were well overdue. The benefits which may potentially arise from the opening up of public procurement had been sought for some time. As legislation is continually introduced and formalised both short and long-term cost savings may at last be realised. Cecchini (1989) refers to five beneficial effects of liberalising procurement:

1 *The static trade effect* – which involves cost savings for buyers as they purchase from the cheapest source.
2 *The dynamic trade effect* – sometimes referred to as the competition effect – wherein there is a downward pressure on prices as a result of competitive bidding by numerous firms for tendered contracts.
3 *The restructuring effect* – which, in the longer term will allow economies of scale, particularly in specific high technology sectors such as computers, telecommunications and aerospace.
4 The savings to be made by private sector buyers who benefit from the lowering of prices by firms serving the public sector.
5 The greater innovation and investment of firms operating in a competitive environment.

These effects, it was argued at the time, would result in a cost saving for the then 12 Member States of Ecu 17.5 billion, equivalent to 0.5 per cent of 1986 EU GDP.

COMBINING THE BENEFITS

So what will these changes actually achieve? It is very difficult to estimate the true effects of changes in competition policy on firms, nations and the EU as much depends on how companies and governments choose to react and adapt their policies in the light of such changes. It is clear, from much of what has been said in this chapter and discussions in Chapter 2, that many Member States do not see eye-to-eye on what is desirable for the effective and smooth working of competition within the Single Market and the improvement of European firms' competitive position vis-à-vis Japanese and US rivals. Relating back to the two different lines being taken by Germany and France, the former promoting more of a *laissez-faire* style approach, the latter looking towards intervention, stark differences in ideology, business structures and doctrine suggest a differing propensity to embrace various aspects of the new competition policy agenda. France believes, for instance, that more funds should be liberated to support EU R&D effort, that public procurement should be opened up with reserved access to EU firms and that 'infant' industries should automatically be given EU protection. They also believe there should be financial incentives for intra-EU co-operation, persuading firms to enter into alliances with other EU nationals and not Japanese and US multinationals. Conversely, Germany has publicly criticised any measures which would hamper competition through increased government intervention in whatever form. While they support the idea of R&D co-operation, they believe this should only be in the area of new primary technology development and not supporting firms financially in their production of new technologies. They are also against protecting infant industries as they believe this dampens competition and results in inefficient organisations unable to compete in the marketplace. According to them, the role of government should be to provide the right conditions for improved competitiveness, not intervention in supporting competitive development.

Nevertheless, despite on-going political uncertainty, as competition intensifies firms will be put under pressure to change their behaviour and be forced to look for ways of improving costs in the short-term and restructuring and sustainable competitiveness in the long-term. This will be achieved in several ways.

Technical efficiency

As firms expand across Europe and raise the volume of their output, there is greater scope for their realising economies of scale. Although these economies may not be realised immediately in sectors beset by over-capacity and high levels of inefficiency, successful firms will be those who can attain a critical mass in production. Equally, the benefits of generating scale economies in functions such as research and development, marketing and finance will add to the advantages of firms who take on the challenge of operating in a wider market. Firms following this strategy, and correspondingly lowering their costs, are likely to squeeze inefficient firms out of the market resulting in a degree of rationalisation. This is likely to be particularly felt in industries which have traditionally been nationally focused and for which the opening up of competition will mean firms facing the harsh realities of competition for the first time. Much more will be said about this in Chapter 7.

Those firms which cannot adjust quickly to the new competitive challenges are likely to atrophy and die. These developments will tend to produce industries in which there are a small number of large players, in other words, oligopolies. While this will perpetuate competition based on innovation and differentiation (and thus enhanced dynamic efficiency) it will also raise the incentive for firms to become involved in market sharing and cartel pricing.

Lowering of costs will also produce a further effect – it gives firms scope to lower their prices. This will benefit customers in both final and intermediate markets. In intermediate markets this means that although there will be a tendency for prices to fall in response to greater competitive pressure, the corresponding fall in costs, partly due to scale economies and partly due to lower input costs, is likely to preserve profit margins. There will also be a tendency for prices to harmonise across Europe as the removal of barriers and the creation of a *Single Market* will converge around the lowest European common denominator.

Parallel trade is likely to play an important part in the process of the harmonisation of prices (*see* Chapter 8). As previously stated, parallel trade involves market intermediaries buying up goods in one country and selling them in another outside of the formal distribution systems created by manufacturers. This is being actively encouraged within the EU as a way of breaking down trade barriers within the single market and accelerating the time for prices to harmonise at the lowest level. Indeed the Commission sees the benefits as so great that any firm who tries to prevent such arbitrage is liable to indictment under Article 85 of the Treaty of Rome.

Dynamic efficiency

As firms expand across Europe, they need to develop the systems and business structures to support their expansionary strategies and overseas operations along with technologically sophisticated products to stay ahead of their leading competitors. Innovation, not only in terms of products but also the systems to support those products, is a critical part of creating a sustainable and defendable competitive advantage. Increasingly, for international firms, emphasis is being placed on the ability to integrate subsidiaries and business activities in far-flung geographic locations. Despite the fact that markets across Europe are harmonising in some senses, the prevailing cultural differences (*see* Chapter 9) continue to support the notion of adaptation. This reinforces the idea that a new era of manufacturing may emerge in Europe based on flexible specialisation rather than mass production. Innovation may, therefore, be concerned with developing new flexible production runs and organisations to support them rather than the development of major capital equipment to lower costs of mass production.

Regardless of the nature of future developments, successful organisations will be those that can innovate and develop their products and systems in response to change. This requires a clear commitment to reinvesting profits in both research and development and business development projects including foreign investment, new equipment, staff training, organisational restructuring and marketing and information systems. Managing the organisation for competitive success is consequently a dynamic process and not simply the search for a competitive formula which works.

As firms in the EU respond to the new internal competitive challenges their ability to compete on an international scale is also likely to be enhanced. The development of skills which allow a firm to respond to local market needs and innovate systems to support the delivery of satisfactory goods and services to support those needs can be transferred from one market to another. Competition within the EU is thus likely to enhance the dynamic efficiency of European firms operating in global markets which may potentially raise their profile, and indeed market share, on an international scale.

CONCLUSION

The creation of a Single European Market depends on much more than simply removing the physical barriers to business. It relies heavily on removing those barriers to cross-border activities which are perpetuated by the anti-competitive behaviour of firms and their national government proponents. The Commission, in recognition of this fact, has begun to take a hard line against firms and governments who support anti-competitive practices. Thus, it has beefed-up European anti-trust legislation and taken action against those who have continued to flout the concept of competition.

Nevertheless, there is a natural dichotomy between the removal of barriers to stimulate competition and the greater incentive this provides for governments to protect local industries and firms from the harsh realities of intensified rivalry. This is particularly true in the case of nationalised industries and 'national champions' who play such an important part in the economic welfare of the individual Member States. This demonstrates the inherent conflict between national goals and directives and those being perpetrated at an EU-wide level. As long as political integration remains a remote likelihood, individual Member State governments will still be motivated, to a degree, by the national benefits which may be derived from protectionist measures.

Some degree of competitive liberalisation is, however, beginning to take effect and the hard line being taken by the Commission is clearly demonstrative of their commitment to stimulating competition in the EU. Governments and firms are beginning to toe the line and are starting to realise that, whether they like it or not, deregulation and competition are going to continue apace and must therefore be catered for and adapted to. In an effort to make this transition as smooth as possible the Commission works with, not against, local anti-trust authorities to ensure that national legislation supports the new Community directives. It is potentially through such co-operation that a coherent stance on competition policy may be achieved – national authorities stamping out activities which work against the public interest of the nation, the Commission reinforcing these directives with rulings against activities damaging to the welfare of the EU as a whole.

What is quite clear, however, is that there is much to be gained from breaking down these barriers and stimulating competition across national frontiers within the EU both in economic and strategic terms. The climate for European competition is changing and is set to change further in response to new anti-trust legislation. There will be winners and losers, but the winners will be those who face up and react to the new dynamism and not those who continue to seek shelter from aggressive competition.

Questions for discussion

1 What would you suggest are the main arguments against such an all-embracing competition policy for firms in the European Union?

2 What potential areas of conflict can be identified between national anti-trust authorities and the European Commission?

3 Certain firms with a national dominant position are considered to be 'national champions' – what are the political problems associated with removing their privileged status?

4 What are the arguments for and against promoting 'Euro-champions' by considering more than just competition in monopoly and merger rulings?

5 Are there justifiable arguments in favour of positive discrimination to support the stimulation of cross-border expansion and new competition?

6 Outline the conflicting interests of buyers, suppliers and governments in public procurement contracts.

7 Are the provisions made for small firms sufficient to enable them to compete against large pan-European players?

8 What do you envisage to be the main barriers to free competition in the future?

CASE STUDY

The European airline industry

Introduction

In February 1991, Virgin Atlantic took its accusations of anti-competitive behaviour by British Airways (BA) to the European Commission. Virgin claimed that BA had exploited its market dominance by anti-competitive pricing on tickets for USA flights. Richard Branson, head of Virgin Atlantic, is quoted as saying 'We believe that British Airways is not just preventing Virgin Atlantic from competing on fair and equal terms, but more importantly, that BA is acting contrary to the best interest of paying customers'.

This case provides just one example of unrest in the European airline industry which has traditionally been characterised by nationally dominant companies. Although there is a common belief throughout Europe, between legislators and companies alike, that the EU needs a more competitive airline industry, there is definitely no common ground concerning how this should be achieved. Should firms within the EU be allowed to grow and become 'mega-carriers' and have a strong position in the world market or will this be detrimental to EU competition?

International regulations

Regulation of the international airline industry dates back to the 1944 Chicago Convention and the 1946 Bermuda Convention, which laid the foundations for air safety regulations, airline routes between nations and regulations on international fares. The Chicago Convention laid down the principle of the *five freedoms of the air* which may be agreed multilaterally (such as under the International Air Service Transport Agreement of 1944), or bilaterally between particular nations:

First freedom – The right of any nation's commercial aircraft to fly over the territory of another state.

Second freedom – The right of any nation's commercial aircraft to land in other nations for technical reasons (refuelling and repair).

Third freedom – The right of any nation's commercial aircraft to set down in another state passengers and freight travelling from the country in which the aircraft is registered.

Fourth freedom – The right of any nation's commercial aircraft to pick up passengers and freight in another country which are bound for the nation in which the aircraft is registered.

Fifth freedom – The right of any nation's commercial aircraft to pick up passengers in a country other than that in which it is registered and set down the same passengers/freight in a third state.

A sixth freedom was subsequently added which is principally the same as the fifth freedom except it provides for taking passengers/freight to the third country destination via the state in which the aircraft is registered. Here the aircraft may be changed.

Not included in these provisions, but an important concept in the current international arena, is the notion of *cabotage* which is the right of a commercial aircraft to pick up and set down passengers/freight within a single state other than that in which the aircraft is registered. More will be said about this later.

The Five Freedoms of the Air is simply a statement of principle and is in no way binding. In order to benefit from these freedoms and attain the right to carry traffic it has been necessary for national governments to draw up bilateral agreements outlining the extent to which these provisions may be applied. Even the first provision has to be negotiated in certain cases. This has resulted in a complex array of bilateral agreements often including maximum capacity restrictions developed on a reciprocal basis. European Union countries, like others around the world, therefore entered into bilateral deals with other nations to secure access to routes between their and other's airports – for their *flag-ship* (mostly state-owned) carriers. This system is essentially monopolistic, with the leading carrier being treated preferentially and thus afforded scope for abusing their dominant position.

Most agreements also make provision for the approval of fares by both governments involved. Tariff co-ordination is also achieved through forums organised by the International Air Transport Association (IATA) – the international trade association for the airline industry.

Lessons from the USA

The USA was the first market to undergo deregulation and liberalisation. Probably one of the largest single markets in the world, given the size of the geographic landmass, it had been blighted for many years by cartel-like and anti-competitive behaviour with customers being penalised by lack of fair competition.

In the first couple of years after deregulation, the market witnessed a large number of new entrants and increased competition resulting in a lowering of prices and greater choice for customers. However, the success story was short-lived. In the first two years after deregulation a large number of small firms emerged who severely undercut the prices charged by the major carriers and served to lower market prices as a whole and thus benefit consumers. However, as price competition continued to dominate competition in the industry, many of the small players found their margins being squeezed and ultimately became vulnerable to takeover by the largest carriers, keen to consolidate their operating position by acquiring landing slots through company acquisition. It is estimated that the leading eight carriers in 1992 controlled 92 per cent of the market. These super-carriers also enjoy control over USA computerised reservations systems, greater bargaining power in ordering new aeroplanes and control over leading hub centres which feed traffic into long-haul flights to Europe and the Far East from all over the USA. It is, therefore, possible to suggest that the long-term benefits to the consumer have been minimal. A USA study in 1988 suggested that prices charged in airports dominated by a single airline were 27 per cent higher than in airports where there was competition.

European airlines, fearful of falling into the same trap are very concerned that they need to bolster their position before the full effects of deregulation become a reality. They are aware that US firms which have survived the deregulation are the large carriers for whom the temporary rise in competitive intensity was an irritant but not ultimately fatal. Further fears concerning lower labour costs enjoyed by Eastern airlines leave European firms with a strong motive to form joint ventures and strategic alliances to preserve prices and protect routes which are being eroded by deregulation.

European Community regulations

It is clear that the structure of the international agreements works against the spirit of competition being pursued in the Single Market. Pressure to change the systems within the EU eventually resulted in the Commission issuing a memorandum in 1984 outlining its concerns, and its wish to liberalise the air transport market and promote competition. Critical to this was the adoption of policies to improve efficiency, reduce tariffs and facilitate access for market entrants.

But the Council of Ministers, charged with drafting new regulations, was faced with an important question. Can European competition policy rules be applied to the airline industry wherein international regulations support the fixing of air tariffs? In 1986, a ruling in the European Court of Justice made this question easier to answer. In the *Nouvelles Frontiers* case (*Ministre Public vs Asjes*) the Court ruled that Article 85 of the Treaty of Rome could be applied to the air transport industry. This landmark ruling set the scene of a new set of rules, designed around existing provision, for liberalisation of air transport.

The USA deregulation experience coupled with differing attitudes towards liberalisation expressed by the 15 Member States of Europe and reform which involved a radical departure from existing legislation, led the Commission to design a multistage process designed to permit a period of adjustment. The first directive adopted by the Council of Ministers in 1987 established the following rules:

1 a relaxation of the rules on pricing, Member States being asked to take into consideration the costs of the airline, the nature of competition in the industry, and the needs of consumers;
2 a progressive reduction in capacity restrictions. Before 1988, capacity on routes was divided equally between carriers (50:50). This was to be altered to 55:45 up to September 1989, and 60:40 thereafter;
3 the introduction of multiple designation permitting more than one carrier to service the same route, thus raising competition;
4 limited fifth freedom rights were deemed appropriate.

The overall impact of these new rules was limited, but it did serve to set the tone for changes to come.

The second package in 1990 contained two important regulations facilitating greater market access and permitting greater flexibility in setting fares. On the first point, new entrants were to be afforded full traffic rights (excepting cabotage). On the second, a system of *double disapproval* was introduced for new fares which exceeded 105 per cent of the *reference fare* (a fare based on economy class return). Only disapproval by both governments concerned could prevent the new fare coming into force. Similarly, double approval was required for fares falling 30 per cent below the reference fare. The United Kingdom Government, through the Civil Aviation Authority, appealed to the Commission in the case of 88 fares which it considered bore no relationship to the carriers' costs. The Commission ruled that 40 of the 88 fares should be disapproved. Unfortunately, by the time the decision was made, these fares were no longer relevant in the individual companies' portfolios. The airlines involved (British Airways, Sabena, Lufthansa, Iberia, Alitalia, Olympic, SAS, TAP and Air France) were simply requested to avoid such pricing policies in the future. The second package also established a timetable for eliminating capacity restrictions, to be phased out by 1 January 1993.

The third package was presented by the Commission in 1991 proposing three new Council regulations to come into force in January 1993. The first outlined regulations for national licences being issued to carriers in accordance with accepted EU criteria – technical reliability and economic viability of the carriers. In order to operate within the EU all carriers are required to have an Air Operator's Certificate and an Operating Licence. This rules that only those operators whose majority shareholdings are held and controlled by nationals within the Member States and whose headquarters is located in the territory of the issuing state can be granted a licence.

The second regulation regarding market access was only partly accepted by the Council in so far as it provided total access to Fifth Freedom operation. However, provisions for *cabotage* and capacity limitations/sharing (removing limitations on the rate of growth of individual carriers) along with 'nursery' protection for new services between regional airports using aircraft with no more than 80 seats, were sent back to the Commission for revision. The Commission also outlined proposals to prevent Member States using capacity/facility shortages to prevent Fifth Freedom provisions and cabotage. This does not mean, however, that the Commission are unaware of inherent problems associated with the infrastructure of the European air transport business, in particular limitations on slots and air traffic control. Legislation providing solutions to these problems are outlined elsewhere. The main intention, therefore, is to remove these issues from the competition agenda which is totally dedicated to providing a free market for air transport. In its revised form, the package made provision for *consecutive cabotage* which allows airlines to fly between destinations in another Member State following or preceding a flight to or from the domestic country. Full cabotage (the ability of a carrier to pick up and put down passengers in a Member State other than the one in which they are registered) will not come into force until April 1997.

The final regulation in the third package replaces that relating to fare controls outlined in the second package. The new regulation covers three key areas:

1 Continued approval of fares by the relevant Member States with an additional overriding rule that fares cannot be disapproved if they are commensurate with organisations' long-term costs, taking into consideration the needs of consumers and the competitive conditions.
2 Double disapproval is to apply to all fares.
3 Where competition on a route is limited and a fare is accepted despite one government ruling against it, that government may ask the Commission to examine the fare. While this is similar to the provisions outlined in the second package, it only related in instances of *limited competition* defined as including:
   (a) instances where there are significant barriers to entry (such as is the case in congested airports where fewer than three carriers operate once a day on the route in question) where public service obligations exist;
   (b) and where there are at most 30 000 seats offered yearly by only one carrier or two operating under a joint service agreement.

However, these regulations alone will not allow for the development of a truly single market. In conjunction with these provisions are issues such as harmonisation of standards (including safety and environmental standards), improved management of existing capacity (incorporating air slots and air transport control harmonisation) and regulations on mergers and acquisitions, also necessary to effect an open market. Indeed, it could be argued that the impact of these new measures has been very limited. While it was expected that airlines would take advantages of the new freedoms and find ways of competing more aggressively with their major EU rivals, the recession, problems with securing mergers and alliances and limitations on slots at leading 'hub' airports have severely curtailed the competitive impact of deregulation.

Recent experience of the airlines

British Airways (BA), one of Europe's dominant airlines, clearly believes that it should be allowed to expand its activities. In 1990, it proposed acquiring a 20 per cent stake of Sabena World Airlines of Belgium (with the Netherland's KLM proposing an equal stake) in order to develop Brussels as the hub of Europe. Basically, for BA, expansion is not achievable by any other means as it has reached full capacity at London airports. The company is therefore keen to secure a further European centre from which to expand its European (including Eastern Europe) and international business. It would also enable BA to regain the Paris and Brussels traffic it was forced to shed, as part of the British Caledonian takeover, through the back door. Although this would give BA scope to develop as a considerable world player, it ignores the fact that such actions work against other struggling UK airlines and, potentially, consumers as it gives the company further scope to exploit its dominant position. Objections of this kind become particularly pertinent in respect of the specific nature of the deal. British Airways and Sabena control 70 per cent of London–Brussels traffic between them and when combined with KLM they have the majority of slots in six airports in a 250 mile radius of London (Farnborough, 1990).

Also at issue is the fact that if the proposed joint venture were allowed to go ahead it would likely spur other arrangements between European airlines aggrieved at having their position in the EU market weakened. This would put the power of inter-EU air traffic into the hands of a small number of large players which would be adjudged to work against the competitive interests of the EU.

Nevertheless, despite the problems of pursuing acquisitions, BA has continued to look to grow through merger both in Europe and the rest of the world. In March 1993 BA acquired a 49 per cent stake in Delta, a German regional airline, which has since been renamed Deutsche BA. This allowed BA to acquire access to 19 German domestic and international routes giving it a strong position to compete against Lufthansa. Later, BA also acquired a 49.9 per cent stake in TAT, a French independent regional carrier. The early 1990s also saw BA enter into negotiations to acquire a 44 per cent stake in the Chicago-based USAir, which would have created the world's largest airline alliances. However, plans were disbanded in 1992 when USAir's major competitors, American, United and Delta, all lobbied the UK government to block the deal unless they were permitted greater access into the UK market, Heathrow in particular. British Airways therefore purchased a 24.6 per cent stake, instead of the desired 44 per cent, within existing US foreign-ownership rules. At the end of 1992, BA's bid for a 25 per cent in Qantas, the Australian national carrier, was granted.

British Airways is not alone in following the acquisition/merger route. Table 5.2 outlines a variety of recent mergers and joint ventures by some of the major European airlines.

Table 5.2. Mergers/acquisitions and joint ventures of European airlines

Acquiror	Target/Partner	Characteristics
British Airways	British Caledonian	100 per cent takeover, 1988 (to consolidate its domestic position).
British Airways	Delta (Germany)	49 per cent stake (to open up routes in Germany).
British Airways	TAT (France	49.9 per cent stake (to open up routes in France).
British Airways	USAir	24.6 per cent stake (to open up USA routes).
Air France	UTA (France)	54.8 per cent stake, 1990 (to consolidate its domestic position).
Air France	Lufthansa (creating EuroBerlin)	Joint venture designed to operate routes in Berlin.
Air France	Air Afrique	16 per cent stake (open up potential in Africa).
Air France	Air Mauritius	13 per cent stake (facilitate links with ex-colony).
Air France	CSA (Czech)	40 per stake (to open up links in the Czech Republic).
Air France	Sabena (Belgium)	37.5 per cent stake, 1992. (Help develop the Brussels hub.)
Air France	Air Canada	Commercial alliance to facilitate access to USA market.
Lufthansa	Lauda Air (Austria)	26.5 per cent stake to help develop joint long-haul services.
Lufthansa	ITAS (travel agency)	26 per cent stake in the travel agency which serves Lauda Air.
SAS*	British Midland	25 per cent share.
SAS	Various	Marketing agreements with small stakes in All Nippon, Thai International, Canadian International and Continental and Northwest in the USA.
KLM	Netherlines (Dutch)	100 per cent takeover. (To consolidate domestic position.)
KLM	NLM (Dutch)	100 per cent takeover. (To consolidate domestic position.)
KLM	Galileo	Major partner (in the international ticket booking system).

*SAS is the jointly owned flag carrier of Denmark, Sweden and Norway.

Regardless of any joint ventures, however, independent airlines in a number of countries have for a long time been at a disadvantage. The well documented failure of Laker airlines in the UK is not merely an issue in the annals of history. The anti-competitive behaviour of rivals to Freddie Laker's airline continued well after the failure of the company. Trans-European Airways (TEA) Belgium's only independent airline was restricted in its coverage by the Belgium government, who wished to protect the activities of the state owned Sabena – the *designated* carrier. Requests by TEA to provide scheduled flights from Brussels to London, Frankfurt, Geneva, Madrid and Paris were continually blocked as they posed a threat to the activities of the national champion. New legislation prevents governments from sustaining such monopoly designations and thus, in theory, opens up the potential for smaller EU independents such as TEA to compete with their larger rivals. However, many of the joint ventures, alliances and mergers now being entered into by the largest players are tying up landing slots and gate facilities at the major 'hub' airports making it difficult for the smaller airlines to compete in anything but niche areas.

Performance of the major carriers

Profitability in the airline industry depends on two important factors: 'bums on seats' – the load factor – and route coverage. The first relies on sophisticated computer booking systems which have been slow to develop in Europe but which are now beginning to take effect with the introduction of Galileo and Amadeus. The second relies on the route allocations and air-space allocated by governments over the last 45 years. Critical to this is gaining access to the leading hub airports and it is this which is driving much of the joint venture and merger activity. By controlling the hubs companies can feed traffic flowing in from smaller regional airports into long-haul routes.

Profitability is also critically dependent on improving efficiency. As state-run concerns, many of Europe's flag-ship carriers have, for years, been 'propped-up' by their governments and protected from the harsh realities of competition. In 1991, for example, Air France benefited from a Ffr 685 million government cash injection. In addition, many airlines have been forced to review their overall strategies. Many have divested peripheral parts of their business (Lufthansa its Penta Hotels division, SAS its International Hotels and Intercontinental groups) in favour of concentrating more effort on growth and development in their core business. Despite this, however, many airlines in 1990 remained unprofitable (*see* Table 5.3). It is perhaps only by following BA's lead and undertaking mass rationalisation (BA making major staff cuts and revamping its marketing in the late 1980s) that profit may be achieved.

Limitations to improving competition

In the EU there remain barriers to full integration, not least the fact that there are 14 separate air traffic control systems, air space is already highly congested and a certain amount of pride exists for national airlines who have dominated Member State markets for so long.

However the Economic and Social Committee have suggested that problems of congestion are overstated (only really posing difficulties at Heathrow and Frankfurt) and what is more important, is the vision of competition:

Table 5.3. Performance in a selection of European airlines (1990)

Airline	Sales (US$m)	Net profit (US$m)
Air France	10 466	(132.1)
Lufthansa	8 963	9.4
British Airways	8 813	170
SAS	5 332	(144.8)
Alitalia	4 592	(81.7)
Swissair	3 779	(15.9)
Iberia	3 695	(137.7)

Source: EIU Travel and Tourism Analyst No. 5, p. 8, 1991.

In the view of the Committee the Commission's approach to competition is very one-sided. It is not a question of competition on each route, but between the networks of the different companies and competition which takes place via the different airports.

(OJE, 1991)

Controlling the impact of competition is therefore more about looking at the spheres of influence of the current players and their networks of activity through various liaisons and joint ventures which suggests more careful control of merger activity rather than liberalisation and market access.

Although Sir Leon Brittan, the European Commissioner responsible for competition suggested that there will be no major mergers in the airline industry which would be damaging to competition by precluding small players from the market, the scale and scope of many leading firms now begs the question of the attractiveness of the market to new entrants. Some attempt at raising the potential for entry have been attempted by the Commission, in particular, opening up access by allocating at least 50 per cent of all unused slots to new operators, if demanded, or enforcing existing carriers which serve routes more than six times per day and use aircraft with less than 200 seats to give up slots to new entrants. Nevertheless, the likelihood is that firms may be persuaded to enter specialised routes and niche markets, but not attempt to enter into the mainstream of operations which is becoming a game for the mega-carriers.

Case Study Questions

1 What would you suggest are the main problems of integrating European Union policy with international legislation?

2 What would you suggest are the major lessons which can be learned from the deregulation experience in the USA?

3 Why do you think that increased competition has not been forthcoming despite the three packages of measures for liberalisation?

4 Why do you think the Council of Ministers were reluctant to permit full cabotage until 1997?

5 Outline the main areas of competition policy which impact on the airline industry?

6 To what extent would you suggest the recent spate of mergers, acquisitions and alliances has facilitated competition across the European Union?

7 What do you foresee as being the future of the small airlines?

8 Outline the major arguments for and against the development of 'Mega-carriers'

9 If you were the Commissioner responsible for competition in the airline industry what proposals would you make for future legislation?

FURTHER READING

Colchester, N. and Buchan, D. (1990) *Europe Relaunched: Truths and Illusions on the Way to 1922*, Economist Books, Hutchinson. This text gives a good review of the problems and challenges of introducing and implementing new competition of policy rules and practical examples of cases where firms have come under scrutiny.

The European Community Report on Competition Policy (1991) provides a detailed overview of the main areas of policy reform and their scope and coverage. Readers may well wish to consult this publication for further information on areas where exceptions have been made to encourage the development of small firms and intra-firm technology transfer.

REFERENCES

Cecchini, P. *The Benefits of a Single Market*, Wildwood House, 1989.

Colchester, N. and Buchan, D. *Europe Relaunched: Truths and Illusions on the Way to 1992*, Economist Books, 1990.

EC Report on Competition Policy, 1991.

Farnbrough, Heather, 'International Aviation and the Airline Industry', *Acquisitions Monthly*, March, 1990.

Hindle, Tim, 'Proof that the Single Market is Here', *Eurobusiness*, Feb, 1990.

Matsura, Nanshi, F. *International Business: A New Era*, Harcourt Brace Jovanovich, 1991.

Official Journal of the European Communities (C339, p. 41 16/12/91).

Pelkmans, J. and Winters, L. A., *Europe's Domestic Market*, Routledge, 1988.

CHAPTER 6

Workplace Issues and Changing Industrial Organisation

INTRODUCTION

Much can be learned about workplace issues from looking at the experiences of different countries. In particular, practices adopted in Germany, Japan, Sweden and the USA have helped to give firms and countries a competitive edge. But how has this been achieved and why have some countries, such as the United Kingdom, not attained the same success? With the progression of the internal market in Europe, creating more competition, such a competitive edge may result in the difference between ultimate survival and success or the failure of a firm. Companies are increasingly looking towards new forms of internal and external organisation which will benefit the company in the Single European Market, and consideration of the 'new Europe' has often been the catalyst for reconsidering the management, organisation and strategy of a firm, and this clearly impinges on the all levels of business activity.

In this chapter, it is argued that there are a number of key external influences brought about by the European integration process which will have an impact on the internal organisation of any business. These external influences include competition policy, social policy, trade union activity, technology, changing working practices and management system standards (*see* Fig. 6.1). In Chapter 5 we dealt with competition policy which will impact on the internal organisation of the firm because of restrictions on the size and competitive behaviour of the firm. This chapter examines the other issues by looking in more detail at the Social Chapter of the Maastricht Treaty, the changing nature of trade unions, the concept of flexible specialisation and at quality standards.

We are arguing, therefore, that the social, political and economic infrastructure of the European Union will itself have an impact on businesses through the various directives of the European Commission and through common standards. For example, a whole series of documents which have become collectively known as the Social Charter and translated into the Social Chapter of the Maastricht Treaty, pull together elements of the EU's social policy which will have an impact on business. Trade unions also have to adapt to a changing environment, to a decade where their power has been reduced, and to the new work and management practices across Europe. There are likely to be new opportunities for new firms in Europe, and new trading relationships between firms often based on new technological advances. Within such systems, management will be looking towards their own roles, towards the roles of the workforce and towards the organisation of their firms, in order to ensure growth and survival. Perhaps the most important movement of the past ten years has been the increased emphasis on quality and quality management systems, with the increasingly widespread adoption of quality standards. All of these interrelated issues are the subject of this chapter, but we begin with the changing social environment in which firms will increasingly find themselves.

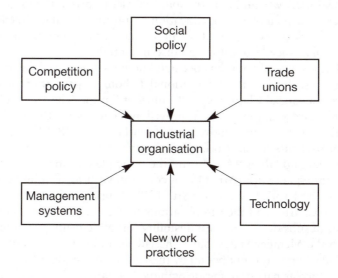

Fig. 6.1 External influences on the organisation of the firm

THE SOCIAL DIMENSION AND ITS IMPACT ON BUSINESS

The social dimension has always been considered as an integral part of the European integration process. The Treaty of Rome stated that there should be an improvement in the working and living conditions of all citizens. The Social Charter and the 47 measures in the EU's Social Action Programme, launched in 1988, were always intended to convince Europeans that the EU had something for everyone. To date, however, very few of the original principles of social action have been or will be implemented, for example, directives aimed at setting-up democratic works councils and mandatory worker participation schemes have never got past the Council of Ministers.

The original idea of a Social Charter was presented by Jacques Delors at the European Trade Union Congress (ETUC) in 1988. The idea was for a set of guaranteed social rights, containing general principles, such as, every worker's right to be covered by a collective agreement, and more specific measures concerning, for example, the status of temporary work. Rather than a document solely about wider social issues and individuals' social rights, the many drafts of the Social Charter and the final Social Chapter of the Maastricht Treaty have all been very business oriented. The recommendations and directives implicit in the Chapter will have an impact on business strategy and on the organisation of work within the workplace. The original Community Charter of Fundamental Social Rights had, as its major aim, the promotion of improvements in living and working conditions within a Single European Market. This remains within the Social Chapter, along with the intention of providing a common set of minimum standards, which every Member State would adopt, helping to create a 'level playing field' in the context of human rights and treatment in the workplace. In addition, one of the priority objectives in the economic and social field is to combat unemployment and to steer the European economy in a direction which will ensure that the completion of the internal market will provide major opportunities for growth and job creation. In order to promote this growth, the Commission has placed much emphasis on education and training and on freedom of movement within a framework of social protection. In particular, the Commission has considered it important to combat social exclusion and discrimination.

The essence of what has become known as the Social Charter is based on the conventions enshrined in the International Labour Organisation and from documents on the European Social Charter of the Council of Europe. The Treaty of Rome, as amended by the Single European Act, contains provisions laying down the powers of the EU, relative, inter alia, to the freedom of movement of workers (Art. 48–51), the social field (Art. 117–122), improvements in the working environment (Art. 118a), the relationship between management and labour (Art. 118b), the principle that men and women should receive equal pay for equal work (Art. 119), a common vocational training policy (Art. 128) and economic and social cohesion (Art. 130). A brief outline of the main components of the Social Charter and their implications for business is given below. As usual, under conditions of subsidiarity, the responsibility for implementing the initiatives outlined below lies with the Member States. Since the UK negotiated an opt out from the provisions of the Social Charter, it is not bound by these minimum standards, although it puts many of them into place as part of domestic employment law.

Right of freedom of movement

It is intended that each citizen of the EU shall have the right to freedom of movement throughout the territory of the EU, subject to restrictions justified on grounds of public policy, public security or public health. The right to freedom of movement must enable any citizen to engage in any occupation or profession in the EU under the same terms as those applied to nationals of the host country, subject to the provision of Community Law. This right implies entitlement to equal treatment in all fields, including social and tax advantages. The unemployed will be supported in searching for employment in a country other than their usual country of residence. Thus, firms experiencing skills shortages have a larger pool of labour from which to draw workers and workers themselves have a wider field in which to search for work. Freedom of movement does mean that there is a greater possibility of migration occurring in the EU and that migration might be balanced but, if a core of economic activity is created, as discussed in Chapter 3, the migratory flow could be one way, leading to congestion, over-crowding and a depopulated periphery.

In order to ensure the implementation of freedom of movement, it will be important for common qualifications to be developed, to ensure that non-recognition of certain categories of qualification of occupational skills are eliminated, and to institute a scheme of credit transfer between institutions and awarding agencies. This is likely to take a long time since, even within Member States, there are seldom clearly defined hierarchies of qualification acceptable to all.

Wages and social benefits applied in a host country must be guaranteed to workers of another EU Member State performing work in the host country concerned. Furthermore, social protection must be extended to all citizens of the EU engaged in gainful employment in a country, other than their country of origin, on terms identical to those enjoyed by workers of the host country. Essentially, this means treating workers moving in the EU much as one would treat workers moving from one part of a Member State to another. The discrimination, in terms of low wage rates and a lack of social benefits, which has, in the past, been practised against those working particularly in northern Europe from the southern European nations, is therefore implicitly barred.

Employment and remuneration

In general, a key principle of the Social Charter is to establish fair remuneration for all employment in the EU. In effect, this means establishing a 'decent' wage. Quite what fair remuneration and a decent wage means has always been open to some interpretation. Whether it will result, over time, in a series of recommended wages in industries or indeed a general minimum wage is likely to be determined more by custom and practice than any Community directive. However, it is clear that whatever interpretation is ultimately reached there will be a set of rules laid down on the basis of which workers, subject to terms of employment, can be assured a degree of equity. To many, though, real equity comes when workers are recognised as in some part responsible for the performance of the firm. The introduction of forms of performance-related or profit-related pay are widely advocated. Tax incentives aimed at promoting this have proved successful in some Member States and advocates suggest that such schemes should be instituted legislatively in large firms.

Improvement of living and working conditions

A general aim of the single European labour market is to lead to an improvement in the living and working conditions of workers in the EU. This relates to the organisation of work, with an emphasis on flexible working time arrangements and establishing a maximum duration of working time per week. Currently there is a wide discrepancy between average hours worked amongst the Member States. Table 6.1 shows both the actual hours worked and the results of surveys about how many hours workers would like to be employed for the EU Member States.

The general aim of a single labour market also relates to all forms of employment rather than just contracts of unfixed duration and, in particular, to contracts of fixed duration, seasonal work, part-time working, temporary work, weekend work, night work and shift work. Every worker residing in the EU shall have a right to annual paid leave and to a weekly rest period.

Living and working conditions are not discrete entities. We all spend a large part of our lives at work. The quality of the workplace, the work we do, the way we are treated and the extent of our own self-determination at work, all have an effect on our general quality of life and of the efforts we make at work. It has long been recognised by the best employers that it is not in their best interests to treat labour as a mere factor of production and that, time spent on considering employee utility in the workplace, is often rewarded by higher productivity and lower absenteeism.

Table 6.1. Average working week in selected countries (hours)

	Actual 1991	Would like
Belgium	35	34
Denmark	36	34
Germany	36	34
Greece	38	37
Spain	38	38
France	36	35
Ireland	37	35
Italy	36	36
Netherlands	34	34
Portugal	40	37
United Kingdom	35	34
EUR12 average	36	35

Source: European Economy, 'Developments in the labour market in the Community', No. 47, March 1991.

Right to social protection

Social Security arrangements will be harmonised in their structure but not necessarily in their value across the EU. The payment of unemployment benefits at the West German level, for example, would encourage people in Portugal never to work again! It is planned that all workers, whatever their status, shall enjoy social security cover proportional to length of service, pay and to their financial contribution to the social protection system. Workers who are unemployed or otherwise excluded from the labour market, shall receive appropriate benefit. Where this is not unemployment benefit and where such a person does not have adequate means of subsistence, they shall be able to receive a minimum income and appropriate social assistance.

Right to freedom of association

Every employer and every worker in the EU shall have the right to belong freely to any professional or trade union organisation of his/her choice. This right shall entail recognition of the right to belong to a trade union. Therefore some governments and some firms which do not allow trade union membership for certain occupations will be forced to reassess their restrictive practices. This general right to trade union membership also extends to the freedom to negotiate and conclude collective agreements (rather than have conditions and pay awards imposed), and the right to resort to collective action including the right to strike. It also relates to the right to renounce the aforementioned rights without any personal or occupational damage being suffered by the person concerned. In other words, it means that if workers refuse to join trade unions, then they have a right to do so, and this implies that closed shops may not be implemented.

The establishment and utilisation of procedures of conciliation, mediation and arbitration for the settlement of industrial disputes is encouraged. Moreover, the Commission seems keen to promote a fuller dialogue between the two sides of industry at a European level. However, the traditional bodies to which workers belong, the trade unions, have often found that their *raison d'etre* is responding to a hostile management. The other side of the coin is, of course, that management has, at times, had to deal with organised unrest. It can be forcefully argued that the best form of relationship, between management and workers, is one which is based on rights. If managers and workers are split by having conflicting objectives – the maximisation of profits as opposed to the maximisation of wages – then it is little wonder that conflict occurs. If workers themselves can be given a fuller role in the operation and outcome of a company this can be eliminated. Thus a participatory role in the firm and a share in profits can improve industrial relations considerably.

Right to vocational training

The intention in the Social Charter is that every European worker shall have the opportunity to continue vocational training during his/her working life. Public authorities, companies and trades unions are to be encouraged to set up and operate continuing and permanent training systems, enabling every citizen to undergo training and retraining throughout his/her working life. Moreover, leave for training purposes and periodical training, particularly as a result of technological developments, are to be encouraged. Every EU citizen shall have the right to enrol for occupational training courses, including those at university level, on the same terms as those enjoyed by nationals of the Member States in the country in which the courses take place.

Right of men and women to equal treatment

Equal opportunities for men and women is another central aim for the single labour market. Equal treatment for both sexes is to be guaranteed and appropriate legislation developed. It is envisaged that action on remuneration, access to employment, social protection, education and vocational training, and career development shall be intensified. However, as has been seen in the UK, despite having had Equal Pay Acts for almost 20 years, the degree to which this is workable depends largely on the responses and behaviour of employers, who still choose to discriminate against women. When it comes to discrimination, either active or passive or through negligence, the scope for avoidance of legislation is enormous.

Right to information, consultation and participation of workers

The European Commission has proposed that information, consultation and participation of workers needs to be developed along appropriate lines, taking account of the laws, contractual agreements and practice in force in Member States. Most importantly, this will apply to firms who have offices and plants in several Member States. In particular, new technology is highlighted as an area which will bring fundamental change and where the workforce should have a degree of determination over its implementation. But it is intended that, ultimately, such provisions involving the workforce shall apply in connection with restructuring operations and/or mergers, which may have an impact on the employment of workers. Thus senior managers may not only be responsible to shareholders for their important policy decisions, but ultimately also to the people they employ.

Little has been suggested directly on the issue of instituting participatory arrangements as a right of workers. Since a basic aim of the EU is to stimulate growth and employment, participatory arrangements have an important role. Work by Professor Martin Weitzman (1984) on profit-sharing shows that there can be employment generating effects in firms which adopt these schemes. Experiences of worker participation in a number of forms, and from a number of sources, show that there are benefits associated with these arrangements. Work by Cable (1988) on alternative participatory arrangements in West Germany, in general, finds benefits from one type of participation or another. Not only does it seem to be in the interest of workers to have a share in profits and/or a role in planning in their workplace, the evidence also shows that it is in the interests of businesses themselves. An involved workforce is likely to judge atmosphere at work in a better light and as such are likely to work harder, be absent less and are less likely to move to other firms, taking their skills with them.

The issue of workers' rights to representation, when employers take decisions, is not central to the Single Market programme. However, there have been a number of proposals (discussed above) intended to increase both worker representation and worker participation. For the Single Market to function effectively and equitably, it is clear that all those having to deal with companies in the EU (shareholders, creditors, customers and workers), can be sure that they are dealing with broadly the same legal structure, and have equivalent rights everywhere in the EU. Although a good deal of progress has been made on many aspects of business law including, the preparation of accounts, the duties of auditors and the disclosure of information, the issue of worker representation has been repeatedly blocked, most notably by the UK government.

Varying degrees of worker participation already exist in the EU. At the beginning of 1988 though, the Commission produced documents suggesting that some form of worker representation on a board of directors or on a parallel supervisory board was required. Member States themselves can choose precisely what sort of system they wish to adopt and some may only decide to pay 'lip-service' to any proposals, even if they do become statute. Surprisingly though, some trade unions have often been wary of co-operative arrangements, profit-related pay and worker share ownership schemes, preferring to see their role as confrontational rather than developmental.

Right to appropriate protection in the workplace

In the workplace, appropriate measures must be taken with a view to harmonising working conditions at the best levels currently provided in the EU, notwithstanding the fact that improvements can and should continue to be made. The minimum employment age shall be fixed at 16 years. One aim is to ensure that young people get a thorough preparation for employment via the provision of vocational training. When at work they should, for a period of at least two years, receive complementary vocational training during working hours, whilst receiving equitable remuneration.

It will be a right of all workers to work in an environment where safe and healthy conditions persist. The Single European Act 1986 gave the EC new powers in the area of health and safety, stating that the objective should be the harmonisation of conditions in this area, while maintaining the improvements made. This means that, in many countries in the EU, health and safety provision needs to be improved significantly. Minimum standards of fire prevention, lighting and ventilation are increasingly being instituted as well as stricter guidelines covering the use of machinery and protective equipment. For example, in November 1989, directives on the minimum standards for workplaces, for work equipment and for personal protective equipment were adopted by the Council of Ministers. However, such legislation also provides for potential difficulties, as it states that health and safety directives shall avoid imposing administrative, financial and legal constraints in a way which would hold back the creation and development of small and medium-sized undertakings and competition.

There is some fear that if harmonisation of minimum standards of working conditions (including health and safety provision) cannot be ensured, new jobs in the EU are more likely to go to the areas of lowest pay and lowest overhead costs. To some extent, the rapid economic growth of countries, such as Spain, may be indicative of this already happening. If this is the case, then it must imply that jobs are being lost in more prosperous areas.

Rights of the elderly and disabled

Every EU citizen in retirement shall be entitled to receive a minimum income giving him/her a decent standard of living. This shall include citizens who, having reached retirement, are not entitled to a pension, for example, because they have never been part of the labour market and who have no other adequate means of subsistence.

Measures will also be taken to ensure the fullest possible integration of the disabled into working life, in particular where vocational training, professional reinsertion and readaptation and social integration are concerned, by means of improving accessibility, mobility, means of transport and housing. The extent to which some of these measures may be at the expense or partial expense of the employer remains to be seen.

Implementation of the Social Chapter

In attempting to standardise social and working conditions across 15 disparate Member States, the EU faces a challenge. In trying to create a level playing field across labour markets, we must recognise that the massive cultural barriers which presently prevent the free movement of capital, are probably greater than any other factor. Nevertheless, the Single Market should be as much about equality of opportunity, both for individuals and for businesses and the Social Chapter provides an outline framework and principles for action.

The implementation of a Social Chapter is the responsibility of the Member States who signed it. It is their task to take such steps, as are appropriate, either via legislation or collective agreement, and to use all necessary resources to fully implement the above social measures. These measures are seen as indispensable to the efficient operation of the Single Market. The Maastricht Treaty provides little more than a statement of principles relating to the Social Chapter and implementation therefore requires commitment from each of the Member States to follow appropriate and effective policies.

Over the next few years, we will therefore see a gradual phasing-in of measures aimed at achieving the aims of the Social Chapter, in all the EU Member States except the UK. The UK's position remains largely unchanged from the influence of Thatcherism. Intervention in labour markets and in the relationship between employers and employees is seen as unnecessary regulation which will ultimately impose increased costs on jobs leading to both uncompetitive industry and higher unemployment. Opponents of that view argue that such an approach is based on a naive neo-classical approach to economics, which sees labour only as a factor of production and will, therefore, result in standards of living for workers falling. The actual outcome of the implementation of the principles behind the Social Chapter will clearly be revealed with time.

The key issue of fuller worker participation in the workplace is, however, still be to be fully considered. It is clear that many of the rights highlighted above can be considerably enhanced by consideration of worker participation. This can be seen not only as a move which can promote better industrial relations, a more stable and satisfied workforce, higher productivity and associated higher profits. It should also be seen as fundamental to democracy within a European context. Democracy is about freedom to choose and about self-determination. Workers spend large parts of their lives in workplaces in which, up until now, there has been little opportunity for participation and self-determination.

As the UK government has be so keen to point out, the implementation of the Social Chapter will impose costs for businesses who are forced to implement some aspects of it. The view of the Commission is that if all firms are expected to implement the same directives, then no firm will be at a disadvantage. The problem here is that firms are beginning from different bases. West German firms which have a long history of worker participation and involvement, are unlikely to be faced with the same transition costs of implementing key directives as a firm in Portugal. Firms in southern Europe, in particular, may be worried that if implementation of the Chapter in the workplace does cost them a significant amount of money, via increased wages and benefits and tougher health and safety procedures, then they might lose some of their relative competitiveness. The EU has always found it difficult to implement social policy and this looks like being no exception.

TRADE UNIONS AND THE SINGLE EUROPEAN MARKET

From the beginning of any discussions about fuller European integration leading to the Single European Market, it was clear that the trade unions from different Member States had different priorities. In West Germany, for example, a key concern has been with the maintenance and proliferation of the idea of co-determination (*see* the case study at the end of this chapter). For trade unionists in the southern European countries, the emphasis has been on narrowing the division between north and south, not only in terms of working conditions, health and safety legislation and wages, but also in terms of broader economic equality.

Nevertheless, European trade unions do have much in common and concerted joint efforts can make significant improvements in the social dimension of the EU and in issues related to quality of life in the workplace. European Union level strategy is primarily undertaken by the European Trade Union Confederation (ETUC). The ETUC has worked as quite an effective vehicle for determining common positions and strategies. Declining trade union memberships across Europe in the 1980s may, paradoxically, have helped foster development and co-operation as trade unions have had to rethink their role and their place in society.

Companies are increasingly establishing links with European partners. Citizens of the EU have the right to work throughout the EU and this will become even easier and indeed, more common over time. It is likely that, for many, there will actually be a need to work in another country. Workers' rights can be lost as they cross national frontiers, unless trade unions engage in similar agreements to firms. One suggestion has been the establishment of the franchise type agreements similar to those made by many firms, where members of one trade union would be protected by another if they moved to a different Member State to work. The 1990s are increasingly becoming a decade of transnational operations. According to some trade unionists it may, in turn, need to become a decade where transnational trade unions are created. Political scientists have long argued that transnational corporations will be important actors in the march towards political integration; conversely, it seems true that a push towards integration could lead to an environment favourable to a transnational labour organisations within the EU, and to transnational wage bargaining.

Large scale economic transformations taking place as a result of the internal market are creating new imperatives in the workplace, including new management systems, new working practices and organisational arrangements, and the adoption of new technology. The appropriate use of human resources and the movement towards a more flexible organisation of working time, therefore, require a new level of understanding between employers and employees. Transnational social dialogue is therefore inevitable and important, and will require careful monitoring in the future.

At the European level, patterns for future bargaining arrangements are emerging. Relationships between the ETUC and UNICE, the European Employers' Association, are generally positive and, with the aid of Community institutions, have produced common statements for action. Branch-level bargaining and company performance related pay agreements are becoming more common with the latter being supported, in some countries, by tax incentives.

The Social Chapter means that trade unions operating in countries where they have lost power in the 1980s, may begin to regain that power if the rights of workers becomes enshrined in Community legislation. But the other trends, outlined above, may also add to the strength of trade unions. For example, in a growing Single European Market, where jobs are being created and where there is a positive ideological climate for trade unions, there may be a resurgence of trade union influence.

Movements towards the Single European Market clearly provide an environment where trade unions can regroup and regain much of their lost power. Moreover, if the Single Market has a general expansionary effect, then employment will rise and increase this influence still further. Trade unions are historically at their weakest at times of high unemployment. But trade unions must recognise that transnational bargaining, changing work practices and the implementation of new technology must be high on the agenda for the 1990s and beyond. Moreover, trade unions will have to move beyond workplace-related issues. With the implementation of new technology and with flexible working arrangements, home working is set to expand considerably. This is likely to be an area of significant female employment and the history of this sort of work is that it is, at best, low paid and, at worst, exploitative. This is just one of the major issues which European trade unions must face.

POST-FORDIST PRODUCTION AND FLEXIBLE SPECIALISATION

The Single European Market represents a fundamental change in the economies of the Member States and in turn in European society. Much of this change will stem from trends in production which may have happened anyway, without the move towards a Single European Market, but which have been accelerated by it. There are complex debates surrounding the future of mass production methods and the key issues are outlined below.

At the outset, if one takes an overview of the European economy, there are trends which appear to be contradictory. On the one hand, the internationalisation of the economy and the trend towards large transnational firms, often working interdependently or oligopolistically (this scenario is often termed *monopoly capitalism*), seems to be vesting economic power in the hands of fewer and fewer institutions. On the other hand, the environmental concerns about mass production (*see* Chapter 10) and a trend away from production line techniques, in the workplace, often termed *Fordist production*, tend to point in the direction of smaller, more flexible firms and divisions. In fact though, both of these trends can co-exist, they are not mutually independent. Although large firms do exist, increasingly their production is being based on smaller scale models such as quality circles, with a significant increase in franchising and sub-contracting. This trend is often termed *flexible specialisation*. Small scale units enable production to be specialised and to meet customers' requirements more accurately, whilst modern production methods, often including new technological modes of operation, enables the unit to be flexible and responsive to changing demands.

Recent experience points to a number of useful indicators which we can use to analyse what has been called the 'new dynamism' apparent in the workplace. Jobs have changed as unskilled manual work has declined and professional occupations expanded. Women now make up a larger proportion of the workforce, even although this is often on a part-time basis. Large corporations continue the trend towards oligopolisation on a worldwide scale and new technologies have radically altered production processes.

In the 1960s and 1970s, according to Braverman (1974), more and more jobs were becoming less skilled, assembly line tasks, as the techniques associated with scientific management, Taylorism or Fordism were being more widely introduced. This meant that tasks were highly regulated, repetitive and became reduced to component elements. Control of production was therefore directly transferred to time and motion managers. Moreover, so called Fordist bureaucracies tended to be very hierarchical, with planning done by specialists and handed down a pyramid of authority for junior managers to implement.

But according to many commentators (e.g. Wood, 1989), we are now living in a post-Fordist era of flexibility in industrial production. Other than the key need for flexibility and adaptability at all stages of business activity, there are five key influences contributing to this trend (*see* Fig. 6.2):

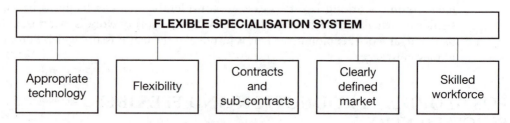

Fig. 6.2 The flexible specialisation system

Appropriate technology

Technologies associated with production, information and communications and in particular, multi-process robotics, computer aided design (CAD) and computer aided manufacture (CAM) have provided many opportunities for reorganising production. In association with reorganisation on the factory floor and many new opportunities for franchising and sub-contracting, many of these developments have made smaller scale, specialised, batch production possible. As the machinery dedicated to fixed assembly operations becomes obsolete, it is often being replaced with multi-purpose capital equipment. The traditional argument that there are benefits of economies of scale underlying mass production, are looking less convincing. In its place is an argument which suggests that economies of scale are being replaced by economies of scope, that is, economies associated with flexible, multi-product production.

Flexibility

The overall philosophy of business in Europe needs to be increasingly flexible. We observe trends towards multi-product production, increased customisation, new demands for quality and environmental attributes, caused by more sophisticated consumer needs and wants. These sorts of trends can only be serviced through more flexible modes of production and working arrangements.

Contracts and sub-contracts

At the limit, flexibility and the need to be responsive means that workers may be needed at one point in time but not at another. The implication of this is that increasingly firms are only employing on a permanent basis, those workers who can be fully employed for the full working week. Part-time working, casual employment and temporary contracts are therefore increasingly common along with franchising and sub-contracting. In many instances, it will be cheaper and more efficient to use external firms, themselves specialised, to carry out particular tasks. Such firms are likely to be relatively small. Moreover, large firms are increasingly operating in this way, recognising that internalising all their tasks is not always the most cost effective mode of operation. The use of small firms undertaking contract work, enables the large firm itself maintain a degree of flexibility and prevent overemployment.

Clearly defined market

In the past, large mass production techniques have relied on mass demand for the product being produced. This meant that production was highly sensitive to changes in aggregate demand and, in particular, to recession. Now, smaller quantities of much more specialised products can be produced profitably because the technology is available to do it and because markets are growing internationally, such that, even the most specialised products are likely to have sufficiently stable markets in terms of demand. A Single European Market accelerates this sort of trend and small enterprises, which may not be able to find a significant market in their own Member State, may find a viable one in the wider European market. This also means that new smaller firms, based on the twin characteristics of flexibility and specialisation, are able to survive alongside their much larger conglomerate counterparts, relying on niche markets, meeting specialised demands and offering a more responsive and personal service.

Skilled workforce

It can also be argued that workers have to become more versatile in the new flexible workplace. This often means that fewer, more skilled workers are employed and they are expected to carry out a wider variety of tasks. Demarcation therefore has no place in the post-Fordist production unit and this is an issue which trade unions will have to address.

The dominant ideology behind the post-Fordist scenario is that new flexible processes work most efficiently where workers themselves take on responsibility for the planning, programming and functioning of their work. It might be argued that this movement towards *functional flexibility* and multi-skilling mirrors best practice within Japanese industry. With workers increasingly controlling their own work patterns, worker motivation can increase, and it is argued that care is enhanced and quality improved. Thus, the devolution of responsibility towards the factory floor can increasingly be seen as part of a total quality management package (we deal with this in more detail below).

A new stage of development?

According to many optimistic commentators, post-Fordism constitutes a new stage of development in the workplace and ultimately in society as a whole. If this is the case then there is the potential to sweep away the dismal prognosis of economists such as Braverman. There may be a return to the notion of a skilled craftworker with a substantial growth of small firms. This is often termed the *Third Italy* phenomenon of small scale, flexible specialisation based on new technology, characterised by the rapid development of new small businesses in north East Italy (*see* Scott, 1988). Flexible organisation and flexible production thus lead to the abandonment of the technical control that Braverman sees as contributing to the degradation of labour.

Implicitly, this new stage of development means the contraction of mass production and a significant change in consumption patterns, where new products designed to suit specialised tastes are made available. But this stage also heralds less secure full-time employment for a substantial part of the workforce. If mass production methods were profitable as a result of the efforts of the labourer and productivity of capital, then a post-Fordist industrial society is likely to maintain profits by bidding down wage rates as competition for employment increases.

The European experience

What evidence there is, concerning flexible specialisation, seems to support the view that this trend is beginning. Table 6.2 shows, for example, that employers expect more flexible working patterns in the future with a shift away from full-time work towards more reliance on part-time employment. The same figures also show a relative decline in unskilled manual work. Sub-contracting has increased somewhat (confirmed by Imrie, 1986) and we can also find evidence that a significant number of jobs are temporary (*see* Table 6.3). There has also been a considerable increase in self-employment and in the number of small businesses in Europe. Many of these small businesses have been artisan in nature, co-operative in organisation and flexible in production.

Comparative studies show that many examples of flexible production systems and total quality management schemes exist in West Germany, Italy and Japan (*see* Piore and Sabel, 1984, for examples). Countries such as the UK seem somewhat backward in relative terms. Traditionally, in countries such as Greece, there have always been a large number of workers who are self-employed and a predominance of small firms. In relative terms, France seems to be hanging on to traditional mass production methods because of the state's powers and its past successes with larger-scale planning. The diverse ways in which post-Fordism can find its way into a new industrial order are well highlighted though in the cases of Italy and (West) Germany.

Table 6.2. Prospective trend of employment in industry (percentage changes in balances)

Country	Expected variation in full-time employment		Expected variation in part-time employment	
	Skilled	Unskilled	Skilled	Unskilled
Belgium	−13	−60	7	−11
Germany	−29	−53	7	−5
Greece	1	−37	27	23
Spain	−10	−41	11	5
France	−13	−35	29	5
Ireland	16	4	5	2
Italy	−45	−64	10	0
Luxembourg	−32	−50	−21	−43
Netherlands	−13	−22	−11	−12
Portugal	2	−19	1	−6
United Kingdom	5	−16	−10	−13
Average	−20	−42	9	−3

Source: EU Business Survey: Ad hoc labour market survey, June 1994.

Table 6.3. Percentage of workers employed under temporary contracts

Belgium	6%
Denmark	10%
Germany	5%
Greece	18%
Spain	31%
France	8%
Ireland	14%
Italy	9%
Netherlands	3%
Portugal	15%
United Kingdom	7%
Average	9%

Source: EU Business Survey: Ad hoc labour market survey, June 1994.

Italy

Much of Italian industry is characterised by flexible networks of small and medium-sized firms, using more and more sophisticated technology to adapt to rapidly shifting markets in a fast growing economy. A tradition of *familialism* and a distinct and large category of artisan firms (helped by certain tax advantages of being 'artisan'), have always been strong in the characteristic tendency away from centralisation in Italy. To some, the survival of these small networks has been based on self-exploitation (i.e. worker-owners paying themselves lower wages than they could get elsewhere) but notions of the ability and wish to exploit oneself have always been hotly debated.

The local government and education system in Italy has also been important. Municipal and regional governments have supported small business development by constructing industrial parks for small producers. They have opened vocational schools in conjunction with associations of artisans and industrialists themselves and, in some cases, have operated regional, shared research centres which is common in countries such as Japan. One of the parallel aims of this sort of investment has been to prevent migration to the cities and the deindustrialisation and depopulation of rural areas. It also seems that this new sort of industrial organisation has been more resistant to macroeconomic fluctuations than the rest of the Italian economy (*see* Brusco, 1983).

Germany

In Germany, flexible changes have more often been centred around larger firms rather than in a network of partnerships and regional conglomerates. Former West German firms are decentralising internally though, with a shift towards customised production. With the rapid adoption of new technology, many of these firms have reconceptualised the relationship between the manufacturing process and the role of workers therein. The approach is away from the facilitating speed of assembly by mass production methods, towards production groups which revolve around common technology, the control of several machine tasks from one computer, and the responsibility for quality control devolved to the associated team of workers.

At a governmental level, it is national state policy rather than localised initiatives which seem to have been important. Policies based on co-determination are now well established and the Social Democrats have always espoused workplace democracy and flexible specialisation. The Christian Democrats have offered state aid for technological innovation based on quality circles which has aided shopfloor technological advances, along with a movement towards post-Fordist production techniques.

The future of mass production techniques

Undoubtedly, mass production is not about to be completely replaced. In industries such as food manufacturing and processing, the trend of horizontal integration and large scale capital expansion continues. Antoine Riboud, Chairman of the French conglomerate BSN, has predicted that there will be only three pan-European food manufacturers by the end of the century. Moreover, the trend of labour intensive mass production continues in the Third World where wages are low, production processes are consequently labour intensive, and environmental concerns are easily overlooked. The 'new international division of labour' has seen many low skilled, repetitive, production line tasks exported to the Third World.

Whilst the trends of monopoly capitalism and post-Fordist production may pull in different directions, they are quite complimentary. Post-Fordism can exist at all levels from EU-based production by small firms to the organisation of labour into small integrated units within the larger enterprise. With a new emphasis on flexible specialisation and total quality management, trends away from the assembly line are set to continue. Where mass production is still appropriate, what activities are left in the advanced industrialised economies are likely to shift to the Third World under the control of transnational corporations. But with a new European market, the number of possibilities for new production processes and new products is increased dramatically. Appropriate production processes for appropriate products is the key to success for enterprises of all sizes. It is tempting to suggest that post-Fordist production is humanising where the assembly line is dehumanising. Certainly, studies suggest that worker satisfaction is increased with movements away from repetitive working, but, in a world of production flexibility, labour may be faced with a new problem: that of uncertain employment. For many, this will increase the attractiveness of self-employment and the establishment of small businesses which will further strengthen the post-Fordist trend. But for others, uncertain, part-time, temporary contracts, subject to competitive bidding, may become the reality of the future.

Production technologies based around flexible specialisation are 'greener', friendlier and potentially less exploitative of the resources needed to produce the final good. Large firms in the global economy are already well established as transnational operators, and so it is the smaller and medium-sized firms who are most likely to face the potential of fundamental change. It is precisely these firms which seem to be adopting post-Fordist production techniques and integrated packages of flexible specialisation. But this change may not accelerate to bring about a *second industrial divide* automatically. The experience of Italy and Germany shows that government and local authority support, technological advancement and the education process are all vitally important. This points clearly towards the sort of industrial policy needed for the 1990s in the EU.

CHANGING MANAGEMENT SYSTEMS AND PRACTICES: THE QUALITY REVOLUTION

The Single European Market means that firms can no longer rely on their existing market to provide them with the profits they need. The increase in competition means that the most efficient firms are the ones which will be able to displace the competition. A key competitive edge revolves around the type of management system adopted in a company and there are moves away from old style hierarchical management, towards devolved decision making and the central importance of quality considerations. The experience, to date, is that firms which adopt such systems can achieve a competitive edge and we are likely to see a further growth in the importance of management systems in Europe. The systems described in this section are all compatible, rather than alternatives to each other, and all revolve around the central aim of increasingly the quality of goods and services.

The importance of quality

Quality is central to the performance of European industry both within and outside the EU. More sophisticated consumer preferences, the existence of written quality standards and, the increasingly common practice, of writing such standards into contracts, all mean that quality is no longer an option, it is central to good business practice. Moreover, quality needs to be seen as a means to an end – customer satisfaction in all aspects of a product or service. Quality should be all-pervasive, covering not only the design, performance and liability of a product, but also the constant improvement of what is on offer.

According to writers such as Deming (1986), quality and productivity increase as variability decreases. There is therefore a need to produce a consistent product of a high quality and this pushes productivity up and reduces costs. Prices can then be lower than they otherwise would be, expanding the market, creating jobs and providing a better return on investment. Deming is an advocate of employee participation in decision making. He claims that management is responsible for 94 per cent of quality problems and that their first step should be to dismantle the barriers which prevent workers doing a good job, by encouraging them to work smarter, not harder.

Too many companies in Europe, and particularly in the UK, still have a poor reputation for quality standards. This is reflected in:

1 import substitution, where Japanese goods are more synonymous with high quality, leading to balance of payments problems and a worsening of problems associated with deindustrialisation;
2 an attitude whereby shoddy work seems to be acceptable because it is always someone else's job;
3 an attitude which sees quality assurance as end of the line inspection, when it is too late – the problem needs to be put right at source;
4 poor management practices, where managers are still operating hierarchical structures with a reluctance to devolve responsibility to those directly associated with processes;
5 resistance to change on the part of management, who too often consider what they are doing to be good practice and are unwilling to re-assess their own management techniques;
6 resistance to change on the part of trade unions, illustrated by the TUC's 1981 guidelines on quality circles, which stated that trade unionists would be opposed to quality circles if they in any way challenged existing trade union machinery or practices.

It is the Japanese who first implemented the ideas associated with a total quality approach, which saw quality as the responsibility of everybody in the workforce. The Japanese have achieved phenomenal success throughout the world in persuading customers that all their goods and services are produced to the highest quality standards. At the same time, in some European companies, there has been a tendency to assume that, however great the Japanese influence on quality, it is something peculiarly Japanese and related to cultural and other factors which cannot be translated into the Western context. Such a view represents an inherent misunderstanding of how to introduce proper quality management systems into an organisation (*see* below).

Quality has to be central to manufacturing and service provision in the post-1992 Europe. There is certainly a growing trend towards integrating quality considerations into all levels of industrial activity. Indeed, total quality is a theme which is beginning to have a major impact across the whole of Europe and this is characterised by:

(a) pan-European co-operation on a number of major projects (e.g. in the aerospace industry), based on shared values about quality standards;
(b) the increasing importance of European and international quality standards;
(c) the establishment of a European quality management foundation (initially funded by 14 multinational corporations), with the aim of creating a positive quality image;
(d) the introduction of quality issues into universities and colleges examining both quality improvement techniques and problem-solving activities;
(e) a particular emphasis on the participative aspects of quality management and the growth of constructive dialogue between workers and management;
(f) a major extension of the importance of quality and the total quality approach to the service sector;
(g) an increase in the number of quality initiatives being undertaken by small and medium-sized firms as the quality approach is rapidly driven down the supply chain;
(h) major developments to improve quality and customer service in the public sector.

These characteristics are all pointing towards a real quality revolution and this is increasingly based around the central concept of total quality management, to which we now turn.

Total quality management

Competitiveness is often measured by three things: quality, price and delivery. It is often a misconception that quality costs extra money in terms of inputs. The theory behind a total quality management (TQM) system is that as quality improves, costs actually fall through lower failure and appraisal costs and less waste. TQM is much more than assuring product or service quality, it is a system of dealing with quality at every stage of the production process, both internally and externally. TQM is truly a system requiring the commitment of senior managers, effective leadership and teamwork. This last facet makes the TQM programme most easily implementable in the sort of flexibly specialised industrial organisation discussed in the previous section.

Whilst the force behind a TQM system has to come from senior management, the responsibility for quality itself belongs to everybody in the organisation. The TQM system requires that every single part of the organisation is integrated and must be able to work together. This is exactly the ethos which is needed for an environmental management system to be successful; the push must come from the top but everyone has a role.

The TQM system (*see* Fig. 6.3) therefore requires co-operation and commitment at all levels. The main elements of the system are:

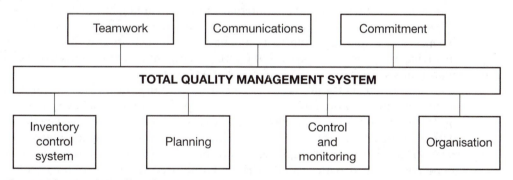

Fig. 6.3 The Total Quality Management system

(i)   *teamwork*: this is central to many parts of the TQM system where workers have to feel they are part of an organisation. In addition, teams of workers will often be brought together into problem-solving groups, quality circles (see below) and quality improvement teams;

(ii) *commitment*: to be successful TQM needs to be truly company wide and therefore commitment is required at the top from the Chief Executive as well as from the workforce. Middle management has an important role to play in not only grasping the concepts themselves but also explaining them to the people for whom they are responsible;

(iii) *communications*: poor communications can result in organisational problems, information being lost and gaps occurring in the system. A good flow of accurate information, instructions and feedback is vital in maintaining the cohesion needed by the system;

(iv)   *organisation*: a cohesive system needs to be an organised one with clear channels of responsibility and clearly defined reporting procedures. Quality related errors can be quickly rectified if an efficient organisational structure is in place;

(v)   *control and monitoring*: the TQM system will not remove the need to monitor processes and sample outputs, neither will it simply control itself. But many organisations use after-the-fact controls, causing managers to take a reactive rather than a proactive position. The TQM systems needs a more anticipative style of control;

(vi)   *planning*: processes need to be planned carefully if they are to be efficient. This usually requires recording activities, stages and decisions in a form which is communicable to all. A clearly defined process reduces the scope for error and provides the basis of an analysis into possible improvements that might be made;

(vii)   *inventory control system*: it is in the storage of raw materials, components or the finished product that quality can diminish. The keeping of stocks is also physically expensive and can lead to cash flow problems. An inventory control system is therefore required to keep stocks to a minimum, whilst ensuring that supplies never dry up. One such system is the *just-in-time* system (*see* below).

A breakdown in any part of the TQM system can lead to organisational gaps where wastage may occur or quality be overlooked. Errors have a habit of multiplying, and failure to meet the requirements of one part of the organisation creates problems elsewhere. The correction of errors is time consuming and costly. TQM can provide a company with a competitive edge, which will be important given increases in competition which the Single European Market implies. This means that managers must plan strategically both externally and internally and that internal strategic planning has to involve everyone in the workplace. TQM is an approach aimed at improving the effectiveness and flexibility of business as a whole and is aimed at eliminating wasted effort as well as physical waste, by involving everyone in the process of improvement; improving the effectiveness of work so that results are achieved in less time and at less cost.

Central to the TQM approach is a need for a change in the attitude and culture prevailing within many organisations. Organisations have to move away from the acceptance of defects and mistakes as if they were just part of life. Divisional, competitive structures within organisations need to be broken down and replaced with committed, co-operative relationships between all employees, who should see themselves as working towards the same goal. Linked with attitude change is the need to create a climate of continuous improvement. Organisations need to ensure that they have information about quality at all times, so that they understand what is happening within any particular process. This moves the culture of the company away from checking whether a particular product or process is working effectively, after the event, to ensuring that one understands and identifies any quality problems early in the process, seeking continuously, to improve performance. It therefore requires everybody, at every level in the organisation, to understand and implement their own responsibilities for the quality management process.

End-of-the-line monitoring, therefore, needs to be replaced by a more effective method of quality monitoring. This can be achieved by the introduction of a Statistical Process Control (SPC) technique. Statistical Process Control involves identifying all the processes in the organisation and what the inputs and outputs are. Once the process is specified, the inputs and suppliers, and outputs and customers, can also be defined, along with the requirements at each of the interfaces. As a product moves from one process to another (even within the same factory), the emphasis is on supplying a semi-finished product to a customer who will have quality requirements: the whole organisation will therefore be full of customer–supplier chains. All processes are monitored by gathering and using data. The intention is to measure the performance of each process and provide any necessary feedback for corrective action as quickly as possible. Statistical Process Control is therefore a strategy for reducing variability, the cause of most quality problems.

Quality circles

A *quality circle* is usually defined as a group of workers, doing similar work, who meet together regularly under the leadership of their supervisor, in order to identify and solve work-related problems, and recommend solutions to management and implement those solutions once they are agreed. Central to any discussion in the quality circle is the key issue of quality of work done. A key feature of quality circles is that people must be invited to join them, not forced to do so. There are no formal rules governing the size of quality circles, but very large groups are difficult to manage and become unproductive. Groups usually range from 3–15 people, but an optimum number is probably 8–10. Commonly, circles meet for one hour per week. The impact of quality circles is to make workers feel needed as well as acting as a monitor on quality and a forum in which new working arrangements can be discussed. Many firms offer bonuses to individuals or groups who can come up with new systems or new practices in their work area which will ultimately save the company money.

Although quality circles can be linked with production line technology, often their use has been associated with a move away from the production line towards team-based production, where several tasks in the production of a good rather than one task is done by a group of people. The best example of this is the movement away from producing a car on a production line to a system where a group of people receive the shell of a car and assemble the whole product to an exact specification to meet the needs of the customer. Such a system was implemented by Volvo in Sweden and is being increasingly adopted by other manufacturers in Europe in the 1990s.

Quality standards

Like the measurement and specification of materials and products, the measurement of quality and of quality systems has become increasingly standardised. In the last decade one British Standard has attracted overwhelming attention: BS5750 was the world's first published national standard dealing with a complete approach to quality management. Internationally, BS5750 is the basis of the European Quality Standard EN29000, and of the International Standards Organisation's ISO9000 series. Such standards set down technical and organisational criteria which help to:

- ensure that goods and services are fit for the purpose and meet a customer's needs
- rationalise, simplify and harmonise manufacturing techniques thus reducing needless variety of duplication and misuse of resources
- provide a means communication and measurement which can be used in the specification of contracts
- provide a means of communication and identification to customers and suppliers
- ensure safety and good health.

As a quality system, BS5750 or ISO9000 involves all phases from initial identification to final satisfaction of requirements and customer expectations. These phases and activities will include:

- marketing and market research
- product design and development
- procurement
- production preparation and process planning
- production
- inspection and testing
- packaging and storage
- sales and distribution
- installation and operation
- technical assistance and maintenance
- disposal after use.

This represents an approach similar to a cradle-to-the-grave system based on the maintenance of quality. That same cradle-to-the-grave approach is common in the assessment of environmental improvement and an environmental improvement programme can be layered on top of a quality-based system such as BS5750 (*see* Chapter 10).

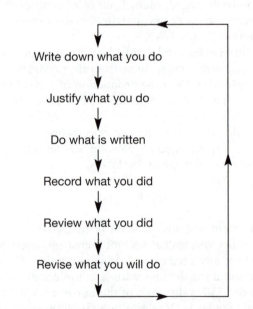

Fig. 6.4 ISO9000/BS5750: A continuing cycle of improvement

The essence of BS5750 or ISO9000 is shown in Fig. 6.4, where it can be seen in terms of a continuous cycle of improvement. The key is to document the quality management system in operation and to justify that system. There is a requirement to adhere to that system, in other words, to do what has been documented. What actually happened in the organisation needs subsequently to be recorded and reviewed, in order that the system can be improved and revised accordingly, and new documentation prepared.

Central to the management of operations certified to such quality standards is the issue of procurement. It is necessary to ensure that any product purchased conforms to a company's own standards, since all purchased materials and components will become part of the purchaser's own product and will therefore affect the quality of output. In order to ensure quality inputs, quality standards are therefore increasingly written into contracts with suppliers, which has the effect of pushing quality down the supply chain. Thus, over time, we will continue to see the spread of quality standards across European industry. Such standards will not be voluntary but rather a pre-requisite for doing business in an increasingly competitive European market.

Just-in-time management

Just-in-time (JIT) management systems are credited to the Japanese who developed and began to use them in the 1950s. Slowly, such management techniques have been adopted but many European firms have been relatively slow to recognise the benefits of such systems. Just-in-time is a programme directed towards ensuring that the correct quantities of materials are purchased or produced at the right time and that there is no waste. JIT fits well under a TQM umbrella and is essentially one type of inventory control system.

Materials and/or services are purchased or generated in exact quantities and just at the time they are needed. The primary objective is therefore to improve quality through the elimination of waste and in turn the system demands that stocks or inventories of raw materials, semi-finished and finished products are kept to a minimum. This results in cost savings for the following reasons:

- less capital has to be invested in inventories
- inventory items do not become obsolescent or deteriorate
- less space is required to keep inventories
- stock control costs are minimised.

The JIT system is not purely about inventory reduction though. It is essentially good management with problem solving, planning and decision making taken further down the ladder of authority. The whole system is often linked with worker incentives, staged promotion systems, performance-related payments, regular retraining and often, in Japan, guaranteed lifetime employment.

The benefits of JIT management systems and techniques are evident in many Japanese firms and increasingly in US and European ones as well. For example, Nissan's automobile assembly plant in Murayama, Japan, schedules its supplies by computer link and updates the schedule every 15–20 minutes. Suppliers deliver between 4–16 times a day, with an on-time delivery performance of 99.9 per cent. This allows Nissan to keep only one day's stock throughout its whole system.

An important outcome of the JIT technique is a programme for improving overall productivity and reducing waste. This leads to cost effective production or operation, and delivery of goods or services, in the correct quantity, at the right time and which exactly meet the requirements of the customer. This is achieved with a minimum amount of equipment, materials, people and warehousing. Once again, a key operational concept is that of flexibility.

In Europe, JIT systems are becoming more popular. Companies like Massey-Ferguson, GKN, IBM, 3M and Lucas have introduced JIT management. In addition, there are many Japanese firms operating JIT systems in their plants in Europe. Just-in-time is, therefore, becoming recognised as being able to provide another competitive edge and for this reason we are likely to see its implementation even more widespread in Europe over time.

Teamwork, consultation and participation

The need to devolve decision making and planning is clear in the two complementary systems discussed above and the advantages associated with participation have been briefly discussed earlier in this chapter. In addition, though, it should be recognised that the use of teamwork as an approach to problem solving has many advantages over allowing individuals to make decisions alone. These include:

- a greater variety of problems can be tackled which may be beyond one single person
- any problem is considered by a wider body of knowledge and experience, and therefore a workable solution is more likely to be found
- the teamwork itself can be satisfying and can boost morale by making participants feel needed
- people involved in making decisions will be happier about implementing those decisions in practice
- recommendations from groups are more likely to be accepted by management because they carry more weight.

When properly managed, teams improve the process of problem solving, producing usable results quickly and economically. It builds up trust, improves communication, improves motivation, develops interdependence and helps workers to identify with the company.

Environmental management and holistic management systems

Environmental issues are discussed in more detail in Chapter 10, but it should be recognised at this point, that environmental management programmes which deal with the reduction of waste, the recycling of necessary waste, the reduction in energy usage, a reduction in pollution and the improvement in the physical environment of the company, are completely compatible with the systems described above. Indeed, the whole approach of an environmental management system has to be integrated and planned and requires corporate commitment. For this reason, many firms are extending their TQM systems to also be environmentally friendly systems.

There is a growing trend now in some circles towards the development of companies which are more integrated, which have a corporate culture and dispose of notions of demarcations and division between workers and management. As part of this, there is often a need for managers to reassess their own management styles and that, in turn, often requires them to look closely at themselves. The ethos of holistic management surrounds the need for managers to be aware of themselves, to spend time on their own personal development and to look closely at their relationship with the people around them.

CONCLUSION

All of the issues dealt with in this chapter are very interrelated. Changing external pressures as a result of European integration are changing the structures of companies, which in turn impacts upon their internal organisation, work practices and management styles. Equally changing management techniques can change internal structures helping a firm to become successful and altering its external appearance. Many permutations like this are possible but they all take place in an increasingly integrated, increasingly technological and increasing legislatory Community.

The dynamics of change over the next two decades will allow firms to reconsider many of their policies and organisational practices, some of which may have been in place since the industrial revolution. Some commentators argue that a second industrial divide is now under way, based on new technologies, flexibility, changing management practices, participatory arrangements, changing ownership of firms and methods of remuneration and environmental concerns. The outcome is likely to be a very different workplace to the divisive, Taylorist, mass production factory, common in post-war Europe.

Questions for discussion

1 To what extent do you think that implementation of the Social Charter is essential to a Single European Market?

2 If working practices and workplace legislation become more and more harmonised, are there any reasons to think that some countries may find themselves losing some of their competitive advantages?

3 Why is education and vocational training seen to be at the centre of workplace developments?

4 What sorts of pressures are impacting on trade unions in the European Union? What is the likely result of these pressures in terms of trade union organisation in the future?

5 Explain the concept of flexible specialisation. What are the main elements in a flexible specialisation system?

6 What sorts of pressures are impacting on management in firms in the European Union? To what extent are these pressures leading to new styles of management being adopted?

7 Why are quality standards increasingly important in the Single European Market?

8 What are the essential elements of a Total Quality Management system? How is this different to a traditional quality assurance system?

9 A central theme throughout this chapter has been the need for teamwork. How do you consider that this might be encouraged?

10 Describe what you consider will be the future structure of European industry in terms of the concepts of flexible specialisation and monopoly capitalism.

11 Given your answer to question 9 what are the main changes we are likely to see in the workplace?

CASE STUDY

Co-determination in West Germany

Although initially resisted by many employers in Germany, co-determination is now supported by most of the large firms in the public and private sectors. Co-determination is founded in German industrial relations law. In companies of more than 2000 employees, there must be supervisory boards where 50 per cent of the representation comes from employees other than management. In addition, works councils which can be, and are, established in companies of more than five people have consultation duties and rights of veto.

The works council is elected by the whole workforce but, not surprisingly, tends to be dominated by trade unionists. In larger companies these representatives may work full-time on council duties. The rights of veto exist over work practices, overtime arrangements, holiday arrangements and over some aspects of employment procedure. However, the council has no direct power enabling it to prevent dismissal although it tends to have influence especially with regard to redundancy arrangements.

In the larger companies the co-determination arrangements on the supervisory board mean that workers can influence the business strategy and plans of the company. At their quarterly meetings all decisions of the management board must go through the supervisory board for approval. However, strict 50 per cent voting rights are generally tightly enforced and a casting vote is always in the hands of a chairperson – a shareholder representative. Even though this right exists, practice of the supervisory boards tends to be to attempt to reach a consensus.

German employers do have some doubts about giving workers so much influence. Not least because worker representatives have to be given access to full information about company strategies and plans. However, with 15 years' experience behind them, employers are well aware of and do promote the positive aspects of the co-determination schemes. These include positive productivity and motivation effects based on an enhanced atmosphere at work, a reduced feeling of 'them and us' and a knowledge of the firms' longer term plans which reduces the tendency to hypothesise for the worse. However, to some extent, in some companies, the supervisory boards may be little more than rubber stamping devices: decisions, in effect, may have been taken by management a long time before they go before the supervisory board. Management is able to present large amounts of seemingly convincing evidence to the board and then press for a decision to be taken quickly in the name of efficiency and progress.

A more indirect benefit of co-determination is that it tends to protect firms and, therefore, senior management from hostile takeover bids and to an extent senior managers have been able to hide behind their supervisory boards at times of possible merger activity. Again, by having a direct link with the workforce via the boards, management is able to provide convincing cases in their favour. On the other hand, where mergers are being discussed they can be done so without worker representatives on the supervisory boards knowing about them.

The abuse of the supervisory boards and the co-determination system by a few firms has led to German unions wanting to increase the extent of the co-determination system. They would like to see the legislation applying to companies with 1000 employees, rather than 2 000, with the shareholders' casting vote being abolished. In turn, the chairperson would be elected by both sides of the supervisory board.

With worker participation firmly on the agenda in Europe, the co-determination schemes in West Germany are being examined rather closely. In practice, at least, the co-determination system offers the greatest potential for employees to influence the traditional firm. Since it is the system which can give the workers most power it is unlikely to find favour amongst all European countries. However, its use by the most successful country in Europe means that, for every firm, it is worth considering. It may actually enhance good management and could have considerable motivating effects and productivity bonuses.

Case Study Questions

1 To what extent do you think that the system of co-determination works because it is enforced within industrial relations laws?

2 In general, what advantages are often associated with worker representation and worker participation?

3 How can co-determination help to protect a firm from adverse external interests in the firm's activities.

4 Do you consider that some sort of co-determination scheme should be instituted legislatively in the European Union?

5 Are there any alternatives to the co-determination system which you think might have superior outcomes? Why?

FURTHER READING

Oakland, J. (1993) *Total Quality Management: The Route to Improving Performance*, (2nd edn), Butterworth-Heinemann. This text gives an excellent overview of total quality management techniques.

Hassard, J. and Parker, M. (1993) *Post-modernism and Organisations*, Sage. This text provides an advanced critique of organisational dimensions of the firm including an analysis of the firm in a rapidly changing and complex world.

Piggot, J. and Cook, M. (1993) *International Business: A European Perspective*, Longman.

REFERENCES

Braverman, H. *Labor and Monopoly Capital: the Degradation of Work in the Twentieth Century*, Monthly Review Press, 1974.

Brusco, S. *Distretti industriali, servizi alle imprese e centri di comparto*, paper presented to the seminar Innovazione Tecnologica, Ruolo della Piccola Imprese ed Intervento del Governo Locale, Turin, 1983.

Cable, J. R. 'Is Profit-sharing Participation? Evidence on Alternative Firm Types from West Germany', *International Journal of Industrial Organisation*, 6, 121–137, 1988.

Deming, W. E. *Out of the Crisis*, MIT Center for Advanced Engineering Study, Cambridge, Mass, 1986.

Imrie, R. 'Work Decentralisation from Large to Small Firms: a Preliminary Analysis of Subcontracting', *Environment and Planning*, 18, 949–65, 1986.

Piore, M. J. and Sabel, *The Second Industrial Divide: Possibilities for Prosperity*, Basic Books, New York, 1984.

Scott, A. J. *New Industrial Spaces*, Pion, 1988.

Weitzman, M. *The Share Economy*, Harvard University Press, 1984.

Wood, S. (ed.) *The Transformation of Work: Skill, Flexibility and the Labour Process*, Unwin Hyman, 1989.

CHAPTER 7

Strategies for Europe

INTRODUCTION

Profound changes in the European operating environment, brought about by the removal of barriers and the new framework for competition, are imposing a need for strategic re-orientation on firms operating within the boundaries of the European Union. Spurred on by two, potentially conflicting, driving forces – efficiency gains and the trend towards market segmentation and increased levels of differentiation – many EU-based firms are devising new organisational structures and strategies. This chapter, having established a 'model' of the strategic management process, attempts to highlight the nature and scope of the new strategies being employed within Europe (and on a wider global scale) and their effectiveness in achieving objectives. Thus, it provides a *benchmark* against which EU firms must judge their strategic performance within this highly dynamic environment.

While there are no simple solutions to achieving competitiveness, this chapter outlines certain prescriptions for improving competitive performance, first through a review of various aspects of the value chain, and then by way of a fuller assessment of the, necessarily, eclectic decision-making process.

Elsewhere, whole books have been dedicated to the subject of European strategic management. Restricting assessment to a single chapter is, therefore, difficult. Accordingly, the chapter is divided into three parts:

1 Analysing the environment;
2 Assessing the firm's position: the value chain explored; and
3 Decision making and Review.

It is inevitable, therefore, that this chapter is longer than the others appearing in this book. This chapter also differs from others in that there is no concluding case study. The text is interspersed with a number of case examples highlighting various experiences of firms operating within Europe. The intention is to demonstrate a wide array of differing strategic problems and solutions which would be hard to achieve in a single case study.

DEVELOPING A STRATEGIC FRAMEWORK

Strategic planning is a complex process which attempts to seek a workable 'fit' between the resources and capabilities of the firm across a wide array of, often, disparate business functions, and an ever-changing operational environment. For the strategic manager, part of the challenge of designing a successful strategy is thus to develop an operational framework for managing the process in an iterative fashion. While every organisation undoubtedly boasts

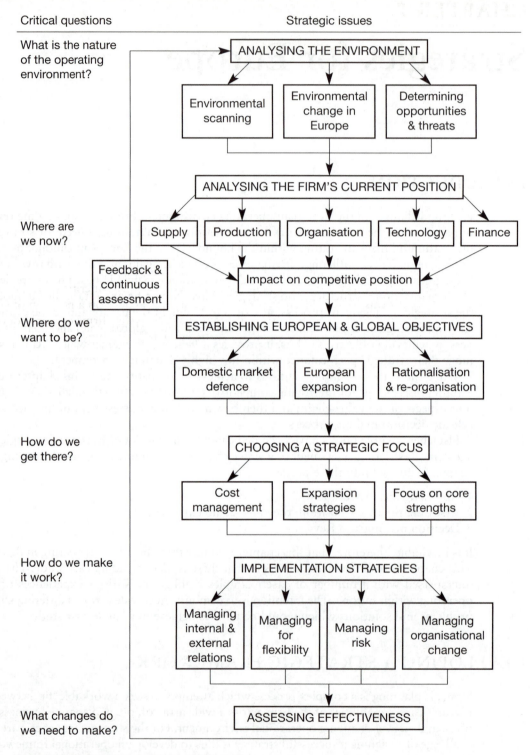

Critical questions   Strategic issues

What is the nature of the operating environment?

ANALYSING THE ENVIRONMENT

Environmental scanning | Environmental change in Europe | Determining opportunities & threats

ANALYSING THE FIRM'S CURRENT POSITION

Where are we now?

Supply | Production | Organisation | Technology | Finance

Feedback & continuous assessment

Impact on competitive position

Where do we want to be?

ESTABLISHING EUROPEAN & GLOBAL OBJECTIVES

Domestic market defence | European expansion | Rationalisation & re-organisation

How do we get there?

CHOOSING A STRATEGIC FOCUS

Cost management | Expansion strategies | Focus on core strengths

How do we make it work?

IMPLEMENTATION STRATEGIES

Managing internal & external relations | Managing for flexibility | Managing risk | Managing organisational change

What changes do we need to make?

ASSESSING EFFECTIVENESS

Fig. 7.1 The strategic management process

its own systems and structures for supporting this process, Fig. 7.1 outlines a typical strategic planning process and acts as the framework for further analysis in this chapter. Strategic managers essentially seek to answer six basic questions:

1 What is the nature of the operating environment?
2 Where are we now?
3 Where do we want to be?
4 How do we get there?
5 How do we make it work?
6 What changes do we need to make?

These six questions form the hub of the strategic management challenge. Within a European context, change brought about by the removal of barriers and the liberalisation of markets at the onset of the Single European Market initiative, and more recently increased competitive pressures brought about by these changes across the 15 Member States, has forced firms operating within Europe to take stock of their current strategic position and develop new strategies for taking on the challenges ahead – defence of their existing position and exploitation of emergent opportunities.

There is no blue-print for success. Different sectors yield different critical success factors, and different firms follow different routes in attempting to develop a position of sustainable competitive advantage. Indeed, it is possible to argue that firms can only develop a sustainable strategic position if they pursue strategies which are unique and innovative and have the potential of affording differential advantages. What is common, however, is the nature of the process followed in developing strategies for European competitiveness and it is the key issues surrounding this process on which the following discussion focuses.

ANALYSING THE ENVIRONMENT

Many of the chapters in this book set the scene of legislative change within the EU and provide the overriding framework in which European strategy formulation takes place. From an operational perspective, however, an understanding of the legislative environment is not sufficient for the development of strategic plans. Organisations require detailed information on countries, markets, industries, competition, culture and business practices, products, demographics and customers from which they may establish the nature of European opportunities and threats and the critical success factors pertaining to their particular market sector. Thus, it is not just the nature and scope of the information, but the way in which this is prepared and interpreted which gives rise to successful strategy development.

Environmental scanning

Environmental scanning, the process of information gathering on external market forces, provides the starting point of any strategic audit. It is not just about characterising the current state of the market and existing competitors, but predicting future changes in demography, culture, politics and technology which will underscore the nature of future strategic decisions and challenge assumptions on which past strategic decisions have been formulated.

Table 7.1 outlines some of the key areas of information sought by most organisations when drawing up strategic plans. These factors establish the current state of affairs in the industry and the market being served and provide a clear overview of the *task environment* for current strategic development. Various information sources exist which may provide firms with data on these key dimensions. Table 7.2 outlines some of the relevant sources for firms operating within the EU.

What is more difficult to ascertain is information on more remote areas of business activity such as culture, sociology, politics, and technology development which might potentially impact on the firm's position in the future. Technology developments (offering product substitutes) often emanate from organisations outside the task environment, making it difficult for firms to predict future changes and developments. Nevertheless, managers need to open their minds to the wider environment if they are to ensure that the strategies developed today lead to on-going success in the markets of tomorrow. The case example of the European television industry typifies change of this nature and outlines the various areas of analysis important to plan successfully in an industry characterised by rapid technology change.

Table 7.1. Critical elements of environmental scanning

Key element	Nature of information
Country	General economic trends including population size and growth, age structure, spending patterns GDP, GNP, inflation, unemployment, productivity, wage rates.
Industry	Key industry indicators including overall size, trends, major players, supply and demand conditions.
Market	Key players within each geographic market, market share, supply and demand conditions, concentration ratios, production and distribution arrangements.
Product	Pricing, promotion, distribution nature of differentiation, technology.
Customers	Customer purchasing habits, buyer behaviour, profiles, price sensitivity.

Table 7.2. Sources of information for European Union environmental scanning

Source	Publisher	Nature of information
Eurostats	EC Commission	Economic indicators, demographics market analysis, industry specific trends.
Panorama of EC Industry	EC Commission	Data on 125 sectors including specific detail on trade associations and contacts.
Company reports	Individual companies	Specific company statistics but also a review of mission statements and strategic direction.
Extel Financial Service	Extel	Available in printed or CD Rom form they provide company financial data, addresses and nature and scope of subsidiary activity.

Table 7.2 continued

McCarthy newspaper & magazine cuttings service	McCarthy	Press cuttings on recent company activity which can include substantial detail on strategic considerations and specific investments, political and market conditions.
Other abstracting services (eg. Ambar)		As above (available in libraries).
Department of Trade and Industry (UK)	HMSO	Country specific information and information on services offered to companies operating abroad.
Embassies		Country specific information, trade contacts.
Banks		Detailed information on countries and specific markets.
Distributors, customers & suppliers		Country, market, competitor, demand conditions.
Chambers of Commerce		Trade associations, market data.
Exhibitions		Company, product and market trends, technology.
Catalogues, trade & technical magazines		Company, product, technology.

CASE STUDY

The European television industry

Market Characteristics

For more than 40 years, most European countries sported two or three television channels provided by state-owned broadcasters and paid for through taxes and licence fees. Some countries, such as the UK and Italy, ventured into the field of commercial television, although their forays were relatively limited and offered only limited additional choice for customers. In some countries, restriction on advertising was severe. In Germany, for example, the two state channels were permitted to take advertising, in five minute blocks, for 20 minutes a day except for Sundays and holidays. The extent of regulation severely curtailed competition both within each country and between countries.

Massive deregulation in the 1980s changed the market dramatically. Technology and political pressures served as the catalysts of change, with satellites and cable diluting the argument that state control of scarce airwaves was in the public interest. Between 1980–1994 the number of European television stations rose from 40–150, with over one third being delivered by satellite. In turn, this led to an explosion in advertising expenditure fuelled by the opening up of new advertising media, and the need for companies to finance their own programme development to fill the vastly expanded airtime (*see* Fig. 7.2).

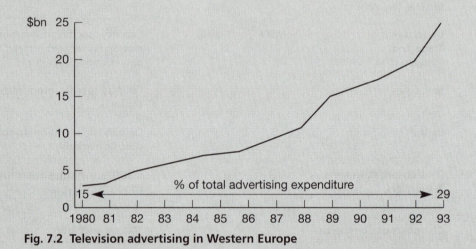

Fig. 7.2 Television advertising in Western Europe

Such change has rocked the television industry Europe-wide. Increased competitive pressures have resulted in financial ruin for some of the leading state-run organisations (Italy's RAI, Spain's RTVE and Germany's ARD and ZDF). The BBC in the UK reduced staffing levels between 1991–1994 by 4 600, representing 20 per cent of its staff. Only those companies that can redress their burdensome cost structures will survive.

But this is not the end of the story. A new wave of technological developments is sweeping through the television industry with telecommunications companies set to reap the benefits of setting up advanced networks and cable optic systems to support the new technology wave in household provision of television services. Computer companies, too, are experimenting with interactive television media designed to provide consumers with greater control over their television watching habits. Long gone are the days when the terrestrial television providers were alone in providing home entertainment.

Nevertheless, the pace of change in Europe remains relatively slow as state-run telecommunications companies continue to monopolise many Member States in the European Union. The UK is the main exception. The privatisation of British Telecom (BT) has opened up the market to major competition from foreign suppliers, American cable firms such as TCI and Nynex spending billions of dollars on fibre optic networks. Industry stalwarts suggest that such expenditure may be misplaced as take-up rates of cable television remain relatively slow, but they ignore such dramatic change at their peril. Slow it may be, but incentives such as undercutting BT's rates for telephone provision by 10–15 per cent have proved an attractive proposition to even the most reluctant consumers.

Such changes have had a critical impact on the UK television and telecommunications market and seriously unsettled the BBC and BT. BT have responded by testing their own video-on-demand services and are clearly aware that failure to explore the potential of the home entertainment market would potentially leave them at a disadvantage in their own back yard. The BBC, on the other hand, believe that there will always be a place for their public broadcast services and while they are attempting to rationalise the organisation and improve their cost base, forays into new technology sectors seem a long way off.

Implications for European Strategy Development

The above example demonstrates some of the complexities facing firms in a highly dynamic industry within the EU:

- Developments in non-terrestrial TV technology are having a profound impact on the industry and changing the nature of the competitive challenge and critical success factors
- Many of the changes taking place are linked to culture (customer demand patterns for substitute forms of home entertainment and their propensity to take-up new technologies), politics (deregulation and liberalisation of state monopolies and the emergence of a new agenda for competition) and technology (which is developing apace and, as Rupert Murdoch suggests, 'galloping over the old regulatory machinery, in many countries rendering it almost obsolete')
- The blurring of industry boundaries with television providers, telecommunications and computer companies all becoming part of a wider 'entertainment' industry.

Failure to address the potential impact on the market both now and in the future, will for any firm, be it a television company, telecommunications provider or computer manufacturer, potentially lead to missed opportunities and limited scope to develop the necessary skills to compete well into the 21st century.

Source: Adapted from The Economist – Feeling for the Future: a survey of Television, 12 Feb 1994,

Environmental change in Europe

In relation to broader issues of European unionisation, consideration of the on-going political and economic development of the EU cannot be overlooked. Table 7.3 provides a brief summary of some of these issues and an overview of their implications for strategy development through the 1990s and into the next millennium.

Gathering information is only the first step in the assessment of the environment. This information has to be analysed in such a way as it provides a clear indication of the real opportunities and threats facing the organisation in its future development. While, at face value, this may appear quite straightforward, the volume and scope of information for a manager researching the 15 Member States of the EU is likely to be significant and the challenge of assessing its impact on company profitability and long-term competitiveness highly complex. Furthermore, when the wider business implications are included, predicting future impact of factors before they exert themselves may be akin to gazing into a crystal ball. Firms often become so absorbed in short-term profit returns that the long-term vision of sustainable competitive advantage within a highly dynamic environment can be overlooked. It is, therefore, essential for firms to define the boundaries of their environmental scanning and assessment in order that the task be made manageable and workable.

Table 7.3. Wider European issues and their potential impact on strategy

Key issues	Strategic impact
Monetary union	If a two-tier Europe becomes a reality, the full benefits of a single currency will not be realised for some time. Adjustment to financial systems will be essential to maximise the gains of a single currency. Transfer pricing mechanisms can be adjusted to maximise financial flows of Ecus and minimise currency transfers into remaining Member State currencies.
Political organisation	Subsidiarity will lead to greater accountability and participation in political organisation at both an EU and national level. The power of lobby groups will rise and with it greater demands on organisations to take due consideration of social welfare issues (such as equality, health, consumer choice and protection).
Social dimensions	Coupled with the above, the new social agenda for Europe is changing firms' decision-making processes. Employee involvement is likely to add further impetus to the erosion of hierarchies and the realisation of flatter organisations with greater consensus and group decision-making across a variety of levels. More project-based team work is also likely to emerge.
Competitive environment	The trend towards alliances and joint ventures is continuing apace producing industry-wide affiliations and networks. Firms are unlikely to survive in the new competitive forum without becoming part of these complex networks. Greater focus on co-operation (rather than competition) will result.
Technology	Increasingly rapid rates of technology change (on a global scale) leading to demands for quicker response times and more flexible means of developing new technologies, including establishing linkages with competitors to share risks and establish common industry standards.
Culture	While cultural harmonisation may never arise, increased opportunities for identifying cultural sub-groups which cross traditional geographic boundaries.

Within a European context, one means of establishing the boundaries is to focus attention on a narrow range of markets or one region within the EU. This may mean concentrating on defence of the domestic market which is an essential priority for all organisations as barriers are removed. It is also important to establish a realistic time horizon for achieving objectives. Firms which imagine that profits can be achieved immediately are likely to be disappointed and possibly pull out of ventures before they have had time to develop their strategic position and realise their potential.

For firms currently operating within the EU, opportunities and threats are critically linked to the changes arising out of the creation of the Single European Market. Figure 7.3

outlines the key issues of change and highlights ways in which these factors are impacting on the European operating environment. The review is not intended to be exhaustive, rather its objective is to provide a starting point for understanding environmental change and the ramifications for future strategy development.

The opportunities of the Single European Market have been well documented. The

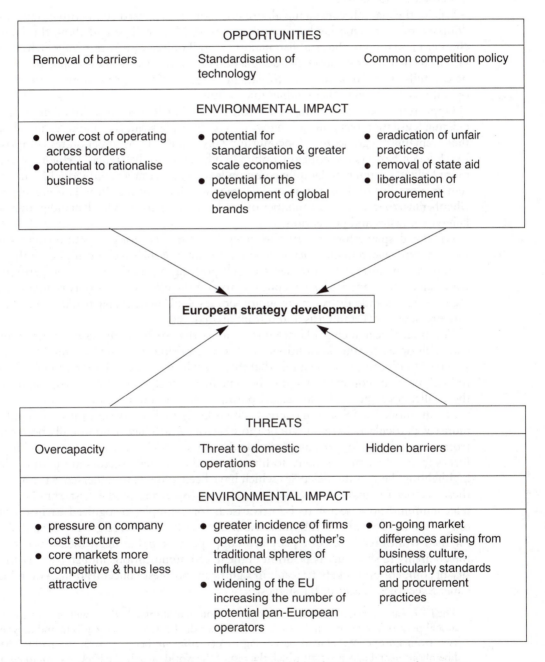

Fig. 7.3 Opportunities and threats within the European environment

removal of barriers between the Member States offers up the potential for organisations to treat the whole of Europe as their domestic market and thus the scope to increase output and thus engender greater scale economies and a more efficient operating position. In reality, however, these opportunities are blighted by the threats facing organisations currently operating in the EU, threats which can limit the scope for firms to fully appreciate efforts at market liberalisation.

One of the main threats facing all organisations is increased competitive activity in their domestic market as market barriers are removed. More will be said about this later in this chapter in relation to the establishment of overall objectives. At this stage, what is important to recognise is that strategies designed to take advantage of new opportunities need to be carefully weighed against the threats involved in diverting effort away from domestic operations and leaving them vulnerable to attack.

Opportunities are also hampered by the hidden barriers between Member States. While existing legislation has gone a long way to remove physical, fiscal and technical barriers, there remains a high degree of incongruity between the 15 Member States comprising the EU. Hidden barriers are critically dominated by cultural differences (which are explained more fully in Chapter 9). Despite common laws of governance, individual Member States remain a product of their history and heritage which means that broad differences between Member States still exist in a number of key business areas such as demand patterns, buyer behaviour, tastes and perceptions.

Equally, despite efforts to establish a level playing field for competition across the EU, local governments remain concerned with protection of their own businesses at the expense of foreign operators. The problems of self-policing mechanisms for competition policy were raised in Chapter 5. They continue to dog the efforts of European organisations in securing access and fair treatment in non-domestic EU markets particularly with regard to procurement, local standards and testing procedures.

The final threat facing EU organisations is that of over-capacity. As firms begin to encroach on each other's traditional territories, raising their output and extending their spheres of influence, it is inevitable that there will be winners and losers. Those firms likely to lose out as the competitive stakes become increasingly intense are those unable to meet the challenges imposed by increased output – namely improved efficiency and business rationalisation. The impact of overcapacity is likely to differ significantly from industry to industry. Particularly hard hit will be those sectors which have traditionally been protected from competition, in particular, nationalised industries which are now facing market forces for the first time as steps to liberalise and deregulate sectors are taking effect and highlighting the vast inefficiencies which have been allowed to underscore the activities of these sectors for many years. British Telecom (BT), one of the first companies in the telecommunications sector to be privatised, for example, recognised early on that the only route to survival was rationalisation. 'Project Royal Sovereign' involved their reducing their workforce by 25 000 people, an unpopular step, but one which was essential for the company to shore up its position in the telecommunications industry where the intensity of competition is likely to result in significant business concentration. As Ian Vallance, Chief Executive Officer of BT suggests:

> The PTTs can't survive indefinitely, and we reckon that ultimately there will only be a handful of global players in telecom, including a couple from the USA, a Japanese group and maybe one or two from Europe. We aim to be among them ... having been through the painful period of liberalisation and privatisation which the rest of the world outside the USA has still to go through, we are corporately equipped to take the lead.

Companies, then, face a complex balancing act between attack (and actively pursuing new opportunities) and defence (protecting existing business operations). Spreading resources thinly between a large number of Europe-wide operations is a dangerous route to contemplate. Aggressive competition in all 15 Member States dictates that each market served must be provided with sufficient resources (financial, managerial and skills) for the organisation to develop a sustainable competitive position within that territory. To preserve the military metaphor, a 'scattergun' approach is likely to produce few prisoners and leave the organisation vulnerable to counter-attack. Alternatively, a failure to exploit new opportunities is also likely to leave a company vulnerable, particularly where major competitors are finding opportunities for growth and expanding their power base. In this sense, attack may be the best possible defence.

Determining opportunities and threats

The elements highlighted in Fig. 7.3, relating to opportunities and threats posed by the Single European Market, only operate at a generic level. In defining appropriate strategies it is important to analyse the specifics of the industry and the markets they serve. It is essential, then, to establish analytical methodologies which allow the incorporation of the widest array of factors possible at an operational level. While various methods of analysis exist, that proposed by Ansoff (1984) provides a useful framework for such assessment (*see* Fig. 7.4). By establishing a profile of the impact of environmental issues (either actual or predicted) on the organisation, managers can decide whether or not the immediate concern should be defence or attack. A model of this kind can allow the incorporation of both generic and specific factors impacting on the operating environment. The ability to adjust the events/issues according to the findings of the environmental scanning process and weight factors according to their impact gives this approach great flexibility.

What is not apparent from the framework is what is meant by 'impact'. Ultimately, most organisations are driven by profit, and an assessment of the impact of an event or issue on the bottom-line is likely to give rise to prescriptive strategy recommendations. In other words, how can we react to the change in our competitive position brought about by such developments in order to maintain or enhance our profitability? In essence, what strategic factors do we need to focus on in order to be competitive in the future?

Finding an answer to this question is not possible without undertaking a strategic audit of the firm's position, not just in relation to its operating environment, but in relation to other firms competing in the industry. Firms do not compete in a vacuum, they compete in a competitive environment which is shaped by the activities of all other players, including not just manufacturing firms, but suppliers and buyers. Some organisations operate as 'leaders' shaping new directions for future development, others behave as 'followers' reacting to the strategic changes initiated by the leaders. Whichever stance the firm takes, it has to shape its strategy around existing competitive forces and rivalry in such a way as to attain a position of competitive advantage which can be defended against attack from other competing firms.

In the following section, we shall look at the notion of competitive advantage across a series of strategic dimensions – supply, production, organisation, technology management and finance (sales and marketing being dealt with in a separate chapter) – and determine how different approaches to these issues afford firms the potential for generating competitive advantage and enhancing their competitive position.

Environment sector	Opportunity/ Threat	Weighting[1]	Importance[2]	Impact on firm's strategies[3]			$\Sigma-$	$\Sigma+$
				S1	S2	S3		
Technology	1							
	2							
Political								
Economic								
Social								
Etc.								
			$\Sigma-$					
			$\Sigma+$					

Note

1 Indicates the degree to which the event is judged to be a threat or opportunity. On an ordinal scale from 1–5, 1 represents a weak T/O, and 5 a strong T/O.

2 Indicates the degree to which the weighted event has, or will have, an impact on the firm's strategies. On an ordinal scale from 1–5, 1 represents little impact, 5 a great impact.

3 The impact each event has on each of the firm's strategies is calculated by multiplying the weighted score by the importance score. A large positive (negative) score represents a strong opportunity (threat).

The row sums indicate the degree to which each event/issue is thought to enhance (+) or inhibit (–) the success of the firm's strategies. The column sums indicate the degree to which each strategy is itself thought to pose a threat or opportunity to the firm given its predicted environment.

Fig. 7.4 The firm's environment threat and opportunity profile (ETOP)

ASSESSING THE FIRM'S POSITION

The value chain explored strategy encompasses a broad array of interrelated business dimensions from procurement through to final customer service, and competitive advantage may be developed through managing any one aspect of the organisation in a superior way to competitors. For example, a superior product technology, emanating from sound technological management, more efficient production processes, efficient procurement of quality raw materials, or more responsive decision making, can all enhance a firm's performance vis-à-vis other rivals in the industry. In the European market of the 1990s, characterised by aggressive competition from both EU nationals and multinational enterprises from the USA and Asia, failure to develop sustainable competitive advantage will ultimately result in business demise.

A useful framework for identifying key strategic aspects of the organisation is the *value chain* (originally developed by Michael Porter, 1982). A summary of the key elements is presented in Fig. 7.5. These various activities all *add value* for customers in the sense that the more effectively these operations are managed the more a customer may be willing to pay for the product or service. A firm is, therefore, profitable if the value exceeds the cost of performing these various functions. In relation to competitors, the firm must therefore provide comparable buyer value but perform the activities more efficiently so as to attain a cost advantage, or perform the activities in a unique way which raises the value to the consumer and thus allows them to command a premium price – the concept of differentiation.

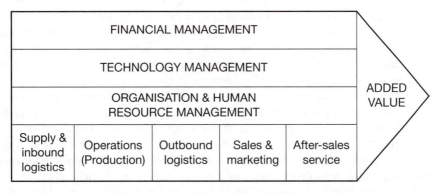

Fig. 7.5 The value chain

The activities performed may be grouped into two categories: those associated with the core activities of on-going production, marketing and servicing are referred to as *primary activities* while those providing inputs, technology, human resources and infrastructure to support the manufacturing function are referred to as *support activities*. Quite clearly, the primary activities draw on a wide variety of support activities in their on-going management.

Firms gain competitive advantage by conceiving new ways of conducting activities, employing new procedures, technologies, inputs or channels of distribution. In other words, firms are a sum of their activities and not just comprised of a series of discrete functions. Managing the organisation is therefore not just about managing functions, but managing linkages between those functions.   More will be said about the integration of various facets of the value chain in the discussion on implementation strategies. At this stage, what is important is to understand how organisation can analyse their current position along various dimensions of the value chain – in essence, their strengths and weaknesses. Issues relating to outbound logistics, sales and marketing and after-sales service are obviously critical to the whole process. However, for ease of assessment they will be treated separately in the following Chapter 8 (European Marketing).

What follows is an overview of various aspects of the value chain and an assessment of the kinds of business practices being employed by European firms in the 1990s. It is only by assessing what constitutes *best practice* (or at least good business practice) that firms can analyse their own position in relation to their leading competitors.

Supply/inbound logistics

The cost and quality of inputs into the production process are a critical aspect of effective and efficient management. Essentially, firms have three options available to them when purchasing raw materials and components:

1 *Buy on the open market.* Here quality and efficiency depend on the buyer power of the organisation (and its ability to dictate prices and quality) and the purchasing relationships established with suppliers. There are obvious risks associated with this approach: the possibility of the supplier going out of business; reliance on quality control methods and delivery schedules; the possibility of the supplier being purchased by a competitor.

2 *Internalise the supply of raw material.* This can be achieved via backward integration and the purchase of upstream organisations or the establishment of raw material processing plants or component manufacturers. Efficiency depends on the ability of the organisation to successfully integrate operations into the overall organisation. The main risk associated with this approach is the inflexibility to choose between alternative sources of supply, which is particularly critical when technology change is rapid and new, more efficient, suppliers emerge in the marketplace.

3 *Quasi-integration.* While quasi-integration is akin to purchasing on the open market, it differs in one key respect. Rather than establishing a buyer/seller relationship, the two companies co-operate to pursue the same ultimate goal of enhancing value for the final customer. Co-operation may take a variety of forms: technological co-operation wherein the companies work together to establish new supply inputs tailor-made to the manufacturer's requirements; supply co-operation, which may involve the mutual establishment of just-in-time (JIT) supply and production scheduling; investment co-operation involving the manufacturer assisting the supplier in improving production capacity or quality to ensure high standards of inputs. To an extent, this approach combines the best of both worlds.

The quasi-integration approach to supply was popularised by the Japanese and has gradually infiltrated operations spanning a wide part of the globe. Such arrangements are now typical in the global car industry and are increasingly being used as a means of cost management in a wide array of industrial sectors from computing to clothing manufacture.

With increased competition in Europe from Japanese manufacturers, many EU organisations have realised that the only way to compete is to mirror Japanese supply techniques and develop co-operative relationships of their own. This has dramatically altered the management demands of establishing and managing inbound logistics operations. As competition in Europe intensifies, firms are realising that low cost procurement is not necessarily the only means of effectively managing inbound logistics. Quality, and the ability to add value to the final product, have emerged as important elements of the sourcing function.

However, while quasi-integration of inputs provides a case of 'best practice', this does not suggest that the recommendation for all firms operating in Europe is to establish co-operative linkages with all of their suppliers. Some organisations depend on a multiplicity of suppliers in sourcing raw materials and components and thus the cost of managing linkages would be preclusively high and would do little to enhance company efficiency. Equally, where supplies are of a commodity nature, the motivation to establish linkages may be less as there is no scope for technology co-operation. Ultimately, the decision is one of balance between careful cost management and quality and co-operative commitment in adding value.

Flexibility of supply was highlighted in relation to integration. Firms which establish or purchase suppliers of raw materials or components can find themselves at a disadvantage where technologies change and independent suppliers react quicker to the new challenges so posed. Similarly, organisations which rely on their domestic market only for the supply of inputs are faced with less flexibility than organisations which adopt a global (or pan-European) sourcing policy. Although domestic sourcing means firms can avoid problems of cultural uncertainty, long distances in distribution channels, exchange rate fluctuations, political and economic risks and tariffs, it also means that firms have less choice over the quality and type of inputs available to them. Global sourcing can provide:

- access to lower cost raw materials and components
- access to raw materials and components not available domestically
- access to higher quality inputs (which may include better technologies)
- less reliance on a small number of possible suppliers which reduces risks.

In the current European market, liberalisation and the removal of barriers has raised the potential for firms to source across a wider market and realise some of these advantages. Take-up of such opportunities has, however, been slow, as cultural uncertainty and exchange rate fluctuations continue to dog the ease with which firms can operate across borders. A move towards a single European currency would undoubtedly facilitate the process although cultural differences and geographic distances will remain. In deciding whether a European or national sourcing policy is preferable, firms invariably make trade-offs: quality against higher distribution costs; technology against lower potential for JIT inventory management; lower risk of using more suppliers against high unit costs associated with re-working defective products.

Importantly, firms need to assess not just what is available, but what might give them an advantage. They thus need to analyse their supply practices in conjunction with other methods employed in their industry sector, test them against key changes in the European operating environment and developments within their own industry, and determine their 'fit' with overall company objectives – whether cost or quality biased. Thus they need to ask:

- What supply practices do we currently employ?
- What supply practices do our competitors currently employ?
- Within the bounds of our current objectives for supply (i.e. quality and cost factors) what strengths and weaknesses are apparent in our existing supply practices vis-à-vis our competitors?
- What changes are occurring in the operating environment which may impact on supply management in the future?
- What are our current strengths and weaknesses in relation to the new demands being posed by changes in the operating environment?
- How can we capitalise on our strengths and address our weaknesses both in terms of our competitors and changes in the operating environment?

Production

Firms are essentially faced with two key decisions when organising and managing their production for Europe:

1 Where do we produce?
2 Who produces?

which incorporate the concepts of centralisation vs. decentralisation and internalisation versus externalisation. Before entering into a detailed discussion of these issues, it is worth commenting briefly on the nature of decision making for production in the context of the Single European Market and assessing the main characteristics of alternative means of servicing European markets.

The removal of barriers between the 15 Member States of the EU has, in theory at least, raised the opportunity for European players to consider the whole market as their 'domestic back yard' and not a series of discrete export markets. This has naturally changed the locational focus of business across the EU (as discussed in Chapter 3) with the central 'golden triangle', spanning southern Germany, France, northern Spain and northern Italy, serving as the economic 'hub' of the whole Community. Location within this hub is attractive given the ease with which the various Member States can be serviced from a centralised manufacturing facility. Over time, however, the lower transportation costs associated with centralised manufacturing may be eroded by the higher costs of operating in a central area where demand for land, labour, energy and materials may raise the costs of production. Equally, centralisation means that organisations may be distanced from final consumer markets and thus find it hard to respond quickly to changes in demand patterns.

The belief that large numbers of European manufacturers will close their existing domestic facilities and build new plants in centralised European locations is far-fetched. Few manufacturing organisations have the flexibility (and resources) to disassociate themselves from their existing supply and distribution networks and co-operative business systems and build new dedicated facilities in countries which are, to them, unfamiliar. Gravitation towards the centre is therefore only likely to be an issue for those organisations adding new capacity to their business, or in non-productive functions of the value-chain (particularly distribution) which are more flexible and easier to re-locate.

While the Single Market has removed many of the barriers between the Member States of the EU, from the point of view of many firms, Member States other than their own, remain foreign markets which can either be serviced by exports, foreign direct investment or contractual relationships. In other words, while business barriers are being eroded, perceptual barriers of operating across the wider EU remain. Organisations may therefore be fully aware of the opportunities provided by the Single Market, but have not yet adjusted their thinking to the point of believing the whole marketplace is their 'domestic market'. Indeed, it could be argued that as long as cultural differences between the Member States remain, they never will.

Firms may therefore choose to:

(a) produce domestically and export their products across the Member States of the EU;
(b) establish (or maintain existing) production plants in other EU countries;
(c) establish joint ventures or contractual relationships with other EU organisations to produce in non-domestic markets.

The decision-making process surrounding the choice of strategy to service non-domestic markets is highly complex and depends on a wide array of factors including costs, physical location, product characteristics, company resources and objectives, cultural considerations and government intervention. Table 7.4 attempts to encapsulate the various factors as a means of identifying critical issues and highlighting the extensive nature of the, sometimes conflicting, elements impacting on final choice.

The foreign market servicing decision is further complicated by the wide array of operational strategies available within each generic group each of which boasts its own set of strengths and weaknesses and thus shapes the ability of the firm to compete effectively with foreign competitors.

Table 7.4. Factors impacting on the choice of foreign market servicing

Costs	Physical location	Product characteristics	Company resources & objectives	Government intervention
Exporting • Potentially high distribution costs from peripheral location. • Adding capacity to existing domestic operations leads to scale economies. • Domestic production costs rise if products for foreign markets need to be adapted for cultural differences due to down-time and re-tooling. • Domestic production costs may be higher or lower than those pertaining in foreign markets due to differences in the local price of resources.	**Exporting** • Known structures and systems in domestic market. • Physical distance from market can raise questions in consumer's mind regarding ability to deliver. • Distance from the market in terms of information and market monitoring (although might be able to overcome difficulties by using the services of market based intermediaries) and thus may not automatically see directions for adaptation and differentiation.	**Exporting** • Large and bulky products preclusively expensive to export. • High-technology products may require technical selling capabilities and after-sales service which may be better achieved by the firm itself rather than relying on third parties. • Highly differentiated products which can command high prices in the marketplace can withstand the costs of transportation although the differential benefits may be best communicated by company employed sales staff rather than those of an intermediary.	**Exporting** • Exporting is generally considered to be the most cost-effective form of market servicing as it involves limited financial outlay. • Effective management of inter-mediaries via co-operative links and the development of good working relationships can substantially raise the costs of exporting. • Firms often continue to export even when economic factors dictate greater involvement due to habit and familiarity. Indirect exporting is generally used by those firms 'dabbling' in foreign markets and selling excess capacity.	**Exporting** • Domestic governments likely to be supportive of exporting as it raises balance of trade and thus likely to provide support packages. • Within Europe, free access to markets means government ability to restrict imports severely limited to safety and consumer welfare issues. • Exporting still not likely to be favoured where access to public procurement contracts desirable due to continued local preference.
Foreign investment • Set-up costs may be high. • Duplication of effort in business functions (eg. finance, marketing personnel). • Local manufacturing costs may be lower. • Shorter transportation distances.	**Foreign investment** • Close to the market and customer needs and wants more obvious. • Operating environment alien in early stages of investment which may lead to cultural misunderstanding.	**Foreign investment** • Offers greater potential for monitoring changing needs and demands and differentiating products accordingly. • Shorter distribution channels for bulky products. • Locally placed for providing technical support. • Closer to foreign customers and thus easier monitoring of competitor technology & differentiation.	**Foreign direct investment** • Foreign direct investment involves maximum commitment to foreign markets and can be highly resource intensive where the investment takes the form of a manufacturing facility. • Only firms seeking to expand international activities in a pro-active manner are likely to contemplate foreign investment. • Firms seeking a fast return on investment may opt for a takeover rather than a greenfield operation due to the existing operation's ability to generate rapid profits.	**Foreign direct investment** • Freedom of capital movements in Europe means freedom of investment without government intervention. • Regional support for investment in economically deprived areas.
Contractual arrangements • Share risks with another player. • High management costs for establishing and maintaining the relationship. • Lower distribution costs because close to the market.	**Contractual arrangements** • Local partner helps overcome cultural and physical distance. • Reliance on local partner may stifle learning and make increased commitment hard to achieve later on.	**Contractual arrangements** • Where product technology is the essence of a company's competitive advantage, contractual arrangements may be less popular as they can lead to technology leakage. • Quality may be difficult to maintain where production is carried out by third parties.	**Contractual arrangements** • Resource commitment can be lowered through contractual arrangements and be spread between more than one firm. • Relies on the ability of organisations to work co-operatively, and choice of partner critical.	**Contractual arrangements** • Favourable attitude towards contractual arrangements shown by EC Commission due to technology sharing potential.

Exporting

The term exporting covers a variety of alternative options including those involving independent intermediaries and those where the firm takes control of all operations. In turn, these distinctions throw up two important issues:

1 there are various modes of exporting for which cost structures and risk vary enormously;
2 different modes of exporting offer the organisation disparate degrees of control.

Exporting via intermediaries: Various types of market intermediaries exist to support the export activities of firms. These involve both intermediaries based in the home country (*indirect methods*) and those in the foreign market (*direct methods*). Each offers a distinct set of advantages to the exporting firm and potential for competitive success.

Overall, it can be argued that indirect methods of exporting yield the lowest levels of foreign market penetration. By operating through the likes of export houses (who buy from the firm and sell products abroad for profit), confirming houses (who sell on behalf of the manufacturer on commission) and buying houses (which buy goods on behalf of the foreign firm) companies depend on the ability of third parties (frequently domestic firms lacking an understanding of the foreign market), to actively sell and promote their products abroad. Whilst modest sales can be achieved through these forms of exporting, they are rarely considered to be ideal by those firms who proactively seek international expansion.

Direct exporting modes include utilising the services of agents (who traditionally do not take title to the goods and sell on commission on behalf of the manufacturer) and distributors (who take title to the goods and sell on mark-up). Because these institutions are based in the host market and employ local nationals they have a broad understanding of the local market, its culture and business practices. This can be an important advantage for firms exporting for the first time with little to no understanding of the foreign market.

Company controlled exporting: In order to improve information flows and control over the product, the company may conduct its own exporting. Direct selling to the end user, establishment of a sales and marketing office or alternatively setting up a sales and marketing subsidiary may all be considered preferable.

Direct selling, wherein the manufacturer services the needs of the customer direct from the home market is not an option open to all manufacturers. A lot depends on the nature of the product and target market. Specifically, this kind of approach is most appropriate where a small number of customers are being serviced with a relatively small number of products, with infrequent, high value orders. Attempting to service a large number of customers across a very wide geographic area would be an administrative nightmare.

Sales offices and sales subsidiaries are separated out as two distinct strategies, not so much because they offer distinct services, but because their legal status differs. Whereas a sales office simply involves locating managers abroad or employing local personnel to operate on the company's behalf, sales subsidiaries are individual companies in their own right. Rather than sell the company's products on commission they, like distributors, buy stock from group manufacturing units and sell it on for profit. Importantly, therefore, sales and marketing subsidiaries provide a channel for internal company transfer pricing.

Licensing and other contractual arrangements

This group of options also comprises a wide variety of alternatives. In particular, it is possible to distinguish between licensing contracts in their various forms and joint ventures (including strategic alliances).

Licensing: Licensing involves a market sale of embodied knowledge to an external producer, in an international context, to an overseas firm. Contracts usually centre on patents and trademarks, legally binding forms of protection which offer firms a monopolistic advantage for a fixed period of time over a particular technology or piece of intellectual property. Various types of contractual arrangement exist which come under the generic heading of 'licensing': turnkey contracts, contract manufacturing, management contracts, sub-contracting and franchising to name but a few. All, however, involve information being provided by the licensor and a resource commitment for manufacturing and production being made by the licensee. In other words, licensing involves the transfer of knowledge via the open market.

Where this takes place across international borders the option typically combines the technical and managerial expertise of the licensor with the market knowledge of the host firm. Theoretically, then, licensing appears to offer a 'best of both worlds' solution to the foreign market servicing problem. Nevertheless, it is often considered to be the third best option principally because financial returns are considerably less than is the case with exporting and foreign direct investment. Remuneration usually involves a one off, up-front payment, plus a percentage of sales revenue or rental payments. Generally, it is reserved for markets where factors militate against the firm choosing any other option, for example, market restrictions, particularly government intervention, and limited resources of the firm prevent other forms of market servicing being followed. Alternatively, licensing may be regarded as a transitory mode offering the licensor the opportunity to test demand and product acceptance and gain knowledge of the workings of the foreign market, or gain a foothold in a highly competitive sector whilst avoiding head-to-head competition.

Notwithstanding these benefits and the fact that licensing involves little financial commitment and perceptually low levels of risk, numerous uncertainties remain. Because licensing involves a market sale of embodied knowledge (technology and management) to a host country producer, there is a risk that the agreement will create a competitor, the licensee using the knowledge in ways which have not been paid for to create new products in competition with the licensor. The danger is loss of technological advantage which is the lifeblood for firms in many sectors.

The growing importance of franchising on a global scale deserves some comment. Franchising, although it is a form of licensing, often appears to be more akin to vertical integration because of the high levels of standardisation between subsidiaries. Rather than elements of company know-how being sold, franchising involves selling a total business concept. It is also a more dedicated approach to earning management fees on an international scale. Whereas many licensing agreements are set up on an ad hoc basis, often initiated by the licensee, franchising involves a committed approach to expanding geographically. In this way, companies like The Body Shop, Bennetton, MacDonald's and Kentucky Fried Chicken have all secured an extensive international franchise network.

The various types of licensing option share one common element: they all depend on the establishment of contracts with independent operators. Control is achieved via contractual arrangements rather than ownership placing great emphasis on the choice of organisation and the establishment of good, legal and workable contracts. This clearly distinguishes this group of strategies from strategic alliances and joint ventures which critically centre on the development of co-operative solutions. Part-ownership in the case of equity joint ventures and strategic collaboration in strategic alliances mean that co-operation supersedes control as the key management focus. Indeed, it is often the failure to co-operate in collaborative ventures, failing to divulge information and using know-how as a bargaining tool which leads to their demise.

Joint ventures: Joint ventures, as typically described, are co-operative business activities between two or more firms, entered into for strategic reasons, involving the creation of a separate business entity under joint control and ownership. Although many joint ventures involve equal shareholdings, this need not be the case. Equally, some joint ventures involve 'passive' partners who invest money in the operation without taking an active role in its management.

As with licensing, joint ventures involve firms pooling their resources and combining critical assets, in particular, technology from the entrant and local knowledge from the market-based partner. Nevertheless, there are many other resources which may add to the synergy of the business linkage: existing customer franchise, complementary product portfolios offering scope economy advantages, service networks, entrenched distribution networks and local business contacts. Joint ventures are not, however, without their risks and high failure rates are common. Conflicting objectives between partners, conflicting business cultures and hidden agendas can all lead to the early demise of the venture emphasising the importance of careful screening and selection procedures. Similarly, continuance of a competitive rather than co-operative ethos in the management of the joint venture means that compromises cannot be reached and common objectives not found.

Strategic alliances have been variously defined. The term is often used to describe joint ventures which do not involve equity investment by the partners and co-operative activities in areas other than manufacturing. But perhaps the most useful definition is that provided by Doz, Hamel and Prahalad (1986) which highlights several facets of strategic alliances which make them different from other collaborative ventures:

- while most joint ventures are between firms of differing sizes and capabilities, strategic alliances are usually formed between firms with similar capabilities and capacities usually from industrialised countries
- companies involved in strategic alliances are often direct competitors operating in the same product and geographic markets
- they are usually entered into for reasons other than market access or the pooling of synergistic resources.

Many coalitions of this nature involve firms based in different geographic regions and consequently operate outside of the artificially developed economic world unions. This helps to spread technologies between major trading blocs which has important ramifications for world technological development.

Foreign Direct Investment

As with the other modes of market servicing Foreign Direct Investment (FDI) involves several distinct forms. Ranging from a sales/marketing subsidiary through to a fully operational manufacturing unit producing the same products as the domestic plant, FDI includes product specific manufacturing units, plants producing components and facilities which simply assemble products in the end-user market.

Sales/marketing subsidiaries and assembly units are usually designed to maximise the benefits of having a presence in the foreign market for the purpose of gathering market information, raising company profile, reacting more quickly to market changes and being better able to secure contracts. Through a foreign market location firms are able to raise confidence about their ability to deliver and service products as they minimise the geographic distance between the source of supply and the customer.

Whatever form foreign direct investments take, firms are faced with a further important decision: do we buy or do we build? That is, they must decide whether it is more profitable to buy an existing operation or establish greenfield facilities. There are several advantages associated with buying firms (Buckley, 1986):

1 rapid market penetration is possible with faster return on capital and learning opportunities;
2 with an existing company, cultural, management and legal difficulties in the early set-up period can be more easily assimilated;
3 the purchase 'package' may include critical assets – technology, skilled indigenous managers, brand names and distribution networks which may compensate for the additional costs;
4 takeovers leave the competitive structure of the market unchanged and do not initiate competitive reaction.

Several problems may, however, be inherent in the takeover mode. First, integrating the foreign operation into the firm, not only in terms of physical systems, but also as regards the management culture and strategic direction of the two, previously independent organisations. This includes the problem of generating good communications systems between the two organisations which is fundamental to integration and co-operation. Second, the purchaser has to evaluate the worth of the assets, which is not always obvious as a result of potential synergies between the assets of the firm and the target acquisition. Finally, the costs of searching for a potential target can be high, adding to the overall cost burden of this strategy.

Regardless of these factors, greenfield facilities are generally favoured by host governments as they provide additional competition, employment and skills. Consequently, some governments offer incentive packages to firms to foster inward investment in economically depressed regions as a means of promoting economic welfare, in particular, employment. Table 7.5 identifies the nature and scope of investment incentives in a selected range of European countries. Greenfield options also give freer choice of location, investment in the most up-to-date technologies and management practices as well as financial commitment which matches existing market potential.

Table 7.5. Investment incentives in a selection of European Union countries

Type of incentive	Spain	Italy	France	UK
Grants	Parts of the country only	Parts of the country only	Parts of the country only	Whole country
Employment subsidies	Whole country	Whole country	Whole country	Parts of the country only
Tax breaks	Whole country	Parts of the country only	Whole country	Parts of the country only
Soft loans	Parts of the country only	Parts of the country only	Parts of the country only	Parts of the country only

Adapted from Maria Brindlemayer 'Comparing EC Investments and Getting the Best Deal', Journal of European Business, November/December, 1990, p. 38.

The strategic alternatives available to firms have been clearly categorised for the sake of analysis. In practice, however, there is a high degree of overlap both within and between generic groups, for example, while joint ventures are grouped together with licensing contracts and other co-operative business arrangements, they may also be regarded as a form of foreign direct investment. Similarly, sales/marketing subsidiaries may also be viewed as forms of foreign direct investment as they involve the establishment of foreign facilities. This demonstrates that boundaries between the modes of market servicing are not clear cut and the distinctions between various strategies which make up the generic modes often blurred. In addition, sales/marketing subsidiaries also demonstrate exporting is not always between a manufacturer in one country and a customer in another, which tends to be the traditional view. Exporting can involve intra firm trade between divisions of the same firm. In 1987, for example, this type of exporting is estimated to have accounted for 35 per cent of total UK outward trade flows.

It is also common for firms to employ more than one strategy at the same time in the same market possibly because different products in the portfolio demand a different approach, but also because different options complement each other in achieving a strong market position, for example, a joint venture may involve a licensing agreement with the partner designed to protect a patented technology or brand name.

Where to produce?

Assessment of strengths and weaknesses in production location invariably involves an analysis of efficiency (production costs) and effectiveness (proximate to market and flexibility to adapt to local requirements). At one level, this involves an assessment of the trade-off between centralised and decentralised production organisation benefits. Centralisation assumes that advantages accrue from conducting business in large-scale centres wherein economies of scale can be achieved in a variety of business functions. Decentralisation, on the other hand, assumes that greater advantages arise from conducting business in the host market where adaptation to the local environment and greater decision-making flexibility through local autonomy permits a higher degree of local sensitivity. Firms may therefore weigh up the strengths and weaknesses of their production organisation vis-à-vis competitors along these two dimensions.

Manufacturing strategies adopted during the last decade, however, point to a second level of analysis which extends beyond simple taxonomies of centralisation and decentralisation. Many modern day production techniques and locational strategies are the product of firms' efforts to combine advantages from both centralisation and decentralisation. Figure 7.6 summarises these strategies and demonstrates that certain approaches to manufacturing permit the achievement of both efficiency and effectiveness in production.

Flexible specialisation (alluded to in Chapter 6) permits highly efficient production in small scale manufacturing units. Again, a product of Japanese manufacturing techniques, production units of this kind, usually relying on computer aided design (CAD) and computer aided manufacturing (CAM), permit greater flexibility to respond to customer demands and service specialised needs profitably. Small batches can be produced cost effectively and thus efficiency does not rely on mass production and the pursuit of scale economies. The box example of Lucas Girling points to how an organisation can be both efficient and effective using decentralised manufacturing based on flexible production techniques.

Alternatively, some organisations, particularly those with existing operations in a number of Member States, are capitalising on the greater opportunities for plant special-isation wherein plant-economies can be achieved by individual manufacturing units concentrating on single products, or a narrow range of the company's portfolio which allows the removal of effort duplication and thus greater plant efficiency. Within the EU, the removal of barriers between Member States and thus the greater freedoms to export mean this approach to production can yield higher benefits than was the case in the past. The box insert on McCains, demonstrates the way in which an organisation with a highly dispersed EU manufacturing base can benefit in this way.

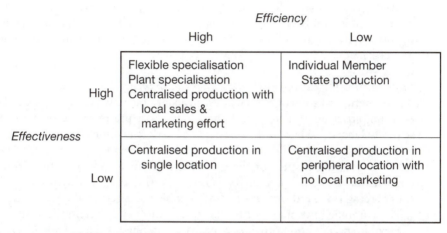

Fig. 7.6 Assessing the effectiveness of production location

Perhaps the most popular route to combining the benefits from centralisation and decentralisation is that which involves the splitting up of the value chain. By centralising production but decentralising distribution, organisations can combine the benefits of scale economies in production with local responsiveness in sales and marketing. More will be said about this in Chapter 8 (Marketing in Europe). At this stage, suffice to say that many organisations are aware that one of the easiest ways to combine efficiency and local mar-ket responsiveness is to treat the manufacturing and marketing functions as discrete entities which can be locationally divided from each other to produce better customer focus in conjunction with rationalisation and efficiency.

CASE STUDY

Lucas Girling

Lucas Engineering Group of the UK produces a wide array of parts and sub-assemblies for the motor industry. Downturn in the UK automotive industry and more exacting standards for components and parts meant that the organisation had to re-develop its strategies in the late 1970s and early 1980s to better fit with changes taking place in the industry including shifts in production away from the UK to other European Community countries by Ford and General Motors.

Lucas Girling, a division of the Lucas Group, manufactures motor breaking systems. Once able to service customers from its UK production sites, it realised in the 1980s that the trend towards close relationship development between car assemblers and component manufacturers meant far greater focus on proximity to customers. It therefore found itself in a position where decentralisation of production, and plant establishment close to major customers, was the only way it could survive in the modern environment of the car industry.

However, the company were keen not to dilute efficiency in production through the establishment of several manufacturing units. Through the adoption of 'flexible specialisation' and computer aided manufacturing, they were able to establish small plants (employing between 40–50 employees) capable of batch size, profitable production. Thus, even with decentralisation they are able to achieve both adaptability and efficiency.

Implications for European strategy development

As competition in Europe intensifies, firms are faced with a complex balancing act: ensuring efficiency on the one hand (which is a pre-requisite of competing in the wider EU market wherein the removal of barriers is improving the potential for efficiency gains) and an ability to cater for changing demand and specialised needs on the other (a growing feature of the competitive environment resulting from increased competition and thus greater focus on marketing effort). Environmental change is thus forcing the hand of firms to find flexible solutions to the production challenge which combine advantages of both centralisation and decentralisation.

Flexible specialisation provides a means of catering for these challenges in an efficient and effective way. It is by no means the only solution, and may be costly in the early stages due to the high fixed costs of establishing computer aided design and computer aided manufacturing systems. Nevertheless, as these competitive pressures are likely to continue, the incidence of this kind of strategic approach is likely to rise and the advantages accruing to those firms which adopt it likely to pose a challenge for those who cannot find equally flexible approaches to European manufacturing organisation.

CASE STUDY

McCains

McCains, the large Canadian food group, had its routes in the potato trading business. With the growing use of home refrigeration, the company identified further opportunities for development in the 1950s in frozen chipped potatoes an area in which it rapidly became market leader. The skills of the company consequently shifted from being a 'potato expert', to being adept at selling frozen food products based on potatoes.

As this necessitated the company establishing strong distribution in the frozen food sector, diversification into other frozen food products was, perhaps, an inevitable move. This was achieved through substantial merger activity as the company bought up small manufacturers of specialised frozen food products.

The McCain corporation today is now clearly positioned as a frozen food group whose products are sold under the McCain brand umbrella across North America and Europe. Its products range from frozen chips, vegetables, fruit juice, pizza, meat product and deserts, all of which have been incorporated into the corporation through acquisition.

From its early forays in frozen potato products, the company has swelled its activities by linking businesses which allow it to capitalise on its core strength as a frozen food producer.

In Europe, as elsewhere, the company expanded its activities through the acquisition of various brands which resulted in its having a wide manufacturing base spanning several Member States of the EU, each focusing on a different product group. This kind of expansion was greatly facilitated by the removal of physical barriers across Europe which means it can now capitalise on plant specialisation.

Implications for European strategy

Unlike some firms, McCains has not re-organised production to benefit from specialisation. The discrete nature of its manufacturing units are a result of its historical growth via acquisition rather than an attempt to organise its business into single product dedicated manufacturing centres. Nevertheless, McCains, like those companies now restructuring for plant specialisation, is able to benefit from greater export freedoms within the EU. The removal of physical barriers between Member States means that these individual production units can be efficiently run as stand-alone production sites without barriers to trade producing an onerous burden on the cross-exporting of goods between EU markets. It also means, that with production sites in a number of countries, McCains are close to its customers and are thus able to carefully monitor changing demand patterns and consumer needs and react accordingly. Again, therefore, the company is able to combine benefits of efficiency and responsiveness.

Using the framework outlined in Figure 7.5, organisations can assess both their and their competitors' manufacturing strengths and weaknesses along the two dimensions of efficiency and effectiveness and discover how well the organisation of their manufacturing compares. Poor performance on either dimension may well force the company to reconsider its manufacturing in line with the approaches outlined above which are becoming more popular across Europe as markets open up and competition intensifies.

Who produces?

Organisations may either choose to produce themselves, or enter into some kind of contractual relationship with another organisation to produce on their behalf (such as a licensing or franchising agreement, sub-contracting arrangement or joint venture).

Critical to the management consideration in this respect is the concept of control. Internalisation of activities (the firm producing itself) implies full control over business functions which is often believed to be a source of advantage as it gives managers free choice over strategies and operational decision making which can be hard to achieve when working with a third party. Nevertheless, firms have to trade off the additional costs incurred in gaining control, both in terms of ownership of business facilities as well as the on-going costs associated with day-to-day management of a full range of business functions, against the benefits of ownership.

Establishing and managing contracts of any sort, involves risks. As soon as an organisations gives up control of an operation (either the use of its technology to a licensee, management practices to a foreign management contractor) it passes on to the third party the responsibility to effectively manage the asset (technology, patent, trade-mark, knowledge) and maintain levels of quality. A number of issues relating to this loss of control need to be written into contracts in order to preserve a degree of control:

- situations under which the contract may be terminated (failure to fulfil obligations)
- geographical/market boundaries for exploiting the asset
- obligations for information sharing in the event of technology/process improvements
- obligations for marketing and promotion
- systems for quality testing.

Without such clear policies, there is always the risk of developing a competitor. It is risks such as this, which make the contractual route to expansion less attractive than those which involve ownership and control of assets. Despite this, however, as outlined in Chapter 5, the European Commission has set out its stall to promote contractual activity between EU players as a means of facilitating technology transfer and thus raise the technology base of European firms per se.

The above appears to suggest that success is linked to control, which may only be achieved through ownership. Relating back to the earlier discussion concerning the success of Japanese firms in the car industry (developing relationships with their suppliers), it is evident that competitive success can be derived from co-operation rather than control with firms focusing on core strengths rather than a wide range of, sometimes unrelated, business disciplines. This has led to an increasing trend in sub-contracting. By 'hiving off' parts of the production process, it is possible to improve efficiency (lowering fixed costs) and raise flexibility (switching between alternative suppliers to adapt to changing demand patterns and technology). An example of this is provided in the case study on the strategies employed by Japanese car manufacturers.

Assessment of the company's position with regard to who undertakes production therefore needs to involve the cost implications associated with contractual relationships as well as control and risks. The associated comparative matrix is shown in Fig. 7.7.

Costs \ *Control*	High	Low
Low	Sub-contracting	Licensing Franchising Management contracts
High	Internalisation of production	Extensive brand licensing

Fig. 7.7 Assessing the benefits of internal v external production

Fig. 7.7 suggests that 'best practice' with regard to the internalisation versus externalisation decision is sub-contracting, the approach affording both cost and control maximisation. Again, however, firms must consider their position not just in terms of best practice, but in terms of the behaviour of their competitors. This approach may, therefore, be a pre-requisite for organisations operating in industries where leading competitors have taken this route, but not in sectors where firms continue to protect their technological and brand advantages (such as in the pharmaceutical industry), where quality control is critical to competitive success or where component inputs and sub-assemblies do not feature. The matrix is also over-simplified. The development of water-tight licensing/franchising/management contracts can also afford high levels of control, particularly for organisations experienced in these operational modes. Many multinational firms have derived great success from the careful management and control of multiple contractual arrangements: Coca-Cola's bottle licensing agreements, McDonald's multinational franchising agreements and Holiday Inn's management contracts all pay testament to the fact that well constructed contracts can result in good levels of control.

CASE STUDY

Japanese car manufacturers

The success of Japanese car producers in the global marketplace owes much to the introduction of flexible production systems.

> ... before you can make things flexibly, you must first make them simple. Simplifying is difficult because each new car is more complex and more costly to develop than the last. So the trick is to get somebody else to develop parts of the car for you – and ideally to build them as well ... Modular manufacturing involves designing and assembling the entire car as a series of sub-assemblies or modules. New modules can be developed directly to replace an existing one, allowing cars to be changed easily.

> (*The Economist*, 29 July 1989)

The contracting out of major parts of the business by leading Japanese manufacturers (exemplified in Figure 7.8) introduced a new dimension into the value chain of large Japanese firms which gives them many advantages over their rivals.

Implications for European strategy development
Within the car industry, the Japanese have set the standard for new production processes which are based on co-operative solutions rather than internal control of business functions. Contract manufacturing also adds to the flexibility of organisations, as assemblers can switch between suppliers (and take advantage of better quality or new technology) or work co-operatively with suppliers to set specifications for new components as the needs of the market change.

Contracting out of parts of the value chain also means organisations can dedicate more time and resource to other value chain activities – technology development, product commercialisation and marketing, all of which are becoming increasingly important within the EU as competition intensifies.

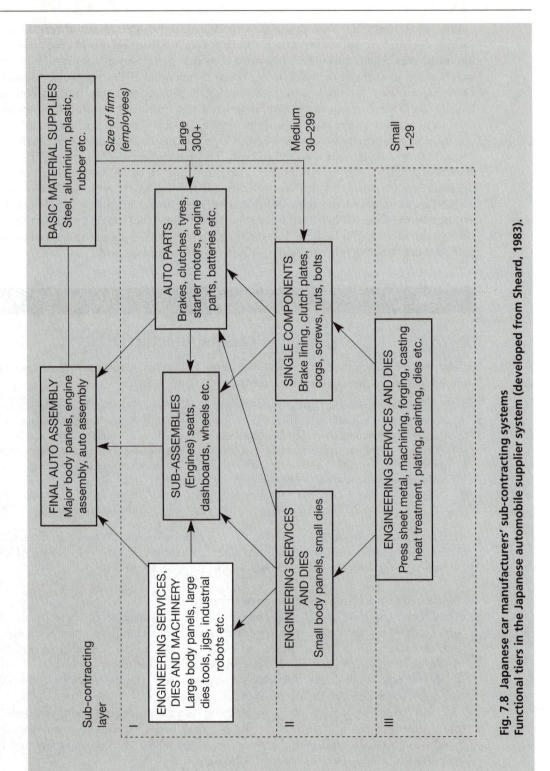

Fig. 7.8 Japanese car manufacturers' sub-contracting systems
Functional tiers in the Japanese automobile supplier system (developed from Sheard, 1983).

Such practices are not limited to the car industry and firms in other sectors, taking their lead from the advantages which the Japanese have demonstrated accrue from this type of organisational practice, are adopting strategies which rely much more on contracting out of key parts of the value chain.

The worst scenario in Fig. 7.8 deserves some comment. Some organisations with well-established brand names are prepared to license their brand for the production of products in which they have no expertise. While this assists the company develop its overall corporate image and raise income the number of these contracts (Gucci, for example, boasting as many as 14 000 before such over-extension resulted in the collapse of the brand name) and the diverse nature of products associated with the brand, heightens the risk of diluting the quality image if any of these products fall below acceptable quality levels.

Importantly, companies must ask themselves:

- Who produces on our behalf?
- What is the rationale behind this decision?
- Who produces on our customers' behalf?
- Why may they have opted for this approach?
- If our approach is different from our competitors, what strengths and weaknesses emerge as a result of our alternative approach?
- On the basis of these strengths and weaknesses, do we need to consider altering the way in which we produce?

Organisation

As the European operating environment continues to change, firms are facing up to new challenges for organisational re-design and re-structuring. A wide variety of forces are coming into play which are changing the way in which organisations view their systems and structures. Some of the critical factors are summarised in Table 7.6 which highlights some of the pervasive forces impacting on industrial organisation and the possible strategic implications.

Again, central to the strategic challenge is the trade-off between centralisation and decentralisation (scale economies versus local responsiveness). Historically, most organisations operating across Europe developed decentralised business structures with a great deal of autonomy being afforded to national operating subsidiaries. The rationale for this approach was country/market diversity which raised demands for local adaptation of both products and strategies to support those products (marketing strategies in particular). Local operating units therefore had to be afforded a high level of decision making autonomy to make necessary strategy changes to cater for local nuances.

With greater harmonisation of business standards and operating conditions across Europe, opportunities have now emerged for organisations to look again at their organisational design and find ways of integrating various parts of the business to achieve greater efficiency through standardisation and the eradication of duplication. But how far should a firms go in establishing common practices? The table includes an important caveat: while some industrial sectors are exhibiting signs of harmonisation and thus greater homogeneity, there remain differences between the Member States in terms of taste, consumer behaviour, needs and wants. Firms therefore have to look at the balance between central-isation and decentralisation not as an either/or decision, but as a continuum where centralisation lies at one extreme, and decentralisation the other. Fig. 7.9, based on the work of Blackwell, Bizet, Child and Hensley (1993) typifies levels of integration across different parts of this continuum.

Table 7.6. Factors impacting on firms' European organisational structures

Critical factors	Likely impact
Europe-wide	
The Social Chapter	Greater attention to: – workplace issues – worker participation – equality.
Greater freedom to operate on a pan-European scale	Business rationalisation and focus on a smaller number of efficient operating units. Greater opportunities to integrate various parts of the European business. Greater opportunities to treat Europe as a single market and effect greater standardisation in business approach (eg. telecommunications, computing, car manufacturing). Remaining cultural barriers between the 15 Member States which makes complete standardisation difficult to achieve (eg. food, electrical goods, services).
International	
The formation of trading blocs	Organisation of the business into regional trading units with individual headquarters in the major triad regions.
The establishment of integrated industry networks	The establishment of joint ventures and strategic alliances as a means of penetrating markets and developing new technologies.
Technological developments	Technological systems now available to enhance business integration and break down the barriers between separate departments and businesses within the multinational.

The most effective organisational structures appear to be those which fall within the middle tier of the continuum affording some advantages of both centralised and decentralised structures – Peters and Waterman's 'simultaneous loose–tight controls'. Recent research on managing international firms (Hedlund and Rolander, 1990) points to the development of global *heterarchies* characterised by multiple centres of control (either functional, geographic or product-based). This involves organisations searching for com-plementarities between the business environment and their operations, using environmental opportunities as a way of complementing their strengths. A heterarchicial firm in Europe may therefore have its financial centre in London (close to the London stock market) its R&D centre in Germany (in a centre of technological excellence where good researchers are abundant), its European headquarters in Paris (responsible for co-ordinating EU-wide strategy development), production units in the UK, Italy and the Netherlands (the latter responsible for distribution co-ordination) and ad hoc teams for global brand develop-ment. No one dimension (product, location, or function) is superordinate. All are given an equal weighting in terms of their contribution to company effectiveness. Within this for-mat, subsidiaries are therefore not just 'outposts' of the organisation responsible for implementing strategies at a regional/market level, they are part of a complex network of learning where experiences and knowledge acquired locally are communicated to the cen-tre as a way of shaping future direction for the corporation as a whole.

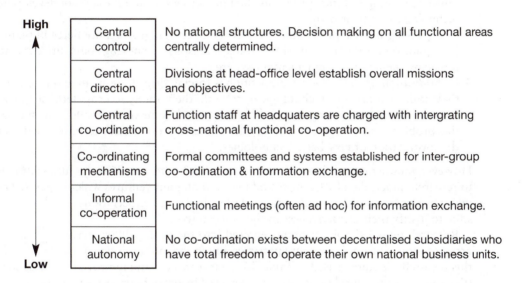

Fig. 7.9 Continuum of business integration

Heterarchies are therefore more task oriented than functionally determined, which enhances their potential for flexibility and responsiveness. The guiding direction is solving common problems, and this is achieved through the sharing of information, knowledge and resources. Hedlund and Rolander (1990) describe organisations such as this as *holo-graphic* with information being stored and acted upon at all levels and not monopolised by strategic thinkers at the centre. But how can such a loose affiliation be integrated? The answer lies in normative mechanisms – 'Corporate culture, management ethics, style and similar concepts become critical in understanding why a heterarchy does not break down into anarchy'. (Hedlund and Rolander, 1990 pp. 25–26). Sophisticated global systems for information exchange and telecommunications now provide a facilitating mechanism for the establishment of these highly integrated, business structures.

A further feature of the heterarchy is the flexibility to establish coalitions with other parties as a means of building synergies in the global (or European) environment. The establishment of co-operative linkages, whether on a one-off basis or as part of a network of synergistic linkages is becoming an important dimension of many firms' strategy development, particularly those in hi-technology sectors. This is changing the organisational challenge for many firms for whom the management of external relationships, and the maintenance of their position within complex global networks, is becoming as important as managing internal relations between different parts of their business.

In the business environment of the late 1980s and early 1990s, several changes initiated greater use of co-operative agreements in international business activity:

1 *The increasing involvement of small firms in international business activity.* The size of firms becoming involved in international activity has steadily fallen over the years as domestic pressures have persuaded many organisations to look for foreign expansion opportunities. Joint ventures permit these firms to reduce their capital outlay and spread risks in international expansion.
2 *Increasing costs of R&D.* The costs of technological development are ever-spiralling upwards making it difficult for individual firms to withstand the costs of developing new technologies on their own.
3 *The growing intensity of competition.* As competition grows more fierce in many markets, joint ventures may be used for strategic reasons – removing competitive threats and replacing them with complementary synergies.
4 *Hybridisation of technology.* Competition is forcing firms to re-focus and rationalise. As they limit their areas of technological strength, their ability to cross-fertilise knowledge between discrete product groups is being restricted. Joint ventures allow them to redress this problem and co-operate with organisations in more diverse technological areas for the formulation of new basic technologies.

However, failure rates for joint ventures remain high. *Business Weekly* (July 1986) alluded to research undertaken by Coopers and Lybrand on joint ventures which suggested that as many as seven out of ten joint ventures fail to live up to expectations – so how is it possible to justify their attractiveness in the modern world?

Research on 4 192 joint ventures entered into the in the 1980s revealed a fairly broad array of motives for joint venture participation in the international arena. The findings of this research are summarised in Table 7.7. Market access and improved business structure (the ability to enter markets which are protected by entry barriers such as excess capacity, tied distribution channels, and the potential to enhance firms' participation in a larger number of geographic regions, attaining a toe-hold in markets from which future strategic encroachment can be developed), technological complementarity (the existence of common goals for technology development and thus the potential to share resources and skills in new product development) and reductions in innovation time quite clearly emerge as the driving forces behind the modern day joint venture. Certain changes in weighting may have occurred since this research was completed, but it is unlikely that the overall picture has changed significantly.

European firms in the 1990s, keen to expand their international coverage and their technological strengths, are likely to continue to see advantages in entering into co-operative business deals with other industry players in an attempt to maximise synergies in their strategy development. Indeed, some proponents of this route go as far as to suggest that joint ventures are essential to long-term strategic success:

Table 7.7. Strategic motivations for joint ventures 1980–1989

Industrial sector	Number of alliances	Technological complementarity	Basic R&D	High cost/ risk	Lack of finance	Reduce time for innovation	Market entry/ monitoring	Market assess/ structure
Biotechnology	847	35	10	1	13	31	15	13
New materials	430	38	–	1	3	32	16	31
Computers	198	28	2	1	2	22	10	51
Industrial automation	278	41	4	–	3	32	7	31
Microelectronics	383	33	5	3	3	33	6	52
Software	344	38	2	1	4	36	11	24
Telecommunications	366	28	1	11	2	28	16	35
Other IT	91	29	2	1	–	28	24	35
Automotive	205	27	2	4	2	22	4	52
Aviation/Defence	228	34	–	36	1	26	8	13
Chemicals	410	16	1	7	1	13	8	51
Consumer electronics	58	19	–	2	–	19	9	53
Food and drink	42	17	–	1	–	10	7	43
Heavy electric/Power	141	31	4	36	1	10	11	23
Instruments/Medical	95	35	2	–	4	40	10	28
Other	76	9	–	35	–	6	8	23
Total	4 192	31	5	6	4	28	11	32

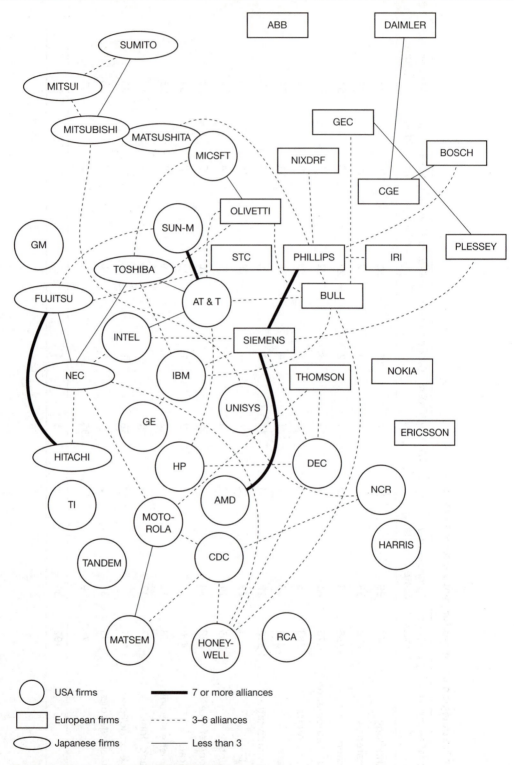

Fig. 7.10 Strategic partnering in the IT sector

In stable competitive environments, the loss of control exacts little penalty. Not so, however, in a changeable world of rapidly globalising markets and industries – a world of conveying consumer tastes, rapidly spreading technology, escalating fixed costs and growing protectionism. Globalisation mandates alliances, makes them absolutely essential to strategy … In the fluid global market place, it is no longer possible or desirable for single organisations to be entirely self-sufficient. Collaboration is the value of the future. Alliances are the structure for the future.

(Bleeke and Ernst, 1993)

Alliances are thus viewed not only as a means of entering new markets, spreading risk, and combining skills for new product development, but an important means of raising flexibility in the development and maintenance of competitive advantage.

The trend in joint venture activity is also likely to be further enhanced by government incentives for joint research projects. The European Strategic Programme for Research and Development (ESPRIT), Research and Development in Advanced Communication Technology for Europe (RACE), Basic Research in Industrial Technology for Europe (BRITE) and European Research in Advanced Materials (EURAM) all favour joint project bids from firms in more than one Member State. The underlying intent is to ensure cross-fertilisation of new technologies between European-based firms as a means of enhancing EU-wide technology strengths capable of competing with Japanese and USA equivalents.

Industry networks provide an extension of this trend towards joint venture development. Certain industrial sectors are now characterised by complex cross-shareholdings, formal equity joint ventures and informal strategic alliances between a wide array of leading competitors, creating networks of business activity wherein organisations are able to address limitations in their capabilities by combining forces with competitors. Many of these alliances are project-based, firms entering into arrangements with others to solve a particular problem, the venture then being disbanded or a further contract negotiated. Figure 7.10 highlights the nature and scope of such networks in the IT industry between 1985–1989, clearly demonstrating the interrelated links between the main players, very few of whom now choose to operate alone outside of this interrelated structure. Indeed, it is possible to argue that those that do are unlikely to derive maximum flexibility in operations, relying solely on their extant, internal knowledge base, skills and competitive advantages. The box insert on AT&T provides an interesting case in point and demonstrates how one firm is using joint ventures to secure a large number of diverse business objectives.

CASE STUDY

AT&T

AT&T, the US telecommunications concern, is the world's networking leader providing communication services and products as well as network equipment and computer systems to a wide array of consumers including individual customers and corporations. Total revenues in 1993 were $67 156 million and net income $3 807 million. With representation in 200 countries worldwide, AT&T can clearly be characterised as a leading multinational.

The telecommunications industry is truly global. Firms regard the world-stage as their marketplace, and thus regional divisions such as the Single European Market simply carve out local operating conditions, but do not deter organisations from pursuing global objectives. In this sense, AT&T is like many of the EU telecommunications concerns, pursuing global operations which will consolidate company efficiency and effectiveness.

AT&T's alliance strategy is largely based on the company's need to learn and rapidly assimilate new technologies, essential for future success in a radically changing environment. Many of the new developments in the industry are based on technologies and knowledge outside of the traditional scope of the organisation. The introduction of fibre optics, wireless communication, microwave transmission, faster microprocessors and new transmission materials have redefined the communications sector and opened up new potential for interaction between computers and communications through digitally-based switching and signalling systems. In order to stay abreast of these changes, AT&T has developed both internal and external systems for technology development and market exploitation based round internal R&D effort, external co-operative technology alliances, increased investment in target markets, and joint ventures with distributors and local handlers.

Table 7.9 identifies a number of alliances entered into by AT&T to re-align its technology focus and re-develop its compentencies to exploit this technology worldwide. Within Europe, deals for consolidating market presence and coverage combine with co-operative links to support the company's move into the next millenium.

The failed joint venture with Olivetti deserves some comment. Essentially, the venture failed due to poor communication between the partners and cultural differences which the established business structures could not overcome. The agreement was carved out such that AT&T was responsible for technology, Olivetti for marketing. On-going rivalry, however, meant that technology transfer was retarded and thus so the implementation of marketing plans. Delays in technology transfer stemmed from AT&T's involvement with Philips, who resented AT&Ts alliance with Olivetti seeing it as a threat to their future agreements in office automation (Zahra and Elhagrasey, 1994). Nevertheless, the venture provided an important learning experience for AT&T not just in terms of learning how to deal with high profile, state-owned, European companies, but in managing networks and interrelated alliances between different industry players.

But this is not the end of AT&T's interests in Europe. The company is also looking closely at building local relationships with national Public Telephony Organisations (PTOs) as a means of gaining access to customer networks throughout the EU who are well placed to service the needs of corporate customers, one of the highest growth sectors within the current global telecommunications industry. These organisations have an advantage over the computer and system integration specialists given:

1 they are privileged players in the European market (due to their historically protected status as sole providers) and are used to dealing with each other;
2 many multinational firms already number among the PTOs' top customers;
3 many are technologically advanced in terms of modern telecoms technology.

There has thus been talk of AT&T entering into a partnership with Unisource (which is jointly owned by PTT Telecom Netherlands, Sweden Telia and Swiss Telecom PTT) which already has national operating companies in all the major markets of

Table 7.8. AT&T global alliance development

Partner	Technology	Intent
NEC	Customised chips and computer-design tools	Learn new core technologies from NEC, increase sales position in Japan.
	Mobile phones	Penetrate cellular phone markets; compatible standards.
Mitsubishi	SRAM and gallium-arsenide chips	Increase sales in Japan: learn new semiconductor technologies.
Italtel	Telecommunications	Expand beachhead in Europe.
NV Philips	Circuitboards	Market and technology access: venture purchased in 1990.
Lucky-Gold Star	Fibre optics, telecommunications, circuits	Entry into Asian markets; technology sharing agreement.
Telefonica	Telecommunications and integrated circuits	Expand production and marketing beachhead in Europe.
Zenith	High-definition television	Apply and learn digital compression technology to set new broadcast standards in the UK and global markets.
Intel	Personal computer networks and integrated circuits	Share manufacturing technology and capacity. Develop UNIX computer operating system for local area networks.
Hoya	Photomarks and semiconductor equipment	Develop ion-beam marks and mask design software in Japan and USA.
Mannesmann	Microwave radio gear and cellular phone technology	Serve as OEM supplier to German firm.
Go Corp.	Pen-based computers and wireless network	Set industry standards for telecommunications power and range.
Olivetti	Personal computers	Failed in 1988.
Eo Corp.	Personal communicator devices	Create new hand-held computers.
Matsushita,	Microprocessors NEC & Toshiba	Encourage new technology standards for Hobbit-based systems.
McCaw Cellular	Cellular telephones	Secure downstream market in the USA.

'Offensive and defensive uses of alliances', Lei, D., Long Range Planning, Vol. 26, No. 4, p. 34 (1993).

Europe. Unisource was established to compete with France Telecom, Deutsche Telecom and British Telecom, all of whom boast significant scale advantages and already developed global linkages and networks.

Implications for European strategy

The case of AT&T enables us to draw out a number of important points relating to current strategic operations in Europe:

(a) Europe is only one arm of many organisations' global business activities. However, learning and experience derived elsewhere can, through careful management, add to a firm's competitiveness within the EU. On this point, it is also worth highlighting the fact that in some industries today, a company's national affiliation is far less important than its ability to react to changing market conditions. Thus AT&T is as well-placed as many of the EU's indigenous players to take advantage of the new freedoms offered in the telecoms industry.

(b) Joint ventures and strategic alliances can enhance a company's position along a number of critical dimensions. Here there is evidence of technology driven ventures (for learning and direct technology transfer), market access driven operations, and co-operative links for 'buying into' existing customer franchises.

(c) Managing linkages on a network basis is far from straightforward. Alliances with one organisation may conflict with objectives of relationships with other players leading to the breakdown of the venture or lack of trust. It is clear then that co-ordination of business linkages needs to be centralised so that firms can assess the impact of new joint ventures on existing business relationships.

(d) In markets where technology change is rapid, individual firms cannot hope to boast strengths in all areas. Linking up with other firms in related business technologies is thus critical to shared learning and the development of an increasingly competitive knowledge base.

But how can organisations assess the best organisational mix for their firm and change their structures accordingly? The emergent approach to solving this problem across Europe lies in greater attention to the management of tasks and functions rather than the management of business units. Thus firms need to react to changes in the environment (outlined in Table 7.6) and provide mechanisms to solve each problem. Some examples of the ways in which this may be achieved are outlined in Table 7.9.

The examples outlined in Table 7.9 demonstrate that there is no simple blueprint and even within functions and tasks, the ability to develop a mix of systems is likely to yield the greatest advantages. The effectiveness of this mix will invariably rest on organisations' willingness to introduce advanced communications systems which will offer organisational flexibility in developing innovative solutions to organisational problems. The box insert on Nestlé offers practical insight into the way one organisation has attempted to solve the problem of achieving a 'balance' in its organisational structure. For many European firms, successful organisational design will necessitate a review of existing structures. Many organisation have, through their historical development, forged structures where primary strategic responsibilities rest at the individual country level. This is partly due to the cultural differences between European Member States, but also the perceptual barriers of

Table 7.9. Task and function organisational development

Task/Function	Organisational implications
Social Chapter requirements	General objectives set centrally, implementation and responsibility charged to local subsidiaries. Co-ordination between groups will enhance shared experiences of implementation.
Business rationalisation	Decisions on rationalisation (which may involve business closure) need to be handled centrally in order that they reflect the needs of the company as a whole and not the concerns of the threatened business which will invariably resist such organisational plans. Consultation across various parts of the groups will be essential in determining the impact on different parts of the firm of business closure.
Greater potential to standardise products for the wider market	Formal integration mechanisms are likely to yield areas where greater homogeneity offers potential for increased standardisation. Where opportunities exist, centrally organised policies for branding and marketing development, possibly handled by a central 'product champion' responsible for the products' success across Europe may provide the best solution.
Continued differences in culture and business practices	Where integrated committees and discussion groups demonstrate little scope for standardisation, the retention of local autonomy to develop products and services for individual customer groups will provide the best approach.

operating across Europe. There remains an ideology among many European managers that the EU can never be a single market. Imbued with knowledge of past wars and conflicts there remains a high degree of uncertainty and mistrust. This is something absent from US and Japanese managers' visions of the Single Market, with evidence to suggest that the US and Japanese are seeing the advantages of a single Europe more readily than their European counterparts.

CASE STUDY

Nestlé

Nestlé is Europe's largest branded goods company. In 1992, group turnover stood at Sfr 54 500 million, 26 632 million of which was generated in Europe. The company is a true multinational enterprise. In 1992 the company boasted 482 worldwide factories in 68 countries spanning the USA, South America, Canada, Australia, New Zealand, the Far East, the Middle East, Africa and Europe.

With such a spread of activities one of Nestlé's major corporate concerns is establishing the roles and responsibilities of both head office and subsidiary managers and the organisational structures capable of facilitating effective management of its extensive operations.

The head office retains control over the company's strategic direction. Essentially it has responsibility for:

- geographic expansion and concentration
- acquisition decisions
- research on world commodities and mandates
- divestment of poorly performing products and non-desirable assets acquired through acquisition
- monitoring of performance reports
- control of money (including in which denomination it is to be held)
- product research (to ensure duplication kept to a minimum)

With this responsibility, the head office operation is able to keep a careful watch on overall business activities and shape the overall direction of the company. A good example of this has arisen recently in terms of the firm's plans for geographic expansion. Greater attention to LDCs (particularly China) as the potential areas for future growth can be directed from the centre. In relation to acquisition decisions, central control enables the organisation to maintain its policy as an independent manufacturer/wholesaler/marketer, avoiding vertical expansion into supply chains (plantations) or distribution networks (retailers).

The importance of controlling acquisitions centrally cannot be overstated. Based on a policy of expansion through acquisition rather than greenfield development, on the grounds that purchasing existing companies with recognised brands and customer franchises is more cost effective than attempting to establish new businesses worldwide, the company is often faced with problems of integrating new businesses into the existing corporate network. This is further hampered by the fact that often acquired businesses do not wholly fit with the company's overall corporate direction and thus require careful post-acquisition management, often involving divestment and rationalisation. For example, following the acquisition of the Buitoni-Perugina operation, the organisation were forced to divest the printing and packaging business which did not fit the organisation's future development strategy. Equally, following the takeover of Rowntree in the UK, the organisation were forced to rationalise production activities in the UK, a contentious issue which could not be charged to local management.

Although this appears to suggest the company is highly centralised, there exist various layers of responsibility and organisational co-ordination below this top corporate level. In the first instance, product groups have been established at head office level to monitor and control the performance of different parts of the portfolio globally. These groups ensure that all subsidiaries are making positive contributions to the head office, and attempt to highlight and solve problems when they arise. At subsidiary level, area managers have great discretion in determining local marketing effort. Local managers have discretion over take-up of new products, being able to refuse their addition into the portfolio if they are considered unacceptable to local market needs. In addition, they are given freedom to adapt products to suit local market conditions as long as the adaptations are not considered harmful to the company's overall objectives. Nestlé's flagship coffee – Nescafé instant – is consequently blended and coloured slightly differently in a wide array of world markets.

In the 1980s, under the control of the Helmut Maucher, the company has continued to devolve power to the local regions and simplify head office procedures in an attempt to make the whole organisation more responsive to the highly dynamic global marketplace. Flatter organisational structures at corporate level and simplified reporting procedures have speeded up decision making. At the corporate level, general managers have been employed who are responsible for different regional groups, rather than different product groups. At the same time, in an effort to ensure that such devolvement of power does not result in less overall control and integration, the company has established policies to bring corporate and subsidiary management closer together:

- Moving individuals between jobs at subsidiary level and jobs at head office level. This encourages permeation of company culture.
- Meetings and training programmes which bring managers from various subsidiaries together. This facilitates the cross-fertilisation of information and knowledge.
- Encouragement of language development so that head office staff can converse with managers in their subsidiaries in at least French and English, and preferably Spanish and German.

European management implications

This brief overview of some of the policies and practices of Nestlé highlights a number of important issues for organisational design and management:

- Many companies now operating in Europe are not only concerned with developing effective systems for Europe, but are looking at their overall global activities. The establishment of regional group managers at corporate level demonstrates Nestlé's awareness of the growing trend towards organising their business according to global regional development and the growing power of the triad. (This theme is re-visited in Chapter 12.)
- Organisations need to find mechanisms for both centralisation and decentralisation. Nestlé's decision to centralise up-stream and support activities (R&D, finance, acquisitions etc.) but de-centralise downstream activities (particularly sales and marketing effort) is not unique. Work by Ohmae (1985) based on Porter's value chain theory, highlighted this tendency. Although it is possible to argue that Europe may provide scope for increased centralisation, continued cultural differences and tastes (particularly for products such as foodstuffs) mean this trend may be slow.
- Integrating mechanisms are a powerful tool to ensure closer co-operation between devolved parts of complex organisations. Regular meetings and briefings and the circulation of staff emerged here as methods by which this may be achieved. Other alternatives might include established systems for information exchange through IT, intra-group newsletters, combined technology forums etc.

European managers must shrug off these beliefs if they are to develop integrated and flexible EU organisations and move away from the traditional 'federation' structures. Michael Porter (1991) suggested that a failure to do so, will not serve European firms well in the new EU operating environment:

> One of the things that Europe 1992 integration will do is hasten the process by which larger European companies move from confederations of subsidiaries to become truly integrated, world-wide competitors. For each product line, there will be a clear home base, with some or many outside the home country. European companies have tended to do well in businesses that are essentially a collection of national markets but not so well in the truly global arena.

Technology management

With technology change featuring so large in the changing global business environment, the challenge of managing technological development deserves some comment. Up until relatively recently many multinational firms took the decision to centralise their global R&D activities for a variety of reasons: first, the need to control the development of new technologies on which the company's future competitiveness may rest; second, economies of scale in R&D where very large amounts of resource can be concentrated into single centres with no duplication of effort; finally, the fear that foreign research departments may be a source of leakage of ideas and knowledge.

Changes in the global environment and the carving up of the world market into three leading global centres, many of which yield 'centres of excellence' in research in particular industries, has changed the thinking of technology managers in many multinational firms. Decentralisation of R&D functions has begun to feature in the strategies of global firms as they seek to derive maximum advantage from a global organisation. The following outline of various types of R&D organisational development, derived by Bartlett and Ghoshal (1990), explain this thinking.

Centre for global: This is the approach typically followed by multinationals (outlined above). While there are advantages in terms of control and scale economies, this approach runs the risk of being insensitive to local market demands in the leading markets of the world.

Local for local: This approach suggests conducting research in all target markets in order that the technologies which are developed match with local market demands. While beneficial in terms of local adaptation, the approach implicitly involves duplication of effort and a tendency for subsidiaries to 're-invent the wheel' in an attempt to maintain the local autonomy.

Locally leveraged: Under this arrangement management can take the most creative and innovative developments from its various subsidiaries and share them with other subsidiaries worldwide. The main disadvantage here is that there are frequently impediments to transferring products from one market to another – particularly cultural differences and local market demand condition.

Globally linked: The final approach (promoted by Bartlett and Ghoshal as the optimum solution to the technology development challenge) involves the establishment of flexible linkages between research teams from various global centres. Structures of this kind allow companies to exploit synergies in technology development at the same time as exploiting local leverage advantages. The major drawback to this approach is the cost of co-ordination and the complexities of managing the linkages on an on-going basis.

None of the approaches, therefore, emerges as adeptly suited to the changing global or European environment. Each has its advantages and disadvantages. This points to managers developing flexible systems which allow them to maximise a variety of advantages from the different approaches, while at the same time minimising the costs and managerial complexities. This may mean having major centres for R&D in a number of key global locations, with a series of local R&D support offices acting more as idea generating centres rather than capital intensive research laboratories.

Technology management is not, however, simply a case of organising R&D facilities. It is about developing systems for monitoring technology advances and ensuring new products are in keeping with customer needs (which will be discussed in more detail in Chapter 8 in relation to product decisions for Europe), ensuring adequate technological systems for competitive production (which was, to a great extent, discussed in relation to new production techniques and the growing propensity of organisations to consider flexible production) and joint ventures and alliances in new technology development (discussed in relation to European organisational issues).

Financial management

Financial management within the context of Europe is inextricably linked to the management of risk and organisational structures which dictate the complexity of financial flows throughout the EU operation.

The management of financial risk centres on two important issues:

1 ensuring payment for goods and services (particularly important for small firms for whom this issue can deter them from expanding across European borders);
2 effective exchange rate management, ensuring the firm is not adversely affected by translation exposure (restating financial statements in the currency of the head office wherein poor performance may be the result of a weakening of currencies and not actual sales performance) transaction exposure (the risk involved when paying bills and receiving payments which involves firms timing their financial flows to coincide with beneficial exchange rates) and economic exposure (involving the pricing of goods, sourcing of parts and investment decisions).

The move towards a single European currency will obviously eliminate exchange risks altogether by ensuring that transactions are conducted in one, rather than several Member State currencies. In the interim period leading to full EU monetary union (assuming this is an inevitable development) protection against such risk rests on the wide array of options available to firms for financing their exports and hedging against financial exposure. A summary of options available to UK firms is provided in Table 7.10. While other countries sport their own institutions for protecting firms against financial risks in international dealings the types of policy and practice are similar.

Financial risk can also be managed through the establishment of joint ventures which permit organisations to share the cost burden of major projects. IBM (USA), Toshiba (Japan) and Siemens (Germany) have entered into a joint venture to develop sophisticated computer memory chips which may become the industry standard for the next decade. The costs of such a venture are obviously high, and while the successful development of a new product will undoubtedly bring prosperity, each individual organisation was averse to taking on the risk alone.

Large firms with a number of EU-subsidiaries also must concern themselves with

Table 7.10. Options for managing financial risk

Option	Characteristics
Pre-shipment finance	
Export Credit Guarantee Department	Where a company is in possession of a suitable ECGD insurance policy (see below), banks are often prepared to advance finance for exports.
Confirming House	Confirming Houses act as principal in the sale of a company's goods to a foreign customer and thus bear the risk of payment default.
Factors	Acceptance by factors is discretionary, and they tend to only back firms with a good domestic record and good exporting prospects. Factors purchase between 70–80 per cent of invoice debts meaning invoices can be turned into cash immediately. The balance is due on receipt of payment and is usually an agreed percent on sales plus an interest charge.
Post-shipment finance	
Bills of Exchange	The seller issues a bill of exchange to the buyer. Once signed by the buyer he is legally obliged to pay the due amount as specified. Can cause problems when the goods are shipped before the bill is signed (particularly in the case of air-freight) or where the buyer decides to return the goods.
Documentary Letter of Credit	A written undertaking by a bank to pay the exporter for his goods providing he complies with the conditions laid down in the document. The bank is therefore responsible for determining the creditworthiness of the customer and not the exporting firm. However, a single mistake in the document or any point of non-compliance means the bank will refuse to pay.
Advance against a Bill of Exchange	When a bank has evidence goods have been shipped, they will negotiate and buy from the exporter the bill of exchange with deductions for interest and commission.
The Export Credit Guarantee Department	Provides insurance for exporters and those financing export credits against political and exchange transfer risks as well as commercial (default or insolvency) risks. These can be negotiated through banks thus avoiding the need to deal directly with the ECGD.
Hedging instruments	
Lead and Lag strategies	Lead strategies dictate collecting foreign money owed before they are due if the currency is expected to weaken and making payments before they are due if the currency is expected to strengthen. With a lag strategy the company will delay making payments if the currency is expected to weaken, or delay receiving payments if the currency is expected to strengthen.
Foreign exchange	Banks will provide forward cover for foreign exchange risk, quoting a price in the domestic currency which must be paid on a certain specified date in the future.
Currency options	Options to buy and sell currency within a given specified time period which can allow for improvements in future exchange rates.

developing effective structures for financial planning and control. There are three basic alternative structures:

Polycentric – in which the head office is treated as a holding company with decisions decentralised to subsidiaries which run as separate profit centres.

Ethnocentric – wherein subsidiaries are treated as extensions of the domestic operation with decision-making and money handling conducted centrally.

Geocentric – where financial planning is conducted globally with some decentralisation of activities and some centralisation.

Relating back to the Nestlé case, it is possible to argue they have adopted a geocentric approach. Subsidiaries are charged with the responsibility of generating profit although this is monitored by head office. The profits generated, flow back to the centre where they are managed in the global interests of the organisation. The subsidiaries are therefore not responsible for decisions about the re-investment of monies locally. Rather new investment directions are the decision of the headquarters.

Two other critical financial planning mechanisms cut across this overall simplified structure and thus deserve some comment:

- funds positioning
- multilateral netting.

Funds positioning relates to the practice of moving monies through internal business networks as a means of minimising tax burdens, exchange translation, and tariff payments. Within international firms, many financial transactions are internal, with business units in one country selling goods and services to subsidiaries in other countries. Indeed, it is estimated as much as one third of all international export transactions are intra-firm. Firms therefore have a high degree of flexibility in moving money around the globe by manipulating their transfer pricing. Within the context of Europe, the most likely incentive for this kind of activity is continued differences in corporation tax between the Member States. In 1991, for example, the corporate tax rate in France was 34 per cent (substantially reduced from 50 per cent in 1988), the UK 35 per cent and Germany 50 per cent (one of the highest levels for any industrialised country).

Transfer pricing allows firms to minimise their tax burdens by 'moving' monies into lower tax states. This is highlighted in Fig. 7.11. The French firm, by raising the prices it charges to its German subsidiary, can effectively move profits from Germany to France, where it will be taxed at the lower rate.

The manipulation of internal pricing dictates organisations have a degree of central control over their financial planning which means that the management of funds positioning for profit maximisation is not possible within polycentric structures. There is also the possibility that firms employing such policies will de-motivate subsidiary managers who continue to exhibit low profit margins although this may be overcome by compiling data for typical arm's-length transactions.

Funds positioning also permits the movement of funds for strategic reasons. Take, for example, an instance where a subsidiary, faced with aggressive price competition in the local region, wishes to reduce prices to maintain market share and levels of profitability. Transfer pricing would allow the firm, in the short-term, to cross-subsidise the subsidiary's activities by charging a lower price for finished goods or components.

Multilateral netting is also relevant to organisations which have a series of international (European) subsidiaries. The cross-transfer of goods and services between subsidiaries

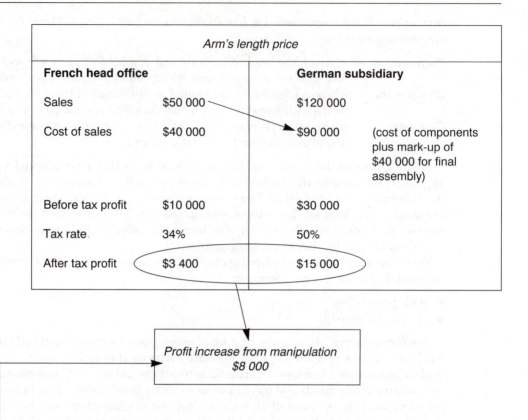

Fig. 7.11 Manipulating transfer pricing to maximise profits and reduce tax burdens

can mean complex exchanges of payment between different parts of the organisation which obviously raises administration costs in financial management. In order to enhance efficiency, certain multinational firms have established clearing accounts in a particular centre charged with making transfers to pay intra-company accounts. This process is based on net flows between subsidiaries, each organisation transferring the money it owes to a central depository (in its own currency) where money is stored and converted at favourable rates and then paid out to subsidiaries. Fig. 7.12 demonstrates traditional and multilateral netting structures graphically. There are various advantages of this approach including:

1 economies in exchange rate management where the clearing account manager can convert large amounts of money at the same time;
2 more rapid payment of accounts which prevents outstanding debts dissuading some subsidiaries to deal with others;

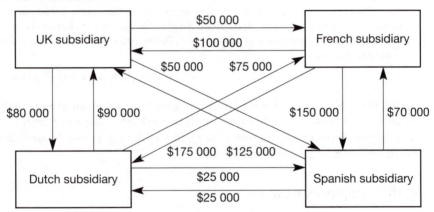

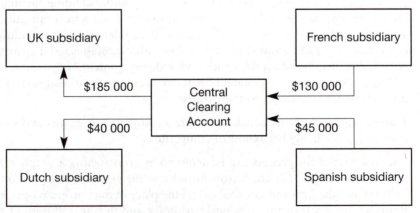

Fig. 7.12 Traditional intra-firm payments v multilateral netting

3 more transparency in money management meaning the head office can see which institutions are compiling large amounts of funds which can be tapped into to support activities in other areas;
4 those units owed money have faster access to their funds and are thus able to react to new opportunities more quickly.

Certain restrictions on netting do, however, exist. Some governments restrict the use of netting for anything other than trade reducing its flexibility as a money transfer mechanism. Others restrict payments until goods have cleared customs. The system also requires co-operation by all subsidiaries. Those which have traditionally balanced their incoming and outgoing payments by delaying account settlement are likely to resist a more centralised approach.

In Fig. 7.12, all financial flows are indicated in dollars. However, many European firms continue to operate different cost accounting systems in their various subsidiaries making cross-comparison of activities and improved efficiency difficult to achieve. Again, European firms may be at a disadvantage here in relation to their Japanese and US counterparts:

> American companies that started from scratch by imposing English as their 'official' language and by installing US-based accounting systems across their European subsidiaries often have a major advantage in this respect over European companies, which have maintained multiple languages and national management accounts. One company, facing severe overcapacity and production-allocation issues, was unable to compare plant economies across Europe because of the different cost accounting systems used in each country. Never before had there been a need to put them on a comparable basis.
>
> (Blackwell, Bizet, Child and Hensley, 1993, p. 363)

Again, there is no blue print for effectively managing financial aspects of the organisation. What is clear, however, is that firms need to establish a degree of centralised control over their financial operations in order they can see 'the big picture' – overall company risks, profit centres and problem areas.

Assessing the company's position

The above review of current issues in the international and European operating environments along the key dimensions of the value chain provides a starting point for assessing the company's competitive position. It is only by understanding the main changes which are taking place in the environment and the industry that a firm can truly establish its own strengths and weaknesses. Not all issues will be relevant in each industry, however, the environmental audit alluded to earlier should have established a clear understanding of critical dimensions within the firm's own industry context.

The challenge now is assessing how the firm compares in relation to its major competitors. There are two stages to this process:

1 assessing the elements which constitute a company's strengths and weaknesses;
2 assessing the likely behaviour of competitors.

The first part of the process can be achieved by constructing a simple matrix such as that highlighted in Fig. 7.13. The factors included in the matrix will depend on the nature of the industry and the firm and key changes taking place in the European operating environment. Ratings of competitors are obviously arbitrary and thus it is important that the matrix is supported by a written description of how the rating was determined for each organisation.

Issues	Dimensions	Rating				
		1	2	3	4	5
Inbound logistics	Cost/Price					
	Relationships					
	Quality					
	Flexibility					
	Reliability					
Production	Cost/Efficiency					
	Local responsiveness/Adaptation					
	Technology					
	Flexibility					
	Relationships					
Organisation	Flexibility					
	Efficiency					
	Mechanism for integration					
	Responsiveness/Local autonomy					
	Centralisation of critical issues					
	Relationships					
Technology	Flexibility in development					
	Responsiveness to local needs					
	Efficiency in R&D					
Finance	Mechanisms for managing risk					
	Efficiency					
	Effectiveness of systems					

5 = a very strong competitive position, 4 = strong, 3 = average, 2 = weak and 1 = very weak

Figure 7.13. Competitor assessment matrix

While such an approach is highly simplified, and has many limitations, it permits a highly transparent means of assessment and visual representation of areas in which the organisation boasts clear strengths and weaknesses. This position then has to be assessed according to the importance of the various dimensions in the current/future European environment. Thus, with cost pressures now facing most organisations as a result of competitive intensity across the EU in the wake of market liberalisation, cost factors must be weighted highly. In addition, as organisational flexibility and the need to adapt quickly to changes in the market and consumer demands becoming pre-requisites for competitiveness on a global scale, flexibility will also derive a high weighting. Alternatively, an issue such as manufacturing technology may be weighted lower if the firm is operating in a sector where production technologies are mostly standardised and local responsiveness may have less importance due to greater homogeneity across Europe post unification. By multiplying the derived ranking by the calculated weighting, a weighted score of competitors' strengths along each dimension can be worked out. Table 7.11 provides an example of this process.

Table 7.11. Calculating weighted scores for competitor assessment of production

Factor	Weight	Rating	Weighted score
Cost/Efficiency	0.8	4	3.2
Local responsiveness	0.3	2	0.6
Technology	0.2	3	0.6
Flexibility	0.7	4	2.8
Relationships	0.6	3	1.8
			9

In this way, an organisation can establish areas of weaknesses which require immediate attention and re-development. However, the business environment is highly dynamic and organisations must also consider future competitor reactions and developments before they can establish optimal directions for strategy development. To do this, they must also pay attention to:

● *firms' core competencies* – areas of business in which competitors display clear comparative advantages which are sustainable in the long-term;
● *firms' likelihood to react* – the changes in strategy they may introduce in response to changes in both competitive activity and industry change;
● *resources* – the extent of competitors' resources and thus their ability to react/develop new strategies;
● *culture* – traditional behaviour of competitors and their overall management culture (eg. centralised versus decentralised, or their propensity to enter into alliances versus a tendency to internalise core technologies and skills).

Information on these types of issues is likely to be limited and analysis along these lines necessarily speculative. However, by monitoring firms along these dimensions there is greater for considering lines of future action and the creation of contingency plans to cope with eventual outcomes.

ESTABLISHING EUROPEAN AND GLOBAL OBJECTIVES

Once firms have undertaken a full review of opportunities and threats, strengths and weaknesses, they will then be in a position to decide on their overall objectives for the future. The immediate concern for most European firms is:

1 How can we defend our existing business operations?
2 Which opportunities should we pursue?
3 How can we rationalise and re-organise to maximise our efficiency?

Defending existing operations

Defence of existing business operations is, arguably, a 'safer' option than considering expansion. Preserving the company's existing profit margins means survival, and concentrating on existing operations is potentially easier than pursuing new lines of action and thus venturing into the unknown.

As many organisations derive the major part of their sales from their domestic marketplace, defence of home territory is likely to be a critical short-term objective for preserving long-term success. Lynch (1994) highlights several conditions under which domestic market defence is essential:

1 Where the company derives a substantial part of its business from its domestic market, and there are major uncertainties in expanding abroad (such as defining clear areas of comparative advantage).
2 Where customers exhibit high levels of loyalty and industry growth rates are low it is desirable to focus attention on keeping existing customers satisfied rather than attempting to generate loyalty among a new customer group.
3 If barriers to entry are difficult to overcome then improving the position domestically is likely to be more advantageous than expanding into other markets which may be more competitive.
4 If competitors have the capacity to 'change the rules of the game' and employ new innovative techniques (such as the introduction of new modes of distribution) or introduce new, more attractive products.

But does this equate with a failure to spread risk? Some would say dependence on a single domestic market brings with it the inability to off-set these risks through business operations in other markets, some of which may throw up better profit potential. However, pursuing opportunities in untried and untested markets which are already well served by competitors also brings risk, particularly if organisations cannot find a 'real' comparative advantage which would give them an edge over foreign indigenous players.

For organisations with extensive European operations deriving profits from a number of individual markets, defence remains an issue. Here, however, it is defence of an existing strategic position rather than defence of a geographic territory which is the concern. In this sense, objectives will be determined by the need to consolidate various dimensions of the business such as:

- overall efficiency in business functions and structures
- improving responsiveness to customer needs and wants
- flexibility to adapt to changes and thus react quicker to defend operations
- improved information systems to permit better monitoring of the environment around which objectives need to be set;
- improved management of relationships to enhance the skills and knowledge development of the firm.

For pan-European firms, therefore, objectives must focus on consolidation of profits and market share through improvements in various elements of the value chain.

However, defence is only one line of action facing organisations within the EU. Opportunities arising from greater freedoms, and possibly greater harmonisation, must also be considered. It is therefore important for firms to derive a balance between defence and attack in order that they maximise the potential from the Single European Market.

European expansion

In order to expand, firms need to ask themselves: why would customers in a foreign country change their purchasing behaviour and buy from us? In other words, what comparative advantages do we have over foreign players? Answering this question is perhaps harder than might first appear. Advantages developed in one country may not be automatically transferable to another. It is important, therefore to analyse the extent to which different advantages can be transferred, before any decision on expansion can be made.

Table 7.12 gives some indication of the nature and scope of different types of competitive advantage and the ease with which they may be transferred between different Member States of the EU. As the table demonstrates, many advantages are difficult or impossible to transfer or may only provide opportunities in the short-term. Expansion is only advisable where opportunities for exploitation and maintenance of advantages are clear cut. (The box insert Marks & Spencer gives some insight into such problems in practice.)

Table 7.12. The transferability of comparative advantage

Source of advantage	Scope for transferability
Product technology (patent protected)	High but may be copied or improved upon as technologies change/improve.
Process technology	High, but again are time dependent. Limited scope for exploitation through exports due to plant capacity and establishing new plant abroad is highly resource intensive.
Quality and systems control in manufacturing	Can lead to cost advantages although additional transportation costs through exporting may erode the advantage. Just in time systems with local suppliers have to be developed abroad in the event of foreign investment which can take time and be difficult to achieve if relations already exist between suppliers and customers.
Productivity	May be linked to production location and therefore only transferable via exports wherein the advantage may be eroded via high transportation costs. Also, may be difficult to sustain in the long-term as competitors have the potential to improve their efficiency by operating in a wider European market.
Marketing expertise	Often the most difficult advantage to transfer as branding, positioning, distribution and promotion often have to be adapted to local market conditions.
Service	Service and customer relations cannot be transferred and require dedicated resources to establish in overseas markets.

CASE STUDY

Marks & Spencer – going into Europe

Marks & Spencer, the UK clothing retailer, continues to enjoy a strong position in its domestic market. Its nationally recognised brand image has developed out of its longevity in the UK marketplace and its continued provision of quality, value for money clothing and its 'no fuss' returns policy.

Based on this success, Marks & Spencer were confident that their early forays into Europe, in response to the opportunities emerging from the removal of tariffs across the EC, could capitalise on their UK reputation. Their establishment of a branch in Paris was seen as a direct means of extending their sphere of influence and capitalising on their well-established image. French nationals visiting London, they believed, would already be well versed in the Marks & Spencer retail culture and they were of the opinion their reputation would precede them.

The reality, however, was far removed from such early hopes. Initial research had already demonstrated that French buying behaviour differed somewhat to that pertaining in the UK. French women, it was found, had a tendency to buy a size smaller than needed which meant due consideration for buttons and zips, and preferred longer skirts than their UK counterparts. Men, on the other hand, showed a marked preference for single back vents in jackets, a wider range of colours in sweaters and jackets and trousers rather than formal suits.

Such research did not, however, prepare Marks & Spencer for low initial acceptance. Despite the number of French tourists travelling to London, only 3 per cent of the French surveyed following poor performance had ever heard of Marks & Spencer and the St Michael brand prior to the store's opening, and the Spartan store design and limited service cover emerged as anathema to French retail purchasing behaviour. The lack of facilities for trying on clothes frustrated French shoppers who were not persuaded that the 'no fuss' returns policy (and the potential for trying on clothes at home rather than in the store) was a preferable way to shop.

Marks & Spencer therefore had to adapt its retailing stance in Paris in order to redress the situation. It introduced changing room facilities, and opted for a product range which was distinctly English and thus serviced a particular market niche, rather than attempting to compete head-on with French styles and couture. The changes have had a marked impact on the success of the organisation in France. One Paris store now sells more merchandise per square metre than any other French department store and is Marks & Spencer's second largest sales generator.

Implications for European strategy development

The experiences of Marks & Spencers highlight a key stumbling block for many organisations venturing abroad. What is successful in the domestic market is not necessarily transferable to overseas markets. Firms must therefore review markets separately and be prepared to make changes in their strategy to cater for local cultures and buying behaviour. Perhaps more importantly, firms must consider what advantages they can develop in overseas markets and not just those advantages which are tried and tested at home.

Rationalisation and re-organisation

One of the central tenets of the Single European Market initiative is the promotion of economic efficiency through provisions for improved economies of scale and, in the longer-term, pressures to innovate and develop new technologies. With this being the case, organisations in the modern environment have no choice but to pay careful attention to the opportunities for rationalisation and re-organisation as a means of enhancing their overall efficiency.

Rationalisation is a highly contentious issue for any organisation as it often means closing down business units and thus creating unemployment. To an extent this highlights a paradox in the Single Market Programme. On the one hand, increased competition will lead to improved business efficiency, lower prices and increased consumer choice, but will also result in there being 'losers' who cannot compete in the new competitive environment and are thus forced out of business.

From a strategist's point of view, the key concern is ensuring their business does not count among the losers and while the decision to rationalise may be painful, it may also be inevitable. In terms of re-organisation, a number of options may be considered:

- expand linkages with other organisations as a means of preserving the existing position and enhancing strengths through co-operation
- work more closely with suppliers and distributors as a means of extending power through the value chain
- join forces with or buy-up the competition to eradicate the threats and internalise business strengths
- re-focus the business on core activities and divest peripheral activities.

On the final point, while the 1970s and 1980s were regarded as the era of diversification, the late 1980s and early 1990s have proved to be the era of focus. Diversification can mean diluting effort in particular areas of business. Different influences on diverse business functions mean it is difficult to establish common objectives and work in an integrated fashion and improve overall company efficiency and effectiveness. Philips, the Dutch electronics giant, provides a good example of an organisation which, as a result of mounting competitive pressures, has re-aligned its business in this fashion. In 1988 it sold its telecommunications business to Alcatel of France, in 1989 it announced the sale of its defence businesses in the Netherlands, Belgium and France to Thomson CSF and, in 1990, it announced the sale of its domestic appliance business to Whirlpool of the USA. This means it can now focus greater attention on its remaining, more focused portfolio, wherein competitive demands, increasing costs of R&D and greater pressures to speed up the process of new product development inevitably mean closer focus.

The box insert on Pilkington Glass provides and example of an organisation that has had to face up to the harsh realities of competing in an increasingly competitive marketplace, re-focusing its business and rationalising production.

CASE·STUDY

Pilkington

Pilkington Glass, is a UK manufacturing organisation with its main production centre located in St Helens in Lancashire. Originally a family-owned domestic producer, the company expanded internationally earlier than many other organisations as a result of the success of its float glass production process which it licensed to a number of leading international manufacturers and exploited through foreign direct investment.

The European glass industry has been beset with difficulties in recent years. The emergence of non-EU competition (with Guardian of the USA establishing a greenfield plant in Luxembourg and Asahi Glass of Japan taking over the German concern, Glaverbel) has put pressure on Pilkington and St Gobain of France, the industry leaders. A downturn in both the car and construction industries has exposed over-capacity in glass production and forced prices down, a situation not likely to improve as the forecast for growth is slow.

This situation has forced Pilkington to rethink its strategy for Europe. It has refocused its production plants on making a narrower range of products for a wider European market. Enabled by greater border freedoms, this approach is expected to enable greater scale-economies of plant, eradication of the duplication of effort and more efficient utilisation of equipment by eradicating production process downtime. To achieve these benefits the firm has been forced to close one of its float glass production lines at its plant in St Helens. Annual cost savings are expected to be substantial, as much as £10 million over two years, permitting the firm to compete more effectively with low cost producers such as Guardian.

But while all this points to greater efficiency in the firm's centralised production location, what of the company's ability to effectively meet demand within the narrower user groups suggested? A change to the company's marketing efforts has also been required – a Europe-wide user specific approach where location will mirror the developments of its major customers (particularly the car producers) which have already moved to Europe-wide production and procurement systems.

The company was also forced to reassess its distribution strategy in the UK. St Gobain, Pilkington's leading competitor in Europe, broke with tradition in 1990 and waived the unwritten agreement not to aggressively compete in Pilkington's home territory by purchasing *Solaglass*, the UK's second largest glass distributor. Pilkington, who had until then resisted the idea of increasing its involvement in domestic distribution, partly due to its protected status, but also because it was committed to the idea of being a cost leader, took three years to realise that defence of their domestic market was essential to long-term success. In 1993, they acquired the UK's largest glass distribution company.

Implications for European strategy

Pilkington, like many other organisations servicing the needs of major customers across Europe, is finding that the only way to survive as market pressures hot up is to stay close to their customers in their sales and marketing provision. Like Lucas Girling, one of the main customer groups comprises the leading car assemblers which are increasingly developing close working relations with their suppliers, relationships which are difficult to manage at arm's-length across geographic borders. Unlike Lucas Girling, however, Pilkington cannot contemplate the establishment of small scale manufacturing units to service the needs of customers in different centres due to the enormous plant economies required to operate in the glass industry. The next best approach is therefore to establish proximate sales and marketing operations which can deal with customer needs and requirements, while maintaining centralised production as a means of preserving economies and profit margins.

Re-organisation alone, is not however seen as sufficient to tackle the challenges. The company has been forced to rationalise its operations and re-focus its activities on a smaller range of products and services in order to maintain levels of efficiency and ensure that it can generate and sustain comparative advantage in all areas of the business. It has also been forced, by an aggressive challenge from its leading competitor, to concentrate attention on defending its home market territory.

CHOOSING A STRATEGIC FOCUS

Strategy development involves the formulation of detailed plans designed to achieve the company's stated objectives. These plans will, invariably, be specific to the individual company, being shaped not only by what is desirable given the current business situation and the firm's existing position, but also what is possible within the constraints of the organisation's existing resources, be they financial or managerial.

Matching assets to competitive drivers

The issue of company assets requires further attention. Strategy development is not just about looking outwards and determining what is required to survive in the competitive marketplace; it also requires looking inwards and analysing company assets. There would be little point, for example, suggesting to a small organisation that as the main *cost driver* in the industry is based on large economies of scale this is the route they need to take. It would be akin to telling a child 'you're too young to understand': in the current circumstances they can do little about it! Equally, however, it would be misleading to suggest that strategy development should be solely dependent on current abilities. This may result in organisations being superbly efficient in the production of products for which there is no market. Successful strategy, then, is about matching competencies to the market, looking inwards and outwards and formulating plans which allow the harnessing (or improvement) of assets to meet changing competitive conditions.

Table 7.13 attempts to highlight the balance between *drivers* of strategy and company assets. The drivers are based on an assessment of those factors now at play in the Community which are having an impact on strategy across three key dimensions: cost leadership, differentiation and focus (Porter's three generic strategies for competitive success). Porter (1985) advocates that the aim of competitive strategy should be to create a defensible position against competitive forces by either defensive or offensive action. The firm should then devise a plan which may include:

Table 7.13. Matching assets to competitive drivers

Assets	Competitive drivers in the EU
Cost related	*Cost leadership drivers*
Access to inputs	Relationships with suppliers. Larger scale production units permitting economies in purchasing.
Appropriate production capacity	Greater potential for scale economies through production in larger units.
Location	Operation of fewer large scale operating units in centres offering cost advantages.
Market coverage	Learning curve effects – the more products sold and the wider the coverage the more likely the company will develop cheaper means of production/distribution.
R&D capability	Shared costs of R&D through linkages with other competitors.
Time to market	Greater flexibility in reaction (either technological or market investment) can lead to first mover advantages.
Brand development	Establishment of Euro-brands can reduce duplication in advertising and raise entry barriers.
Differentiation related	*Differentiation drivers*
Technological know-how	Continuous product development required to stay one step ahead of the competition in aggressively competitive markets.
Firm/product reputation	Creates barriers to foreign entry and raises loyalty among existing customer franchise.
Distribution channel	Can protect against entry. Innovation in distribution can change the rules of the game and customer purchasing habits. Joint ventures give access to closed distribution channels.
Market knowledge	Customer awareness essential for targeting differential effort particularly for servicing small specialised markets with specific needs now possible/desirable in the new Europe.
Service network	Differentiation through service becoming more important as products standardise (particularly in industrial sectors).
Marketing personnel	Personnel with wide experiences of European market able to generate better awareness of areas for standardisation and adaptation.
Integration	Either with internal units or partners can lead to better responsiveness, improved knowledge and greater flexibility to add value through different parts of the value chain.
Focus related	*Focus drivers*
Geographic spread	'Cherry picking' of markets which offer greatest potential gives rise to better resource allocation.
Portfolio focus	Focus on core strengths means excellence in one area rather than fair performance in several which generally results in easier defence.
Managerial skills	Current management skills may not always transfer to new businesses outside of geographic and product sphere.
Genera	*General cost drivers*
Information technology	IT as a means of integrating business organisations and improving efficiency.
Financial capacity	Shapes amount of money available for new investments.
Culture	Centralisation potential enhanced through the opening up of borders – may not fit with company culture.
Government/union relationships	Government and union goodwill can facilitate expansion/contraction objectives.

Based on Verdin and Williamson (1994) 'Successful Strategy: Stargazing or Self-examination', European Management Journal, *Vol. 12, No. 1. p.12.*

1 positioning the company so that its capabilities provide the best defence against the competitive force;
2 influencing the balance of competitive forces through strategic moves;
3 anticipating shifts in the factors underlying the competitive forces and responding to them.

Thus the key to successful competitive strategy is to establish a position which is less vulnerable to attack from competitors, whether established or new, and less vulnerable to erosion from the direction of buyers, suppliers and substitute goods. While the specific operational strategies followed by each firm are likely to differ, Porter established three generic lines of action:

● cost leadership, achieved where a firm can sustain a cost advantage through, for example, exploiting economies of scale, proprietary technology or access to raw materials
● differentiation, which involves developing a positioning of uniqueness along a dimension which is valued by customers, for example, product uniqueness, service uniqueness delivery uniqueness
● focus, which relates to the choice of a narrow competitive scope which may be a narrow geographic market or product 'niche' in which the organisation can either become a cost leader or exploit differential advantages.

It is clear from Table 7.13 that a review of assets alone is misleading. A company may, for example, believe that it boasts a very strong management team as all of its people have good qualifications and a good track record. However, within the Single European Market, it is pan-European experience and knowledge of markets, from which an understanding of standardisation versus adaptation may be derived, which is likely to bring most success, and not just paper qualifications and a track record in one area of the business. It is thus exploitation of assets which fit with overall market and industry drivers which will lead to a position of sustainable competitive advantage.

Reviewing critical lines of action

Having established a clearer understanding of what can and cannot be achieved given existing resources, it is possible to establish a list of critical areas of action. Some objectives may be more urgent than others given the nature of change in the European/industry operating environment leading to different time-frames for defensive or aggressive strategy development. Similarly, gaps identified in competence across parts of the value chain will determine areas of focus for development in the immediate future.

At this point it is worth looking back at some of the critical themes within the Single European Market which are likely to provide the foundation for this assessment. Figure 7.14 summarises various strategic alternatives for achieving the different types of European objective – defence, rationalisation and expansion. As highlighted earlier in the chapter, these three lines of action are not mutually exclusive and certain strategies may permit the achievement of objectives along a variety of dimensions.

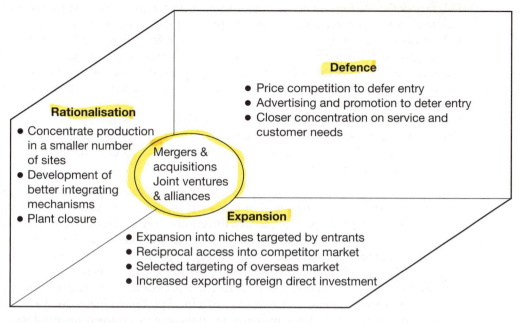

Fig. 7.14 Strategies to reach European objectives

Defence strategies will invariably take precedence over attack/expansion. It is important to protect existing profit margins for the good of all company stakeholders, (shareholders, staff and customers). Defence strategies, however, do not come cheap, and it can prove expensive to sustain businesses where profit margins are already slim. Price and advertising/promotion wars, while potentially protecting the firm from encroachment in the short-term, cannot be sustained in the long-term without concomitant cost reductions. Companies need to ask themselves whether they wish (or can afford) to enter into a series of aggressive moves and countermoves, particularly if the new entrant (or potential entrant) has deeper pockets and a wider resource base on which to draw.

Within the context of Europe, the downward pressure on prices resulting from the opening up of markets will make defence of markets on prices alone a very dangerous route to contemplate. But doing nothing is equally as dangerous. Sitting back and wondering what will happen if and when a competitor takes an aggressive stance and moves into existing territory runs the risk of being undermined in competition for existing customers. Pre-emptive defence, through expansion into niches, increasing customer service, thus emerge as preferable.

Joint ventures and alliances provide an interesting case as they can permit improved competitiveness across the three dimensions. Defence may be achieved by considering co-operative links with potential competitors such as:

1 *Licensing* – agreeing to produce a product for another company (in return for an up-front fee and royalty payments) instead of facing up to competition from the product in the market.

2 *Cross licensing* – refers to examples in which both firms license a product (or products) to their foreign 'partner'. This not only helps deter entry, but also reduces development costs in the long-term as the two organisations do not duplicate the research efforts of their 'partner'.

3 *Acting as distributor* – rather than face competition from a new product line, provide the distribution network for the competing firm wishing to enter the market.

4 *Bilateral marketing agreements* – which can vary from simple bilateral deals wherein each party sells the products of its partner in its own domestic market, to more complex agreements (such as that outlined in *The Economist* report on the European internal market in July 1988) wherein the agreement between a French pet food company and a Dutch rival involved:

(a) the two companies taking a one third stake in their partner;
(b) exclusive market rights for its own and its partner's products in domestic territory;
(c) the formation of jointly owned marketing subsidiaries elsewhere in Europe;
(d) a jointly run research centre.

However, it would be wrong to assume that all firms can strike up co-operative agreements with potential entrants as a means of protecting themselves from new entry. Marketing and licensing deals, whether operating in one direction or on a bilateral basis, are more likely to occur where there is complementarity between products (and thus the potential for extending the product range) rather than direct competition where the products of the new entrant might potentially cannibalise the products of the incumbent.

Extending beyond defence, joint ventures also permit expansion into new markets through the existing systems and structures of a local player. As highlighted earlier, this can substantially reduce problems in learning (particularly cultural uncertainty) and can enhance the spread and development of the organisation on a Europe-wide scale without the need for major investment in new facilities. Equally, alliances offer potential for rationalisation, particularly in research functions, where the pooling of resources lowers the R&D bill for co-operative partners.

All of these co-operative routes provide one further strategic advantage: they allow firms to internationalise their outlook without necessarily internationalising their business. In other words, even in the simplest case of licensing in technology from a foreign player, organisations are able to learn more about operations outside of their traditional sphere of influence and, in so doing, develop a broader understanding of the nature and scope of the European marketplace. This may potentially give them an edge in their own domestic back yard.

Mergers also provide a powerful mechanism for expansion, and at the same time lead to greater industry-wide rationalisation and potentially more efficient utilisation of resources. Equally, they also provide a defensive option – buying up the competition rather than facing competition head on. Relating back to Chapter 5, Table 5.1 highlighted the on-going trend in merger activity across the EU. It is possible to suggest that this trend is demonstrative of the wealth of advantages accruing from this kind of option for firms involved in defence, expansion and rationalisation.

Before moving on it is worth spending some time considering the polarisation of industry. Many industrial sectors are now dominated by large firms at one end of the scale, operating across a wide range of sectors, and small firms at the other operating in specific niches. Calori (1991) believes this means companies will have to choose between becoming one of the big players (growing to a critical size) or focusing on one or a small number of niches in which they can re-inforce their competitive advantage. To this end, the medium-sized generalists will be vulnerable (and possibly the target of takeovers by those firms seeking to become large dominant players). Calori goes on to suggest that this trend is a result of:

1 the rise in technical and marketing investments;
2 the tendency towards stronger market segmentation;

which may mean that even the largest players in the future will have to differentiate their products to match the demands of different segments becoming 'differentiated generalists'. Consequently, the battles between differentiated generalists and niche players (either in single or multiple niches) will take on more importance than the traditional battles between cost leaders and differentiators.

Developing a strategy

It is only once a firm has identified its strengths and weaknesses, determined market opportunities and threats, and undertaken a review of possible lines of action available to it given its resources that it can work out its strategy for Europe. There is clearly no magic recipe for success, and some firms, despite careful analysis, will still find themselves struggling as the competitive conditions change. What is important, however, is that they build strategy out of their analysis and not out of whims and misguided perceptions or habit. As the marketplace continues to change, so firms must adapt their strategies and systems to cater for the new challenges.

A useful way of finalising strategic options is to consider a range of scenarios which can be tested according to their potential to generate profit and 'fit' with overriding company objectives. Profit estimates are never easy to make, particularly when the proposed area of development is intangible, such as improving co-operative links with suppliers. Equally, changes to one area of the value chain may have knock-on effects in other parts of the business. Analysis of options must, therefore, include a review of potential impacts across all areas of the business as a means of discovering how a change in one area may have a positive or negative effect on another, for example, improving just-in-time and quality delivery systems in inbound logistics will have a powerful impact on production flows (improving stock-management costs) and reduce the number of defects. In turn, this will impact on the sales and service function. Thus, a move in just one area of the value chain will have far reaching ramifications for other business functions. Even allowing for highly subjective assessments of potential profit impact, contemplating different potential outcomes of strategy development is a useful mechanism for comparing across different lines of action and determining the most appropriate strategies.

One further issue on strategy choice also deserves comment. Few firms are completely stand-alone entities; most have links with other organisations be they distributors or formal 'partners'. It is, therefore, critical that all strategies gain acceptance and support from third parties and partners. It is useful at this stage to enter into a consultation process to ensure that all parties working on behalf of the firm are agreed that the options being proposed are the right ones. History points to numerous examples of firms which have changed their strategic orientation only to find that their new line of attack is out of keeping with the objectives of business associates. This is nowhere more apparent than in areas of marketing strategy, companies changing elements of the marketing mix without consulting their foreign distributors who are then charged with adapting their own strategies to the new product or pricing policies of the principal. Changes made independently of other interest groups run the risk of damaging relations and local market effectiveness.

IMPLEMENTATING STRATEGIES

Having decided upon a line of action, firms are then charged with the task of effective implementation. Implementation is essentially about understanding a corporation's overriding objectives and ensuring that operations and resources are contributing to the effective delivery of strategy. It is far beyond the scope of this chapter to review all options for successful strategy implementation. What is possible, however, is to pinpoint a number of key dimensions raised by the review and provide some discussion on how firms can address these as they develop their European strategies for the next millennium.

Managing internal and external relations

The formulation of relationships, whether between buyers and sellers or between firms competing in the same industry is increasingly becoming a feature of the European environment. This raises questions over the most effective means of managing relationships and getting the best out of co-operative alliances and joint ventures.

The literature on alliances is awash with recommendations for effective management and ways of overcoming the traditional pitfalls associated with co-operative business development. Table 7.14 summarises many of the main issues which are traditionally discussed with regard to the management of alliances. Although much of what is included in Table 7.14 is derived from the literature on equity joint ventures, the recommendations apply equally to all kinds of co-operative agreement. Essentially, the key determinant is co-operation, which may mean organisations developing a new mind-set and culture, moving away from traditional managerial objectives which are more normally based on systems and structures for competition. Equally, successful management of co-operative business deals is about establishing systems and structures for integrating the joint ventures into the company's overall strategic objectives. Table 7.15 provides a checklist of critical issues which need to be incorporated into the process of managing co-operative links. Some of these issues are reflected in the Box insert on the Davidson-Marley joint venture.

Extending beyond the notion of managing one-off strategic alliances is the issue of *network management*, now part of the vocabulary of leading EU organisations. These organisational designs have their roots in the Japanese *Keiretsu* systems (discussed in more detail in Chapter 12). The OECD (1992) suggested:

> Networking is an attempt to obtain economies of scale or scope by changing the balance of activities between those carried out within the firm and those which are performed externally. The overall result has been the growth of organisational forms which have some of the characteristics of integration combined with decentralisation.

and went on to identify three main network alternatives:

1 a wide intra-group affiliated or *Keiretsu* network;
2 networks with hub firms and supplier networks;
3 R&D networks, consisting of co-operative R&D relationships (highlighted with respect to the IT industry earlier in the chapter).

Implementing a network strategy, while including elements of relationship management alluded to above, also involves organisations re-designing internal linkages and relationships, focusing on the extent to which each unit or person adds value to the company. Based on the work of Vandermerwe (1993) and Reeve (1990), it is possible to establish a

Table 7.14. Recommendations for effective alliance management

Stage	Recommendations
Determining the need for co-operative alliances	Concentrate on strategic gaps. (e.g. technology, distribution, quality of inputs co-operative alliances local market knowledge).
	Ensure venture is being entered into for positive strategic reasons and not just because the firm feels obliged to jump on the bandwagon.
	Ensure joint venture fits with firms' overall objectives (defence, expansion and rationalisation).
	Look beyond economic and technical acquisition to learning, knowledge and skill acquisition.
	Consider risks and resource pooling.
Partner selection	Cast the net widely. Don't just enter into ventures with known organisations (e.g. existing suppliers) because they are there. Review various alternatives to find best match.
	Look for synergies and complementarities. If firms are too closely aligned, there is the risk of on-going secrecy and a lack of transparency.
	Assess company culture as well as economic factors. Look at traditional lines of action and historical developments.
Selection & negotiation	Bring everything to the table, as a way of building trust. If you are honest and open, then partner more likely to follow suit.
	Determine the importance of the JV to the partner. If it is peripheral for them, but significant for you, different commitment balances may lead to problems later.
	Look beyond obvious objectives and try and determine if the partner has a hidden agenda (e.g. pre-emptive strategy leading to full takeover). If you suspect hidden motives say so.
	Set realistic objectives. The early stages of the venture are likely to require a lot of adaptation and re-negotiation so don't expect a quick fix.
Management	Involve people in both organisations across a wide array of functions. The more people involved and committed the stronger the relationship.
	Be prepared to re-negotiate and adapt. As partners learn about each other the balance of power and decision-making may have to change and overall objectives be re-formulated.
	Don't hold hostages unless you can do this on a mutual basis. If you hold back technology or knowledge without the partner having a hostage in return, the venture will fail.
	Invest good people. If the skills and knowledge of the managers is marginal, so will be profits.

Table 7.15. Checklist for co-operative business management

Objectives
1   Do we understand the major goals of our partners?
2   Have we established clear contributions, responsibilities and obligations?

Financing
3   Have we established equity contributions which are realistic and affordable?
4   Are we certain about how each partner will finance the co-operative operation?

Markets
5   Are we clear about lines of demarcation between customer and geographic markets and are these in keeping with EU competition rules?

People & management
6   Have we decided who is going to be responsible for the business (or who will comprise the board of directors in the case of an equity joint venture)?
7   Do we have procedures for selecting managers and is this sufficient for ensuring the right kind of people with the right kind of commitment?
8   Are there systems in place for technical/managerial training to support staff in the new venture?
9   Have we adequate systems for strategic planning and implementation?
10   Do we have adequate control and information systems for monitoring and facilitating the business?
11   Do we have systems in place for reviewing the success or otherwise of the alliances?
12   Are our management systems flexible enough to allow for re-developments of objectives and partner contributions?

Technology
13   Have we made provision for protecting patents, trademarks, technical secrets, brand names?
14   Have we made provision for sharing information in the event of one partner re-developing/improving the technology?

Finance
15   Have we established common accounting principles and standards including the declaration of dividends?
16   What systems are in place for auditing and reviewing performance?
17   Do we have appropriate systems in place for transferring monies efficiently?

General
18   Have we established clear conditions for failure and disbandment (including the distribution of any assets)?
19   Do we have mechanisms for settling disputes?

Based on Young et al (1989) interpretation of the UNCTC's Guidelines for Effective Joint Venture Management.

number of recommendations for organisations seeking to move from traditional to networked structures within the EU. These are presented as Table 7.16. Essentially, the table summarises much of what was discussed in relation to organisational design for Europe and best practice in financial management.

Table 7.16. Moving from traditional to networked structures

Key elements	Location/level	Recommendation
Strategic objectives	Pan-European	Set guiding principles at headquarters level which are filtered to local operating units for interpretation. Establish integrating mechanisms through strategic sub-groups and project teams. Establish a culture of co-operation which permits/initiates co-operation at a divisional level for extending market coverage and core skills.
Sourcing	Pan-European	Extend sphere of influence in supplier market through linkages and thus develop deeper control of supply activities in the value chain.
Production	Regional/local	Balance scale economies against speed, efficiency, quality and local production costs to generate maximum efficiency. Devolve control over production where asset specificity low (where control of technology, production quality, inventory management or distribution can be equally effective in contract manufacturing operations).
Organisation	Pan-European	Establish teams for working on a pan-European basis, sharing information and reducing duplication in knowledge generation and implementation. Rotate managers between different parts of the organisation o disseminate culture and knowledge. This should include time at the head office.
Finance	Pan-European	Centralised systems for financial co-ordination and improved transparency in accounting systems.
Sales and marketing	Regional	Devolve power to subsidiaries to market and service the needs of individual customers to maximise customer focus and the ability of subsidiaries to operate as profit centres.

CASE STUDY

Davidson-Marley BV

Background to the two parties

Marley PLC is one of the leading manufacturers of building materials in the UK with several international manufacturing subsidiaries. While the main areas of its business are in the construction industry, the company also boasts a well-established operation supplying quality components to the UK car industry.

The car industry has changed significantly in recent years. Many companies are now looking to sole sourcing of many of their supply needs as a means of simplifying buying processes and tying in organisations to meet their specific needs. Time frames for delivery and product development are also shortening, and there is a growing trend towards closer integration of supply and assembly and the pursuit of common goals and adding-value objectives. Manufacturers are also devolving design responsibilities to their suppliers for sub-assemblies, in return for single supplier status.

Davidson Instrument Panel is only one of 33 divisions of the US, Textron conglomerate. With its two sister companies, Interior Trim and Exterior Trim it makes up Davidson-Textron. Davidson-Textron is the largest supplier of instrument panels to the US market.

For some years Marley operated as a licensee of Davidson, using its technology to produce instrument panel skins and foam injections.

Ford approaches Marley

Marley had been producing instrument panels for Ford Sierras in the UK for some time. With the development of its plant in Genk, in the Netherlands, it approached Marley about the possibility of supplying instrument panels for their new world car. However, Ford's policy was clearly outlined as one of global sourcing and, although Marley was keen to develop its automotive business (and thus reduce its dependence on cylicial demand patterns in the construction industry), it was aware that it did not have the capacity, alone, to provide a global sourcing solution for Ford.

Marley were also concerned about the risks associated with the venture. There was no guarantee that the Ford venture would be successful.

The initiation of the joint venture

Against this backdrop, the possibility of a joint venture seemed attractive to Marley. It would allow them to reduce their risk, and it would extend global sourcing potential for Ford. For Davidson, there were equally sound reasons for contemplating an alliance. They were keen to expand their business beyond the USA, particularly in Europe where they had little presence.

The venture also offered Marley a number of associated benefits, not least the potential to learn about new manufacturing and business techniques from Davidson which had a proven track record of flexible manufacturing, workforce flexibility, team-work and total quality management.

Location of the plant

Plant location was carefully considered. The first objective was to locate near to Ford so that just-in-time delivery could be successfully implemented. However, the companies were also aware of the importance of establishing in a position proximate to other car manufacturers which would potentially open up its market to new opportunities. The Born site, 45 minutes from Ford, is also close to Volkswagen, Audi, Mercedes and NedCar and although these companies currently source much of their instrumentation internally, the joint venture is well-placed to take advantage of any change in their policies. Marley have, therefore, also established a small marketing company responsible for assessing new business opportunities.

Getting the management right

It was decided by both parties to employ a local manager with considerable experience in manufacturing. As it was deemed important for the organisation to 'fit into' the local culture, it was believed important for a local to drive the company's development. The recruited human resource manager and facility manager were also Dutch, the former boasting experience in a Japanese subsidiary in the Netherlands. These three individuals were charged with the responsibility of recruiting the 150–200 strong workforce, although strategies for recruitment, training and responsibility had been decided on earlier by representatives from the two parents. This led to some conflict in the early stages between the local managers and the parents, the former finding it difficult to operate freely within the strict guidelines established by the owner organisations.

Both parents committed skilled workers to the venture for a period of time to facilitate the smooth transfer of technology and know-how. It was strongly felt that this process should be rapid so as to allow local managers to quickly take on a feeling of ownership.

With local managers responsible for the long-term development of Davidson-Marley BV, there is a belief that they will carve their own career paths within the 'child' organisation, separate from concerns about the future development of the two parent groups. This is believed to severely reduce the likelihood of conflict between the two parents.

Organisational structures

Davidson-Marley BV is a flexible organisation, with flat structures (no more than four hierarchical layers) organised on the basis of team-work and shared responsibility. Much training takes place 'on-the-job' by associates which were sent to Davidson's Canadian plant for an initial period to learn about the systems and structures to be employed. Workers are involved in all aspects of the business with training courses being run on the company's relationships with its parents, customers and the country.

The company, through its flexible manufacturing technologies and sequential delivery procedures is focused on lean manufacturing and distribution. In order to enable a fuller understanding of the demands of their prime customer, employees are also sent to the Ford plant to understand the nature of Ford's production processes and thus their customers' demands. This is helping to strengthen links between Davidson-Marley and Ford.

Joint venture survival

Both of the parents of the joint venture are aware of what it takes to make a joint venture work:

1 shared objectives (a joint mission);
2 co-operation as equals (based on parity, no domination or paternalism);
3 openness, mutual trust and respect of others as persons and their values, capabilities and objective understanding of their intentions;
4 building on each other's strengths;
5 reducing each other's limitations;
6 each has something the other needs (resources, access, etc.);
7 pooled capabilities and resources permit taking on tasks neither could alone;
8 two-way flow of communication (breakthrough of communication blocks);
9 mutually perceived benefits;
10 commitment of leadership and middle management to find some shared values, without ignoring the fact that they are not identical;
11 co-learning flexibility;
12 a win-win orientation.

Implications for European strategy development

The above review of the Davidson-Marley BV joint venture raises a number of important points:

1 Many firms in the modern environment are reluctant to go into new ventures alone. In such a highly competitive environment, sharing risks can bring great rewards and mean individual companies are not unduly exposed to problems associated with business failure.
2 Managing joint ventures is far more than simply identifying joint opportunities. It is about committing resources and effort to attain mutually beneficial outcomes. This requires time, effort and good people. A failure to dedicate sufficient resources will ultimately result in failure.
3 A critical aspect of a successful joint venture is its people. Not only does the venture require good management, but in a European context, managers who can successfully operate in the local environment. By recruiting local managers into the venture, Davidson and Marley were demonstrating a willingness to be adaptive to local cultural nuances. Neither firm is Dutch, and therefore some degree of personnel sensitivity at an operating level is essential.
4 Equity joint ventures of this kind involve the creation of a separate entity which needs to develop a personality and business culture of its own. It is interesting to note that one of the only areas of conflict which has arisen is that between the parents and local management. By attempting to enforce tight rules on the local operation the parents have frustrated the process of the company developing its own way of doing things. Nevertheless, the parents have shown a degree of sensitivity here recognising that once managers from the parent firm have transferred their knowledge and know-how, they should leave the business up to the managers on the ground.

5 The final checklist in the case suggests that European managers proposing a joint venture must keep in mind the purpose and intent of the venture as the business develops. It is only in this way that they can preserve the longevity of co-operation without seeking ways of sub-optimising and using the venture for their own ends.

Based on two case studies:
Schuler, R. and Van Slujis, E. (1992) 'Davidson-Marley BV: Establishing and Operating an International Joint Venture' *European Management Journal*, Vol. 10, No. 4 December, pp. 428–436; and
Schuler, R., Dowling, P. and De Cieri, H. (1992) 'The Formation of an International Joint Venture' *European Management Journal*, Vol. 10, No. 3, September, pp. 304–309.

Managing for flexibility

The description of 'network management' leads us on to consider the notion of flexibility. Successful implementation of strategies in Europe throughout the next decade will dictate firms designing structures for flexible and creative strategy development and implementation. Change in the EU is rapid, partly due to the new agenda for Europe-wide business, and partly due to increasing competitive threats in the global environment which mean shorter technology/product life-cycles and thus more rapid changes in the European competitive environment.

Long gone are the days when firms could develop a technology, protect it with a series of patents, launch it internationally, and live off the benefits until the patent was close to expiry. Reverse engineering, resulting not only in the 'copying' of technologies, but often improvements on it, means reliance on patents to secure long-term sustainable advantage is risky to say the least. More important, in the modern world, is the design of systems and structures which permit continuous technological improvement as a way of staying one step ahead, or at least level with, the other players in the game.

Similarly, as production techniques are changing, and mass production no longer the only means of efficient manufacturing, scale advantages are being eroded by flexible specialisation in production. When this factor is coupled with a resurgence in the marketing field (discussed in the next chapter) of satisfying the demand of specific groups of consumers, rather than attempting to generate markets which afford scale opportunities, flexibility in customer servicing, possibly through adaptation, is re-emerging as a prerequisite of competitive success.

Strategic managers must review the way in which they view their asset base. It is no longer a case of summing up the scale and dominance of fixed assets, it is a case of developing flexible assets, many of which may be intangible:

1 Buyer power, relating to the scale of purchasing may be superseded by co-operative links with suppliers prepared to offer similarly attractive deals to smaller companies with whom they strike up long-term relationships.
2 Economies of scale in manufacturing may be superseded by flexible specialisation where productivity rates can be matched and advantages enhanced through closer proximity to customers and shorter distribution channels.

3 Reliance on patents and trademarks may be undermined by co-operative R&D developments which gives firms access to a wider knowledge pool and new technologies.
4 Relationships with a number of distributors or bilateral marketing arrangements may offer firms wider distribution coverage than those who have sunk resources in establishing their own distribution networks. It also permits the flexibility to swap partners or distributors as market conditions/customer buying behaviour changes.

Managing for flexibility is therefore about determining the most effective balance between fixed and flexible assets, which may mean divesting parts of the business in favour of developing looser affiliations with third parties and partners.

Implementing strategies flexibly is therefore about 'stage managing' the organisation of the value chain, but not necessarily owning its constituent functions. A good example of this is provided by Mexx, the Dutch fashion company as outlined in the box insert.

CASE STUDY

Mexx and the fashion clothing industry

Mexx is a relatively young and dynamic international fashion company operating in the casual clothes segment of an increasingly competitive and turbulent market. During its 12 year history, it has faced a number of important changes in the market, not least the growing trend for competitors to copy new designs dictating careful management of lead times to sustain competitive growth.

Clothing production across Europe decreased in volume by 10 per cent between 1986–1989, although the value of production rose gradually. This is not a reflection of a decrease in industry activity, but a move towards international subcontracting with many firms, keen to lower costs as a means of retaining profit margins, turning to non-EU marketplaces for the major proportion of their manufacturing activity.

Scale has never been an important factor in the world clothing industry. The industry remains fragmented with large numbers of small manufacturers in most of the world's markets. Flexibility is, however, critical, particularly in today's competitive markets where response times, fashion change and the need to produce small batches to cater for variable demand (in both quantitative and qualitative terms).

In the developed markets, leading players have had to develop flexible organisations, which has mostly been achieved through subcontracting. By managing networks of small subcontracted production units, orchestrated through tight centralised control and exploited through regional or centralised marketing efforts, the Italians, for example, were able to carve out a very strong position within the EU garments industry.

New production technologies also promoted greater reliance on flexibility as the core concept for success. Team working and the use of computer aided design and computer aided manufacturing meant organisations could speed up response times and lower the overall minimum efficient scale of manufacturing and thus respond to increasing market segmentation.

Given the need for more rapid response, distribution systems have also changed. Many agents, have begun to sell from stock to meet their clients' short-term demands, making them more akin to importers and wholesalers than agents intermediating between suppliers and wholesalers.

Within this context, Mexx developed a strong position in the market in the 1980s through its concentration on design and wholesale activities. With no manufacturing facilities of its own, the company outsourced all its production to manufacturing plants in Hong Kong, India, Taiwan and Japan. The company also employed a policy of *forward ordering*, orders being placed on the basis of reviewed samples, so that each garment when produced already had a target market. In this way, the company could keep its inventory to a minimum.

In the mid 1980s, the company consisted of a headquarters in the Netherlands, a co-ordinating company in Hong Kong, and sales companies in the Netherlands, Germany, Belgium, the UK, France, Denmark and the USA some of which had developed partnerships with Mexx, the Mexx managing director and the local MD being co-owners. In turn, in 1986, all co-owners of the distribution companies became shareholders of the Mexx corporation. Seven agents/distributors, independent members of the group, operated outside of these territories. The roles of responsibility for these various departments were as follows:

The headquarters — responsible for design, production co-ordination and perpetuating the overall image of the group.

Hong Kong centre — in charge of production administration, quality control and delivery schedules.

Sales companies and agents — responsible for local marketing, sales distribution, logistics and financial planning. With no common ownership they retained a high level of independence.

Despite the cross-shareholding and interdependence of the various parts of the group there remained problems with communication. Sales managers argued that the product mix reaching them was not capable of satisfying the demands of customers within their own region, the head office design department being fashion product orientated rather than consumer need driven. Thus, there was an apparent mismatch between collections, pricing and advertising. At the same time, the on-set of the Single European market was raising pressures for improved cost-management and centralisation of production and services.

In 1989, therefore, the company decided to re-organise its business. Finance, distribution and transport functions all passed to headquarters control, along with greater co-ordination of marketing effort. Head office brand managers were employed to oversee the various product lines, liaising between the central design departments and local sales managers. Two separate regional headquarters were set up – Mexx Europe and Mexx America, on the basis that demands in the two areas were different enough to justify separate treatment.

A central warehouse policy was also fostered with distribution being centred in Germany and the Netherlands, the company closing down distribution centres in the likes of Denmark, Finland, and Norway. The operating freedoms offered by the Single Market had to be harnessed to produce better efficiency in distribution on a pan-European basis.

European strategy implications

Mexx provides a good example of a flexible organisation which orchestrates its European business operations without full ownership. Subcontracting of production to the Far East and partnership with distributors give the organisations a degree of control, but not the risks involved with owning and managing a broad base of fixed assets.

The case also highlights the importance of greater centralisation in the wake of the Single Market initiative both for competitive effectiveness and economic efficiency. Essentially, Mexx has abandoned its 'confederation' style structure, with a great deal of decentralisation of decision making to regional operating units, in favour of a more centralised co-ordinated organisational structures which monitors and integrates business units.

This does not mean that the company has taken decision making authority away from the sales subsidiaries altogether. What it does mean is that the organisation has a clearer understanding of the different needs of each subsidiary and can thus find areas of commonality and areas of important difference which may serve as the central driving knowledge behind the organisation's design function.

Developed from Open Universiteit, The Netherlands, Strategic Issues for Management in an Integrated European Context 1993.

Managing risk

The issue of financial risk was raised in an earlier section, where it was stressed that organisations are well advised to consider utilising the various mechanisms available for reducing financial risk – both in relation to exchange rate fluctuations and non-payment. Up until now, however, the concept of political risk has been ignored. While it is reasonable to assume that political risk will be far less a factor in managing operations on a pan-EU basis than it would be in managing operations in eastern Europe (discussed in Chapter 11) where continued political uncertainty is likely to have an important bearing on the types of strategy employed, it would be false to assume that political factors have no bearing on implementing strategies in EU markets.

Without political unification, the EU remains a series of 15 Member States with varying political interests and objectives. Although evidence points to greater alignment of political goals between the Members, there remain differences in terms of such factors as:

- inflation
- interest rates
- attitudes towards imports and investments (along the lines of the hidden barriers discussed earlier)
- attitude towards foreign firms in relation to procurement (a continuing hidden barrier)
- per capita income
- skills of local workers
- effectiveness of public administration.

There also exists a degree of mistrust between countries in the EU, a throw back to Europe's turbulent history, littered with wars and disputes, which continue to tarnish individuals' attitudes towards their fellow statesmen. In terms of strategy implementation, it can therefore be very difficult, as an outsider, to attain equal treatment in other EU Member States. This may mean, for example,

- customer mistrust over the firm's ability to deliver or provide quality service
- poor government relations leading to difficult negotiations regarding available land for investment
- problems of gaining access to procurement contracts
- priority given to local firms by distributors.

Overcoming these barriers, thus improving the effectiveness with which strategies may be implemented, can be achieved by ingratiating the company with the local government, local firms or customers. Changing brand names such that they sound local, investing money in local community projects/charity work, sourcing raw materials and components from local firms, producing as much of the product as possible locally, hiring and training local personnel – can all assist in ensuring fair local treatment and easier access to the market. The Japanese (as discussed in Chapter 12) have used this technique very successfully to establish themselves in Europe.

Risk may also come from over committing the company to new projects. There is the temptation, as market barriers come down, to try to take advantage of all available opportunities immediately. Against the back-drop of *first-mover* advantages, there is sometimes the fear that a failure to react quickly to new opportunities will mean missing out in the long-term. For firms with deep pocket advantages this kind of option can be financed by cross-subsidising across different parts of the global business. For smaller national or regional companies, it may mean a recipe for disaster. Gradual development – organic growth rather than the addition of large major investments – will invariable give rise to greater stability, and also avoid the risk of being taken over by a competitor keen to extend his powers further.

On balance, it is impossible for firms to grow and develop in the modern operating environment without taking some risks. Sitting by and watching it all happen will not produce the necessary returns to support either avenues of defence or attack. But companies must try to implement strategies in a phased way so as not to jeopardise various parts of the business at the same time. Thus, if the risk does not pay off, the company still has stable operating units which will support future development.

Companies must also be prepared to pull out of business operations which are a potential threat to their operating base. All too often, the time and effort which goes into developing a new product or business makes managers reluctant to say when enough is enough. They therefore go on supporting the operation long after it is economically viable.

Managing organisational change

It would be remiss, in a chapter on strategies for Europe, not to mention the issue of business re-engineering and to discuss its place in implementing strategies for European competitiveness. Strategic research typically demonstrates that most problems relating to strategy emerge in the implementation and not the formulation stage. It is the processes which the firm employs and not the functions it manages, which give rise to successful strategy implementation.

Business process re-engineering may be defined as:

the management of tasks designed to meet stated business outcomes through the design of processes within and between organisations.

With this in mind, it is perhaps not surprising, given the growing complexity of organisational structures characterised by diverse subsidiaries and multiple business relationships, that a concept such as business process re-engineering has emerged in recent years. Organisational demands are now such that traditional functional management systems are no longer suitable to cater for today's management demands which centre on deriving a balance between co-ordination and decentralisation.

Managing change, in this sense, is therefore about managing the company architecture to facilitate the way in which strategy is delivered. This does not just mean improving processes at a functional level (although this may be a critical strand in improving overall company performance) but looking at the business as a series of complex processes which require close co-ordination and integration. A company may, for example, through re-engineering of its manufacturing processes, improve its overall productivity manifold. It may not, however, be able to sell the efficiently produced end-product due to its misconceptions about market needs and changing customer demands. From discussions throughout this chapter it is quite clear that various processes are at play in an organisation: those which can be centralised and determine overall strategic direction and those which are decentralised functions and relate to the tasks performed at a regional level.

Earl and Khan (1993) identifies four distinct types of process:

1 **Core processes** – commonly the primary activities of the value chain which drive the delivery of added value to customers. Critical here is management of business throughputs, identifying inefficiencies and simplifying processes.
2 **Support processes** – the secondary activities of the value chain including systems for accounting, technology management and human resource functions.
3 **Business processes** – which centre on managing links with organisations beyond the scope of the firm – distributors and joint venture partners.
4 **Management processes** – planning and control processes.

Quite clearly, this type of approach to management mirrors much of what has already been highlighted in the chapter giving rise to cross-functional business teams (as proposed by the concept of heterarchies), management of internal and external relationships and flexibility.

The concept of business process re-engineering is still in its infancy and companies and theorists alike still debating the semantics of what it means and where it fits in the overall strategic management process. It is far beyond the scope of this chapter to review current thinking, although it is important to draw out two critical lines of thought which demonstrate process re-engineering's relationship to strategy implementation:

● it is usually conducted by project teams, independent of the formal strategic planning process;
● most business process re-engineering advocates suggest that it is a policy for massive structural change, and in this sense does not comfortably fit with models of strategic change which tend to be based on learning and incremental change.

From this perspective, business process re-engineering is not a central tenet of formal strategy development processes, but a system for providing the flexible assets for strategy implementation alluded to above. It is, therefore, an important adjunct to managing strategy change, but not the strategic change process itself. Without a change in architecture, it is unlikely that many organisations will be able to successfully implement the types of strategies necessary for competitive success in the EU, already alluded to in this chapter. Thus, the recommendations for flexibility highlighted in Table 7.16, which take into account cost drivers (implying a degree of centralisation and co-ordination as well as relationship development for extending skills and technology), differentiation drivers (which promote local responsiveness) and focus drivers (which determine pursuit of excellence in targeted business spheres), can only be achieved by European organisations prepared to shrug off the mantle of functional management and adopt a more flexible approach to management which embraces the interdependence of tasks, roles, people, departments, functions and business units.

ASSESSING EFFECTIVENESS

Strategic planning is an iterative process requiring continuous adaptation and reformulation. This has never been more the case than in today's business environment wherein the pace of change, both environmental and technological, is far more rapid than has ever been the case before. Firms which rest on their laurels of past strategic success are unlikely to be the winners of the future.

Evaluation is critical and feedback loops need to be established to ensure that unprofitable strategic outcomes are re-evaluated rapidly so that the firm does not expose itself to undue risks. Criteria for assessment can be divided into two categories:

- quantitative measures such as export market share, return on investment, sales growth, profitability
- qualitative measures such as improved quality perceptions by customers, better relationship management, improved goodwill.

Quantitative measures, while requiring a considerable amount of effort in compilation and analysis, are obviously easier to amass and assimilate than qualitative measures which dictate targeted research effort, both within and without the organisation. Nevertheless, a failure to accurately measure outcomes will invariably result in misguided perceptions on the success or otherwise of strategic moves and make the re-development of new strategies difficult.

Also at issue is the time-frame for evaluation. Poor performance of UK firms in recent years has often been attributed to *short-termism* which hampers the effectiveness of their strategic planning worldwide. Concerned about share performance and the reactions of the city there is a tendency to set strict time-frames for profit realisation in new ventures and pull out of ventures before they have realised their true potential. Competing with the likes of the Japanese, who measure effectiveness via market based measures rather than pure profit related measures, UK firms are restricted in their ability to plan organically and long-term.

CONCLUSION

Change in the European (and global) operating environment is causing organisations to carefully re-think their strategies. Traditional success factors such as scale economies and patent protection are now being challenged as the pace of change and development speeds up. Today, strategy is more about the development of systems and structures for enhanced flexibility than the pursuit of effective performance in individual divisions.

Managing strategy is a highly complex task which requires enormous amounts of information gathering and handling on both external environment and the internal resources and capabilities of the firm. With new, sophisticated, IT systems available to organisations, this process should, however, become easier. However, it requires careful management and should be treated as a business development issue in its own right.

A recurrent theme throughout much of this chapter is the need to derive balance in strategic objectives: between defence and expansion strategies, between centralised decision making and decentralised autonomy at the regional level, between standardisation and adaptation. While there is clearly no blueprint for achieving these complex balances, it is evident that firms with rigid structures, pursuing strategies based solely on internal strengths and ignoring the opportunities offered by relationship development across the value chain, are likely to find themselves without the flexibility to adapt to the new competitive environment in which they operate.

Similarly, as European environmental change continues to drive prices and costs to ever lower levels, breaking down traditional *confederation* structures (in which devolvement of power to local operating units dominates) and integrating more of the business centrally is likely to become a pre-requisite of success in modern day Europe.

Questions for discussion

1 On balance, would you suggest that the Single Market has resulted in more opportunities than threats for firms operating on European soil?

2 Why do you think that protecting the domestic market is potentially more critical than expanding across Europe?

3 What can European firms learn from Japanese management practices to improve their position within the new operating environment of the European Union?

4 Why is competitor analysis so critical to ensuring that future plans lead to competitive success?

5 Why do you think so many European firms have adopted a *federal* style approach to organising strategy development for Europe?

6 What are the implications for firms moving beyond 'federal' style to pan-European strategy development?

7 Why might you suggest flexible assets are more important than fixed assets in the modern European environment?

8 How can firms expand if the competitive advantages derived in domestic operations are not transferable to other European Union markets?

9 What would you suggest are the main advantages of flexible business structures?

10 What are the challenges for firms in developing flexible business structures?

Case Study Questions

1 Would you suggest there is any one lesson to be learned from all the case studies presented in this chapter?

2 Based on the two cases of Lucas Girling and McCains, what would you suggest are the best recommendations for production re-organisation within the European Union?

3 The case example on Japanese subcontracting highlights the complex layers of a subcontracting network. What would you suggest are the main advantages and disadvantages of adopting this kind of approach?

4 Based on the case study of AT&T, suggest how the complex network of joint ventures has allowed AT&T to improve its competitiveness within the European Market.

5 Extending out of the review of AT&T (and Fig. 7.10 which highlights industry networks in Europe), to what extent will technology firms in the future be able to manage their own destiny?

6 The Nestlé case highlights an organisation which has adapted its structure to better cater for changes taking place in the European Market. What lessons may other firms derive from this kind of move?

7 What would you suggest are the management difficulties associated with altering the company's business structure?

8 How could Marks & Spencer have better prepared itself for entering into the French market?

9 What are the ramifications for European businesses, such as Pilkington, which are undertaking programmes of rationalisation?

10 Why would you suggest Pilkington was so slow to react to the threat posed by St Gobain's encroachment on the domestic market?

11 What lessons for successful joint venture management can be derived from the Davidson-Marley case study?

12 What facilitated Mexx's development of a flexible network structure for its European operations?

13 From the Mexx case study, and other case examples in the book, outline the main arguments for and against the movement towards flexible networks.

FURTHER READING

The area of Europe strategy is now well documented and the following is, therefore, a select list of books exploring some of the issues presented in the text in further depth.

Dudley, J. (1993) *1993 and Beyond: New Strategies for the Enlarged Single Market*, Kogan Page. This text highlights the different areas of strategy development from a theoretical perspective and provides a detailed review of the practical challenges of doing business in Europe in the 1990s.

Lynch, R. (1994) *European Business Strategies: the European and Global Strategies of Europe's Top Companies*, Second edition, Kogan Page. This text gives an insight into the strategic development of a wide array of organisations from various sectors.

Bartlett, C.A., Doz, Y. and Hedlund, G. (1990) *Managing the Global Firm*, Routledge. This text provides a series of articles (emanating from a global conference on the subject) focusing on business change and redevelopment in the modern world. Although the focus is not primarily on strategies for Europe, the text provides a rich backdrop of critical thinking on business redevelopment.

Thurley, K. and Wirdenius, H. (1990) *Towards European Management*, Pitman Publishing. This text is primarily geared towards an academic audience and covers such issues as the meaning of European management, the study of management practice, the gap in management theory, the management of change and enterprise management.

Calori, and Lawrence, (1990) *The Business of Europe: Managing Change*, Sage. This text is particularly useful for those wishing to understand further the way in which firms need to move from 'federalist' to pan-European management systems. One particular chapter stands out as critical: 'European Developments in the 1990s: Managerial Views and Implications'.

REFERENCES

Ansoff, H. I., *Implanting Strategic Management*, Prentice Hall International, 1984.

Bartlett, C. A. and Ghoshal, S., 'Managing Innovation in the Transnational Corporation', in Bartlett, C. A., Doz Y. and Hedlund G. (Eds) *Managing the Global Firm*, Routledge, 1990.

Blackwell, N., Bizet, J. P., Child, P. and Hensley, D., 'Shaping a Pan-European Organisation', *McKinsey Quarterly*, No. 2, pp. 94–111, 1993.

Bleeke, J. and Ernst, D., *Collaborating to Compete*, John Wiley and Sons, New York, 1993.

Brindlemeyer, M., 'Comparing EC Investments: Getting the Best Deal', *Journal of European Business*, Nov/Dec, p. 38, 1990.

Business Week (21 July, 1986) 'Corporate Odd Couples', pp. 100–105

Calori, R., 'European Developments in the 1990s: Managerial Views and Implications', in Calori, R. and Lawrence, P. *The Business of Europe, Managing Change*, Sage Publications, 1991.

Doz, Y., Hamel, G. and Prahalad, C. K., 'Controlled Variety: A challenge for human resource management in the MNC', *Human Resource Management*, Vol. 25, No. 1, 1986.

Earl, M. and Khan, B., 'How New is Business Process Redesign', *European Management Journal*, Vol. 12, No. 1, March 1993, pp. 20–30.

The Economist, 'Feeling for the Future: A Survey of Television', 12 February, 1994.

The Economist, 'Survey of Europe's Single Market', July 1988.

Hedlund, G. and Rolander, D., 'Action in Heterarchies: New Approaches to Managing the MND', in Bartlett, C. A., Doz, Y. and Hedlund, G. (Eds) *Managing the Global Firm*, Routledge, 1990.

Lynch, R., *European Business Strategies: The European and Global Strategies of Europe's Top Companies*, Kogan Page, 1994.

OECD (1992), *Technology and the Economy*, Paris.

Ohmae, K., *Triad Power: the Coming Shape of Global Competition*, Free Press, 1985.

Porter, M. E., *Competitive Advantage: Creating and Sustaining Superior Performance*, Free Press, 1985.

Porter, M. E., 'Towards a Dynamic Theory of Strategy', *Strategic Management Journal*, Vol. 12, No. 2, pp. 95–112, 1991.

Porter, M. E., *Competitive Advantage of Nations*, Macmillan, 1990.

Reeve, T., 'The Firm as a Nexus of Internal and External Contracts', in Aoki, M., Gustafsson, B. and Williamson, O. *The Firm as a Nexus of Treaties*, Sage, 1990.

Sheard, P., 'Autoproduction Systems in Japan: organisational and locational features', *Australian Geographical Studies*, Vol. 21 pp. 49–68, 1983.

Vandermerwe, S. 'A Framework for Constructing Euro-networks', *European Management Journal*, Vol. 11, No. 1, March, 1993.

Verdin, P. and Williamson, P., 'Successful Strategy: Stargazing or Self-examination?', *European Management Journal*, Vol. 12, No. 1, March, pp. 10–19, 1994.

CHAPTER 8

Marketing in Europe

INTRODUCTION

Even for firms who are not actively involved in expanding their activities across the new Single Market, 1992 spells change for their marketing departments. As the internal market breeds more competition the stakes are bound to change and marketing strategies need to adapt if firms are to protect their market share and customer base. Whether firms like it or not, 1992 has provided the foundation for readjustment, reassessment and a new strategic focus.

While at the outset of the Single Market initiative, many theorists alluded to greater opportunities for pan-European standardisation of products (brands), services, distribution and promotion, the growing reality in the newly formed dynamic marketplace is that firms need to focus their strategies and realign their business objectives to cater for the increasingly demanding needs of customer sub-groups. The argument that focus strategies are likely to produce better rewards than the pursuit of scale economies has turned the tables on organisations which have relied for so long on mass production and mass marketing. Closer analysis of the specific needs of smaller customer groups means a renewed focus on marketing effort, particularly market segmentation and differentiation. However, problems remain in terms of operationalising strategies along these new dimensions, not least because differences between markets prevail.

This chapter follows on directly from the last chapter on strategies for Europe. It was highlighted there that marketing and sales are an important part of the value chain of business activity and as such are subject to readjustment in the new European business environment. Given the important place of marketing in the strategic re-organisation of firms, it is appropriate to give this one element separate treatment.

As with the chapter on strategy, it is difficult to do justice to European Marketing within a single chapter. So much has been written about the subject that it is hard to fully reflect all the issues within the obvious constraints here. Nevertheless, this Chapter, which focuses on the changing face of marketing understanding in the current business environment, by diverging from many traditional texts on the subject, should provide food for thought which extends student knowledge of a newly emerging discipline.

THE CURRENT STATUS OF MARKETING

In theory, the underlying ethos of marketing has never changed. The concept concerns finding out what customers want and delivering it. This led to Peter Drucker's observation that effective marketing should make selling unnecessary. If the firm produces what the customer wants, then demand already exists and active sales effort is not required. While most firms embrace this thinking in theory, many have failed to establish systems and structures to facilitate the processes required to achieve these ends in practice. Marketing has therefore become more synonymous with sales and promotion or, in some instances, strategic management.

At present, marketing as a discipline is undergoing review. Through the recession of the late 1980s and early 1990s many marketing departments came under severe pressure and careful scrutiny. The large budgets traditionally afforded to marketing departments were criticised and marketers accused of being a drain on company resources. These accusations were fuelled by a lack of innovation and product development with few new successful products carving out a successful position in the highly competitive recessionary markets.

In response, several organisations have been forced to re-think the principles on which their marketing operations are based. Essentially, they have been compelled to re-define what marketing means in an environment which is dominated by retailer power, multiple inter and intra-firm relationships, shorter product life-cycles and more aggressive competition. This has led to the establishment of a new paradigm for future marketing development (McKenna, 1991) based on:

1 *Knowledge-based marketing* – which stresses the importance of market review and analysis, company review and analysis and environmental scanning. With a vast armoury of knowledge marketers are better prepared to integrate the customer into the product development process (ensuring products are developed for specific customer needs and strategies), to identify niches which the company can own, and develop an effective infrastructure of suppliers, intermediaries and partners to enhance learning and technological knowledge.
2 *Experience-based marketing* – which focuses on interaction, creativity and connectivity – working with customers and suppliers to develop products and services which are tailor made to individual needs. The development of feed-back loops to process changing needs is also stressed.

Two important issues emanate from this new thinking: the focus is on processes and not functions and there are doubts raised over the usefulness of advertising which is more about selling mass-produced goods to a mass market than identifying customer needs and developing products to cater for them. On the first point, there is now emerging evidence of new marketing organisation structures. Instead of focusing on functions such as advertising, sales and promotion, firms are devolving systems based on brand development, innovation and delivery system improvement: new marketing departments are likely to be process and task based rather than functionally organised.

These changes clearly parallel those taking place in other parts of the value chain and their successful development will depend on the willingness of organisation to embrace the concept of 'flexibility'. In a recent interview Philip Kotler, one of the pioneers of marketing theory suggested:

> Too many companies are inside-out thinkers, not outside-in thinkers. They are product centred, not market-centred ... Many companies today, especially technology-driven companies, still think that the lab designs all the products. I would counter that good products are designed in the market place ... I would go further and say that the customer should have a major role in designing the products ... Outside-in companies take their clues from the marketplace. They spot unmet needs and translate them into business opportunities. They define target groups and develop a value-delivery system that is superior to competitors who are serving the same market.

> (Kotler, 1994)

So has marketing had its day? The answer is definitely 'no'. Given that competition has intensified and firms are now having to look more closely than they have before on targeting customer needs (possibly in small pan-European niches) the role of marketing is critical to success in the modern environment. However, those firms which will survive the severe competitive pressures will be those who are prepared to adopt new forms of marketing based on tasks and problem solving rather than traditional marketing functions. Successful firms will therefore be those that are prepared to go back to basics: to look at marketing as a means of building bridges between customer needs and firm strategy.

With this as the backdrop for discussion, it is important in a chapter on European marketing to reflect the changing attitudes taking place in marketing departments across the European Union and focus on good practice in marketing – not old practice in marketing.

DEVELOPING A MODEL FOR ANALYSIS

The traditional view

With change in the field of marketing, it is essentially to consider marketing along new dimensions. The traditional view of marketing was that it could be split into four critical functional areas: product, price, place and promotion – the now familiar four Ps of the marketing mix. These aspects are presented in Fig. 8.1.

Fig. 8.1 The Four Ps of the marketing mix
Source: Kotler, 1986, p. 69.

Marketing departments were charged with the responsibility of managing these elements and planning strategy accordingly. However, as has been suggested, departments organised in this way have, in recent years, failed to deliver. This kind of structure has perpetuated the idea that marketing is about managing discrete functions rather than tasks. Competitive pressures, more complex organisational interactions and changing market demands mean that this type of functional organisation no longer reflects the changing needs of society particularly in the EU where increased competition and the adoption of new, more flexible strategies, suggests a renewed vision of marketing as supporting flexibility by interfacing between the firm and the market.

Developing a new framework

It is therefore preferable to consider a new framework for reviewing current and future marketing effort within the context of the European environment based on tasks and processes. A proposal for such a framework is depicted in Fig. 8.2.

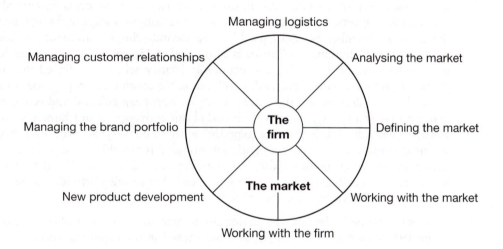

Fig. 8.2 A new framework for marketing

Fig. 8.2 reflects the thinking that marketing is about establishing links between the marketplace and the firm. The key tasks and marketing elements are not linked together in any kind of sequential process. They need to be flexibly managed on an iterative basis – conducted by project teams and work-groups comprising managers from a variety of business disciplines and across European cultures. The future role of the marketing department, therefore, will be one of co-ordinator: responsible for managing teams and groups, setting overall objectives and missions and acting as a conduit for information exchange and learning. It is possible to suggest, therefore, that the marketing department (which will probably retain its position in the centralised head offices of European firms) will be a microcosm of the head office itself, responsible for steering marketing directions and setting central aims and objectives, but devolving decision making to inter-disciplinary and cross-cultural project teams responsible for developing and implementing tactical plans for the tasks at hand and local sales and marketing offices responsible for designing effective operational strategies at a market level.

This framework provides the starting point for reviewing European marketing strategy. However, it is worth commenting on some of the general features of European marketing before looking more closely at these dimensions.

Trends in European marketing

Two key concepts, traditionally associated with strategic marketing, are receiving new emphasis in the European environment of the 1990s:

1 the trade-offs associated with standardisation versus adaptation;
2 identification of customer target groups which can be 'owned' by organisations.

Standardisation versus adaptation

There are two divergent lines of thinking as regards marketing products and services in the Single European Market. The first is that there will be increased opportunities for standardisation of product offerings as markets converge. Thus firms will be able to find trans-European product and service solutions and common ways of doing business across the different Member States of the EU. The second school of thought provides a direct corollary to this thinking. As Europe is comprised of 15 separate countries, each with their own national identity, culture and economic framework, it is believed that market-by-market adaptation will be preferable to looking for common Europe-wide solutions.

Much, then, depends on the extent to which European cultural and economic convergence becomes a reality. More will be said about convergence in Chapter 9 on culture in Europe. Generally, it is impossible to predict whether convergence will result from changes in European legislation and competition although it is possible to suggest that there is evidence of growing commonality in behaviour, and potentially the emergence of pan-European customers. Paitra (1995) suggests that people's attitudes across Europe are becoming similar along a number of dimensions:

1 *Money* – while budgeting and saving dominated the behaviour of many individuals in the 1950s, by the 1980s Europeans had turned into consumers, spending money (for hedonistic pleasure) and getting into debt.
2 *Revolt against the father* – paternal authority, which dictated hierarchical and authoritarian family structures has been supplanted with informal families with more open and liberal structures. With this trend, authority has given way to increased affability and a search for well-being.
3 *Search for autonomy* – European consumers have become more autonomous. They no longer feel a need to 'belong' and this has resulted in changed purchasing behaviour with brand loyalty arguably a thing of the past.

Assuming that greater commonality in behaviour will ultimately result in greater potential for standardisation has its draw-backs. While the trends outlined above are very real, there remain differences between countries along these dimensions. Some Member States have altered faster than others, which means that differences still prevail. Assuming that all consumers are the same is as dangerous as thinking all are different. Equally, it is possible to interpret these developments from a different perspective. Consumerism leads to more discerning and demanding customers. They are not just concerned with acquiring goods, they are also interested in purchasing products which provide 'solutions' to their needs. Second, the idea that paternalism is breaking down means that consumers expect organisations to prove themselves – through sound economic performance. Finally, the fact that individuals are searching for autonomy means they are looking for uniqueness in product offerings and a high degree of variety. The above suggests that European consumers in the future will increasingly demand differentiated products which raises questions over the ability of firms to standardise their product and service offerings on a pan-European scale.

Identifying target customers

European firms in the past tended to pursue organisational strategies based on decentralisation and localised differentiation and adaptation. This feature was discussed in Chapter 7. Adaptation to local market needs implicitly assumes high levels of local sensitivity to culture and demand patterns. What it fails to afford is an assimilation of common demand patterns across geographic boundaries. In modern day Europe, where firms are being forced to balance efficiency with local responsiveness, this type of marketing organisation is clearly inefficient. Pursuing a process of geographic segmentation is not a recipe for effective and efficient marketing effort. Paitra (1995) went on to conclude that while there are growing commonalties in behaviour this does not equate with pan-European homogenisation. However, greater harmonisation of behaviour between different groups within each Member State means that trans-European consumer segments are emerging, displaying similar needs and wants.

Implications for European marketing effort

What the above discussion suggests is that in the current European environment the parameters which traditionally established the basis of marketing effort no longer apply. Therefore, the debate on pan-European mass marketing (and standardisation) versus differential marketing (and local adaptation) need not concern the marketer. Marketing strategy development is about designing appropriate customer solutions in the here and now, and therefore if marketing managers get their homework right, research markets appropriately and identify needs (which may be common across some markets), the debate is of little relevance to success. Too many managers, in recent years, have become hung-up on the notion that to be successful means treating markets as separate entities. Good marketing practice in the 1990s and next millennium will necessarily need to look to pan-European customer solutions and common areas of demand.

The product/market-specific nature of these choices must be stressed. Some markets may be better served by mass-marketing (particularly industrial markets where consumer buying patterns are based on technological issues rather than individual desires) and others by differential marketing (potentially consumer markets wherein a number of varying subgroups displaying different needs and buying behaviour are apparent across European nations). The decision of which approach is preferable is therefore product/market determined, and no one single prescription is possible. Both approaches are likely to exist together in the new European environment.

What the two approaches will distinguish, is the objectives followed by European organisations. Those which can identify large-scale Euro-consumer segments are likely to pursue cost leadership strategies, focusing their efforts on economies of scale and improved business efficiency. Conversely, those for whom the identified target groups are smaller and varied, will concentrate their efforts on differential focus.

The view *'Think global act local'*, while theoretically sound, is difficult to operationalise. Many European organisations are now talking about this concept around the boardroom table but few examples of firms which have fully embraced this new thinking have yet emerged. Therefore, much of what appears in this chapter is prescriptive, based on propositions of change, but offering few practical examples of where change has, as yet, been achieved. The rationale for taking such an approach is the fact that theorists and business practitioners alike are generally agreed that change to a pan-European way of thinking is the only effective of way of managing their marketing efforts (and strategic development) in the Europe of the future.

However, as the discussions in this chapter will attempt to demonstrate, this is a far from easy strategy to implement and operationalise. There remain differences between countries in terms of technological acceptance, laws on advertising and promotion, pricing conventions and established distribution channels. Thus the opportunities for raising efficiency through servicing the needs of common sub-groups is likely to be difficult to realise, at least in the short-term.

ANALYSING THE MARKET

Chapter 7 provided a fairly comprehensive discussion of the requirements of a strategic audit. The information sources and tools for analysing markets are equally applicable to the marketing department. However, it is worth commenting on a number of other issues for market research which are likely to become more important in Europe in the future.

Customer research

The research tools and techniques referred to in Chapter 7 primarily looked at market-based research – the nature of the environment in which products are being sold or which offer opportunity for business development. What was not considered was the problem of cross-country comparison of statistics, much of which is gathered locally using different conventions and reporting practices. For example, differences in demographic data, educational qualifications, family groups, social trends, advertising and promotional spending exist between Member States making meaningful comparison very difficult. However, help in this area does exist: the European Society for Opinion and Marketing Research (ESOMAR) publishes material to assist in reviewing market research data from the fifteen Member States.

With customer focus taking on renewed emphasis in the European marketplace, it is important to consider *customer-focused research* techniques as it is these which will shape understanding of common patterns of purchasing behaviour, needs and requirements. In industrial markets, Europe-wide research may pose few problems. There are generally fewer numbers of customers involved and this raises the potential for organisations to work closely with individual companies. Entering into an on-going dialogue with customers, not just as a means of determining their buyer behaviour, but more importantly to understand their businesses and thus critical areas of adding value can be done relatively easily, although it does demand time, resources and a proactive desire to truly co-operate and not merely pay lip-service to the idea of becoming more involved in an interactive buyer–seller relationship. More will be said about developing good relationships with customers and intermediaries later in this chapter. Here, it is important to recognise that failing to co-operate and work closely will invariably result in less trust and mutual inter-dependence and thus a failure to fully embrace the new challenges of targeting effort at designing solutions to customer problems.

In consumer markets, the problems of market research are manifold:

1 *Language barriers* pose real problems for identifying commonality of behaviour between different nationals. This does not just refer to difficulties in translation, but also com-parability in meaning, which is linked not just to the words used but semantic differences in understanding between different nations;

2 *Sensitivity of questioning.* The different peoples of Europe will demonstrate a different willingness to impart information. The Greeks, for example, will not be concerned about giving information on their income, whereas the British are very sensitive about the money they earn and the implications this has for their being stratified into different social groups.

3 *Different research techniques.* Many modern day market research techniques are the product of American marketing activity and centre on individuals' ability to talk about feelings and emotions. Some country nationals, however, find this difficult to do and pre-fer more factually-based research questions than those which require them to express feelings.

4 *Cultural differences.* With cultural differences between the Member States being so sig-nificant, and culture permeating the way in which groups and individuals behave and think, questionnaire responses from different nationalities need to be considered within their own cultural context. A failure to do this may well lead to misinterpretation of the real meaning of research findings.

5 *Suspicion.* In some countries, there is growing suspicion about the usage of information gathered through marketing research which is leading to a growing reluctance to par-ticipate in research exercises.

Although the EU is awash with marketing research agencies, many of these are nationally based. With growing emphasis on pan-European marketing, the popularity of locally based organisations is likely to dwindle in favour of research institutions geared up to oper-ating across the Member States. In this way, the agencies are charged with the responsibility of overcoming the difficulties of producing information which is comparable across Member States and not the firm itself.

Database marketing

Databases are increasingly being used to store useful information on actual and potential customers which can be continually up-dated to provide a framework for changing demand patterns and customer requirements. Some of the most sophisticated databases developed to date are those of the catalogue companies who track the purchasing behav-iour of their customers and therefore are able to distinguish buying patterns and lifestyle characteristics. This means that it is easier for them to distinguish different buying groups to the extent that many companies have now differentiated their product offerings by introducing a number of s naller, specialised catalogues, deliberately designed to cater for the needs of smaller sub-segments.

Databases are also critical to direct marketing, which is becoming popular in today's competitive markets (more will be said about this later). It was highlighted in the introduction that some theorists are now questioning the effectiveness of mass advertising (given the exorbitant costs associated with promoting goods in this way) and the rationale for spending large budgets on promoting, often indistinguishable, product features. Kotler (1984) reports that Tony O'Reilly, the CEO of Heinz, is planning to drop television advertising in the UK in favour of direct marketing to heavy users. While this is a marked divergence from traditional practice in the food sector, it is perhaps a sign of things to come. Marketing budgets need to be wisely spent, and it may be preferable to consider marketing more as an information gathering and review function than a promotions exercise.

Database marketing allows organisations to take a long-term perspective of their relationship with customers. By continually up-dating information the identification of key trends is easier to see and thus creative business solutions easier to develop. The only problem with database marketing is customer suspicion and resistance. The concept smacks of a 'Big Brother' mentality, with behaviour being monitored by agencies over which the individual has no control. While some customers may find it appealing to be sent a special promotion for a restaurant just before their birthday suggesting 'Celebrate your birthday in style' – others consider this an invasion of privacy. Therefore, the use of information gathered needs to be treated with great sensitivity and considered in the light of cultural norms and acceptance.

Life-style analysis

Increasingly market researchers are turning to lifestyle analysis as a means of generating a clearer picture of their customers' behaviour and thus their tendency to purchase different types of product. This kind of assessment, frequently referred to as *geodemographics* is typically based on analysing residential neighbourhoods on the assumption that purchasing power and usage behaviour is strongly related to the type of neighbourhood in which they live. Geodemographic analysis, unlike other traditional means of classifying groups (usually along class dimensions) offers a richer picture of individual behaviour with around 40 different classifications being identified. It thus allows organisations to more closely tailor their marketing efforts to different groups. Therefore, this kind of approach, like data-basing marketing, is likely to yield greater opportunities in the European context for focusing on the needs of smaller target audiences.

The European Union dimension

Firms in the EU must change the focus of their research effort along a number of important dimensions depicted in Fig. 8.3. Essentially, they need to change from a market-by-market analysis of Member States to a Europe-wide view of interrelated markets, they need to look at ways of identifying both commonalties and differences, they need to review the effectiveness of highly decentralised organisational structures and look at new ways of identifying and solving marketing problems.

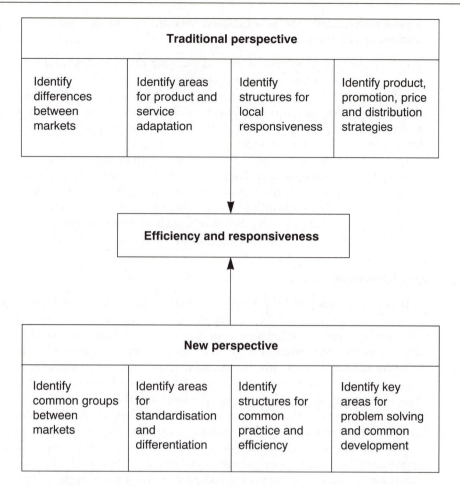

Fig. 8.3 The new objectives of European marketing research

DEFINING THE MARKET

Based on the above discussions of marketing demands in the new EU, it is clear that the concept of 'market' no longer equates with 'Member State'. Markets therefore need to be re-defined to reflect customer target groups. However, this raises a number of important problems with regards to effective marketing operations:

1 customers exhibiting similar demands may be broadly dispersed geographically thus raising costs of distribution and service;
2 some customer groups may fall outside of the company's typical sphere of expertise and experience;
3 the different countries in which consumers exist may have different distribution structures which means high levels of adaptation of logistics systems across Member States;
4 divergence in rules on advertising and promotion may make standardisation difficult;

5 price differentials may exist between the different markets again complicating the issue of standardisation and common practice.

It is here that the problems of operationalising the *'Think global act local'* proposition begin to emerge. While, in theory, offering products and services to common customer groups across the EU is attractive, in practice it requires new thinking on managing and organising marketing effort on a Europe-wide scale. The European Commission's attempts at removing these barriers, some of the successes to date and the ramifications for marketing effort require closer scrutiny.

Despite asserting at the outset that the marketing mix is no longer a useful tool for considering the challenges of marketing in a unified European context, the following analysis, which parallels much of the writing on the issue of European marketing, focuses on the Four Ps. There are two justifications for this: they provide a useful framework for identifying differences between Member States; such an analysis will allow a closer assessment of the problems involved in viewing Europe along these dimensions.

Technical differences

Differences between technical standards across the 15 Member States of Europe were, in the past, a major hurdle to achieving European integration. By providing different sets of rules and regulations in different countries they perpetuated the need for product adaptation. Thus they prevented firms from treating Europe as a Single Market.

Technical regulations, product standards and testing procedures have all played an important part in supporting the lines of demarcation between markets. Nationally established standards, designed to protect the interests of the people in terms of health, safety and the environment are now being replaced with EU-wide standards designed to eliminate the differences and assist in the development of a single market for technologies.

The effect of technical differences was to encourage firms to produce their various products in plants based in end-user markets. This kind of duplication often resulted in sub-optimal plants and supported company inefficiency. Cecchini (1989) highlighted the specific nature of these costs. His typology is shown as Table 8.1. With the convergence of technical standards there is scope for firms to rationalise their production, centralise activities, improve plant efficiency and thus make considerable cost savings.

Table 8.1. A typology of costs resulting from divergent costs and regulations

For companies
- duplication of product development
- loss of potential economies of manufacturing scale
- competitive weakness on world markets and vulnerability on European markets as companies operate from a narrow national base

For public authorities
- duplication of certification and testing costs
- not getting value for money in public purchasing whose non-competitive nature is often reinforced by national standards and certification

For consumers
- direct costs borne by companies and governments means higher prices
- direct and larger losses due to industry's competitive weakness and inefficiency structure

Source: Paolo Cecchini, '1992: The Benefits of a Single Market' Wildwood House, p. 26, 1989.

With so many different technical standards applying across industry, the achievement of a harmonised set of rules and regulations for all sectors is likely to take a long time. In order to speed up the process and ensure that EU firms are not discriminated against when operating outside of their own Member State, simply because they offer products based on different technical specifications, the Commission introduced a three-tier approach to harmonisation based on mutual recognition, standardisation and common reporting procedures.

Mutual recognition

First, in order to facilitate the 'right' of firms to operate across the EU, mutual recognition (discussed in Chapter 2) has been introduced. This stipulates that each Member State must give access to goods accepted as fit for sale in other countries. In effect, this ruling reduces the need for the Commission to make undertakings on an individual product basis. Nevertheless, there remain two key issues which mean that mutual recognition alone is not sufficient to eliminate technical barriers:

(a) Countries are still able (under Article 36 of the Treaty of Rome) to restrict access to those goods which do not meet their 'essential requirements'. This means that products can be barred access on the grounds that they infringe local rules on health, safety and environmental protection grounds.
(b) Because, historically, standards have been different and goods are often required which are compatible with existing equipment and systems – barriers will prevail until the Commission undertakes to set common standards for the EU as a whole.

Standardisation of essential requirements

Second, then, the Commission has undertaken to standardise the essential requirements rulings in a number of areas. While this does not provide exacting standards for individual products it provides guidelines for what is and is not considered acceptable. Within the overall framework individual companies are afforded a degree of freedom in deciding the most appropriate products for meeting new requirements.

This approach permits a degree of harmonisation to be achieved more rapidly than attempting to set specific product standards which may prove ephemeral. In addition, the Commission has introduced new European Standards which act in much the same way as present national standards such as DIN (in Germany), BSI (in Britain) and AFNOR (in France). While these standards are not legally enforceable, they are used as a yardstick for assessing quality and are promoted to consumers as the signs of acceptability. In this sense, they provide strong incentives for compliance and a stimulus for firms to adapt their products to comply with EU-wide standards.

The European Committee for Standardisation (CEN) and the Committee for Electrotechnical Standardisation (CENELEC) have embarked on a programme of establishing common EU benchmarks. Their work is likely to continue for some years as they promote long-term technical harmonisation. Because they do not enforce legal change upon firms, they allow organisations to adapt gradually to the new reforms. This involves not only manufacturers of goods adapting to new technologies in their new product development programmes, but also organisations gradually introducing new standards into their companies in the form of new equipment purchases. This is likely to promote a smooth period of transition and ultimately facilitate a natural progression to the harmonisation of technical standards.

Mutual information procedures

Finally, the Commission has introduced mutual information procedures which require national authorities to inform the Commission of any changes in regulations and standards. The Commission is empowered to block these changes, in favour of EU-wide regulations, if they are deemed to raise barriers to market entry and competition.

In addition to these across-the-board provisions the Commission, through the Council of Ministers, has also introduced new legislation for specific industries seriously hampered by continued differences.

The obvious question is: have these changes had an effect on the capability of firms to operate across the EU unhindered by technical barriers? To answer this question, it is worth looking at a specific example.

The pharmaceutical industry was, for decades, seriously hampered by protracted testing and registration procedures in the various Member States. These could take as long as three years and seriously curtailed the effective market life of the product, thus impacting on profit. Wu (1988) referred to this as the 'drug-lag'. In an attempt to overcome these problems, the Commission introduced a number of measures:

1 a centralised procedure for drug authorisation across all Member States for certain medicines (mandatory for all biotechnology products);
2 a decentralised procedure, based on the concept of mutual recognition of national marketing authorisations.
3 the establishment of a centralised regulatory body – the Medicines Evaluation Agency.

Based on the above, companies can now gain simultaneous authorisation for their drugs across the Member States of Europe and can also apply for registration in any country deemed to exhibit the least amount of regulatory red tape. Chaudhry, Dacin and Peter (1994), who conducted research into the impact of regulatory change on the European pharmaceutical industry, reported that nine out of 14 managers interviewed suggested the changes would be beneficial to operating across Europe. They highlighted such issues as the increased speed of product registration (and thus improved patent protection), the centralised body reducing duplication of effort, and greater choice to either go through the central body or pursue a policy of mutual recognition. The disadvantages associated with change (highlighted by the remaining five managers) concerned: making it easier for foreign firms to penetrate EU markets, and increased bureaucracy with centralised registration.

From this perspective, it is possible to argue that legislative change designed to limit the problems of operating across the EU are having an impact. While some firms are fearful of the changes (and possible increased centralised bureaucracy), on balance, the outcome appears favourable and, if this industry reflects changes taking place in other sectors, hidden barriers such as these are apparently eroding.

The potential for European pricing

Unlike technological issues described above, some firms see the harmonisation of pricing as detrimental, not beneficial, to their overall operations, potentially eroding the opportunities for price discrimination. However, it is important for marketers to develop pan-European solutions to their pricing problems as markets open up. Price differentials across the Member States of Europe dictate that managers need to gauge the extent to which differences in prices charged between different subsidiaries can be sustained (Simon and Kucher, 1992). As buyers turn more and more to pan-European sourcing there is the threat that firms will lose the potential to offer products at different prices in different locations, with important ramifications for overall company profitability.

Price is an important aspect of product positioning. Prices are decided, not just as a means of deriving profit, but as a means of giving signals to customers about the quality and nature of the product being offered. Therefore, if managers adopt a single pricing policy for Europe, the common price may mean a product being positioned in an upper segment in one market and a lower segment in another. Differences in competition between markets also impact on price. As each Member State of Europe is characterised by a different competitive structure (with different local firms coming into play) local operating units need to have a degree of freedom to decide on the most appropriate pricing level in the current circumstances. Equally, different channel structures and degrees of retailer power between Member States also impact on the amount of mark-up required by distributors and retailers, and thus ultimately prices in final consumer markets.

Table 8.2 highlights different cost/price positions across a number of Member States in 1986 for a number of banking products. The differences are significant and question the feasibility of attempting to harmonise prices on a pan-European scale. Dutch mortgage companies, for example, which charge the lowest price for their mortgages, would not be advised to offer their products at similar prices across the Member States. Although this would mean their having very competitive rates, consumer perception would be of a 'cheap' product, with doubts over firms' ability to offer necessary levels of quality and service professionalism. Equally, it would mean Dutch firms not taking advantage of the potential to charge higher prices elsewhere in Europe and thus raise levels of profitability.

Table 8.2. Relative cost-price positions* for banking products

Country	Consumer credit	Credit cards	Mortgages
Belgium	−41	74	31
Spain	39	26	118
France	105	−30	78
West Germany	136	60	57
Ireland	n/a	89	−4
Netherlands	31	43	−6
United Kingdom	121	15	−20

* percentage discrepancies from price of average lowest four producers.
Source: European Commission.

In an attempt to encourage the erosion of price differentials, the Commission are actively encouraging parallel importing. Parallel trade involves market intermediaries buying up goods in one market (where prices are low) and selling them in another (where prices are higher) at below the going market rate. This deters manufacturers from charging different prices in different markets and exploiting those markets where price elasticity is lower and consumers are prepared to pay the higher price. This is possible in markets where there is a greater need for the product or where the overall market rate is higher and competitors have failed to lower the price through aggressive price competition, preferring to preserve profit levels.

Clearly, there are disadvantages to manufacturers from intermediaries conducting parallel importing. Dudley (1990) highlights the following list:

- average selling prices will be lowered reducing manufacturers' profitability regardless of whether or not they sell products across the EU
- the price consumers are prepared to pay for additional intangible product features is reduced as it is discounted against local competitors, which may be damaging to the product's image and its position in the market
- the manufacturer loses control over where and to whom its products are sold which again can be damaging to the product's image as it may be sold on to retail outlets which do not match the product image and market position
- traditional market intermediaries lose confidence in manufacturers as they see their services being side-stepped; targeting marketing expenditures becomes difficult as the direction of investments is distorted by parallel trade. For example, a company may raise its investment in a particular sector to find that it is being out-competed by its own products in the same market.

While manufacturers may be frustrated by this practice, the Commission are keen to promote it to the extent that Article 85 of the Treaty of Rome permits the Commission to take action against any firm who tries to prevent intermediaries from parallel importing. The overall benefits to the EU, as they see it, are a reduction in EU-wide prices, which benefits consumers, and a convergence of prices which helps to enhance the idea of a 'level playing field'.

With or without parallel trade, differences in prices between countries in certain industry sectors are likely to prevail, raising questions over the most effective solutions to the new European pricing problem. Simon and Kucher (1992) talk about the development of a *European price corridor*. Price differentials, they suggest, are narrowing, as a result of both price increases in lower price countries (as manufacturers see the potential to earn larger profit margins) and price reductions in other countries where competition and cross-border arbitrage are dictating lower market prices. Their recommendation is that firms need to adjust their European pricing policies to fit this corridor, rather than establish a standard price for all Europe-wide activities. They propose the following steps:

1 Determine, for each country, the optimal price level based on competitive conditions, channels of distribution, consumer buying behaviour and desired product position.
2 Find out whether parallel imports (cross-border arbitrage) occur at these prices.
3 If price disturbances are expected, identify a price 'corridor' and adjust prices accordingly.

Ultimately, each company's goal is to maximise profit and not simply pursue a policy of arbitrary alignment. However, it is impossible to judge the ramifications of price changes on the company at large at subsidiary level which argues for more centralisation of pricing at head office level where an overall picture of price differentials can be monitored and managed. Therefore, while subsidiaries need the freedom to dictate appropriate prices, the ultimate decision on overall policy should come from the centre.

In the short-term, at least, the European environment appears to offer up little potential for price standardisation and harmonisation. However, there is the possibility (indeed the necessity) for organisations managing prices on a Europe-wide scale to ensure that profit potential is maximised and price differentials exploited. If managed well, price differentials are a potential advantage, not a threat.

Differences in distribution

One of the key economic changes facing many firms in the EU is the growing dominance of retail chains. In the UK, for example, retailer dominance has restricted profit margins for even the largest multinationals and the growth in own-label brands is changing customer behaviour and eroding brand loyalty.

Although supermarkets and large retail chains have made an impression in most European countries, restrictions imposed by governments in some Member States, designed to support the continued existence of local specialist stores have limited the extent to which large dominant groups have developed. For example, strict planning and regional coverage regulations imposed in Belgium, and the Netherlands have severely restricted the growth of the dominant retailers. In France and Spain questions have also been raised recently regarding planning permission for large out-of-town developments which have the potential to offer 'one-stop shopping' solutions to customers and draw business away from smaller stores and town centre shops. In the UK, over the last year, questions of this kind have also been raised with planning permission being refused to large groups to develop retail parks in conveniently sited out-of-town locations. Nevertheless, the five largest retailers in the UK account for approximately 60 per cent of the market, in Germany about 45 per cent and in Sweden 80 per cent. Therefore, while recent curbs may be slowing down the rate of concentration, the situation in most markets is one of considerable retailer power.

The proliferation of discount stores is also affecting the traditional small retailer. As many of these are wholesale type operations, cutting out the middle-man and dealing directly with end customers, they are able to charge prices far lower than many retailers who are consequently forced out of business. They are also squeezing the profit margins of other big retailers who, in turn, are putting pressure on manufacturers to lower prices even further. In this competitive bonanza, only the dominant are likely to survive.

The power of retailers, like other issues discussed above, differs considerably from market to market. This means that it is hard to standardise distribution strategies across the EU. Therefore, while it may be appropriate to enter into long-term relationships with retailers in the UK (where five retailers account for 60 per cent of the market), maybe through producing own-label goods, in Italy, where small family businesses still prevail, with no chain controlling more than two per cent of the market, operating via locally based distributors may continue to be preferable. Once again, there is little potential for pan-European standardisation of distribution effort, although common practices may be applicable between markets.

Perhaps more importantly, however, in the new environment, recognising that common customer groups exist across Member States means diverting attention away from traditional channels of distribution based in individual countries. In Chapter 7, issue was made of centralisation of distribution functions as a means of better serving geographically dispersed EU customers. The removal of barriers between Member States means that this kind of distribution organisation is now feasible. BICC VERO, for example, part of the BICC group of the UK, involved in construction and electronic cables, opened a central warehouse in Metz in France in 1991 which offers the firm lower transportation times (with a seven day delivery policy) and proximity to major centres of electronic excellence. Multilingual workers also enable the central distribution facility to operate effectively with customers from a variety of EU markets. For a company such as BICC, whose manufacturing facilities are located on the periphery of the EU, this move is understandably attractive and affords the company distinct advantages in operating on a pan-European basis.

The BICC example raises an important point in EU marketing understanding. Whereas in the past, effectiveness of marketing effort was seen to depend on the existence of nationally/regionally based sales and marketing offices responsible for adaptation of the marketing mix at a local level, recent moves have witnessed a shift towards increased centralisation of distribution functions. This tends to suggest a shift away from traditional marketing thinking based on managing the 'Four Ps' locally towards increased emphasis on effective logistics organisation on a pan-European scale. Although this does not necessarily mean firms closing their local sales and marketing offices (which can serve as important listening and learning posts for identifying changes in customer needs) it is demonstrative of a change in focus and prioritising of tasks.

Alternatively, other firms have demonstrated that the complexities and costs associated with customer dispersion can be effectively handled through alternative logistics management tools such as just-in-time (JIT) delivery systems which allow maximum efficiency in servicing a broad market. Berghaus, the UK producer of speciality performance outdoor clothing has established JIT stock response systems (backed by flexible production techniques) which has allowed it to restructure its relationship with European retailers. Retailer reluctance to stock large quantities of goods, particularly those which only sell in specific weather conditions, meant it was difficult to maximise the potential from market integration when large shipments were viewed as the only cost-effective means of servicing the market. New systems mean the company has been able to shorten delivery times from 6–12 weeks to one week and relax minimum order quantities to a single garment. This shifts stockholding risk away from retailers which makes Berghaus a far more attractive supplier.

Advertising and promotion legislation

Although advertising is on the agenda for pan-European legislation, national rules on advertising behaviour still dominate. These include such areas as:

1 limited media availability for such things as tobacco, alcohol and pharmaceuticals;
2 limits on the number of hours available for television advertising (Germany for example, adopting a policy of *block advertising* rather than spot advertising which means only certain times of the day are set aside for advertising and thus adverts are not interspersed between programmes as they are in France, Italy and the UK).
3 limits set on the amount firms can spend on advertising;
4 rules regarding misleading advertising;
5 rules regarding superiority claims;
6 codes of conduct on advertising to children.

In the short-term, then, scope for standardisation of promotion may be limited. In recognition of this fact the Commission are introducing legislation to determine EU-wide rules. An important part of the new reform is liberalisation of broadcasting for both television and radio. In the case of television, Directive 89/552 includes rulings on cable and satellite coverage, an area where expansion may not only provide an outlet for increased demands on television advertising time, but also scope to reach a pan-European audience.

The growing propensity of magazine publishers to develop international products (in translation) is also providing greater potential for pan-European coverage in promotion of some products. Equal potential theoretically exists in the case of newspapers, although few publishers have reacted to the opportunities. The *Financial Times* and the *European* are major exceptions. Further penetration in the future may be expected.

European strategy implications

What much of the above discussion assumes is that organisations already have a number of diverse European activities which require re-organisation and assimilation. But what of firms which are only just beginning to explore non-domestic EU markets or small organisations which lack the resources to contemplate the additional costs of operating on such a grand scale? The decision of appropriate market scope and coverage is a complex one for any firm to make and requires careful consideration of a number of key factors:

1 Are individual country markets sufficiently large to sustain our business expansion efforts? If not, what regions might we first consider?
2 To what extent do we need to build close relationships with customers and intermediaries to secure access for our products? If it is large, where do we start and what time-frame do we need to consider for future expansion?
3 How different are distribution systems in the different Member States? If considerable, is there any potential to transfer learning between different markets and regions?
4 Does the company have any existing knowledge of operating in a certain fashion? If so, in which markets would the firm be best able to exploit existing skills?

The key task for European expansion is prioritising market entry and marketing development. Even if a firm has identified trans-European customer groupings, it is impossible to develop the systems and structures to service all these customers in the short-term. Efforts must be focused on getting the right systems and structures in place to manage effort in each distinct region before rolling out into other Member States. By identifying commonalties between markets (cultural and economic clusters) and opportunities for transferred learning between different regions, the roll-out process is simplified.

One final question deserves attention: is the 'think global act local' prescription workable in practice? From what has been said, it is evident that Europe is carved into a number of discrete geographic territories across which technologies, prices, distribution channels and advertising legislation differ markedly. The EU is not a single market in the sense of there being opportunities for adopting a unified mix of marketing policies which are appropriate across all markets. In order to manage this diversity firms have to be prepared to adapt their strategies on a market-by-market basis. This need not, however, mean losing sight of Europe-wide objectives.

The tendency of organisations to view Europe along the four dimensions of the marketing mix outlined above tends to obscure the real challenges of marketing in the modern EU. It perpetuates the process of geographic compartmentalisation and makes it difficult for firms to adopt a pan-European vision for development. By suggesting that marketing is solely concerned with managing elements of the marketing mix assumes that marketing is a decentralised function best managed at a local level. Within this structure, it is impossible to adopt pan-European marketing strategies, as individual subsidiaries continue to pull in different directions. It is, therefore, critical that modern marketing departments drive from the centre. This does not mean taking marketing mix decisions away from the subsidiaries (who need to be given the freedom to manage local differences) but establishing a centralised management and co-ordination function responsible for identifying key tasks and co-ordinating Europe-wide marketing policy. The different layers of this process are outlined in Fig. 8.4.

What Fig. 8.4 attempts to encapsulate are the differences between headquarter control, co-ordination and vision (which centre on tasks and problem solving) and local subsidiary implementation (concerned with functional marketing issues). Also included is a 'middle-tier' of common projects. This tier is the linchpin of the process, wherein the exchange of information provides the foundation for overall marketing developments and the identification of commonalties and differences. It is at this level that the firm can solve common problems and identify common needs and establish a framework for its Europe-wide marketing developments.

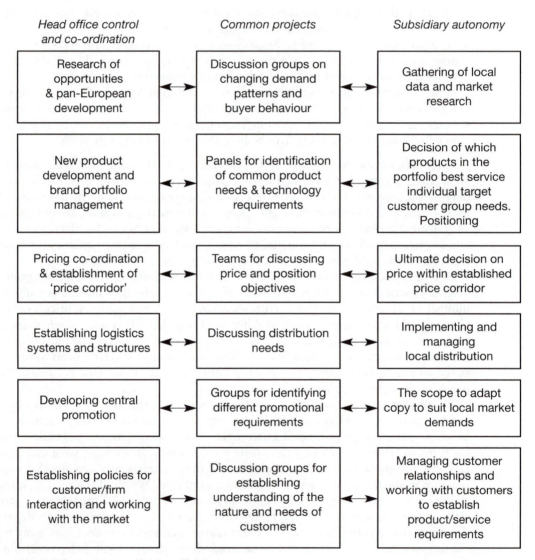

Fig. 8.4 European marketing divisions

WORKING WITH THE MARKET

There is a growing belief in the area of marketing that customers want solutions not products. As consumerism has developed in Western economies customers have become more discerning and demanding of suppliers and are continually looking for products which add more value (whether this be aesthetic, technological or performance and quality). This has important ramifications for organisational structures. Vandermerwe (1994) suggests:

> Value in today's terms can only be created when knowhow connects to knowhow, i.e., when people and corporations (within and across industries) come together, to add to the lifestyles and corporate bottom lines of their dedicated markets.

No longer is it possible for firms to produce and sell, they must enquire and provide which means re-thinking the way in which they interact with their market and develop structures which permit market-driven decision making rather than company directed. It also means changing the mind-set of the organisation to think in terms of customer benefits rather than tangible products. A bank, for example, does not want to purchase a computer system. What it wants is a tool which facilitates financial planning and permits the establishment of a sophisticated customer database. The bank customer, on the other hand, wants a solution which spans his/her day-to-day financial transactions including deposits and withdrawals, the payment of bills, ease of access to his/her money at any time, services for foreign travel and holidays, credit and loans, etc. Therefore, producing standardised goods for mass consumer markets appears to hold less sway than developing solutions for the individual – making the customer king and being sensitive to individual requirements rather than those of the general populace.

Customer identification

The first important thing a firm must do, is identify its customers. This is not as easy as it first appears. It is not only the final consumer firms need to concern themselves with, they also have to consider the role of intermediate purchasers such as wholesalers, distributors and retailers, all of whom have a role to play in the ultimate success of the product in the marketplace. Once an intermediary purchases goods from a manufacturer, he takes title to those goods and therefore has the freedom to choose how and to whom they are sold. If the intermediary is not clear about the manufacturer's intentions, it is possible that he will fail to sell to the desired customer target groups which has important ramifications not only for the success of the product, but also perceived differentiation. It is therefore critical that firms not only attempt to develop relationships with final customers, but also intermediaries. By working together, manufacturers and intermediaries have the potential, together, to add value.

Managing relationships with intermediaries

Research conducted by the Industrial Marketing and Purchasing Group in the 1980s focused on the problems of developing good relationships with intermediaries. Much emphasis was placed on designing systems to facilitate co-operation rather than concentrate on control mechanisms. There is much scope for conflict between manufacturers and intermediaries as both are seeking to maximise profits at the expense of the other. Conflict may arise for a number of reasons:

1 Intermediaries and manufacturers may disagree on price. Intermediaries may cut prices in order to move stock, lowering the returns for the manufacturer.
2 Conflicts arise in the way the product is marketed. Intermediaries, based on their closeness to the market and understanding of customers, sometimes perceive products as uncompetitive which gives them less incentive to promote them. Equally, helpful advice made by the intermediary to the manufacturer is frequently ignored as it fails to fit with the manufacturer's understanding of the product and competition based on experience from other countries.
3 Intermediaries fear over-performance. By promoting a product and achieving a certain level of business, the intermediary can encourage firms to establish their own distribution functions, removing their business from the intermediary.
4 The intermediary is often faced with divided loyalties. Dealing with a number of competing products means the intermediary is not solely dedicated to the manufacturers' product which dilutes the amount of selling effort provided by the salesforce. Generally, they sell those products which earn them the highest commission or for which there is a strong demand generated by high promotional expenditure, a high degree of attractiveness (be it brand name or technological sophistication) or greater reliability.

Conflict can be overcome through one of two methods, control or co-operation. Control involves a series of rewards and sanctions based on targets set by the manufacturer. Although they can prove successful in raising performance, they do little to nurture good relations between the two parties as they continue to support a buyer–seller type relationship. In so doing, the individual parties continue to sub-optimise. While the intermediary may be inclined to improve sales performance, there will be little incentive for him to improve additional complementary functions such as information gathering and dissemination which can be critical to future strategic planning for the manufacturer.

Co-operation emerges as the most favourable approach, wherein the manufacturer works closely with the intermediary, setting price levels which are acceptable to both parties, giving, receiving and acting on information, and providing adequate support and incentives. While many firms assume that operating via an intermediary involves handing over the product at the docks or market border, nothing could be further from the truth. The challenge facing firms in the Single Market, particularly small firms for whom utilising the services of the intermediary is their only available option, is to establish and preserve good relations. In the longer-term this may involve technical staff placements in the foreign firm although the acceptability of this approach, in turn, depends on the development of good relations in the short-term.

The Industrial Marketing and Purchasing Group alluded to the notion of *tripartite* relations in international industrial marketing, the manufacturer, the distributor and the customer all becoming involved in the decision-making processes. Without this kind of relationship, it is impossible to effectively adopt a customer-oriented approach which embraces the duopoly of customer management: good relations with the intermediary on the one hand (to encourage them to work closely with consumers) and knowledge of and communication with the consumer on the other (either directly or via the intermediary) as a means of ensuring that products and services are tailored to provide solutions. The complexities of tripartite customer management are highlighted in Fig. 8.5.

While the above research centres on relationship management in industrial markets, there is no reason why these concepts cannot be equally transferred to consumer markets. Companies need to ensure they work closely with customers (by researching their needs and wants and understanding their purchasing behaviour) and develop good relations with retailers. If marketing managers are going to actively pursue the advantages which accrue from working with their customers to provide more tailor-made solutions and added value, intermediaries need to be incorporated in the value chain of the firm, whether they be internal or external to the organisation. At one level, this would appear to suggest greater vertical integration within the value chain (gaining greater control over the firm/customer interface through ownership of distribution and marketing functions), although as was stressed in Chapter 7 and above, control can be equally achieved through co-operation and relationship management.

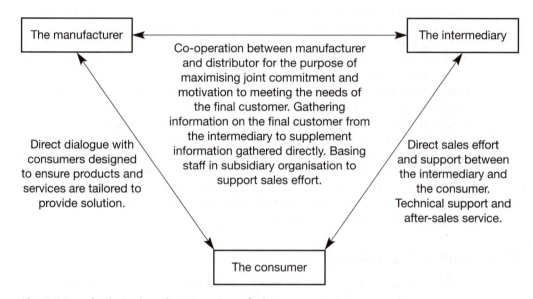

Fig. 8.5 Developing tripartite customer relations

WORKING WITH THE FIRM

Organisational structures

Marketing departments in recent years have been accused of working independently of other functions within the organisation, of becoming islands without linkages to other departments. Arguably, however, it is not the marketing departments themselves which are to blame, but the organisational structures in which they operate. Peters (1990) suggested that organisational structures have lagged behind strategies, which means that the philosophy of getting closer to the customer is not being supported by organisational restructuring, structures acting as impediments not facilitators to this new way of thinking.

Within strictly compartmentalised hierarchies, marketing departments, which may be adept at identifying the needs of customers and targeting products, are frustrated by the failure of internal systems to permit group-wide value adding. With R&D departments and production operations ploughing their own furrow, it is inevitable that knowledge of markets will not be translated into improved product offerings. The various functions within the organisation therefore require review if European firms are to respond to the new environmental challenge.

So how can firms react? The first issue to stress is that all departments should be working in the same direction – to satisfy the needs of targeted consumers. This means the marketing function transcending other business operations and not merely being an adjunct to them. Indeed, some proponents of customer-oriented marketing have gone as far as to suggest that everyone in the organisation needs to adopt a marketing role, thinking how their particular function relates to the needs of customers, both internal and external. If guided by a marketing department which is freed from the ties of its island status and permitted to operate across functions, various departments may be able to more clearly align their activities with the pursuit of customer value-adding.

The notion of customer focus, both internal and external, is reminiscent of Total Quality Management (TQM) principles. This is, perhaps, not surprising. Some theorists have argued that TQM is, in essence, a management tool for developing systems for internal and external marketing improvement. While it is way beyond the scope of this chapter to outline the varying arguments in this debate, it is useful to understand the parallels. Quality is driven from the top, through mechanisms to integrate and reinforce the notion of the customer as king, to remove inefficiencies and draw the organisation together to meet a common purpose. New marketing challenges demand the same: an all-embracing ethos of customer orientation designed to find solutions to problems not products to sell. This can only be driven by the top and through re-organisation of the company into more cross-disciplinary groups charged with the responsibility of managing across functions, and not perpetuating functional inefficiency.

Cross-functional involvement

Marketing departments have to become involved in the design and manufacturing functions. New product development needs to be driven by market forces, not the whims of technical staff. There have been numerous examples of firms which have produced highly innovative products, but without a clear target market in which to sell them. Equally, there is no point in the marketing department identifying and targeting numerous niches which demand the production of small batches of highly differentiated products if the production department is geared up for mass production.

The latter point raises an important problem in the modern organisation. Many European firms have out-dated production and management systems. Production processes developed for world markets of the 1960s and 1970s, where the object was to produce mass market goods for mass market consumers, afford few advantages in the modern environment where customisation dictates more flexible production runs based on computer aided design and computer aided manufacturing systems and flatter, flexible organisational structures based on team work and inter-disciplinary co-operation. De Meyer and Ferdows (1991) reporting on the results of the 1990 European Manufacturing Futures Survey suggest:

> Integrated CAD and CAM is still far off for many respondents. Only half have both CAD and CAM. Only half have some kind of integration between them. Job rotation across functional borders is not yet common practice.

(De Meyer and Ferdow, 1991, p. 28)

Making the necessary adjustments is, however, not straightforward. Whereas the marketing function is a relatively *soft* discipline in which change and new ways of thinking can be adopted quickly, company organisation and production, are *hard* disciplines which are far less flexible and require major investment before change can be achieved. The marketing department cannot, therefore, work alone in achieving the objectives of pan-European marketing and improved customisation. Directives must come from the top with senior managers finding ways of altering organisational structures and functional competence to support new developments.

NEW PRODUCT DEVELOPMENT

It was stated above that marketing departments need to work more closely with R&D departments to ensure that the products which are developed are those which cater for the changing needs of target customers and different needs of varying customer segments. In recent years, high failure rates in the introduction of new products have led departments to be very risk averse, with most 'new' products emerging being merely extensions of existing product lines and not truly new and innovative offerings.

The marketer's role in new product development is therefore about providing a link between the market and the design department, with customers and R&D technicians both being involved in the process. It also requires involving senior management, as changes in customer demand and purchasing patterns may have serious implications for future business objectives and directions. Figure 8.6 attempts to highlight the varying degrees of involvement of different players in different stages of the design process and thus the role of marketing departments in the new product development function.

Although the processes described in the figure are highly simplified, it is easy to see the rationale for presenting the marketing department as the linchpin in the new product development process. They are the conduit of information between the market, and the firm and the various departments involved in the new product development process. Taking on a pivotal role means broader involvement of various *stakeholders* which can be further facilitated by project teams which bring members of all groups together at the same time to discuss and attempt to solve mutual problems.

The above apparently suggests that new product development is purely finding out what customers want and then delivering it. It is possible to suggest, however, that customers do not always know what they want, or at least cannot articulate it in concrete terms. So what then? Some theorists are now talking about the concept of *market sensing*. Robertson (1994) suggests market sensing is about:

> Designing a product that consumers did not explicitly request. The challenge of course is to get out in front of consumers; to extrapolate and infer future customer needs. Yet traditional forms of marketing research seldom seem to provide the insight necessary to engage in creative marketing.

Thus new product development is also about having visions. This does not merely mean innovative researchers doing their own thing, but marketing managers exploring trends in customer purchasing and demand more broadly – 'living' with consumers in such a way that their emerging needs become explicit to the supplier organisation before they have become apparent to them. This is a far from easy task, but organisations which master the art have the potential to create markets, rather than create products.

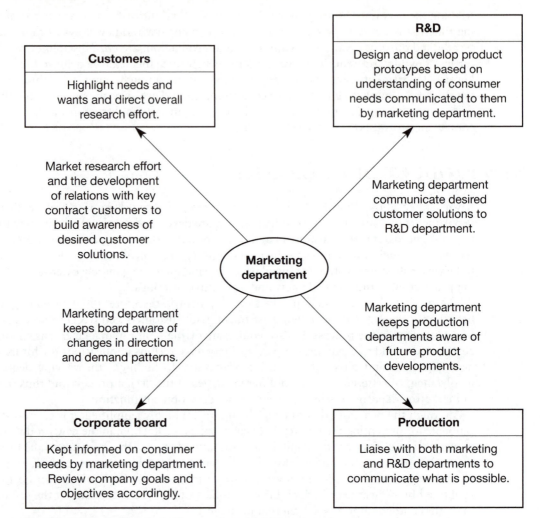

Customers

Highlight needs and wants and direct overall research effort.

R&D

Design and develop product prototypes based on understanding of consumer needs communicated to them by marketing department.

Market research effort and the development of relations with key contract customers to build awareness of desired customer solutions.

Marketing department communicate desired customer solutions to R&D department.

Marketing department

Marketing department keeps board aware of changes in direction and demand patterns.

Marketing department keeps production departments aware of future product developments.

Corporate board

Kept informed on consumer needs by marketing department. Review company goals and objectives accordingly.

Production

Liaise with both marketing and R&D departments to communicate what is possible.

Fig. 8.6 Marketing's role in the product development

Highlighted in Chapter 7 was the issue of R&D organisation, which deserves some further comment here. It was suggested that different markets, given their different economic and social structures, may well give rise to diverse marketing requirements and product solutions. Centralised R&D, therefore runs the risk of being insensitive to local demand conditions, although highly decentralised R&D tends to result in firms 're-inventing the wheel' in their developments for different consumer groups. Co-operation between research departments in different European centres was therefore viewed as a preferable means of ensuring that local markets are catered for, ideas emanating from developments in one area being communicated to the group and tested against conditions in other markets where they may potentially prove as successful. This kind of thinking re-affirms the importance of the marketing department's information exchange role in the research and development process. By combining forces, different marketing subsidiaries around Europe can compare their knowledge and experience of different customer segments in the various

Member States and demonstrate areas of similarity and difference which can either be communicated to centralised development centres or decentralised units in different countries which may then work co-operatively rather than independently.

MANAGING THE BRAND PORTFOLIO

Branding issues have changed significantly in recent years in the grocery sector with the proliferation of own-label branding. Although the concept was relatively slow to take off at first, with consumers wary to accept own-brand labels, believing them to be inferior to the branded alternatives, focus by the retail chains on quality and value for money has resulted in increased acceptance. In the UK, for example, when Sainsbury's introduced its 'Classic American Cola' in April 1994, within weeks it had achieved almost 25 per cent market share for take-home cola against industry giants Coca-Cola and Pepsi. Trends such as this are putting increased pressure on branded manufacturers to look to new ways of reducing costs and sustaining the quality image of their products.

Barwise and Robertson (1992) suggest that development of European brand portfolios will develop as firms pursue four principal objectives:

1 to establish global brands
2 to pursue multiple segments
3 to counteract the growing power of retailers
4 to raise scale economies.

The concept of global brands

On the first issue, while the notion of standardisation versus adaptation was discussed in some detail earlier in the chapter, the idea of global branding was never fully pursued. The tentative conclusion drawn earlier was that, while marked differences remain between markets, there is the potential to identify common customer groups between Member States which means that there is potential for trans-European brand development. Mars, which had developed a Europe-wide portfolio based more on local adaptation than standardised brand development, recently standardised the brand names of its ranges in Europe. The Treets and Bonitos brands were harmonised under the M&M's umbrella, and Marathon bars (sold in the UK) were pulled under the common global brand-name – Snickers.

That there is potential for pan-European brand development is undeniable, and those firms which are prepared to shed the mantle of marketing-mix based marketing development are likely to see the advantages. Thus, the issue is not one of standardisation or adaptation, but global branding backed by local adaptation of operational strategies.

The pursuit of multiple segments

The second point, highlights the growing difficulties facing firms in developing products for different customer segments. As was highlighted earlier, the inflexible nature of production technologies often makes it difficult for firms to introduce differentiated offerings for a variety of different market segments (and thus develop brands to cater for differing needs). This has led many firms to acquire brands which can fill identified 'gaps' in the company's brand portfolio. Acquiring brands also means acquiring production facilities, and thus it brings with it two clear advantages: it means firms can add new brands without diluting the overall image of their existing portfolio and it means organisations do not have to face the problems of manufacturing down-time or inflexibility in production.

Responding to retailer dominance

With retail concentration increasing across Europe, and branded producers intent on managing costs more effectively, broad brand portfolios raise the bargaining power of manufacturers vis-à-vis dominant retailers. Offering more lines means being able to charge higher prices without being de-listed, raises the potential to command greater shelf space and facilitates relationship development as it is in the retailers' interest to deal co-operatively with organisations servicing their needs across a variety of diverse product ranges.

Heightening the potential for scale economies

Finally, scale economies in marketing can arise when companies are handling more branded products. Different ranges of products can be distributed together, the salesforce can handle larger volumes and promotional efforts can be cross-subsidised.

Developing brand portfolios for Europe

But how can European firms develop their brand portfolio? Essentially, there are three basic alternatives available to them:

1 extend existing brands into new markets;
2 purchase new brands through acquiring existing firms;
3 enter into joint ventures and alliances to raise the power of the combined group.

It is the second of these issues which is proving particularly attractive in the EU. This is the result of two important features of brand acquisition:

1 It is relatively cost effective. Buying an existing brand is comparatively cheaper than attempting to establish a new brand which requires considerable advertising backing to establish awareness and acceptance (although this obviously depends on the price paid).
2 More is better than less. By acquiring different brands firms gain additional leverage, particularly when dealing with dominant retailers.

Obviously, options such as this are not open to smaller firms, for whom concentration on a single brand, or narrow portfolio is preferable. Firms cannot afford to be in the middle ground. Either they must specialise in developing and sustaining a strong position in a small number of target areas, or develop an extended portfolio. Those which fall between the two stools are likely to become the targets for takeover activity of the larger players. Lynch (1994) suggests that only those firms with advertising budgets of at least US$60 million for three years are in a position to consider building and supporting brand portfolios of the scale suggested above. Therefore, it is likely to remain a preserve of multinational enterprises and not smaller European organisations. Nevertheless, the challenges for brand development, in Europe whether by multinationals or small specialist firms are the same:

1 to establish a product which has a distinct image and offers consumers clearly defined differential advantages;

2 to maintain levels of quality and service;
3 to establish brand names and supporting advertising which have general rather than national appeal;
4 use price as a means of positioning the brand effectively;
5 clearly communicate brand objectives to third parties and partners.

A failure to focus on the above list of factors diminishes the effectiveness of brand development and ultimately may lead to misconstrued signals and market failure. Branding is therefore about establishing a clear picture in the minds of target customers and intermediaries of what the brand represents and why it is a preferable purchase solution to other products or services available in the market.

Before moving on it is important to highlight the issue of corporate branding, particularly as it relates to the activities of service firms. Unlike goods, services are intangible, which means they cannot be seen, touched, or tested prior to purchase. This obviously raises doubts in customers' minds over the ability of the firm to provide the 'right' kind of solution to their needs. Many service firms, anxious to overcome such uncertainties, have turned their attention to corporate branding as a means of providing consumers with 'cues' regarding reliability and quality. This is nowhere more apparent that in the banking industry, where advertising campaigns are intent on promoting corporate symbols and images synonymous with service professionalism, quality and reliability.

MANAGING CUSTOMER RELATIONSHIPS

Managing on-going relationships centres on four objectives:

1 managing quality;
2 providing service;
3 understanding repeat purchase;
4 effective communication with customers.

If we are to accept that modern marketing is relationship marketing, then managing these relationships is a critical function of the current day marketing department. A failure to deliver on time, an inability to cope with after-sales servicing, and a failure to understand why customers come back (or don't) means the organisation does not have a foundation on which to build consumer loyalty and long-term meaningful relationships with their market.

Managing quality

An important problem immediately arises when considering quality management: what is it and how can it be measured? There are no simple answers to this, and in many ways the only reliable means of measuring quality is through consumer research on past purchases. This gives manufacturers some indication of how well a product is performing relative to customer expectations. Post-purchase questionnaires are becoming a popular tool for monitoring opinions about quality issues. Satisfaction of product features and performance, and indication of faults and complaints can all be assessed using this technique.

Providing customer service

Providing service poses a completely different set of problems. For intermediaries, service quality is often measured in terms of a company's ability to deliver on time. Alternatively, from a consumer's point of view, service is more about providing adequate after-sales support to cope with breakdowns or product failure.

The importance of delivery can be regarded in relation to future demand. Where a manufacturer fails to deliver on time, whether because of the firm's inability to secure adequate stock or respond rapidly enough to orders, or where there are unexpected problems such as dock strikes and poor weather conditions, the likelihood of the customer trading with him again is remote. This introduces the notion of the *cost of lost sales* into the management equation. In order to prevent this happening, firms have a number of options available to them:

1 they can establish a more centralised distribution facility which is better placed to respond quickly to orders;
2 they can employ more flexible manufacturing and distribution techniques;
3 they can rely on the services of locally-based intermediaries to hold stock on their behalf (although problems of delivering to intermediaries will remain).

Regarding the provision of after-sales service, again manufacturers have a number of options:

1 establish their own after-sales service provision in the local market (usually through local sales and marketing offices);
2 employ a team of Europe-wide trouble shooters prepared to go to any location within the EU at short notice (only really feasible where the number of customers is small);
3 rely on the services of market-based intermediaries.

On the final point, Valla (1986) notes that intermediaries can, and do, provide effective service support, although the extent to which this will raise customers' perceptions of quality is linked to the extent to which the supplier and intermediary can develop good, co-operative working relations. This point deserves a little more comment. It would be wrong to suppose that intermediaries do not provide an effective link between the manufacturer and the customer. Although establishment of foreign-owned operations gives manufacturers control over the quality of service they provide, intermediaries, through their longevity in the market and knowledge of customers derived over a number of years, may be better suited to deal directly with consumers. Foreign intermediaries can provide firms with a *surrogate* presence in the market and many are highly adept at handling major accounts and important clients. Intermediaries can provide a number of important services for the manufacturer:

1 *providing warehouse facilities* – building and breaking bulk;
2 *distribution* – utilising existing channels to reach foreign customers;
3 *providing market intelligence* – gathering and passing on information to the manufacturer on which future strategies may be based;
4 *providing a visible market presence* – increasing awareness and confidence by having a physical market-based representation;
5 *managing relationships* – between manufacturer and customers;
6 *administrating* – responding to enquiries, taking and processing orders;

7 *providing customer service* – technical advice and repairs along with advice on product usage (for end users), product storage and display (for retailers);
8 *minimising cultural distance* – serving as a learning post for the company to understand the foreign market and, when staffed by local managers, a means of reducing the foreign image of the firm and overcoming local language barriers.

Consequently, the role of intermediaries in service provision should not be underestimated.

Understanding repeat purchase

Firms need to continually enquire of their efforts: why do customers buy from us again? Understanding relationships with customers is not just about identifying needs, but also understanding how those needs are satisfied (or not as the case may be).

Effective communication

Managing customer relationship also relates to sales and promotional efforts. Direct selling costs are constantly increasing which means firms are continually looking for new methods of promoting their products. A study conducted by McGraw-Hill in 1990 highlighted the average cost of a sales visit in EU markets. These ranged from a high in Denmark of $1 439.62 to a low in Ireland of $128.18 per visit. Based on their evaluation that it takes six visits to secure a sale, the cost of single sale in the UK worked out at $1 822.99. With this in mind, it is unsurprising that there has been increased focus on direct marketing techniques: catalogue sales (which are being used in markets as diverse as clothing and electrical goods), direct mail (which is now abundantly used to sell books, retail financial services, records, tapes and compact discs) direct response and telephone selling (both of which are used to sell a wide variety of products and services).

Direct mail techniques are principally designed to replace the retail outlet for those goods which are traditionally sought through this channel. With the growing power of retailers and the consequent pressure on profit margins for many manufacturers, direct marketing offers an alternative medium where the selling overheads are lower and thus profits potentially greater.

As the various media replace bricks and mortar investment in retail chains, a large number of geographically dispersed customers can be reached at a relatively low cost. In this respect there is great scope within the EU for firms to reach the 325 million people in the Single Market. The success of this approach, however, depends on consumer acceptance of these techniques. Several factors suggest that replacing traditional retail channels holds great advantages:

● the movement of women into the workforce has cut down on available shopping time
● characteristic hassles of shopping – traffic congestion, parking problems and high costs of public transport
● movement of people out of the cities into the suburbs reducing the tendency for people to visit major cities during non-working hours.

In non-consumer sectors where catalogue sales have become increasingly common, the basic underlying advantage is ease of ordering. A 'phone call and rapid delivery have replaced visits to dealers who may or may not hold the required stock. By centralising warehousing in large regional centres the catalogue companies can hold more stock elim-inating (or at least reducing) the likelihood that products are not available. Equally, the economies of operating large warehouses enables them to withstand the transportation costs.

However, there are problems associated with cross-border payment collection and han-dling, and while transnational efforts have been attempted, their success to date has been relatively limited. Different VAT rates (particularly on clothes) also make it hard for com-panies to operate across European borders, as do data protection rules. Some cross-border potential is also limited by legislation. For instance, there is a ban on life insurance adver-tising across borders by way of direct mail. There are also barriers in terms of consumer acceptance. For example, some people may be reluctant to order a product which they can-not see or touch. Having to return the good if it is not acceptable and having to wait up to 28 days for delivery may also deter consumers from embracing methods of this kind. Equally, in the case of direct mail, the growing amount of 'junk mail' received by people may reduce the impact as the degree of overload means that none of it is read or digested. Nevertheless, the increased number of catalogue firms emerging across Europe and the number of companies turning to direct marketing techniques is testimony to the growing acceptance of distance selling methods and opens up potential for more industries to experiment with these kind of selling media.

Table 8.3 shows the percentage change of direct mail in Europe up to 1988 which not only illustrates its growing importance as a marketing tool across the EU, but also the scope for development in a number of countries where levels are relatively low.

Table 8.3. Direct mail in Europe

Country	% Change in 1988	Volume (millions)	Items per head	Rank order items/head
Germany	7.6	3 607	58	3
France	5.2	2 500	46	8
United Kingdom	8.6	1 766	32	10
Spain	n.a	980	26	11
Netherlands	14.7	780	56	4
Switzerland	2.9	638	96	1
Belgium	4.3	556	55	6
Sweden	5.9	541	66	2
Italy	n.a	435	8	13
Denmark	4.4	235	47	7
Norway	4.7	225	56	4
Finland	9.6	216	43	9
Portugal	0.0	85	9	12
Ireland	−0.1	20	5	14
Greece	n.a.	8	<1	15

Source: Service Postaux Europeens. SPE Service Guide to European Direct Mail, Amsterdam, 1988.

What of the future of advertising? With advertising costs continuing to rise, and European margins continuing to shrink, can the large advertising budgets, so typical in the 1970s and 1980s be sustained through the next decade? Appelbaum and Halliburton (1993) suggest that advertising in Europe in the future will, contrary to this thinking, become even more important. They base this thinking on three important factors:

1 *Growing retailer dominance.* In order to secure shelf-space in supermarkets, manufacturers will be forced to raise the attractiveness of their products and prove to retailers that significant demand for the products exists.
2 *Increased competition.* Firms are looking more and more towards differentiation as a means of securing advantages. Differentiation dictates organisations clearly communicating product/services differences to their customers.
3 *Increased levels of internationalisation.* Advertising is critical to the support of Euro-brands.

This obviously diverges from the underlying principles which have led Heinz to abandon its television advertising in favour of targeted direct mail. However, perhaps the underlying principles are the same. Competing firms need to find innovative ways of promoting products to their customers. This may either be achieved through innovative advertising campaigns which capture the imagination of the customer, or through innovative means of advertising, which give the firm a differential edge over other industry players.

MANAGING LOGISTICS

Logistics is the management of product and information flows from the sender to the customer in such a way that quality is maximised and costs minimised. Some mention was made of inbound logistics in Chapter 7. Here, more attention will be paid to logistics functions between the manufacturing process and the final consumer.

Like other tasks highlighted in this chapter, logistics management is an integral part of the firm's value chain. Establishing the right systems and structures for managing the movement of physical products and information between the firm and the marketplace has the potential of adding value to customers. This means asking a number of important questions:

1 How efficient are our existing logistics systems?
2 Where can we make cost savings in our existing systems?
3 Are there implications for stock handling and inventory control?
4 How effective our existing systems in providing customers with sufficient levels of service?
5 Do the failures in our current logistics system raise questions over plant location and warehouse sites for Europe?
6 To what extent do we want to externalise elements of the logistics process (warehousing, order handling, complaints handling, servicing transportation etc.)?

Answering these questions, firms need to bear in mind important changes which are taking place in the European environment:

● Customers are becoming more demanding in relation to delivery times. As leading firms adopt more flexible production and stockholding techniques, this raises the stakes for effective delivery and service.
● Pan-European sourcing is a growing phenomenon. Firms need to put in place systems which allow them to service the diverse needs of various parts of customer organisations which may by highly geographically dispersed.
● Product diversity. As companies continue to differentiate their product offerings, targeting pan-European customer groups, there are new demands for pan-European logistics solutions.

- Pressures to rationalise. As borders have opened up firms have recognised much duplication of effort between markets which has resulted in a period of rationalisation and realignment.
- Harmonisation of transport regulations. This is opening up the potential for more Europe-wide solutions to logistics problems.
- Increasing propensity for firms to contract out. Firms are likely to look in the future towards the services of large European logistics organisations capable of handling the firms' distribution and logistics requirements on a Europe-wide basis.

Some aspects of logistics management in the new Europe have already been implicitly raised in the chapter:

- adoption of more flexible production techniques (computer aided design and computer aided manufacturing) as a means of servicing diverse markets
- introduction of just-in-time delivery systems to more rapidly respond to customer requirements
- centralisation of warehousing to facilitate distribution to the various corners of the EU.

Logistics management in the future will not just be about reacting to poor performance in delivered service (such as lowering the times between order and delivery, ensuring products reach customers in one piece, ensuring orders are processed effectively, lowering the batch size for efficient delivery, systems which simplify the placing of orders) it will be more about delivering benefits to customers. This means that innovative logistics can provide a means of adding value to customers, in much the same way that innovative products might. Logistics functions therefore need to be as tailor made as the products which they are serving, building customers into the process and not simply viewing them as the final depository for goods.

LOOKING TO THE FUTURE

This chapter has highlighted an important problem in developing appropriate marketing systems for future Europe-wide marketing effort. Business structures need to change if marketing departments are to be given the freedom to operate creatively and flexibly as Europe changes. It is perhaps not surprising that the conclusion to this chapter mirrors the conclusions drawn in the last. Marketing is only one element of the firm's value chain activities all of which now need to be developed in a creative and holistic manner.

Value-adding activities can only be as effective as the systems on which they are based and as many European firms continue to perpetuate functional divisions there remain concerns over the ability of European firms to effectively compete in today's global markets.

CONCLUSION

It is impossible to consider the issue of marketing in a European context without paying attention to changing thinking regarding the marketing concept per se. This chapter has suggested that firms must review their marketing efforts in line with renewed thinking which stresses relationship marketing and customer focus rather than product and organisational driven marketing effort.

Consequently, the Four Ps of marketing emerge as antiquated and unable to provide adequate solutions to meet the needs of demanding European customers. Firms must shed their traditional belief that marketing is about adapting products and services, promotion, distribution and pricing on an individual market basis and embrace the challenge that Europe offers for segmentation, branding, relationship development, innovation and logistics – tasks which require a high degree of flexibility and innovative potential.

While change in thinking poses few conceptual difficulties, change in business structures is essential if firms are to react to these challenges and find meaningful customer solutions. Marketing departments alone cannot achieve these goals, and it is possible that organisations will continue to question the effectiveness of their marketing managers' efforts if they do not provide the right business environment for the effective implementation of flexible, task-based strategies.

Questions for discussion

1 Explain why concentrating on differences between the Member States is detrimental to taking a European view of marketing.

2 Why are the Four Ps of marketing management considered to be a less than useful tool for managing marketing effort across the Single Market?

3 What advantages do you think accrue from marketers working more closely with their customers?

4 Why would you suggest project groups and inter-disciplinary teams are important in the modern marketing organisation?

5 Why do you think that organisational change has lagged behind strategy change?

6 What prescriptions would you offer for developing structures to facilitate marketing effort in the new European environment?

CASE STUDY

Benetton

Company history
Benetton began as a small family business in Treviso in Italy in 1965. Ten years earlier, Luciano had begun selling his sister's knitted-sweaters to shops in the local regions, and as they had continued to meet with approval, and differed in many respects from other knitwear available locally, the establishment of a manufacturing plant in 1965 was an inevitable move. Supported by brother Gilberto, who handled company finances, Luciano was established as company chairman and his sister, Guiliana, head of design. A long-standing family friend, Elio Aluffi was given responsibility for manufacturing. In 1983, Aldo Palmeri, a senior manager at the Bank of Italy, was recruited by Luciano Benetton to oversee Benetton's growth from a local sweater manufacturer to a major knitwear manufacturer. Based on the existing

company culture, Palmeri embraced the challenges of turning a national producer and retailer into a multinational firm. In 1989, he left the company, following disagreements over company strategic direction. However, two and half years later he was invited back and, has since worked closely with the Benetton family to take the organisation from an international to a multinational giant.

Manufacturing and sub-contracting

Growth in demand for Benetton products quickly outpaced company capacity. Before the company was even legally registered, demand exceeded production and thus Benetton, like so many other Italian garment manufacturers turned to sub-contracting as a way of increasing output. Sub-contracting has three primary advantages: it reduces the social contribution paid out to workers (and thus increases margins) it allows Benetton great flexibility in manufacturing and it reduces depreciation. The garment industry, like many other fashion industries, is cyclical in nature. Small sub-contractors can react much quicker to changes in demand than could a large inflexible manufacturing unit. This means that Benetton can make last minute decisions and adapt rapidly to changes in market demand patterns.

Relationships between sub-contractors and Benetton are based on trust. The company has no written contracts with only quality specifications being presented to sub-contractors in written form. Quality is obviously essential to the long-term success of the organisation, and firms which cannot meet the demands imposed by Benetton are dropped. Those which continue to produce at the quality levels determined by Benetton stay loyal, and many refuse to work for other manufacturers.

Despite the flexibility of the system, the meteoric rise of Benetton, has caused problems for balancing growth in business with growth of the sub-contractors. Without their growing with the organisation it would have proved very difficult for Benetton to sustain levels of performance. Benetton have, therefore, actively encouraged the growth of their suppliers and supported developments (sometimes financially) wherever possible.

In addition, the various entrepreneurs all work together to solve common problems. It is not unusual for group meetings to be held between entrepreneurs to discuss major corporate problems and difficulties and draw on the brain power of a wide pool of individual managers.

Within Benetton's own manufacturing units (of which there are now three, all close to the company headquarters) CAD and CAM systems have been employed. This allows the company to design and produce up to 2 000 different garments a year with the existing software and cut 15 000 garments every eight hours. It also means reduced wastage and improved efficiency.

More recently, the company has begun to look to ways of increasing manufacturing operations outside of Italy, which is believed to be a rather limited approach in such a diverse global marketplace. For example, they have developed a joint venture with a Japanese company as a means of becoming more involved in production (without full ownership) for markets outside of their traditional dominant sphere of Europe. The development of the joint venture involved their identifying a partner, establishing a licensing deal, teaching the partner about the workings of the typical Benetton network and then formalising the arrangement into a joint venture. The

Japanese partner – Seibu, like Benetton, uses a system of sub-contracting (utilising the services of firms in China and Hong Kong) which market in Japan through Seibu's department stores. Seibu also acts as a local agent, running the retail networks of entrepreneurs and managing some 300–400 stores of their own.

Product innovation and development

The company has always focused on innovation. In many ways, it is its hallmark. In 1972, the company changed one of its central processes. Rather than dyeing the yarn, it turned its attention to dyeing garments, a process which could be completed in two hours for each batch. This helped the company to respond quickly to differences in retail demand. In addition, a wool softening technique (first identified in a firm in Scotland) has supported Benetton's ability to differentiate itself from its leading competitors.

Benetton's design processes remain centralised, even for the products sold through the emerging joint venture companies.

Agents and sales

The Benetton company runs a peculiar system of target country agents – around 80 in total – who are supported by Benetton in their commercial activities. They are independent entrepreneurs, and not employees of the company. They take the risks and make the investments and control market-by-market activity.

Benetton store owners thus deal directly with the agents and not Benetton itself. This means that Benetton's commercial department has remained relatively small, with concomitant cost advantages in organisational operation. Shop owners consult with the local agents on a continuous basis:

- regarding shop sites and whether there is room for a new retail outlet;
- location of the stores;
- merchandise;
- on-going strategy.

Benetton, through its agents, permit a fairly high degree of freedom in locally offered product range although tight control over prices and promotion are maintained by the Benetton group.

Agents attend two collections per year from which they select a range of garments for recommendation to their store owners. This forum is not only a presentation but an opportunity for the agents to come together to exchange information on products, prices, retail trends, the competition and product designs. It is, therefore, an important information gathering exercise for the whole group. Later, production schedules are planned on the first 5–10 per cent of orders received. Stores also sell what are termed *flash* and *reassortment* products. The first relates to products which are based on competitor designs (produced at short-notice to undermine the effectiveness of competitor activity), the latter on a number of garments in the company's basic range. Thus, while store owners have the ability to choose those products deemed most appropriate for their customer target group, shops around the world offer a common core of products which helps to bind company identity.

Agents essentially act as the bridge between the Benetton organisation – Luciano in marketing and Guiliana in design – and customers in the marketplace. They work with the shops in their local area and support localised development of the Benetton brand and image. In the early days, all agents were Italian, conversant with Benetton operations. This, however, is likely to change as the company gears itself up to working in an ever growing number of highly diverse marketplaces.

Store owners have to agree to comply with overall Benetton objectives for image and high standards. While some people allude to the Benetton retailing concept as a franchised operation, the Benetton group are adamant that it is not. It is, they assert, a unique system employed only by them. Unlike in traditional franchising formats, retailers pay Benetton no royalties on on-going sales and no fee for the use of the Benetton brand name. Store owners are responsible for their own individual investment, and while they are given the right to purchase goods exclusively from Benetton, they are responsible for their own premises, including all furniture and displays (although these have to match Benetton specifications). Annual sales targets are set for all stores.

International logistics

With such a complex network organisation Benetton are aware of the importance of establishing sophisticated logistics networks to integrate the diverse parts of their business. Controlling the activities of agents is obviously a logistical problem as so much decision-making is decentralised. However, the company have established an information system to support communication between the market and the organisation. There were fears, however, in the early 1990s that this information system was no longer satisfactory. They are exploring new information gathering techniques to ensure rapid market feedback from their stores using point of sale (POS) computer systems to monitor day-to-day sales in terms of volume, price, type of garment, styles, colours etc., as a means of ensuring that their development at head office level is aligned to national differences in demand.

Benetton has a central warehouse in Italy which manages all of its stock for the European (and global) market. This mean Benetton bills clients directly and there is no middleman. Thus, the agents do not take title to the goods. The size of the warehouse also means there are great economies of scale to be had in central handling.

Pricing

Prices are usually set at head office level. It is expected that between 75–80 per cent of all merchandise will be sold at full price. This leaves some discretion for discounting during sale periods (two of which are held each year). Generally, pricing policies are linked to Benetton's market position as a global brand leader combined with a premium pricing policy. Research has indicated that price does not play an important part in the purchasing decision. In 1983, a crisis in the garments industry was identified at one of the company's biannual collections. It was decided collectively at this meeting (between Benetton head office staff and local agents) that it would be preferable for Benetton to occupy a higher position in its markets worldwide.

Sales in Benetton stores are not like elsewhere. The main agents dictate the structure of mark-downs (between 10–15 per cent for current stock and up to 50 per cent for last season's range).

Branding

With such a clear focus on developing and sustaining the company's brand image it is unsurprising that Benetton refuses to allow other organisations to use its brand name internationally. Although *selling the brand* would invariably derive considerable revenue, fears that such a policy would dilute company image and quality perceptions mean that the brand is protected at all cost. This is why standards for Benetton 'franchisees' are so exacting, and failure to meet standards liable to result in enforced closure of stores (or non-renewed contracts in sub-contracting). There is a firm belief that a worldwide brand cannot be sustained and supported without protecting the cherished brand name. This thinking extends to store development, where layout and style are important means of translating the brand and company image to customers on a unified basis. Specialised exclusive shops support the development of image, which retailing through independent chain stores and boutiques could not achieve.

Advertising

Benetton's advertising campaigns in the early 1990s were perhaps more noted for their controversy than the products they were promoting: this was deliberate. The culture at Benetton is to provoke. This is part of their on-going policy of innovation and new development. Without provocation there can be no change. Therefore, this was extended to customer communication, to make people sit up and think about political and social issues, to make them identify with a company which is prepared to provoke and move forward, a company which is not afraid to stand out of line and say 'I am different'.

Benetton do not, however, advertise their products, they advertise their corporate culture, the thing that embraces the organisation and draws it together. It would be impossible to reflect the ranges of clothes sold in Benetton outlets in an advertising campaign, which would therefore do little for establishing company image across cultures. The solution – 'The United Colours of Benetton' is a reflection of a number of critical corporate issues: a dedication to colour and design, a global philosophy and vision and a forward thinking and progressive firm prepared to stand out from the crowd, and a firm clearly centred on the people it serves.

Organisation

Benetton provides an excellent example of a firm which has embraced the challenge of network management. Its organisational complexity is based on relationship management not ownership, trust not contracts, and an entrepreneurial mind-set geared to group problem solving and flexibility. Managers are concerned not about personal development, but achieving group goals.

However, the only way for such a system as this to work effectively is to ensure that directions are centrally steered and relationships centrally managed. Thus while Benetton has carved out a highly fragmented structure of business operations based on, often, loose affiliation, the corporate headquarters establishes tight control over group-wide activity. Design, pricing, promotion, and advertising are all co-ordinated at the centre, with limited amounts of discretion being afforded to local managers in the day-to-day running of operations.

This, however, poses problems for an organisation which has grown so quickly, not so much due to the fact that the control mechanisms are not effective, but due to the fact that centralised control is essentially still handled by the original family members, particularly relationship development, which is proving an increasing burden on a small number of individuals. Therefore, as Benetton continues to develop internationally, it is likely that expansion of head office management will follow. In turn, as the firm is increasingly becoming involved in a wide array of highly diverse markets it is important for increased regional management. Expert managers in Italy are no longer able to handle the complex diversity of Benetton's operations in world markets.

The essence of network companies is that their flexibility allows them to evolve rapidly, and this is certainly the case with Benetton. Therefore one cannot rule out the possibility of sub-contracting arrangements expanding out of Italy and Europe and joint ventures becoming more popular as the organisations encourages the management of related networks by close partners. One thing is clearly certain, the company will not stand still.

Case Study Questions

1 To what extent do you think Benetton is prepared to take on the marketing challenges in the new European Union?

2 What advantages and disadvantages are apparent as a result of the company's policy of sub-contracting?

3 What logistical challenges do you think will face the company in the future?

4 Has Benetton, to your mind developed effective organisational structures for handling business diversity across the European Union?

5 To what extent do you think the organisation at Benetton allows the firm to take a customer-focused view of marketing development?

6 How effective would you suggest Benetton's advertising campaigns have been in communicating the image of the company?

7 Are there any lessons which this case raises for other organisations operating on a trans-European basis.

FURTHER READING

Halliburton, and Reinhard, (1993) *European Marketing: Readings and Cases*, Addison-Wesley. This text is a compendium of 'seminal' articles on the subject of European marketing, in particular, 'Pan-European Marketing – Myth or Reality', 'Standardisation of Marketing in Europe', the Euroconsumer, Myth or Reality', 'The European pricing time bomb and how to cope with it', 'Toward a new millennium – a new perspective for European marketing'.

Lynch, R. (1994) *European Marketing: a Guide to the New Opportunities*, Kogan Page.

Bleeke, and Ernst, (1993) *Collaborate to Compete*, John Wiley & Sons. This text provides both a theoretical and practical look at the way in which collaborative strategies can enhance competitiveness.

REFERENCES

Appelbaum, U. and Halliburton, C., 'International Advertising Campaigns: the Example of the European Food and Beverage Sector', *International Journal of Advertising*, Vol. 12, No. 3, September, 1993.

Barwise, P. and Robertson, T., 'Brand Portfolios', *European Management Journal*, Vol. 10, No. 3, September 1992.

Cecchini, P., *The Benefits of the Single Market*, Wildwood House, 1989.

Chaudhry, P., Dacin, P. and Peter, P., 'The Pharmaceutical Industry and European Community Integration', *European Management Journal*, Vol. 12, No. 4, December, pp. 442–453, 1994.

De Meyer, A. and Ferdows, K., 'Removing the Barriers in Manufacturing', *European Management Journal*, Vol. 9, No. 1, pp. 22–29, 1991.

Dudley, J. W., *1992: Strategies for the Single Market*, Kogan Page, 1990.

Kotler, P., *Marketing Management: Analysis, Planning and Control* (5th Edn), Prentice Hall, 1986.

Kotler, P., 'Reconceptualising Marketing: an Interview with Philip Kotler', *European Management Journal*, Vol. 12, No. 4, December pp. 353–361, 1994.

Lynch, R., *European Business Strategies The European and Global Strategies of Europe's Top Companies*, (2nd Edn), Kogan Page, 1994.

McKenna, R., *Relationship Marketing*, Addison-Wesley, 1991.

Paitra, J., The Euro-Consumer, Myth or Reality, in Chris Halliburton and Reinhard Hunerberg (Eds) *European Marketing: Readings and Cases*, Addison-Wesley, 1995.

Peters, T., 'Liberation Management: Necessary Disorganisation for the Nanosecond Nineties' Alfred Knopf, 1990

Robertson, T., 'New Developments in Marketing: A European Perspective', *European Management Journal*, Vol. 12, No. 4, December, pp. 362–365, 1994.

Simon, H. and Kucher, E., 'The European Pricing Time Bomb and How to Cope with it', *European Management Journal*, Vol. 10, No. 2, June pp. 136–145, 1992.

Valla, J. P., 'Industrial Firms in European Markets: the French Approach to Europe', in Peter Turnbull and Jean-Paul Valla (Eds) *Strategies for International Industrial Marketing*, Croom-Helm, New York, 1986.

Vandermerwe, S., 'Building Seamless Service Structures: Some Whys, Whats, Hows', *European Management Journal*, Vol. 12, No. 3, September, pp. 280–286, 1994.

CHAPTER 9

Culture in Europe

INTRODUCTION

While the removal of physical barriers and the development of a European Union-wide competition policy are all designed to create a Single European Market some observers are concerned that cultural differences will prevent the realisation of a homogeneous market for goods and services. *Cultural difference* is a term which is frequently bandied about by both academic theorists and business practitioners alike but is an issue which tends to receive scant attention. Although most people understand the generic implications of different cultures whether or not they understand the specific features is more questionable. If managers in the new Europe are to embrace the challenge of operating in a multi-cultural environment it is important that they understand something more than the mere fact that markets are different.

It is not possible within the confines of a single chapter to describe *culture in Europe*. Indeed, it is arguable whether any theoretical text could come close to explaining what constitutes the difference between the fifteen Member States. Understanding culture is dependent on first hand observation and experience. This chapter is not, therefore, designed to provide readers with everything they need to know about culture in Europe. Rather it is concerned with providing pointers to those elements of culture which need to be considered by managers developing their European business. With this in mind, this chapter, which develops on from discussions in Chapters 7 and 8 on European strategic issues, seeks to answer four basic issues:

1 What is culture and how will it impact on the strategies of European firms?
2 How can firms analyse cultural differences?
3 What are the main challenges of managing across cultures in the EU?
4 What systems and strategies can firms put in place to help overcome the uncertainties of European cultural difference?

CULTURE AND ITS IMPACT ON MANAGEMENT

Its [culture's] influence for organisational behaviour is that it operates at such a deep level that people are not aware of its influences. It results in unexamined patterns of thought that seem so natural that most theorists of social behaviour fail to take them into account. As a result, many aspects of organisational theories produced in one culture may be inadequate in other cultures.

(Triandis, 1983, p. 139)

The above quotation highlights one of the main problems with analysing culture from a theoretical perspective. As theorists are so steeped in their own cultural norms and ways of thinking it is difficult for them to fully understand the cultural context of foreign countries' business practices. It has been argued in recent years that modern day business theories, most of which are the product of American (and latterly European) business school research, lack validity when applied to the global scene as they fail to take into account the nuances of different business practices and norms around the world. It is therefore important, before proceeding to a review of cultural issues pertaining in a European context to highlight a critical caveat: analysing culture is not just about assessing how different cultural groups differ from one's own; it also involves looking to new ways of thinking and behaving and embracing new possibilities for conducting business outside of one's domestic territory.

Culture is essentially about people, and the way in which they behave as a result of their background and group affiliation. The reason why culture is so important to business strategy development is the fact that different cultural groupings (national cultures, regional cultures, ethnic cultures, family cultures, gender cultures, age cultures, occupational cultures and corporate cultures) all impact on how efficiently and effectively organisations can 'get the job done'. Essentially, how corporations understand and manage their people. Within the context of the EU, the clear concern in the current environment is understanding the behaviour of people from different parts of the newly formed union. By understanding their background, and what shapes their behaviour, it is possible for organisations to identify both similarities and differences, and thus opportunities for standardisation and adaptation of products, services and EU-wide business practices.

Managing culture poses a difficult challenge to individuals as they tend to view opportunities and threats, strengths and weaknesses, from their own cultural perspective. The old adage: 'You can't put an old head on young shoulders' typifies this kind of limitation: knowledge and understanding is a product of our own experiences. Generally, as individuals are so wrapped up in their own culture, it is difficult for them to develop an open attitude which transcends their own norms. Eliminating this lack of cultural sensitivity or what Lee (1966) called 'self reference criterion' (SRC) allows the development of strategies based on host market needs and wants and not those pertaining to the domestic market. Lee proposes a four step approach to minimising SRC when planning for cultural difference:

1 determining the problem or goal in terms of home country culture, habits and norms;
2 determining the same problem or goal in terms of host country culture, habits and norms;
3 isolating the SRC influence on the problem and how it complicates the issue;
4 redefining the problem without the SRC influence and solving it according to the specific foreign market situation.

This suggests looking carefully at factors which dictate behaviour of organisations and people in foreign markets – but what kinds of factors need to be incorporated into an understanding of cross-cultural management?

Kroeber and Kluckhohn (1952), identified 164 definitions of culture – summarising the collective findings in the following observation:

> Culture consists of patterns, explicit and implicit, of and for behaviour acquired and transmitted by symbols, constituting the distinctive achievement of human groups, including their embodiments in artefacts: the essential core of culture consists of traditional (i.e. historically derived and selected) ideas and especially their attached values; culture systems may, on the one hand, be considered as products of action, on the other as conditioning elements of further action.

This complex definition brings with it three important distinguishable factors:

1 Culture is not innate, but learned. In other words, people are not born with an understanding of culture. It is rather something they acquire through the socialisation process.
2 It is shared, communicated and transmitted by members of a social set and defines the boundaries between different groups. This point interacts with the first factor in that it is through reinforcement within the social group that culture is learned.
3 There are various facets of culture, many of which are interrelated, for example, social organisation may well be reflected in business organisation and underscore power play and organisational structures.

These elements have important ramifications for the European manager. First, managers can, and indeed must, learn about the culture in each foreign market in which they operate. As culture can be learned it need not remain a *black box* within the management function. Second, as culture is determined by group behaviour an awareness of group dynamics can be an important part of understanding cultural norms, particularly organisational structures employed in different Member States. Finally, the fact that different elements of culture are interrelated highlights the importance of identifying the individual facets and the way in which they interface with each other. What managers therefore need is a framework for assessing cultural differences across boundaries.

ANALYSING DIFFERENT CULTURES

Identifying cultural clusters

Probably the most famous study on cultural difference, and the most commonly used framework for analysing cultures, is that proposed by Hofstede (1983) based on research conducted between 1967–1973. Hofstede's original research included a sample of 116 000 business personnel from over 70 different countries – the largest organisational study ever conducted. In analysing the data, Hofstede derived four basic dimensions which explained half of the variance in countries' mean scores:

Power distance: Focuses on how society deals with inequalities between people in physical and educational terms. Countries with a high score are those which feature broad differences between individuals in terms of power and wealth.

Uncertainty Avoidance: This index relates to the extent to which countries establish formal rules and fixed patterns of life (such as career structures and laws) as a means of enhancing security.

Individualism: At the high end of the scale are those societies where ties between individuals are very loose versus those societies where individuals are born into *collectives* which support and foster development in return for loyalty – essentially, personal freedom versus group loyalty.

Masculinity: The more 'masculine' a society the more it values assertiveness and materialism. Less concern is shown for quality of life. 'Femininity' relates to caring and concern for people. The index also reflects the extent to which societies distinguish between the roles of men and women.

The scores for each country describe its unique position against the others. No two countries are identical, although there are similarities. By plotting pairs of dimensions it is possible to identify groupings of countries. Figure 9.1 (which plots uncertainty avoidance against power distance) and Figure 9.2 (which plots masculinity–femininity against individualism–collectivism) demonstrate this across two of the possible six matrices which can be developed using Hofstede's data. The Uncertainty avoidance versus Power distance matrix shows five (albeit arbitrary) groupings of countries for the 15 Member States (Japan and the USA being included as comparators). While it is possible to identify, from this, certain regional groupings, with similarities apparent between Nordic countries, Anglo countries, north European and southern European Member States, the boundaries are far from clear. Austria appears as an outlier, with a very low power distance index (i.e. little difference between individuals in terms of power and wealth, which leads to the assumption of low class differentials). Belgium, on the other hand, shows greater similarity to Greece, Portugal and France, which clearly distinguishes it from other nations in its immediate regional locale (the Netherlands and Germany in particular).

In terms of Masculinity–Femininity versus Individualism–Groupism, again regional groups can be established – Anglo-American, north European, Nordic and southern European – but again outliers emerge. Italy, for example, shows more affinity with the north European states than southern. Japan provides an interesting example along these two dimensions. It stands alone in terms of the masculinity index, which suggests great delineation between men and women in Japanese society.

More recently (1987), Hofstede has also included a further dimension into his pioneering work on culture: long-term versus short-term orientation. Long-term relates to such values as thrift and perseverance, while short-term values include respect for personal tradition, social obligations and 'saving face'. Generally, East Asian cultures show the most long-term orientation (Japan with an index of 80, Hong Kong 96) European and American cultures figuring quite low in the rankings (the UK exhibiting an index of 25, Germany 29, the Netherlands 44 and Sweden 33).

But what does all this mean to European management? As the groupings between the two assessments of crossed pairs are not the same, it is difficult to suggest overall groupings which can be used by managers to carve-up Europe into a number of similar areas. Research conducted by Ronen and Shenkar in 1985, reviewing 8 cluster studies over the previous 15 years, found that four common areas had been used to analyse differences between nations:

1 the importance of work goals;
2 fulfilment and job satisfaction;
3 managerial and organisational variables;
4 work roles and interpersonal orientations.

By compiling the findings of the different research efforts, Ronen and Shenkar were able to derive eight country clusters (shown in Fig. 9.3) with only four countries not fitting into any cluster – Brazil, Japan, India and Israel. Not all theorists agree with their findings. However, there exists a degree of uniformity between these findings and the country clusters which emerged from Hofstede's dimensions determining that the EU comprises a number of discrete areas which display certain cultural similarities:

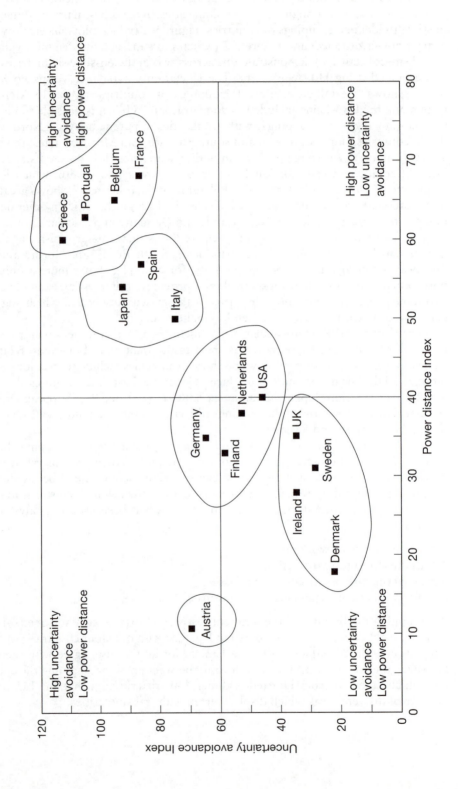

Fig. 9.1 Uncertainty avoidance v Power distance

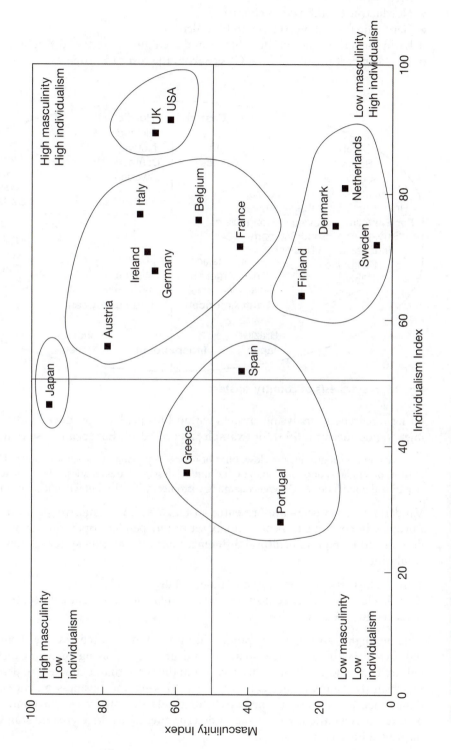

Fig. 9.2 Masculinity–femininity v Individualism–collectivism

- Anglo (with the UK and Ireland exhibiting more similarities to the USA than other EU Member States)
- Nordic (the Scandinavian countries)
- Germanic (including Austria and Sweden)
- Latin European (the southern States and including France and Belgium)
- the Near East (distinguishing Greece from the rest of Europe).

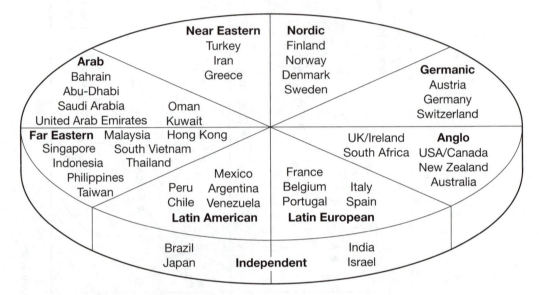

Fig. 9.3 A synthesis of country clusters

Other researchers, analysing clusters within Europe, have produced rather different findings. Vandermerwe (1993) for example, identified six European clusters with:

> ... customers geographically close, but not necessarily living in the same country. They will have the same or similar economic, demographic and/or lifestyle characteristics, which cut across cultural and national boundaries ... Differences among customers will exist, but will not be nationally determined.

Vandermerwe's clusters are presented in Fig. 9.4. Vandermerwe went on to suggest that Europe will continue to be a complex set of independent operating areas, not necessarily determined by regional cultural differences but by a market system dominated by certain similarities:

1 mass clusters with common consumer needs;
2 niche clusters wherein consumers have similar but not identical needs;
3 local and specialised clusters.

This highlights an important point. Cultural analysts often involve themselves in highlighting differences between nations and groups, focusing on what distinguishes one culture from another. While this is useful in the sense that it can help to demonstrate areas in which the company needs to adapt its thinking and business practices, it can also be dangerous. It can obscure the search for similarities which, in the context of the Single Market, may be the pivotal issue in determining areas for increased standardisation and improved business efficiency.

Fig. 9.4 Six European clusters

Before moving on, one further piece of research defining cultural clusters should be mentioned. Hall (1976) distinguished between cultures according to communication and understanding. He suggested:

> A high context-communication or message is one in which most of the information is either in the physical context or internalised in the person, while very little is in the coded, explicitly transmitted part of the message ... A low-context communication is just the opposite; i.e. the mass of information is vested in the explicit code.... Although no culture exists exclusively at one end of the scale, some are high while others are low.

(Hall, 1976, p. 91)

In high context cultures, therefore (Japan, China and Arab countries, for example), the spoken word relays most of the meaning of the communication. By contrast, in low context cultures (the USA and the UK for instance) the external environment, situation and non-verbal communication play an important role in the communication function. From a managerial point of view, this tends to mean that in low context cultures much emphasis is placed on formal documentation and legal processes rather than covert agreements and co-operation. This raises an interesting point for strategy development. Companies operating in EU countries displaying a low context culture (the UK, in particular and West Germany, to a lesser extent) which have traditionally placed limited emphasis on the historical, social, cultural and governmental factors impacting on business, will be forced to undertake wider research than has traditionally been the case. Chapter 7 pointed to the need for companies to look beyond simple economic and market factors in analysing the Member States and highlighted the critical aspect of cultural assessment in the environmental auditing process. Without this, a UK company, for example, would not be aware of the ramifications of French government involvement in business. It would be easy to conclude that this practice is simply a deliberate attempt to preserve protectionist measures while in reality, the practice is deeply embedded in the country's history wherein the extensive Romanic influence has carved out a culture based on centralisation and common law. As a consequence, central law is deeply embedded in France's culture, making legal documentation less of an issue in contractual arrangements. This is reflected in the number of lawyers per 100 000 of the population: 114 in the UK, 77 in West Germany and 29 in France.

Cultural change

Much of the above analysis suggests assessing various cultures at a point in time. What is of equal importance is understanding how cultures change over time. Culture may change slowly as a result of evolution, or may change quite rapidly in response to internal strife or exogenous factors. Culture contains an inherent contradiction (Robock and Simmonds, 1989): on the one hand individuals are keen to protect and preserve their own culture which suggests a degree of constancy. *Ethnocentrism*, the natural belief that one's own culture is superior to that of others, tends to perpetuate the existence of cultural barriers. Concerns that the Single Market will dilute individual country sovereignty (and the power of national state rule) also extend to worries that centralised decision making will not account for individual country nuances. Some observers argue that these fears will manifest themselves in growing nationalistic tendencies as individuals attempt to preserve their domestic cultural norms within the new Europe. This, in itself, asserts a change in attitudes and behaviour which serves to highlight the converse case: dynamism of the environments in which culture exists means that individuals will react to the challenges imposed by grouping together large masses of people with different social norms. Cultural change is therefore inevitable.

Each culture will yield a different propensity to change. Some cultures will readily accept new ideas, innovations and products while others will put up a great deal of resistance. Much depends, then, on the proportion of the population likely to accept change. Rogers (1962), proposed five categories of people within each society, ranked according to their willingness to adopt new innovations (*see* Fig. 9.5). Where societies are made up of a large number of innovators then they are likely to be highly progressive and dynamic as change is accepted readily. They are also more likely to yield higher levels of innovation as individuals not only accept new developments, but demand them as a matter of course. Alternatively, some societies yield a lot of resisters curbing the potential for change.

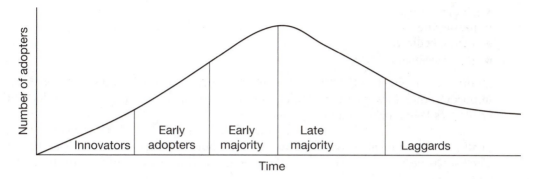

Fig. 9.5 Product adopter categories

The diffusion theory suggests that innovators and early adopters – the risk takers in any cultural group – secure the fate of new developments. If consumers in these adoption groups regard the product as acceptable their attitude is likely to be mirrored by individuals in the other adoption groups. Acceptance slowly works through society until, ultimately, even the most resistant individuals find that common opinion has swayed their thinking.

The case of the hole in the ozone layer may serve to highlight how this process works. Originally, when it became clear that chlorofluorocarbons (CFCs) were creating a hole in the ozone layer, a number of individuals immediately reacted to this news by boycotting sales of aerosols which had this damaging effect. These people, many of whom formed pressure groups, were able to convince others that changing their buying behaviour of aerosols was necessary if everyone was to work together to save the planet. In turn, the manufacturers of aerosols were also persuaded by the behaviour of the innovators and early adopters (and government pressure) that attitudes were changing and thus developed more environmentally friendly aerosols in readiness for (and adding to) the acceptance of the early majority.

This case is particularly interesting as it incorporates not only the changing attitude of customers for a particular generic product, but also the changing behaviour of manufacturers prepared to adapt in the face of dynamic market conditions. In this instance, the manufacturers who originally refused to change their behaviour, or who were slow to react, lost market share in favour of those who had made a more rapid adjustment to the exogenous pressure.

The degree of nationalism displayed by a culture may also have an important bearing on the willingness to change. Those societies characterised by high degrees of nationalism tend to resist any new developments introduced from outside their immediate environs. Furthermore, this may be directed specifically against a particular nation or culture which is seen to challenge the status quo. Highly nationalistic attitudes tend to sustain barriers between individual nations and cultures.

Developing a model for analysing Europe

The previous, albeit highly limited, review of critical strands in cultural determination and assessment, provides a general context for looking at European cultural issues. It fails, however, to provide a clear framework for analysing culture which, as suggested earlier, comprises a wide array of elements:

- national culture
- gender culture
- age culture
- regional culture
- organisational culture

all of which interact to determine the way in which individuals and groups behave. It is important, therefore, to establish a common framework before proceeding to look at the challenges facing firms in a European context.

Murdock (1945) developed an elaborate list of 70 *culture universals*, which are present in all societies and which arguably make up the whole cultural environment (*see* Table 9.1). The list has been reproduced here as it serves as a useful checklist of features for any cross cultural analysis.

Table 9.1. Cultural universals

Age grading	Food taboos	Music
Athletic sports	Funeral rites	Mythology
Bodily adornment	Games	Numerals
Calendar	Gestures	Obstetrics
Cleanliness training	Gift giving	Penal sanctions
Community organisation	Government	Personal names
Cooking	Greetings	Population policy
Co-operative labour	Hairstyles	Postnatal care
Cosmology	Hospitality	Pregnancy usages
Courtship	Housing hygiene	Property rights
Dancing	Incest taboos	Propitiation of
Decorative art	Inheritance rules	supernatural beings
Divination	Joking	Puberty customs
Division of labour	Kingroups	Religious rituals
Dream interpretation	Kinship nomenclature	Residence rules
Education	Language	Sexual restrictions
Eschatology	Law	Soul concepts
(after life)	Luck superstitions	Status differentiation
Ethics	Magic	Surgery
Ethnobotany	Marriage	Tool making
Etiquette	Mealtimes	Trade
Faith healing	Medicine	Visiting
Family	Modesty concerning	Weaning
Feasting	natural functions	Weather control
Fire making	Mourning	
Folklore		

Source: George P. Murdock 'The Common Denominator of Cultures' in the Science of Man in the World Crisis, Ralph Linton (ed.) New York: Columbia University Press, 1945, pp. 123–142.

To assess all these various facets of culture would be a highly complex task. However, individual elements can be isolated as key variables in certain situations; for example, if a company were to consider selling housing finance in a foreign market it may wish to consider the following elements: family, inheritance rules, kingroups, law, marriage, property rights, and residence issues. In so doing it would become aware of specific elements of the foreign culture associated with family groups, their homes and the laws surrounding ownership and residency. Arguably, however, these factors are too specific, and a more generalised understanding of the people and their environment may provide a more realistic management tool.

Many academics in recent years have preferred to opt for a more generic, framework which provides key headings for closer assessment. A typical framework is provided in Fig. 9.6. However, by analysing along these dimensions there is a tendency to only observe differences and not areas of commonality which can be translated into the adoption of workable business practices for the EU. It is, therefore, important to adopt some kind of 'model' which allows managers to observe the nature and scope of both differences and similarities and assess the way in which these impact on different parts of the business, for instance.

- doing business with suppliers and partners
- managing intermediaries
- managing subsidiaries
- identifying markets
- developing products to suit needs and wants.

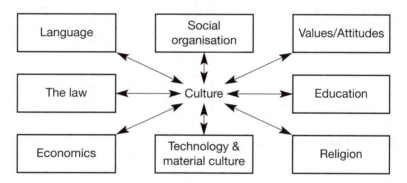

Fig. 9.6 Generic aspects of the cultural environment

An attempt to encapsulate various elements of cultural analysis is provided in Fig. 9.7, which provides the foundation for analysing cultures within the context of the EU.

Political and legal culture, although absent from the list of factors shaping national identity obviously have an important to role to play in shaping culture. Many of these distinguishing features were highlighted in Chapters 2 and 3 and shall therefore not be re-iterated here. Suffice to say, at this point that differences between Member States continue to prevail, despite efforts by the Commission at unifying countries' political ideologies and levels of economic development. Based on historical developments of economic systems and political structures, it is unlikely that convergence will, at least in the foreseeable future, lead to greater harmonisation of cultures.

Figure 9.7 shows social organisation cutting across all levels of cultural understanding. Within cultural groups there are a number of smaller social organisations which have an important bearing on how people think and behave. Families, schools, and social hierarchies all serve to define people's roles and functions within their own social groupings.

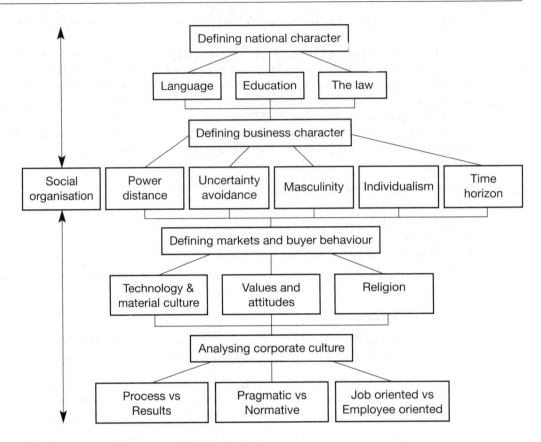

Fig. 9.7 A model for cross-cultural assessment

Social organisation

The family

The family clearly provides the central hub of most individuals' social sphere and it is here that many cultural values and norms are instilled. Leadership roles in the family differ by situation. Fathers may be referred to for major financial decisions, mothers for decisions about the day-to-day running of the house, and older siblings about school issues and relationships. However, as children grow older, develop their expertise in particular areas and formulate opinions, the likelihood of their becoming involved in joint decision making and consulted on major family issues increases. Furthermore, the scope for conflict between adults and children increases as children grow older and develop attitudes which differ from those of their parents and siblings. All this may be seen to parallel situations encountered in work and social organisations later in life, with the family serving as an important learning ground for group behaviour.

Social groups at work

Organisations differ widely between countries and dictate differences in attitude and behaviour within the workplace; for example, meetings, decision-making processes, work delegation, leadership roles, communication and promotion issues are all shaped by cultural factors and group norms pertaining in different societies.

For managers engaged in joint activities with foreign partners or with indigenous managers based in their own subsidiaries understanding these factors can be important for the smooth running of the organisation. Misinterpreting the informality of French managers at meetings or the tardiness of Italians, who find it more rude to terminate a current meeting than be late for their following appointment, may lead to a bad atmosphere for decision making and may, ultimately, result in a failure to secure a deal or operate in an harmonious manner.

Although these factors appear small and relatively trivial, all too often it is the combined effect of factors such as these which result in the demise of joint ventures between firms from different cultures and the failure to secure deals. Communication fails because managers give off signals which can be wrongly interpreted by their foreign colleagues. More will be said about this in the following sections.

CHALLENGE OF CROSS-CULTURAL MANAGEMENT IN THE EU

Introduction

Van Dijck (1995) suggests that the challenges of managing across cultures in Europe is changing significantly. At one level, there is the perpetuation of differences in national identity, at another, there is greater harmonisation of business practices and approaches. He summarises the main factors impacting on the European *transnationalisation process* as follows:

1 substantial increases in cross-border activity;
2 increased mobility of graduates and managers in the 1990s, and into the next millennium, placing pressure on educational systems based on trans-European not national thinking;
3 greater competition between firms in the EU;
4 greater need to balance the divergent objectives of increased strategic efficiency and better servicing the needs of customers in diverse geographic regions;
5 closer attention to managing diversity and finding transnational solutions;
6 a move by MNEs towards network structures in organisational development;
7 the trend towards a social Europe which will effect changes in employment conditions and practices.

Much of this cuts across the discussions presented in Chapters 7 and 8 and clearly re-iterates the notion that managing cultures in Europe is more about analysing culture from the point of view of finding a 'European way of doing things' rather than an exercise in identifying differences and potential barriers to operating across the 15 Member States.

Van Dijck's thinking also incorporates two divergent schools of thought. On the one hand, there are those that believe that business cultures across the globe are converging as internationalisation is resulting in technological similarities, homogenisation of customer tastes and the interdependence of nations. Those supporting this viewpoint believe that technology, market conditions and organisational structures have a more pervasive effect on management styles and processes than culture. Conversely, there are those that believe that management styles continue to be culture specific – and although they bow to the notion that there are increasing similarities in technology, production techniques and communication, they assert that human resource management, personal interaction and values and attitudes continues to differ markedly between different cultural groups.

Van Dijck's suggestion that there are both elements of convergence and divergence (the former in the area of strategies, the latter in terms of values and behaviour) shows that both sides of the debate have a valid point. Convergence is apparent in some business areas, but not others. The convergence–divergence debate therefore lacks validity in the context of Europe. It is not an 'either/or' situation, it is a matter of degree and strategic focus. By considering the framework for strategic management developed by the McKinsey Consulting Group (the 7-S Framework depicted in Fig. 9.8) it is possible to suggest that there is evidence of convergence in the 'hard' functions of structure, strategy and systems, but continued divergence in the soft-elements of skills and style. Shared values, on the other hand, are more likely to be company-specific and shaped by corporate, rather than national cultural norms.

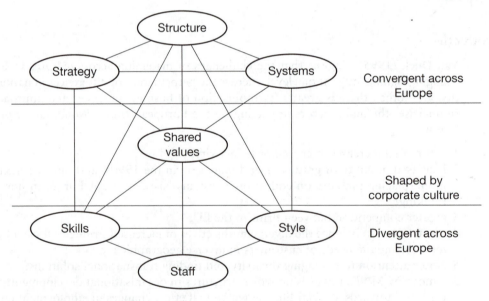

Fig. 9.8 McKinsey 7-S framework

DEFINING NATIONAL CHARACTER

Language

Language refers not only to the spoken word, but also to the language of things, space, time, and relationships. Language is a key element in the *cultural mix* as it provides the medium through which social norms are transmitted and perpetuated and the means with which people relate to each other. In a business sense language forms the hub of communication between managers from different cultures, which in turn acts as a means of firm-to-firm communication, and company to customer communication both in terms of personal contact and promotional effort.

The spoken language

Within the EU there are continuing arguments regarding the adoption of a common language. Over time, English has become the accepted language of international business principally because it is the most widely spoken language in the developed Western world. Some countries, however, are less than happy about conducting business in another language as they feel this puts them at a disadvantage. This is hardly surprising as most people feel more confident communicating in their first language wherein they fully understand the nuances of the idiom.

Alternatively, in a foreign tongue, there is the risk that a literal translation of a word or phrase will not have the desired meaning and thus not communicate what was intended. This was certainly the case in General Motors' advertising campaign 'Body by Fischer (corpse by Fischer) and the 'Nova' brand name (it doesn't go). Equally, Hertz's slogan 'Let Hertz put you in the driving seat' translated into Spanish reads 'Let Hertz make you a chauffeur' which quite clearly communicates a different message (Ricks and Mahajan, 1984). Certain countries are keen, therefore, to foster the idea of 'when in Rome do as the Romans'. While this approach is accepted in marketing communication effort on the basis that 'the customer is king', manufacturers accordingly adapting their approach, there is less common agreement that this should be the line taken in business to business communication.

The main resisters to this approach are those countries whose managers lack language skills and whose education system, correspondingly, does not promote high levels of language learning. The UK, Italy and Ireland, in particular, and Spain, Portugal and France to a lesser extent, are dominated by individuals who have no second European language (*see* Table 9.2). This is often attributed to their highly nationalistic attitudes and high levels of ethnocentrism. Whatever the reason for their poor language skills, however, there seems to be a growing awareness of the need to develop language training at both a national level as part of the school curriculum and within the business environment.

Table 9.2. Percentage of people who can follow a conversation in another language

Country	Number of languages			
	0	1	2	3+
Belgium	50	22	18	9
Denmark	40	30	25	6
Germany	60	33	6	1
Greece	66	27	5	2
France	67	26	6	1
Ireland	80	17	3	–
Italy	76	19	5	1
Luxembourg	1	10	47	42
Netherlands	28	29	32	12
Portugal	76	14	8	2
Spain	68	26	5	1
United Kingdom	74	20	5	1

Source: Eurobarometer 1989.

Even if English does become the dominant language, the failure to learn other languages may put individuals operating outside their own EU market at a disadvantage. Communicating in the language of the host may be seen as a symbol of co-operation, faith and trust.

Thus the effort in itself may be regarded as a way of communicating with foreign partners or customers. Equally, some people argue that it is impossible to understand other elements of culture without comprehending the medium through which that culture is perpetuated. In this respect, musicality, intonation and phraseology all serve as secondary communication signals which are lost on those with no grasp of the language.

The language of time

The language of time includes response times for a written communication, punctuality at business meetings, the time it takes to make a decision, formal schedules and deadlines. All communicate different messages in different societies. In France, punctuality depends on the importance of the person being kept waiting with 15 minutes being the acceptable barometer. In Germany, people are expected to be on time, and any degree of lateness is considered unacceptable. In Britain, a degree of flexibility exists regarding punctuality and it is almost accepted that people will be late for meetings. In a social context, it is considered rude in the UK to be on time and if the host stipulates 8.30pm, it is expected that his guests will turn up nearer 9.00pm.

The language of space

The language of space concerns personal surroundings and also the environment in which we live. The old adage 'an Englishman's home is his castle' holds much store in this respect. In the UK space acts as a surrogate for social class and position. One would expect the chief executive of a large organisation to have the biggest and most impressive office and people with large houses are viewed as being higher up the social class ladder than those with smaller properties. This is not the case in France where the size of an office or a home does not reflect class or status. Many families, particularly in Paris and other large cities, live in relatively small apartments which are conveniently sited rather than larger properties in the suburbs, as is the case in Britain. Alternatively, in the workplace, the French are more likely to lay space out so that it facilitates interaction rather than promoting positions of dominance.

Education

Education is often considered to be the backbone of society where individuals are prepared for their role within the workforce. Different educational systems across Europe show a polarisation of opinion regarding the benefits of vocational versus pure academic training. Both systems offer advantages: the vocational system prepares students within the school environment for their job role in society while the academic approach provides the building blocks of learning on which employers may build.

What is more important than the simple choice of system is that education is fully integrated into the country's economic environment. In the traditional industrialised society, labour demand is roughly triangular with a narrow peak of top management, a broader band of middle management and a wide base of skilled and semi-skilled workers. In countries which have moved to a more tertiary economy, this shape changes as their is greater demand for skilled professional workers which demands a corresponding readjustment of the education system. John MacGregor, Secretary of State for Education in the UK summarised the central role of education in society in the following statement made to the *Sunday Times* in August 1989:

> If we are going to achieve continued economic performance and higher standards of living ... and also enable more and more people to fully exploit what life can offer today, then we have got to ensure that our education system delivers our capacity to be competitive, and to take full advantage of this fast-changing world.

The European Commission (1993) has suggested that without increased commitment to education and training, the advantages of the Single Market will accrue to the most highly educated and dynamic who will be persuaded to move to areas where the best jobs and conditions are available. In order to avoid a 'brain-drain' from the periphery to the centre, countries need to look carefully at their education and training provision over the next few decades. The Commission, too, believes it has a role to play in monitoring and supporting a new agenda for education as a means of improving the overall skills-base of the EU, essential for the future development of Europe within the global arena. In 1988, Jacques Delors raised the issue of giving every worker in the EU the right to continuing training throughout his/her working life – a policy which has been readily adopted by some countries, but rejected or ignored by others. This focus on vocational education and training is likely to continue, particularly with new technologies and work practices demanding different skills of trained workers across the 15 Member States.

While it has been argued that reluctance to embrace new measures for improving training is the result of fears of trained workers being poached by other companies, the reality is more to do with the historical development of different Member States' educational systems. The German education system is often regarded as the best in Europe, with a highly integrated combination of schools, vocational training and management development. As many EU countries strive to improve educational provision the German system is proving to be the ideal role model. The fact that only around three quarters of German students over the age of 16 remain in secondary education is not a reflection of poor educational attainment – at this age, many individuals enter into vocational training programmes. These are run jointly by the state and over 500 000 approved registered training companies. Even though the cost to firms is large the benefits of training the workforce in appropriate skills is apparently justifiable.

The ethos of company-formal learning in Germany is also extended to management development programmes in which managers are encouraged to continually improve their skills by attending courses covering various disciplines from product and function specific courses to those more concerned with objective management techniques. With this historical background, it is arguable that Germany is well placed to deliver the kinds of people needed to work in the new Europe.

The UK, on the other hand, which arguably has one of the poorest records for education and training for a developed Western economy, was, for many years, accused of producing high numbers of individuals leaving the education system with poor standards of literacy and numeracy. The Education Reform Act 1988 was therefore designed to introduce a number of measures to improve both school and post-school learning. The underlying intent is to provide a system which provides opportunity, choice, motivation, flexible response to changing work demands, a spirit of enterprise, realisation of potential and employer investment in qualifications. This last point is a change of direction for UK education which has traditionally been operated independently from business and commerce.

Training and Enterprise Councils (TECs) have been established in England, Local Enterprise Councils (LECs) in Scotland, which act as linchpins between training departments and employers. A network of training in firms is also to be controlled by Industry Training Organisations. National Vocational Qualifications (NVQs) have also been introduced to allow individuals to acquire levels of competence and manage their own training development within their specific job. However, these have been severely criticised for failing to address critical theoretical underpinnings, raising questions over their real effectiveness as a 'development' tool.

Equally, the *laissez-faire* approach to training, with employers responsible for the majority of training, is raising fears over short-termism in training. It is argued that employers see training as a cost, not an investment, and are therefore only concerned with 'doing the minimum' – training individuals for specific tasks rather than broadening their knowledge base and skills. Training has also been severely affected by the recent recession, with employers cutting back on training budgets and showing a reluctance to invest in their workforces, viewed more as a dispensable commodity rather than a critical asset.

The UK case contrasts markedly with that in France. Successive governments in France have, over the last couple of decades, demonstrated a clear commitment to training and education and have given the right to training to all working people. A statutory minimum requirement has been established for training provision. In companies with 10 or more employees, 0.15 per cent of the wage bill must be dedicated to training (of which 0.3 per cent must be channelled into training young workers and 0.2 per cent external training centres for employees on training leave). Many companies spend more than the minimum, the estimated average in 1990 being 3.2 per cent of the wages bill. Consultation between employers and employees takes place at least twice a year to discuss training plans although this can lead to frustrations as the workers only have a voice, but not a say, in future training needs. Greater government intervention, therefore, produces higher standards and better commitment than is the case in the UK.

Nevertheless, the UK is not alone in suffering problems with on-going training and development of its workforce. In Italy, for example, large number of people leave the formal education system without attaining the school leaving certificate. To combat this problem the *150 hour system* allows workers to attend school in work hours to complete the required qualifications to attain the certificate. This clearly reduces the potential for vocational training and development as time is dedicated to school rather than post-school qualifications. Other factors also militate against vocational training: the small-size of many firms makes the cost of providing in-house training schemes preclusively high; the failure of the government to provide any incentives, such as tax concessions, limits the attractiveness of in-house courses; and the focus of trade unions on job security and higher wages overrides the issue of vocational training.

Italian trade unions objected to apprentice schemes as being a form of cheap labour, and initiated their demise. However, recent incentives have been offered to firms to employ young workers on a short-term basis before taking them on as full-time employees or allowing them to return to the labour market. Over 70 per cent of these young workers are taken up by the large number of small firms prevalent in Italy.

Focus on vocational training for Europe by the Commission reflects the growing awareness that Europe must prepare individuals for new work practices and improve their skills within the workplace if EU firms are to survive in the increasingly competitive world marketplace. The objectives of the FORCE action programme, which ran between January 1991–January 1995 underline this thinking:

1 develop transnational training projects with extensive exchange of information, experience and people, to improve Europe-wide skills necessary for tackling the challenges posed by the Single Market programme;
2 assist in designing training systems which respond to market needs by better identifying skills gaps and forecasting skills requirements;
3 encourage more innovation in training management;
4 provide information on the best continuing training available;
5 persuade organisations of the importance of training.

The ease with which these objectives can be met at the level of the individual Member States will be critically determined by the current state of the nation's educational provision and thus its history, educational culture and overriding political will. This may well mean countries such as the UK being forced to re-consider the effectiveness of market forces in delivering effective training. A failure to do so will inevitably lower competitive potential and possibly induce staff movement to areas offering better provision for life-long learning and skills development. This will probably be most acute among top managers and technicians (who may be more cosmopolitan and accept the challenges of working in a different culture – and a different language) which will further accentuate skills shortages in particular regions.

Law

The diverse nature of the legal frameworks pertaining to the 15 Member States of the *EU* has, for a long time, served to reinforce the differences between nations. As different laws and regulations continue to apply on an individual national basis, true harmonisation and the development of a Single European Market is still a long way off. The law provides formal guidelines for shaping cultural norms and the seriousness of penalties incurred through failure to comply with the law, dictates that they are strictly adhered to by the majority of the population.

Although the law is dynamic and is adjusted according to the changing needs of each society, the rate of change is often slow which can, in some instances, serve to retard changing attitudes and beliefs. For example, recent changes in UK law, where rape is now recognised between husband and wife, reflects the changing attitudes towards the role of women in UK society and the institution of marriage. The idea of 'conjugal rights' which dominated thinking for so long has now been challenged and was considered to be a long-overdue change in thinking by many women.

Another reason why law is constantly changing is the fact that it is never clear cut. Often, important test cases emerge which challenge existing legal guidelines and serve as a catalyst for change. In these instances, adjustments to the law are made either as a result of outmoded thinking or the fact that loopholes restrict their implementation. Although this suggests that ultimate harmonisation of Community law is achievable as each Member State is used to making adjustments and adaptations, the process is likely to be far from easy.

Changes which occur on a national level do so gradually as a result of the fluidity of the culture. Very few new laws are introduced and imposed on the people without changing attitudes and beliefs. The introduction of compulsory helmet wearing on motorbikes in various Member States and more recently compulsory seat-belt wearing in the UK were met with a degree of resistance and resentment. Even though in both these instances there were pressure groups actively promoting legal change, large numbers of the populace felt that it did not reflect their own attitudes. However, the fact that dissatisfactions were soon forgotten and behaviour rapidly adapted in accordance with new legal requirements suggests that harmonisation will necessarily involve major short-term upheavals but passive acceptance in the medium-term.

Increasingly, Community law is taking precedence over national law as the European Court of Justice continues to raise its status – particularly in ensuring that nation states and their institutions abide with changing directives and new EU-wide legislation. Problems have arisen as many laws are based on compromise, and as the gap between the ideal and the compromise position for many Member States is so great, the introduction of major concession to cushion the blow of legislative change only serves to undermine the power of any new legal enforcement.

DEFINING BUSINESS CHARACTER

Relating back to the work of Hofstede, it is useful to look at differences between the 15 Member States in terms of Power distance, Uncertainty avoidance, Masculinity versus Femininity, Individualism versus Collectivism, and Management time frames.

Power distance

Figure 9.9 plots the Power distance indices for the 15 Member States and includes those pertaining to the USA and Japan as a means of comparison. As mentioned earlier, organisation of society, including the family, the school and the workplace, have an important bearing on the extent to which people accept and expect that power will be distributed unevenly. Thus, the index measures the extent to which individuals look up to their elders (parents, teachers, line managers) versus the extent to which they are encouraged to have a free-will; student-centred learning versus received wisdom from teachers; consultation with workers and joint decision making versus an acceptance of being told what to do.

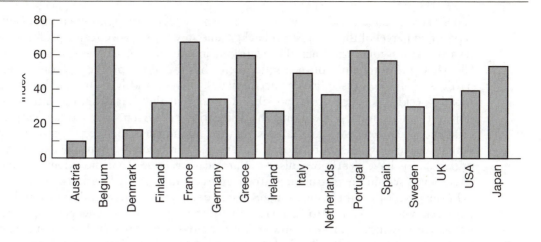

Fig. 9.9 Power distance index for the European Member States and their leading competitors (excluding Luxembourg)

Austria exhibits the lowest power–distance score of the group, followed by Denmark, Ireland and Sweden. Austria, Denmark and Sweden, which feature legally mandated co-determination procedures for business, tend to have flat organisational structures, decisions being made more by consensus than imposed by top-level management. Germany too, has recently adopted co-determination policies for management (as outlined in the Case study in Chapter 6) which may partly explain its relatively low score. Equally, as decisions are shaped in German firms by clearly defined rules, the exercise of personal command is unnecessary. Conversely, the same cannot be said of the UK which has continued to reject Social Charter initiatives to move towards increased worker participation. How then can the UK's (and Ireland's) relatively low score (which is the same as that of Germany) be explained? Hofstede (1983) suggested UK organisations are akin to 'villages' with decisions based on negotiation rather than command. Therefore, although the UK has no formal structures for co-determination and employee involvement, this suggests there is an inbuilt culture of co-operation and negotiation. He also suggests that UK firms display no decisive hierarchy, which rather belies the fact that many UK firms are ordered into clear lines of organisation from top management, through middle management to blue-collar workers. The answer to this apparent paradox lies in the nature of class divisions in society which dictate job status, but not necessarily ultimate decision-making authority.

Class relates to the social stratification of people within society which has an important impact on various facets of a country's culture, particularly buying behaviour, social aspirations, work and career objectives and the balance between upper management, middle management and blue-collar workers. Labelling particular social classes and drawing clear boundaries between groups of people based on something as arbitrary as their class is often a highly contentious issue. People's view of themselves often differs from others' perception.

People often assume that income and personal worth are surrogates for social class, but this is not always the case. While there is a general parallel between income and class there is not a perfect match. Class groups often manifest themselves in the various institutions within the education system, for example, the Grandes Ecoles in France and Oxford and Cambridge in the UK support the idea of social elites, which are not so prevalent in other societies. Job status may also serve as a surrogate for social class. In Germany, engineers and those with a technical background are the most highly thought of within society. This is part and parcel of their industrial background in which service sector professionals are regarded as less important than those working in industry. The converse case is true in the UK where the dominance of the service sector has raised the profile of professional jobs, particularly in such disciplines as accountancy, finance and law. By establishing a clear social 'pecking order', it is possible to suggest that class may support a high Power–Distance index perpetuating the delineation between people and the acceptance of differences between distinct social sets but does not, in itself, dictate the balance of power within business organisations. Power distance is therefore not about the extent to which organisations have clearly organised hierarchical structures, but the extent to which different levels within these structures are given freedom to make decisions.

In the UK, for example, many operational decisions are decentralised to middle-level managers who are known to be invested with the skills and knowledge in specific functional areas, whereas in Germany, many decisions are centralised at top-management level, but made in consultation with worker representatives. Therefore, it is apparent that different business structures can lead to similar Power–Distance scores. It is therefore not just the scores themselves which managers need to concern themselves with, but what it is about the way companies in that country do business which leads to the score.

For the EU countries scoring high on the Power–Distance index, Portugal, Spain, France, Greece and Belgium, other factors come into play in determining their autocratic business methods. In the southern European states – Spain, Italy, Greece and Portugal, the dominance of the family as the central focus of the individual, and resultant paternalistic business practices means lines of authority, established in the home, are perpetuated in the workplace. Although decision making may be shared in the firm (as in the family), there is an acceptance of senior authority which is bound by trust and loyalty and not formal contracts. France, on the other hand, which exhibits the highest Power–Distance score, shows a marked tendency for centralisation of decision making and, while there is a degree of informal networking, management is often considered to be dictatorial and highly formalised. This is linked to the country's political regime of centralised authority reflected in business organisations through strict pyramidal hierarchies held together by strong unity of command and formal rules.

It is worth noting at this stage the value for Power–Distance in Japan. It is a commonly mis-held conception that Japanese management practices, which promote team-work and bottom-up management, implicitly mean flat organisational structures and consensus decision making. This is not necessarily the case: although workers are encouraged to identify and help solve work related problems, and management is receptive to their ideas and suggestions, decisions are made by senior managers who are highly respected and looked up to by the workforce.

Uncertainty avoidance

Figure 9.10 plots the Uncertainty–Avoidance indices for the 15 Member States, Japan and the USA. High scores of Uncertainty–Avoidance reflect the extent to which society attempts to shape rules and laws to provide safety, security and deal with ambiguity. Conversely low scores reflect the extent to which individuals are comfortable with uncertainty and risk taking. Again, Uncertainty–Avoidance manifests itself in different social organisations. At home, differences between curiosity about the unknown versus suspicion; the propensity of individuals to display emotion; levels of anxiety and stress. At school, acceptance of broad tasks and unstructured learning versus highly structured formalistic learning with clear timetables and curricula. At work, a desire for formalised rules and little risk taking versus great flexibility and high risk taking.

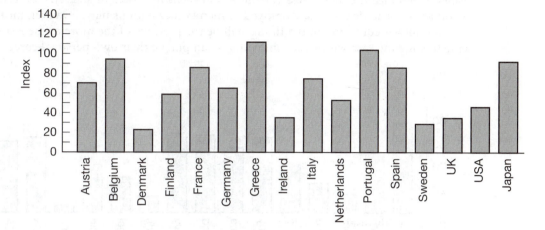

Fig. 9.10 Uncertainty avoidance index for the European Union member States and their leading competitors (excluding Luxembourg)

Greece and Portugal, and to a lesser extent, Belgium, France and Spain exhibit high scores for Uncertainty–Avoidance. As was highlighted earlier, the Romanic influence on certain of these nations, with centralised nationwide laws being established for common governance, means cultures have been shaped wherein individuals and institutions expect to be guided by the rules and stipulations of the state or the organisations in which they work. Therefore, individuals not only welcome direction and orders, they depend on them.

Conversely, Denmark, Ireland, Sweden and the UK exhibit low levels of Uncertainty–Avoidance. Hofstede (1995) suggests that in the Germanic part of Europe (including the UK) which inherited their civilisations 'never succeeded in establishing an enduring common central authority'. Hofstede also argues that Uncertainty–Avoidance is linked with Roman Catholicism, with nations dominated by the Catholic ethos showing higher scores due to their strict adherence to religions codes of conduct.

Masculinity–Femininity

Figure 9.11 shows the indices for Masculinity–Femininity for the 15 Member States of Europe, Japan and the USA. Again, the graph shows broad differences across the Member States of Europe. In the home, the school and the workplace, masculine societies promote competition, performance outcomes, reward-based systems, assertiveness and decisiveness. Feminine societies on the other hand promote relationships, co-operation and compromise and a focus on life qualities rather than outcomes.

Austria, Germany, Ireland, Italy and the UK exhibit the highest scores along this dimension. Career aspirations and profit orientation drive individuals and companies. Performance is highly rewarded and class structures often promote an ethos of upward mobility – although this can be difficult to achieve as class systems tend to be self-perpetuating. In the UK, however, the 1970s and 1980s witnessed a move by many citizens from working class to middle class status. Many observers have attributed this to the opening up of higher education to all in the 1960s and 1970s, through the system of student grants which meant equal access for the less affluent members of society. The proposed introduction of student loans, employed in many other nations may, however, mean that access to higher education in the future will be the preserve of the more affluent and will serve to stifle the ease with which individuals can pursue their own personal career goals.

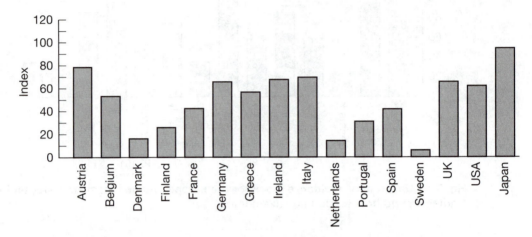

Fig. 9.11 Masculinity v Femininity index for the European Union Member States and their leading competitors (excluding Luxembourg)

Conversely, in Scandinavian countries such as Sweden, Denmark and Finland, much more emphasis is placed on the quality of work life and the well-being of workers rather than the maximisation of profit. This is not to suggest, however, that goals are not important: rather that they are achieved through encouragement rather than driven by necessity.

Also important in understanding differences between Masculine and Feminine Societies is countries' attitudes to women at home and at work. Across the EU, attitudes are being shaped by Social Charter provisions to improve equality in the workforce. However, countries are starting from very different perspectives. Thus, for some embracing these new directives will be relatively easy, while for others a great deal of change will be required, not just in terms of policies and practices, but also as regards overriding attitudes towards women in society.

Germany demonstrates the highest degree of chauvinism. The view of women as housewives and 'nest builders' still holds and was allowed to continue up until recently through an absence of sex discrimination laws. However, Germany may be forced to redress their attitudes, not only because of new Social Charter regulations but as a result of changes in age structure of the population. Table 9.3 shows the age structure for the 12 Member States in existence in 1989. It clearly shows Germany's population as one of the most rapidly declining in the EU. Given their attitude towards women in the workplace, this does not auger well. It is likely, in the future, that women will be required to make up the short-fall of professional workers in many sectors requiring reassessment of education and training for women. This will not, however, be achieved without a corresponding change in attitude and the rate of change will depend on how entrenched these are within society and the rate with which the country responds to Social Charter provisions for equality.

Nevertheless, despite Germany's entrenched beliefs about women, they have well-developed systems for women taking maternity career breaks, holding jobs open up to three years after the birth of each child.

Table 9.3. European Union population by Member State (in 000's; percentages in parentheses)

Population	1995		2000		2010		2020	
Belgium	9 915	(3.0)	9 880	(2.9)	9 687	(2.9)	9 387	(2.9)
Denmark	5 169	(1.5)	5 176	(1.5)	5 073	(1.5)	4 776	(1.5)
W Germany	61 359	(18.6)	61 160	(18.4)	58 585	(17.7)	54 704	(16.9)
Greece	9 973	(3.0)	10 115	(3.0)	10 300	(3.1)	11 149	(3.4)
Spain	40 094	(12.2)	40 746	(12.3)	41 193	(12.4)	40 699	(12.5)
France	57 060	(17.3)	57 880	(17.4)	58 763	(17.8)	58 664	(18.1)
Ireland	3 500	(1.1)	3 471	(1.0)	3 412	(1.0)	3 347	(1.0)
Italy	57 585	(17.5)	57 610	(17.3)	56 408	(17.1)	53 484	(16.5)
Luxembourg	374	(0.1)	375	(0.1)	375	(0.1)	369	(0.1)
Netherlands	15 329	(4.7)	15 716	(4.7)	16 101	(4.9)	16 160	(5.0)
Portugal	10 819	(3.3)	11 140	(3.3)	11 473	(3.5)	11 814	(3.6)
United Kingdom	58 144	(17.6)	58 858	(17.7)	59 391	(17.9)	59 838	(18.4)
Europe	329 321		332 127		330 761		324 381	

Source: European Commission.

The UK displays the highest proportion of women in the workforce, despite the appalling provision of childcare for working women, and is regarded by some observers to have successfully fostered a non-discriminatory working environment for women. The country has recognised the economic necessity of introducing women into a wide spectrum of functions and this has, in theory at least, resulted in greater opportunities for female workers. Certain sectors, however, such as engineering, remain bastions of male dominance and even sectors which have theoretically embraced the new equality can boast few women in top management positions.

Has the UK, then, merely paid lip-service to changes in rules on equality? The answer to this question is by no means clear cut, but some consideration should be paid to the rate with which attitudes change. Among the older generation, who grew up in the belief that women should stay at home and bring up the family, there remains a tendency to discriminate. The impact of changing legislation which has stamped out overt discrimination has tended to obscure the clear boundaries of what does and does not constitute a discriminatory action. In terms of job applications and promotions, for example, a lot of factors other than sexuality may be used to decide between two candidates which can obfuscate whether or not any discrimination was involved in the final decision.

The potential for covert discrimination will always exist, but with each new generation the entrenched attitude that women should concentrate on being wives and mothers is slowly eroded. What this suggests, then, is that attitudes cannot be changed overnight and take time to filter through society as each generation fosters a new cultural code amongst its young. On this understanding, the UK may rather be regarded as being on the road to removing sexual inequality rather than simply paying lip-service to the problem.

Table 9.4 sheds some interesting light on attitudes towards the role of men and women in society in the 12 Member States in 1987. Although the UK ranks second (behind

Denmark) in its progressive view towards equality in work between men and women, it still has a long way to go to eradicate a continuing belief that women should stay at home and men should go to work. The data suggest that up to 18 per cent of the UK population continue to hold this belief although this is far less than in Luxembourg and Ireland where 39 per cent of the population are estimated to think this way and Germany where the equivalent figure is 32 per cent.

In these countries attitudes towards women must change if they are to embrace the new social charter directives on equality. France, like the UK, welcomes women in certain professions but not others. While they are well represented in the service sector, personnel functions, law and finance, there remains a bias against women in industry. Spain continues to show a polarisation of opinion towards women. Unqualified men in particular feel threatened by qualified women, particularly as they are readily accepted into management positions to fill the gaps produced by the acute shortage. Women in management roles is not a new phenomenon in Spain as family firms have automatically passed control onto women where there are no male heirs.

Table 9.4. Views on the roles of men and women in society

	Both have an absorbing job and share roles equally	The wife has a less demanding job and does more of the housework	Husband has the job and the wife stays at home
Belgium	34	30	25
Denmark	53	26	12
Germany	26	34	32
Greece	43	28	23
France	45	29	24
Ireland	34	20	39
Italy	42	31	25
Luxembourg	20	30	39
Netherlands	43	28	23
Portugal	43	24	25
Spain	47	19	28
United Kingdom	48	31	18

Source: Eurobarometer, 1987.

This has also been an issue in the Italian market where the 'family' takes preference over issues of sexuality. Although many firms have grown beyond the family, the Italians continue to value women in management and leadership roles and have correspondingly developed favourable maternity leave provisions and child care facilities. As countries and companies respond to changing demographics and begin to actively encourage more women in top level jobs, more consideration of career breaks to allow them time with their young children, retraining after their return to work, and crèche facilities for pre-nursery children for those women who either choose not to take a career break or who cannot afford to do so, is essential.

Scandinavian countries, given their high 'Femininity' bias, are unsurprisingly supportive of women in their businesses. Women fit easily into institutions which encourage good living standards and are encouraged to pursue their careers in parallel with their family lives. Childcare facilities in organisations are common and career paths take into account career breaks for maternity and childcare.

Individualism–collectivism

Figure 9.12 outlines the indices along the Individualism–Collectivism dimension for the Member States of the EU, Japan and the USA. In the home, this will mean differences between: self-interest versus group harmony, self-actualisation versus respect, the expression of personal opinions versus acceptance of group norms. These are translated in the education process to distinguish between learning how to learn versus learning how to do, and in the firm between task dominance versus relationship dominance, and a view of other workers as assets versus other workers as group members.

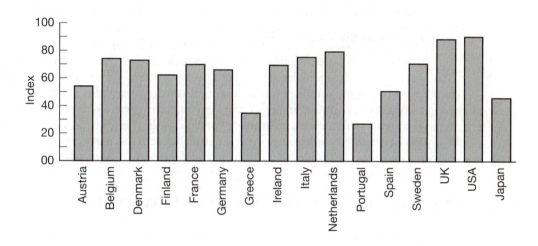

Fig. 9.12 Individualism index for the European Union Member States and their leading competitors (excluding Luxembourg)

The UK exhibits the highest score along this dimension. The UK, which in this respect is possibly more akin to the USA than other Member States, encourages an individualistic ethos. Great store is placed on such management values as *entrepreneurship*, industry champions and individual effort. People are encouraged to operate alone, and often, can only get on at work by usurping others and competing for jobs and recognition. Various other Member States show slightly lower, but still significant scores showing a tendency towards individualism rather than collectivism. The two clearest exceptions are Greece and Portugal, where collectivism is assumed to dominate. Hofstede (1995) argues that individualism is positively correlated with economic performance and national wealth, which possibly suggests the low scores for these two Member States.

Japanese management practices (of which more later) are generally accepted to differ markedly from those pertaining in the West along this dimension. Teamwork and group effort has often been ascribed as one of the driving forces behind their success and Western firms, adopting elements of Japanese 'best practice' have attempted to introduce teamwork concepts into their organisations with varying degrees of success. To what extent this will change the behaviour of people in Western European society is debatable, but it does raise the issue (discussed later in this chapter) of the continuing practice for firms to adopt new management practices outside of their traditional spheres of cultural practice.

Time horizon

The issue of *short-termism* was raised in Chapter 7. The UK has, for several years, been accused of taking a short-term view of planning and development which tends to lead to fire-fighting and strategies which can make a quick return rather than those which will ultimately result in long-term competitive success. Japan on the other hand has traditionally been thought of as taking a long-term perspective on decision making, looking to attaining a long-term sustainable business position rather than short-term profit. It is not surprising, therefore, that the index for the UK is 25 and that for Japan is 80. Similarly, the figures for Germany, the Netherlands and Sweden are 31, 44 and 33 respectively.

Much here relates to the way in which business interacts with the financial community. Japanese industrial groups – *keiretsus* – include at their core banks and financial intermediaries. This means Japanese firms tend to benefit from favourable terms for borrowing which allows them to take a longer view of investments and projects. Nevertheless, this alone does not give society its long-term cultural affinity. Stability at work, and individual commitment to the organisation (rather than self-development) also aid the continuity of management decisions and an ability to promote long-term goals which individual managers can see through from inception to ultimate conclusion. In Western nations, where individual worth is measured by outcomes, there is a tendency to try to make a fast impression and look for short-term profitable solutions which do not necessarily bring long-term success.

DEFINING MARKETS AND BUYER BEHAVIOUR

These aspects of culture are treated separately from those relating to national identity as many of them cut across the Member States and potentially define sub-cultures and groups which may differ from dominant cultural norms. Discussed here are issues relating to technology and material culture, attitudes and beliefs and religion.

Technology and material culture

Trappings of society

Material culture relates to the way in which people regard material possessions and wealth and often serves to communicate important messages about different societies. Furnishings and trappings also make important statements about individuals in certain materialistic cultures such as the UK and Germany. This is often manifested in one-upmanship between friends and colleagues where individuals compete through their acquisitions of new technologies and gadgets to assert their social standing.

In other cultural groups, particularly those of southern Europe, the family, relationships and friendships are considered more important than material 'things'. The 1980s is regarded, in retrospect, as the decade of materialism. 'Yuppies' developed as an important sub-group in many European societies even those which are traditionally associated with non-materialistic cultures. Buoyed by the healthy economic development of the mid-1980s many young people throughout Europe found themselves with large disposable incomes, a dream for European marketing men wishing to capitalise on the economic boom. These groups also perpetrated an acquisitive culture as they acted as innovators and early adopters in the acceptance of many goods.

Some cultural observers assert that the material culture of the 1980s will give way to a concern about quality of life in the 1990s and indeed there has been some evidence of this. Constructively utilising leisure time and greater concern about the environment and the people in it are expected to be more important than who owns what. This is likely to produce a shift in emphasis from the manufacturing to the service sector which supports the notion that internationalisation in the service sector will become an increasingly common phenomenon.

There are also differences in material culture according to age. The success of products and services such as Levi Jeans, Swatch Watches, McDonald's, Sega Computer Games and Nike sportswear is often attributed to the notion that there is a global youth sub-culture – a pop culture – which exists irrespective of differences in language and social acclimatisation in the local state.

Pay and remuneration

Material culture also dictates the way people regard pay and remuneration for work. In most Western European cultures people generally accept that the harder they work the greater will be the remuneration. Those people who desire more economic wealth are therefore likely to work longer and harder. Equally, employers who require extra effort from their employees, greater commitment of more loyalty can achieve their goals through providing the right economic incentives. This might take the form of favourable overtime conditions, pay rises, a better company car, or additional peripheral benefits such as pensions and private medical insurance.

Values and attitudes

Values and attitudes refer to commonly held beliefs about a variety of issues, which in turn determine common behavioural patterns. More specifically, values are the standards by which things may be judged and serve to shape people's beliefs and consequently their attitudes. This is probably the most illusive area of culture as values and attitudes only become apparent through inter-personal communication and interaction. There are no formal rules and guidelines, but the unwritten frameworks may be just as powerful in determining behaviour.

'The best thing about the British is their sense of humour!' This is a belief the British hold about themselves, but how do others view them? Mole (1992) suggests the Germans think they are idle, the Spanish regard them as arrogant and the French as chauvinistic. In return, the English think that the Germans are arrogant and pushy, the French are not to be trusted and the Spanish idle. A major stumbling block to achieving a Single Market, and managing across cultures, may therefore turn out to be unqualified attitudes and beliefs by each Member State about its neighbours. Many of these feelings lie deep within the core of each society and are often based on past historical events, feuds, wars and misunderstandings. While firms operating on a pan-European scale will, over time, overcome some of these preconceived notions through their dealings with institutions from other Member

States, it is more the attitudinal block to viewing Europe as a Single Market which is likely to hamper true integration.

It is perhaps important at this stage to consider the concepts of ethnocentrism and polycentrism and their effects on pan-European management. Ethnocentrism refers to the belief that one's own group is superior to others. Daniels and Radebaugh (1995) suggest there are three types of ethnocentric behaviour:

1 Differences abroad are ignored as managers are so steeped in their own cultural norms that they cannot see beyond their own social group. This kind of ethnocentrism demands careful review of foreign cultures and an opening up of attitudes before successful foreign operations can be achieved.
2 Managers are aware of environmental and cultural differences but do not translate these into the establishment of new worldwide (or Europe-wide objectives). This may result in under-performance in overseas markets and demands a strategic re-think of strategy on a wider scale.
3 Management is aware of differences but believes they can re-educate foreigners to adopt something new. While this kind of ethnocentrism can produce positive results through the introduction of innovative products or business practices which may give the firm an edge over indigenous companies, it may be dangerous. Foreigners may show high resistance to change, particularly if it means diverging from their own norms, ethics and morality.

Quite clearly, ethnocentrism can result in managers failing to identify the differences, with a lack of *cultural fluency* (familiarity with different norms and practices) hampering progress in the Member States. But what of the converse case. Polycentrism assumes that cultures are all so different that all decision making should be decentralised and left to managers in individual Member States who are then free to adapt products and practices according to local customs and norms. The most extreme case, however, ignores the potential for standardisation and harmonisation and ultimately may result in inefficiencies and a loss of overriding control. Equally, if the practices adopted become so localised, there is little scope for the firm to innovate or behave as a change agent.

This returns us to the on-going debate in Europe on the benefits and disbenefits of centralisation versus decentralisation. Whereas, before this was analysed from a strategic point of view, the cultural focus here points to the fact that managers in Europe must not just look for differences. It is imperative they look for similarities between different cultural groups and common business behaviours, which may cut across national boundaries, but which may serve as the starting point for establishing *transnational* European objectives rather than multi-market solutions based on simple adaptation.

Religion

Religion provides a foundation for attitudes, beliefs and values. Christianity is the cornerstone of European culture, with other religious sects such as Muslims and Hindus providing important cultural sub-groups. Religion shapes material culture within society. Catholicism tends to support an acquisitive society as it has traditionally been associated with greed and material wealth. The Protestant ethic encourages thrift with economic reward coming from hard work. In both cases, wealth is regarded as a measure of achievement which has the effect of perpetuating class divisions wherein people make value judgements about others based on their opulence and outward display of affluence.

Religion also affects male/female roles within society and family groups. Various examples of these kinds of influences can be cited:

- Catholics continue to prohibit birth control which tends to result in large family groups
- under Islam, women are expected to stay in the home and play the role of wife and mother
- Islamic people have a sacred obligation towards parents which often results in tightly knit extended families
- Muslim men may have more than one wife although the women are expected to remain monogamous
- Jewish people have a strong sense of family loyalty and decision making tends to be more democratic than is the case in various other groups.

While factors of this kind serve to shape the boundaries of cultural sub-groups they also provide sources of conflict. Some of the main problems arise as many laws and social provisions are designed specifically for the dominant cultural streams, alienating the sub-groups. Education, for example, is frequently regarded as an area of contention. Formal teaching of subjects such as history and religious education and the informal learning which takes place in schools as part of the hidden curriculum are often solely concerned with supporting the development of the dominant culture while ignoring the needs of sub-cultures.

Although cultural norms may be perpetuated through the home, many sub-groups feel that their culture is threatened by the lack of formal educational reinforcement. They tend to react against this by congregating in large regional community groups which helps them to sustain their cultural affinity through community as well as family life. What this means, however, is that a lot of sub-groups fail to integrate into society which is often thought to be the cause of racial/religious tension.

There are also other areas where EU policy may affect some of the sub-groups; for example, the Islamic principle of encouraging women to stay at home is out-of-keeping with the social charter which actively discourages this kind of 'sexist' attitude. It is unlikely, however, that the Islamic community will ever be directly tackled on such an issue as their religion will always be respected. Again, however, issues of this kind provide scope for tension between dominant and sub-cultures.

ANALYSING CORPORATE CULTURE

Corporate culture clearly differs from national culture. It is the product of the firm's history and development which may, for multinational organisations, be an amalgam of experiences in a number of national marketplaces. It is, therefore, unique to the individual organisation and carves out a path for behaviour and practices which may be distinct from other firms operating within the same locale. Essentially, there are two schools of thought on managerial styles and corporate culture:

1 management style is the product of levels of technology and economic development;
2 management styles are directly linked to the culture of the society in which the organisation operates.

On the latter point, it is possible to distinguish different types of management styles according to Hofstede's dimensions of national culture (*see* Table 9.5). While the corporate

Table 9.5. Corporate culture and management styles

National cultural characteristics	Business structure	Corporate culture	Management style
High power distance	Hierarchical structures with power determined by level in the pyramid.	Centralised decision making and control.	Authoritarian and coercive.
Low power distance	Flat organisational structures – heterarchies possible.	Decentralised decision making and consultation of lower managers and the workforce.	Democratic and open to ideas.
High uncertainty avoidance	Formalised structure (possibly hierarchical) functional structures with much centralisation.	Job specialisation and clear delineation of individual job roles and functions.	Dependence on documentation and written rules.
Low uncertainty avoidance	Loose organisational structures – task oriented and teamwork with high decentralisation.	Job mobility and little attention paid to titles and roles. Generalism encouraged.	Freedom afforded to individuals to take responsibility and make decisions.
Individualistic	Line functions support individual effort. Often hierarchical with clear lines of career development.	Encourages entrepreneurship and competition between employees. Low loyalty and high inter-company mobility.	Freedom to express opinion. Encouragement of innovative thinking.
Groupist	Flat organisation structures and focus on interdisciplinary teams and functions.	Encourages co-operation and common purpose – usually established at the top but communicated through management levels.	Process oriented, focus on encouragement and involvement at lower levels (although not always decision making power).
Masculine	Functional departments made accountable.	Reward systems based on profit. Low loyalty.	Aggressive/results oriented.
Feminine	Process orientation.	Focus on worker welfare leads to consultation and communication. High loyalty.	Decisions made on the basis of common communication and understanding.

Based on Lachman, Nedd and Hinings, 1995.

cultures and management styles are highly simplified for the purpose of analysis, it is possible to project different corporate and business cultures for firms operating out of countries on the basis of this thinking; for example, compare France, Italy and Sweden. Each of these countries exhibits different scores along the four dimensions proposed by Hofstede. By plotting these scores for the four countries, and assuming that they have an impact on company culture for firms with their main operating base in each of these Member States, it is possible to compare corporate cultures pertaining in firms from each nation. This is demonstrated in Fig. 9.13.

Theoretically, at least, it is possible to distinguish between different corporate and management cultures according to national affinity. Swedish firms, therefore, are expected to demonstrate decentralised and democratic decision making with high levels of worker consultation, common communication and understanding. Managers are also given freedom to make decisions outside of formal rules and are encouraged to think innovatively. French firms on the other hand are expected to show high formality in their rules and structures, authoritarian and coercive management practices. While innovation is encouraged, this can only take place within the strict regulatory rules. Consultation is encouraged, although not necessarily the basis of ultimate decisions. Finally, Italian firms are likely to show similar characteristics to their French counterparts, with rather less emphasis on authority and coercion and more emphasis on results and profit.

Even those with only a cursory knowledge of the workings of European firms will be aware that there is some validity in these distinctions with firms from the various countries highlighted exhibiting characteristics in line with these distinctions. However, suggesting that all firms within each country display all these characteristics to the same degree would be misleading.

Multinational, or even trans-European firms, which have been exposed to different cultures as part of their normal day-to-day business practices (either through working with intermediaries, selling to final customers, acquisition of foreign organisations, joint ventures and alliances) are likely to have adopted a corporate culture and managerial ethos which is distinct from other companies operating purely within a single nation state. It is, therefore, possible to suggest that multinational organisations are likely to be more akin to each other than they are to other organisations within the nation in which they are headquartered. This relates back to the first point above, and suggests that levels of development and common experience can shape companies as much as domestic national characteristics.

Obviously, then it is difficult to characterise organisations without 'getting inside' and learning first hand what systems and practices they have adopted as a result of their experiences and historical development. Nevertheless, it is possible to characterise 'types' of organisation along certain dimensions: process versus results, pragmatic versus normative and job versus employee.

Process versus results

Peters and Waterman (1982) argued that strong cultures are more results oriented than weak ones and vice versa. By a *strong* culture, they were referring to the degree of homogeneity in perceptions about practices and ways of conducting business according to the norms of the firm. There are various advantages and disadvantages associated with strong cultures (Hannagan, 1995) which are highlighted in Table 9.6.

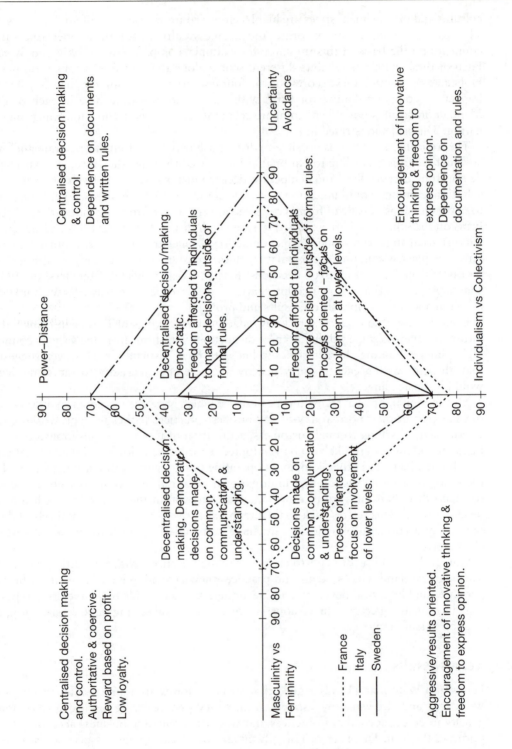

Fig. 9.13 Corporate cultures and management styles for France, Italy and Sweden

Table 9.6. Advantages and disadvantages of strong cultures

Advantages	Disadvantages
Goals are easier to achieve as the culture drives all employees not just towards the same ends, but to the same ends via the same means.	Although goal alignment may be easy to achieve, the goals may not be the right ones. They may be unethical or uneconomical.
With everyone pulling together, organisations tend to be more efficient with less time wasted in conflict and disagreement.	Strong cultures do not always give rise to motivation. UK public sector organisations, for example, have very strong cultures but are notoriously bad at motivating staff. It is
Leads to high levels of employee motivation. There is 'comfort' in working for an organisation with clearly defined ways of doing things even if these are idiosyncratic.	possible to argue that strong cultures can generate a variety of different attitudes towards the organisation not all of which are conducive to motivation.
Organisations with strong cultures often incorporate practices which make working for them rewarding such as participation in decision making, again determining good motivation.	Organisations can become too introspective and wrapped up in their history and fail to focus on the present and future development. Changes in the operating environment can mean that old rules no long apply.
Strong cultures tend to learn lessons from past experiences and learn the best ways of doing things.	There remains the question of causality. Does a strong culture result in good performance, or does good performance help to strengthen company culture?

Based on Hannagan, 1995, pp. 250–251.

Pragmatic versus normative

This essentially measures the degree of customer orientation displayed by the organisation. Pragmatic organisations tend to drive from the centre, whereas normative organisations tend to be driven by functions lower down the value chain (sales and marketing in particular). This is obviously a fundamental issue in modern day Europe wherein firms are grappling with the problem of balancing centralisation and decentralisation (efficiency and market responsiveness). To an extent it is possible to argue that all European firms are demonstrating a trend towards more pragmatic management styles as they endeavour to find ways of improving their marketing effort in the EU market which is increasingly competitive and challenging. Without an outward looking focus on customers it is impossible for them to survive.

With this thinking in mind, it is clear that this cuts across all of the national managerial determinants discussed above and suggests that there is the possibility of 'Euro-firms' developing which display common cultural characteristics and business norms. This tends to support the argument that culture ultimately can converge in business activity across the EU.

Job versus employee

Some organisations consider their workforce purely as an economic asset, expendable at any time. Others are more concerned about the welfare of their employees and consider not only their job role, but their personal well-being. Differences of this kind obviously have a bearing on the way in which managers liaise and co-operate with staff lower down the organisation, training and individual development. Implicitly, differences of this kind impact on motivation and loyalty.

Within the context of the EU, it is again possible to argue that things are changing. The Social Charter has set out a number of guidelines which require organisations to shift their thinking about employees and look more closely at working conditions. Culture change is therefore likely to result as organisational thinking converges and firms begin to look at their workforce not just in terms of the jobs they perform but in terms of social duty. It is possible to argue that the UK, which has shown such great reluctance to embrace the new Social Charter, has done so not due to its lack of concern about workers, but because of its cultural bias. Many firms in the UK, partly as a result of the cyclical nature of the economy which has been beset by several recessions over the last couple of decades, and partly due to high levels of employee mobility, have not developed systems and structures for long-term nurturing of their employees' well being. The demands of the Social Charter, therefore, dictate major cultural change among UK organisations which is fuelling resistance to the new proposed legislation.

MANAGING ACROSS CULTURES IN THE EUROPEAN UNION

There is no doubt from the above that Europe is, and will remain, a marketplace in which cultural differences prevail. Strategic management for Europe, then is about matching organisations not just to one, homogeneous environment, but to several, culturally distinct environments of the Member States.

It is perhaps the term 'Single Market' which has been popularised to describe the current state of the EU, and discussions of *homogeneity*, which have obscured the real challenge of managing across cultures in Europe. It is unlikely there will ever be a truly single homogeneous market in the EU in the sense of there being a single, homogeneous culture. While this has led to some to argue that the proposed benefits of the Single Market – greater opportunities for achieving scale economies, improved efficiency and a stimulus for innovation – can never truly be realised, they are perhaps missing the point. The cultural diversity of Europe need not be considered as a barrier to achieving Europe-wide objectives, but a facilitator of achieving improved competitive advantage.

Porter (1990) developed a model to explain the competitive advantage of different nations. While, in the past, advantages were assumed to result from comparative advantage in factors of production, growing evidence in the world economy that factors of production are mobile, means that these give only transitory advantages, and do not support long-term competitive advantage. Porter therefore focused on four key aspects of national environments which support the development of different national advantage. These are depicted in Fig. 9.14.

While culture is not explicitly included in the model, it is assumed that cultural differences work through the four key variables. Indeed, Porter argues that culture is often the result of economic conditions:

> ... the primary reason behind the Japanese preference for close and long-lasting supplier relationships in the automotive industry is economics, not culture. A deeper investigation shows that close vertical relationships are necessitated by just-in-time production which, in turn, was invented as a result of a factor condition – the severe shortage of factory space in Japan.

(Porter, 1993 p. 178)

The EU is a marketplace, and not a locus for competitive advantage. Each country within the EU boasts a different set of conditions (factor, demand, competitive and relationship) which dictates its comparative advantage vis-à-vis other Member States. In essence, it means that various nations offer up different locational advantages and disadvantages.

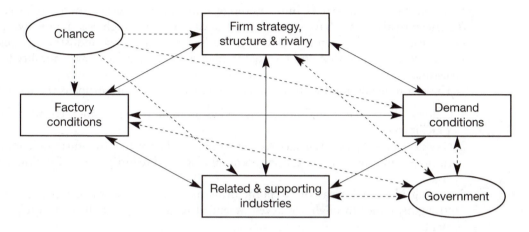

Fig. 9.14 The determinants of national competitive advantage

European firms, which have the freedom to re-organise their businesses across the Member States are therefore well placed to tap into the advantages (many of which are culturally determined) of the various EU nations. From this point of view, European firms have the ability to strengthen their Europe-wide (and international) competitive advantage as a result of cultural diversity. But how can they achieve this? Relating back to Chapter 7, much issue was made of the growing importance of flexibility, and without wishing to labour the point, it is important to re-iterate this in relation to cross-cultural management.

Flexible organisations have the potential to maximise benefits from different business practices and national economic conditions through a variety of means:

1 locating businesses in markets where factor conditions are favourable leading to cost advantages and efficiency;
2 operating in non-domestic markets where demand conditions are more favourable and profit potential apparent. This critically involves the identification of common patterns of demand and sub-markets which are likely to cut across national boundaries;
3 the development of relationships with suppliers can improve the quality and efficiency of inbound logistics. Europe-wide sourcing facilitates this process. Companies can build relationships with suppliers in other Member States which show a high propensity for co-operation and long-term relationship management;
4 joint ventures, strategic alliances and mergers allow firms to internalise not only the knowledge and learning of organisations from other Member States (and thus potentially benefit from their comparative advantages) but also new business practices.

Effectively, they can improve their position along all four dimensions of Porter's 'diamond' of competitive advantage by developing on a pan-European basis.

One point, not hitherto mentioned, but critical to managing across cultures, is that culture is industry dependent. While this chapter has reviewed culture from both a national and company perspective, it is also important to recognise that cultural determinants impact differently from industry to industry. For example, Porter goes on to suggest that advantages which can benefit one industry, can be destructive in other industries and cites the case of Sweden's tendency for risk aversion (i.e. high uncertainty avoidance). Risk aversion has put the Swiss biotechnology industry at a disadvantage relative to its American rivals as they have shown a reluctance to invest in high-risk, innovative areas of research and development. Conversely, the Swedish insurance industry has benefited greatly from risk aversion and resulted in high investment returns and stability for local investors.

The recommendation for firms managing across cultures in Europe is therefore this:

1 Cultural difference should not be viewed as an inhibitor of competitive advantage but a facilitator.
2 Having established critical success factors in its industry, the firm must look at national cultures and economic conditions across Europe and identify areas of national advantage.
3 Having identified areas of strength, firms must devolve ways of tapping into these strengths, either through the development of relationships or through foreign investment.
4 Identify commonality in demand conditions between markets as a means of ensuring maximum coverage for common products and brands.
5 Be prepared to be flexible and adaptive, but don't lose sight of Europe-wide objectives. In other words, adapt where it is essential to do so, but standardise wherever possible.

The latter point is likely to be difficult to achieve for European firms which have traditionally viewed Europe as a series of discrete markets which require separate treatment. As alluded to in Chapter 7, high levels of decentralisation have characterised the Europe-wide activities of many firms which, in the past, viewed this as the most appropriate way of dealing with foreign market differences. Despite this, however, as firms are moving more towards networked structures, with subsidiary managers coming together to voice their concerns, they are finding that common problems and opportunities exist across a large number of markets and the potential for standardisation (particularly in cross-market niches) greater than first thought possible.

Whether or not, then, European culture becomes more homogeneous, is of little concern. By developing a flexible approach to European strategic management, firms can turn differences into competitive advantage. However, there is some concern that in the current environment, firms showing the greatest aptitude for this approach to pan-European management are the Japanese and Americans who are therefore out-competing Europeans on their own soil. Here, too, however, change within Europe opens up new potential for cultural learning. Exposure to Japanese management practices, either through competing against them, or working with them, has resulted in a worldwide move towards the adoption of some of the factors which have arguably led to the Japanese 'miracle' in recent years.

ADOPTION OF NEW BUSINESS PRACTICES

While this chapter is on European business culture, it would not be complete without a review of Japanese management practices. The meteoric success of Japan in the world economy in recent years has led many businesses to ask: what makes the Japanese so successful?

Much has been written about the success of Japan in recent years, researchers looking for clues as to why the Japanese have been able to outperform their Western counterparts. Much of this research has focused on cultural differences between Western and Japanese management practices which are depicted in Table 9.7. For the sake of convenience, 'Western' management practices are grouped together, although as has already been demonstrated, distinct differences do exist on a country-by-country basis. Nevertheless, it is possible to make certain generalisations at a generic level.

Oliver and Wilkinson (1992) identify four groupings of factors characteristic of Japanese industry:

1 Manufacturing methods (including Total Quality Control, Quality Circles, In-Process controls such as Statistical Process Control, Just-in-Time delivery and management systems and Continuous improvement – *Kaizan*)
2 Organisational structures and systems (including Management accounting) which does not simply inform but forces improvements, R&D lead by powerful *Susha* (project leaders) and flatter organisational structures
3 Personnel practices (including lifetime employment, longer working hours and commitment to consultation and improvement).
4 Wider social, political and economic conditions (incorporating enterprise unions, buyer–seller relationships, government support and economic structures including an integral banking system).

All of these reflect how different cultural norms in Japan have impacted on the way in which the Japanese do business. In terms of manufacturing techniques, for example, while the systems employed are not unique to Japan, many of them being introduced with US aid packages and technology transfer deals after the Second World War (particularly quality control techniques) they were enthusiastically implemented by Japanese managers after being adapted to suit the Japanese cultural preference for group and teamworking. Thus, it is not the systems in themselves which have offered great scope for 'good practice' but the way in which they have been adopted into the culture.

Japanese manufacturing techniques

Japanese manufacturing techniques constitute the most tangible elements of the Japanese business system. They are essentially concerned with quality and efficiency and the improvement of competitiveness and thus it is unsurprising that it is these, more than any other aspects of Japanese management, which are now being adopted by Western firms. Table 9.8 outlines the nature and scope of the most commonly followed systems in this respect.

Table 9.7. Japanese-style management v Western-style management

Japanese style	Western style
Organisational principles	
1. The firm viewed as a collective body; total devotion of the individual to the firm (i.e. joining the firm, not hiring on by contract).	1. Functionalist organisation of individuals as specialists.
2. Human centred, not functionalist centred organisation.	2. Co-operative work system based on a thoroughgoing division of labour; subdivision and standardisation of jobs.
3. Stress on co-operative teamwork.	3. Pyramid-shaped bureaucracy.
4. Indeterminate job description and job standing (authority and responsibility); generalist orientated.	4. Clearly defined job description and job standing (authority and responsibility).
5. Japanese style adaptation of modern bureaucracy.	5. Employment of contract (give and take commercial exchange).
Decision making and communication	
1. Collective decision-making (bottom-up consensus type decision-making as seen in the *ringi* system).	1. Top-down decision-making and one-way orders (no consideration given to opinions at the lower echelons.
2. Verbal and non-verbal communication (*nemawashi* or behind the scenes manoeuvres; information transmitted by implicit understanding, gut decision ...).	2. Autocratic authority at the top; expanded power of the bureaucracy.
3. Collective work performance system (common room system; total membership participation & planning).	3. Individual responsibility and competition (fair-play principles).
4. Exemption from responsibility (seat of authority is obscure; no one takes responsibility).	4. Strong owner consciousness (the company President is also a hired hand).
5. Separation of ownership and management (no real power in officers' meetings and general stockholders' meetings.	5. Legal armament by lawyers (legal specialists).
6. Japan Inc. (collusive relationships of government, business and labour).	
Personnel system/labour management	
1. Life-long employment (no layoffs but there is flexibility by means of part-time and temporary employees).	1. Employment of people needed only at times when needed; layoffs in bad times.
2. Seniority-based promotion system (evaluations for promotions are quite comprehensive; they stress not just work results but incentive and effort as well and also reflect capability).	2. Wages are job compensation according to competency (efficiency system) with no relationship to age and seniority.
3. Seniority wage system (stress is placed not just on compensation for labour but on overall exhibition of ability); stress on fringe and welfare benefits.	3. Seniority system at times of promotion and layoffs.
4. Extensive employee training and education.	4. Labour unions are functionally organised by craft and job type; unions safeguard the individual's life and rights.
5. Enterprise labour unions; co-operation between labour and management.	5. Much tension between labour-management relations.
Human relation and values	
1. Groupism (the group comes first; value on the group; the individual is devoted heart and soul to the group) mutual dependence.	1. Individualism (ultimate value on the individual; devotion and loyalty to the group are weak).
2. Concurrence of the firm's goal and the individual's life goal (devotion to the group; prestige, sense of security, and morale pursuant to participation; co-prosperity idea; love of company spirit).	2. To the individual the firm is nothing more than a means to obtain wages and to the firm the individual is a piece of machinery, a tool.
3. Stress on harmony in human relations (emphasis on feelings and motives, warm human relations, mutual consent of all members and linking of hearts).	3. Human relations in the workplace are simply artificial relations for work purposes; relations cease outside of the company.
4. Egalitarianism in substance (little chance for class discrimination; small earning differentials).	4. Egalitarian in form (strong class consciousness, competition for equal opportunity).
5. Strong desire for the elevation of quality and efficiency.	5. Purpose of life resides in the family and leisure, strong community consciousness.

Source: 'Can – Should – Japanese Management Practices be Exported Overseas?', Hafiz Mirza, The Business Graduate, January 1984.

Table 9.8. Japanese manufacturing techniques

Manufacturing technique	Overview
Total quality control	The de-specialising of the business function. Responsibility for quality remains in its 'natural' place, namely where production is performed. It incorporates all business functions with the aim being customer satisfaction both internal to the organisation (downstream business units) and external to the company (intermediaries and final customers).
Quality circles	These are small groups, usually between five–ten people who meet voluntarily to try to find ways to improve quality and productivity. Members are trained in statistical analysis and problem solving techniques.
Statistical process control (SPC)	This system is used to assist in the control of production processes in order to achieve less variation in output and ensure quality. SPC involves operators periodically sampling their own production not with a view to accepting or rejecting it, but in order to produce a chart of how the process itself is behaving. In addition to reducing scrap and reworking costs, minimising variation in components can significantly improve product performance.
Just in Time (JIT) production	'The JIT idea is simple: produce and deliver finished goods just in time to be sold, sub-assemblies just in time to be assembled into finished goods, fabricated parts just in time to go into the sub-assemblies and purchased materials just in time to be transformed into fabricated parts' (Schonberger, 1982). The system requires predictable and planned demand, or production flexibility to cater for changes in demand.
Kanban production system	This system involves containers for holding stock and cards for initiating production. This means that the amount of stock in the system can be varied by altering the number of cards in the system. In this way materials are pulled through the production process according to the demand for final assembly rather than pushed through by an inflexible production plan.
Flexible working	In Japanese firms this includes team working (or cellular manufacturing). This is facilitated by multi-skilled workers who can be rotated between jobs. The system simplifies workflow, allowing workers to be moved to alleviate bottlenecks and ensure a continuous flow of production.

Organisational structures

Organisational structures are, arguably, more ephemeral and difficult to replicate. They are reflective of family values and the country's national identity. It is often assumed that Japanese organisations are flat, with management being by consensus. This is rather mis-leading. Many Japanese organisations exhibit hierarchical characteristics, with decision making coming from the top. Although there is great talk of a 'bottom-up' approach to management (the *ringi* system) this is more about consultation and involvement than lower level decision making. There is a strong belief that workers have the potential to improve the quality of their work and thus they are encouraged to participate in problem solving, usually through the formation of teams. Team work is essentially the hallmark of the Japanese organisation. It not only involves bringing people together to solve common problems and work on group activities, but manifests itself in common goals and commitment by every individual to the company's welfare.

Team work is also fundamental to flexible manufacturing and TQM. As increased global competition is placing more emphasis on local responsiveness, market segmentation, differentiation and product quality firms need to develop more flexible manufacturing systems and quality programmes to respond to the new demands. Part of the team work ethos prepares individuals for a variety of functions within the workplace. Through *cross-training*, workers can stand-in for absent co-workers and respond quickly to changes in models and production runs. Used in conjunction with flexible manufacturing technology (computer aided design and manufacture), firms employing a team work ethos have the potential to change product models more than a dozen times a day. Similarly, team work enables TQM initiatives by providing a forum for problem solving and continuous improvement.

It is unsurprising then, that many Western firms, keen to pursue TQM principles, are moving towards team development and management. However, for many of them, introducing these techniques is proving difficult because it cuts across cultural norms. Many Western firms (as was highlighted earlier) are based on an *individualistic* rather than *collective* culture, which means teamwork is anathema to the underlying work ethic. Teams challenge individual power and authority and thus their introduction fuels resistance.

However, suggesting that differences centre on a clear distinction between collectivism and individualism is over-simplistic. Personal leadership in Japan is regarded highly, and many leading Japanese companies have attained their position in world markets as a result of strong leadership. Equally, many Western firms have pursued a policy of co-operation and teamwork for many years and while they have not considered this to be directly akin to Japanese-style management, the effects are markedly similar.

It is also wrong to assume that individualism is not conducive to good business practice. The benefits of individualism have been well-proven in Western organisations. The notion of entrepreneurial spirit is not only welcomed, it is actively encouraged as the tendency for individuals to compete against each other frequently gives rise to the development of new ideas. In the commercial organisation this means new products and technologies which have a positive impact on the national economy.

Nevertheless, individualism has its drawbacks. First, it tends to promote mobility between organisations as employees attempt to build impressive work records and move up the management ladder at a faster rate than their peers. This produces managers with broad general management experience but limited knowledge and understanding of the workings of an individual company. Nevertheless, mobility can mean that Western managers are exposed to a wide array of differing business practices as they move between organisations. This mirrors the situation in Japan, to some extent, although here mobility tends to be controlled within organisations by senior managers rather than at the personal level.

Second, it dilutes continuity in management with new personnel frequently replacing old and constantly moving business departments in a different direction. This can be unsettling to the workforce and overall morale with concomitant adverse effects on productivity. Finally, individualism may make it difficult to build co-operation both within and without the company. With co-operation between business departments and between organisations becoming an increasingly important feature of global business activity, there is a case for concern regarding Western managers' ability to adapt from a competitive to a co-operative mentality.

In Chapter 7, much emphasis was placed on the competitive success of Japanese firms accruing from the close business relationships developed with suppliers. Although inter-firm collaborations in Japan are centred on the *Keiretsu* (linked group) business system, which is a product of Japan's historical development, the basic elements of the system are being replicated by Japanese firms within the EU through collaborations with local firms, but more importantly, with Japanese suppliers who have followed the lead of the major producers and located production within the EU (*see also* Chapter 12). The success of these linked groups (based on mutual inter-dependence and trust) is prompting many EU firms to find new ways of working with their suppliers. Technical and business collaborations between suppliers and buyers for problem solving and the mutual development of components and inputs are becoming more prevalent within the EU as firms seek to capitalise on established business links to enhance competitive advantage. These linkages have, in turn, led to the development of JIT systems between unrelated firms.

Planning time frames

The idea that the Japanese take a longer perspective in planning was alluded to earlier. Management accounting procedures differ radically from those typically found in Western organisations. Systems are based more on products and market share than profit. This leads to activity based costing programmes rather than cost-plus and permits greater flexibility to adapt to changes in the external environment.

However, it is possible to over-emphasise the long-termism of the Japanese economy:

A far-sighted Japan and a myopic America make a tidy contrast, but one with little basis in fact. By and large, Japanese managers are at least as much obsessed with short-term results as their American counterparts ... They have arrived where they are today, not by rigidly adhering to pre-determined long-range strategies, but by paying scrupulous attention to performance on a monthly or even weekly basis – performance measured not against a three-or five-year plan, but against budget, against return on sales, against competitor performance.

(Ohmae, *McKinsey Quarterly*, Spring 1982, pp. 2–3)

Thus it is more the difference in approach to measuring profits rather than profit concerns themselves which distinguish between Japanese and Western firms. Whereas Western firms tend to concentrate on return on investment (ROI), Japanese organisations concentrate on return on sales (ROS).

Communication and employee involvement

Japanese personnel practices centre on co-operation, not mere compliance. The concept of *collectivism*, which starts in the family, and is mirrored in businesses, relies on mutual interdependence and loyalty. Groups are based on strict hierarchical models based on seniority systems in which individuals respect and look up to their elders.

Loyalty is promoted through involvement and consultation. Loyalty brings with it a sense of belonging, a common purpose, and high levels of motivation and commitment. In Japan, this is also facilitated by life-long employment (although this is no longer guaranteed in many Japanese firms) which gives individuals a sense of security and heightens their commitment to the organisation.

Japanese companies see their workforce as an asset. Core-workers are protected and nurtured and although they go through tough recruitment and selection procedures, in return they enjoy secure contracts and attractive remuneration packages. Nevertheless, profit-linked bonus schemes can result in broad differentials in pay between boom and slump periods.

Traditionally, many Western organisations have shown a limited propensity to involve employees in decision making. The main exceptions to this are provided by the Nordic countries, and more recently, Germany. The Social Charter is attempting to redress this situation and create a more harmonious relationship between management and workers. Much resistance has been displayed by Western firms in the adoption of employee involvement despite the apparent quality and productivity payouts.

The UK has been vehement in its criticism of this proposal, partly due to the fact that it seen as rejuvenation of union activity through the 'back door'. The Conservative government of the 1980s worked hard to dilute the power of UK trade unions in an effort to eradicate union interference in working practices which frequently led to industrial action and lost output. Their criticisms, however, appear to have missed the point. Employee involvement is not so much about empowering the workforce to take action against management, but to provide an environment in which employees are encouraged to take a greater interest in the long-term success of the organisation. Nevertheless, a shift to this way of thinking necessitates cultural change and shrugging off *individualistic* tendencies in favour of a more *collective* approach to management. The cultural barrier argument again seems to hold some sway.

Emerging examples of successful employee involvement within the EU suggest an approach somewhat different to that employed by the Japanese. The German systems of worker participation relies on the involvement of workers in decision making, which acts contrary to the intentions of the Japanese approach. Whereas the Japanese are concerned with employees playing a part in identifying and solving problems on the production line to reduce the number of defective goods produced, the German system is geared more towards real empowerment, giving workers a voice in company-wide decisions. Teams are more loosely supervised and workers actively encouraged to work under their own initiative. In essence, then, the Germany system, by empowering employees in this way, is combining both the benefits of co-operation and teamwork with individualism and entrepreneurship – adapting systems to suit local cultural conditions.

Training and development

Japanese companies stress life-long learning and multi-skilling as central to the development of their workers. As the demands on firms in Europe are changing and increasingly requiring more flexible manufacturing and work practices, teamwork and multi-skilling are essential if firms are to remain competitive. This means training the workforce in a variety of skills so that they can react quickly to changes in models and production runs. Harnessing the knowledge and expertise of in-house managers can reduce the cost of such training considerably. SP Tyres in Birmingham, a company which has introduced teamwork and flexible manufacturing has introduced extensive training programmes very cost effectively:

> This is because most of it is done relatively inexpensively in-house by multi-disciplinary teams, led by senior managers. These teams take responsibility for training other members of staff, often in areas outside their occupational expertise.

(*Financial Times*, 3 January 1990)

The Commission's efforts to improve EU training and its commitment to life-long learning clearly reflects the recognition that without systems in place to improve the skills of workers the EU is likely to be beset by problems of skills shortage and structural unemployment. Lessons from Japan are clear: improve the skills of the workforce, or run the risk of losing the competitive battle. In the current European environment, however, high levels of unemployment and company lay-offs in the early 1990s as a result of recessionary conditions (but also increased business rationalisation as a result of the Single Market initiative), act against the development of employee commitment, raising some doubts about successful development of vocational training programmes, at least in the short-term.

Wider economic considerations

Close liaison between government departments and industry in Japan, facilitated by the culturally determined co-operative ethos of the Japanese business system is anathema to many EU Member States (the UK in particular) where a *laissez faire* system of Government has resulted in little intervention and control of industry. The Commission, through its identification of key industries and intention to 'back winners' in terms of technological development (information technology, new materials, biotechnology and energy) appear to be pursuing a system of industrial development based on *managed* growth. This is more in keeping with Japan's view of economic development than that which has characterised much of Europe in the past. Nevertheless, few systems have been developed to facilitate working linkages between the Commission and industry which begs the question of the overall effectiveness of the proposed intentions. Giving industrialists greater voice in the design of policies and strategies is the only way of replicating the kind of co-operation and mutual understanding apparent in Japan.

The term *Japan Inc.* has often been used to describe the interrelated nature of Japanese industry, society and government. The Japanese *Keiretsu* groups, broad based conglomerates which stem from the activities of large wealthy industrial families, have produced a marketplace dominated by large conglomerates with complex cross-shareholdings and directorships. Each *Keiretsu* involves a wide array of disparate industries including manufacturing organisations, banking institutions, trading companies and service firms. There is, therefore, great potential for synergy within the *Keiretsu* groups as skills and resources can be drawn from a wide pool of industrial and commercial activity. The 22 existing groups account for a substantial proportion of the economy, are extremely influential and constitute the international face of Japan.

But this is not the full picture: outside the *Keiretsu* groups the economy boasts a very high proportion of small firms and family firms which make up half of the employment in Japan. They enjoy long-term relationships with the *Keiretsu* groups although they are vulnerable and tend to suffer in periods of economic down-turn. As these firms are sub-contractors and suppliers to the major economic groups, they are a significant feature of the total Japanese business system. A key feature of the *Keiretsu* group is the integral nature of the banking sector. With banks being part of the conglomerate, tied in to the successes of the group, Japanese firms tend to enjoy more favourable banking rates than their economic counterparts. In addition, the *Keiretsus* have strong links with powerful state bureaucracies which involves joint decision-making and consultation. This gives the main economic groups a leading voice in industrial policy and development which ensures political policy takes into account the needs of industry and commerce.

In Europe, banks remain removed from industry and an instrument of Government economic policy. Although German banks have formed close links with some of the larger German MNEs, this kind of relationship development tends to be the exception rather than the norm in the EU. Unlike their Japanese counterparts, EU banks have little incentive to offer low cost capital loans, firms providing a major source of income on loans granted. Without some provision being made for redressing the situation it is arguable that Japanese firms will always be able to reap the benefits of their integrative system and exploit the greater competitive advantages so offered.

The lessons to be learned

Important lessons are being learned by multinational managers as they are exposed to the different business practices utilised in other countries of the world. In terms of Japanisation, Graham (1988) identified three levels of business practice permeation into Western economies:

Direct Japanisation: Japanese companies setting up operations in the West, training workforces and establishing links with local suppliers.

Mediated Japanisation: The attempt by Western firms to emulate Japanese business practices in the belief that they may improve the competitive standing of the organisation.

Permeated Japanisation: The adoption of similar strategies and investment patterns including government support programmes.

Although the focus in this section has been on differences in Japanese versus Western management practices, this picture can be regarded more broadly. The three mechanisms outlined above serve as the conduits for learning and change in business practices on a global scale. Firms are now looking beyond the systems and structures developed in their own marketplace and towards global best practice. They are adopting systems and techniques from a variety of organisations – either their competitors or their partners – to improve their standing in European (and world) markets.

From this point of view it is difficult not to argue that multinational firms are changing culturally. While their behaviour may be partly attributable to national characteristics in their domestic market, this can no longer be seen as the only driving force behind corporate culture and management practices. Managing across cultures in the context of the EU is therefore not only about looking at different national markets, or European companies, but looking at global business cultures and managerial practices and learning how other organisations are solving problems and facing up to the new strategic challenges being posed by global environmental change. In this way, firms can draw on a wide pool of experience and proven behaviour as a means of deriving ways of improving their competitive position.

Research on Japanese management, and prescriptions for its adoption in the West, have tended to highlight the difficulties rather than the opportunities and have often tried to find mechanism for 'transfer' of techniques, rather than focus on learning opportunities. Their conclusions have frequently centred on the fact that it is impossible to replicate Japanese management practices as they rely on subtle ambiguities of culture, different ways of thinking (which often means they cannot be precisely defined) and an acceptance of constant dynamism of processes (Fry, 1991). Some have also tended to implicitly assume that everything about Japanese management is better than anything the West can offer. This is clearly not the case. Rather, many Japanese firms, through incorporating effective business techniques into their culture have been able to perform to very high standards.

The message then is that European firms may have a lot to learn, both from each other and their international competitors or collaborators. The Japanese have never been frightened of learning from the West. Their business practices are continually evolving, and often draw on Western input. Peters and Waterman's best selling book *In Search of Excellence* (1982), which describes the strategies employed by the most successful US Corporations, sold 50 000 copies in two days of being launched in Japan, and Ohmae (1982) reports Japanese managers remarking on similarities between their companies and the 'excellent' ones in the USA.

The challenge, then is to adopt 'best practice', regardless of its source. Successful firms from individual countries do not have a monopoly over best practice they have simply derived a good fit between efficient business techniques and company culture. This means adapting systems and techniques to fit existing company values and norms. Even the Nissan business operation in the UK is not solely based on Japanese style techniques, being a combination of 'the best of Japanese and British strengths to create a harmonious and productive working environment' (*Guardian*, 8 September 1987).

Differences lie in approach rather than practice. IBM, for example, which for many years pursued strategies which have now been labelled 'Japanese' was described by Basset (1986) as following strategies 'exactly the opposite of the Japanese method'. This conclusion was drawn on the basis of IBM's promotion of Individualism rather than Collectivism, which seemed to be in stark contrast to the Japanese ethic. However, the underlying intent of their strategic programme was improved efficiency and quality, and while they employed different means to the same ends, it is possible to argue that while processes may differ, ultimate outcomes are the same. Thus, while there may be some validity in the statement 'Japanese and American management is 95 per cent the same and differs in all important respects' (Takeo Fujisawa, co-founder of the Honda Motor Company) it is important not to lose sight of the fact the differences matter far less than the opportunity for learning.

But how can companies ensure that they have systems and mechanisms in place for acculturation and learning? Recently, the literature has been awash with articles concerning the development of 'Euro-managers' (international managers) who are able to operate across boundaries and who are adept at introducing change into organisations.

EURO-MANAGERS – RESPONDING TO CULTURAL DIVERSITY

Leading EU multinationals are increasingly turning their attention to training managers for European cross-cultural management as a means of attaining competitive advantage. Awareness that managers need to be able to operate across cultures is leading to a new agenda for the establishment of career paths and new demands for skills and learning. Sending successful domestic managers abroad to conduct the activities of the firm in foreign markets has, for a long time, been considered less than ideal. Failure of ex-patriate managers (and their early return to their domestic base) is thought to be attributable to a variety of factors, in particular inappropriate selection processes (based on technical skills and a proven track record rather than personal characteristics which may lead to rapid acculturation and flexibility), inadequate training and preparation (which often fails to develop self-maintenance skills such as stress management and psychological health) and lack of experience in developing working relations with foreign personnel (not fostered internally through staff rotation or considered important in the employment of staff where technical skills again dominate considerations).

Equally, growing numbers of joint ventures and strategic alliances within the EU are posing new management challenges which traditional thinking fails to address. Successful managers need to be aware of the specific challenges posed by alliances which are distinct from those pertaining in wholly-owned operations. Multiple ownership, multinational affiliation, tendencies to protect rather than share information, and the existence of hidden agendas all demand a sensitivity to business which is much more to do with co-operation than competition, a role for which many high flying managers are ill prepared.

The European business environment is growing ever more complex. The notion of 'think globally (or Europe-wide) but act locally' means managers now have to have at their fingertips a thorough understanding of the environment in which they operate, and an ability to assimilate complex operations to determine areas of commonality. Wills and Barham (1994) suggest that successful international managers share a number of important traits:

1 *Cultural empathy* – an ability to 'get into the heads' of the people they deal with from other cultures. This requires putting aside one's own assumptions when dealing with foreign managers or customers and opening up to alternative perspectives and ways of behaving.
2 *The power of active listening* – cultural empathy depends on an ability to listen and to absorb what is being heard. This means not thinking of a response before the other person has finished talking. In this way, it is possible to learn how others look at things from a different perspective. It also requires managers to look for 'hidden meanings' and covert thinking.
3 *A sense of humility* – an acceptance that you can learn from others and your own mistakes.
4 *Self-awareness* – demonstrating emotions improves the openness of interactions and helps to build trust between parties.
5 *Emotional resilience* – a failure to express emotions is not the same thing as emotional resilience. The failure often stems from an individual suppressing their emotions. Emotional resilience refers to the ability to express emotions and deal with difficult situations without the emotion hampering the effectiveness with which a situation is handled.
6 *Risk acceptance* – emotionally resilient managers tend to view the concept of risk differently from other managers. They accept that cross-cultural dealings expose them to risk and thus they develop: mechanisms for understanding levels of discomfort, survival techniques, ways of learning from the outcomes (whether they are positive or negative).
7 *Emotional support of the family* – the family providing a 'comfort zone' and a place for alleviating stress and supporting the challenge of risk and complexity.
8 *Curiosity to learn* – an active interest in seeking out the new and unfamiliar. Learning by doing and continually adding new layers of knowledge to old.
9 *Orientation to time* – 'living in the here and now'. Making the most of existing opportunities and not pondering on what has passed or what is to come except to learn from past experiences and plan for the future. Essentially, they are controllers of their time and not servants to it.
10 *Personal morality* – taking responsibility for decisions and, through a respect for people, encourage empowerment of others.

With such an extensive list of personal qualities required for managing across cultures it is not surprising that the task of developing good managers into good international managers is highly complex. It is not just about developing managers in job functions, tangential to their private and personal lives, but developing them as people to cope with the complex environments in which they operate. So how do firms encourage the development of such managers in practice?

As Europeanisation of activities increases, so too will the challenge of Europe-wide human resource management. Whereas marginalisation of personnel issues has been common in the past, even in many major multinational enterprises, advantages can accrue from incorporating new personnel initiatives in the overall strategic plan for Europe. Creating career paths which include operating in various Member States, developing reward schemes which reflect cross-cultural learning, emphasising language learning by providing in-house programmes as well as recruiting good language graduates and greater attention to personal attributes rather than technical skills in recruitment all have the potential to foster the development of Euro-managers. Nevertheless, there is a reluctance on the part of many firms to embark on training programmes when employee mobility is so high and job security so low. To date, many individuals of this nature have been sourced from the small open economies of Belgium, the Netherlands and Sweden where language skills and experience of working overseas are a result of relatively small domestic markets and high levels of foreign business involvement. But this is not the only answer.

Tijmstra and Casler (1992) suggest managers need to go through four distinct aspects of learning: awareness, knowledge, skills and attitudes. Knowledge, they argue, is a *hard* element which can be delivered through training courses on such issues as:

- the European business environment (socio-political, economic, business sector and technological)
- European management dynamics (the diversity of business cultures and variations in management values)
- the Europeanisation process (transnational structures, transnational processes, European identity and cross-cultural communication).

Conversely, awareness, knowledge, skills and attitudes can only be shaped through on-the-job experience and exposure to other cultures.

Training of managers is therefore imperative at both a pre-occupation and post-occupation level. Educational institutions have an important role to play in preparing individuals for the new Europe. Emphasis in secondary education on language learning and a renewed vigour in business schools to adopt a wider European perspective (to include links with industry at a Europe-wide level) will also better prepare individuals for the challenges ahead and aid the development of necessary skills for cross-cultural management on a Europe-wide scale. At business school level, this means not just the bland *internationalisation* of courses (in which all too frequently international elements are 'tacked on' to existing course provision) but an integrated systems which prepares managers along a number of dimensions:

- foreign language aptitude
- exposure to students from other cultures
- significant numbers of non-domestic faculty
- exchange programmes which permit individuals to study in a foreign country
- knowledge-based courses which provide a review of key management issues (and not just theoretical models and constructs)

- texts and case studies which reflect the experiences of business in other EU (/international) countries
- transnational experience of educational provision in other countries.

Within the company, providing opportunities to work in (or with people from) other Member States is required so that individuals attain the *soft* experiential elements required for the development of good European managers. Project groups and inter-department cross-cultural team work, coupled with longer stays in a foreign location are essential. So too are well-defined career paths which incorporate job rotation for attaining European exposure.

What is needed is a universal commitment on the part of the state and industry to promote increased awareness and learning. Education, technical and management training and systems to allow the attainment of broad experiences by individuals can provide firms with critical resources for competitive success.

CONCLUSION

Cultural differences pertinent to managers within the EU cover a wide array of factors blanketing the state of intellectual development of the people and the state of commercial development of the nation. As culture is learned and not innate, there appears to be no reason why managers cannot embrace the challenge of learning about foreign cultures and their implications for doing business in other Member States.

Although it is easy to reject the study of something as non-specific as cultural difference, failure to address the issue can be costly. If advertising campaigns, business strategies and business meetings do not cater for these differences and thus offend or antagonise individuals or institutions, fail to convey the desired messages, or break local laws, then the cost to the firm can be enormous. Lost sales, failure to secure a contract, fines and lost opportunities can all arise as a result of business being conducted without due attention to the local cultural environment.

While cultural differences may be regarded as a barrier to the achievement of a truly harmonised single market, they do not act as a barrier to doing business abroad. By adapting to local cultural conditions firms can operate successfully across the Member States of Europe. Indeed, it is possible to argue that the divergence of cultures across Europe actually offers EU firms an advantage over their international competitors as it permits scope to identify national strengths and weaknesses and develop strategies which tap into these critical resources. Equally, exposure to different cultures provides opportunities for learning new ways of doing business and improving company performance. The rich cultural mix of Europe therefore needs to be regarded as an asset and not a barrier to improving Europe's position in the world economy.

Obviously, managing across cultures requires firms to adjust their strategic thinking. While, in the past, firms believed that mass decentralisation of decision making to subsidiaries in the various Member States of Europe allowed more effective management at the local level, it is important to develop structures which, while sympathetic to market differences, concern themselves more with similarities and commonalties.

One of the biggest hurdles ahead for most firms will be changed thinking: a new view of what Europe has to offer and how this can be tapped for competitive success; a willingness to learn and develop within a Europe-wide context; greater flexibility in management structures and business practices; new recruitment and training practices which provide scope for the development of European managers.

Overriding these issues are changes which are taking place on a global scale which are re-shaping business practices within the context of international competitive advantage. It is, therefore, not possible to assume that cultural change in the future, either for the individual or the firm, will merely be a product of changes taking place within the confines of the Single Market. To this extent, it is important for firms to keep one eye on developments in the rest of the world when they are planning for future success within their new domestic back yard.

Questions for discussion

1 Why is cultural understanding so important to managers of cross-cultural business organisations?

2 Why is concentrating on cultural differences only less beneficial than identifying commonalties *and* differences?

3 What common perceptions to you hold about other European Union cultures?

4 Why might it be dangerous for you to assume that your perceptions of other cultures are adequate to conduct business in foreign markets?

5 What is the usefulness of identifying cultural clusters across different Member States?

6 Why would it be wrong to suggest that corporate culture is simply a reflection of national cultural identity?

7 To what extent do you think Japan's success can be attributed to its cultural identity?

8 In what way might European firms be able to turn cultural diversity into competitive advantage?

9 How well do you think you measure up to the list of qualities required to be an international manager?

10 If you are weak on any of the dimensions necessary for being an international manager, how would you attempt to overcome these difficulties?

11 In what way might European managers be able to affect cultural change within their organisation?

CASE STUDY

Germany and the United Kingdom, a cultural perspective

Introduction
In many respects, Germany and the United Kingdom share much of their heritage. Both countries, like so many others in Europe, are a product of an amalgam of different economic and political forces emanating from different nations throughout

both countries' histories. It is not surprising therefore that there is a degree of commonality between these two nations. But what is the extent of this commonality and how might it affect the way in which companies from each country do business in each other's national markets?

Germany and the United Kingdom – an economic perspective

Central to the German market is the fact that it retains the highest level of manufacturing GDP in the European Union – just under 40 per cent – the largest for any OECD nation. This, in turn, explains many other facets of German society. Germany spends proportionately more per employee on R&D than any other Member State (between 1981–1985 UK firms spent £200 per employee, French firms £300 and German firms £400). The high status of technical personnel within the business community, and training schemes for their development, also reflects the industrial focus and serves to strengthen commitment towards industry and technical excellence. However, such technical mindedness is not without its drawbacks. While excellent at developing new technologies, the Germans are often accused of failing to exploit these technologies fully in the marketplace. The problem lies in the commercialisation of new innovations, the development function within the R&D process, where lack of marketing expertise means that there is an unrealised gap between market needs and product development.

One other element of the German business culture is worthy of comment as it has such an important impact on the state's commercial development. The very close liaison between the banks and industry gives Germany a long-term view of planning and strategic development. As bank loans are made at very favourable interest rates, businesses can contemplate taking out major loans for investment in new technologies, new plants and overseas expansion without having to generate short-term profits to cover the loans. However, in recent times, high costs of production in the German market have meant companies looking to take their investment monies abroad.

The UK, by contrast, is dominated by short-termism. However, this may not be solely attributed to high interest loans. The UK Stock Market is often accused by UK managers of perpetuating a short-termist attitude as publicly quoted firms' performance is monitored so closely by City analysts. Any downfall in share performance is immediately seen as a sign of failing rather than an indication that the firm is investing in its future. The failure of UK firms to invest in R&D and training may also be explained in these terms.

Germany and the United Kingdom – the Hofstede perspective

Figure 9.15 compares Germany and the UK along the four dimensions of Hofstede's research. It is clear that the two countries are very similar along the power distance and masculinity indices, but show considerable differences along the uncertainty avoidance and individualism dimensions.

But why the differences? It is possible to argue that the UK's business culture is now more based on an American rather than European model. Sharing the same (or at least very similar) language and displaying similar political and economic systems based on the exploitation of capitalist principles the UK has forged a cultural path which has moved it away from its European neighbours. Germanic culture, on the other hand, the product of Bavarian influence, has shaped a markedly different set of principles in relation to individualism and uncertainty avoidance. But how does this manifest itself in business behaviour?

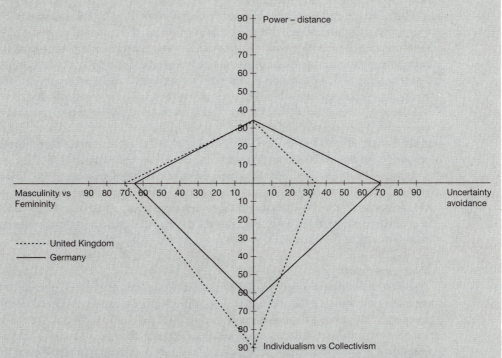

Fig. 9.15 A comparison of Germany and the United Kingdom along Hofstede's four dimensions

Personal relationships

Personal relations count for a lot in Germany. Business is frequently based on trust and 'seeing eye to eye' and this tends to form the cornerstone of negotiation. The British on the other hand place great store on affability and, generally, they only like to work with people they like.

The difference between these two perspectives is this. The Germans are more prepared to work at relationships than the British who tend to recoil from dealing with people they do not get along with. This has important ramifications for the way people behave and interact at work. The Germans will persevere with colleagues and will attempt to build bridges and long-term relationships. This leads to stability in organisations and less movement of staff between business functions (unless for the purpose of gaining broader experience). This assists in continuity of management and the building of teams as well as close working relationships with partners and customers. This does not mean, however, that the Germans are closed to outsiders.

Germans tend to be better at building new relationships than the British, who, once they have established working partnerships (either inside or outside of the firm) are reluctant to change. Once they have developed a network of contacts, they are keen to preserve it and not extend it. This is why so many foreign firms are frustrated by their failure to gain contracts with UK clients. It is not because their products are inferior, or can offer no added value, but because they are happy to preserve the status quo. Conversely, the Germans will shop around for new products, new customers, new suppliers, new relationships.

This tends to result in relatively slow decision making by UK managers. Although this appears to contradict with the short-termist attitude alluded to earlier, because of the importance of getting to know people, UK managers are reluctant to make a decision without first understanding what people stand for. However, it is important to note that this kind of decision making time frame is short by comparison with southern European nations which are notorious for protracted and lengthy decision making.

Based on this kind of longevity, the British tend to be more faithful than the Germans. They do not change supply lines rapidly or delist products and there is a tendency for them to give second and third chances to suppliers. If the British like a person, then they will often turn a blind eye to failings.

Because of the highly individualistic culture, with UK managers (or sales people) you can deal with the individual. They have the authority to make decisions and secure deals. By contrast, as much German decision making is centrally determined, it is harder to negotiate with German managers who refuse to bend rules and operate within tight limitations.

Communication

The British tend not to get to the point quickly. They find launching into business negotiations without first establishing some kind of rapport very difficult to do. They may talk about the weather, the state of the economy, or crack a few jokes, as a means of breaking the ice before getting down to the matter in hand. The German mentality is the total opposite. They believe that business relationships can only be developed by talking business, and therefore get to the point very quickly. Differences also exist in how directly managers from different countries express themselves once they have got to the point. The British have a great tendency to couch difficult issues in terms and phrases which dilute the impact – soften the blow. This may mean the British saying 'yes' when they actually mean no. The Germans, on the other hand are very direct, even to the point of being brusque. It is this difference which has often led to British managers thinking the Germans they are dealing with as rude. They expect to hear a softer, more cushioned response, instead they may just hear an outright 'no'.

Rules and regulations

The German management system is steeped in rules and regulations. Everything is boiled down to specifications, contracts, documentation and the minutiae of small print. This can slow down the process of negotiation, and is frustrating for those intent on building relationships and mutual co-operation. Take, for example, a UK company which tried to enter into an inward licensing deal with a German chemical manufacturer. The UK company were keen to develop a relationship which would allow them to add-value for customers. Their focus on people, rather than systems, meant that they wanted to talk to a variety of people in the German organisation and get to know them on a personal level – particularly marketing and sales people who would be charged with the responsibility of getting the product into the market and thus developing the new product's potential.

The German company, on the other hand, were eager to finalise the specifications and technical details and continued to send financial and legal representatives to the meetings. They believed there was little point in their potential partner talking to the sales staff until they had finalised the legal transfer of the technology and the financial targets. They also couldn't see the point of introducing more people into the meetings until the existing team had achieved its purpose. The result – a lack of trust, a failure to fully communicate and, ultimately, the failure of the venture. Communications is thus clearly more than just talking to people, it is about understanding different information and exchange requirements, which in this case did not happen.

Conclusion

What is apparent from this cursory overview of some of the differences between Germany and the UK is that the two countries show very different behaviour patterns in the way they conduct business which have the potential of complicating the way in which people from outside of the nations deal with them. Cultural sensitivity is critical to ensuring that such differences do not pose problems and result in a failure to consolidate contracts and relationships.

What is also apparent is that there are a number of contradictions between different facets of each country's culture. This partly stems from the fact that cultural analysis, which always tries to reduce things to their simplest level, is not wholly sufficient in providing a framework for assessment, but also relates to the fact that culture is so complex and deep-seated in a society that it manifests itself in very subtle and not always apparent ways.

Case Study Questions

1 How would you explain the various differences in personal relationships and communication from the perspective of Hofstede's four cultural dimensions?

2 What impact do you think that each country's economic and political culture has on manager behaviour?

3 What are the main similarities between the two cultures and what are the main differences?

4 How would an American firm, say, entering Europe for the first time adapt its way of business to cater for the nuances of UK and German cultural norms?

5 What would you suggest are the main challenges likely to be encountered by UK and German managers when dealing with each other?

FURTHER READING

Jackson, T. (ed.) (1995) *Cross-Cultural Management*, Butterworth-Heinemann. This text explores the general use of culture in depth. Chapters of particular interest include 'Transnational management in an evolving European context', 'Business of international business in culture' and 'Management learning for Europe'.

Mole, J. *Mind Your Manners: Culture Clash in the European Single Market*, the Industrial Society. This text, full of anecdotes and examples, takes a look beyond theoretical issues of culture and into the practical ramifications of doing business with people from other backgrounds.

Kenichi Ohmae (1982) *Mind of the Strategist: Art of Japanese Business*, McGraw-Hill. This text provides a thought-provoking, analytical and critical view of Japanese management practices and styles.

Randlesome, C. (1992) *Business Cultures in Europe*, Heinemann. This text provides a comparative study of different cultures in Europe with emphasis on political, economic, legal and educational differences.

REFERENCES

Basset, P., *Strike Free: New Industrial Relations in Britain*, Macmillan, 1986.

European Commission, *Social Europe*, 1993/1, European Commission, 1993.

van Dijck, J., 'Transnational Management in an Evolving European Context', in Terence Jackson (Ed.) *Cross-Cultural Management*, Butterworth-Heinemann, 1995.

Fry, E., 'Subtlety and the Art of Japanese Management' *Business Credit*, October, 1991.

Hall, E.T., *Beyond Culture*, New York, Doubleday, 1976.

Hannagan, T., *Management Concepts and Practices*, Pitman Publishing, 1995.

Hofstede, G., 'National Cultures in Four Dimensions: a Research Theory of Cultural Differences Among Nations', *International Studies of Management and Organisation*, Vol. 13, Spring-Summer, p. 52, 1983.

Hofstede, G., 'Cultural Difference in Teaching and Learning', *International Journal of Intercultural Relations*, Vol. 10, pp. 301–320, 1986.

Hofstede, G., 'Managerial Values: The Business of International Business in Culture', in Terence Jackson (Ed.) *Cross-Cultural Management*, Butterworth-Heinemann, 1995.

Kroeber and Kluckhohn, *Culture*, Vintage Books, 1952.

Lachman, R., Nedd, A. and Hinings, N., 'Analysing cross-national management and organisations: a theoretical framework', in Terence Jackson (Ed.) *Cross-Cultural Management*, Butterworth-Heinemann, 1995.

Lee, J. A. 'Cultural Analysis in Overseas Operations', *Harvard Business Review*, March–April, pp. 106–114, 1966.

Mole, J., *Mind Your Manners: Culture Clash in the European Single Market*, The Industrial Society, 1992.

Murdock, G. P., 'The Common Denominator of Cultures', in *The Science of Man in the World Crisis*, Linton R. (Ed.) Columbia University Press, pp. 123–142, 1945.

Ohmae, K., *Mind of the Strategist: Art of Japanese Business*, McGraw-Hill, 1982.

Oliver, A. and Wilkinson, S., *The Japanisation of British Industry: New Developments in the 1990s*, (2nd Ed.), Blackwell, 1992.

Peters, T. and Waterman, R., *In Search of Excellence*, Harper and Row, 1982.

Porter, M.E., *Competitive Advantages of Nations*, Macmillan, 1990.

Porter, M. E., 'A Note on Culture and Competitive Advantage: Response to van den Bosch and van Prooijen', *European Management Journal*, Vol. 10, No. 2, June 1992, p. 178.

Robock, S. H. and Simmonds, K., *International Business and Multinational Enterprises*, Irwin, 1989.

Rogers E. M., *The Diffusion of Innovations*, The Free Press, p. 76, 1962.

Ronen, S. and Shenkar, O., 'Clustering Countries on Attitudianal Dimensions : A Review and Synthesis', *Academy of Management Journal*, September p. 449, 1985.

Tijmstra, S and Casler, K., 'Management Learning for Europe', *European Management Journal*, Vol. 10, No.1, March, pp. 30–38, 1992.

Triandis, H. C., 'Dimensions of Cultural Variation as Parameters of Organisational Theories', *International Studies of Management and Organisation*, Vol. 12, No. 4, pp. 139–169, 1983.

Vandermerwe S., 'A Framework for Constructing European Networks', *European Management Journal*, Vol 11, No. 1, March, 1993.

Wills, S. and Barham, K., 'Being an International Manager', *European Management Journal*, Vol. 12, No. 1, March, pp. 49–58, 1994.

CHAPTER 10

Environmental Issues and Environmental Management

THE CHALLENGE FOR EUROPE

Since the 1960s, there has been a growing interest in the environment, or more specifically in the damage being done to the environment, in Europe and North America. The process of European integration has brought the transnational nature of the environmental problem to the forefront. The hole in the ozone layer and global warming is the result of not one country's action but that of many. Acid rain, which is polluting rivers and lakes and damaging forests, often emanates from one country and is deposited in another. European integration therefore offers an opportunity for transnational cooperation and this has been reflected in a multitude of European Community environmental legislation, much of which is already in place. Much more legislation is planned for the 1990s and beyond and a large amount of this will affect the way in which every business is run and the way in which managers must recognise their responsibility, not only to a company, but also to the environment in which it operates. Perhaps more importantly, many of the more recent initiatives on the environment, emanating from the European Commission, have been market driven and are voluntary. These are dealt with in detail towards the end of this chapter, but collectively their impact is to demand that businesses take on more responsibility for environmental damage and approach environmental management in a more proactive way.

The effects of different industrial sectors upon the environment vary enormously. At one end of the spectrum we might put the oil companies whose very business is environmentally damaging and at the other end we might put retailers and the service sector who have less of a direct impact on the environment, although who, in most cases, could still make environmental improvements through recycling and improved transportation policies. There is still much confusion both for consumers and companies about what constitutes an environmentally friendly product or operation, and the 'green revolution', to date, has provided few answers, although many misrepresentations, particularly in the area of product marketing, have been exposed. To give just one example, in mid 1990 ICI, was forced to withdraw an 'environmentally-friendly' label from a range of cleaning products which it was marketing, after Friends of the Earth pointed out that the manufacture of the main ingredient, soda ash, is a highly energy intensive process with extremely polluting discharges. A spokesperson for ICI said that the products were given the label because they were based on sodium bicarbonate, listed in the Green Consumer Guide as 'environmentally friendly'. Some of the confusion over what constitutes an environmentally-friendly product will undoubtedly be put right over the coming years by the introduction of the European Union Eco-labelling scheme.

Everything which consumers, companies and other institutions do will have some impact on the environment. Even substances which, in their final form, are environmentally benign may have been unfriendly in their manufacture especially if that manufacture was energy greedy. They may have been produced using non-renewable resources and may also pose problems after they have been used and come to be disposed of. If we take what is commonly called a cradle-to-the-grave view of products, where we examine their environmental impact through their life-cycle from raw material usage to disposal, then there are few, if any, products which will not have some negative impact on the environment. The key question is therefore not how we completely eliminate environmental damage, but how we reduce it over time and how we achieve a state of balance such that the amount of environmental damage done is repairable and therefore sustainable.

It is generally accepted that the world cannot go on using the resources of the planet at the present rate. But there is a *free rider problem* at work. Everyone thinks that there should be something done, but many people just assume that everyone else will do it and, since their individual impact is minute, it will not matter to the environment. The trouble is that when too many people or firms think in that way then nothing is ever achieved. The world has scarce resources and only limited capacity to deal with the pollution caused through production and consumption. The ability to deal with that pollution is also being reduced as we strive for further economic growth by, for example, cutting down forests which help to control carbon dioxide emissions.

Industry, particularly in the developed world, must increasingly take into account the costs of the effect of its operations on the environment, rather than regarding the planet as a free resource. In the past few companies have counted the costs of the pollution which they discharged into the atmosphere, and the debate has now turned to legislation aimed at forcing companies to comply with certain standards and taxing firms which pollute. The so-called *polluter pays principle* is now central to Community legislation. The implication here is clearly that prices will rise for consumers as firms experience increased costs associated with environmental improvements. Less energy consumption and more efficient use of resources are obvious targets for improvement and should not conflict with industry's aims since their attainment can actually reduce costs. Certain metals are already recycled and a thriving, and at times profitable, recycling industry has been established across Europe.

Many of the products now considered to be environmentally hazardous were at the time of their discovery regarded as an invaluable resource. The best example of this has been the use of chlorofluorocarbons in refrigerators which have since been found to be a major ozone-depleting agent. Predicting a product's long-term impact on the environment is a difficult process and, until recently, has rarely been done. This will change as firms are forced to consider cradle-to-grave management of their products and as we increasingly give the benefit of doubt to the welfare of the planet. Moreover, industry has a responsibility to ensure that its products are less harmful to the environment and there is a need to push along a very steep environmental learning curve.

Governments across Europe and the Commission have all been implementing increasingly stringent environmental legislation. There is even renewed debate within the EU's Fifth Environment Programme (*see* below) about the provision of information about products and processes available to the public. The statutory bodies which do exist with responsibility for monitoring the environmental performance of companies have limited resources and powers in most cases. Companies themselves have often, in the past, been shown to be ignorant of current environmental legislation, particularly with regard to EU environmental directives and legislation on issues such as waste disposal, air pollution and water quality. However, such ignorance is not an excuse for non-compliance. Moreover, non-compliance which can be attributed to negligence cannot only result in fines but also occasionally in imprisonment for company directors.

In the USA the Environmental Protection Agency (EPA) is an independent environmental body with significant power. In 1980, the US Congress passed the Comprehensive Environmental Response, Compensation and Liability Act, better known as *Superfund*. Under the provisions of the Act, companies must report potentially toxic spills and releases greater than a clearly defined minimum. Violations of this are criminal offences with penalties of up to one year in jail and fines of up to $10 000. Superfund also deals with uncontrolled hazardous waste sites, where previous or present owners and operators of a site must help to pay for whatever remedial action is necessary. If the previous firm has gone out of business the EPA has often managed to obtain funds from companies which sent the waste there for treatment or disposal in the first instance.

In the UK, by contrast, Her Majesty's Inspectorate of Pollution adopts an approach of constructive engagement with companies rather than fining them for pollution violations. In 1988/9 the number of visits by HMIP inspectors to registered works was fewer than 500. In 1986/87 there were 3 129 contraventions of the Clean Air Act 1968, but local authorities only brought 153 prosecutions. More recently, the National Rivers Authority (NRA) has been tougher though. In 1989, the English NRA fined Shell £1 million for an oil spillage in the Mersey.

The rapid growth of public environmental awareness in recent years has placed new pressures on industry. These pressures can take many forms as individuals collectively exercise their environmental conscience as customers, employees, investors, voters, neighbours and fellow citizens. However, whether it is due to intellectual fatigue with environmental issues, a lack conviction that an individual's own actions will have an impact or a reluctance to reduce private consumption for public welfare, many individuals seemingly prefer to pass their responsibilities on to those parties that they feel can make a significant impact. The two major parties that the public perceive can make a difference are government and industry. Given an inherent public reluctance to reduce their own levels of consumption, it is apparent that government and industry must respond in order to effectively protect the environment.

THE EUROPEAN SITUATION

As a major part of the industrialised world, economic activity in Europe is responsible for much of the environmental damage facing the planet. Human activities have resulted in the introduction of numerous chemical contaminants into the global environment, many of which are man-made and have no natural sources. Contamination of the environment has reached global proportions with trace metal and organic pollutants being detected in even the remotest parts of the northern hemisphere. Issues, such as climate change and ozone layer depletion, emphasise the global scope of the impact of environmental degradation.

There is insufficient room for a full review of environmental pollution in this section but an analysis of selected statistics concerning atmospheric pollution and waste is able to paint a broad picture from a European perspective.

ATMOSPHERIC POLLUTION: THE GREENHOUSE EFFECT

The naturally occurring abundance of greenhouse gases such as water vapour, carbon dioxide, methane, chlorofluorocarbons and nitrous oxide exert a warming effect on the earth by absorbing radiation emitted by the earth's surface. Continuing increases in concentrations of greenhouse gases due to human activities are therefore warming the atmosphere and leading to global climate change. Carbon dioxide emissions are a primary contributor to the enhanced greenhouse effect. Table 10.1 demonstrates how it is the developed world which is largely responsible for this trend.

Table 10.1. Emissions of carbon dioxide to the atmosphere from human activities, 1988 (1 000 000s tonnes carbon per annum)

Region	Fossil fuel combustion	Land use changes
North America	1 481	112
Europe	1 268	0
USSR	896	35
Asia	1 054	687
Africa	141	367
South America	135	579
Australasia	63	32

Source: Environmental Data Report, UNEP, Blackwell, 1991.

Atmospheric concentrations of carbon dioxide are increasing globally but concentrations are higher in the northern hemisphere due to a greater density of industry and energy generation. Fossil fuel combustion, in order to create electricity, has trebled since 1950 and the burning of forests not only produce carbon dioxide but also destroy one means of absorbing the gas.

In Europe, carbon dioxide emissions continue to rise steadily. The EU alone accounts for around 12 per cent of the world's carbon dioxide emissions. Within the EU there are also wide differences, but what is clear from Table 10.2 is that most of the problem emanates from the most developed part of the EU. However, one should also note the extremely high level of emissions from the USA compared with the EU average.

Table 10.2. Carbon dioxide emissions from fossil fuels, 1990

Country	Total emissions (Mio t CO_2)	Per capita emissions (t CO_2)
EUR12	3 086.0	8 411
Belgium	107.5	10 781
Denmark	53.7	10 446
Germany	1 039.0	13 098
Greece	74.2	7 332
Spain	214.8	5 514
France	374.0	6 595
Ireland	31.6	9 020
Italy	398.9	6 917
Luxembourg	11.0	28 672
Netherlands	158.1	10 572
Portugal	40.2	4 069
United Kingdom	583.0	10 156
Austria	57.0	7 391
Finland	59.0	11 833
Sweden	55.9	6 426
Norway	32.0	7 544
Switzerland	44.0	6 555
USA	5 021.0	20 086
Japan	1 060.0	8 580

Source: Eurostat, Basic Statistics of the Community, 1995.

The hole in the ozone layer

The ozone layer in the stratosphere provides protection from harmful solar ultra-violet radiation. Ozone contains three atoms of oxygen whereas the atmospheric oxygen molecules contain two atoms. The effect of the mass use and emission of chlorofluorocarbons (CFCs) and nitrogen oxides has been to break down ozone, allowing the harmful radiation through into the atmosphere. This has increased the incidence of radiation-induced skin cancer. Chlorofluorocarbons have commonly been used in solvents, aerosol propellants and refrigerants and, not surprisingly, we find most use of these in the developed world (*see* Table 10.3). The Montreal Protocol Conference in 1990 decided that CFCs would be completely phased out by the year 2000, but much damage has already been done and this case does illustrate how industry often produces chemicals without first knowing their full impact on the environment.

Table 10.3. Consumption of chlorofluorocarbons, 1986

Country	tonnes per annum
Africa	18 485
North America	353 680
South America	22 618
Asia	163 367
Europe	369 939
Australasia	15 200

Source: Environmental Data Report, UNEP, Blackwell, 1991.

Urban air pollutants

Air pollutants that are prevalent, particularly in industrialised cities worldwide include sulphur dioxide, nitrogen oxides and carbon monoxide as well as harmful trace elements such as lead. These pollutants cause respiratory diseases and are therefore a threat to human health. Table 10.4 shows emissions of two of the most harmful gases from a number of different countries:

Table 10.4. Emissions of sulphur dioxide and nitrogen oxides from man-made sources, 1988 (1000s tonnes per annum as SO_2 and NO_2)

Country	Sulphur dioxide	Nitrogen dioxide
USA	20 700	19 800
Belgium	414	298
Czechoslovakia	2 800	950
Denmark	241	249
France	1 216	1 655
Germany (East)	5 208	1 008
Germany (West)	1 300	2 850
Hungary	1 218	259
Italy	2 410	1 700
Netherlands	278	522
Poland	4 180	1 550
Portugal	204	122
Sweden	199	316
United Kingdom	3 664	2 480
USSR	17 650	6 290

Source: Environmental Data Report, UNEP, Blackwell, 1991.

There are significant differences in emissions within Europe and this is often reflected by differing means of energy generation and different agricultural policies (see Table 10.5). Emissions of sulphur dioxide into the atmosphere often return to the land as acid rain. It is interesting to see that Sweden produces very little sulphur dioxide but it suffers greatly from the acidification of its water and forests. Much of this emanates from the UK, a significant generator of sulphur dioxide. The main source of nitrous oxide emanates from road transport and highlights the need for more environmentally aware transportation policies across the EU.

Table 10.5. Sulphur oxide and nitrous oxide emissions by sector, 1985

Country	Fuels, energy production	Oil refining	Energy combustion	Manufacturing processes	Road transport
Sulphur oxide					
Belgium	48.1	8.8	25.2	13.9	4.1
Denmark	72.4	1.2	18.4	4.7	3.3
Germany (West)	66.8	6.2	18.0	6.4	2.6
Greece	74.7	5.5	16.2	3.5	0.1
Spain	77.6	4.4	12.0	2.9	3.1
France	41.2	15.1	30.0	7.1	6.7
Ireland	56.0	0.4	39.3	1.2	3.1
Italy	56.7	7.1	26.3	6.2	3.6
Luxembourg	22.1	0.0	26.7	47.8	3.4
Netherlands	35.7	40.9	7.3	10.6	5.5
Portugal	43.4	6.5	34.8	11.8	3.4
United Kingdom	78.3	3.2	14.8	2.5	1.2
EUR 12	66.3	6.8	19.2	5.0	2.9
Nitrous oxide					
Belgium	20.3	1.9	11.7	8.5	57.5
Denmark	54.9	0.6	4.7	1.8	38.0
Germany (West)	30.7	1.0	8.4	5.2	54.7
Greece	48.0	1.2	2.7	9.1	39.0
Spain	31.7	1.5	4.7	8.0	54.0
France	16.1	1.1	7.7	6.8	68.2
Ireland	42.0	0.5	9.6	6.2	41.7
Italy	28.1	1.7	7.4	8.0	54.0
Luxembourg	10.1	0.0	3.1	38.5	48.2
Netherlands	28.6	4.2	6.0	3.7	57.5
Portugal	14.5	2.3	11.3	12.7	59.1
United Kingdom	40.2	1.9	14.1	0.6	43.1
EUR 12	30.7	1.5	8.8	5.4	53.6

Source: Corinair-EC, reprinted in Eurostat, Basic Statistics of the Community, 1992.

Wastes

Population growth, increasing urbanisation, industrialisation and rising standards of living have all contributed to an increase in the amount of waste generated in most countries. Moreover, many countries are faced with dealing not only with a greater volume of waste but also more hazardous waste materials. Wastes which arise from virtually all human activities can be classified with respect to their source. The major categories include household and consumer wastes, industrial, agricultural, extraction, energy production and sewage wastes.

Industrial process wastes encompass a very wide range of materials but an important feature of these wastes is that a significant proportion are regarded as hazardous and as such require special treatment and disposal (*see* Table 10.6). The main industrial sectors producing hazardous waste are the chemical sector, mineral and metal processing industries and the engineering sector. Estimates of the amount of hazardous waste arising in the EU vary between 20–50 per cent of all waste depending on the exact definition used. Much hazardous waste is moved between countries, particularly from industrialised to developing nations where there are neither the resources nor the knowledge for their safe disposal.

Table 10.6. Production of hazardous wastes in selected countries, 1985

Country	(1000s tonnes per annum)
USA	265 000
China	2 900
India	36 000
Belgium	915
Denmark	125
France	2 000
Germany (West)	5 000
Hungary	5 000
Netherlands	1 500
Spain	1 049
Sweden	500
United Kingdom	2 000
Australia	300

Source: Environmental Data Report, UNEP, Blackwell, 1991.

COUNTING THE COSTS OF THE ENVIRONMENT

The use of the market mechanism to distribute goods and services in the West, with its consequent stress on property rights has contributed to the environmental degradation which we have experienced. Much of the environment (particularly the air and atmosphere) is treated as a free good since no individual owns it and there are no assigned property rights to it. Firms and consumers have therefore made excessive uses of environmental resources both as an input and as a source of output (or sink). This can be illustrated in Fig. 10.1.

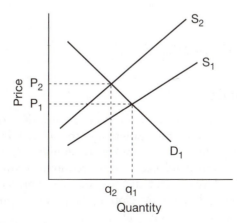

Fig. 10.1 Using the market mechanism to deal with environmental damage

Suppose that a firm produces a good and in the process of doing so it pollutes the air around it. Traditionally, and ignoring legislation which might or might not exist, the firm can do this freely since no one owns the air. Assume that the demand for the product is D_1 and the production and marketing costs of the firm imply that it is willing to sell along a supply curve given by S_1. Essentially, S_1 is drawn based on only the private costs of the firm, that is, those which it must pay in a monetary form. But the pollution imposed on the local community imposes a cost on them and on society as a whole. If the firm was required to internalise those costs, either by paying a tax to pollute based on an estimate of the social cost that that pollution imposed (the tax might subsequently be used to clean up the pollution), or by the use of legislation banning the pollution meaning that the firm would have to invest in a new non-polluting process, then its own costs would rise. The firm's willingness to supply at any particular price would be reduced and S_1 would shift backwards to S_2. The equilibrium in the market would shift from p_1q_1 to p_2q_2. Thus less of the good would be produced at a higher price.

The premise upon which EU and Member States' environmental legislation has largely been based is the 'polluter pays principle'. In other words this is a notion that public money should not be used in clearing up or avoiding pollution but, as described above, that polluters themselves should face those costs. From a welfare point of view the difference between a firm compensating a local community for the pollution it creates and the community paying the firm not to pollute is purely distributional. But from an ethical perspective it is often argued that the polluter pays principle is superior.

We might extend the sort of analysis described by Fig. 10.1 to the economy as a whole. Since most processes will impose at least some negative impact on the environment, the fact that the environment has not been properly costed and treated as a free good over time has meant that we have produced too many goods. Moreover, we might hypothesise that mass production techniques which have enabled firms to produce more and more goods and to charge lower prices have been particularly damaging. Indeed this is largely confirmed by evidence.

The implication which then arises is that Western economies have developed using a particular model and in a way that has caused significant and often irreparable damage to the environment. It is further argued that that sort of development is not sustainable into the future and it is the concept of sustainable development to which we now turn.

SUSTAINABLE DEVELOPMENT

The future economic model?

The belief which lies behind the concept of sustainable development is that there is a trade-off between continuous economic growth and the sustainability of the environment. Over time, growth causes pollution and atmospheric damage. The concept of sustainable development stresses the interdependence between economic growth and environmental quality. It is possible to make development and environmental protection compatible by following sustainable strategies and by not developing the particular areas of economic activity that are most damaging to the environment.

The Brundtland Report, commissioned by the United Nations to examine long-term environmental strategies, argued that economic development and environmental protection could be made compatible, but that this would require quite radical changes in economic practices throughout the world. They defined sustainable development as 'development that meets the needs of the present without compromising the ability of future generations to meet their own needs'. In other words, mass consumption is not possible indefinitely and if society today acts as if all non-renewable resources are plentiful, eventually there will be nothing left for the future. But more importantly than that, mass consumption may cause such irreparable damage that humans may not even be able to live on the planet in the future.

The challenge that faces the economic system is how to continue to fulfil its vital role within modern society whilst working towards sustainability. Complying with the principles of sustainability cannot be achieved overnight. However, both for entire economies and for individual businesses, there is hope that it can be achieved within the timescales which appear to be necessary if environmental catastrophe is to be avoided.

Sustainable development is made up of three closely connected issues:

Environment: The environment must be valued as an integral part of the economic process and not treated as a free good. The environmental stock has to be protected and this implies minimal use of non-renewable resources and minimal emission of pollutants. The ecosystem has to be protected so the loss of plant and animal species has to be avoided.

Equity: One of the biggest threats facing the world is that the developing countries want to grow rapidly to achieve the same standards of living as those in the West. That in itself would cause a major environmental disaster if it were modelled on the same sort of growth experienced in post-war Europe. There therefore needs to be a greater degree of equity and the key issue of poverty has to be addressed; but it seems hypocritical for the West to tell the Third World that it cannot attain the same standards of living and consumption. What therefore is the solution?

Futurity: Sustainable development requires that society, businesses and individuals operate on a different time scale than currently operates in the economy. While companies commonly operate under competitive pressures to achieve short-terms gains, long term environmental protection is often compromised. To ensure that longer term, inter-generational considerations are observed, longer planning horizons need to be adopted and business policy needs to be proactive rather than reactive.

The Brundtland Report concludes that these three conditions are not being met. The industrialised world has already used much of the planet's ecological capital and many of the development paths of the industrialised nations are clearly unsustainable. Non-renewable resources are being depleted, while renewable resources such as soil, water and the atmosphere are being degraded. This has been caused by economic development but in time will undermine the very foundations of that development.

The Brundtland Report calls for growth which is environmentally and socially sustainable rather than the current situation of unplanned, undifferentiated growth. This means reconsidering the current measures of growth, such as gross national product (GNP), which fail to take account of environmental debits like pollution or the depletion of the natural capital stock. While concern about the depletion of materials and energy resources has diminished since the 1970s there is nevertheless now concern surrounding the environment's capacity to act as a sink for waste. For example, bringing developing countries' energy use up to the level of the developing world's would mean an increase in consumption by a factor of five. Using present energy generation methods the planet could not cope with the impact of sulphur dioxide and carbon dioxide emissions and the acidification and global warming of the environment which would be consequential.

One major obstacle preventing sustainability from being achieved is the overall level of consumption. However, western consumers are apparently reluctant to significantly reduce their own levels of consumption. While increasingly, governments are adopting economic instruments such as taxes, subsidies and product labelling schemes to reduce and channel consumption toward more environmentally friendly alternatives, industry itself must be encouraged to further increase environmental efficiency.

Sustainability challenges industry to produce higher levels of output while using lower levels of inputs and generating less waste. The problem that remains is that while relative environmental impact per unit of output has fallen, increases in the absolute level of output, and hence environmental impact, have more than offset any gains in relative environmental efficiency. However, if we examine the ways in which environmental efficiency has been improved, then we can begin to understand some of the key practical elements with which sustainability may be better promoted.

The corporate response to sustainable development

Companies are faced with a challenge of integrating environmental considerations into their production and marketing plans. There is always an incentive, however, for profit-maximising firms seeking short-term rewards, to opt out and become a free rider (assuming that everyone else will be environmentally conscious such that their own pollution will become negligible). However, EU environmental legislation is increasingly plugging the gaps which allow this to happen and firms attempting to hide their illegal pollution are now subject to severe penalties. Even before then though, businesses should recognise that it is not only ethical to be environmentally friendly, but with the growth of consumer awareness in the environmental area, it will also be good business.

Firms clearly have a role to play in the development of substitutes for non-renewable resources and innovations which reduce waste and use energy more efficiently. They also have a role in processing those materials in a way which brings about environmental improvements. For many products (e.g. cars and washing machines), the major area of environmental damage occurs in their usage. Firms often have the opportunity of reducing this damage at the design stage and when new products are being developed there is a whole new opportunity for considering both the use and disposal of the product.

Given the internal and external demands to improve the environmental performance of a company, those companies that achieve high standards of environmental performance will benefit in a number of ways. In order to realise this competitive advantage, companies must seek to develop management strategies which will improve their environmental performance and address the environmental demands placed upon them by government, the EU and stakeholders. By incorporating the increasingly important environmental dimension into the decision making processes of the firm, managers can seek to reduce costs and exploit the opportunities offered by increased public environmental concern within a dynamic marketplace. Such a strategy must be proactive and honest. It may also involve a degree of education and campaigning such as that undertaken by The Body Shop. But more than anything, it must be ethical.

The general principles of such a strategy are embodied within the International Chamber of Commerce Business Charter for Sustainable Development. The key elements to this strategy are embodied in sixteen *Principles for Environmental Management*. Companies are encouraged to endorse the following aims:

1 *Corporate priority* – to recognise environmental management as among the highest corporate priorities and as a key determinant to sustainable development; to establish policies, programmes and practices for conducting operations in an environmentally sound manner.

2 *Integrated management* – to integrate these policies, programmes and practices fully into each business as an essential element of management in all its functions.

3 Process of improvement – to continue to improve corporate policies, programmes and environmental performance, taking into account technical developments, scientific understanding, consumer needs and community expectations, with legal regulations as a starting point; and to apply the same environmental criteria internationally.

4 *Employee education* – to educate, train and motivate employees to conduct their activities in an environmentally responsible manner.

5 *Prior assessment* – to assess environmental impacts before starting a new activity or project and before decommissioning a facility or leaving a site.

6 *Products and services* – to develop and provide products and services that have no undue environmental impact and are safe in their intended use, that are efficient in their consumption of energy and natural resources, and that can be recycled, reused, or disposed of safely.

7 *Customer advice* – to advise, and where relevant educate, customers, distributors and the public in the safe use, transportation, storage and disposal of products provided; and to apply similar considerations to the provision of services.

8 *Facilities and operations* – to develop, design and operate facilities and conduct activities taking into consideration the efficient use of energy and raw materials, the sustainable use of renewable resources, the minimisation of adverse environmental impact and waste generation, and the safe and responsible disposal of residual wastes.

9 *Research* – to conduct or support research on the environmental impacts of raw materials, products, processes, emissions and wastes associated with the enterprise and on the means of minimising such adverse impacts.

10 *Precautionary approach* – to modify the manufacture, marketing or use of products or services to the conduct of activities, consistent with scientific and technical understanding, to prevent serious or irreversible environmental degradation.

11 *Contractors and suppliers* – to promote the adoption of these principles by contractors acting on behalf of the enterprise, encouraging and, where appropriate, requiring improvements in their practices to make them consistent with those of the enterprise; and to encourage the wider adoption of these principles by suppliers.

12 *Emergency preparedness* – to develop and maintain, where appropriate hazards exist, emergency preparedness plans in conjunction with the emergency services, relevant authorities and the local community, recognising potential cross-boundary impacts.

13 *Transfer of technology* – to contribute to the transfer of environmentally sound technology and management methods throughout the industrial and public sectors.

14 *Contributing to the common effort* – to contribute to the development of public policy and to business, governmental and intergovernmental programmes and educational initiatives that will enhance environmental awareness and protection.

15 *Openness to concerns* – to foster openness and dialogue with employees and the public, anticipating and responding to their concerns about the potential hazards and impacts of operations, products, wastes or services, including those of transboundary or global significance.

16 *Compliance and reporting* – to measure environmental performance; to conduct regular environmental audits and assessments of compliance with company requirements and these principles; and periodically to provide appropriate information to the Board of Directors, shareholders, employees, the authorities and the public.

EUROPEAN INTEGRATION AND THE ENVIRONMENT

The original Treaty of Rome was concerned with stimulating economic growth and contained no specific reference to the environment. Since then though, EU environmental policy has developed in line with general concern in Europe and the deteriorating environmental position in which Europe finds itself. By 1990, 160 pieces of environmental legislation had been passed covering pollution of the air and water, noise pollution, chemicals, waste, environmental impact assessment, the prevention of industrial accidents and wildlife protection.

However, few Member States have been able to fully enforce Community legislation. Denmark is probably the only country with a consistently good record and the southern European countries have consistently bad records. Once again this highlights the emphasis often given to economic growth rather than environmental protection, with the primary aim of countries such as Spain and Portugal being the attainment of similar living standards to the rest of the EU.

The Single European Act gave environmental policy a boost stating that there is not only a need for such legislation but that the laws should meet three key objectives:

● preservation, protection and improvement of the quality of the environment
● protection of human health
● prudent and rational use of natural resources.

These objectives must be met by applying four principles:

● prevention of harm to the environment
● control of pollution at source
● the polluter should pay
● integration of environmental considerations into other EU policies (all EU policies are now required to take the environment into account).

The Internal Market Programme has added a new note of urgency to environmental problems. The relationship between economic growth and the environment has returned to centre stage. Clearly, there exists a major opportunity with industrial and legislative restructuring to put into place the appropriate financial and regulatory mechanisms that would make the internal market environmentally sustainable. The extent to which this happens will be seen over time, but the Single European Act also provides the necessary constitutional basis for a forceful environmental response. Perhaps the strongest part of this is the requirement that policy makers should make environmental considerations a component of all the EU's other policies.

In 1992 the EU's Fifth Environmental Action Programme was introduced. The first environmental action programme, in 1973, set out a number of principles which have formed the basis of environmental action in the EU ever since. The aims are clearly set out, stating that:

1 Prevention is better than cure.
2 Environmental effects should be taken into account at the earliest possible stage in decision making.
3 Exploitation of nature and natural resources which causes significant damage to the ecological balance must be avoided. The natural environment can only absorb pollution to a limited extent. Nature is an asset which may be used but not abused.
4 Scientific knowledge should be improved to enable action to be taken.
5 The polluter pays principle; the polluter should pay for preventing and eliminating environmental nuisance.
6 Activities in one Member State should not cause environmental deterioration in another.
7 Environmental policies of Member States must take account of the interests of developing countries.
8 The EU and Member States should act together in international organisations and also in promoting international environmental policy.
9 Education of citizens is necessary as the protection of the environment is a matter for everyone.
10 The principle of action at the appropriate level; for each type of pollution it is necessary to establish the level of action which is best suited for achieving the protection required, be it local, regional, national, EU-wide or international.
11 National environmental policies must be co-ordinated within the EU without impinging on progress at the national level. It is intended that implementation of the action programme and gathering of environmental information by the proposed European Environment Agency will secure this.

(Source: Official Journal of the European Communities: OJ C112 20.12.73)

The main activities of the EU in the environmental policy arena, until 1987, were centred on the application of nearly 200 command and control directives in areas as diverse as lead in petrol and aircraft noise. More recently, in realising that environmental policy is of little use unless enforced, EU environmental policy has given increased emphasis to the improved enforcement of existing legislation. Emphasis has also shifted from the use of traditional command and control instruments in environmental policy to the application of economic market based instruments such as the proposed carbon tax, and voluntary agreements such as the eco-labelling and eco-management and audit schemes (*see* below). The aim of such measures is to encourage change in all sectors of industry and society, in a more general way than can be achieved through the use of tightly defined legislative instruments. The use of economic instruments and voluntary measures is seen as a complement rather than a substitute to the more traditional application of command and control measures.

The EU view of the future of environmental policy and its interface with industrial development is clear. With some 340 million inhabitants, the EU is the largest trading bloc in the world, and is therefore in a critical position to take the lead in moving towards sustainability. The Commission accepts that tighter environmental policy will impact on the costs of industry, however, increasingly a high level of environmental protection has become not only a policy objective of its own but also a precondition of industrial expansion. In this respect, a new impetus towards a better integration of policies aiming at consolidating industrial competitiveness and at achieving a high level of protection of the environment is necessary in order to make the two objectives fully mutually supportive.

These views are given more substance within the Fifth Environmental Action Programme. While this programme sets out the likely developments of EU environmental policy in a general sense, a number of specific measures relating to industry are included. Perhaps most importantly the commitment of the EU to strengthen environmental policy is underlined. The EU shares the view that urgent action is needed for environmental protection, and that many of the great environmental struggles will be won or lost during this decade. Further, it states that achieving sustainability will demand practical and political commitment over an extended period and that the EU as the largest trading bloc in the world must exercise its responsibility and commit itself to that goal.

For industries and companies that are facing a rising tide of environmental legislation, it is essential that attempts are made to find out about and then positively address the legislative pressures which they are under. However, the Fifth Environmental Action Programme focuses on the improved enforcement of existing legislation rather than the adoption of new legislation. To some extent this should allow industry to take stock of the rapid increase in environmental legislation that has taken place in recent years and to focus on achieving compliance with existing legislation. Despite the stated objective to concentrate on the effective implementation of existing policy, there are many pieces of environmental legislation in the EU policy-pipeline which are awaiting final adoption. Many of these measures have fundamental implications for business, the need to track forthcoming legislation therefore remains essential.

Furthermore, the Maastricht Treaty and the Fifth Environmental Action Programme require that environmental policy should be fully incorporated into all other EU policies. Therefore while it may become easier to track the development of policies which are explicitly environmental, it will become more difficult to monitor the development of environmental policy throughout the activities of the Commission as a whole. The establishment of the European Environment Agency which will collect data and monitor compliance throughout the EU could help to disseminate information to all interested parties. In the meantime, the delay between the release of Community legislation and its subsequent implementation in Member States offers vital time for planning for those companies who monitor the development of European environmental policy in order to avoid the costs and exploit the opportunities which are undoubtedly generated.

The strategic significance of the EU's views cannot be overstated. By taking a long-term EU-wide perspective and accepting that industrial competitiveness is enhanced by tight environmental legislation, the policy framework within which all European companies must participate will reflect these views. Some companies, some regions and some nations will benefit. If the views of the EU are correct, the economic prospects of the EU as a whole will benefit and the environment will certainly benefit. However, at the company level realising these benefits will not be automatic, strategic planning and proactive responses to the changing policy climate are imperative if success is to be secured. Information must be gathered, its implications assessed and the necessary action taken in a systematic and integrated way.

Tackling environmental problems always requires a concerted and co-operative effort and in the EU success will depend on the extent to which Member States are politically committed to the environmental philosophy and the extent to which they are willing to co-operate. The balancing of the economic growth/environment trade-off is likely to determine the Europe wide success of any policies, but there also needs to be concerted and co-operative political motivations. There will be those who will therefore argue that the attainment of an effective and concerted environmental policy in Europe will require political and economic union. However, the EU and national governments legislate over environmental protection and police offenders, significant environmental improvement will only be attained with the co-operation and commitment of producers. There is therefore a need for firms to institute environmental management practices and it is to this issue that the rest of this chapter is devoted.

ENVIRONMENTAL MANAGEMENT

The company level strategy

Companies are beginning to realise that environmental issues need to be addressed for a number of reasons, including consumer pressure, potential cost savings, legislation and ethics. There is therefore growing interest in the area of environmental management. Environmental considerations are likely to be a source of quite profound changes in business practices. With this in mind there are a number of questions which companies should ask themselves:

1 Is the company meeting its existing environmental commitments?
2 Is the company adhering to environmental legislation and what will be the impact on the firm as environmental legislation becomes more stringent?
3 Is concern for the environment integral to each company operation?
4 Do managers and workers see environmental improvement as a goal and in what ways are personnel being encouraged to be more involved?
5 Does the company have the capacity to evaluate the environmental impact of its processes and products including packaging and distribution channels?
6 Are there new product opportunities which the company could exploit which would have less of an environmentally negative impact?
7 How vulnerable is the company to environmental changes such as climate change?
8 What financial and organisational constraints are there which might prevent environmental improvement taking place?
9 How are the company's competitors placed in terms of environmental accountability and can the environmental performance of the firm be turned to a competitive advantage?
10 Does the company have a systematic approach to management which can be used to integrate environmental issues across the organisation?

The answers to these questions provide the firm with the basis of a strategic plan for the environment. An environmental policy can be developed from these questions and it can be circulated to company personnel, suppliers and vendors, and the public. The environmental policy sets out the context for future action. There is no single model and the policy will reflect a company's structure, location, industrial sector and business culture. If such a document is published then it is important that the plan is adhered to, thereby providing an all important environmental ethos around which the company must operate.

All aspects of a company's operations, from accounting and purchasing, to product design, manufacture, sales, marketing, distribution and the use and disposal of the product will have an impact on the environment and the environmental policy should reflect a recognition of this. The policy needs to be comprehensive and detailed but it should not contain statements or targets which the firm cannot hope to achieve. This will do more harm than good if exposed. The content of any policy will vary from firm to firm and be influenced by the activities of that organisation. However, there are some general principles which can be applied to the content of the policy statement:

1 Adopt and aim to apply the principles of *sustainable development* which meet the needs of the present, without compromising the abilities of future generations to meet their own needs.
2 Strive to adopt the highest available environmental standards in all site locations and all countries and meet or exceed all applicable regulations.
3 Adopt a total 'cradle-to-grave' environmental assessment and accept responsibility for all products and services, the raw materials you use and the disposal of the product after use.
4 Aim to minimise the use of all materials, supplies and energy and wherever possible, use renewable or recyclable materials and components.
5 Minimise waste produced in all parts of the business, aim for waste free processes and where waste is produced avoid the use of terminal waste treatment dealing with it, as far as possible, at source.
6 Render any unavoidable wastes harmless and dispose of them in a way which has least impact on the environment.
7 Expect high environmental standards from all parties involved in the business including suppliers, contractors and vendors and put pressure on these groups to improve their environmental performance in line with your own.
8 Be committed to improving relations with the local community and the public at large and where necessary introduce education and liaison programmes.
9 Adopt an environmentally sound transport strategy and assess the general infrastructure of the company.
10 Assess, on a continuous basis, the environmental impact of all operations and procedures via an environmental audit.
11 Assist in developing solutions to environmental problems and support the development of external environmental initiatives.
12 Preserve nature, protect ecological habitats and create conservation schemes.
13 Accept strict liability for environmental damage, not blaming others for environmental damage, accidents and incidents.

Environmental policies should identify key performance areas and form a sound basis for setting corporate objectives. They need to be detailed enough to demonstrate that the commitment of the company goes beyond lip-service. A clearly defined environmental policy should be implementable, practical and relate to the areas in which the company wishes to improve its environmental performance. In particular when designing an environmental policy the organisation needs to think hard about how it is going to quantify its objectives and measure its environmental performance.

For a policy to be implemented, personnel with special responsibilities for environmental performance will have to be found. Many companies in Europe have found that the best way to achieve this, in the short run, is to appoint a main board environment director. This person will be there to champion the environment and will need some very important personal skills as well as legitimacy. Such legitimacy is often achieved by the publication of the firm's environmental policy.

There are three very clear roles which an environmental director can take on.

1 *Taking a strategic view*: promoting minimal environmental impact from products and processes and developing an integrated and comprehensive approach.
2 *Raising the profile of the environment*: coordinating educational effort within the company, developing partnerships with customers, other companies (particularly suppliers), environmental pressure groups, legislators, the EU and national government.
3 *Putting policy into practice*: the establishment of company monitoring systems and environmental audits, the establishment of environmental improvement plans, involving all personnel and making them accountable and responsible for the environmental performance of their business and taking anticipatory action which is central to good environmental performance.

The initial stage in the implementation of an environmental approach at a firm level must be for a firm to establish exactly how well or how badly it is performing environmentally. An increasingly common way of achieving this is to have the firm environmentally audited.

Environmental auditing

The first environmental audits can be traced back to the USA, where US corporations adopted this methodology during the 1970s in response to their domestic liability laws. Such audits are now common among US industry and growing in importance in Europe. Environmental audits are usually carried out by teams which include lawyers, economists, engineers, scientists and environmental generalists drawn from industry, government and consultancy. The US Environmental Protection Agency has been instrumental in promoting environmental audits in the USA and has published policy guidelines which recommend going beyond the minimum legal requirements to identify actual and potential environmental problems.

There is some confusion over terminology still, but environmental auditing is generally seen as a check both on the environmental performance of a company and on the performance of the management system (*see* below) which should be designed to bring about improvements in that performance. In the first instance the firm needs to establish a baseline against which to measure future audits and this is commonly referred to as the environmental review. The environmental review follows many of the procedures of an audit as laid out below. However, strictly speaking an audit measures the attainment or non-attainment of some target objectives whereas the environmental review simply provides an initial assessment of the environmental performance of the company.

The environmental audit consists of a regular, independent, systematic, documented and objective evaluation of the environmental performance of an organisation. It should measure how well organisations, management and equipment are performing with the aim of helping the company management to safeguard the environment. It also provides management information which can be used in the control of environmental practices and in assessing compliance with company policies which include meeting regulatory requirements. It should be stressed, however, that within the task of environmental management there is a role for everyone in the organisation.

The overall aim of environmental auditing is to help safeguard the environment and minimise the risks to human health. Although auditing alone cannot achieve that, it is a powerful managerial tool and the key objectives of the environmental audit are:

1 to determine the extent to which environmental management systems in a company are performing adequately;
2 to verify compliance with local, national and European environmental and health and safety legislation;
3 to verify compliance with a company's own stated corporate policy;
4 to develop and promulgate internal procedures needed to achieve the organisation's environmental objectives;
5 to minimise human exposure to risks from the environment and ensure adequate health and safety provision;
6 to identify and assess risk resulting from environmental failure;
7 to assess the impact on the local environment of a particular plant or process by means of air, water and soil sampling; and
8 to advise a company on environmental improvements it can make.

There are a number of benefits to firms in having an environmental audit undertaken. These include assurances that legislation is being adhered to and the consequent prevention of fines and litigation, an improved public image which can be built into a public relations campaign, a reduction in costs (particularly in the area of energy usage and waste minimisation), an improvement in environmental awareness at all levels of the firm and an improvement in overall quality. On the other hand, there are some potential disbenefits of the audit. These include the initial costs of the audit and the cost of compliance with it and the temporary disruption of plant operations. It is also vital that management sees that the recommendations of the environmental auditor are adhered to, otherwise an audit report could be incriminating in a court case or insurance claim.

All environmental audits involve gathering information, analysing that information, making objective judgements based on evidence and a knowledge of the industry and of relevant environmental legislation and standards. There is also the need to report the results of the audit to senior management with recommendations and possible strategies for the implementation of the findings. This all needs considerable preparatory work as well as follow up time in order that the findings are accurate and comprehensive. Ideally, therefore there needs to be three clear stages to an audit (*see* Fig. 10.2).

Environmental audit stages

The first, the pre-audit stage will aim to minimise the time spent at the site and to maximise the audit team's productivity and will involve:

1 Planning the nature and scope of the audit and providing a framework for setting goals and objectives, developing strategies for their achievement and specifying accountability for accomplishing the work and scheduling the audit process.
2 Selecting members of the audit team and allocating resources to the strategies and policies determined in 1 above. The audit team will consist of people chosen for their expertise not only in environmental matters but also having knowledge of the industry in which a company operates. An assignment of audit responsibilities should be made according to the competencies and experience of the team.
3 Getting to know the industry and company to be audited. A useful strategy here is to use

pre-survey questionnaires submitted to management in order for the audit team to familiarise themselves with the type of instalment, the site and the location. It will also focus the minds of management on what will be required of them during the audit.

4 Questionnaires may also be sent to a representative sample of the workforce (to be filled out in confidence) asking about key issues such as communications, planning, health and safety and working conditions.

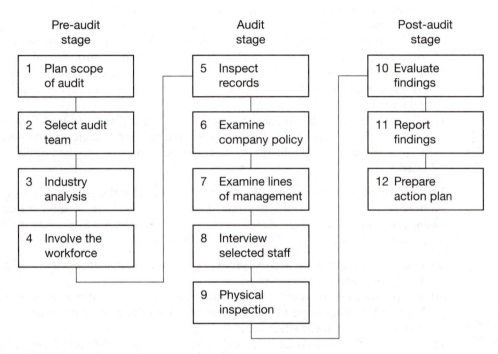

Pre-audit stage	Audit stage	Post-audit stage
1 Plan scope of audit	5 Inspect records	10 Evaluate findings
2 Select audit team	6 Examine company policy	11 Report findings
3 Industry analysis	7 Examine lines of management	12 Prepare action plan
4 Involve the workforce	8 Interview selected staff	
	9 Physical inspection	

Fig. 10.2 Stages of an environmental audit

The second stage is the on-site audit itself. This will include:

5 An inspection of records kept by the company, certificates of compliance, discharge consents, waste licences etc.

6 The examination of inspection and maintenance programmes and the company's own policy on what to do in the event of spills and other accidents. Auditors will have to assess the soundness of the facility's internal controls and assess the risks associated with the failure of those controls. Such controls will include management procedures and the equipment and engineering controls that affect environmental performance.

7 Examining lines of management and responsibility, competence of personnel and systems of authorisation. There needs to be a working understanding of the facility's internal management system and of its effectiveness.

8 A confidential interview of selected staff at all levels of operation with a view to collecting information, particularly in the area of the effectiveness of systems and waste management.

9 A physical inspection of the plant, working practices, office management systems and surrounding areas including a check on safety equipment, verifying the company's own sampling and monitoring procedures, investigating energy management systems and where necessary taking samples of waste, liquids, soil, air and noise.

The final stage of the audit will involve:

10 Confirming that there is sufficient evidence on which to base and justify a set of findings and evaluating the audit information and observations. Such evaluation will involve the audit team meeting to discuss all facets of the environmental audit.

11 Reporting the audit findings in written form and in discussion with the management of the audited company. This entails a formal review of the audit findings to avoid misinterpretation and discussion about how to improve the environmental performance of the firm based on the audit report. Management is thus provided with information about compliance status and recommendations regarding action which should be taken.

12 This will often result in the development of an action plan to address deficiencies. This will include assigning responsibilities for corrective action, determining potential solutions and establishing timetables. Recommendations for the next audit may also be made.

The environmental audit is more likely to be successful if the general ethos of the firm is supportive to the success of the programme and the welfare of the company. To this extent it is useful to consider some key characteristics which will provide the foundation for a successful programme. These factors will include:

(a) comprehensive support for the programme throughout management and particularly by senior management;

(b) acceptance that an auditing programme is for the benefit of management rather than a tool of individual performance assessment and is a function which, in time, will improve management effectiveness;

(c) the recognition that useful information will come out of the audit programme and that information needs to be shared and acted upon;

(d) the commitment to considering the comments and suggestions at each level of the organisation's management and workforce and encouraging responsible participation;

(e) a commitment to establishing systems for managing and following up on results;

(f) clearly defined roles and responsibilities and clear operational systems;

(g) the recognition of an integrated approach where the auditing system is linked to a wider management system.

Much stress needs to be placed on the idea that audits should be seen by management as a positive help rather than a threatening or hostile exercise. The company must create a culture, led by its main board directors, which recognises the positive benefits of the audit and sees it as good day-to-day management practice. Management must feel that they own the audit and even though some external expertise may be used, it is an activity which is promoted and driven internally rather than externally.

Environmental auditing in Europe

In the Netherlands, the concept of environmental auditing has been known since 1984, although Dutch subsidiaries of American owned firms had used the technique before then. The Confederation of Dutch Industries promotes environmental management within companies, encouraging interaction between government and industry and providing guidelines. Environmental auditing in the Netherlands is largely confined to the largest of industries but the Dutch expect that good practice by large, successful firms will be emulated by small and medium-sized firms. In the Dutch Shell group, the requirements for environmental auditing vary but the general principles have been published. Shell regularly conducts health, safety and environmental audits worldwide for agrochemicals formulation and environmental audits of oil and gas explorations take place every three years. Partial internal audits of plants takes place annually with a full external audit taking place every three–five years.

In Norway, factories are required to establish and maintain an internal environmental control system, supervised by a government agency. Environmental auditing is not legally required but a number of companies practise environmental auditing on a voluntary basis. Within the Norwegian company, Norsk Hydro, every major installation is audited once every two years, lasting between three–five days in each case.

In the UK, the CBI has published a set of environmental auditing guidelines. These stress the practicalities of undertaking an environmental audit and stress the need to implement audit recommendations and continue monitoring processes. The Labour Party has stated in its programme for a greener environment that it believes that environmental auditing should be made compulsory within EU company law.

The number of companies operating audit programmes in the EU will grow whether or not environmental auditing legislation is implemented. Demands from groups such as environmentalists or local communities will lead to pressure on companies not only to undertake environmental audits but also to disclose the results of those audits. The increase in auditing activity is also likely to lead to more standardisation of auditing practice and environmental standards. However without the development of an overall integrated environmental management system, environmental auditing will be a mere palliative.

The European Union eco-management and audit scheme

Whilst the first stance of the Environment Directorate of the EU has always been to encourage firms to improve standards of environmental performance, without waiting for regulation, there is nevertheless a growing amount of European environmental legislation and directives. Moreover, the EU has been keen to establish common environmental standards and systems for environmental reporting. One such system is embedded in the eco-management and audit regulation.

At the end of 1991, the Commission approved a proposal for a Council Regulation to establish an EU eco-management and audit scheme which would be open for voluntary participation by industrial companies. The Regulation was published in March 1992. The eco-management and audit scheme provides a framework for companies to think ahead, assess their own environmental impacts and commit themselves to a policy of reducing them. It also encourages firms to keep the public informed by regularly making statements and reporting progress. At the present time the eco-management and audit scheme is voluntary and administered by individual Member States but many expect the system to become compulsory for larger firms in time and the Council has retained the right to introduce compulsory registration. Member States themselves also have the right to adopt a compulsory registration system for certain industrial categories if they feel this is beneficial.

The objective of the scheme is to promote improvements in the environmental performance of industry by encouraging companies to:

- establish and implement environmental protection schemes;
- carry out regular, systematic and objective evaluations of the environmental performance of these systems; and to
- provide information about environmental performance to the public.

The purpose of the scheme is not to confirm compliance with legislative requirements (although this must be achieved), nor is it aimed at awarding best practice or performance. The scheme aims to recognise efforts to improve environmental performance over time given a baseline established by an environmental review of the firm. The scheme highlights the need for a continuous cycle of improvement.

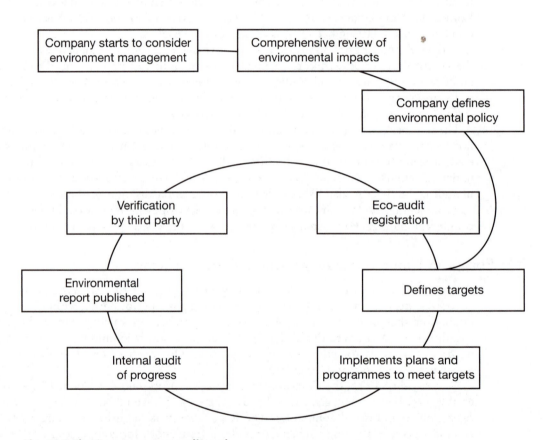

Fig. 10.3 The European eco-audit cycle

In order to join the eco-audit system a firm has to adopt and adhere to an eco-audit cycle (*see* Fig. 10.3). Essentially this requires the firm to:

- define an environmental policy, based on an overall review of the environmental impacts of its activities
- set targets for achievement within a set time

- put into place plans and systems to achieve these targets and include provisions for the constant monitoring of these
- periodically audit to assess progress
- report the audit findings to the public and have these findings verified by a third party
- set new targets for further progress and repeat the procedure.

There is a need to establish systems based on the environmental review which:

- assess and manage the environmental impact of the activities
- manage the use of energy, raw materials and water
- minimise waste
- consider the selection and design of products and processes
- prevent accidents
- include staff in consultation and provide motivation and training
- inform and involve the public.

Essentially, the audit assesses this system and evaluates performance in relation to the environmental review and the operation of the system as defined and documented. The results of the audit have to be considered by senior management and any necessary revisions to the company policy, objectives, targets, action plans and systems made.

All of these steps can be internal to the company, if there is sufficient expertise available to perform the various tasks adequately. Indeed the intention of the eco-management and audit scheme is that the discipline of having to follow these steps should help the company better manage its own environmental performance. However, there are also important external aspects to the scheme.

The eco-management and audit scheme requires that an external environmental statement is prepared based on the findings of the audit or initial review. Validation of this statement must be made by external accredited environmental verifiers. The validation will confirm that the statement has covered all of the environmental issues relevant to the site in enough detail and that the information presented is reliable. The validation process involved the examination of relevant documentation, including information about the site, its activities, a description of the environmental management system and details and findings of the environmental review or audit. This would normally be followed by an inspection visit to the site and preparation of a verifier's report.

In order to join the eco-management and audit scheme a company has to be able to demonstrate that this sequence of events has taken place, and that sensible targets have been set towards which the firms should make progress. The approved independent and accredited environmental verifier (AEV) will have checked that the audit process was carried out properly and that the environmental report is a true and fair view of the company's environmental performance. Application can subsequently be made for inclusion in the eco-management and audit register of companies. In order to continue to be registered companies have to continue the eco-audit cycle and maintain commitment to improving environmental performance. Any lapse will result in the removal of a company's name from the register.

Environmental Management Systems and Total Quality Management

There are some very strong links between Total Quality Management (TQM) Systems discussed in Chapter 6 and Environmental Management Systems. At the centre of each is the need for an integrated and committed approach. We saw in Chapter 6 that competitiveness is often measured by three things: quality, price and delivery and that the theory behind a TQM system is that as quality improves costs actually fall through lower failure and appraisal costs and less waste. Waste reduction will also help the firm to become more environmentally friendly. Total quality management is much more than assuring product or service quality, it is a system of dealing with quality at every stage of the production process, both internally and externally. TQM is a system requiring the commitment of senior managers, effective leadership and teamwork. This last facet makes the TQM programme compatible with the integrated and comprehensive approach required if a firm is to be serious about environmental issues. Indeed, if we view damage done to the environment as a quality defect then a TQM approach to environmental management is entirely compatible with principles of sustainable development.

The TQM system requires that every single part of the organisation must be able to work together. As well as teamwork there therefore needs to be commitment, organisation, planning and effective communications. A breakdown in the organisation leads to gaps where wastage and environmental damage may occur or quality be overlooked. Errors have a habit of becoming multiplied and failure to meet the requirements of one part of the organisation creates problems elsewhere. Managers must plan strategically both externally and internally and that internal strategic planning has to involve everyone in the workplace.

Total quality management is an approach aimed at improving the effectiveness and flexibility of business as a whole and is aimed at eliminating wasted effort as well as environmentally damaging physical waste by involving everyone in the process of improvement; improving the effectiveness of work so that results are achieved in less time and at less cost. One practical way of achieving the human involvement in the system is to move to a system of devolved work practices and quality circles (*see* Chapter 6).

Whether or not an environmental management system is ultimately successful may depend, in part, on factors outside the control of the firm. But, apart from the existence of a growing legislatory framework aimed at directing firms, the most significant determinants of success will be commitment, careful planning and the development of a responsible culture. There has to be good reasons for instituting an EMS and they need to be thoroughly explained and discussed with everyone involved in the firm, including, workers, shareholders and customers.

Over time, the aim must be to develop a positive culture surrounding environmental management and its constituent parts. Here there is a very important role for managers; they need to start thinking about more holistic management approaches and the EMS and TQM system can easily constitute the core of that. Reward and recognition provide the incentives to maintain the EMS culture. That is, reward directly related to performance for the workforce and recognition by customers, shareholders, pressure groups and regulatory authorities for the company as a whole. This can help workers to develop a sense of pride in their company which in turn feeds back into commitment.

THE CRADLE-TO-GRAVE APPROACH TO ENVIRONMENTAL MANAGEMENT

Product design managers are increasingly examining ways in which the total life-cycle of a firm can be managed to ensure that potential environmental damage is minimised. In other words, they are looking to create an enclosed resource loop where waste is recycled and even the product itself is recycled at the end of its use. Natural ecosystems operate in a similar fashion so that the waste from one process feeds into another as a nutrient. Traditional environmentally damaging production and consumption works more in a linear way such that inputs and outputs are not connected and possible environmental improvements are missed. One alternative is cradle-to-grave management where companies have to recognise their wider responsibility and manage the entire life-cycle of their products.

Many companies are recognising their responsibility in this area in terms of what has been termed product stewardship. This involves:

1 examining the design of a product and considering how efficient it is;
2 considering the energy sources, raw materials and components used in the product;
3 deciding whether they might be substituted by alternatives which are more environmentally friendly;
4 examining the production process itself and considering whether a more energy efficient and less polluting process innovation might be found;
5 re-examining the disposal of the product and the waste from its production in terms of recycling and returning the used materials to the production cycle after use; and
6 reconsidering the after sales service and packaging of the product and ensuring that adequate information is provided for its safe and energy efficient use and environmentally friendly disposal of waste caused by consumption of the product.

It is relatively easy for firms to target their internal systems and make changes to improve the environment. The part of cradle-to-grave management which is probably hardest to achieve is the return of materials from the consumer waste stream, for example, only 2 per cent of consumer used plastic is recycled in the EU owing to a lack of an effective collection infrastructure combined with underdeveloped markets for recycled plastics. One solution is for companies to take action and to construct their own recycling infrastructure. Many environmentalists would like to see the reintroduction of deposits on glass bottles for example.

The European Union eco-labelling scheme

Over time, eco-labelling schemes have been devised in a number of countries in an attempt to promote the use of production methods which are less harmful to the environment. The first such scheme was introduced in West Germany in 1978. Canada, Japan and Norway established their own schemes in 1989. The schemes were also introduced to prevent, often spurious, environmental claims. In countries such as the UK, where eco-labelling developments have been part of the EU development, environmental claims have been covered by advertising standards. For example the UK Advertising Standards Authority (ASA) has criticised companies for failing to substantiate claims of environmental benefits and the ASA has issued the British Code of Practice on the use of Environmental Claims which includes five basic principles:

(a) full documentary evidence must be held for all claims made;
(b) claims should not be absolute unless there is convincing evidence that a product will have no adverse effect on the environment;
(c) the basis of any claim should, if possible, be clearly explained;
(d) the cloaking of claims in extravagant language should be avoided as this will only cause consumer confusion;
(e) spurious claims should not be made.

Germany's Blue Angel eco-labelling scheme is probably the world's best established programme. Launched in 1978 by the German government, it now has almost 4 000 products carrying the label. The organisers of the scheme claim that 80 per cent of German households are aware of the scheme and it receives widespread support from manufacturers. Like the EU scheme, the label is not restricted to domestic made goods. The Japanese multinational, Konica, was the first company to win a Blue Angel label for use on a photocopier, for example. Many firms are aware that they cannot be without the Blue Angel award because the public sector, and many large German companies, will make every attempt to only buy products which carry the label.

The objectives of the EU's eco-labelling Regulation, agreed at the end of 1991, are to promote products with a reduced environmental impact during their entire life-cycles and to provide better information to consumers on the environmental impacts of products. These must not be achieved at the expense of compromising product or workers' safety or significantly affecting the properties which make the product fit for use. The EU scheme is designed to reduce confusion by providing an authoritative and independent label to identify those goods, with the lowest environmental impact in a particular product group. That is not to suggest that those products are environmentally benign, but simply that their environmental performance is superior to those products in the same group, which do not have a label. The scheme should also encourage the production and sale of more environmentally responsible products and so aid the impact of consumption on the environment.

The label should affect all businesses along a supply chain even if some suppliers cannot use the label themselves. This is because suppliers will have to provide detailed information about their own components and their manufacturing process, in order that the suppliers of the end product can apply to use the eco-label, on the basis of a life-cycle assessment. Thus, in time, the label may become a minimum standard, specified by an increasing number of buyers, who practise green procurement policies.

All products, excluding food drink and pharmaceuticals, are potentially eligible for an eco-label if they meet these objectives and are in conformity with the EU's health, safety and environmental requirements. Products comprising substances or preparations classified as 'dangerous' under EU legislation will also be barred from receiving an eco-label along with any product manufactured by a process likely to cause significant direct harm to humans or the environment.

The EU scheme issued as a Regulation applies directly to all Member States and is EU-wide. It is a voluntary scheme and self-financing. It assesses individual products and their manufacturing processes so that a multi-product firm will have to make multiple applications if they would wish all of their products to have eco-labels. The criteria for the award of an eco-label is ever tightening, such that upon application for the renewal of an eco-label, producers cannot assume that just because their environmental performance has remained unchanged, it will be awarded the label again.

Judgement of the products must be made on the basis of a cradle-to-grave analysis or life-cycle assessment (LCA). The assessment matrix in Fig. 10.4 must be used in setting criteria for the award of an eco-label. This will require account to be taken, where relevant, of a product group's soil, water, air and noise pollution impacts, waste generation, energy and resource consumption and effects on eco-systems. These impacts must be assessed in the pre-production, production, distribution, use and disposal stages. The criteria established for the award of an eco-label within a product group must be precise, clear and objective so that it can be applied consistently by the national bodies which award the eco-labels.

National competent bodies who are independent and neutral, actually award the eco-labels for products. They are made up of representatives from industry, government, environment pressure groups and consumer groups and the body has to reflect the full range of social interests. These bodies act as a kind of jury and assess the environmental performance of the product by reference to the agreed general principles and specific environmental criteria for each product group.

Environmental fields	Product life-cycle				
	Pre-production	Production	Distribution	Utilisation	Disposal
Waste relevance					
Soil pollution and degradation					
Water contamination					
Air contamination					
Noise					
Consumption of energy					
Consumption of natural resources					
Effects on ecosystems					

Fig. 10.4 European Union eco-labelling scheme indicative assessment matrix

The use of an eco-label is not necessarily open to any product. The first step is to get a particular product group accepted as suitable for the award of a label. It may be the case that a particularly polluting group of products will not be open to such an award. Requests for the establishment of new product groups may come from consumers or industry itself and are addressed to the competent body in the Member State. The competent body if it so wishes can ask the Commission to submit a proposal to its regulatory committee. In any event the Commission will consult with interest groups and take advice from a range of sources. If it is decided that a particular product group will be open to the award of an eco-label then this will be announced in the Official Journal of the EU. This process is outlined in Fig. 10.5.

Following applications from manufacturers or importers of a particular product for the award of an eco-label, the national competent body has to notify the Commission of its decision relating to the award of an eco-label, enclosing full and summary results of the assessment. The Commission will then notify other Member States and they usually have 30 days to make reasoned objections to the recommendations. If there are no objections the award proceeds and a contract to use the label for a specified time period is drawn up. Lists of products able to use the eco-label are published. In the case of any objections and disagreement the Commission acting through its advisory or regulatory body of national experts

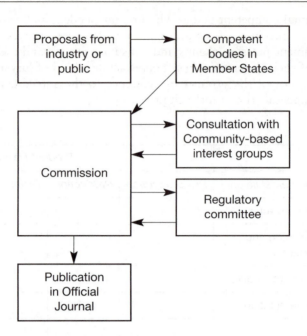

Fig. 10.5 Selection of new products

will make the final decision. This procedure is summarised in Fig. 10.6 Companies applying for an eco-label have to pay a fee to cover administration costs and a fee is also charged for the use of the label if awarded. Companies which succeed with their applications can only use the eco-label in advertising the specific products for which it was awarded.

The whole process of LCA used in the eco-label assessment process is fiercely controversial. The key issue here is the amount of depth to which companies are expected to subject their products. To undertake a complete LCA with accurate assessment of all the environmental impacts of a product would be very expensive and time consuming and like environmental impacts cannot be guaranteed to be 100 per cent accurate because of a lack of scientific knowledge in many areas. On the other hand anything short of this sort of approach is open to criticism and might easily be destroyed by competitors or interest groups which were not involved in the process. In time the LCA will need a much more focused definition if it is to be successfully implemented and form the long term criteria for the award of eco-labels.

It is clear from the EU eco-labelling Regulation that a full life-cycle assessment is not actually needed. Products must be able to satisfy the criteria laid out for each product group and therefore any application for an eco-label need only to address these key areas and show that there is no additional significant harm done by the manufacturing process. This has led many environmentalists to criticise the EU scheme on the basis that only a piecemeal LCA is needed. Indeed many have gone as far to suggest that this is not true life cycle assessment and that all the Regulation demands is that firms jump through some predetermined hoops.

Companies which are keen to identify their more environmentally friendly products within their marketing strategy will also be aided by the EU's eco-labelling scheme which will be able to confer a recognised accreditation for a particular product. It will not be

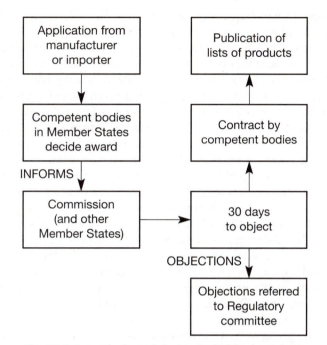

Fig. 10.6 Award of eco-label to individual products

enough therefore to make minor changes to a product and call it environmentally friendly since environmental impacts need to be assessed from cradle to grave. Increasingly consumers' attentions will be based on corporate performance as well as individual product profiles and therefore any strategy will have to focus on the widest possible aspects of environmental impacts. Companies who take the environment seriously need therefore to adopt a proactive environmental marketing strategy which is much more holistic than the narrower marketing so often employed by more traditional firms.

CONCLUSION

The environmental revolution has been gathering momentum and speed since the 1960s and has developed rapidly in the 1980s. Environmental considerations are likely to form an integral part of commercial normality and indeed competitiveness in the future. Definitions of business success are likely to include the assumption of zero negative impact on the environment at the very least. A competitive advantage can be achieved not merely by keeping abreast of environmental developments but also by initiating change within an organisation and responding with new environmentally friendly products and production processes. Indeed growing consumer awareness and environmental pressure groups are likely to ensure that firms which do not take action on the environmental front will lose market share. With increased competition as a result of European integration, environmental management will provide firms with a competitive edge.

Governments will increasingly seek to make the polluter pay and one consequence of this is that some industries and products may simply disappear. But ultimately, the success of environmental improvement will be determined largely by the responsiveness of business. That is not to suggest that legislation is a bad thing, indeed it can act as the impetus to a firm thinking about instituting a proper environmental management system. In addition, increasing legislation and government expenditure to increase environmentally related expenditure might be seen as a win-win situation. It stimulates the economy without leading to the pollution problems often associated with growth. Moreover, a shift in expenditure from the military to promoting security on the environmental front is possible.

Increasing environmental legislation at the European level will also act to stimulate research and technological innovation in the area of environmental improvement. For companies, the key to survival will be the development of environmentally compatible products and processes. Companies looking to prosper in the 1990s are already rethinking their corporate policies ahead of legislation, which is inevitable. Those companies are contributing towards a global shift towards sustainable development, but much else is still to be done. An important shift is taking place in EU policy. In the future there will be less command and control instruments and more reliance on market measures including voluntary schemes such as the eco-management and audit scheme and the eco-labelling scheme. However, like BS5750, such voluntary standards are likely to become the norm and increasingly written into contracts, and European firms need to think carefully about how they are going to move towards meeting the requirements of such standards.

Questions for discussion

1 Examine Table 10.3. What can you say about emissions of pollutants between East and West Europe?

2 What are the consequences of the Third World countries attaining the economic development and standards of living of the industrialised countries?

3 In general how can a firm turn an expensive environmental management policy into a competitive advantage?

4 How would economic theory suggest that a pollution problem is tackled?

5 Do you consider that a sustainable development model of economic development is possible?

6 In what ways does European integration help to control pollution? What sort of steps are being taken with the European Union?

7 What key steps can companies take to improving the environment?

8 In what ways does cradle-to-grave management mimic natural ecosystems? Why might this be of benefit to the planet?

9 How can industry be encouraged to institute environmental management systems?

10 What is meant by the *free rider problem* and why is this central to problems surrounding the environment? What solutions are available to avoid this problem?

11 To what extent do you think new voluntary standards published by the European Union will become the norm for European business?

CASE STUDY 1

The Body Shop International

Background

The Body Shop was founded in March 1976, when Anita Roddick opened her first shop in Brighton. Before 1976, working for the United Nations, she had travelled around the world and met people from a number of different cultures. Observing how people treated their skins and hair, she learned that certain things cleansed, polished and protected the skin without having to be formulated into a cream or shampoo. When she started The Body Shop, Anita Roddick aimed to utilise these raw ingredients such as plants, herbs and roots in products which would be acceptable to consumers. Only six years later she was described by the International Chamber of Commerce as 'the inventor of sustainable retailing' (Williams and Goliike, 1982).

The first shop was basic and initially sold only 15 lines. They were packed in different sizes to fill up the shelves and to give the customer an opportunity to try a product without buying a large bottle – a principle which remains today. A refill service operated which allowed customers to refill their empty bottles instead of throwing them away. Although this was clearly an environmentally friendly strategy, it was also initially implemented to cut down the costs of packaging.

Today, The Body Shop's principal activities are to formulate, manufacture and retail products which are primarily associated with cleansing, polishing and protecting the skin and hair. The underlying aims are to conduct that business ethically, with a minimum of hype and to promote health rather than glamour. Naturally based, close-to-source ingredients are used wherever possible and ingredients and final products are not tested on animals (Wheeler 1992). Packaging is kept to a minimum and refill services are offered in all shops. Packaging, in the form of plastic bottles, can be returned to shops and is recycled into The Body Shop's carrier bags.

The Body Shop's full range now contains over 300 products. The organisation trades in 41 countries and employs around 6 000 people, either directly or in franchises. Senior management in the organisation is committed to the encouragement of positive change. The aim is to establish a new work ethic, that will enable business to thrive without causing adverse damage to the environment, at both the local and the global level. There is an emphasis placed on not selling products which have an adverse effect on sustainability. That is, those which consume a disproportionate amount of energy during manufacture or disposal, generate excessive wastes, use ingredients from threatened habitats, which are obtained by cruelty, or which adversely affect other countries, especially in the developing countries.

It is claimed that the company is not a major polluter, nor a major user of energy and raw materials. Manufacturing at its principal site, Watersmead, in West Sussex, produces no airborne emissions and only 23m^3 of waste water per day. Energy consumption by the entire UK operation (including distribution and retail outlets) is responsible for only 0.003 per cent of total UK emissions of CO_2 (around 18 000 tonnes per annum). And the use of plastics in packaging represents only 0.01 per cent of total EU demand (Wheeler, 1992). Nevertheless environmental strategies are at the centre of The Body Shop's approach to business. Moreover, the organisation has been so successful in raising the profile of the environment both within and external to the business that it is endlessly cited as being the leading business, worldwide, in this field. Even though the organisation itself would argue that there is still more to be achieved, this case study examines the practices and systems which have enabled The Body Shop to reach this leading position.

Commitment and policy

One of the most apparent characteristics of The Body Shop is its commitment to environmental and social excellence. This is often attributed to Anita Roddick herself and whilst many of the principles are hers, the truth is that commitment in the organisation exists not only at board level but throughout the whole organisation. Everybody is encouraged to contribute to environmental improvement. The ultimate aim of The Body Shop is to include environmental issues in every area of its operations but, at the same time, the organisation rejects environmental opportunism which has often paralleled the green marketing strategies of more cynical firms.

At first, The Body Shop did not commit itself to a formal strategy or programme of environmental improvements. Action was taken when environmental problems were identified. This approach tended to increase employee involvement and reduce bureaucracy. However, with the continued growth of the organisation, it has been necessary to move to a more systematic approach, setting targets and planning for environmental improvement.

The overriding factor for The Body Shop is the perception of a moral obligation to drive towards sustainability in business (Roddick, 1991). It is impossible to measure progress towards this ideal without a detailed policy statement followed by a systematic process of data gathering and public reporting. Hence, auditing activities are considered absolutely essential to the company's long-term mission to become a truly sustainable operation. In other words, aiming to replace as many of the planet's resources as are utilised. That fundamental aim translates into a wish to play a full part in handing on a safer and more equitable world to future generations. The fundamental basis of this goal is a commitment to the broader concept of sustainable development. It is the strong belief of The Body Shop that the moral burden of achieving sustainability in business should become the principle driving force behind business in the future.

Environmental management and environmental auditing

The only real way to achieve the environmental improvement is to take a systematic approach to achieving its aims through an appropriate management structure and to periodically assess or audit progress, measuring the extent to which targets and basic objectives are being met. For that reason environmental auditing has a very high profile at The Body Shop. On the main site, it involves all staff and managers in continuous data collection, frequent reviews of priorities and targets (on a department by department basis) and an annual process of public reporting of results. The process extends to all retail outlets in the UK, and during 1993/94 it was being replicated in all overseas franchise operations.

In parallel with the need for environmental auditing, there is a need to put in place management systems capable of achieving targets and adhering to environmental policy. The Body Shop maintains a very decentralised system of environmental management. A corporate team of Environment, Health and Safety (EHS) specialists acts as a central resource for networks of environmental 'advisers' and coordinators in headquarters departments, subsidiaries, retail outlets and international markets. Environmental advisers and coordinators are usually part-time, fulfilling their role in environmental communications and auditing alongside normal duties.

When in 1991 The Body Shop carried out its environmental auditing, it did so in line with the draft version of the EU eco-management and audit scheme, publishing The Green Book, laying out its report to the public on its environmental performance. Early on, it was decided that the most important areas of environmental concern at The Body Shop were energy efficiency, waste management and product life-cycle assessment. Although the retail outlets fell outside the scope of this auditing procedure, other assessments have been or are being conducted in these areas. All UK shops, for example, were given an 'eco-audit' checklist covering their most important environmental issues. This was supplemented by training programmes on environmental improvement for Shop Environmental Advisers (SEAs).

Case Study Questions

1 Outline the ways in which The Body Shop manages its business so as to promote the concept of sustainable development.

2 How is the importance of commitment to environmental achievement achieved at The Body Shop?

3 Why do you think The Body Shop undertook its environmental audit in line with the European Union eco-management and audit scheme?

4 Do you think that the environmental management system in The Body Shop is transferrable to other businesses in other industries?

CASE STUDY 2

Environmental management in the hospitality and tourism industries

The success of tourism relies to a great extent on the quality of the environment where it takes place. Tourism is therefore influenced by the environment, but it must also be recognised that the environment is equally influenced by tourist activities. Tourism therefore requires proper planning and management and the industry itself has a responsibility to respond to the environmental challenge for its own well being as well as the well-being of society as a whole. Moreover, tourist activities today can destroy the potential earning capacity of a tourist destination in the future. Evidence from Germany suggests that up to 20 per cent of tourists who consider that the environment of their destination is damaged are unlikely to return (Boers and Bosch, 1994).

The hospitality industry, particularly in the developed world, must therefore take into account the costs of the effect of its operations on the environment, rather than regarding the planet as a free resource. In the past few companies have counted the costs of the pollution which they discharged into the atmosphere, and the debate has now turned to legislation aimed at forcing companies to comply with certain standards and taxing firms which pollute. The so called *polluter pays principle* is now central to legislation in the EU therefore. The implication here is clearly that prices will rise for consumers as firms experience increased costs associated with environmental improvements. Less energy consumption and more efficient use of resources are obvious targets for improvement and should not conflict with industry's aims since their attainment can actually reduce costs.

Tourism policy

Tourism has been selected as a priority area within the Fifth Environmental Action Plan, both because of the industry's significant environmental impact, and the relevance of the action at a EU level. For tourism there are three key areas of action which the Commission would like to encourage:

- better planning, development and management of mass tourism especially in coastal and alpine areas;
- sustainable tourism development and the development of different types of activities and products in other areas;
- changes in tourist behaviour and raising visitor awareness.

As part of this plan there are a number of initiatives taking place within the LIFE programme established by the Commission in 1992. Projects which contribute to the development and implementation of environmental policy are encouraged particularly where these include innovative demonstration projects such as land use planning and the use of 'clean' technologies, awareness campaigns and the provision of technical assistance. Within this framework the LIFE programme seeks to stimulate a planned approach to tourism development, especially in supporting actions which respect the natural environment.

Within the tourist industry, the Commission is also encouraging information networks, where hotels, restaurants and the transport sector can share solutions and strategies for overcoming damage caused to the environment. This voluntary cooperation is very important if the whole tourist industry is to become more environmentally responsible. Nevertheless there will still be a great emphasis placed on governments and local authorities to ensure that future planning applications for new tourist facilities meet newer and tougher environmental requirements.

Another specific action the EU will support is the drawing up of a code of behaviour for tourists. The aims of such a scheme would be to get service providers to educate their customers and ensure that they are aware of the environmental impact of their activities. In effect it requires the industry itself to take more responsibility for visitor management. Moreover, by drawing up a practical guide, tourists can feel more of a part of the environment they are enjoying, and help to protect it for future generations. It is likely that such a strategy involving the industry and its consumers will be central to devising and delivering new tourist products and facilities.

Sustainable development and sustainable tourism

There is increasing concern that tourism can damage the environment. Holiday packages have led to overcrowding, over-exploitation and depletion of resources in many regions of Europe. This has led to both environmental and cultural damage in those regions where traditional industry has largely been replaced by tourism. The environmental situation is particularly disturbing in the Mediterranean where coastal areas have seen rapid growth in both tourism and manufacturing industry.

However, the tourist industry will find itself having to respond to increasing pressure from the Commission to improve its environmental performance. It will be directly affected by directives on environmental impact assessment, the quality of bathing water, waste management and control of emissions. The Commission's proposals for the urban environment stresses the need to develop a planning strategy for urban tourism. Moreover, through the use of its structural funds, the Commission is able to support regional action programmes which improve the environment. Such programmes are increasingly integrated schemes which include participation from all industries including tourism.

According to The Tourism Society (1991), sustainable tourism challenges us to view the use of our precious natural and built resources in a creative way. It is important to recognise the real relationship between economic activity and environmental concern. In recognising the *polluter pays principle* there is a need for new charges for tourism management purposes. In addition however, we must recognise that the concept of sustainable development encompasses wider issues than just the environment.

The industry response to sustainable tourism

According to the results of monitoring by the World Travel and Tourism Environmental Research Centre there is evidence to suggest that many companies are adopting programmes to improve their environmental performance (Hawkins, 1994). This is partly motivated by a growing awareness that the industry's own interests are at stake and an increased emphasis put on environmental attributes as an element of non-price competition.

The following seven Principles for Sustainable Tourism were drawn up in May 1991 by the Secretary of State for Employment's Tourism Task Force. They form a useful basis for the growth and development of the industry.

1 The environment has intrinsic value which outweighs its value as a tourism asset. Its enjoyment by future generations and its long term survival must not be prejudiced by short term considerations.
2 Tourism should be recognised as a positive activity with the potential to benefit the community and the place as well as the visitor.
3 The relationship between tourism and the environment must be managed so that it is stable in the long term. Tourism must not be allowed to damage the resource, prejudice its future enjoyment or bring unacceptable impacts.
4 Tourism activities and developments should respect the scale, nature and character of the place in which they are sited.

5 In any location, harmony must be sought between the needs of the visitor, the place and the host community.
6 In a dynamic world some change is inevitable and change can often be beneficial. Adaption to change, however, should not be at the expense of any of these principles.
7 The tourism industry, local authorities and environmental agencies all have a duty to respect the above principles and to work together to achieve their practical realisation.

Recognising the urgent need to support moral and ethical conviction with practical action, the hotel industry has established the International Hotels Environmental Initiative to foster the continual upgrading in the industry worldwide. With the co-operation and participation of individual companies, hotels and related organisations, the initiative endeavours to:

1 Provide practical guidance for the industry on how to improve environmental performance and how this contributes to successful business operations.
2 Develop practical environmental manuals and guidelines.
3 Recommend systems for monitoring improvements in environmental performance and for environmental audits.
4 Encourage the observance of the highest possible standards of environmental management, not only directly within the industry but also with suppliers and local authorities.
5 Promote the integration of training in environmental management among hotel and catering schools.
6 Collaborate with appropriate national and international organisations to ensure the widest possible awareness and observance of the initiative and the practice it promotes.
7 Exchange information widely and highlight examples of good practice in the industry.

Clearly every company within the hospitality industry can begin by improving its own environmental performance. In this first instance, organisations can develop environmental policies, assess their environmental impacts through reviews and audits and develop comprehensive environmental management systems.

FURTHER READING

Welford, R. and Gouldson, A. (1993) *Environmental Management and Business Strategy*, Pitman Publishing. This text takes the form of a practical guide to the subject and includes discussions on European environmental legislation, environmental auditing, environmental management systems, green marketing and eco-labelling.

Welford, R. (1994) *Cases in Environmental Management and Business Strategy*, Pitman Publishing. These case studies on environmental management include leading companies in Europe such as IBM, The Body Shop, British Telecom and Volkswagen-Audi.

Welford, R. (1995) *Environmental Strategy and Sustainable Development: The Corporate Challenge for the 21st Century*, Routledge. This text provides a more radical approach to corporate environment management including a critique of traditional environmental management systems and in depth consideration of sustainable development, life-cycle assessment, ecological auditing, auditing for sustainability and bioregional dimensions of environmentalism.

Welford, R. (1996) *Corporate Environmental Management*, Earthscan. This text gives a particularly in depth discussion of the various elements of a corporate environmental management strategy including environmental management systems, associated standards, environmental policies, environmental performance measurement, environmental auditing and environmental reporting.

Welford, R. (1996) *The Earthscan Reader in Business and the Environment*, Earthscan. This text gives a review of some of the most important writings on the subject of business and its interrelationship with the environment.

REFERENCES

Boers, H. and Bosch, M., *The Earth as a Holiday Resort: An Introduction to Tourism and the Environment*, Institute for Environmental Communication and Netherlands Institute of Tourism and Transport Studies, Utrecht, Netherlands, 1994.

Hawkins, R., 'Towards Sustainability in the Travel and Tourism Industry', *European Environment*, 4, 5, 1994.

Roddick, A., 'In Search of the Sustainable Business', Ecodecision, 7, 1991.

The Tourism Society, *Sustainable Tourism: Development in Balance with the Environment*, A Tourism Society Memorandum, 1991.

Williams, J. O. and Goliike, U., *From Ideas to Action, Business and Sustainable Development*, ICC Report on the Greening of Enterprise, International Chamber of Commerce, London, 1982.

Wheeler, D., 'Environmental Management as an Opportunity for Sustainability in Business – Economic Forces as a Constraint', *Business Strategy and the Environment*, 1, 4, 37–40, 1992.

CHAPTER 11

Central and Eastern Europe

TRANSITION AND CHANGE

As an important part of Europe, we cannot fail to give some consideration to the huge changes which continue to occur in Central and Eastern Europe and their impact on European businesses. The transition to the market mechanism, the liberalisation of trade and closer links with the European Union have opened up vast, potential markets in Europe. The size of the population alone (*see* Table 11.1), indicates the revenue which can be earned from the sale of basic consumer products in Eastern Europe. Over time, as markets develop and living standards increase, the size and sophistication of markets will grow. Many firms are making investments in these markets now in the expectation of rapid growth some time in the future.

Table 11.1. Population of Eastern Europe, 1993

Country	Million
Albania	3.2
Bulgaria	9.0
Czech Republic	10.3
Slovak Republic	5.3
Hungary	10.6
Poland	38.3
Romania	23.0
Slovenia	2.0
Other Yugoslav Republics	23.5
Baltic States	8.0
Russia	147.4
Ukraine	51.7
Other CIS Republics	73.0

European Economy, Special Supplement, Eastern Europe, 1992.

As can be seen from Table 11.1 the smaller countries of Central Europe have populations similar to the size of Belgium and the Netherlands and there is considerable interest in Hungary and in the Czech Republic, in particular, in examining the economies and models of development of their Western counterparts. Overall, despite the large populations involved, markets are underdeveloped because of low living standards. The transition from centrally planned to market economies will only occur with further upheavals, which might actually lower living standards still further (particularly if the reforms lead to very high levels of unemployment), and so the markets are likely to take many years to mature.

For some businesses though, they see an advantage in entering the market at an early stage in order to build their own infrastructure of suppliers and customers, thereby giving them a first mover advantage when faced with competition later.

One characteristic of many of the Central and Eastern European economies is that the structures of their economies are relatively underdeveloped compared with their EU counterparts. Table 11.2 demonstrates that the primary sector is often relatively large compared with the EU average and that service sectors are relatively underdeveloped.

Table 11.2. GDP by sector, 1993

Country	Agriculture and Forestry	Industry and construction	Services
Romania	23.7	44.4	31.9
Bulgaria	9.3	42.3	48.3
Czech Republic	5.6	61.2	33.1
Slovakia	5.7	60.1	34.2
Hungary	5.7	40.7	53.6
Poland	7.6	39.5	52.9
Russia	10.0	56.0	34.0
EUR 12	5.7	32.8	61.5

Sources: National sources and Economist Intelligence Unit Country Reports (1995).

One effect of the economic and political reforms, which will be discussed in detail later in the chapter, is that as inefficient and uncompetitive industries are being forced to close on the removal of state subsidies, the quantity of output falls and unemployment increases. Table 11.3 shows that in the early years of reform national output fell considerably. Such statistics fail to demonstrate, however, that significant differences exists between the different Central and Eastern European economies. Table 11.4 shows GDP per head in various countries showing that standards of living are often quite disparate.

Table 11.3. Economic growth

Country	1990	1991	1992	1993
Romania	−5.6	−12.9	−13.6	1.0
Bulgaria	−9.1	−11.7	−5.7	−4.2
Czech Republic	−1.2	−14.2	−6.6	−0.3
Slovakia	−2.5	−14.5	−7.0	−4.6
Hungary	−3.9	−11.9	−4.3	−2.3
Poland	0.2	−7.6	2.6	3.8

Sources: National sources and Economist Intelligence Unit Country Reports (1995).

Table 11.4. GDP per head, US$, 1993

Slovenia	9 000
Czech Republic	7 800
Hungary	5 400
Latvia	5 200
Slovakia	5 100
Russia	5 050
Estonia	5 000
Poland	4 950
Bulgaria	4 750
Lithuania	4 400
Ukraine	3 950
Romania	2 850
Albania	1 800

Sources: National sources and Economist Intelligence Unit Country Reports (1995).

The institutional changes required to move a previously planned economy to a market oriented economy are huge. State enterprises which were often monopolies must be converted into organisations able to operate in the market. Financial institutions must be established to support these organisations and to provide them with the capital to function in the market. This must be done in a two stage process. First, institutions must be separated from the core governments with its role redefined and its revenue base secured. Second, private ownership may then be introduced and extended to create, at least in theory, an incentive structure to yield better results in the management of assets. These fundamental institutional changes, required for the transition to the market economy make the problem of transformation in Central and Eastern Europe quite different from the development problem of raising per capita incomes in poor market economies.

Constitutional arrangements are also a problem in Central and Eastern Europe. The roles of various levels of government and the relations between them are a source of tension. Disputes concerning jurisdiction, authority to raise taxes and property rights at a local level continue to lead to disagreements and uncertainty. There remains a shortage of individuals who are capable of managing local governments and introducing reforms at the local level. Most of the people most able to perform such tasks are often discredited by association with old regimes or the Communist Party.

Cultural and psychological change should not be underestimated either, particularly for those who have lived their lives through and invested their energies in the old systems, the changes are often quite distressing. The wide gap between the aspirations to Western living standards and the reality of what is likely to be achieved in the near future is also a source of discontent. However, governments realise that they must maintain the support of the population so that they can continue with the reform process and see it through to some sort of conclusion. A factor which makes this particularly difficult is the large number of ethnic and nationality conflicts that weaken the cohesion of central governments and delay economic reform.

THE EASTERN BLOC PRIOR TO TRANSITION

The Comecon Customs Union

Comecon was established in 1949 to co-ordinate the economic and development activities of its member countries and thereby seek to make the whole greater than the parts. The member countries were Albania (expelled in 1961), Bulgaria, Cuba (from 1972), Czechoslovakia, German Democratic Republic (from 1950), Hungary, Mongolia (from 1962), Poland, Romania, USSR and Vietnam (from 1978). Comecon has been likened to the EU and, although it was a customs union, the size of its secretariat was much smaller than the EU. It did, however, co-ordinate scientific and technical co-operation. Much like the structure of the European Commission, it had divisions which covered agriculture, fuel, machinery, chemical industries, metal production, food manufacturing, transport, construction, foreign trade, post and telecommunications, standardisation procedures, statistics, finance and currency, health and civil aviation.

Traditionally, most of the trade of the Comecon countries was with each other and the Soviet Union dominated that trade. Certainly, for the smaller countries of Comecon, the USSR was their biggest trading partner. With the reforms in Central and Eastern Europe, and the virtual collapse of areas of the former Soviet economy, most of the former Comecon countries are developing trading relationships with the West. The largest beneficiary of this is Germany, which as a united country, not only has all the traditional links with the East, but also has the industry to produce the products and is geographically in an optimum position. Leaving aside the contribution of former East Germany, West Germany alone exports six times the amount that the United Kingdom does to Central and Eastern Europe. Indeed, West Germany exports more to these markets than all the other EU countries put together.

Comecon suffered from many problems which the EU has also had to deal with. One of the key issues was always the extent of the integration between those countries which should occur. Bulgaria, being among the less developed countries in Comecon, always argued for greater integration and mutual assistance to bring it up to the levels of the more developed Comecon partners. Hungary and Poland always argued for a more flexible approach with a slower integration process, whilst former Czechoslovakia was reluctant to see significant integration take place. It was in the area of foreign trade with Western Europe and the USA that the greatest divergence of opinions were to be found. Romania, Poland and Hungary have long had important trading links with the USA and this was not always popular with the Soviet governments, of course.

As the traditional Comecon arrangements fell fallen apart, trade and economic ties with the West have increased and there has been much discussion relating to new trading alliances. Poland, Hungary and the Czech and Slovak Republics would all like to become full members of the EU. Implicitly, the association agreements, making these countries associate members of the EU, which were all virtually identical, represents an attempt on the part of the EU to encourage a little sister organisation to itself, being a prelude to possible full membership sometime in the future (but probably not before the end of the century). The countries which have particularly suffered from the new realignments in Europe are the non-European members of the former Comecon system, who have lost some of their important trading links with countries which were more economically advanced. Mongolia, Cuba and Vietnam are now faced with their own new set of problems as a result of the reforms.

STRATEGIES FOR TRANSITION

The market economy

The transition from a centrally planned economy to a market economy entails the creation of the rights to own property, which is central to any market mechanism and which is required to facilitate privatisation and joint ventures. It also requires the establishment of a network of modern legal and financial services. Large scale foreign investment will flow mainly to countries which can establish an effective financial and legal system, and where safeguards on ownership and property are well established. The development of such infrastructures is an ongoing process but early in its transition period, for example, Poland established its stock exchange in the building once occupied by the Communist Party Central Committee.

In order to maintain stable economic conditions each country must create an institution framework for maintaining macroeconomic control. There are three main requirements here:

1 the establishment of a secure government revenue base adapted to the institutional framework of the market economy;
2 creating a strong monetary control regime that will allow some flexibility in financing budget deficits without requiring support from income policies; and,
3 ensuring that a coherent exchange-rate strategy supportive of macroeconomic stability is in place.

One of the main problems is ensuring the secure revenue base for the government and its associated institutions. In the past, all government revenues were heavily dependent on state enterprises. During the early liberalisation programmes revenue was buoyant but more recently the sums of money paid to the government to buy the most successful of the former state owned companies has dried up because they have all been sold. Therefore introducing fair, broadly based tax systems and ensuring that revenues are actually collected, with the support of the electorate is an important longer term programme.

Poland, the Czech Republic and Hungary have been most advanced in developing an infrastructure for the market economy and, aided by their borders adjacent to Austria and Germany, are best placed for attracting investment from the EU, USA and Asian countries, attracted by low wages, proximity to the EU markets and a relatively skilled workforce. Eastern European banks, building societies, insurance companies and other institutions have been modelled on existing European structures and new economic and financial legislation has been deliberately designed to be compatible with existing Community legislation.

Privatisation

The process of privatising a state owned economy is entirely different to privatising state enterprises in an otherwise capitalist environment. Looking to the UK as a model, which has been done by some economists in the East, will therefore only provide a partial solution. It took the UK government ten years to privatise 50 companies with the help of some of the most sophisticated financial and legal institutions in the world. In Poland alone there were 8 000 such companies in 1991. Many smaller companies have simply been auctioned off. In the early stages of the privatisation programme in Poland, it took a year to privatise five medium-sized companies. The sale of large companies which dominated the command economy, has required fundamental changes to property laws. Given that privatisation has already been slow, the sheer size of the former State sector in the Central and Eastern Europe (*see* Table 11.5) indicates the enormous task which still lies ahead.

Table 11.5. State ownership of industry by country , 1990

	Percentage of value-added
Czechoslovakia	97
USSR	97
Poland	82
Hungary	65
France	17
Italy	15
United Kingdom	12
US	2

Source: Independent on Sunday, July 1991.

In most countries though, there has been a recognition that the privatisation process will be a long one. After a wave of spontaneous privatisations which have resulted in foreign buyouts of potentially profitable firms the stance has become more pragmatic. In Hungary, for example, an official list of 20 or so companies to be privatised is issued from time to time but every company is open to bids being made and case by case negotiations can take place at any time.

Privatisation processes are often divided into *small scale* and *large scale*. The former comprises the transfer to private ownership, small state owned or cooperative enterprises. Small scale privatisation had in fact begun in Central and Eastern European countries under old communist regimes. The rapid acceleration in small scale privatisation is changing the situation with regard to the exchange of goods and services, de-monopolising trade and subjecting it to free market rules. For foreign investors this is an important development since it means that for the first time they have the same access to the new private firms as other domestic suppliers.

In the case of large scale privatisation the difficulties involved are augmented by the lopsided structure of the former communist economies. In 1989, large enterprises accounted for over three-quarters of the national product in these countries. For large scale privatisation to achieve its desired results, a whole series of conditions need to be fulfilled. First, there has to be in existence entrepreneurs, with substantial capital resources and access to dynamic management skills who can restructure and rationalise these large firms. What is lacking in the region is both sufficient funds and management expertise. Thus, it is often towards foreign investment which governments are forced to look. Many large enterprises remain in the public sector though because buyers simply cannot be found. However, the need to privatise relatively inefficient firms more rapidly has led to the need for mass privatisation methods. Table 11.6 outlines how this process has been managed in selected countries.

Table 11.6. Mass privatisation methods

Specific features	Czech Republic	Hungary	Poland	Russia
Principal method	Vouchers.	Cheap loans.	Shares in intermediary funds.	Vouchers.
General features	Vouchers issued for KCR 1 000 1st and 2nd wave. All citizens over 18 entitled to participate. Complex series of bidding processes to convert vouchers into shares. Effected either directly or via private investment funds acting as intermediaries.	Assistance provided in the direct purchase of shares by means of interest-free loans repayable over 5 years. All citizens over 18 eligible.	Shares will be distributed through National Investment Funds. All citizens over 18 eligible. Cost US$15. Number of shares received for this price depends on subscription to funds.	Vouchers issued for free. All citizens over 18 entitled to participate. Vouchers converted into shares through auction process or through private investment funds.
Number of companies included	1 804	Up to 70	At least 400	Over 5 000
Value of companies included	US$8.75 billion.	Not yet known (280.6 billion HUF).	Not yet known (60 000 billion Zloty).	Not yet known.
Restrictions on subsequent disposal of shares	No.	Yes.	No.	No.
Extent to which controlled or market-driven	Market-driven.	Controlled.	Controlled.	Market-driven.

Source: Adapted from Howell, J., Understanding Eastern Europe: The Context of Change, Kogan Page, 1994.

The privatisation processes are clearly underway in all Central and Eastern European economies. The pace of change is very uneven both between countries and within countries when we examine the scale of operations. Of crucial importance is still the question of political stability. However, such political stability and the privatisation process are actually inseparable. One has to realise that privatisation holds the ultimate key to the burial of all traces of central planning and communist regimes. Consequently, those who believe in a clean sweep are now urging an acceleration of privatisation and the conservatives are doing everything in their power to slow the process down.

Where foreign investment has been at its greatest, so we have seen most progress made towards privatisation. In turn, foreign investors are drawn primarily to the countries which have gone the furthest along the privatisation path. This has kept the momentum up in countries such as Poland, the Czech Republic and Hungary but has compounded problems associated with the sale of state assets in countries such as Bulgaria and Romania.

Inflation and currency convertibility

There is a very strong link between inflation and currency convertibility. If inflation is high then the only way for a country to remain internationally competitive is to continually devalue its currency. Moreover, with prices rising quickly, people become unwilling to hold on to currency because its value declines. Therefore over time, currency, whilst maintaining its use as a medium of exchange domestically becomes almost worthless externally and cannot be exchanged for stable (hard) currencies. This, in turn, means that without hard currency a country will lose its ability to import the goods it wishes. Moreover, hard currencies themselves become the medium of exchange particularly on parallel (black) markets. Their purchasing power becomes great because they become a 'passport' to buying the goods a consumer wants.

In order to become internationally competitive and be able to both import and export goods which will lead to growth and industrialisation, currencies therefore need to become convertible and thus the control of inflation is central. Table 11.7 shows the problems which have been experienced by Eastern European countries with respect to price levels. In addition, the move towards the market mechanism also works against the stability of prices, since the basic functioning of the system replaces the ubiquitous physical queues of the centrally-planned system with higher prices which are simply a form of financial queuing.

Table 11.7. Inflation (percentage changes in the index of consumer price increases

Country	1990	1991	1992	1993	1994
Bulgaria	21.6	333.5	91.1	72.8	77.4
Czech Republic	10.0	58.0	11.1	21.0	9.7
Slovakia	10.0	58.0	9.0	23.0	13.9
Hungary	30.0	35.0	23.0	22.5	17.6
Poland	249.3	60.3	43.0	35.3	31.9
Romania	5.0	344.5	199.0	295.0	225.9
Russia	5.0	90.4	1534.0	877.0	552.0

Sources: European Economy, Special Supplements, Eastern Europe, 1992 and 1994.

Productivity and prospects of unemployment

It is estimated that about one third of Central and Eastern Europe's industrial production is up to international standards, that one third will have to be abandoned and that the rest can survive with restructuring (European Parliament, 1990). There is likely to be some job creation in those sectors where production has been restricted (e.g. construction and services) but, in general, Table 11.8 shows that unemployment has become common since the end of central planning. That is not to suggest that central planning cured unemployment. A characteristic of that system was massive underemployment, in other words, most people had jobs but many were not employed fully or efficiently in them.

Table 11.8. Unemployment

Country	1992	1993	1994
Bulgaria	15.6	15.9	13.4
Czech Republic	3.0	3.6	3.0
Slovakia	1.0	14.0	13.9
Hungary	12.2	12.1	11.0
Poland	13.6	16.1	16.6
Romania	8.4	10.2	10.8

Source: European Economy, Supplement A, No. 8/9, 1994.

Most of the production in Central and Eastern Europe comes from the large conglomerate enterprises or combines, established by governments and formerly under the direct control of ministries or administrative districts. Most of the combines are to be privatised and demerged. Since the average size of production units within the combines is often considerably larger than in Western Europe, a degree of rationalisation is inevitable. Where privatisation is planned shares are likely to be divided amongst workers, managers, domestic investors and foreign investors. But the most successful parts of the combines have been susceptible to purchase by EU, USA and Japanese industrial groups.

Technological underdevelopment in the East is the main reason for the productivity gap between the East and West. Growth in the Eastern economies has been led by the needs for capital equipment in former Comecon countries. This has resulted in a neglect of consumer goods and little investment in new production technology. According to the Deutsche Bank (1990) overall productivity levels in former East Germany are about 47 per cent of the West German level and Wharton Economic Forecasting Associates (1990) estimate labour productivity at 40 per cent of the West German levels. There is no reason to suggest that the other Central and Eastern European countries will have levels significantly different to these.

In many Central and Eastern European countries, the right to work was guaranteed and every worker had some rights to choose his/her job under the centrally-planned system. The latter part of this was subject to considerable control however, because of particular shortage areas and a degree of regional planning. Nevertheless, this policy has resulted in a well trained workforce in the East, with 85 per cent of all workers in former East Germany, Poland and Hungary having completed some form of vocational training. This percentage is higher than in any EU Member State.

Unemployment has become an inevitable consequence as workforces are rationalised and plants close. During the transitional stage it is difficult to forecast the levels to which unemployment might climb but estimates range from 12–40 per cent of the workforce, depending on the country under consideration. Lower unemployment levels are obviously expected in the countries more able to react to change and which already have at least a rudimentary market system in place. Hungary would therefore be expected to suffer considerably less than Bulgaria for example.

Mass unemployment is less likely in the longer term because of the upturn which is expected after the transitional period. In particular, investment in the private sector and, in general, infrastructure development will have a favourable effect on the employment situation. In the building sector there is already a genuine shortage of labour and in particular industries such as light and electrical engineering, where skilled workers are in demand there has been very little evidence of any downturn.

It was foreign nationals in the East who were the first to be hit by the wave of dismissals and redundancies in the early 1990s. Linked to this was a growing wave of xenophobia and nationalism. The most prevalent nationalities working in East European countries have been Vietnamese, Cubans and Angolans. In countries such as former East Germany it was common to find Poles and in Hungary, Bulgarians have often found jobs. In other words, there was a migration from the poorer East European countries to the more wealthy. These people too have often been sent back to their countries of origin. Subsequently it was women who were made redundant. In countries such as former East Germany 75 per cent of women's jobs were traditionally reserved for them. Upon reform such rights to work have been lost.

The environment

It has been a characteristic of the discussions surrounding the recent events in Central and Eastern Europe, that environmental issues have loomed large. This is not only because of the general increasing awareness of environmental problems in these countries in particular, but also because many countries' own pollution problems are directly linked to the situation in the former centrally planned economies. Scandinavia and Austria, in particular, have often complained about their own levels of imported pollution. Former East Germany, in particular, is suffering from a severe environmental problem only part of which is its own making. Prevailing winds bring pollution from Russia, for example, which is subsequently deposited in Poland and Germany. Increasingly, such pollution is being identified as a threat to human health and a barrier to inward investment.

There has been a legal basis for environmental protection in many Central and Eastern European countries. However, often key polluting industries, such as energy generation, were exempted from the standards. In addition monitoring technology was poor and overall compliance with the legislation was low.

In recent years, the environmental problems in Central and Eastern Europe have increased substantially. The air, water and soil in the East have become heavily polluted and endanger general health and the natural environment. According to the former GDR Ministry for Environmental Protection (1990) the main causes of this environmental situation are:

1 Many years of maintaining an energy and structural policy characterised by large-scale use of brown coal, heavy industry involving intensive use of energy and raw materials, high energy consumption and outdated production processes.
2 Long-term neglect of environmental management and low funding for environmental protection measures.
3 The underdevelopment and underproduction of environmental protection technology.

High levels of air pollution are mainly a result of the energy policy of the centrally planned economies. Prior to reunification, the GDR's energy consumption was 25 per cent higher per person than in West Germany, and was the third highest in the world, for example. High sulphur content brown coal accounts for about 70 per cent of the energy sources used and the present structure of industry is one where there are many energy intensive production systems. In general energy conversion technologies are outmoded and inefficient, for example, fifty per cent of steam generators are over twenty years old.

If sulphur dioxide emissions are examined per unit of area then we find that former East Germany has the highest emission levels in Europe and whilst West Germany has reduced its emissions by half since 1980, they have increased in the East by 20 per cent. In the worst affected countries such as former East Germany, Poland and Czech Republic emissions of sulphur dioxide affect over 30 per cent of the population directly and in certain areas, with the highest levels of air pollution, the number of respiratory diseases among children has more than doubled in the last 15 years and now stands at about 50 per cent. The number of children suffering from endogenous eczemas has also risen sharply to about 30 per cent in heavily polluted areas. Such high levels are also taking a toll on the natural environment with many forests already severely damaged and some completely dead in Poland and the Czech Republic.

However, the level of nitrogen oxide emissions in Eastern Europe has often been lower than in Western Europe. This is mainly due to the fact that, since the beginning of the 1980s, goods transport has been shifted from the roads to the railways and waterways. This could be a lesson for future EU policy on transport, perhaps.

The main reasons for relatively high levels of water pollution are: untreated effluent from key industries, the discharge of organic waste products from agriculture and the uncontrolled disposal of domestic waste. On top of this, air pollution often adds to water pollution through the deposition of atmospheric pollution as is the case with acidifying pollutants.

In 1988, in the GDR, 91.3 million tonnes of industrial waste and secondary raw materials were produced, of which 36.9 million tonnes were reprocessed, representing a reprocessing level of only 39.9 per cent. The technology necessary to reduce the volume of waste or to provide preliminary treatment to eliminate pollutants hardly exists in Central and Eastern Europe and those which are available do not meet international standards. The pollution of the environment by uncontrolled and inappropriate waste disposal occurs mainly through contamination of the groundwater. This problem is further exacerbated by the fact Central and Eastern European countries have often imported waste from the West for treatment. Over the ten years before reunification the GDR imported about 5 million tonnes of waste annually including 650 000 of toxic waste and more than 200 000 tonnes of sewage sludge from West Germany alone.

When we consider the possible scenarios for the implementation of future environmental policy objectives, the outlook is quite bleak for industry. A study from the chemical industry, for example, suggests that a 25 reduction in the most polluting capacity is needed to bring about a 50 per cent reduction in the pollution associated with the industry (Deutscher Bundestag, 1990). If the aim is to try to preserve as much of industry as possible, whilst moving gradually towards EU environmental standards, substantial reinvestment in new environmentally acceptable technologies will be necessary. This presents an extra cost which will have to be borne by anyone buying existing plants and makes such acquisition more unattractive. When the massive productivity disadvantage associated with Central and Eastern European production, estimated at only 50 per cent of West German productivity, is taken into account there is little incentive to buy up existing plants.

The source of the greatest pollution in Central and Eastern Europe is, of course, industry and we know that industry is at a huge competitive disadvantage compared with its Western counterparts. With low productivity, old machinery and equipment, there is already limited incentives for inward investment. Having to live in poor environmental surroundings is a major disincentive to Western businesses wishing to move into Central and Eastern Europe.

The situation in the East provides a good example of the environment-economy trade-off discussed in Chapter 10. There is a need to make industry more competitive in the East and there is also a need to improve the environment. Achieving the latter objective will mean putting restrictions on firms and forcing them to invest in more expensive environmentally friendly capital equipment and therefore the two objectives conflict. When a decision has to be made as to which objective to prioritise the decision has come down every time in favour of economic development. One strong argument which has been put forward is that only with a developed economy is one able to tackle the environment. Many disagree of course.

The introduction of market forces, international competition and the reduction of state involvement will nevertheless remove the safety net which previously protected business in the East. But the environmental scenario in the longer run (despite the short run social and economic ramifications) may be not be all bad as a result of this. Outdated and inefficient firms which are also the most significant polluters are likely to close first and will automatically improve the quality of the environment. In addition, the power of consumers should not be disregarded. With the large Green movement firmly in place in Eastern Europe, new industries are less likely to be as environmentally damaging. To some extent, it may be ironic that greater economic growth will actually make new investment and environmental protection more feasible in the longer run, even if pollution increases in the short run. On the other hand, experience from the West indicates that environmental protection requires state intervention and the backlash against any type of planning in Central and Eastern Europe may mean that the process is not as rapid as it might otherwise have been.

The transition period may also bring about beneficial environmental effects. In the West, for example, it has been found that one of the major barriers to the adoption of energy efficient technology is a desire to avoid disruption, and that the most promising developmental route is the incorporation of new environmentally friendly technology where changes in the production process are going to happen anyway. An intense period of change therefore holds great potential for environmental improvement although this will be limited by the lack of short term finance and wider economic constraints.

The role of small businesses

The privatisation of the large industrial units may be less significant in the long run than the development of small and medium-sized businesses. This is vital for industrial takeoff. In former East Germany in 1988, there were 3526 industrial enterprises with an average of 900 employees. At the same time there were 47 826 West German enterprises with an average of 190 employees (Handelsblatt, 1990). In 1990 the share of enterprises with less than 800 employees in East Germany was 25 per cent whereas, in the West, it was 68 per cent. Moreover, during the last fifteen years industrial concentration in Central and Eastern Europe has increased whilst in the West it has remained constant. This has been characterised by significant vertical and horizontal integration in the East as opposed to substantial increases in subcontracting and franchising in the West.

A significant small business sector carries an immense potential of making an economy not only prosperous but also distributes that prosperity to a larger segment of a country's population. Moreover, small business tends to be less environmentally damaging. The lack of significant social benefits in Central and Eastern European countries is already driving people into enterprising ways of generating incomes and the abundance of new small businesses to be found in any large town in Central and Eastern Europe is the beginning of the development of an enterprise culture.

Much can be learned from the development of small businesses in Europe and particularly from the work of local authority development agencies in countries such as the UK and Italy. Again there is an apparent contradiction between the creation of a market economy and the need for government (particularly local government) support and planning. In the EU local governments have been successful in creating and supporting business parks, managed workspaces, small business advisers, co-operative support networks, grants and low interest loans. In many cases projects have built upon local resources and skills and where appropriate have been linked to such things as local tourism or the particular ethnic mix of a region. These types of developments are being considered by governments in Eastern Europe and in some regions, are in their early stages of development. However, there is limited availability of finance and venture capital and therefore for a significant development of new business to take place, we return to the need for a financial and legal infrastructure.

Foreign investment in Central and Eastern Europe

Up until the First World War, foreign investment was a very important feature of the economies of the countries in Central and Eastern Europe. Foreign owner assets were an extensive part of the manufacturing sector and over half of mining production. During the First and Second World Wars, the liberal regime that had allowed this to happen was tightened and much foreign owned property was placed under state control. Prior to and during the Second World war the majority of firms still under foreign control were expropriated and assigned to German companies. Eventually, during the nationalisation programme between 1944–1950, control was placed in the hands of the communist governments.

In the 1960s the state control of production remained binding but some communist governments began to see that there might be certain advantages in foreign investment and it began to be accepted that limited investment could help with some of the problems of relative underdevelopment. Most of the inward investment centred around co-production activities however, where control was still held by the state. Towards the end of the 1970s it became clear that these types of arrangements had not brought with them the hoped for technology transfer and associated benefits, and regulations were loosened still further. Even this move did not bring with it significant new investment though because Western companies were still reluctant to invest in countries which they perceived to be politically unstable.

There can be little doubt now that all countries (including Albania) in Central and Eastern Europe are in favour of attracting foreign investment. It is hoped that foreign investment will help to speed up the process of modernisation in industry, improve productivity and increase output. However, these views are based on a number of important premises. One of the most important of these is the anticipation that foreign investment will bring with it new technology and new management methods. The experience to date is that in virtually all cases, the better organisation introduced in factories belonging to foreign firms has led to rapid increases in labour productivity and that the technology transferred (although not perhaps the most up-to-date) has been more modern than those hitherto used. Nevertheless, it can be argued that such technology transfer is a short run palliative and not a long run solution to the problem of technological advance. What economies in the East need for longer term development is their own research and development capabilities and the domestic manufacture of advanced technology.

The countries of Central and Eastern Europe are also banking on foreign investment in helping to improve their balance of payments problems. It is central therefore that foreign investment brings with it the capability for export growth and import substitution. A further bonus of foreign investment is that it creates greater market competition. It provides one effective method of breaking down the old state monopolies although it also runs the risk of foreign firms simply replacing the activities of domestic companies which, because foreign companies are using more efficient labour saving technology, can lead to an increase in net unemployment. Growth in competitiveness is, however, a major factor in forcing down production costs.

The benefits brought by foreign investment should not obscure the fact that there will be less welcome facets to this sort of activity. The governments of all countries confront a key dilemma: if legislation is restrictive, foreign capital will go elsewhere; if it is too liberal, profits will be removed abroad. This gives foreign firms some very strong bargaining power with which to play off different countries looking for new investment. We also see that foreign investment is concentrated in specific locations. Rather than invest in the most underdeveloped parts of the region it is clear that foreign firms prefer to pay somewhat higher wages in order to operate in the most developed and favourably situated locations. This in itself, is leading to Central and Eastern Europe's own core and periphery problem.

For many big Western companies, expansion of their sphere of operations through the establishment of branches in Central and Eastern Europe, is regarded as a key aspect of strategy, often more important than immediate returns on capital. By moving towards the East now, many firms are seeing their investments as lower than they would have to be in the future and as providing them with a first mover advantage as those economies begin to grow significantly. Added to this, the technical advantages which foreign investors bring with them are a source of economies of scale and these, in turn, make for reductions in production costs and increases in income. We have seen, in a number of cases, the transfer of basic and even stood-down products to the East, at low costs.

Another key strategic aim of Western firms is to open up new markets. Changing patterns of demand and more sophisticated tastes are expected over time and foreign investors want to be in the marketplace ready to supply them. One of the means by which foreign investors often create market penetration is through the creation of their own distribution facilities. Many Western firms are buying up retail outlets and making strenuous efforts to build a retailing network, which, apart from the immediate financial advantages, facilitates the marketing of their products.

The prospects for future foreign investment in Central and Eastern Europe depend on a number of factors. To date, Western governments have been very supportive of such investments and have provided help in identifying markets, locations and partners of new investment programmes. Whilst the West continues to see mutual benefits to such developments, investment is likely to remain relatively high. Increasingly though, because of their initial associate membership of the EU the favoured locations are Poland, the Czech Republic, the Slovak Republic and Hungary. Prospects for foreign investment also depend crucially on internal developments in recipient countries. The rapid introduction of social and political mechanisms similar to those in the West will be to the long-term advantage of both countries and foreign proprietors. However, the democratisation process is far from smooth. Disintegration of the communist system should not be equated with a victory for democracy. One of the principal factors in the downfall of communism was the power of nationalist sentiment and we have seen major problems associated with ethnic partitioning, particularly in the former countries of Czechoslovakia and Yugoslavia.

In the economic field we will no doubt see the continuation of systematic change. But the privatisation processes that now enjoys widespread popular support may eventually provoke negative social feedback if they lead to the foreign control of industry. Foreign investment strategies need to bear this in mind.

There is little doubt that in the future the situation in Central and Eastern Europe will continue to evolve in a way which is favourable to foreign investors. This will encourage an increasing flow of new investment into the region and foreign owned enterprise is likely to become the main vehicle for the modernisation process. Economic growth and structural change should therefore proceed with greater momentum so long as political stability can be achieved. Over time we will see Central and Eastern European economies more closely interlocked economically with the EU and the wider world markets which may involve fuller membership of the EU.

EUROPEAN UNION INTEGRATION

As the traditional markets for Central and Eastern European economies have declined so their attention has been focused more heavily on the stronger Western European countries. Table 11.9 shows that during the early stages of the transition process there was a significant switch in trade patterns towards the EU in particular. This switch reinforces the need for Central and Eastern European countries to become more and more integrated with the EU.

Table 11.9. Percentage of total trade accounted for by the European Union

Country	1988	1989	1990	1991	1992
Exports					
Bulgaria	5.8	6.7	10.4	15.7	30.8
Czech and Slovak Republics	24.2	25.7	32.0	40.7	49.5
Hungary	22.5	24.7	34.2	47.6	49.5
Poland	30.3	32.1	46.8	55.6	55.6
Romania	24.0	26.7	31.4	34.2	32.5
Total	22.5	24.5	33.5	44.6	48.2
Imports					
Bulgaria	16.7	16.5	14.8	20.7	32.6
Czech and Slovak Republics	17.7	17.8	32.1	34.3	42.0
Hungary	25.2	28.5	31.5	40.4	42.4
Poland	27.2	33.8	42.5	49.9	53.1
Romania	6.2	6.1	19.6	27.4	37.5
Total	19.2	20.8	27.8	39.5	44.7

Source: United Nations, Commission for Europe, 1993.

Although during the 1970s there were discussions between the EU and Comecon relating to trading agreements and areas of co-operation no formal agreement was ever reached. It seems that the Soviet Union, in particular, often viewed links with the EU as detrimental to its own interests. Nevertheless, bilateral trading links between individual countries did take place, despite the fact that, from 1970, individual EU members were not supposed to enter into agreements without prior consultation with the European Commission. Romania was granted special trading concessions with the EU in 1973 because it was categorised as a developing country.

In 1986 though, the Soviet Union finally recognised the existence of the EU as a trading bloc that could negotiate as a single entity on behalf of its Member States. In 1989, a ten year trade and economic co-operation pact was signed between the EU and the Soviet Union. It meant that EU trade barriers to Soviet exports would be reduced and that collaboration on a range of activities would be permitted, including environmental protection, nuclear power station safety and technology transfer. At the same time the EU dropped its quota restrictions on Poland and Hungary.

Since the reforms in the Eastern Bloc took place, the EU and its Member States have increased the amount of aid going to Eastern Europe. In particular, EU projects such as TEMPUS and the UK know-how fund have been established to pay for training, the transfer of skills and know-how and management development in the East.

Poland, Hungary and former Czechoslovakia were amongst the first countries in the former Comecon alliance to make clear their wish to join the EU. Whilst there is considerable political will to see an expanded EU, the prospects of early entry into the EU are nevertheless remote. Within the EU as presently constituted, there are heavy costs associated with structural adjustment in the economies of the Objective 1 areas, which should make them more compatible, economically, with the rest of the EU. The inclusion of new countries which are even less developed, could simply not be afforded if a similar structural strategy was adopted. In addition, before more countries with a large agricultural sector are included in the EU, it is commonly accepted that significant reform of the Common Agricultural Policy would be needed.

Nevertheless, in the longer term there is a prospect of a EU much increased in size. With the membership of Austria, Sweden and Finland into the EU, as well as some of the East European countries some time in the future, it is easy to envisage an EU of over 20 nations. Indeed, admission of Central and Eastern European countries to the EU has a good number of supporters. Those advocating the widening rather than the deepening of the EU are keen to see the integration process not only include the remaining non-EU countries in the European Economic Area (EEA), but also the less developed countries whose economic development could be accelerated by being part of a wider single market. The idea of extending membership in the first instance to Poland, Hungary and the Czech and Slovak Republics will also have the backing of those who fear dominance of the EU by Germany. There are, however, three major obstacles:

1 fears that too rapid enlargement of the EU could weaken its cohesion and make it too cumbersome to function efficiently;
2 fears that the costs of integrating countries in Eastern and Central Europe would be prohibitively expensive if the same sort of regional policy operating via structural funds was to be continued;
3 a view that the EU should deepen its integration process first before any new (relatively poor) members are admitted, leading to the barriers to entry being greater in the long run.

Because of these problems we are unlikely to see a full membership package agreed for a number of years. But there is likely to be growing support for an arrangement of an interim nature. Some sort of new status somewhere between associate membership and full membership might be constructed where Central and Eastern European countries have some, but not all, of the rights and practise a degree of economic co-ordination which stops well short of monetary union. Countries in this category would not be entitled to grants on normal terms from the agricultural and structural funds, but this might be offset by smaller contributions to the EU budget and being allowed to maintain some import restrictions. For foreign investors there would be the manifold benefits of the consequent institutional linkages with the EU and the direct gains to be reaped in the sphere of production as a result of easier exports to the West. The advantages associated with the cheapness of labour in the East would manifest themselves in full, leading to more employment and output opportunities.

An indispensable condition for the continued inflow of foreign investment into Central and Eastern Europe is the creation of a favourable business infrastructure through the introduction of appropriate laws and regulations. Current legislation and fiscal arrangements are increasingly mimicking Community legislation, and membership (in some form) of the EU would further increase certainty in this area. On the other hand, close integration of economic policies with the EU (which may be required for a fuller membership arrangement) may not always be favourable to Central and Eastern economies, since these policies are increasingly centred around tight monetary and fiscal policies which might be less compatible with the rapid growth strategies which the region desires.

In October 1991, Jacques Delors called on the EU to prepare for an EU of 24, or even 30, members. His answer to the collapse of the economic system in Eastern Europe and the growing demand from EFTA countries for EU membership was to devise a system of so-called *concentric circles* with the present EU membership at the centre, the EFTA countries in the second ring and Central and Eastern Europe in the outer ring. Those circles were to be linked with association agreements. These ranged from the agreement on the EEA for the EFTA countries (*see* Chapter 3) to the co-operation agreements signed with Poland, the Czech and Slovak Republics, Romania, Hungary and Bulgaria. The first stage of integration was well under way in 1995 as Sweden, Austria and Finland eventually joined the EU.

The association agreements

The association agreements, initially negotiated between the EU and Poland, former Czechoslovakia and Hungary in 1991, build on the bilateral trade and economic co-operation agreements that the EU had struck with a number of Central and Eastern European countries in the latter 1980s. Although the association agreements which have now been extended to Bulgaria and Romania (with plans for agreements with the Baltic states), do not guarantee automatic entry into the EU some time in the future, they do implicity lay out a model of development which sees the development of trade in and with the East as a prerequisite to a wider EU. Before full entry into the EU is considered though, the EU is keen to see a 'little sister' relationship develop, whereby the Central and Eastern European economies develop in tandem with each other, creating their own internal markets which, in time, would allow them to enter into an EEA agreement. This would mirror the development of the EFTA countries leading up to ultimate EU membership.

The initial three association agreements negotiated were essentially the same document. Whilst this reflected the EU's wish to act equally between Poland, former Czechoslovakia and Hungary and to emphasise the need for the countries to develop together, it also indicated that the EU was viewing this bloc as a single economic entity. Not surprisingly, this did not please countries such as Hungary which saw themselves as better prepared for EU entry and more economically developed than their neighbours.

The association agreements cover a ten year transition to mutual free trade. They provide a basis on which trade can be expanded from its very low basis. However, the EU may not have been as generous as the Central and Eastern European countries may have wished. There is no timetable for EU membership in the agreements and there is no written commitment to provide particular levels of aid and investment funds. The EU is keen to make it clear that it cannot afford the sort of integration costs which Poland, the Czech and Slovak Republics and Hungary require. In addition, the agreements do place some limits on three sectors of production which are important to the East, namely, steel, textiles and agriculture and although these will be relaxed over time, they do suggest that the EU is more of a fortress than it will openly admit.

The need for new investment and the role of the European Union

There is little doubt that the new democracies of Central and Eastern Europe are still struggling to develop mature political systems and stable banking and commercial frameworks. Privatisation has not been easy but in most countries is now progressing well and investment continues to be drawn into the countries (although perhaps at a slower rate than one once might have imagined). Nevertheless some countries such as Romania are still suffering from political uncertainty, which in turn, discourages the new investment so much needed. The events which have occurred in the Yugoslav Republics simply remind us that there are still ethnic tensions which in many cases exploded after the grip of communism was released.

The view of the EU has been that the way in which to enforce and encourage democracy in the East lies in creating certainty and development through economic and financial instruments. The Rome Summit of December 1990 approved the establishment of the European Bank for Reconstruction and Development (EBRD) to assist economic recovery in East Europe. The EBRD draws on £7 billion of capital from 41 countries and provides financing for a combination of investments in new infrastructure and private investment in Eastern Europe.

In 1992, the EBRD board approved 54 investment projects in the year with a total contribution from the EBRD of Ecu 1.2 billion. However, only Ecu 126 million was disbursed as loans and equity injections. The bulk of approved EBRD projects have, to date, not surprisingly, been in the Czech Republic, Hungary and Poland. Up to the end of 1992, private investors had put $7 billion into these three states, but little elsewhere in the other 22 countries in which the EBRD operates.

Rapid changes in the make up of countries such as Poland is making the job of the EBRD easier, for example, in that country private sector enterprise already accounts for well over 50 per cent of GDP and it is, therefore, easier both to find matching funding and eligible projects for EBRD support. However, up until now financing arrangements with the existing international organisations, banks and agencies have dominated and there have been few projects which have lent money to fledgling local entrepreneurs directly. But, given the EBRD cost structure and organisation, it is not able to make profitable loans of under Ecu 5 million and this cuts out a number of locally based investment projects.

The EBRD's initial emphasis on co-financing western projects and on financing numerous technical studies may have done less for the countries of Central and Eastern Europe than we might have hoped was possible from the EBRD. A more innovative approach, and a less bureaucratic style, within the organisation is needed if it is to accomplish its primary aim of helping to foster local private initiatives. The typical sort of deal which the EBRD has supported to date has been like that of the Ecu 102 million contribution to Volkswagen's Ecu 3 490 million investment in Skoda in the Czech Republic. It was hardly risky or innovative and could easily have been served by traditional commercial banks. This lack of risk taking and forward looking innovation has been the main criticism of the EBRD to date.

DOING BUSINESS IN CENTRAL AND EASTERN EUROPE

The underdeveloped economic and physical infrastructure, the lack of management skills, the underdeveloped market mechanism, low levels of national income and problems associated with currency convertibility in Central and Eastern Europe all mean that traditional methods of doing business which are common in the EU are often not transferrable to the East. This section therefore reviews methods of doing business in that region which are particular to the situation to be found there. Although many of these methods are used outside Central and Eastern Europe as well, they are particularly appealing to both governments and firms.

Joint venture agreements

Joint venture agreements have existed in some Central and Eastern European countries for a considerable length of time but were always limited to the Western firm having a shareholding of not more than 49 per cent in the enterprise, with the exception of Hungary where, since 1977, foreign firms have been allowed to have majority shareholdings. Traditionally, the Western partners' contribution has been in the form of cash, production licences, manufacturing know-how, machinery and components and Eastern partners have contributed land, buildings and equipment. As the transition of Central and Eastern Europe continues, many more sophisticated joint ventures are occurring. Governments in the region have been actively encouraging joint venture activity as a means of averting unemployment, gaining inward investment and technology transfer and in order to sell part stakes of conglomerate firms, aiding the privatisation process.

The most important consideration in a joint venture is the selection of a partner. Sharing management is difficult, so careful consideration has to be given to finding a partner that has complementary skills or resources. Often joint ventures are categorised into three categories dependent on management style:

1 *Shared management* – the specific joint venture is managed jointly by both parent companies on an agreed basis.
2 *Dominant management by one partner* – one parent company takes over responsibility for the management of the whole joint venture (this has been common in Central and Eastern Europe).
3 *Independent management from either partner* – a separate devolved management structure is set up with day to day autonomy, responsible solely for the running of the joint venture.

Killing (1982) found that independent management outperformed the others and shared management had the poorest performance. This suggests a positive relationship in a joint venture framework between performance and devolved, independent management. It is understandable that in the early history of joint ventures in Central and Eastern Europe, dominant management from the West has been common, but with the development of management skills in the East, the aim should be towards the adoption of independent management.

Compensation trading

Compensation trading has always existed between West and East under the titles counter-trading, parallel deals, linked deals, reciprocal trading or barter trading. In the main, compensation deals exist when the Western supplier agrees to accept at least part of the payment for goods supplied in terms of Eastern goods. Counter purchase and buy back arrangements are also common where Western equipment is sold to the East to establish a plant and as part of the contract a percentage of the goods produced by the new plant are bought back by the equipment supplier.

There are obvious advantages of compensation trading on both sides of the agreement. For the Western firm, the contract may be lost if compensation trading is not considered. For the Central or Eastern European firm, it provides them with one outlet for their products and alleviates some of the need to find hard currency for their transactions. However, Western firms have to be careful not to be left with goods that they cannot resell or which require a significant amount of marketing expenditure to sell.

Selling know-how

There is a great need to develop expertise and use new technology in Central and Eastern European countries. Many firms in the East are keen to buy know-how from the West. Often this know-how will be in the form of licences to use a particular production process, item of technology or particular branded product. The licence will be paid for in a number of ways, varying from a lump-sum to some kind of sliding scale or royalty, with a preference in the East for the latter.

Technical co-operation agreements

A typical industrial co-operation agreement involves some type of co-production and the exchange of know-how, raw materials and components between Eastern and Western partners. There may be an element of joint assembly or the supply of semi-finished products to be finished in a different country, perhaps close to the market. The advantages claimed for such arrangements are economies of scale, the ability of Western manufacturers to produce at lower costs (particularly on the wages front), technology transfer to the East, and the ability of Central or Eastern European firms to gain expertise.

Some of the most successful co-operation agreements have been in the field of automobiles. This is partly because the product can be broken down into component parts and the production of semi-finished goods and separate assembly plants is common. The best known examples include the agreement between Hungary and Volvo (Sweden) to assemble the Lapplander cross country vehicle and the agreement between Romania and Renault (France) to manufacture a car under licence using a mixture of French and Romanian components.

STRATEGIES FOR CENTRAL OR EASTERN EUROPEAN FIRMS EXPORTING TO THE EUROPEAN UNION

Given the transitory nature of the Central and Eastern European economies and a relative lack of investment funds, at least in the short run, it is useful to consider what strategies are open to developing firms wishing to sell into the biggest market in the world – Europe. Only by competing on a European-wide scale are such firms likely to be able to survive and grow in the long run and in turn generate the much needed wealth in the East.

We saw in chapter 7 that marketing is related to the identification of consumer needs and wants and the delivery of products and services with the best strategic fit to satisfy such customer demands. Successful strategies are those which provide this 'fit' more efficiently and effectively than competitors. Their development depends on careful management of controllable variables within the marketing mix – products, prices, distribution and promotion.

The challenge for Central or Eastern European firms is to produce products using appropriate technology and to manipulate marketing mix variables to provide a match between their products and consumer demands in areas of market opportunity in various EU markets.

Product policies

Despite the fact that some commentators argue that there is a trend towards commonality in needs and wants on a global scale, there still exists a diverse array of cultures which demand strategic planning on a country-by-country (and even region-by-region) basis. Sensitivity to local markets and product adaptation will, therefore, be a key strategic objective for Central or Eastern European firms planning to do business in the EU.

Since adaptation impacts on production, there would seem to be a need for short production runs and flexibility in manufacturing. For many large multinational corporations with dedicated mass-production capital equipment, such flexibility can be hard to achieve. This gives rise to opportunities for small and medium-sized firms prepared to invest in new technologies to support a flexible (yet often specialised) approach. This is likely to include computer aided design [CAD] and computer aided manufacture [CAM]. The concept of flexible specialisation, as discussed in Chapter 6, thus replaces scale economies as the main drive behind producing competitive products. This does not imply less efficient resource use, since with careful planning and the adoption of appropriate technology, economies of scale can be replaced with economies of scope, that is, economies associated with multi-product production.

It is clearly not possible for most developing firms to invest in costly CAD and CAM due to their limited resources, but this is not the only way in which flexible specialisation can be achieved. Given relatively low wage costs in Central and Eastern Europe, it should be possible to achieve a degree of batch specialisation in the production of less technologically sophisticated products.

Adaptation and specialisation may not, however, always be essential. Central or Eastern European firms may also do well by trading on the cultural characteristic of their products. Many consumers in Western Europe are attracted by ethnicity. This is particularly true amongst the middle classes where spending power is at its greatest, for example, Polish and Russian vodka is being treated with much interest as it finds its way onto Western markets.

It must be recognised, however, that the *ethnicity dividend* will not exist for all products. In the area of high technology products a 'made in Poland' label, for example, may not be quite so attractive.

Alternatively, there may be scope for mass production in basic commodity-intensive type products. Combined with low wage costs, firms can exploit low-cost inputs and achieve low pricing strategies in EU markets. In this area competition is likely to be fierce but Central or Eastern European firms do start with some comparative advantage because of their lower production costs, largely resulting from lower wage levels.

Pricing policies

Most companies use different prices in different markets reflecting not only different market conditions (taxes, tariffs, price controls) but also differences in marketing strategy. As policies associated with the Single European Market begin to take effect, it is likely that prices will harmonise to prevent arbitrage, as organisations shop around the EU for the cheapest deals. Such harmonisation is likely to be at the lower end of the price scale, where differentiation and brand loyalty are harder to achieve, increasing demands on production efficiency.

At the low technology, basic commodity end of the market, the key element in buyer behaviour is price. Customers accept that they are trading-off added-value (quality, technological sophistication and service) for a low price purchase. Such positioning also reduces the need for large advertising budgets to establish highly differentiated products. Since Central or Eastern European firms, with their limited resources, will find it difficult to find large promotional budgets, they need to differentiate their marketing strategy by placing heavy reliance on price competition.

Aggressive price competition places further emphasis on production efficiency and cost minimisation for firms in order to protect margins. For firms to be competitive in the long run, they need to earn sufficient profits to provide resources for reinvestment in research and development and production technology, and achieve a sufficient volume of sales in order to remain competitive and sustain their position in the market.

A possible problem associated with low-pricing strategies emerges with possible adverse competitive reaction. Increased sales effort by other low priced producers – particularly large firms who can subsidise such effort from more profitable products in a diversified portfolio (the character of many developed Western firms), should make Central or Eastern European firms wary of entering markets dominated by such powerful firms or, if they do so, of pricing below competitive market rates.

Alternatively, for products with a high level of ethnicity or similar specialisation, firms may be able to charge higher prices as the ethnicity factor itself adds perceived value to the product. This will depend, to some extent, on the product's image, supported by appropriate packaging and promotional activities. Entering markets with relatively low prices will permit firms to establish a significant market share, but in the longer run firms may wish to raise prices and test the upper-limits of the price scale as products gain acceptance.

Distribution policies

The choice of marketing channel for distribution of goods abroad is critically dependent on the foreign market servicing decision employed to enter international markets. That is, whether the firm decides to export, license or invest in production overseas. Given available investment capital for Central or Eastern European firms, certain options may be ruled out. Foreign direct investment (FDI) in wholly-owned production facilities, requiring major capital outlay is not feasible. However, this does not rule out FDI altogether. It could be possible for firms to enter into a joint venture by acquiring a minority equity stake in a European manufacturing firm.

Whilst joint ventures offer a number of advantages, not least entering the EU with relatively low outlay and gaining much knowledge of the market through the experience of the partner, they depend on each party offering the other something which would be difficult for them to do themselves. Clearly a foreign partner can offer market access and knowledge to the Central or Eastern European firm, but given the low-technology factor of potential products, that firm may lack the necessary complementary benefits, restricting this option to products which are culturally attractive.

Similar arguments can be levelled against licensing. Licensing involves the sale of knowledge (usually technology based) to a foreign manufacturer lacking the technical expertise and financial resources to produce the product itself. Patent protection of products restricts access to the option of simply copying the product. Consequently, licensing tends to be associated with the manufacture of high technology goods and provides little room for exploitation by small manufacturers without significant financial resources.

Much emphasis is thus placed on exporting strategies and associated marketing channel structures. There are three basic marketing channel types available to firms:

1 traditional marketing channels, which involve employing the services of indigenous market intermediaries (wholesalers/distributors, sales agents and retailers);
2 vertically integrated channels, wherein the manufacturer internalises the stockholding, distribution, selling and information gathering functions, and less commonly, retail operations; and
3 horizontally integrated channels, which involve the setting up and management of distribution channels by a number of producers.

Each alternative displays a very different cost structure. Vertical and horizontal integration involves capital outlay in the form of set-up costs and requires on-going management outlay. Again, given the limited financial resources of Central or East European organisations it is unlikely that such investment will be possible in the short term.

Moreover, operating via market intermediaries has the added benefit of providing a good source of market research information and experience of the market, which in the early stages of international expansion is critical for developing marketing strategies. Over time, through gradual expansion, increased profitability and market share, firms may wish to dedicate more resources to their exporting effort, internalising critical functions, particularly locally based sales and marketing activities. The major benefits of internalisation stem from the greater ease with which information flows within an organisation (as opposed to between firms) and the positive impact this has on flexibility, rapid reaction to changes in the market and the increased control over the activities performed.

Promotion policies

Central or Eastern European firms lack detailed knowledge of European markets and are likely to seek the help of intermediaries who process that knowledge. Where manufacturers employ the services of indigenous intermediaries they may need to target four different sets of promotional literature:

(a) information directed at wholesalers aimed at persuading them to stock their product;
(b) information for wholesalers' sales agents to use to sell to retailers;
(c) promotional literature for retail outlets designed to persuade consumers to buy at the point of purchase; and
(d) direct advertising to end users to generate demand.

The key benefit of using an intermediary is that manufacturers can pass on the responsibility for wholesalers' sales agents' literature, and that designed for sales support in retail outlets to the wholesaler.

Although in low-technology sectors firms may wish to play-down the country of origin of their products, with products with a high cultural character the promotion of Central and Eastern European goods may be as much about emphasising the 'made in Poland' or 'made in Hungary' labels as anything else. It is in this area that there is a role for government in promoting their countries and in facilitating general trade fairs, and perhaps even subsidising generic country-specific advertising in the Western Press, which is likely to be prohibitively expensive for all but the largest firms. We might term this sort of approach, macro-marketing and it does seem indispensable for the success of Central and Eastern European reforms.

Another powerful tool for promotional activities is to sell to and use the business contacts of the large Central and Eastern European expatriate communities which exist throughout Europe and North America. Market networking of this kind may be critical in creating relationships with intermediaries and also, through goodwill, may be a way of establishing joint ventures and strategic alliances in the EU.

There are clearly opportunities for developing East European firms to expand into the EU. Although the available strategies may be more limited for firms due to the associated problems of shrugging off inefficiencies, which are a by-product of an era of central planning, careful management of the various marketing mix elements and an openness to take on board the best of Western production techniques and management styles, where these are implementable and appropriate, gives scope for European expansion. If attention is paid to the production of products which are responsive to changes in consumer demand across Europe by adopting the principles of flexible specialisation, Central or Eastern European firms may well find that they are not at a significant comparative disadvantage compared with their Western counterparts.

The early stages of developing marketing strategies for EU markets relies on a commitment to listening and learning. First, listening to firms in the market, particularly intermediaries whose services Central and Eastern European firms will undoubtedly look to in the short term, and, second, learning about cultures and consumer demands in an attempt to manipulate market mix variables to the best effect, are the immediate challenges ahead.

The Single European market will be both large and growing but at the same time dynamic and sophisticated. Many cultural differences and differentiated tastes will remain and indeed as incomes rise, so too will demand for non-standardised products. In both the production of goods and in the marketing strategies adopted, the most successful Central and Eastern European firms are likely to be those who adhere to the principles of flexible specialisation.

CONCLUSION

Central and Eastern European industry has been and in most areas still is, uncompetitive and unproductive. The East has a well trained flexible workforce, and growing links and integration with the EU will provide, in itself, a major boost to growth. However, as much as two-thirds of Central and Eastern European industry is under severe strain during the transitional period and rationalisation is causing high levels of unemployment. Moreover, in the short term at least, with increased domestic spending power and the development of the market mechanism, both inflation and unemployment are likely to provide problems. Despite the highly trained workforce, challenges include the need to retrain workers and managers and to provide both a physical and professional infrastructure capable of dealing with a market mechanism.

In the past, most of Central and Eastern European trade has been with its fellow Comecon members and particularly with the Soviet Union. The region will remain an important market but its relative significance will fall because of the Soviet Union's own problems. Export efforts must therefore be shifted towards the West, but this will mean a heightened need for industrial restructuring and the development of support networks and effective distribution systems in those countries. Joint ventures to aid technology transfer are clearly a positive way forward for the development of a new manufacturing industry.

Questions for discussion

1 Why are Western businesses getting involved in business arrangements in Central and Eastern Europe despite the underdeveloped nature of their economies?

2 Outline the basic requirements for the successful transition of a centrally-planned economy into a market economy.

3 Explain the close link between the control of inflation and currency convertibility.

4 Outline what you would expect to be the pattern of unemployment in Central and Eastern European countries over the next few years.

5 Is there a straightforward trade-off between environmental protection and economic development in the East?

6 Why is the development of a small business sector important in Central and Eastern Europe?

7 How might methods of doing business differ in Central and Eastern Europe to those in the European Union. What are the reasons for these differences?

8 Outline the strategies available to Central and Eastern European firms wishing to export to the West.

CASE STUDY

Economic development and environmental performance in Hungary

This case study has been adapted from: 'Economic development and environmental performance in Hungary', Sandor Kerekes and Richard Welford, *European Environment*, 3, 2, 1993.

The Central and Eastern European region is living through a period with no parallel in history up to now. Many specialists from around the world are offering advice and guidance with a view to a rapid transition to a market economy. Such a rapid transformation does have a number of advantages but if we look carefully at the political, social and environmental ramifications of such a transformation we would argue that there is a need for a slower gradualist approach advocated by Kindler (1992) and Van Zon (1992). Here, we attempt to prove the necessity of a gradual transition, taking into account achievable economic development and the interests of environmental protection.

Those recommending fast progress, the so-called shock therapy or quick fix approach, generally underestimate the significance of the small income-generating capacity of the region's economies and its parallel, small income-accumulating capability, which is especially apparent when we take into account the burdens originating from indebtedness.

There will also be growing political tensions arising out of the quick fix approach. Rapid economic development is only possible if the conditions for fast technological transfer are created. But, because of low income levels and a very low modern capital base, rapid forms of technological transfer can operate only through foreign investments which also bring with them social tensions. Moreover, with the world recession, it is increasingly apparent that the initial euphoria directed towards the East has been short lived.

In comparison with the other Central and Eastern European countries, Hungary is in a relatively advantageous position being much further down the line towards the market economy with foreign confidence relatively high. The practical failure of the reforms of 1968 have led to a re-examination of economic thinking and this has provided favourable conditions for privatisation and foreign market entry. Hungarian managers are familiar enough with Western management methods to be able to adapt them right away, and this is helped by a culture which is much more liberal, tolerant and adaptable than in the neighbouring countries. Another advantage which Hungary has over its neighbours is that the establishment of the institutional system necessary for the operation of the market economy (the banking system, stock exchange etc.), began some time ago and is now relatively well developed. Budapest is fast becoming the financial centre of the region with significant inward investment from the EU, USA and Japan.

The environmental challenge

In 1993, the impact of the world recession on Hungary was compounded by the instability of the neighbouring countries and the virtual economic collapse of the former Soviet Union. But in spite of unfavourable conditions and the initial failures, there are increased expectations that the current developmental path will work and these expectations themselves encourage the acceptance of the market economy amongst the population and an increased willingness for foreign companies in to invest in the region. Of course, these expectations have their environmental risks. First, the greater probability of a successful transition to a market economy in comparison to the other countries of the region, could lead to a temptation to follow the Western consumer model above all others. We know that this model is unsustainable and environmentally damaging. To some, those sorts of levels of consumption may seem unachievable, but the population does aspire towards Western consumption patterns and high levels of energy and raw materials consumption needs to be avoided. We need therefore to avoid a development path which would put huge pressure on already inefficient energy production. Second, these expectations are naively short term and the government's response is increasingly short termist, trying, understandably, to rectify problems such as growing unemployment. Longer-term thinking and strategic planning consistent with sustainable development have perceptibly fallen into the background and there is a need to rectify that situation.

The economic situation therefore encourages many of Hungary's policy makers to take the view that there is no possibility or need for anything other than the management of current problems (the debt crisis, unemployment, inflation etc.) and if these variables can be controlled then the market will solve structural problems as well. However, we know from the experiences of the market-driven UK economy of the 1980s, that such expectations overestimate the power and flexibility of the market and in particular continue to treat the environment as a free good unless the *polluter pays* principle can be forcefully applied.

We would argue that what is not being given enough emphasis are the longer term problems such as improving the environmental performance of industry, the question of utilisation of natural resources and the problems of environmental protection and nature conservation. Undoubtedly, urgent action is required in the area of environmental management for two reasons. First, the transformation offers an excellent opportunity to achieve environmental aims at the lowest cost, with many of the most polluting industries closing in the competitive marketplace. Second, a growing number of new enterprises are appearing in the developing open economy. It would seem timely to introduce environmental measures which these firms can adapt to at the outset. Without this sort of initiative it will be very difficult to estimate and control the environmental effects of these small and medium-sized enterprises.

Environmental protection

A common way of assessing the degree of environmental protection in an economy is the measurement of environmental protection investment in an economy as a share of GDP. Given the traditional structure of the Hungarian economy we should expect this figure to be relatively high, if protection were at the same level as we find in Western Europe, for example. We know that in heavily polluting branches such as mining, metallurgy and the chemical industry, environmental protection investments have been significant (although at lower levels than in the West). However, in high earning branches such as tourism and the retail sector, environmental investments are virtually non-existent. However, now there is a real danger that the heavily polluting branches will simply not be able to keep up with their environmental investment and environmental protection in what is the crisis sector for the environment. Because of social tensions it is also increasingly likely that more of a blind eye will be turned on such industry in order to improve its chances of existence. Like the rest of the world it is environmental protection investments in the water industry which dominate. However, these too may be threatened.

Because of the transitional nature of the Hungarian economy, use of the important *polluter pays principle* runs into difficulties not only from the bankrupt branches but also from those sectors which are top of the list for privatisation. Pollution taxes and controls are too often seen as an impediment to the sales of assets to the private sector. In addition, the question as to whether new private owners should have to pay the costs of pollution created in the past, or whether the state should take on this burden (which it cannot) is still unresolved and continues to add more uncertainty to the move towards the market economy. The dominant ideology at the moment is therefore one of do nothing, pushing environmental considerations further down the country's agenda.

The environmental impact of foreign trade

The success of transition depends to a large part on the Hungarian economy's productive capacity. Hungary's greater political stability compared with the surrounding countries, is largely thanks to the relatively positive achievements of the economy. The role of foreign investment is vital to the continued transformation of the economy through vital technology transfer. However, such foreign investment has been significantly lower than that hoped for and it is a characteristic of all the East European economies that foreign investment has actually been quite sluggish. There is still a fear of economic colonialisation bringing with it not the best technology, but industry more associated with environmental damage than environmental improvement, as environmental protection tightens in the West (Kaderjak and Lehoczki, 1991).

However, to date new investment has not been dominated by investment in the most polluting branches. Indeed, the bulk of new investment has been in retail and other service sectors which are generally accepted as less environmentally damaging. Nevertheless, one has also to be wary about assuming that much of the foreign investment in sectors which are not regarded as heavily polluting are in fact environmentally friendly. In the tourism sector, for example, we are increasingly aware of the environmental damage done through increased energy and water consumption and the generally harmful effects of the vast number of tourists now entering the country and particularly, Budapest.

The future of Hungarian environmental policy

What the government can achieve is clearly limited by the Hungarian economy's indebtedness, increasing unemployment and loss of markets. With falls in GDP the government is further hampered by a decreasing budget with which to invest in environmental improvements and in any case these are of a lower priority than issues such as privatisation. For environmental protection to be a success, it also requires the support of enterprises and society as a whole and again we would point to other priorities.

Such phenomena are typical of any underdeveloped region. Too often the quality of the environment only becomes important when a threshold material quality of life is attained. In Hungary, due to deteriorating living conditions, the significance of the environment and even of people's own health is driven into the background compared with consumption. To challenge the implicit societal resistance which this implies, it is important to challenge the view that environmental protection is first and foremost a financial question. A pre-condition of successful environmental policy is the creation of strong societal support.

In addition, because of the transformation of the Hungarian economy, future environmental policy will have to be based largely on decentralised instruments. This will be aided if people actually adopt a 'not in my backyard' approach which is so commonly derided elsewhere. A municipal approach will therefore be more successful than directives from central government. Indeed this approach is occurring in Hungary with local government taking over more responsibility for planning. Hopefully, this will lead to a more rational use of resources and the achievement of a greater consensus between the public and producers. There is still a role for central government, however, in putting in place an institutional system to protect the public interest.

Finally, we must recognise that environmental and technological risk is of a fundamentally different nature to that existing in the West. Therefore, the sort of environmental policies adopted in the West may not be applicable in Hungary in the short run. Poor living conditions and not environmental damage constitute the most serious risk to human health in Hungary at present. Whilst Western economies have had the luxury of embarking on environmental policies within a framework of democracy, a functioning market economy and an up-to-date technological infrastructure, this is not the case in Central and Eastern Europe. Nevertheless, the environment does matter in countries such as Hungary and whilst the ideas and principles of sustainable development remain the same, their implementation will have to be different. However, it is our assertion that effective environmental protection measures are simply not consistent with the quick fix approach. Such an approach will continue to sideline environmental issues. A gradualist strategic approach needs to be developed with the co-operation of the population, if we are to begin to deal with the environmental problems of the region.

Case Study Questions

1 Do you agree that a gradualist approach to economic development in Hungary is superior to a 'quick fix' approach?

2 Do you agree with the contention that the Western-style consumer model is unsustainable?

3 Why are Western-style environmental policies not necessarily appropriate to Central and Eastern European economies?

4 Outline the environmental impacts of foreign investment in Hungary.

5 Outline the apparent conflict between the *polluter pays principle* and the wish for a speedy privatisation process.

6 If you were a Hungarian policy maker, what priority would you give to environmental issues compared with other areas of policy?

FURTHER READING

Howell, J. (1994) *Understanding Eastern Europe: The Context of Change*, Ernst & Young and Kogan Page. This text provides a broad overview of the changes taking place in Eastern Europe and their implications for business including an assessment of the relative attractiveness of different Central and Eastern European countries.

Dobosiewicz, Z. *Foreign Investment in Eastern Europe*, Routledge. This text contains a discussion of foreign investment strategies in Eastern Europe.

REFERENCES

Deutsche Bank, 'Volkswirtschaftliche Abteilung', *DDR-Special*, January, 1990.

Deutscher Bundestag, 'Die Energieversorgung in der DDR', *Info-Brief*, February, 1990.

European Parliament, *The Impact of German Reunification on the European Community*, Research and Documentation Paper, 1990.

GDR Ministry for Environmental Protection, *Konzeption für die Entwicklung der Umweltpolitik*, Berlin, 1990.

Handelsblatt, *Die Deutsche Wirtschaftsgemeinschaft*, March, 1990.

Kaderjak, P. and Lehoczki, Z. S., *Economic Transition and Environmental Protection: Foreign Investment and the Environment in Hungary*, Budapest University of Economics, Department of Business Economics Working Paper, 1991/5.

Killing, P. J., 'How to Make a Global Joint Venture Work', *Harvard Business Review*, 120–127, 1982.

Kindler, J. et al, *A Study of the Environmental Protection Bill from an Economic Viewpoint*, Regional Environmental Centre for Central and Eastern Europe, Budapest, 1992.

Van Zon, H., *Alternative Scenarios for Eastern Europe*, Commission for the European Communities, Science Research and Development, Forecasting and Assessment in Science and Technology, FOP 226, 1992.

Wharton Economic Forecasting Associates, 'Die Wirtschaftslage in der DDR', *Trend*, March, 1990.

CHAPTER 12

Europe in the World Economy

INTRODUCTION

As the European Single Market develops into an economic reality it is inevitable that this will impact on the world economic order. Although Europe was, for many years, a loose affiliation of countries belonging to the European Community and the European Free Trade Association (EFTA), nothing compares with the coherence which '1992' and the Single European Act have begun to initiate and the emergence of a new *European Union*. The wider market which the EU has now become, although not fully exploited by all firms to date, offers new potential for European companies to expand and raise their stature on a global scale.

For many years the fragmented nature of Europe – consisting of a number of relatively small, highly distinct national markets – was believed to be one of the major causes of poor competitiveness of European firms. The barriers to operating on a pan-European scale, restricting firms to domestic market operations hampered the development of large firms and the realisation of economies of scale. With the removal of barriers the scope for expanding across Europe has heightened, and with it comes the new hope that EU firms will develop their capabilities and secure their position as leading multinational enterprises.

The potential for European firms to strengthen their standing in international markets poses a threat to multinationals around the world. Japan and the USA, two of the world's major trading blocs, originally saw the creation of a unified Europe as the throwing down of the gauntlet by the European Commission heralding the start of major competitive warfare. Policies for restricting competition from outside the EU in the early round of developing the internal market were also regarded as the foundations of a 'Fortress Europe' which threatened to engender anti-competitive reactions from the Japanese and Americans.

The realisation by the Commission (encouraged by anti-protectionist Member State governments) that shielding Europe from the rest of the world would be damaging in terms of a new global order of business activity, resulted in a relaxation of external competition policy. Europe has, therefore, come to look less like a fortress and more like a rejuvenated trading area ready to take a more active role as the third leg in the world triad of economic power next to the USA and the Far East.

The trend towards unification is similarly dominating economic issues in other areas of the world. The North American Free Trade Agreement, uniting the USA, Canada and Mexico, is designed to facilitate free trade between the countries and promote economic activity and efficiency across the American continent. Greater co-operation between countries in the Asia-Pacific regions (including Japan, Australia, Hong Kong, Singapore, Korea and Malaysia) is also signalling greater coherence among the countries comprising one of the key areas in the new world order. The implications of these trends on global economic activity and thus the future success of European firms is central to understanding the long-term implications of economic union.

ECONOMIC UNION AND THE EMERGENCE OF A GLOBAL TRIAD

Free trade and the benefits of economic groupings

After the Second World War the benefits of free trade took on greater significance as many countries, keen to promote more global co-operation after such a protracted period of unrest, fostered the development of multilateral organisations to promote freer movement of goods on an international scale. The General Agreement on Tariffs and Trade (GATT) was formed in 1947 as a means of promoting the expansion of international trade through tariff reductions and the elimination of quotas and other non-tariff barriers. GATT operates in two ways:

1 on the basis of reciprocity. Negotiating lower tariffs for countries' exports in exchange for a lowering of domestic tariffs;
2 through 'the most favoured nation rule' – which dictates that countries should apply their lowest tariff to all importers.

To date, GATT has organised eleven multilateral rounds of tariff negotiations for manufactured goods, and in the last round, extended its concerns to international trade in services. This helped to foster rapid expansion in world trade which reached a peak in the late 1960s. Since the oil crises of the 1970s and through the more recent world recession, the emergence of new protectionism, particularly non-tariff barriers such as anti-dumping legislation, voluntary export restraints, import licensing, government subsidies and reciprocity arrangements, has undermined the power of GATT to the extent that its role as an international force for trade promotion has recently come into question.

The International Monetary Fund (IMF) was established alongside GATT in 1947 to facilitate the promotion of international trade by encouraging members to set 'orderly' exchange rates and avoid the use of foreign exchange controls and other monetary restrictions which limit the availability of currencies to finance trade and investment.

The United Nations Conference on Trade and Development (UNCTAD) was established in 1965 to support the economic interests of the less developed countries. Its work centres on three key concerns:

1 market access for manufactured goods. These concessions are in addition to those granted by GATT and are specifically designed to ensure that less developed countries do not lose out as the major world powers increase their global dominance;
2 controlling world prices of commodities through the extension of International Commodity Agreements to stabilise less developed countries' foreign exchange earnings as well as producers' incomes;
3 the need for financial assistance and technology transfer from the developed world.

Despite the attempts made by UNCTAD, however, to promote international trade in the less developed world, their plans have been thwarted through lack of co-operation from the developed countries.

At a regional level, the promotion of free trade centres on the creation of economic unions. These unions can be classified according to the degree of economic integration they support.

Free trade area

A group of countries that agrees to removal all trade barriers – tariffs, quotas and non-tariff barriers – is known as a *free trade area*. Each country retains discretion in establishing trade barriers with non-members. Examples of free trade areas include EFTA (European Free Trade Association), LAIA (Latin American Integration Association) and ASEAN (Association of South East Asian Nations).

Customs union

As well as adhering to the removal of all trade barriers, customs unions have a common external policy on international trade with non-members. Examples include the Central African Customs and Economic Union, and the East African Customs Union.

Common market

Common markets are those which, along with the removal of trade barriers and the adoption of a common external policy, also remove all restrictions on competition between countries. Therefore, foreign establishment and free movement of people, capital and equipment are all central elements. The EC, at the end of 1992, provided an example of an integrated group of countries with common market policies and principles. Other examples include the Arab Common Market.

Economic union

An economic union is formed when the individual member countries agree to forego unilateral control over economic decision making and policy. Characteristically this involves a unified monetary system and fiscal and monetary policy, a single central bank, and a unified international trade policy. With the realisation of a single currency in Europe being actively pursued through the establishment of convergence criteria and a timeframe for full economic union (set out in the Maastricht Treaty), the development of Europe from a *Community* to a *Union* is nearing achievement – and hence the change in terminology.

Economic and political union

The most extreme form of economic integration is the economic and political union where individual member countries agree to common control from a central government. The major example of this kind of union is the USA.

Various economic groupings and the degree of economic integration pertaining to each group in 1991 are shown in Table 12.1. The eagerness of countries to affiliate themselves to an economic group stems from the various benefits offered by economic integration.

Elimination of trade restrictions between countries promotes country specialisation in certain products and industries. The theory of comparative advantage asserts that under free-market conditions countries specialise in the production of goods and services which can be manufactured at a comparatively lower cost than in other countries rather than attempt to produce all goods and services domestically, promoting trade and welfare.

Table 12.1. Some examples of economic integration

Group	Type	Members	Population (m)	GDP $bn	GDP per capita (US$)
Latin American Integration Association (ALADI)	Free Trade Area	Argentina Bolivia Brazil Chile Columbia Ecuador Mexico Paraguay Peru Uruguay Venezuela	380.9	1 018.1	2 673.0
Association of South East Asian Nations (ASEAN)	Free Trade Area	Brunei Indonesia Malaysia Singapore Philippines Thailand	322.7	345.7	1 971.0
European Community (EC)	Common Market	Belgium Denmark France Germany Greece Ireland Italy Luxembourg The Netherlands Portugal Spain UK	345.9	6 101.955	17 642.0
European Free Trade Association (EFTA)	Free Trade Area	Austria Finland Iceland Lichtenstein Norway Sweden Switzerland	32.8	824.3	25 164.0
North American Free Trade Agreement (NAFTA)	Free Trade Area	Canada Mexico USA	363.3	6 404.161	17 628.0

Source: World Development Report, 1993 (Washington D.C.: The World Bank).

The picture of economic integration in the world economy obviously now differs from that presented in Table 12.1. In 1993, the European Community was re-defined as the EU (a reflection of the attempts of the Maastricht Treaty to foster closer economic integration) and, in 1995, the accession of Finland, Sweden and Austria to the EU changed the balance between the EU and EFTA. Switzerland, which applied for Union membership in 1992, is likely to follow shortly, which leaves only two powerful countries within EFTA – Norway and Iceland. Nevertheless, even these countries are incorporated into the new economic union to a degree. The European Economic Area (EEA), which was established in 1992, meant that EFTA countries were accepted into the Union in all but name. They implicitly agreed to embrace the fundamental principles of the internal market programme.

Economic integration features two important economic effects. Liberalisation of trade between countries within the bloc promotes trade (trade creation) and through increased competition as well as specialisation enhances efficiency. Conversely, the expansion of trade within the bloc may potentially take place at the expense of trade with non-member countries (trade diversion) the balance between these effects determining to what extent the creation of an economic union is beneficial to its members.

Many observers have concluded that, on balance, the creation of the EU has had a beneficial effect on world welfare (El-Agraa, 1988). Trade creation effects have been apparent within the EU but, perhaps more significantly, the creation of the single market has also catalysed inward trade from non-EU members. Although a degree of trade diversion has been apparent (for example, the adverse effects felt by the Caribbean sugar industry following the UK's entry into the EEC in 1973) its extent has been limited by a lowering of tariffs (through GATT) and through trade deals with non-EU member regions (EFTA and the Lomé Agreement Countries in particular). Furthermore, the potential effects of specialisation – decline of whole industries in individual Member States (inter-industry specialisation) – has not been apparent as intra-industry specialisation (the concentration on particular sub-products) has dominated post-unification re-organisation.

The global triad

The growing trend towards the development of economic unions is having a powerful effect on the shape of international trade and investment. Ohmae (1985) argues that the economic world is now dominated by three major markets, Japan (and the newly industrialising countries of Asia), North America (including the USA and Canada) and Europe (including EFTA countries). As Japan improved its position in the world market, other industrialised countries and regions, whose governments were lobbied by firms in sectors with a marked increase in Japanese imports, began to look for new ways of shielding their domestic industry from the new competitive threat. As membership of GATT prevented the imposition of increased tariffs, alternative methods of protection were required to respond to the demands of Western firms.

Non-tariff barriers can involve a variety of restraints. Page (1990) proposed the following classification of types of protection:

● international agreements such as international cartels (e.g. OPEC) and market sharing agreements (such as those which are common in the steel, textile and shipbuilding industries);
● national/regional controls on trade such as import quotas, anti-dumping duties, certificates of origin, voluntary export restraints and government imposed restrictions on the purchase of imports;

- other national/regional controls such as health and safety, technical and product standards, domestic subsidies, customs clearance procedures and patent laws.

While the restrictions in the latter group may be designed to protect the well being of the nation or economic group, those in the second category, in particular, are specifically designed to limit the inflow of trade.

To the extent that non-tariff protectionism imposes new hurdles to business and detracts from the benefits of free trade, its impact on world trade may be considerable. But simply concentrating on international trade flows ignores the growing levels of foreign direct investment now characterising global business. Indeed, as shall be discussed in more detail later in this chapter, trade barriers act as an important inducement to foreign direct investment and partly explain the rapid growth in world FDI. Between 1983–1989 world FDI outflows grew by 28.9 per cent compared with a 9.4 per cent growth in world exports and a 7.8 per cent in world GDP.

EUROPE AND THE GLOBAL TRIAD

The need for a European Union

In much the same way that global oligopolies involve a small number of large dominant companies, the new world economic order is dominated by a relatively small number of major trading blocs. The growing propensity of countries to affiliate themselves with large economic unions reflects increased awareness that large unrestricted markets give rise to internal efficiency and economic welfare which has a bearing on outward trade and investment flows. The USA, which has been identified as an example of economic and political union, has been in the forefront of world trade and investment for a long time. Although recent years have witnessed sharp erosion of its dominance, particularly in those sectors which have been encroached upon by the Japanese, its long-standing success is thought to be partly attributable to the coherence of the integration between the individual states and the size and stature of the US market which provides a strong platform for future economic development.

Indeed, the success of the USA as a world power and the benefits accruing to US firms from their being free to operate in such a wide market are often believed to have contributed to the greater competitiveness of US firms over their European counterparts. The larger scale of US firms gives them greater scope to attain economies of scale and more resources for future investment, and the scale of the USA market provides a wider pool of personnel on which to draw. One of the important motivations, then, for developing the Single European Market has been to emulate the USA's high degree of integration in an attempt to give firms freer access to a wider market, promote internal efficiency and strengthen the position of Europe vis-à-vis the other leading world trading blocs.

Taking the analogy of the global oligopoly one stage further, aggressively competitive actions by one party are matched by equally aggressive counteractions by others. It was not surprising, therefore, that signals by the EU of increased economic integration and consolidation led to reactionary threats by the Japanese and Americans of renewed protection against European imports. Fearing that greater internal efficiency would lead to more effective competition, as firms are able to attain greater scale economies and improve their dynamic efficiency and thus their innovatory expertise (*see* Chapter 5), there were rum-blings among US and Japanese industrialists, keen for their governments to shield them from the potential new threat, of a new round of world protectionism. Added to this belief were reports emanating from Brussels which seemed to suggest that along with the new internal freedoms from competition across the EU, external trade policies, in the short-term at least, would be designed to protect the EU from external pressures in an effort to allow firms and industries alike to strengthen their position in the new Europe.

Notwithstanding any efforts being made by the Commission to shield EU firms from external trade, evidenced by a reassessment of rules on dumping, increased attention to 'rules of origin' and a renewed effort to ensure *reciprocity*, the report of a strict anti-competitive, external trade policy was not unanimously supported by all EU Member States. Some countries that were traditionally open to external competition found this new protectionism running contrary to their own national policies and indeed, contrary to internal EU competition policy, which was keenly promoting free competition and restrict-ing any form of protectionism as detrimental to the promotion of efficiency. No country was more against a protectionist external trade policy than the UK, and Margaret Thatcher, Prime Minister at the time, in her critique of the Community presented in Bruges in 1988, is quoted as saying:

> My fourth guiding principle is that Europe should not be protectionist. It would be a betrayal if, while breaking down constraints on trade to create the Single Market, the Community were to erect greater external protection. We must make sure our approach to world trade is consistent with the liberalisation we preach at home.

Mrs Thatcher's comments are in keeping with the principle that protectionism stifles eco-nomic growth as it allows industries to avoid adjusting to changes in international competition, consumer demand and new technologies, a principle keenly supported by the Conservative party during its government throughout the 1980s. Nevertheless, some would argue that this approach has not served to promote adjustment by UK industry which has, in many sectors, atrophied and died in the face of aggressive competition. Added to this, the Japanese success story, which is one of rapid economic development and world expansion, partly rests on its strict protectionist stance. Import substitution policies allowed Japan, at an early stage of its development, to reduce its dependence on developed countries and establish its own industries to produce the goods which were previously imported. The continuance of this strategy after the development of a strong economic base is less easy to explain.

Porter (1990) argues that protection only works under three conditions. The first is domes-tic rivalry, which acts as a surrogate to international competition and stimulates efficiency. The second is the development of competitive advantages in the domestic market which can be transferred and sustained internationally. Finally, success depends on protection being implemented for a limited period as, in all cases, it ultimately serves to delay competitiveness. Japanese protectionism may be explained in these terms: firms in protected sectors faced aggressive internal, often oligopolistic, competition between the *keiretsu* groups, the large trading groups which encompass firms across a variety of industries. The nature of compe-tition also served to militate against firms competing on price and encouraged innovation and differentiation, two competitive advantages which could be transferred to international mar-kets. Over time, this allowed Japanese firms to climb the quality ladder in their products and services. Finally, although protectionism has historically been a feature of the Japanese mar-ket, they have begun to embrace a more liberalised stance to foreign trade and investment.

This is particularly the case in industries in which the Japanese have failed to capture global markets such as chemicals and pharmaceuticals. The underlying intention is to promote domestic competition to stimulate competition and promote innovation and product development – the first stepping stone to developing global products and brands. Nevertheless, cultural factors in the Japanese market, particularly the complexity of the Japanese intermediary market means that restrictive barriers remain for foreign investors.

The case of Japan, then, while not discouraging protectionism outright, provides some potential ground rules for the EU concerning which sectors should be afforded a degree of protection and for how long. What is less clear, however, is how a common external trade policy will affect trading links between the EU, trading blocs and other world regions. In 1987 the signing, finally, of the US–Canada free trade agreement was shrouded in accusations that moves of this kind were serving to create trading blocs in which internal trade was facilitated, external trade was made more sensitive (often being based on the notion of reciprocity and 'tit-for-tat' agreements), and countries outside the blocs isolated further. The overall effect is the concentration of trade in highly-developed economic regions. Increased momentum for the creation of the Single European market and common agreement of directives for economic activity fuelled the argument that there is a dominance of economic power in the leading industrialised countries (Ohmae's global triad) which is potentially damaging to the global balance of trade and investment as it excludes those outside the core – the less developed countries in particular.

External European Union trade policy – the establishment of Fortress Europe?

In the run up to 1992 there was evidence of more stringent EU rules on dumping and 'rules of origin' and increased effort to ensure reciprocity. In addition, such agreements as voluntary export restraints (VERs) came to play a key role in European policy and added to the arguments levelled against the EU that the Single European Market was concerned with building impenetrable walls to those outside the Union.

Dumping

Various definitions of dumping exist, many of which refer to the exporting of goods at prices below the cost of production. Other definitions, however, focus on the fact that dumping is the charging of different prices in various markets without these differences being supported by variances in costs. These two definitions are clearly very different; the former concerns prices which are set below cost the latter prices which are lower than those in other markets, specifically the domestic market. Indeed, Penrose (1990) asserts: 'It does not necessarily, or even usually, mean that sales are made "below cost" in order to drive out competition' (p. 181).

Although pricing below cost suggests anti-competitive behaviour, charging different prices in different markets is less obviously 'unfair'. There are good reasons why a firm cannot standardise prices on a global scale:

- competitive conditions differ on a market-by-market basis, which often makes local adaptation a prerequisite of competitive success. Different costs of factor inputs, different levels of local competition and differences in the price elasticity of demand for goods between countries, prevent firms establishing common market prices;
- a higher degree of intra-industry trade between divisions of multinational firms distorts

the assessment of prices. Efficiencies of internalised business functions arising both from horizontal and vertical integration makes it difficult to determine what may or may not be deemed a 'fair' competitive price.

While the use of anti-dumping law in the EU's external trade policy was specifically designed to prevent anti-competitive behaviour through unfair pricing, in theory it was not intended that it should be used as a protectionist weapon against import competition from the rest of the world. However, the breadth of the criteria on which rulings are based gives the Commission scope to use anti-dumping laws for a variety of reasons. If it can be proved that a European company is being injured by a foreign firm and also show that a foreign competitor is selling goods either below the price charged in the domestic market or below the cost of production plus a reasonable mark-up, under GATT rules, the Commission is empowered to force the firm to raise its price or pay import duties on its goods.

The rules for determining the existence of dumping employed by the Commission address both definitions of dumping: different prices being charged in different markets and exports which are sold below the cost of production plus a reasonable mark-up. Thus, there is scope for the Commission to use the rulings in instances where the proof of 'unfair' practice is not clear. Accusations levelled against the Commission in the run-up to 1992 that procedures were distorting the results by overstating source country production prices and understating EU prices suggest that the laws were being used for protectionist reasons rather than promotion of fair competition.

Added to this, GATT rulings against dumping were developed around commodity products and thus fail to address the problems of calculating prices for highly differentiated products which change rapidly and where costs involve the allocation of research and development, marketing, advertising and promotion expenditures. The complexities of the required calculations and the various market-by-market distortions suggest that there is no guiding line between what can and what cannot be construed as dumping. Indeed, Colchester and Buchan (1990) assert that 'within GATT rules the creative dumping-inquisitor can demonstrate just about anything' (p. 201).

Around 100 accusations of dumping are levelled against non-EU firms every year by companies who are aggrieved by the harsh realities of foreign competition. Arguably, many of the complaints, particularly against the Japanese, reflect a lack of EU competitiveness rather than abuse by the foreign firm. 'The anti-dumping code, used in the modern world, confuses what is methodically cross-subsidised with what is horribly competitive' (Colchester and Buchan, 1990, p.202). With this being the case there is the fear that abuse of anti-dumping legislation will lead to retaliation by foreign governments whose firms have been wrongly penalised.

Anti-dumping legislation is particularly relevant to firms from less developed countries wherein a Catch-22 situation often arises. Competitive advantage for firms from less developed countries centres on their low-cost production which is reflected in low prices in export markets. However, by exploiting their low-cost base in Europe, firms run the risk of being reported to the local authorities for 'unfair' pricing and dumping. While promoting exports is essential to less developed countries improving their economic performance, they are prevented from utilising their comparative advantage in the most effective way within the EU. This highlights the tension between anti-dumping and competition law. The former is a limit on competition, the latter specifically designed to promote it, leading to inevitable conclusions that the importing firms is discriminated against.

The EU, like other nations shows a propensity for calculating costs differently between importing and domestic organisations. It is common for legislators to deduct more over-head from incoming goods but to calculate domestic costs on the basis of directly related selling expenses only. Similarly, domestic goods are often ajudged according to average costs (which takes into account higher selling costs over time) whereas imported goods are judged according to the import price on actual transactions. Twenty cases were brought before the Commission between 1990–1991. This led to the imposition of dumping duties of as much as 85 per cent (for tungsten lamps)

Rules of origin and local content

Legislation against the import of certain goods is complicated by the fact that it is often dif-ficult to establish rules of origin. If, for example, an anti-dumping duty has been levied on a particular US product, the question to be answered is what makes the product American? Adjudging a good to be American simply because it emanates from a US manufacturing plant may be misleading. The good may have been assembled in the USA from components manufactured elsewhere. In 1968, the EU's definition of origin was established as being the place where the good underwent its last major transformation. Even this, however, is open to a degree of different interpretation and therefore more specific rulings have been established on an industry by industry basis, many of which include stipulations of the extent of *local content* – that is the amount of component input sourced from local man-ufacturers. Several industries can be identified where specific local content rules have been applied:

● radios and televisions are considered European where 35–45 per cent of their value is added in the EU;
● figures of up to 90 per cent have been suggested for establishing that Japanese cars made in Europe are considered to be European;
● low-tariff access for cars made in EFTA countries must have 60 per cent EFTA content;
● integrated circuits are required to be *diffused* (etched onto blank silicon wafers) in Europe to be regarded as European.

The final point addresses the issue of *screwdriver* plants which have been set up in some instances to side-step restrictions on trade. These plants, under the guise of local manu-facturing centres, involve minimal value adding and may arguably be regarded as 'windows' to free imports rather than centres for manufacture. Rulings against this kind of activity are essential to ensure that external restraints do not engender abuse through internalisation of business activities. This raises a second issue: trade barriers have the effect of persuading firms to locate their manufacturing within the EU, which restricts imports and raises the amount of local investment. This brings with it a range of benefits from increased employment, through technology transfer, to local education and training, which can have a marked impact on less developed EU regions.

Some observers argue that external policy which restricts trade, and the imposition of local content rules, are a clever ploy by the Commission to encourage (or force) foreign firms to invest in Europe and thus boost economically depressed regions. Rather than make it harder for firms to compete this kind of policy may reinforce the competitiveness of for-eign organisations as they gain a stronger foothold in Europe from an internal position than they could have achieved as outsiders. This will be discussed in more detail later in this chapter where the specific implications for Japanese and US firms are assessed. Suffice to say at this point that it may actually intensify competition for indigenous European firms rather than protect them from it. While this is in keeping with promoting competition and efficiency it is not the desired outcome for firms who report cases of dumping to the Commission in an attempt to shield themselves from the harsh realities of low-price competition or where the Commission imposes local content rulings to cushion indigenous firms from foreign competitive pressure.

Foreign firms have, however, responded positively to local content rules. Toyota agreed to reach 60 per cent local content by August 1993 at its UK plant, and 80 per cent by August 1995. This has led to major local content commitments by Japanese firms in the EU which are far higher than corresponding amounts in the USA. For example, in the production of television sets in the USA, Japanese firms source only 28 per cent of their components locally, while in Europe this figure is 70 per cent.

Reciprocity

The determined attitude of the Commission to promote reciprocity is reflected in the communique of the European summit presented in Hannover in 1988. The duality of their approach, on the one hand promoting a free-market stance and on the other ensuring that freedom of access is afforded reciprocal access to foreign countries for European firms, is by no means congruent with a liberal external trade policy.

> The community must be open to third countries and must negotiate with these countries where necessary to ensure access to their markets for Union exports. It will seek to preserve the balance of advantages accorded, while respecting the identity of the internal market of the Community.

> (Colchester and Buchan, 1990, p. 192)

This raises two important implications:

- first, countries which fail to offer reciprocal access will discriminate against and give impetus to a round of global protectionism;
- second, international trade will become increasingly dependent on bilateral trade agreements secured between Europe and other trading blocs.

While the General Agreement on Tariffs and Trade (GATT) has attempted to remove bilateralism since its inception in 1947 through the adoption of a policy of multilateralism involving common agreements between a large number of countries, economic integration and the formation of powerful trading blocs have turned the theory of international agreements full circle. Bilateralism was originally rejected for the way in which it distorts world trade through preferential agreements established between (usually developed) countries, which results in some firms operating at a clear disadvantage vis-à-vis their international counterparts. In an attempt to harmonise the foundation on which world competition is based, improve efficiency, economic welfare and world trade, GATT proposed a solution to the problem of developing international agreements which involved a common multilateral approach. The tendency for reciprocity to foster bilateralism, then, may be seen as a retrogressive step working contrary to GATT principles. Although large economic groups have superseded the individual countries involved in bilateral bargaining in former times, the basic issues remain the same: international trade will be free to those countries who are willing to open their doors to foreign trade thus putting competition back in the hands of government authorities rather than market forces wherein true efficiency lies.

Voluntary agreements

Legal, under GATT rules, is the potential of nations to protect certain industries through tariff manipulation by raising tariffs in one area, but compensating importing countries in other areas. However, with tariffs between developed nations already being low, it is difficult to effect real balancing effects through these mechanisms. This has led to the introduction of voluntary agreements wherein the importing country asks the exporter to agree to quota restrictions. This protects local firms and permits them to earn higher than normal profits than would otherwise be the case.

Voluntary agreements form a key part of modern non-tariff protectionism. Voluntary export restraints (VERs) are the major type of agreement under this banner. The underlying motive for their implementation is pre-emptive: failure to reduce the level of exports is likely to result in unilateral restrictions on imports by the host country. Economists generally agree, however, that protectionism of this kind, which is bilateral and involves restrictions on the quantity of output, is more damaging than tariffs. Whereas tariffs directly raise the price of a particular good and thus deter imports, limitations on quantity reduce supply and indirectly raise prices. Under these conditions not only do firms become inefficient through lack of competition, but restrictions are levelled against the lowest-cost producers which biases the allocation of resources towards less efficient manufacturing organisations. Because restrictions of this kind are not unilateral and involve imposing limits on exports they do not come under GATT rules. This may partly explain their growing attraction as a means of protection in recent years.

The car industry provides a good example of the use of voluntary trade restrictions in the EU. As far back as 1980 all European imports of Japanese cars were subject to VERs. France and the UK established fixed levels of market share (3 per cent and 11 per cent respectively) while Italy, Spain and Portugal arranged fixed quantity agreements (3 200, 2 000 and 1 000 cars per year respectively). These temporary measures were designed to cushion the industry through a period of readjustment to the increasingly competitive world market for cars. The continued imposition of these restrictions over a protracted period of time brings into question the effectiveness of VERs as a way of promoting industry adjustment. Like so many forms of protection there is a clear case to suggest that by limiting competition authorities perpetuate inefficiency. Although data is available in the case of the car industry, many arrangements are not publicised and the secrecy which surrounds agreements makes it difficult to judge the true economic impact of this kind of policy measure.

Within the bounds of the Single European Market the bilateral nature of VERs is not viewed favourably and it is likely that the future will see them being centralised. Given the wide differences between the restrictions imposed by various countries the process of standardising the level of European 'quotas' is likely to be met with a great deal of resistance.

Fear or fortress?

In the mid to late 1980s the concerns of the Americans and Japanese, in particular, that the creation of the Single European Market heralded the laying of the foundations for Fortress Europe were not unfounded. The Japanese had good cause to shout *unfair discrimination* in the light of their being singled out as a target for the Commission's new external policies. Action against many of their industrial exports, particularly in high-technology sectors, suggested that the new Europe was not going to welcome further encroachment by competitive Japanese imports. Equally, the Americans feared that the development of new standards for Europe would be made without their knowledge thus leaving them at a considerable disadvantage in respect of new-product development for Europe. Strict rules on reciprocity and discrimination against particular goods based on arbitrary taste judgements further fuelled the fear that Europe was becoming a bastion for indigenous firms.

Although specifically targeting protection against the Japanese is permissible with such policies as voluntary trade restrictions, it is not in keeping with GATT rules on dumping and rules of origin. While many countries, France in particular, lobbied their government to ensure that the opening-up of the EU did not mean that the advantages were equally applicable to Japan and the newly industrialising countries (NICs), the Commission was wary of implementing policies which would strain relations with GATT.

The EU appears to be divided into two halves – those countries who favour protection and those countries who promote 'free market' principles. The effect is that contradictory demands are placed on the European Commission which cannot be reconciled to the benefit of all. In deciding what is best for Europe, and this includes sustaining good trading relations with other major economic regions and working within the bounds of GATT rules, a more thorough examination of the specific impact of 1992 on trading areas is essential.

JAPAN AND THE ASIA-PACIFIC REGION

The effects of 1992 on Japan – promoting good Europeans

The singling out of Japan as the principal target for EU external trade policy stems from the growing strength of Japanese exports in world markets. Table 12.2 shows the value and share of the top 25 ranked exporting countries in 1989. The list includes 11 of the 15 Member States of Europe (excluding Greece, Portugal Ireland and Finland) and compares their performance with Japan and the USA. It is interesting to note that the top six countries did not change their ranking over the period and thus despite the world's growing interest in the international activities of Japan and its growing dominance of global markets, the reality is that Japanese merchandise exports have grown in line with other leading industrial nations. Nevertheless, the Japanese growth rate over the decade 1979–1989 was rather higher than those of the other leading nations (168 per cent compared with 100 for the USA, 99 for Germany, 78 for France and 76 for the UK) although it falls far short of that enjoyed in the newly industrialising countries of Hong Kong, Taiwan and Korea (even allowing for high values of re-exports).

However, the real crux of international competitiveness depends not only on export market share, but on the commodity composition of this share (Buckley, Pass and Prescott, 1992). In this respect, the competitiveness of Europe appears to be declining even more rapidly. Table 12.3, although now outdated, clearly shows one of the main concerns which led the architects of the EU to establish new rules and principles to improve the standing of European firms in world markets. As Japan was clearly leading the way in those sectors with *strong demand*, that is high-technology sectors with much future growth potential, giving them a foundation for sustainable competitive advantage over the USA and Europe (profits in the short-term being re-invested in future development), it was clear

Table 12.2. Leading exporters in world merchandise trade 1979, 1989 and 1992

1979	Rank 1989	1992	Exporters	1992 Value $m
1	1	1	USA	447 440
2	2	2	Germany	429 290
3	3	3	Japan	339 991
4	4	4	France	235 938
5	5	5	United Kingdom	190 059
6	6	6	Italy	180 015
8	9	7	Netherlands	138 957
10	7	8	Canada	133 447
11	10	9	Benelux	122 961
27	11	10	Hong Kong	119 512
34	14	11	China	86 200
29	13	12	Korea	74 790
22	12	13	Taiwan	67 763
13	16	14	Switzerland	56 549
19	18	15	Spain	64 495
12	15	16	Sweden	55 598
9	24	17	Saudia Arabia	51 711
32	17	18	Singapore	49 604
7	8	19	Former USSR	48 836
25	22	20	Austria	44 412
37	20	21	Mexico	42 700
17	19	22	Australia	42 439
		23	Malaysia	40 709
		24	Denmark	39 548
26	21	25	Brazil	36 207

Source: Direction of Trade Statistics Yearbook, 1993, pp. 2–7.

that something had to be done to stimulate competition in the EU. Worries over Japan's growing strength in high technology sectors was heightened at this time given Japanese growing involvement in primary research, that is the development of new basic technologies. While in the past most Japanese research had centred on the improvement of existing technologies and effective commercialisation programmes, efforts were being made to bring Japan into the forefront of basic world research efforts. Government supported programmes offering grant money and preferential conditions to private firms intent on embarking on basic research programmes, particularly in the targeted areas of software engineering, development of new materials, biotechnology and biomaterials clearly raised the stakes for technological development and continual improvement in the EU.

One of the motivations for restricting Japanese trade is to give European firms a 'breather' period; time to adjust to new high-technology world competition without the pressures of aggressive rivalry. But, as has already been argued, the lack of competition is believed by many economists to hamper, not facilitate, innovation and technological development (*see* Chapter 5). Perhaps more importantly, however, external restrictions are encouraging Japanese firms to invest in the EU as a means of bypassing the trade restrictions being levelled against them.

Tariff barriers have traditionally been cited as one of the major motivating factors persuading firms to locate production abroad. Non-tariff barriers work in exactly the same way. Rather than face the external barriers then, many Japanese firms have decided to locate their production within the EU and bypass the barriers altogether or enter into collaborative arrangements with EU firms as a way of securing a market presence and local involvement. In the field of consumer electronics, an industry in which Japan has attained a position of global dominance, the first foreign investments in Europe were made in the 1970s as an effective means of servicing local markets with colour televisions. Most of these early investments were greenfield, dedicated to single product production, although latterly most firms have extended their local production portfolio to include video recorders, compact disc players, microwave ovens and the like. Many of these moves were made in response to actual or predicted trade restrictions, and with the on-set of the Single European Market assured access to the wider EU market has facilitiated business development. This has led to firms creating strong networks across Europe rather than being content on concentrating production in single locations. According to the work of Strange (1992), Sony Corporation has established a number of dedicated manufacturing facilities throughout the EU, while Matsushita Electric has set up a network of subsidiaries to manufacture and supply components as well as entering into a number of joint ventures with Philips, the largest EU competitor. The need to co-opt local organisations in the development of EU strategies is gaining greater prominence in Japanese firms' strategies for Europe as this enables market access without disturbing the competitive balance of the market, provoking competitive reaction by incumbents. Hitachi and Toshiba's approach of fostering collaborative links with EU firms is testament to this kind of thinking.

Table 12.3. Changes in export market share (%)

	1968–1973	1973–1979	1979–1985
Industry total			
Europe	−1.83	+0.24	−1.44
USA	−3.63	−0.17	+1.73
Japan	+1.61	+0.85	+5.37
Strong demand			
Europe	−3.43	−0.56	−2.54
USA	−4.96	+0.57	+1.24
Japan	+2.21	+0.70	+7.14
Moderate demand			
Europe	−1.19	−0.29	-2.42
USA	+4.61	−0.99	+0.21
Japan	+2.85	+1.64	+5.66
Weak demand			
Europe	−1.67	+1.70	+1.93
USA	−1.55	−0.09	−1.05
Japan	−0.71	−0.40	+1.85

Source: European Commission.

Thus while the use of non-tariff measures was potentially seen as a way of protecting the new Europe from further Japanese encroachment, exactly the opposite has happened. The Japanese have reacted to the implicit challenge posed by the Single European Market Act and have augmented their European investment to ensure that they have a strong position inside the fortress. Sony Corporation's founder, Akio Morita, is reported as saying in the run up to 1992: 'Japanese are not fools. Japanese industry will move technology to Europe'. Although the early response of the Japanese to 1992 was tinged with pessimism, this has given way to a realisation that the advantages offered by the Single European Market can be exploited from the inside. Japan's direct investments in Europe rose dramatically from around $7 billion in 1987 to $9 billion in 1988, and over $14 billion in 1989. Furthermore, as Table 12.4 highlights, the proportion of Japanese outward direct investment flows going to Europe has almost doubled over the period.

Table 12.4. Japanese outward direct investment 1984–1989

	1984	1985	1986	1987	1988	1989
Total $million	4 700	12 200	22 300	33 400	47 000	67 500
% Europe	12.3	15.8	15.5	19.7	19.4	21.9
% North America	34.0	45.0	46.8	46.0	47.5	50.2
% Other Areas	28.4	27.5	27.3	19.3	21.3	15.7

Source: Ministry of Finance, Financial Statistics Monthly, 1990.

The data presented in Table 12.4 also demonstrates the maintained momentum in foreign direct investment in the USA. Increased activity in Europe has not been at the expense of American investments. With the global triad being the key seat of global economic activity, balance of activities across the triad is being actively pursued. Supported by the high value of the yen throughout the late 1980s, Japanese firms have been able to react positively to trade restrictions and embark on a programme of foreign direct investment in both the USA and the EU.

From a position within the 'fortress' Japanese firms have the potential to exploit the advantages which accrue from establishing local production facilities. For example:

- *Closeness to the market* – this involves not only geographic proximity which makes delivery easier, but also closeness in the sense of shortening the communication links between the market and the manufacturer for the diffusion of information.
- *Better market information* – related to the above point, gathering market information on which marketing strategies are based is easier at first hand. In turn, this also helps firms adapt more quickly to changes in market conditions (demand, consumer behaviour, competition) and adapt products and strategies accordingly.
- *Stimulating demand* – there is often assumed to be a *presence effect* in foreign investment where the introduction of new competition into the market serves to raise overall levels of market demand.
- *Raises image and local identity* – one of the major problems for firms doing business abroad, particularly in highly nationalistic countries, is their 'foreignness'. This manifests itself in a lack of understanding of the local culture (*see* Chapter 9) and also the image of the company held by local customers. Firms with a local manufacturing presence often come to be considered as 'local firms'.

- *Access to public procurement* – in a similar way that barriers to competition between the 15 Member States within the EU made it difficult (or nigh impossible) for non-indigenous firms to gain access to public procurement, non-EU firms may only win contracts if they have a local market presence.

Despite these additional advantages, many observers suggested that once Japanese firms were forced to face up to the higher wage rates pertaining in the EU, as opposed to their domestic and offshore production locations, much of their competitive advantage would be eroded. This presupposes that Japanese imports secured market penetration through low pricing strategies, enabled by low cost production, a fairly naive view given the trend by Japanese companies towards more sophisticated technologies and higher quality.

Arguably, however, Japanese firms' strength in Europe goes beyond the simple advantages traditionally associated with local production. Part of Japan's outstanding competitive success is often attributed to the development and exploitation of business networks. In the domestic Japanese market this centres on the *keiretsu* (linked group) structure, coalitions of diverse organisations – manufacturing firms, banks and trading companies – interlinked through crossholdings of shares, interpenetration of directorships, linked business fora and ongoing business relationships based on mutual trust and co-operation. Several advantages are adduced to this kind of business organisation: co-operation involving the sharing of risks and resources and resulting in minimal duplication of effort; intense competition between and within groups made all the more aggressive by firms ability to pool resources; synergy from grouping together divergent industries and exploitation of small firms and intermediaries who are forced to bear much of the burden of aggressive competition. In recent years, many Japanese firms have focused their international strategies on developing global resource networks for goods, humans, money and information in an effort to ensure that the competitive advantages developed at home are being translated to the international business arena.

Global goods networks have increased rapidly in recent years. Once export oriented companies have moved from the establishment of sales subsidiaries abroad to the creation of dedicated manufacturing facilities in many of the world's key markets. In the last five years, these networks have been extended further to incorporate other business functions such as procurement, new product development and even basic research. Money networks have been facilitated by the establishment of financial subsidiaries abroad, in the USA, Europe and Asia. Almost 70 new subsidiaries were established between 1986–1990, approximately 30 of these appearing in Europe (JCED, 1991).

The development of human networks on a global scale is reflected in the number of foreign employees as a percentage of total organisational workforces. The ratio of foreign employees rose from 10.17 per cent in 1985 to 15.53 per cent in 1990, and the average number of foreign employees in Japanese parent companies rose from 1.2 per cent in 1985 to 6.6 per cent in 1990. In terms of communication networks, Japanese industries have actively up-dated and extended their computer networks on a global scale to take account of their increased foreign involvement.

With rapid global expansion, many Japanese companies have developed overseas regional headquarters. Multinational giants such as Honda and Cannon fostered the idea of the *four headquarters system* in the late 1980s based on the notion that regional business centres were essential in Japan, the USA, Europe and Asia if firms were to realise true global potential. The objective of serving the four centres with separate 'headquarters' is to adapt to different local requirements while exploiting the advantages of being a multinational enterprise (that is balancing the benefits offered by both centralisation and decentralisation).

This trend towards the development of global heterarchies (as opposed to hierarchies where single, centralised head offices dictate the strategies of the organisation) is not, however, restricted to Japanese multinational firms. As the competitive stakes have risen in many developed markets the need for local responsiveness has given way to the establishment of locally dedicated subsidiaries by many multinational enterprises. The new global challenge therefore centres more importantly on local adaptation and flexibility as opposed to global scale economies. This is not to suggest, however, that economies of scale are no longer at issue in the strategic development of multinational firms. Within each of the major world regions, particularly the economic groups which make up the global triad, business volume is substantial which suggests that economies can be achieved within each economic group. Furthermore, those elements of the business which can be effectively centralised will continue to be managed centrally from the regional headquarters. The national head office may therefore take on a new role in the modern international business arena – nurturing a common business culture and overall corporate strategy and encouraging business integration through the establishment of working parties and problem solving teams between the various international subsidiaries.

Decentralisation does not stop at sales and marketing and manufacturing, the trend is also evident in the area of research and development. While centralised research and development departments characterised multinational enterprises for many years, mostly because of the high costs associated with research and the obvious problems of duplication of effort, many firms are now seeing new opportunities in decentralising efforts and establishing regional R&D departments. This was discussed in Chapters 7 and 8. As Japanese firms increasingly internationalise their research and development efforts they are clearly developing the organisational networks which facilitate this kind of management.

With Japanese firms' long-standing ability to integrate business organisations and develop integrated networks, there is some ground to suggest that they are better placed to develop and exploit multinational heterarchies than their western counterparts from the USA and Europe. Consequently, by actively encouraging Japanese firms to locate their production within the EU, the Commission has facilitated the process of international network development, and thus they may have shot themselves in the foot. For France and, to a lesser extent Spain, Italy, Portugal and Greece, countries which have actively lobbied the Commission to restrict Japanese involvement in the EU, the imposition of high external trade barriers have caused a degree of concern. Conversely, however, the actions of the Commission have played into the hands of countries such as the UK which not only reject protectionism as damaging to the ethos of free competition but have actively encouraged Japanese inward investment.

Britain not only accepts Japanese investment, it actively encourages it. The government has, on many occasions, sent out officials to talk to Japanese businesses and highlight the attractiveness of the UK as an investment location. Japanese investment has thus increasingly become a key element in the UK's regional development policy. Areas with high unemployment and declining industries have been bolstered by major industrial investments by Japanese firms. The most visible investments were those in the car industry with the Nissan plant in the north east of England and the Toyota plant in the Midlands. These, arguably, saved two highly depressed areas from serious regional atrophy. Added to this, the contribution of Japanese exports to the UK balance of trade figures, particularly during the depression of the late 1980s and early 1990s, was actively welcomed.

The fear that this open door policy would severely raise competition within the EU was probably overstated. There had already been a great deal of inward investment activity by the Japanese, keen to build global networks rather than rely on international trade to enhance business volumes. Sony Corporation, with eight Western European subsidiaries, asserted that it had complete freedom to operate on a pan-European scale well before the realisation of the 1992 directives (Charles Smith, 1988). The Single European Market has merely catalysed the rate of investment for Japanese firms in much the same way that internal EU investments have been stimulated by the need to think and plan on a wider European scale. Furthermore, non-tariff barriers may be less of an inducement to EU investment than first imagined. MITI suggested, in the late 1980s, that the anti-dumping threat was receding as increasing numbers of Japanese exports were competing on advanced levels of technology rather than price as firms moved up the quality/technology ladder.

For the Japanese, the problems imposed by the new protectionism are by no means insurmountable. They are even confident that, given time, they can meet the imposed local content rulings. Nissan achieved a 70 per cent local content ratio at its UK plant within two years of manufacturing while Matsushita's vacuum cleaner plant in Spain buys 80 per cent of its components locally. Early fears that local industry was, in some cases, unable to support the quality of inputs required have waned as firms have either developed close working relationships with indigenous suppliers or encouraged their Japanese suppliers to invest within the EU. While the first case relies on firms developing business networks with indigenous firms, promoting the local economy, the second suggests that local content rules have invoked vertically-integrated investment by Japanese suppliers, further stimulating inward investment. Japanese automotive component manufacturers and electronic component suppliers have been attracted to the EC by the presence of the Japanese automobile and electronic appliance manufacturers without whom EU investment would probably not have taken place.

> Some (e.g. Ikeda Bussan and the Nissan venture) are essentially part of a larger operation; some (e.g. Calsonic) have developed a wider customer base including European companies; some (e.g. Alps Electric) were asked to establish EU facilities by their customers; and some (e.g. Tabuchi Electric) simply reckoned on picking up trade from both Japanese and European companies.
>
> (Roger Strange, 1992, p. 17)

Simple foreign direct investment data, however, belies the extent to which the Japanese are now becoming involved in the Single European Market. Local sensitivities – in the sense of upsetting the balance of competition and antagonising governments as well as responsiveness to local markets and cultures – have resulted in a growing number of joint ventures and strategic alliances as a way of securing market access (such as in the case of Honda's alliance with the Rover Group in the UK), fostering closer links with customers (e.g. Yamazaki Mazak in the machine tool sector), and establishing links for the development of new technologies (such as Fujisawa-Smith Kline, Yamanouchi-Eli Lilly and Fujisawa-Fisons KK in the pharmaceutical industry). To a great extent, then, growing Japanese involvement in Europe, while partly attributable to trade restrictions and the fear of a fortress Europe, must be seen within the context of multinational growth. The strategies being employed by Japanese firms are little different to those now being employed by European and US multinationals in their efforts to secure strong international business networks in the three major regions of the world. As the global triad has become the centre of the greatest proportion of world trade and investment (despite, not necessarily because of global economic integration) the need to attain a global balance of activities for multi-national enterprises is clearly apparent.

The singling out of Japan as a target for renewed protectionism therefore appears hard to justify, although some would argue that their greater competitiveness makes it difficult for indigenous firms to adjust to the new competitive pressures imposed by the creation of the Single Market. The high value of the yen, which has given Japanese firms the necessary investment capital to strengthen operations on a pan-European scale and invest in the latest manufacturing technology in modern plants with greater potential for efficiency, has undoubtedly added to the competitive burden of European firms. Similarly, the efficiency of Japanese management systems and practices, which permit higher levels of productivity as well as more coherent business networks, adds a further challenge to indigenous EU firms. When this is coupled with renewed efforts in the pursuit of new technologies, with the level of Japanese R&D spending having rise from 1.9 per cent of GNP in 1971 to 2.8 per cent in 1987, there is perhaps some cause for concern. Nevertheless, as ways of overcoming the imposition of market barriers is part and parcel of the challenge facing multinational companies, grounds for finding new measures of protectionism are hard to find. Although Japan, for many years, was reluctant to join GATT, fearing the implications of removing tariff barriers, recent affiliation provides the armoury to prevent being singled out by EU (and the USA) external trade policy. This adds to the inevitability of Japanese competition in Europe and stresses the need for European firms to match levels of competitiveness rather than attempt to find measures to shield themselves from it – measures which may ultimately prove ephemeral.

One thing which the European Commission perhaps overlooked was Japan's propensity to adapt and work with government policy rather than react against it. Gaster (1992, p. 42) suggests that while the Commission may be reluctant to accept that they have policies on inward investment:

> ... they have clearly had a tremendous impact on executives making decisions about the level and form of their involvement in Europe. Perhaps the most important point of all is that, in the end, the approach adopted in Europe seems very familiar to Japanese investors. There have been very few public complaints. Just as Japanese firms accepted guidance from MITI or their Japanese Ministry of Finance in the past, they are now willing to accept it from host governments elsewhere.

The newly industrialising countries

The newly industrialising countries have faced similar challenges to the Japanese. South Korea, Taiwan, Hong Kong and Singapore frustrated by USA protectionism experienced secular trade expansion within the region, developing closer links and business relations with each other. This strengthening of intra-group trade is sometimes adduced to the development of the Single Market and while the latter has obviously had an impact, a degree of caution is necessary in interpreting the trend. Throughout the 1980s, companies from these regions have been concerned with trade with and investment in the EU. They have been similarly frustrated by the imposition of trade restrictions and many have turned to EU investment as a means of consolidating and expanding their European presence.

Unlike many of the Japanese multinationals, however, those from the NICs often lack the resources to establish major investments within the EU although this does not prevent them taking advantage of the Single Market. Other strategic alternatives are available to them: establishing alliances with European and non-European firms to secure EU access; establishing operations in nearby locations such as East Europe or North Africa where treaty access to the EU allows firms to exploit their specific expertise (using cheap, skilled labour). There are, of course, exceptions. Companies such as Samsung and Tatung have developed greenfield manufacturing facilities within the EU which not only give them a strong base from which to develop their European business but also give them access to European design and R&D facilities.

ASEAN countries

ASEAN is different from most economic blocs in that the primary motivations for unification is to improve the countries' export position rather than to remove barriers between the trading nations. With the exception of Singapore (which has extensive off-shore manufacturing activity) the group primarily relies on exports of raw materials.

Over the past few decades ASEAN has also been concerned with maintaining adequate flows of inward investment rather than looking to expand their business into the EU. ASEAN is a major industrial exporter to OECD countries. It supplies the world with 95 per cent of its hemp, 85 per cent of its rubber, 75 per cent of all tropical hardwoods, 83 per cent of its palm oil 67 per cent of its tin and 60 per cent of its copper (Richards, 1991). Nevertheless it suffers relatively high costs (particularly in Indonesia and the Philippines). Lack of local competition, stifling a drive towards efficiency, means that for a less developed region the major traditional competitive advantage of low cost manufacturing is not apparent. This has led to a new drive for regional integration (the ASEAN Free Trade Area, AFTA) in an attempt to expose firms to increased competition thereby lowering prices and increasing global competitiveness through improved prices and delivery. Greater integration should also lead to higher levels of inward investment as it raises local efficiency and thus confidence among investors.

In 1984, ASEAN trade with the EU accounted for only 11 per cent, while EU trade with ASEAN was as little as 1 per cent. EU imports are primarily basic commodities and the EU has not been averse to imposing trade restrictions against imports – textiles and processed agricultural products being the most obvious examples (Richards, 1991). While improvements in this position are desirable, and negotiations being made with the EU accordingly, there are grounds to suggest that the favoured option for ASEAN firms is to concentrate on other areas, particularly East Europe and Mexico both of which alternatives offer the potential of associated access to the developed regions. Alternatively, restructuring at home and improving competitiveness of exports and expanding economic relations with other Asia-Pacific economies may prove preferable. This last alternative is already occurring due to the rapid growth throughout the region fostered by trade restrictions being imposed in many developed regions.

A CASE FOR FURTHER ASIA–PACIFIC UNIFICATION

Although the development of a Pacific Asian Economic Community has been resisted by many economies because of the dominance of Japan, it is now being given serious consideration. If this were to occur the result would be three major trading blocs of comparable size: Europe with a total product of $6.2 billion (the EU accounting for 76 per cent), North America $5.9 billion (the USA accounting for 90 per cent) and Asia Pacific $3.7 billion (Japan accounting for 76 per cent). The number of Asia-Pacific countries with high and rising per capita GDP has recently grown: while in the 1970s only Japan and Australia demonstrated high per capita GDP, Hong Kong, Singapore, Malaysia and Korea have developed rapidly promoting greater comparability between the regions and thus greater possibility for integration. Unification of these economies and the development of a common external trade policy, potentially threatens the ability of European and North American firms taking advantage of the high growth rates and rapid expansion within the region. The reciprocity implications of the on-going trend towards closer economic integration on a global scale cannot therefore be overlooked in the current plans being established by the EU. The long-term threat of evoking reactionary measures in the Asia-Pacific region from current trade policy must be taken seriously if these markets are to be open to EU firms in the future.

North America

The Effects of 1992 on the USA – demand for transparency of technical standards

> The United States does not want to be forced to set up plants in Europe in order to sell there. It wants access to US exports.
>
> (Colchester and Buchan, 1990, p. 197)

This suggests that, unlike the Japanese, the Americans are not concerned with establishing manufacturing facilities within the EU as a way of sidestepping external trade restrictions. However, this rather belies the evidence which demonstrates that while they may be reluctant to invest in Europe they have made a concerted effort to ensure that they have a strong internal base from which to exploit the advantages of the Single European Market. Table 12.5, which compares US outward direct investment data between 1982–1992, highlights that its EU investment position has more than doubled over the period.

Table 12.5. US outward direct investment position by country 1982–1992

	$millions 1982	1992	1992 % of all countries
All Countries	207 752	486 670	100
EUROPE	92 449	239 389	49.2
EC (12)	71 712	200 535	41.2
Belgium	5 549	10 771	2.2
France	7 391	23 257	4.8
Germany	15 463	35 393	7.3
Italy	4 316	13 605	2.8
Netherlands	6 760	19 114	3.9
United Kingdom	27 537	77 842	16.0
Canada	43 511	68 432	14.1
Japan	6 407	26 213	5.4

Source: Survey of Current Business, August 1987, August 1991 and July 1993.

It would therefore seem that the USA is rather more vociferous in its complaints against the Commission's trade policy than the Japanese. The reaction of US firms to the shoring-up of external trade barriers shows a similar trend to the Japanese – increased levels of inward investment in the EU. When this is compared with Table 12.4 which shows similar figures for Japan, US firms emerge as having invested more than their Japanese counterparts in both absolute and relative terms. Once again, the UK emerges as the major recipient of inward investment, reflecting its liberal attitude towards competition. Conversely, Germany appears as a major investment region for US firms which is a marked difference on the Japanese picture. Traditionally, much of the investment activity has been concentrated in a small number of EU countries. In 1982, France, Germany, the Netherlands and the UK accounted for 80 per cent of US inward investment. By 1990, however, the same four countries comprise only 65 per cent of the total, reflecting the growing awareness of US firms of the need to develop pan-European networks.

A sectoral breakdown of investment also shows that sharp increases in investment have occurred in those sectors which are expected to be affected most by the Single European Act. Whereas sales of US subsidiaries in Europe rose by 39 per cent in all sectors between 1985–1987, in pharmaceuticals they rose by 70.4 per cent, motor vehicles by 93.5 per cent, finance (excluding banking) 110.9 per cent and business services 109.1 per cent (Dunning, 1990). The initial impetus of the creation of the Single Market clearly had a marked impact on levels of US business activity within the EU. Since 1986, however, there has been a slow down in growth rates (between 1987–1990 the corresponding growth rates in investment position are 34 per cent for all industries, 27 per cent in the car industry, 43 per cent in pharmaceuticals, 86 per cent in finance and 100 per cent in business services) but the increases remain significant.

Like the Japanese, the Americans are concerned about local content and rules of origin, although whereas the Japanese were concerned about not being able to maintain quality levels, US concerns reflect an outrage that changes made in Europe should have such an insidious effect on the activity of US firms. Specifically, their objections are addressed against the singling-out of certain sectors for discrimination. The ruling that semiconductors are only considered European where they are 'diffused' in Europe was regarded as blatant enforcement of EU manufacturing for US semi-conductor manufacturers. Equally, asserting that European television programming should be sourced from Europe 'wherever practicable' hit a nerve with the Americans who resented the Commission directing their attack at the film/television industry which is considered to be one of the main areas of US strength.

More importantly, American concerns centre on the issues of standards and reciprocity. Because they are on the outside, US officials fear that new European standards will be developed behind closed doors, specifically to exclude US exports. There are some grounds for this fear as the USA has been denied access to CEN and CENELEC, the European standards-setting bodies. This makes it difficult for US firms to make the necessary technological adaptations to ensure their products meet future European specifications. The rejection of any involvement is particularly galling for the USA as the American National Standards Institute is, in theory at least, open to Europe. Nevertheless, those American firms which have invested in the EU and consequently treated as 'indigenous' will have access to all standards information suggesting US fears are overstated.

The financial service sector has provided a test case for reciprocity between the USA and Europe. Within the EU, the stance which has been taken in financial services is 'mutual recognition of home country control', which allows all EU-based firms free access to other Member States, firms being regulated by domestic, not host country, regulations.

Conversely, in the Canada–USA Free Trade Area, the system adopted is one of *national treatment reciprocity*, which asserts that firms are regulated according to host country rules. If the Commission decided to take the purist view of reciprocity and insist the Americans provide mutual recognition in the same way as is expected in the 15 Member States of Europe, this would effectively mean the USA bending the rules to accommodate EU firms. The US banking system separates commercial and investment banking. By letting European banks who do not observe this distinction operate freely in North America, the Americans may find their firms at a disadvantage vis-à-vis their European rivals. It is hardly surprising, therefore, that the Americans are intent on preventing mutual recognition of home country regulations. Ultimately, *national treatment with effective access* was settled upon, which recognises that tight US restrictions should be relaxed enough to effect market entry by European firms, but from then on, local operation comes under local rules. This agreement is in keeping with GATT guidelines on trade in services, agreed in Montreal in early 1989.

Reciprocity rules, as with anti-dumping regulations, may potentially be levied against individual countries or sectors. This makes them a highly flexible means of regulation and an active forum for bilateral bargaining. Notwithstanding these issues, many US multinationals have long-established European investments and manufacturing facilities. Ford, General Motors and IBM, for example, have well-developed manufacturing and marketing networks throughout Europe to the extent that they are no longer considered expressly American. These firms are as well placed as their European counterparts to exploit the proposed benefits of the Single Market. Some observers even argue that their long-standing experience of operating across national state borders in their domestic marketplaces them in a stronger position to benefit from the Single Market. When this is coupled with their size, as compared with the 'national champions' of Europe, who dominate individual countries but who, in many cases have not developed as Euro-champions, it is apparent that there are major opportunities to be reaped for US multinationals. Nevertheless, intensified competition within the EU (and other developed markets) has brought with it new competitive challenges, specifically the need for local responsiveness and business flexibility. To an extent this dilutes the scale advantages achieved by US multinational giants and reinforces a growing need for businesses to adjust on a global scale to take account of the different needs pertaining in the various regional centres.

Whereas Japanese firms have traditionally been against takeovers as an effective means of market penetration American firms have been very active in this area. Table 5.1 showed the dominance of the USA in European takeovers and revealed how over 26 per cent of all acquisitions in the EU in 1993 were made by US firms, compared to 18.7 per cent for France, 10.3 per cent for West Germany and 13.8 per cent for the UK. The figure for Japan was 0.8 per cent, reflecting their reluctance as aggressive corporate acquirors, which can be partly attributed to their limited domestic experience of takeovers (brought about by fears of disunity) as well as the fact that in many high technology sectors, similarly developed target firms were often not apparent. For US firms, the motivations for takeover have tended to centre on market access as well as acquisition of critical assets such as extant distribution systems and customer franchises and brand names.

As the US has experienced a decline in its relative economic power in recent years it too has become aware of the need to strengthen its position globally. Enhancing international networks and improving technological development are high on the business agenda. High levels of defence spending and low tax rates during the Reagan years led to a large government deficit which is still taking its toll on the economy. Although the US has traditionally been against intervention in the economy, taking a neo-classical, free trade stance on economic development, there are now strong pressures to initiate more careful planning of industry. With global competitive pressures continually rising and the EU and Japan clearly targeting innovation and development in a number of key technology areas, the USA is reviewing its overall industrial strategy for the future. Highlighting areas of potential growth – automation, computing, advanced materials, medical technology and thin-layer technology – and diverting R&D support away from the defence and space industries (under public control) into more private initiatives is testament to the government taking a more proactive stance in long-term development of the economy. Examples of major research initiatives include (Fortune, 1991):

1 Sematech, launched in 1987 and awarded $200m a year, focusing on methods, materials and equipment for advanced semiconductors.
2 National Centre for Manufacturing Sciences (NCMS), initiated in 1986 and awarded $80m a year, concerned with improving machine tools, software, machine methods and new materials.
3 Microelectronic and Computer Technology Corp. (MCC), launched in 1983 and awarded $60 million a year, involved in improvements in advanced computing, software, CAD and CAM.

Concerns over the strengthening of economic groups on a global scale has also led to the creation of the Canada–US Free Trade Area and on-going negotiations to form the North American Free Trade Area to include the USA, Canada and Mexico.

The Canadian position

Canada has always operated in the shadow of the USA. With a population ten times smaller than the USA and an economic focus on commodities and semi-processed materials its position in the world economy is unable to match that of its dominant neighbour. Its foreign trade has, historically, been dominated by the USA. In 1979 the USA accounted for 69 per cent of total Canadian exports; by 1989 this value had risen to 75 per cent. The bilateral flow between Canada and the USA is now the largest trade flow in the world between two countries, a situation which is likely to intensify as the policies of the Canada–US Free Trade Agreement take effect. Table 12.6 reinforces the dominance of the USA and also highlights its export position in other leading global markets. Japan is Canada's second largest export market accounting for 6 per cent of total outflows, a position which has changed little since 1979.

Table 12.6. Canada's main export markets, 1979 and 1989 compared

Country	1989 %	(1979) %
USA	74.6	(68.7)
Japan	6.0	(5.9)
United Kingdom	2.5	(3.8)
China	1.9	(0.9)
W Germany	1.3	(1.9)
Netherlands	1.0	(1.7)
France	0.9	(1.0)
Korea Rep	0.9	(0.6)
Benelux	0.9	(1.0)
USSR	0.8	(1.2)

Source: Statistics Canada.

The EU as a whole accounts for more than Japan (8 per cent) although its relative position has fallen from 11 per cent in 1979 (Papadopoulos, 1986). The UK has continued to decline in relative importance. By contrast, Canadian investment in the EU has risen as Table 12.7 demonstrates.

Table 12.7. Canadian stock of outward direct investment assets by region 1984 and 1989

Country	1984 Value C$m	%	1989 Value C$m	%
USA	32 151	67.8	50 122	62.7
EU	5 862	12.4	14 661	18.3
Other W Europe	512	1.1	1 013	1.3
Other developed countries	945	2.0	2 368	3.0
Rest of world	7 951	16.7	11 761	14.7
Total	47 422	100.0	79 925	100.0

Source: Statistics Canada.

The Canadian government viewed '1992' as presenting an opportunity for Canadian companies to expand their European operations to reverse the situation wherein Europe has remained a neglected area by Canadian firms.

> Penetration of this vast and sophisticated market will enhance any company's competitive position in the global market place. Success in the European market, however, demands the ability to respond rapidly to changing technological and business conditions. Few Canadian businesses will be able to prosper in the EC if all they do is maintain an arms-length trading relationship.

(Executive Summary, *Moving into Europe*, External Affairs and International Trade, p. 19)

In order to achieve the depth of involvement deemed necessary to penetrate the European market the Canadian Government has been urging companies to establish alliances with European partners in order to save time and money and allow the local partner to provide the necessary local knowledge, resources and finance necessary to promote success. Recent examples of the establishment of such alliances include IAF Bio Chem with Glaxo of the UK in drug research, Dowty Canada's participation in the European Airbus consortium, Desjardins Group with Confederation Nationale de Credit Mutual in France in insurance and other financial services and Labatt Brewing with Biorra Moretti and Prinz Brau of Italy.

Shared fears that Europe would become a 'fortress' following the establishment of the Single European Market are potentially one reason why Canadian investment has increased in the region. Equally, some Canadian firms share US fears regarding exclusion from the new harmonisation of technical standards although the growing propensity of Canadian firms to enter into global strategic alliances for the purpose of innovation and new technological development make this problem less severe than at first sight (Buckley, Pass and Prescott, 1993). The UK currently accounts for two-thirds of Canada's investment in the EU a position which reflects the cultural affinity of the two countries and the historically developed business links from days of the commonwealth. This position has also increased in recent years rising from 7.2 per cent in 1984 to 11.9 per cent in 1989. Capitalising on these business links and utilising the UK as a doorway to the EU is an active policy of many Canadian firms. French Canadians are also able to build on historical links with French companies as a means of consolidating and expanding European business.

The Canada–US Free Trade Agreement and the North American Free Trade Area

In 1989 Canada and the USA finally signed the Canada–US Free Trade Agreement which had been under discussion for some time. This formally recognises the inter-dependence between the two economic regions which has been growing since the Second World War. This is the second major attempt made by the two nations to liberalise trade flows. As long ago as 1854, steps were taken to establish free trade, an agreement being signed between the US and the UK representing Canada's interests. The agreement was binding until 1866 when the USA abrogated the agreement in reaction to the UK's involvement in the US Civil War. Politically, Canadian attitudes towards free trade have run the full gamut of opinion: the Liberals actively rejected establishing formal ties with the US, in the 1950s (under Diefenbaker) attempting to divert 15 per cent of Canada's trade with the USA to the UK and in the 1970s (with Trudeau) developing the *Third Option Policy* aimed at diverting Canada's trade partners. These attempts had little impact on the economy, and the USA trade and investment dependence continue (Papadopoulos, 1986). The Conservatives, on the other hand have continued to support the idea as offering substantial benefits to the Canadian economy. The Americans have, over many years and through various Governments, continued to support the idea of trade liberalisation – arguably because they have less to lose – but also due to the fact that it is in keeping with the free market ethos they so actively encourage.

The first real attempt to establish more harmonised rules between the two nations was the 1965 Canadian–US 'Autopact'. For the Canadians the effects were significant: massive rises in employment in the Canadian car industry and 80 per cent of Canada's output exported to the USA. The major benefits of free trade were adduced to be: real gains for consumers by eradicating price distortions, greater scope for exploiting economies of scale and reorganisation of industry to more efficiently use resources and exploit comparative advantage. Latterly, fears about increased American protectionism were the main impetus for renewed talks on developing the Free Trade Area. Although existing conditions were relatively open (80 per cent of Canadian exports to the USA and 70 per cent of US exports to Canada being duty free with the average tariff on the remainder only 0.7 per cent on Canadian goods and 3.8 per cent on US goods) the American deficit, low domestic demand and a weak American dollar all raised the threat of renewed protectionism. Nevertheless, there was evidence through the 1980s of an increase in non-tariff protectionism. Between 1980 and 1986 50 countervailing actions (employed where unfair government support is adjudged to have been given to exporting firms) and anti-dumping actions (where goods are thought to be offered below cost) were filed against Canada (Rugman and Anderson, 1989).

Even with the signing of the Free Trade Agreement, disputes still continue to prevail in trade between the two nations. Canadian trade in raspberries, pork, steel rail, replacement parts for paving equipment, beer and softwood lumber have all come under scrutiny for anti-dumping and countervailing actions. Furthermore, fish landing rights and automobiles have also witnessed disputes based on a broader definition of *protectionism* not specifically related to particular behaviours (Stevens, 1992). Similarly, the Canadians are lodging complaints against American imports, carpets and drywall for building being two cases in point. Thus, while many restrictions have been removed, the two states are far from being a single market.

Some North Americans argue that the continuance of trade disputes results from the limited impact of the directives designed to promote free trade. Comparing American policies within the Canada–USA Free Trade Agreement with those which have been developed to create the Single European Market has led some to conclude that the directives don't go far enough. The clarity of objectives and future direction of business within the EU brought about by the comprehensive package of directives covering all major industries is seen as 'all embracing'. This permits identification of real advantages rather than simple expressions of 'greater opportunities' which tends to be the case with the Canada–US agreement (Buckley, Pass and Prescott, 1993). The main provisions of the Canada–US Free Trade Agreement are outlined in Table 12.8. The outlines are indicative of an opening-up of markets in much the same way that the removal of physical, fiscal and technical barriers liberalise markets in the EU. What is lacking, however, is any evidence of establishing guidelines for creating 'a level playing field' through a common competition policy and it is perhaps this which potentially dilutes the impact as compared with the EU initiative.

Table 12.8. The Canada–USA Free Trade Agreement

Sector	Main provisions
Manufactured goods	Removal of all bilateral tariffs starting on 1 January 1989 over a maximum period of ten years.
Automotive	USA–Canada Auto Pact continues. Canada's embargo on imports of used cars to be eliminated. Duty remissions to be phased out. To benefit from tariff exemption, at least 50 per cent of the value of goods must originate in North America.
Agriculture	Elimination of tariffs on agricultural trade within 10 years and the agreement not to use direct export subsidies on bilateral agricultural trade.
Energy	Restrictions on exports of Canadian oil and gas can be imposed, however, any reduction in exports to the USA must be proportional to the total supply of oil and gas available in Canada, without price discrimination.
Banking	Canada is to eliminate restrictions on acquisition of Canadian assets by USA banks. Canadian banks will receive equal treatment under USA Securities law.
Financial services	Improved access and competition; national treatment for financial institutions.
Road haulage, maritime & air transport	No change, but further restrictions ruled out.
Other services	Liberalised access to enhanced telecommunications, computer services, tourism and architectural services.
Government procurement	Exclusion of national preference on government contracts worth more than $25 000; exceptions for defence procurement.
Direct investment	Restrictions on establishing new firms relaxed; extension of national treatment.
Technical standards	Harmonisation of technical standards based on the GATT code.
Emergency action	More stringent standards for the application of arbitration emergency safeguards. Establishment of a dispute settlements mechanism and an independent arbitration panel.

Source: External Affairs, Canada.

Negotiations have also been concluded which extend the Canada–US Free Trade Agreement to include Mexico – the North American Free Trade Area. Mexico, like Canada, relies heavily on the USA for its exports. In 1990, 69 per cent of all Mexican exports went to the USA, although only 1.2 per cent to Canada. Given this dependence, Mexico approached the USA to secure a free trade pact; this was rejected on the grounds that with the USA running two free trade pacts in parallel, the USA would be the only country to have free access to both markets giving them greater bargaining power. Consequently, Canada became involved in the negotiations to work towards a *pluralist* agreement giving equal access to the three markets for all participants.

The inclusion of Mexico in the Free Trade Area does, however, pose certain problems. It implicitly means two industrialised economies linking themselves with a less developed country with low wage levels. There is the potential threat of plant closures in both the USA and Canada and relocation in Mexico where cost savings can be made as a result of low labour costs. Special duties and taxes for firms investing along the Mexican border have already resulted in a spate of multinational enterprise investment in the region. Equally, investment in the region by non-American multinationals permits access to the whole market, a situation which is less than desirable for both the US and Canada as they fight off the effects of the recent recession. Nevertheless, the low wage argument has, perhaps, been overstated by some observers. Although Mexico boasts low wages, it is a low productivity economy with relatively high unit labour costs. For Canada, though, the prospect of plant closures does not bode well. In the wake of the signing of the Canada–US Free Trade Agreement Canada has already experienced a number of plant closures as some US firms have closed their branch operations in Canada in favour of following a more centralised approach to their American manufacturing. With trade barriers eliminated, there is no longer a need to maintain separate facilities in Canada to side-step tariff barriers. Lower production costs in the USA as opposed to Canada may potentially intensify this trend. The further threat to industry from low cost manufacturing advantages in Mexico is seen as very real by the Canadians.

These difficulties are further compounded by low levels of investment in Canada. While Canadian firms are actively expanding their business in the USA through local investment, few US firms are investing in Canada, further diverting business out of the Canadian region. Using Canada as a gateway to America may also hold little appeal for non-American firms as a result of continued trade actions by the USA against products originating in Canada. Multinational firms may prefer to establish subsidiaries in the US – the ultimate target market – to avoid combating such restrictions and ensure that the business is centred in the hub of the economic region. A lot may rest on the case against Honda cars which have been adjudged to contain less than the required 50 per cent local content (i.e. 50 per cent of the costs incurred in Canada) and are thus being restricted access to the USA.

Despite these concerns, on balance the North America Free Trade Area is considered to offer greater opportunities for its members, stimulating competition, promoting efficiency and providing a forum for the development of new technologies. More importantly, scale economy gains from the elimination of branch plants and duplication offer further efficiency gains. Trade diversion is expected to be small due to the size of existing bilateral flows between the countries and overall inward investment is expected due to the growing need for international firms to secure a presence in the region to ensure they are not treated as outsiders.

Bilateral bargaining and the new world economic order

External restrictions are particularly detrimental to firms from the less developed world who have relied for so long on the multilateral agreements through GATT negotiations to secure access to the major world markets. The growing trend towards bilateral agreements between the major trading blocs threatens trade for firms from the LDCs whose governments lack the political and economic clout to make the necessary bilateral deals to permit access and favourable trading conditions. Here the focus is very much on developing good relations with triad members and attempting to establish special trading deals (such as those secured under the Lomé Convention) as well as enabling inward investment to strengthen the economic base, benefit from education and technology transfer and build domestic capabilities to improve the competitiveness of their products on a global scale.

But the less developed world is not the only potential loser in the new world economic order where trading bloc protectionism is a very real threat to global trade (and investment) flows. While the imposition of non-tariff barriers may look attractive to solve immediate problems in a regional economy, the backlash from other trading blocs and the imposition of reciprocal trading restrictions may be highly damaging for triad group firms, many of whom operate on a truly global scale. Figure 12.1 gives some indication of intra-triad trade flows for 1992. The figure highlights that the triad (including EFTA nations) accounted for 60.9 per cent of all global trade activity in that year. The USA shows a trade surplus with Europe, but a deficit with Japan (which has led to much of the USA's concerns over greater access to Japanese markets). Equally, Japan has a trade surplus with Europe.

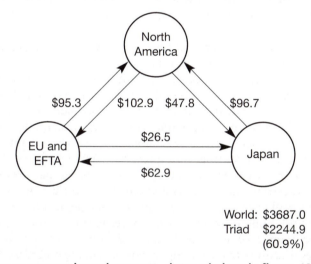

World: $3687.0
Triad $2244.9
       (60.9%)

Fig. 12.1 The macroeconomic environment – intra-triad trade flows, 1992 ($ million)
Source: International Monetary Fund: Direction of Trade Statistics Yearbook, 1993, Washington.

Figure 12.2 shows intra triad direct investment stocks and flows in 1992, demonstrating the importance of intra-triad investment on a world scale. Over 50 per cent of all Japanese outward direct investment stocks (that is the value of overseas assets) now lies within the triad, the corresponding figures for North America and the EEA being 20 per cent and 33 per cent respectively. Although Japanese investment in Europe remains relatively low compared with its position in the USA, levels have grown significantly in recent years. As the growth in world FDI continues to outpace that of exports these figures must be regarded as significant in the balance of economic activity on a world scale. The scale of FDI in the triad, 98 per cent of all world FDI flows, should not be understated.

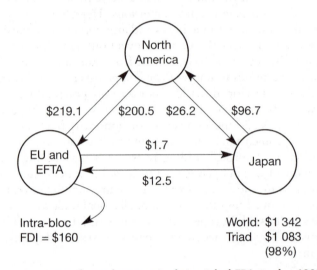

Fig. 12.2 The macroeconomic environment – intra-triad FDI stocks, 1992 ($ million)
Source: UNCT World Investment Report (1991).

Considering the volumes of trade and investment now concentrated in the triad it is unsurprising that such concentration of economic activity is changing the strategic focus for many multinational enterprises. Most MNEs focus attention on attaining a global balance in their business activities. Although for many years they have been concerned with spreading risk by having a diverse international portfolio incorporating a wide spectrum of countries between the East and West, developed and developing world, the trade (and investment) diversion effects of economic union means that the balance increasingly being sought is between the three triad powers of Asia-Pacific, the USA and Europe.

Part of the reasoning behind the drive for a global balance is gaining access to the largest industrial and consumer markets in the world as well as benefiting from regionally initiated R&D programmes either internal to the firm or through government initiatives. These trends point to two important issues for multinational enterprises: they must ensure that the amount of attention being paid to integration of the domestic region does not divert efforts away from developing business in the other leading regions; and they need to ensure that their domestic governments do not impose policies which are detrimental to their welfare and survival. This does not mean that firms should lobby governments to increase protectionism; the focus should clearly be on ensuring policies which promote growth, efficiency and technological development. The main caution against imposing greater protectionism is the retaliatory impact it is likely to engender.

For smaller firms from the developed world, the challenges are no less significant. Concentration on consolidating business or securing a broader position in the domestic region rather than attempt to expand on a global scale may theoretically be the most attractive option. This permits exploitation of the advantages being offered by greater harmonisation within economic blocs and prevents organisations facing up to protectionism and trade restrictions. Nevertheless, as many historical trade patterns were developed on the basis of colonial links and cultural affinity trade with non-bloc members may be significant in the business portfolio of smaller companies. This reinforces the need for openness between the trading blocs and while they have less bargaining power individually than multinational enterprises, pooling their efforts through trade associations and representative bodies suggest they have a powerful voice to influence governmental actions.

So much depends on the on-going relationships between the triad group as well as relationships developed (on a bilateral basis) with outside countries and regions. Where protectionism is used ill-advisedly, that is to specifically block trade or make investment more difficult, retaliatory action is inevitable. A recent case of this may be seen with MITI's white paper, drafted in the early part of 1993, to combat accusations levelled by the USA that Japan's trade surplus with the USA is unacceptable and must be reversed. It argues that Japan is already more open than other countries imposing an average tariff on mining and manufactured goods of only 2.7 per cent compared to 4.2 per cent in America and 4.6 per cent in Europe. While Japanese critics argue that slow growth at home is being combated by renewed export activity, the Japanese are keen to point out that the recent rise in Japan's surplus with the USA may be explained by such factors as a decline in demand for expensive imports due to Japanese recession, and the fact that the Japanese and US economies are out of balance in terms of demand patterns: strengthening of the US economy meant increased demand for Japanese imports, while demand for foreign goods in Japan resulted in decline. MITI goes on to argue that the surplus will diminish of its own accord as recovery from recession will draw in high levels of foreign goods, increased exports back to Japan from overseas subsidiaries and greater attention to the bottom line and short-term planning by Japanese companies. Nevertheless, the Clinton administration is intent on opening up Japanese markets and have threatened reactionary measures if planned levels of US export growth to Japan are not met.

Such a clear example of bilateral bargaining and bipartite dealing raises questions over the long-term effectiveness of GATT. With economic blocs continually concentrating their efforts on the triad, enthusiasm for GATT negotiations has undoubtedly waned. It is hoped that the new World Trade Organisation (WTO), due to take over from GATT in 1996, and with powers which extend the control of world FDI flows, will be able to re-assert its authority on the new global business order. Some talk has been made of extending the NAFTA which would enable the accomplishment of many objectives which GATT has failed to achieve. Latin American nations have turned to the NAFTA as a potential way forward for their future development and possible emergence as developed countries. Some talk has also been made regarding the inclusion of East Europe and New Zealand which would extend the power of the group as well as further changing the pattern of world business. If the new WTO fails to effectively control global activity further impetus to affiliation with trading blocs would be at issue for non-triad member countries particularly those in the Asian region where the current loose affiliation of nations is insufficient to challenge the coherence of the new emerging giants. Although the future is shrouded in uncertainty, what is eminently clear is that the future of global business will centre on how countries, both within and without the major trading blocs, adjust to the new world economic order.

CONCLUSION

The creation of the Single European Market is one of the most spectacular attempts at promoting economic integration the world has ever seen. Talked about for so long, from its inception through its development to the beginning of its implementation and the problems therein experienced, the metamorphosis of Europe has had a high public profile in the world economic arena. At each stage of its development the world has been able to see the opportunities and threats posed by changing legislation and policy, and in response establish codes of practice for reacting, to and living with, this new rejuvenated union of countries. It is partly the public nature of the developments and partly the economic inter-dependence of countries in the developed world which have seen proposed responses run the gamut from reactionary protectionism to increased levels of foreign direct investment.

Although there remain doubts about how the Single Market will ultimately affect the global balance of power, two things are clear. First, decisions cannot be made within the EU without the likely reaction of foreign firms and governments being taken into consideration. Failure to predict a reactionary measure being made by the Japanese or US governments, for example, in response to a change in EU policy may mean that while European firms may reap the benefits within the Community, they pay the price in wider global markets. Second, for 'trade restrictions' read 'investment incentive'. Whereas the balance of trade around the globe once characterised the relative economic power of nations, this is no longer the case. Increasingly trade flows are being replaced with FDI, not only because of restrictions imposed on imports, but because firms are keen to establish a presence in the three major economic centres now dominating the world economy. It is no longer sufficient to analyse international business, or indeed the effects of something as far reaching as the creation of the Single European Market, without assessing the impact on global investment and the continual erosion of national boundaries. As trade restrictions have, for many years, been apparent in international business dealings the creation of trad-ing blocs and the apparent new world protectionism, while posing new challenges for firms, does not undermine rates of internationalisation. Some would argue that the new barriers will have little significance in the shaping of global business which is being dom-inated by increased competition rather than the emergence of trading blocs. If the growing tendency for firms to establish links with competing firms through strategic alliances and joint research projects, the importance of these artificially imposed barriers may be less than at first imagined. This suggests that concentrating on the simple taxonomies of trade and investment fails to highlight some of the important strategic developments now tak-ing place on a world scale, developments which are not regional or country-specific but more dependent on industry-specific considerations.

Questions for discussion

1 Are the arguments put forward to support the practice of protectionism in any way justifiable?

2 What recommendations would you make to countries which are currently not part of the major world economic groupings?

3 It has been suggested that protectionist measures designed to provide favourable economic conditions for European Union firms has actually raised the stakes of

competition by promoting inward investment by major international firms. Can you think of any ways the European Union could provide a degree of protection for firms in nascent technology areas which would not have this kind of impact?

4 Japan has been accused of dumping on various occasions because the prices being charged within the European Union are deemed to be below costs. To what extent do you think this is justifiable?

5 Do you think the suggestion that Japanese and US firms are better placed to take advantage of the opportunities of the Single Market are realistic?

6 Will lack of transparency of technical standards really hinder US firms in a significant way?

7 To what extent do the newly industrialising countries pose a threat to indigenous European Union firms?

8 What are the prospects for less developed countries in the new world economic order?

9 What are the future prospects for the new World Trade Organisation given the changing patterns of world business?

CASE STUDY I

The world car industry

Introduction

The global automobile industry is one of the most visible sectors in the world economy. The international strategies of the leading firms have shaped production techniques and international business activity in a way which is unparalleled in any other business sector. The firms which have now come to dominate the industry are transnational in nature, cutting across the globe and developing business systems which have fostered the growing interdependence of national states on a global scale. The industry is a clear example of a global oligopoly – the largest 10 firms account for 76 per cent of all world production with 96 per cent emanating from the top 20 producers. Through the industry's development, location of production has been shaped by the power play between firms and governments. Tariff and non-tariff barriers were able to explain a great deal of foreign direct investment in the early days of internationalisation, although in more recent years governments' desire to secure car production within their domestic markets has led to firms playing governments off each other in an attempt to secure major investments. This has led to a growth in the relative power of the car producers as they have been able to secure the most beneficial conditions for their operations through government incentives and more favourable operating conditions.

Although it would be easy to regard the effects of the automobile industry in terms of the major producers, it is important to be aware of the linkages which exist within the industry. Car producers themselves are principally *assemblers* and many raw materials and components are sourced from external companies. This splits the production process into a number of constituent parts: the provision of raw materials (steel, rubber, glass, textiles, plastic) the manufacture of components and parts (bodywork, components and engines) and final assembly and manufacture. It is for these reasons that so many governments are keen to attract inward investment by the leading car manufacturers as the impact on the economy, through the development of links with local suppliers, can be significant. Nevertheless, all constituent functions need not be located in the same area and as competition in the industry increases, there is an increasing trend for firms to look for optimum location advantages at a functional rather than business level.

The global picture

The relative dominance of global regions has changed dramatically in recent years. The effects of the growth in the Japanese (and more latterly NICs) car industry has had a powerful effect on the world balance of activities. The USA, in particular, has suffered as a result; while the USA accounted for 51.4 per cent of world production, this figure had fallen to 19.2 per cent in 1989. By contrast, the Japanese car industry which accounted for a meagre 1.3 per cent in 1960, boasted 25.5 per cent in 1989. On balance, the EU's position has changed little, although within that there are various winners and losers. The UK for example has suffered a sharp decline from 10.4 per cent in 1960 to 3.7 per cent in 1989 (a level which comprises a high proportion of foreign-owned production), while Spain has raised its position (albeit again through inward investment) from 0.3 per cent in 1960 to 4.6 per cent in 1989. Production is principally concentrated in the global triad although growth in Korea suggests that future competition may also come from the developing world. The dominance of the triad is also reflected in international trade flows, with 96 per cent taking place within the triad. Western Europe accounts for 50 per cent, although approximately three quarters of this total is intra-European.

Japan's spectacular penetration of the global car industry began in the 1970s when they were able to exploit low cost production advantages on a global scale. By 1987, almost a quarter of all cars sold in the USA were Japanese, the corresponding figure for the UK being 9.7 per cent. This relatively lower level reflects the imposition of voluntary export restraints (VERs) by the EU. Conversely, the USA shows relatively low levels of international trade in the car industry (1.9 per cent of total production in 1987), partly as a result of the scale of the domestic market, but also because of the continued production of large (high fuel consumption) cars which have limited appeal in other world markets where fuel prices are considerably higher. Latterly, producers have reduced the size of American produced cars with growing costs of running vehicles, although before this adjustment, high import penetration by Japanese and European car producers in the late 1970s and early 1980s was a response to the growing need for smaller more fuel efficient cars.

The production process

In the early days of the car industry, competitive success rested on the notion of mass production. The techniques fostered by the Ford Motor Company (which has led to the term 'Fordist' production) of mass produced, highly standardised goods, led to the rapid growth of the car industry as it made automobiles affordable to the masses. While this technique of production offered major scale economy advantages, it lacked the potential for differentiation as it was so rigid. Setting up equipment for the production of adapted models involved a protracted period of down-time which essentially detracted from the benefits being offered by the system. Additionally, the need to recoup massive research and development costs was only seen as achievable through a focus on mass production. Costs are not, however, equally divided between the constituent production functions. Finally, assembly, which demands the greatest proportion of labour input, is the most costly accounting for as much as 23 per cent of the total costs of vehicle production. The costs involved with the production of engines and transmission on the other hand can be as little as eight per cent of the total cost. These issues have important ramifications for the location of production, although they cannot be considered in isolation. The quality and training of the labour force is also at issue and acts as a further key factor shaping world investment decisions.

As the structure of the global industry has gravitated towards a global oligopoly, where price competition is inherently ruled out as detrimental to all players, firms have begun to look more towards differentiation as the major source of competitive advantage. The first moves in this direction were made by the Japanese who were intent on finding production methods which combined the benefits offered by mass production but permitted greater flexibility in manufacturing systems. The system they employed, the *lean production* system, focuses more on computer aided design and manufacturing, team works, just-in-time delivery systems, close liaison between manufacturers and their suppliers. This not only facilitates pursuance of competition based on differentiation but also allows shorter innovation periods for bringing new products to market. It is estimated that in 1989 it took Japanese companies 47 months to bring a new model to market compared to 60 months for US manufacturers. In order to enable this, close relationship with customers has also been a priority to ensure that product developments reflect changing demand patterns in the market. Local production is one way of facilitating this kind of strategy, although reliance on suppliers for providing market information is also a key element in the ongoing process of new product development.

Trade protection and economic union

Governments have the power to influence the car industry in two ways: through the impositions on trade and investment in the local region and through support given to local producers. In the early days of the industry's internationalisation, tariff barriers were actively used to protect domestic markets and impose limits on the volumes of imports. This was the major cause of early direct investment in the industry. Today, however, tariff levels are relatively low: the common EU tariff is 11 per cent, with 3 per cent in the USA and no import tariff in Japan. Conversely, the use of non-tariff barriers has risen in recent years, particularly in response to Japanese encroachment on an international scale. The agreement of voluntary export restraints with the EU limits Japanese imports to 11 per cent of domestic sales in the UK, 3 per cent in France, 3 200 cars in Italy, 2 000 in Spain and 1 000 in Portugal. There has been increased pressure for the EU to establish a common policy towards Japanese automobile imports although conflicting attitudes by the various Member States makes a common approach difficult. France, Italy and Spain are keen to retain high levels of protection to enable their industries adjust to the increased competitive pressures imposed by the Single European Market. This has led to tensions between France and Italy (in particular) and the UK which has continued its open door policy to Japanese inward investment providing a gateway to the rest of Europe.

Local content rules and rules of origin have been employed by both the EU and North America dictating that products sold in the local market contain a certain proportion of locally produced components. This (along with the voluntary export restraints) has had a powerful influence on Japanese direct investment in both the USA and Europe. In the EU, the local content figure has been set at 80 per cent (although the French have continually pushed for 100) and 50 per cent in the USA.

In terms of support of local industry, Western European firms, especially France, the UK and Italy, have taken an interventionist approach to facilitating the development of their domestic car industries. Direct ownership of vehicle producers such as Renault in France, Rover in the UK and Alfa-Romeo in Italy was an important feature until the late 1980s when firms were privatised as a result of EU competition policy rulings. All firms received enormous subsidies and preferential treatment through protectionist measures, although the net result was arguably less successful than desired. These firms were often accused of being inefficient and slow to respond to changes in market demand. Since their privatisation, the Rover Group has exploited its links with Honda of Japan and dramatically improved its position in the UK market through product innovation and aggressive marketing efforts; Renault while decreasing its overall output, has become more streamlined and efficient; Alfa-Romeo has been taken over by Fiat and incorporated into a larger, more powerful organisation. The Japanese government, although active in the support of the car industry in the 1950s and 1960s through high import tariffs and restriction of foreign involvement in the local industry, has recently rescinded its position, limiting its involvement to the negotiation of voluntary export restraints. Today, government involvement is most evident in the provision of incentives for inward investment. The Toyota plant in Kentucky in the USA, for example, was offered an incentive package worth $325 million.

The European Union car market

Before the inception of the Single Market, the major limitations to efficiency were outlined as follows:

- different levels of taxation on vehicles between the 15 Member States ranging from 12 per cent in Luxembourg to 200 per cent in Denmark and Greece. Further differences in tax rebates on company cars limit market integration;
- different technical standards between countries reinforced by local mandatory safety rulings. Unique rear reflectors in Germany, yellow headlight bulbs in France, reclining drivers' seats in West Germany, right hand drive and dim-dip lighting in the UK. In addition, different testing procedures mean duplication of car tests between countries;
- state aid supporting national champion car companies which distorts competition as it removes free-market principles.

It is estimated that up to five per cent of the industry's unit costs (Ecu 2.6 billion) could be saved if these differences were removed. Greater scale economies and lower development costs would result from the harmonisation of taxes and standards and the removal of state aid (Cecchini, 1988). While the focus here is on the effect of the removal of barriers, it is likely that the real issues will centre more on the effects of foreign competition, Government-supported domestic competition and, ultimately, the effects of over-capacity in the industry.

As has already been suggested, the European car industry is highly parochial with the greatest proportion of trade being inter-EU. To this end, for most firms the centre of production activity is the domestic market and while some firms are redressing this balance (Volkswagen, the most international European company having raised its proportion of overseas production from 25–30 per cent between 1982–1989) others have further concentrated production at home (Fiat having reduced overseas production from 20 to 7 per cent in the same period).

French producers have provided the greatest support for EU induced protection against Japanese competition. Peugeot-Citroen, formed through a Government induced merger between the two companies in 1975 and later extended through the acquisition of Chrysler's European operations in 1978, has had problems integrating the various combined organisations and is actively in favour of permitting European firms a period of adjustment in the face of new competitive pressures. Renault, for so long the French government's national champion, benefited in the past from major government cash injections. Facing up to new competitive pressures, and in order to facilitate greater company efficiency, the firm has sold off its major US activities to Chrysler and closed its Mexican plant.

While most European producers have only limited operations in the USA (production being mostly cited in South America) US producers manage a powerful presence in the Single Market. Ford has, since the early developments of the EU, been concerned with developing and consolidating its activities within Europe. As early as 1967, Ford reorganised its European operations, then concentrated in separate markets (the UK, West Germany and Belgium) and formed Ford Europe wherein European plants developed specialist roles within the company's broader, transnational organisation. Activities were later developed to include production in Spain. Reorganisation and rationalisation now dominate the company's European activities as it looks towards greater efficiency gains in an effort to stay afloat in a highly saturated marketplace. General Motors' European activities have, for a long time, been concentrated on two subsidiaries, Vauxhall in the UK and Opel in West Germany. Like Ford, the company opened a manufacturing plant in Spain in the late 1980s and is now looking towards greater efficiency and rationalisation as the way forward in the 1990s. Much of this is due to Japanese competition in the EU (as well as local indigenous activity) and concerns building new component supply plants and developing new distribution networks as well as extending product ranges (through acquisition) to incorporate the luxury car market (Ford now owning Jaguar and Aston Martin and General Motors, Lotus).

Japan's early encroachment on the European car sector was based on exports from Japanese car plants. The price competitiveness of these exports was dependent on large-scale flexible manufacturing and the close networks developed with suppliers –

advantages which off-set the high variable costs associated with transportation. Government resistance towards the growth of Japanese imports has, however, induced inward investment in the EU enabling firms to achieve a further global objective: to locate production close to the market to more effectively adapt products to customer requirements. Although investment in Europe was slower than corresponding developments in the USA the major producers, Honda, Nissan and Toyota have all secured a strong presence in the region through investment activity. Honda was the first firm to make a move, signing a joint venture agreement with British Leyland (then part state-owned) which has since, following privatisation, become the Rover Group. In 1986, Nissan started production in the UK, later followed by Toyota in 1989. Honda's decision in the late 1980s to build a dedicated, wholly owned construction plant in the UK potentially jeopardises the joint venture with the Rover Group and signals the firm's intention to further develop its own activities within the new Single Market.

The overall picture for the EU indicates that in 1990, Ford had 10 per cent market share, General Motors 11 per cent and the Japanese producers 10 per cent (compared with 16 per cent for Volkswagen 13 per cent for Peugeot, 10 per cent for Renault and 15 per cent for Fiat). With such high levels of foreign involvement, the European market is a key centre of world competition. The growing development of linked networks by both the Japanese and Americans through vertical investment (by the car producers themselves in the case of US firms and linked suppliers in the Japanese case) is demonstrative of growing pressures in the sector. This has led some economists to suggest that industry rationalisation is inevitable. Joint ventures between European producers, in an attempt to combat growing competitive pressures and enable enhanced technology to be developed, are likely to continue as over-capacity threatens the long-term survival of some manufacturers. Six European producers, Fiat, Peugeot, Renault, Rover, Volkswagen and Volvo have set up a joint research programme, Volvo and Renault have cross-shareholdings and Fiat and Peugeot have a joint research project for developing engines and steering systems. Company mergers may also be a reality. With Honda potentially relinquishing its ties with the Rover Group, Volkswagen has expressed an interest in buying the company if it were put up for sale by British Aerospace as a way of establishing a stronger foothold in the UK market.

European protection of the EU car market is set to continue until 1998. Until then Japanese firms are permitted no more than 17 per cent of EU market share. Bilateral agreements between individual Member States and the Japanese car producers will be gradually removed up to the 1998 deadline as the individual freedom of Member States to control their own destiny passes into the hands of the Commission. This gives European car producers until 1998 to restructure their industries and adjust to the new competition.

The USA car market

Ford and General Motors (GM) have long dominated US activity. Both firms have recently undergone major reorganisation and contraction of plants in an effort to rationalise domestic activity and face up to the new challenges, particularly those posed by Japanese encroachment. Ford has doubled its plant capacity in Mexico as a way of lowering overall production costs and gaining greater competitive advantage in serving its domestic market. Between 1978–1989 employment in the US automobile industry fell by 24 per cent.

As with the EU, trade restrictions imposed by the US government induced Japanese firms to invest in the USA. In 1991, there were over 15 Japanese manufacturing subsidiaries in North America, representing all the leading manufacturers (Nissan, Honda, Toyota, Mazda, Mitsubishi, Subaru and Suzuki). Some of these activities are based on joint ventures with indigenous firms such as Toyota and GM and Mitsubishi with Chrysler although increased capacity and the later establishment of wholly-owned operations (in the case of Toyota) are testament to increased involvement and market penetration. Raised local content requirements have also seen firms establish component plants as well as inducing investment by Japanese component suppliers intent to capitalise on their established links with Japanese producers on a world-wide scale. Technology joint ventures with Japanese firms have attained substantial importance in the strategies of US car manufacturers. For example, Ford owns 24 per cent of Toyo Kogyo (Mazda) which supplies transmissions, and the North American Ford Escort was developed jointly with Mazda which sells a version of the car under its own brand name outside of the US. These linkages assure that growing technological leadership by the Japanese is harnessed and exploited to good effect.

In the late 1980s and early 1990s the USA experienced rising levels of car imports from the newly industrialising countries based on aggressive price competition enabled by low manufacturing costs in Korea. Success led to the establishment, by Hyundai of a manufacturing plant in Canada although product unreliability and declining demand meant that in 1990 the plant was only operating at 40 per cent of its planned capacity. Equally, rising labour costs in Korea led to an erosion of their main competitive advantage leading to major challenges to their future development as a world car producer.

The Japanese market

Unlike the other two triad regions, the Japanese indigenous market is devoid of foreign competition. This is partly a result of continued Japanese protectionism as well as the complexities of the Japanese industry which acts as a deterrent to inward investment. The major exceptions are the niche producers, particularly those operating in the luxury car sector who are able to satisfy a gap in the market which has only relatively recently been filled by Japanese car manufacturers. Whereas in the past the Japanese concentrated on 'middle range' cars – those affordable by the masses – recent product portfolios have been extended to include luxury cars. This enabled some specialist producers the chance to gain a foothold in the market.

Summary and conclusions

The world car industry is clearly dominated by firms based in the global triad. Although some emerging competition has, in recent times, come from the newly industrialising countries, these threats have not had a major impact on the balance of world output dominated by the developed country multinationals. Trade in the industry has been severely curtailed by governmental policies and given rise to major investment initiatives by the leading players which have enhanced their local competitiveness through market proximity advantages. Vertical investments have also been evident which has allowed firms to deepen their involvement in the regions served. A growing characteristic of the industry is the number of joint ventures and strategic alliances being established between the major producers, partly for the purpose of market access, but mostly for the development of new technologies. When coupled with changing production techniques and growing demands for flexibility, the future challenges facing car producers demand reorganisation of business and rationalisation on a global scale. The trend towards economic integration and the establishment of trading blocs on the one hand acts counter to the development of global networks by making the physical flow of intermediary and finished goods more difficult, but on the other, promotes deepening regional involvement and the potential to reorganise activity within the various trading blocs. To this extent, triad members may come to look like miniature global economies where business is organised to take advantage of inter-regional diversities and opportunities.

Questions

1 To what extent will new production techniques in the car industry alter the organisation of world manufacturing?

2 Will European firms be able to counter the threat of Japanese encroachment when voluntary export restraints are removed?

3 How will over-capacity in the European market affect the global industry for automobiles?

4 What will be the future prospect for international joint ventures?

5 Do you think that the producers in the newly industrialising countries pose a serious threat to the world marketplace for cars?

6 Are there any lessons to be learned from the changing world order in automobile manufacturing for producers in other industrial sectors?

7 What do you expect the international car industry to look like ten years from now?

CASE STUDY II

The world semiconductor industry

Introduction

Semiconductors are a critical intermediate good in the production of many of today's sophisticated technologies. They are not, as is popularly assumed, solely employed in the electronics industries, but have broad applications across numerous industries. Although they are now a common part of our world, semiconductors are a relatively young product, only emerging in the late 1950s. However, growth and development in this field has been spectacular with increased miniaturisation and extended their usage through such diverse products as televisions, robots and guided missiles.

Japan's dominance

Japanese encroachment on the industry began as late as 1975 when, backed by the Ministry of International Trade and Industry (MITI), Japanese firms began to extend their international reach in the industry. By 1985, Japanese firms had become world leaders in the sector. Much is attributed to MITI's involvement in encouraging R&D and providing active support to domestic producers through subsidies, loans and favourable interest rates. Furthermore, protection of the industry was supported which meant that the industry could develop in the early years without having to face up to aggressive competition.

By 1989, Japanese firms accounted for 42 per cent of the world market, the United States 26 per cent and Europe a mere 12 per cent. (Germany representing 31 per cent of this total, France 19 per cent and the UK 16 per cent.) Problems in Europe were also compounded by increasing numbers of NICs becoming involved in semiconductor production, South Korea, Malaysia, Thailand and Hong Kong in particular.

With demand rising dramatically, the dominant firms in the world market have carved out a powerful niche in this newly emerging market. Demand was also fuelled by technological changes, which resulted in lower prices, making the new technology affordable for all kinds of consumer technologies.

Production processes

With technologies changing rapidly, one of the problems now facing firms in the industry is continual up-grading of plant and equipment. The technologies on which basic semiconductors are founded have developed rapidly raising demands for quality and sophistication and necessitating new production technologies. In addition, while some products can be mass produced, some chips require high levels of customisation making flexible manufacturing a pre-requisite of successful operations.

A further feature of development is the ever-shortening product life-cycles associated with semiconductors which can make newly developed products obsolete very quickly. Firms, therefore, have to react quickly to changes in technology and follow processes of continuous improvement if they are to sustain their position in the marketplace. Japan, with its policies of continuous development and total quality management have therefore been able to capitalise on their manufacturing technologies and processes to sustain their position in the market.

The story in Europe

European firms were very slow to react to changes in technology in the semiconductor industry. In the early days, Japan was not seen to pose a threat, and therefore firms engaged in little technology development. It was not until the mid 1980s that European organisations found it essential to take steps to combat the growing power of the Japanese. However, without the same time advantages in the market, even the largest European firms found it hard to bridge the gap between their antiquated technologies and processes and those emerging out of the Pacific Rim.

In the late 1980s, therefore, Philips and Siemens engaged in major investments to improve their semiconductor manufacturing capabilities. However, both found it hard to match the pace of development and by 1991, Philips had discontinued its $1bn megachip project (a joint development project with Siemens for the production of 4M DRAM memory chips), preferring to concentrate on manufacturing specialised semiconductors to meet its own internal needs (and those of its partners) for the production of audio, video, medical, household and telecommunications equipment. The effort to catch up appeared hopeless, the Japanese beat them to the market every time.

Consequently, with little capacity of its own, Europe relies heavily on Japanese imports and semiconductors produced by Japanese firms on European soil. Companies also rely heavily on Japanese production techniques and raw materials in developing their own semiconductors, which further reinforces European reliances on Japan.

The role of government

With semiconductors now being a major element in today's new technology industries, it is unsurprising that governments have involved themselves in protecting and nurturing domestic/regional industries. There are three potential ways of attempting to secure more control over semiconductor production activity:

1 promote manufacturing by indigenous companies;
2 encourage inward investment;
3 purchase semiconductors and concentrate on end-usage.

Europe has involved itself in all three of these areas. On the first issue, the Commission has targeted a large amount of money at supporting research and development in the EU through the creation of such projects as EUREKA. One of the largest projects funded out of this was the European Semi-conductor Research Programme which was afforded Ecu 3.8bn. However, as the above argument suggests, the results from EU firms' increased involvement in semiconductor development have been disappointing.

Second, the EU has, through local content stipulations and anti-dumping duties made it very hard for Japanese firms to export to the EU, or establish only screw-driver plants. In 1989, the Commission ruled that for semiconductors the rule-of-origin be defined by the location of wafer fabrication, and not the location of final testing and assembly of chips. According to this definition, chips which are not fabricated in the EU are subject to a 14 per cent tariff. In 1990 the Commission also levied dumping duties of up to 60 per cent on the import of DRAMS.

On the final point, it is evident that the European Commission have also encouraged final product development, through the granting of R&D support monies for electronic product development.

Future of the European semiconductor industry

Based on the above brief description of the current state of play between the Japanese and European markets for semiconductors, several questions need to be raised about the future of the European semiconductor industry. With little expertise in the production of semiconductors, and the market changing so rapidly, reliance on the Japanese is inevitable.

The only future scope for development by European firms appears to be in specialised applications for customised usage (either in-house or within technology alliances), however, even here the Europeans are reliant on the Japanese technology. Restrictions on trade, which have brought Japanese producers to the marketplace has an important implication here. By 'persuading' Japanese firms to invest in local plant, the Commission has effectively derived a means of encouraging technology transfer. Although many alliances in the past in Europe have been between indigenous European firms, there is no reason why those in the future should not be between Europeans and the Japanese. In this way, EU organisations can enhance their learning and develop better in-house capabilities for developing semiconductors for end product usage.

This raises an interesting point. Whereas originally, the Japanese relied on Western firm technology for improving their industrial base, by promoting inward licensing agreements for technology transfer, the shoe now appears to be on the other foot. By actively encouraging inward Japanese investment (and possibly joint ventures with major Japanese players) technology transfers are now flowing from East to West.

Case Study Questions

1 Why do you think European Union firms did not see the Japanese as being a real threat in the semiconductor industry?

2 What critical factors enhanced the development of Japanese supremacy in this field?

3 How effective do you think European legislation will be in ensuring that European firms do not lag behind in semiconductor technology?

4 Have the tables really turned between the East and the West?

FURTHER READING

Kenichi Ohmae (1985) *Triad Power: the Coming Shape of Global Competition*, Free Press. Although written in 1985, this text provides an interesting and (still) relevant overview of the way in which global competition is changing and the strategic challenges this poses for organisations. Particular emphasis on relationships between trading blocs makes this text a valuable read.

Burgenmeier, and Mucchiellie, (eds.) (1991) *Multinationals and Europe: Strategies for the Future*, Routledge. This text provides a good review of the challenges facing European multinationals as a result of the Single European Market initiative. The text includes materials of both general and company specific nature which means it is relevant to both the theorist and practitioner.

REFERENCES

Bartlett, C. A. and Ghoshal, *Managing Innovation in the Transnational Corporation* in Bartlett, C. A., Doz, Y. and Hedlund, G. (Eds) *Managing the Global Firm*, Routledge, 1990.

Buckley, P. J., Pass, C. and Prescott, K., *Servicing International Markets: Competitive Strategies of UK Firms*, Blackwell, 1992.

Buckley, P. J., Pass, C. and Prescott, K., *Canada–UK – A Study of Trade and Investment Bilateral Relations*, Report prepared for the Canadian High Commission, 1993.

Burton, J., 'Single Market Changed Swedish Priorities', *Financial Times*, 21 February , 1990.

Cecchini, Paolo, *1992: The Benefits of the Single Market*, Wildwood House, 1988.

Colchester, N. and Buchan, D., *Europe Relaunched: Truths and Illusions on the Way to 1992*, Economists Books, 1990.

Dunning, J., *European Integration and Transatlantic Foreign Direct Investment: The Record Assessed*, paper presented at the UK Academy of International Business, 6–7 April, Strathclyde, 1990.

The Economist, 'A Survey of Business in Europe', 8 June 1991.

El-Agraa, A. M., 'The European Community' in El-Agraa, A. M. (Ed.), *International Economic Integration*, Macmillan, 1988.

Gaster, R., *European Industrial Policy*, Study Papers, Committee on Foreign Affairs, US House of Representatives, June 1992.

Japan Committee for Economic Development, Kigyo Hakusho, White Paper on the Corporation, JCED, 1991.

Matsuura, Nanshi, F., *International Business: A New Era*, Harcourt Brace Jovanovich Inc, pp. 110–111, 1990.

Ohmae, K., *Triad Power*, Free Trade Press, 1985.

EAITC (External Affairs and International Trade in Canada) (1991), *Moving into Europe*.

Page, S. *Trade, Finance and Developing Countries: strategies and constraints in the 1990s*, Harvester Wheatsheaf, 1990.

Papadopoulos, *Canada and the European Community: An Uncomfortable Partnership?*, The Institute of Public Policy, Montreal, 1986.

Penrose, E., 'Dumping – Unfair Competition and Multinational Corporations', *Japan in the World Economy*, 2. pp. 181–7, 1990.

Porter, M. E., *The Competitive Advantage of Nations*, Macmillan, 1990.

Richards, Howard, *Developing Relations Between the European Communities and the Association of South East Asian Nations*, European Research, January 1991.

Rugman, Alan and Anderson, Andrew, 'Business Concerns about Implementing the Free Trade Agreement', *Business Quarterly,* Spring 1989, pp. 23–26.

Smith, C. 'One Big Market at a Price', *Far Eastern Economic Review*, 5 May 1988, p. 131

Stevens, Mary-Anne, *Canada, the Free Trade Agreement and US Trade Actions*, paper presented at the Euro-Asia Management Studies Association Annual Conference, Bradford, 27–29 November 1992.

Strange, Roger, *A Political Economy Framework for the Analysis of Direct Investment Strategies,* paper presented at the Euro-Asia Management Studies Association Annual Conference, Bradford, 27–29 November 1992.

INDEX